INTERNET PROGRAMMING

Kris Jamsa, Ph.D.

Ken Cope

JAMSA
P·R·E·S·S™

...a computer user's best friend™

a division of Kris Jamsa Software, Inc.

Published by
Jamsa Press
6366 W. Sahara Ave.
Las Vegas, NV 89102
U.S.A.

For information about the translation or distribution of any Jamsa Press book, please write to Jamsa Press at the address listed above.

Internet Programming

Printed in the United States of America.
98765432

ISBN 1-884133-12-6

Publisher
　Debbie Jamsa

Copy Editor
　Larry Letourneau

Composition
　Caroline Kinsey

Cover Design
　David Ewen
　Phil Schmauder

Proofer
　Rosemary Pasco

Technical Editor
　Kris Jamsa

Indexer
　Carl Koch

Cover Photograph
　O'Gara/Bissell

Illustations
　Communication Designers, Inc

Table of Contents

Internet Programming

Chapter 3
An Introduction to TCP/IP 60

Chapter 4
Understanding the Internet Protocol 74

Chapter 5
Understanding the Transport Protocols 103

Chapter 6
SLIP versus PPP 124

Chapter 7
Understanding the Socket Interface 154

Chapter 8
Understanding the Windows Sockets API 180

Chapter 9
Understanding the Domain Name System 219

Chapter 18
Visual Programming on the Internet 485

Chapter 19
Spiders on the Web 525

Chapter 1
An Introduction to Computer Networks

If you already understand computer networks, you can use this chapter as a quick review. If you are familiar with network terms but not the underlying principles, this chapter takes the covers off, so to speak, and shows you a network's moving parts (mostly bits and bytes). If you are new to networks, this introduction presents, one step at a time, essential information about networks you need to understand as an Internet programmer. In the preface to his definitive book, *Computer Networks*, Prentice Hall, 1981, Andrew S. Tanenbaum states:

> *"The key to designing a computer network was first enunciated by Julius Caesar: Divide and Conquer."*

As it turns out, your key to understanding networks is the same principle. At first glance, you may find networks—especially the huge, worldwide Internet—very intimidating. Thus, understanding networks may seem like an impossible task. However, if you use Tanenbaum's "divide and conquer" technique to break this task (or topic) into smaller tasks (or subtopics), you will easily understand each subtopic and, after a brief period of time, have a thorough grasp of underlying network principles.

For example, to understand network communications among 100 computers, you would first study how two computers talk to each other. Likewise, you don't need to try to understand how thousands of Internet networks interact. Instead, you can simply study how two or three networks communicate with each other.

Initially, the amount of network information you need to absorb may seem overwhelming. However, just as you eat a large meal one-bite-at-a-time, you can easily digest networks one-idea-at-a-time. For this reason, Chapters 1 and 2 divide the subject of networks into several bite-sized pieces of information. As you absorb these pieces of information, you will obtain a solid understanding of networks and conquer an otherwise intimidating learning curve. By the time you finish this chapter, you will understand the following key concepts:

- What a computer network is
- The difference between a network and an internet
- How computers communicate with each other
- Communication switching uses switch boxes to route electronic signals

- ◆ Packet switching breaks messages into smaller pieces for transmission
- ◆ Network topologies specify how a network connects computers
- ◆ How network administrators connect networks
- ◆ The conceptual components of a network

Defining a Computer Network

In its most basic form, a computer network is simply two computers that communicate with each other. Of course, most networks consist of more than two computers. However, the principles of network communication are the same for two, three, or even 1,000 computers. If you understand how two computers communicate, you have the foundation to understand how 1,000 or more computers communicate.

Networks usually fall into one of two groups: local area networks and wide area networks. A *local area network* (LAN) connects computers located near each other. In some cases, "local" means within the same room or building. In other cases, "local" refers to computers located several miles apart. In contrast, *wide area networks* (WANs) consist of computers in different cities, states, or even countries. You can refer to WANs as *long-haul networks* because of the great distance the information they exchange must travel. As you may know, the Internet consists of thousands of networks worldwide. However, for your programming purposes, you can treat the Internet as a single network.

Connecting Two or More Networks

When you connect two or more computers so they can communicate, you form a network. You can also connect two or more networks and form an *internetwork* (or *internet*). Figure 1.1 illustrates the relationship between networks and internets. The Internet (spelled with an upper case "I") is the largest and most widely known internetwork in the world. The Internet connects more than 20,000 computer networks in 130 countries. Thousands of different computer types exist within this internetwork. These computers use a wide variety of network software. Luckily, as you use and even program the Internet, you can ignore such differences. The programs you will use, as well as the software libraries your Internet programs will access, hide most of these differences from you!

To begin learning the basics of Internet programming, you should view the Internet in terms of individual networks. After you grasp the fundamentals of a single network, you can apply that knowledge to understanding a network of networks—such as the Internet.

How Computers Communicate

A network, in its simplest form, is two computers that communicate with each other. As such, to understand networks, you must understand how computers communicate. The following paragraphs will introduce you to a variety of communication terms and concepts.

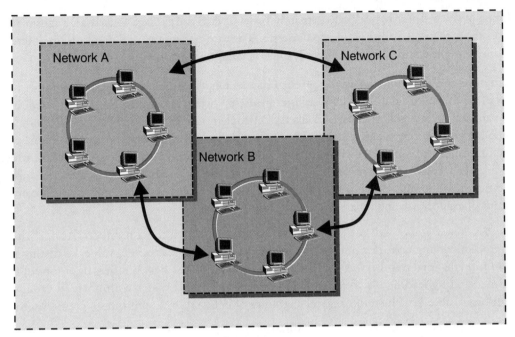

Figure 1.1 The relationship between networks and internets.

Conceptually, computer communication is similar to human communication. All humans use language to communicate. And all languages consist of the same basic components: letters and symbols which combine to form words or ideas. Regardless of the language you speak, to communicate ideas and information, you form sentences from words.

Similarly, computers use a language composed of *binary (base 2) digits* (symbols) that represent either a 1 or a 0. Computers combine 1's and 0's to form *bytes* of data (words). Computers transmit multiple byte combinations (sentences) to communicate meaningful information. To fully understand computer communications, you need to understand *binary numbers*.

The ultimate purpose of computer communications is to transfer information to people. Although computers easily understand 1's and 0's, binary data is practically impossible for people to read. As you will learn, computers map binary data to letters and numbers that people can read. The following paragraphs will show you how to easily convert data for use by humans and computers.

Understanding the Language of Computers

When you create a program, the computer represents your data as a series of binary digits or *bits*; each bit, in turn, represents either a 1 or a 0. The language of computers consists of 1's and 0's only. As an applications programmer, you may never have dealt with binary data. However, as a network or Internet programmer, you will occasionally need to read, interpret, and store binary information.

Normally, you will need to work with data at the bit level when you package your data for transmission across the network. In other words, to understand how to transmit your data across the Internet, you need to understand how to represent some data in binary format.

Computers use electronic signals to represent data as binary numbers. Each binary number consists of a string of 1's and 0's. Many computers use a 1 when an electrical signal is present on a wire and a 0 if the signal is absent. Conversely, people normally use *decimal (base 10) numbers*. Although you can convert binary (base 2) numbers to decimal numbers, the process is time consuming and error prone. As such, you may want to use *hexadecimal (base 16) numbers*, which provide a convenient middle ground between binary and decimal numbers. If you are serious about Internet programming, do yourself a favor and buy an inexpensive calculator that can convert decimal, hexadecimal, and binary numbers.

Internet Programming will use the term *hex* to refer to hexadecimal numbers. As does the C programming language, this book will add the *0x* prefix to hexadecimal values to distinguish them from decimal numbers. Also, this book will always show hex numbers in groups of two digits including leading 0's. *Internet Programming* will display binary numbers in groups of eight bits. Table 1.1 illustrates several examples of decimal, hex, and binary counterparts.

Decimal	Hex	Binary
10	0x0A	00001010
100	0x64	01100100
255	0xFF	11111111
512	0x0200	0000001000000000
500	0x01F4	0000000111110100

Table 1.1 Examples of formats for decimal, hex, and binary numbers.

Many Internet documents identify, or specify, data in terms of bits. For example, a Request for Comment (RFC) might tell you that a particular data field is 16 bits wide or that a particular bit pattern identifies a special network message. As you develop Internet programs, you will need to refer to many such documents. Learn to view, or think of, your data in terms of bits and bit patterns. Otherwise, you will find many important Internet reference documents difficult to read.

Reviewing Decimal, Hex, and Binary Numbers

Every programming language lets you manipulate numbers and characters. You may be familiar with ASCII, the American Standard Code for Information Interchange. *ASCII* assigns unique values to each letter of the alphabet, punctuation symbols, and so on. When your programs display information (such as a name) on a computer screen, they internally represent the information using ASCII codes. Likewise, when your programs send information to the printer, they actually send ASCII codes to the printer.

As you examine ASCII reference tables that map ASCII numeric values to the corresponding symbols, you will find that most tables specify the ASCII numeric values in both decimal and hexadecimal. ASCII reference tables use decimal and hexadecimal numbers because programmers use these tables. Although most programmers equate an ASCII character with a byte (eight bits), the ASCII encoding system is really a 7-bit data-encoding scheme for computers. Table 1.2 shows the ASCII codes for the first five letters of the English alphabet. The table shows each code in its character, decimal, hexadecimal, and binary format.

Character	Decimal	Hex	Binary
A	65	0x41	01000001
B	66	0x42	01000010
C	67	0x43	01000011
D	68	0x44	01000100
E	69	0x45	01000101

Table 1.2 Examples of ASCII codes in character, decimal, hex, and binary formats.

As a personal-computer (or PC) programmer, you may be more familiar with the *extended-ASCII* character set. Extended-ASCII codes use an 8-bit pattern to represent data. Using the eighth bit, your programs can use extended-ASCII codes to display special characters such as box drawing characters (⌐, ⌐, ∟, ⌐, and so on). For the sake of simplicity, this book will use the term *ASCII* to refer to extended ASCII.

Today, most computers use eight bits to represent a byte. As discussed, hexadecimal provides a convenient way to represent a byte of data. Hexadecimal is the base 16 numbering system. Hexadecimal digits consist of the numbers 0 through 9 and the letters *A* through *F* (or *a* through *f*). As shown in Table 1.3, it takes four binary digits to represent 16 values. Using two hexadecimal digits (four bits each), you can represent an 8-bit byte.

Decimal	Hex	Binary	Decimal	Hex	Binary
0	0x00	0000	8	0x08	1000
1	0x01	0001	9	0x09	1001
2	0x02	0010	10	0x0A	1010
3	0x03	0011	11	0x0B	1011
4	0x04	0100	12	0x0C	1100
5	0x05	0101	13	0x0D	1101
6	0x06	0110	14	0x0E	1110
7	0x07	0111	15	0x0F	1111

Table 1.3 The hexadecimal (base 16) numbering system.

Since a byte is the smallest unit of data that your program can process, your programs will always work with some combination of 8-bit data units. The largest number that eight bits (11111111) can represent is 255 (base 10) or 0xFF (base 16). A two-digit hex number can represent the 256 different values a byte can hold, as well as every possible extended-ASCII code.

If you don't usually work with binary information, try to view byte data as two-digit hex values. With ASCII codes, a byte can represent any character in the English language. If you understand the implicit relationship between an ASCII code, a two-digit hex number, a byte, and eight bits, you can more easily manipulate your data as you package it for use on a network.

For example, you know that every two-digit hex number represents a byte (or eight bits) of data. As such, when you need to use binary values, you can easily convert a two-digit hex number to eight bits of binary information. Also, if your data is text, you can use hexadecimal-ASCII codes to easily convert each text character into an 8-bit binary number.

However, you will appreciate hexadecimal numbers most when you convert data in the opposite direction—from binary to text. If you use hexadecimal values when you convert binary data to text, each two-digit hex number will represent one byte of data. Using ASCII codes, each byte will represent a text character. After you convert your data into text or character strings, you can easily use this data in your applications.

Figure 1.2 shows the transformation of binary computer data into information readable by people. The computer represents data as a series of 1's and 0's. To start, you can convert each combination of eight bits into a two-digit hexadecimal number. Next, you can use ASCII codes to translate each two-digit hexadecimal number into a character of text.

Binary Computer Data	01001000	01001001	00100000	01001011	01000101	01001110
Hexadecimal Programmer Data	0x48	0x49	0x20	0x4B	0xB5	0x4E
ASCII Text User Data	H	I		K	E	N

Figure 1.2 Translating binary data to text.

Each day, people use decimal numbers to count money, quantify test results, and much more. As such, people are comfortable using decimal numbers. At first, you may feel uncomfortable using hex and binary numbers to represent your data, especially if you usually work with text. However, the more you work with binary and hex numbers, the more natural these numbers will feel to you.

As an Internet programmer, you must work with binary data. As you develop Internet programs, you will find that hex numbers let you more easily manipulate binary numbers and bytes of data. As you become proficient with binary and hexadecimal numbers, you may better understand low-level, Internet programming concepts.

UNDERSTANDING COMMUNICATION SIGNALS

Computers communicate in a binary language that consists of 1's and 0's only. As an Internet programmer, you need to know how to communicate in that language also. The following paragraphs briefly describe how computers use electronic signals to represent binary data. It is not essential for you to understand this information in detail. However, if you are curious how computer hardware transmits binary data, you may find the following paragraphs interesting.

Regardless of the language or languages you speak, you use words and sentences to communicate with other people. Instead of words and sentences, computers use electronic signals. Your words and sentences consist of letters, numbers, and symbols. Computers communicate with electronic signals that represent 1's and 0's.

Electronic signals come in two basic forms: *digital* and *analog*. Because computers can easily represent digital signals using 1's and 0's, computers normally use digital signals to represent data internally. As an Internet programmer, however, you may find analog signals more interesting. Computers typically use analog signals when they transmit data to one another across a network. View analog signals as waves, much like those you see in an ocean. For example, Figure 1.3 shows a simple analog signal.

Ocean Wave   Electrical Wave

Figure 1.3 A simple analog signal.

Note: *The process of creating signals is a subject for people interested in electronics—not programming. This book will not discuss the production of electronic signals.*

The number of times a wave occurs in a fixed time interval (such as one second) defines the wave's *frequency.* Analog waves can vary in frequency. For example, one electronic circuit might generate 100 analog waves per second. Another circuit might generate 1,000 waves per second. As such, you can say the circuit that generates 1,000 waves per second has a higher frequency than the circuit that generates 100 waves per second.

Many electronic circuits are capable of generating both signal frequencies. In other words, a single electronic circuit might be able to generate 1,000 analog waves per second and then change the signal frequency to 100 waves per second. This process of varying the frequency of analog waves is called *frequency modulation* (FM) or just plain *modulation.* For example, Figure 1.4 shows two analog signals. As you can see, the left signal has more waves than the right signal. In other words, the left signal occurs with greater frequency than the right signal. As such, the left signal is a higher frequency signal. When computers use binary code to transmit information, they commonly use a high frequency analog signal to represent a 1 and a low frequency signal to represent a 0.

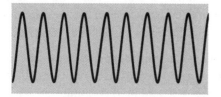
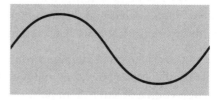

High Frequency Signal   Low Frequency Signal

Figure 1.4 *Analog signals with different frequencies.*

Telephone lines use analog signals to carry information. Your computer uses a modem to translate binary data into an analog signal for transmission over a telephone line. Modems use frequency modulation to represent binary data. The term *modem* is shorthand for modulator/demodulator. A modem transmits binary data by representing a 0 as a decreased-frequency signal and a 1 as an increased-frequency signal. In other words, to represent binary data, the modem *modulates* the frequency of an analog signal. Figure 1.5 shows how the letter *A* (ASCII 0x41 or binary 01000001) appears as an analog signal created by a modem. When a second modem receives this signal, that modem *demodulates* the analog signal and converts it into 1's and 0's that your computer understands.

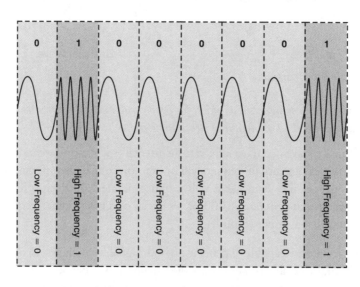

Binary: 01000001   Hex: 0x41   ASCII: A

Figure 1.5 *The letter A represented as an FM signal created by a modem.*

How Computers Transfer Data

When computers communicate with other devices, computers transfer data in *parallel* or in *serial* format. Most PCs use parallel communication for transferring data to their printers. Parallel communication simply means you simultaneously transfer data across multiple lines or wires. To send a byte (eight bits) of data over a parallel cable, the computer sends the eight bits over eight wires at the same time. Parallel communication uses lines connected in parallel, as shown in Figure 1.6.

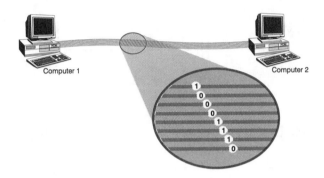

Figure 1.6 *Two computers connected for parallel communication.*

As shown in Figure 1.6, parallel communication lets the computer use eight wires to transfer an entire byte at one time. In contrast, serial data transfer occurs over one wire, one bit at a time. Normally, networks use serial communication to transfer data from one computer to the next. Serial communication requires bits of data to line up behind each other. For example, Figure 1.7 shows the binary number 10001110 being transferred between two computers. As you can see, the bits will arrive one at a time.

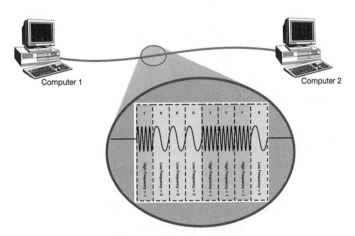

Figure 1.7 *Two computers connected for serial communication.*

Computers use different methods to transfer data over wires. You should understand three important terms that network professionals commonly use to describe these methods of transfer: simplex, half-duplex, and full-duplex communication. *Simplex communication* occurs when data flows in one direction only. *Half-duplex communication* lets data flow in two directions, but only one direction at a time. *Full-duplex communication* lets data flow in both directions simultaneously. Figure 1.8 shows the difference in data flow between systems that use simplex, half-duplex, and full-duplex communication methods.

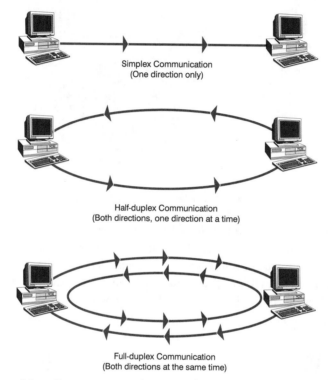

Figure 1.8 Patterns of data flow in simplex, half-duplex, and full-duplex communication.

UNDERSTANDING COMMUNICATION SWITCHING

To perform data transfers, networks use *communication switching*. Communication switching lets hardware devices share physical lines of communication. To understand communication switching, consider telephone communications.

Suppose, for example, no one shared telephone lines. To create a telephone system that lets you avoid sharing (communication switching) lines, you will need to connect a wire between your telephone and each telephone you may ever call. Thus, if you wish to call 1,000 different people, you will need to plug 1,000 wires into the back of your phone. Since adhering to such a principle is not very practical, most people share phone lines with their neighbors and co-workers. Likewise, networks use communication switching. The two common methods of communication switching are circuit switching and packet switching.

UNDERSTANDING CIRCUIT SWITCHING

Circuit switching creates a single, unbroken path between two devices that want to communicate. While these two devices talk, no other devices can use this path. However, when the two devices finish talking, they release the communication path, so other devices can use it. In other words, circuit switching lets devices share lines of communication, but each device must wait its turn.

A simple example of circuit switching is an A-B switch box that many people use to connect two computers to a single printer. In order for a computer to send data to the printer, you must toggle the switch to form a single, unbroken path (a circuit) between the computer and printer. This type of path, or circuit, is a *point-to-point connection*. As shown in Figure 1.9, only one computer at a time can use the printer.

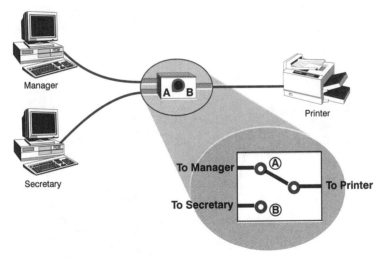

Figure 1.9 An example of circuit switching using an A-B switch.

UNDERSTANDING PACKET SWITCHING

Most modern computer networks, including the Internet, use *packet switching*. In fact, you can refer to the Internet as a *packet-switched network*. In a packet-switched network, programs break data into pieces, called *packets*, and transmit them between computers.

Consider the following two methods of transporting people. Suppose you need to transport a group of 50 people from one side of a town to the other. You can use a bus to transport everyone at the same time, or you can load your group members into any number of separate automobiles. Assume you can use many different streets to travel from one side of town to the other. If everyone travels by bus, they travel the same path—the path followed by the bus. If group members drive to the destination in separate cars, they might follow the same path, but not necessarily.

In the this example, the group of 50 people is like 50 bytes of data. In a packet-switched network, you can transmit your data (group of people) in a single packet (bus). You can also transmit your data in multiple packets (separate cars). Just as the bus and cars in the example can follow different paths to the same destination, packets in a packet-switched network can follow different network paths to reach the same network computer.

To compare packet-switching and circuit-switching configurations, assume you break the communication path in each type of configuration. For example, in the circuit-switch shown in Figure 1.9, when you move the switch connection to the "B" side of the switch box, you break the connection between the printer and the Manager computer. As a result, the Manager computer cannot print. A circuit-switched system requires an unbroken path for communication.

Conversely, in a packet-switched network, data can flow along multiple paths. For example, in Figure 1.10, data can travel between the Home and Office computers using several different routes. Breaking one path does not necessarily mean your data will be unable to reach its destination.

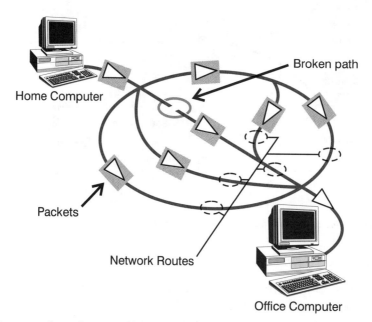

Figure 1.10 Data traveling along a packet-switched network.

On the surface, a packet-switched network seems rather simple and straightforward. Programs just send the packets out, tell them to travel in only one direction (simplex communication), and let packets find their way to their destination, right? Well, not quite—remember that most computer networks consist of more than two computers.

A packet-switched network will have multiple paths between many computers. Data can travel in both directions. As such, each packet must carry its destination address. (Packets usually carry the address of their source computer also.) As you will learn, understanding packet addresses is an essential part of programming the Internet.

UNDERSTANDING NETWORK TOPOLOGIES

As you can imagine, you have an unlimited number of ways to connect computers. The more computers you have—the more options you have. Each connection creates a new path for data to follow. *Network topology* refers to a network's shape or geometric arrangement of computers. Topology gives you a way to compare and classify different networks. The three most common topologies are the star, ring, and bus.

Since the Internet is an internetwork (interconnecting networks), you may come across all of these topologies on the Internet. The following paragraphs briefly describe each of the most commonly used topologies. By understanding the differences between topologies, you will more easily understand much of the network literature you are likely to encounter about the Internet.

UNDERSTANDING A STAR TOPOLOGY

In a *star topology*, all computers (nodes) connect to a central computer or hub. Direct connections between two computers (other than a hub computer) do not exist in a star topology. Figure 1.11 shows a computer network using a star topology.

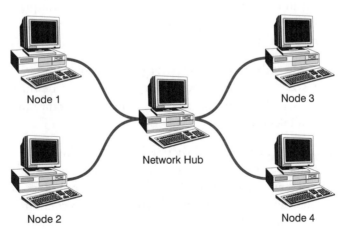

Figure 1.11 A star topology.

Although Federal Express delivers packages and not computer data, their package delivery system is similar to packet transfers in a star topology. Federal Express initially ships all packages to a central company location in Memphis, Tennessee. From there, Federal Express re-ships each package to its ultimate destination. As you can see in Figure 1.12, the Federal Express distribution network looks like an exploding star.

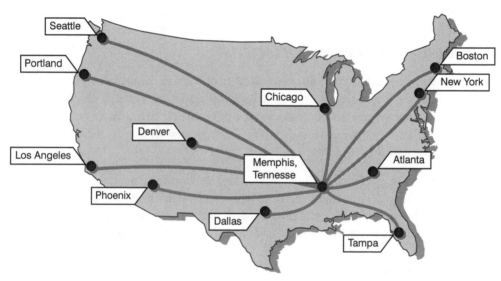

Figure 1.12 *The Federal Express distribution network shaped like a star.*

If Federal Express used a point-to-point delivery system, they would transport packages from each sending point to each destination point. Their package distribution network would look like a spider's web. Such a system would require many more Federal Express airplanes and trucks. Each path in the spider-web network would require its own delivery vehicle, or Federal Express would need an extremely complex delivery schedule.

Using a star topology, Federal Express ships all packages to a central location. At the central head-quarters, Federal Express collects all shipments and sorts packages by destination. The following day, Federal Express ships, at the same time, all packages destined for the same location. The system is simple, efficient, and effective.

In a similar way, data packets in a star topology travel to a central hub. The central hub then re-transmits the packets to their destination address. The major advantage of the star topology is that a communications breakdown between any computer and the hub does not affect any other computer on the network. For example, think of a computer-hub communications breakdown as a blizzard in Buffalo. Although Federal Express may not be able to ship packages to or from Buffalo, Federal Express can deliver packages to all its other sites without any delay. The major disadvantage of the star topology is that if the central hub breaks, you are in big trouble—a broken central hub brings down the entire network.

UNDERSTANDING A RING TOPOLOGY

In a *ring topology*, the network has no end connections. In other words, the network forms a contiguous ring (an unbroken path, but not necessarily circular) through which data can travel. For example, from any point in the network, you can travel in one direction and eventually return to your starting point. Because of this circular link, data in a ring topology flows in only one direction around the ring. Figure 1.13 shows a computer network using a ring topology.

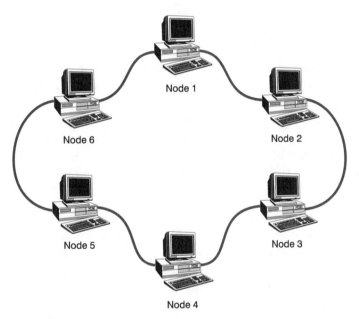

Figure 1.13 A ring topology.

Unlike the star, a ring topology requires an unbroken path between all computers on the network. A break anywhere in the ring will cause all network communications to stop. Another weakness in ring topologies is that data passes every computer on the network. As such, any computer on the network can be used to eavesdrop or spy on the data circulating throughout the ring.

UNDERSTANDING A BUS TOPOLOGY

A *bus topology* uses a single transmission medium called a bus. All computers in such a network attach directly to the bus. Normally, a coaxial cable serves as the transmission medium in a bus topology. Figure 1.14 shows a computer network in a bus topology configuration.

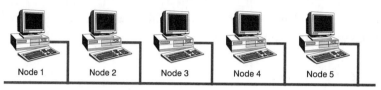

Figure 1.14 *A bus topology.*

In a bus topology, data can flow in either direction. Bus topologies require you to attach special end connectors (terminators) to both ends of the bus (cable). Like a ring network, a physical break anywhere in the bus causes all network communications to fail. Network security is weak in bus and ring topologies for the same reasons—data passes every computer on the bus.

COMPARING NETWORK TOPOLOGIES

In the last section, you learned some of the differences between star, ring, and bus topologies. For example, you now know that in a star topology, a break between a computer and the hub does not affect network communications. You also know that in a ring and bus topology, a break anywhere in the network path causes all network communications to stop. These characteristics would seem to favor a star topology. However, the hub in a star topology is a rather sophisticated device. In many cases, the hub may be another computer. As such, you need to consider this question: *Which is easier to repair—a broken computer or a broken cable?* In most cases, it is probably easier, faster, and more economical to repair or replace a cable.

While the hub remains functional, a star topology has several distinct advantages over a ring or bus topology. However, when the hub fails, the cost (in both time and money) to resolve the problem can be significant. To compare network topologies, network integrators and administrators must weigh different factors. For example, because cables are cheaper than computers to repair or replace, many network administrators prefer to use ring or bus topologies rather than a star topology. As an Internet programmer, you will not need to consider the advantages and disadvantages of network topologies—you will have to program for them all. However, to program effectively, you need to understand the basic differences between the topologies.

UNDERSTANDING BUS ARBITRATION

Regardless of network topology, when two computers try to transmit (or talk) at the same time, data collisions occur. Using *bus arbitration,* computers resolve disputes over which computer can use the bus and when. The two most commonly used methods of bus arbitration are *collision detection* and *token passing.*

UNDERSTANDING COLLISION DETECTION

Many parents teach their children to look both ways before crossing a street—that is, look before they walk. When a network bus uses collision detection for arbitration, computers on the bus listen before they talk. That is, each computer listens to the bus before transmitting data. If a computer hears another computer talking on the bus, the computer must wait until the other computer finishes before it transmits any data. Unfortunately, despite these rules, two computers occasionally transmit data at the same time.

Because accidents (two computers transmitting at the same time) happen, collision detection systems require that a transmitting computer listen to the bus while it is sending data. If the transmitting computer hears data on the bus that is not its own, it must stop sending data and wait a short, but random amount of time before resuming transmission. The random delay provides the network equivalent of "Oh, no, you go first."

When computers listen for network activity before transmitting, they use *carrier sense collision avoidance*. In other words, the computer listens to (senses) the carrier (network bus) to determine if anyone else is communicating. When computers listen for other activity while they transmit, they perform *collision detection*. Computers that use both technologies employ *carrier sense collision detection* (CSCD).

UNDERSTANDING TOKEN PASSING

Token passing systems avoid data collisions by requiring all network computers to obtain permission before they transmit data. To obtain permission to transmit, computers grab a special data packet called a *token*. Think of the token as a permission slip. The permission slip tells the computer that it can transmit data. The permission slip or token travels in an endless path between all the computers on the network.

You might compare a token passing system to a room (network) full of people (computers) seated in a circle with one wireless microphone (token). The people in the room pass the microphone in one direction so everyone gets a chance to hold it. If a person wants to talk (transmit), that person waits until it is his or her turn to hold the microphone. Nobody talks without the microphone. If the person who receives the microphone has nothing to say, he or she simply passes the microphone to the next person.

Just as two computers occasionally transmit at the same time in a collision detection system (despite the rules), token passing systems occasionally lose the token. All token passing systems include technology to detect and recreate lost tokens. Otherwise, all network communication would end each time the token disappeared. As you have learned, a computer grabs and holds the token when it needs to transmit data. However, when the computer finishes, it must re-transmit the token. The token will continue on its path through the network. Eventually, every computer on the network will get a chance to grab and hold the token if it needs to transmit data.

NETWORK TOPOLOGIES VERSUS NETWORK TECHNOLOGIES

You have learned the basic differences among three types of network topologies: star, ring, and bus. Many people use the term *topology* when they really mean to refer to a specific technology.

For example, Ethernet, ARCNET, and IBM Token Ring are three popular and widely used network technologies. You should understand that there is a difference between network topologies and network technologies.

Ethernet is a technology developed in 1973 by a team of researchers, led by Bob Metcalf, at the Xerox Palo Alto Research Center (PARC). You can configure Ethernet networks (or Ethernets) in either a star or bus topology. Typically, if you use coaxial cable as the transmission medium, you will configure the network as a bus. If you use twisted-pair wiring (such as the wire used to connect your telephone to the telephone jack in the wall) for the transmission medium, you will normally configure the Ethernet as a star.

ARCNET is actually an acronym for Attached Resource Computer NETwork. ARCNET is the local area network (LAN) first introduced by the Datapoint Corporation in 1968. Like Ethernet, you can configure ARCNET networks in either a star or bus topology.

IBM Token Ring is an interesting mix of topologies. As the name implies, IBM developed the token ring technology that uses token passing for bus arbitration. IBM Token Ring technology is a hybrid (mix) of star and ring topologies. IBM Token Ring uses a star topology with an IBM device called a Multi-station Access Unit (MAU) as its central hub. However, IBM Token Ring networks also use a ring topology. Each computer on the network uses two cables to connect with the hub. The computer transmits data to the hub on one line and receives data from the hub on the other. As such, an IBM Token Ring network forms a contiguous ring in the shape of a star. Figure 1.15 shows how data flows in an IBM Token Ring network.

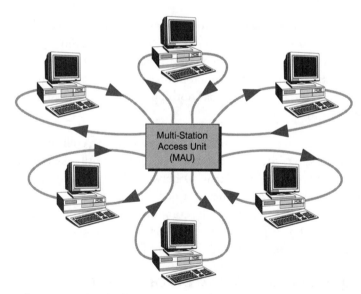

Figure 1.15 Data flow in an IBM Token Ring network.

CONNECTING COMPUTER NETWORKS

As you have learned, the Internet is an internetwork—a system of interconnected networks. Internetworks do not take the form of a particular topology. An internetwork connects networks regardless of their topologies and technologies.

Internetworks commonly use special devices called repeaters, bridges, routers, and gateways to connect independent networks. Local area networks occasionally use these devices to extend connections within a local area network. Although you don't need to know how each of these devices work, you should understand their function.

WHAT IS ATTENUATION?

If you have ever dropped a pebble into a puddle of water, you may have noticed how the wave ripples become smaller as they travel further from where you dropped the pebble. Likewise, the further an analog signal travels, the smaller or weaker it becomes. If there were any objects in the puddle of water, you may have noticed how those objects caused the wave pattern to further dissipate. In a similar fashion, resistance and noise in network transmission lines weaken analog waves. Engineers refer to this signal deterioration as *attenuation*. As you have learned, computers use analog waves or signals to transmit data across networks. Networks use repeaters to overcome attenuation problems.

UNDERSTANDING A REPEATER

As its name implies, a *repeater* copies or repeats signals that it receives. However, a repeater also amplifies all received signals before re-transmission. This means a repeater increases the size of analog waveforms it receives. By increasing the size of the waveform (without changing its frequency), a repeater eliminates the signal loss or attenuation that the waveform experienced during its journey to the repeater. In short, a repeater strengthens an incoming signal before sending the signal on its way. By strategically placing repeaters along a network bus, engineers can extend the distance between adjacent computers.

Long-haul networks may contain many repeaters. Ethernets also frequently use repeaters to extend the length of the bus cable within a local area network. That is, network administrators use repeaters to avoid attenuation problems when they connect two pieces of the same network. In other words, although you can use a repeater as part of an internetwork connection, you can also use repeaters within a single, stand-alone network such as a LAN.

UNDERSTANDING A BRIDGE

A *bridge* interconnects two networks that use the same technology (such as Ethernet or ARCNET). A bridge is more sophisticated than a repeater. For example, assume a bridge interconnects two networks called "Eastside" and "Westside." The bridge will examine all packets on each network data bus. When the bridge sees an Eastside packet destined for an address on the Westside network, the bridge transfers the packet from the Eastside network to the Westside network. The bridge will not transmit a packet to the Westside network if the packet's destination address is on the Eastside network.

In other words, a bridge acts like a traffic cop at a busy intersection beside a bridge that crosses a river. The traffic cop (the bridge) asks the occupants of each vehicle (the Eastside packet) where they want to go. If the occupants specify an address on the other side of the river (Westside address), the traffic cop directs the vehicle across the bridge (to the Westside network). If the occupants specify an Eastside address, the traffic cop waves the vehicle through the intersection. The traffic cop (bridge) only redirects traffic (packets) destined for an address located on the other side of the river (a Westside address).

USING A BRIDGE TO IMPROVE PERFORMANCE

In addition to interconnecting networks, bridges often boost performance, reliability, and security. For example, you have learned that a collision detection system requires a computer to delay transmissions after a data collision occurs. As you add more computers to a network, the number of data collisions rises.

More collisions occur because more computers are trying to transmit data packets at the same time. Like cars on a freeway, packets represent network traffic. As you know, the more cars (packets) you have traveling on the freeway (data bus), the greater the number of collisions. As you attach more computers to a network, data traffic increases. In some cases, traffic can increase to the point that network performance begins to suffer. In effect, traffic jams begin to occur.

Sometimes, you can add a bridge to solve performance problems that result from heavy traffic. In effect, a bridge divides one crowded local area network into two or more networks. For example, suppose the Eastside and Westside networks were originally part of the same local area network. The bridge (traffic cop) keeps Eastside packets on the Eastside network and Westside packets on the Westside network. Eastside packets don't clog the Westside network and Westside packets don't clog the Eastside network. In other words, due to the bridge, the traffic on each network decreases and, as a result, performance increases.

USING A BRIDGE TO IMPROVE RELIABILITY

Network administrators often use a bridge to create two or more smaller networks—even if performance is not a problem on their network. As you have learned, in a ring or bus topology, a single break in the data bus stops all network communications. By partitioning a single LAN into multiple LANs (connected by a bridge), network administrators reduce the impact of a break in the data bus.

For example, consider the imaginary Eastside and Westside networks again. Assume that a network administrator added a bridge to a single local area network to create the two networks. A break in the Eastside network data bus would cause all Eastside network communications to stop. However, computers on the Westside network could continue to function normally—except they could not communicate with any Eastside network computers.

By adding the bridge and dividing a single LAN into two networks, the network administrator improves reliability for the entire network. For example, a single break only affects half the network—not the entire network. Network administrators may repeatedly sub-divide networks until they reach an acceptable level of reliability.

Using a Bridge to Improve Security

As you have learned, in bus and ring topologies, data passes each computer on the network. As such, any network user can utilize a special electronic device, called a *network analyzer*, to intercept and examine data packets on the network. Depending on the type of network, you can use software to accomplish the same task.

Network analyzers, either hardware or software, help network professionals troubleshoot network problems. Network professionals analyze network traffic for a variety of reasons. For example, they may monitor traffic to help identify traffic problems such as congestion. In other cases, network analyzers monitor packets to help a programmer debug a network program. These are legitimate reasons for monitoring network traffic. Unfortunately, network analyzers can present a security problem for a network administrator if the network carries sensitive information.

A bridge will not prevent unauthorized monitoring. However, a network administrator can use a bridge to divide a local area network into secure and unsecured LANs. In that way, the network administrator can restrict the flow of sensitive data to one LAN and thereby reduce the data's vulnerability to tampering or monitoring.

Understanding a Router

A *router* transfers or routes data between networks. Although a router can transfer data between networks that use the same technologies, routers commonly transfer data between different technologies such as Ethernet and IBM Token Ring. Since the Internet consists of thousands of networks that use many different technologies, routers are an essential part of the Internet. A router has an address on the network; a bridge does not. This difference is the key to understanding the difference between a bridge and a router. Networks frequently use a router as an intermediate destination.

In other words, a computer can send a packet destined for another network to a router. The router will transfer the packet to the other network. On the other hand, a bridge must examine all data on the bus to determine which packets to transfer between networks. As such, computers never send packets directly to the bridge—doing so is unnecessary. A router never examines a packet on the data bus unless the packet contains the router's address.

Understanding a Gateway

Gateway is a generic term that can refer to three types of network entities. You can refer to a router as a gateway. When you use the term in this way, a gateway is identical to a router as described in the previous paragraphs. A gateway can also refer to something called an *application gateway*.

Application gateways translate data that specific network programs use. The most common type of application gateway is one that e-mail applications use. For example, you can use MCI Mail to send e-mail to someone on a private company's local area network in another state. Your e-mail message might travel from MCI Mail to the Internet and from the Internet to the destination LAN. At each interconnection, an application gateway (for e-mail) would translate your message into a format suitable for further transmission.

As you will learn in Chapter 2, networks use a set of rules, called *protocols*, for all data transmission. Different types of networks use different sets of rules. The third type of gateway translates data from one set of network protocols to another.

Understanding the Structure of a Network

The previous sections introduced a lot of important concepts and definitions. However, most of the discussion focused on the physical structure of networks. In this section, you will start to explore some of the design concepts that underlie a network's physical structure. As you read the following paragraphs, you should try to relate network design concepts to a network's physical or hardware elements. If you want to be an effective and proficient Internet programmer, you need to understand a few basic network design concepts and how these concepts relate to the hardware elements that make up a network.

Understanding Conceptual Components of a Network

Conceptually, network designers divide a network into two fundamental components: *network applications* and a *network communication subsystem*. Network applications use the communication subsystem to transmit data across the network. In other words, the communication subsystem is the vehicle that delivers your data. If you want to be a successful Internet programmer, you must understand how this subsystem works. That is, you need to know how to drive the network data-delivery vehicle.

You may come across literature about the Internet, or networks in general, that refers to a network's communication subsystem as a communications subnet, a transmission system, or a transport system. The term *transport system* probably comes closest to the total idea of a network communication subsystem. The subsystem's primary responsibility is to *transport* data and messages between network computers and applications.

As an Internet programmer, you will develop programs that communicate with other applications across the Internet. For these programs to function effectively, they must use the network communication subsystem to transport your application data across the Internet. As such, understanding the network communication subsystem is critical to your success as an Internet programmer. The best way to understand network communications is to view the subsystem from the perspective of a network designer.

UNDERSTANDING COMMUNICATION SUBSYSTEMS

As you have learned, communication switching lets computers and networks share physical lines of communication. You should understand, however, that communication switching concepts focus on the communication process, not the purpose of the communication. For example, telephone companies form a network that uses communication switching techniques. Telephone networks use a form of circuit switching. On the other hand, computer networks almost always use packet switching—the Internet is no exception.

Packet switching networks consist of two basic subcomponents: the switching elements and the transmission lines. As an Internet programmer, you will send data across the Internet over transmission lines and through the network's switching elements. A packet switching network is much like a railway system. The rails over which the trains travel are like the transmission lines. The trains are like packets. Railway switches (switching elements) exist at various points along the railroad. By changing these switches, railroad engineers control the destination of each train (packet) that passes through the switching station (element).

The switching elements within the communication subsystem can consist of a host computer or a device (such as a bridge or router). Usually, you can consider a switching element to be any device that helps a data packet find its destination. Internet literature may use any of the following terms to refer to network switching elements: interface message processors (IMP), communications computer, packet switch, node, or data switching exchange.

As you build your understanding of network structures and their designs, precise terminology becomes critical. *Internet Programming* will use the term *packet switch* to refer to switching elements within the Internet. However, you should understand that a packet switch can be a host computer, bridge, router, or some other device that performs similar functions.

Transmission lines consist of the physical elements that connect packet switches. Internet literature often refers to transmission lines as circuits, communication channels, or just plain channels. When referring to data in the context of its movement across a network, Internet literature may refer to a transmission line as the *data stream*. You should understand that data stream refers to the data riding on (or being transferred over) the network's transmission lines. Internet and network literature may refer to transmitting data across the Internet as "pumping data into the channel" or "sending data across a circuit." You should understand that these phrases and others mean placing your data on the transmission lines for delivery to another network destination.

UNDERSTANDING COMMUNICATION SUBSYSTEM DESIGNS

In his book *Computer Networks*, Andrew S. Tanenbaum identifies two basic designs for communication subsystems: *point-to-point channels* and *broadcast channels*. In Section 2, you will learn that the design of your Internet applications depends on the type of channel used to transmit data. Applications that use point-to-point channels are significantly different from applications that use broadcast channels. In a point-to-point communications network, designers connect host computers so that data passes from one packet switch to the next. In a broadcast communications network, all packet switches on the network receive all packets of data.

UNDERSTANDING BROADCAST CHANNEL DESIGNS

Network designers classify broadcast-channel designs in terms of how the network allocates the communications channel for use by attached hosts. You can refer to these designs as *static* and *dynamic* allocation methods. Static allocation assigns each host computer a specific time slot and a specific period of time for data transmissions. This time period is static or unchanging. In a computer network, static allocation is inefficient. Each computer controls its assigned time slot. Even if a computer has no data to transmit, no other network computer can use this time slot.

Typically, networks use dynamic allocation methods to allocate the communication channel. When the network controls access to the communication channel dynamically, any computer with data to transmit can use the channel. Two words describe the key design issue in a dynamically allocated broadcast channel: *bus arbitration*. Network designers can use a centralized or decentralized method for dynamic allocation of a broadcast channel.

Network professionals use the terms *centralized* and *decentralized* to describe bus arbitration methods with which you are already familiar. For example, centralized dynamic allocation uses a token passing system for bus arbitration. As the need arises, allocation of the broadcast channel (permission to transmit) changes or is dynamic. The token controls permission to transmit. The token is the centralized authority that determines which host may transmit—no host can transmit unless it possesses the token.

When you hear or read the term *decentralized dynamic allocation*, think collision detection. In a decentralized design, each host must determine if it's okay to transmit. There is no central authority, such as a token, that grants permission. Data collisions are inevitable in a decentralized design. As such, a decentralized dynamic allocation design requires a collision detection system.

PUTTING IT ALL TOGETHER

You can compare programming the Internet to driving a car. You don't need to be an automotive expert to drive a car. Likewise, you don't need to know how to design networks to program the

Internet. However, an automotive mechanic can more easily spot problems and take steps to avoid further complications than someone who does not understand automobile engines and transmissions. By understanding certain aspects of network design, you can avoid problems within your Internet applications and more easily diagnose errors when they occur.

This chapter introduced you to computer networks in very general terms. In Chapter 2, you will learn important network design concepts that will help you understand the Internet's powerful network engine—the TCP/IP protocol suite. However, before you move on to Chapter 2, make sure you understand the following key concepts:

- ✓ Two or more interconnected computers, capable of communicating with each other, form a computer network. Two or more interconnected networks form an internetwork—an internet.

- ✓ Communication switching is a technique that lets computers share physical lines of communication.

- ✓ Packet switching is a form of communication switching that transmits information in self-contained units of data called packets.

- ✓ Network topology refers to the physical shape or geometric pattern of computer connections in a network. Common topologies include a star, ring, and bus.

- ✓ Network administrators use repeaters, bridges, routers, and gateways to connect networks.

- ✓ Conceptually, a network consists of two basic components: applications and a communication subsystem.

Chapter 2
Understanding Network Architecture

When an architect designs a skyscraper, he or she never tries to work out all the details in one sitting. The architect doesn't sit at a drafting table and draw one blueprint that specifies the building's exterior dimensions and facade, floor plan, use of construction materials, wiring, plumbing, and so on. The design task would be overwhelming, and the resulting blueprint would be far too complex and confusing to be useful to any of the contractors who would actually construct the building. Instead, the architect breaks the design task into simpler steps.

Rather than developing one comprehensive blueprint that incorporates everything, the architect drafts a series of blueprints, each of which covers one small aspect of the building's construction. For example, the architect might draft one blueprint per building floor. Likewise, as an applications programmer, you usually design and build extremely sophisticated and complex programs using small, simple, modular blocks of code.

As you have learned in Chapter 1, you can use this "divide and conquer" approach for more than just design tasks. For example, you can conquer a difficult learning task, such as understanding the Internet, if you divide it into easily manageable subtasks. In other words, each component within the Internet, by itself, is not too difficult to understand. However, if you try to digest the entire thing at once, the complexity will likely overwhelm you.

As you may know, if you carefully define and maintain the interface between code modules (the parameter list), you can make extensive changes within a module without affecting any other code module in your program. Network designers build networks using similar principles. The term *network architecture* refers to the modular format and design structure of a computer network. The term describes how network developers piece together network components to build the network. By the time you finish this chapter, you will understand the following key concepts:

- Network concepts are easier to understand than network terminology
- Protocols define rules that network software must use to send and receive data
- The ISO/OSI network model describes networks as layers of functionality
- Each layer in a network performs a well-defined function
- The client/server model simplifies the development of network software

UNDERSTANDING NETWORK TERMS AND CONCEPTS

If you want to increase your knowledge and understanding of networks, pay close attention to network terminology. When you hear or read an unfamiliar term, take time to learn what the term means. Frequently, an unfamiliar term may refer to a network concept that you already understand. Protocol discussions are especially notorious for confusing people unnecessarily. Build your knowledge and understanding of networks as you would build your software. Use small, well-defined conceptual blocks. Make sure you understand each block before you add another. Use multiple sources of information, such as different books and magazines. Tap the knowledge of your co-workers. Network concepts are actually much easier to understand than network terms.

After you grasp a network concept, look for other terms that describe the concept. The more sources of information you access, the broader your exposure to the many different terms used to describe the same concepts. Remember, an unfamiliar term may describe a familiar concept. Network professionals often use network terminology casually or imprecisely. You can avoid a lot of confusion if you build a solid foundation of network concepts. One of the most important concepts to grasp is the network protocol—what it is, how it works, and why you need it. Nearly every chapter in this book contains a discussion of network protocols in one context or another.

A BRIEF HISTORY LESSON

Between 1977 and 1984, network professionals developed a network-design model called the Reference Model of Open Systems Interconnection (OSI). As you may know, in an *open system,* the design or features of the system are not proprietary. In other words, you can obtain complete details about the system and freely use them for your own purposes. In fact, the open system designers want you to read and use their specifications. In short, open systems provide the documentation and hooks you can use to create programs that use or extend the system.

Quite often, computer professionals use open system designs to promote standards across the computer industry. In other words, by making a system design open and freely available, the developers hope more people and companies will adopt the design. If enough companies build products that use the design, the design features become a de-facto standard.

The network professionals that developed the OSI model derived the model from a proposal by the International Standards Organization (ISO). Founded in 1946, the ISO sets international standards in all fields except electrical engineering and electronics. The ISO oversees more than 160 technical committees, as well as 2,300 subcommittees and working groups. The ISO includes standards organizations from more than 75 countries. The American National Standards Institute (ANSI) is the United States' member in the ISO.

Network literature commonly refers to the Reference Model of Open Systems Interconnection as the ISO/OSI model. The ISO/OSI acronym acknowledges the ISO's contribution to the creation of the model. To many network professionals, the ISO/OSI model represents an ideal network.

EXAMINING THE ROAD MAP

To create modular, reusable software, application programmers use a variety of design methods, such as structured programming or object-oriented programming. To achieve similar objectives, network designers use a design method called *layering*. In short, network designers place different functionality into each layer. The bottom layer, for example, contains basic communication functionality. The network designers place a second layer on top of the basic communications layer that may add error detection. By building upon each layer's functionality, the network designers create functional networks comprised of layers that are easy to understand. The ISO/OSI reference model represents a network as layers of functionality.

This chapter examines the ISO/OSI network model from a programmer's viewpoint. You should understand that the ISO/OSI model represents a pattern that developers can use to design networks—the ISO/OSI model itself is not a design specification or blueprint for a specific network. In Chapter 3, you will read about the TCP/IP protocol suite—the Internet's powerful network engine. Your knowledge of the ISO/OSI network model will help you understand the TCP/IP protocol suite. As you will discover, the TCP/IP protocol suite departs from the ISO/OSI design guide in several areas. However, to understand these departures and appreciate their significance, you first need to understand the ISO/OSI model.

UNDERSTANDING LAYERING

The ISO/OSI model uses layers to organize a network into well-defined, functional modules. Network designers use the model's descriptions of these layers to build real networks. However, as you will learn in Chapter 3, depending on a network's purpose, a designer may change the number of layers, layer names, and layer functions. As a result, even a network built from the ISO/OSI model can vary quite significantly from the model or from other networks built from the model.

In a layered network, each module (or layer) provides specific functionality or services to its adjacent layers. In addition, each layer shields layers above it from lower-level implementation details. In other words, each layer only cares about its interface to the next layer in the network. Figure 2.1 shows the layers in the ISO/OSI network model. As an applications programmer, you may not view your software as vertical layers of modularity. However, the concept of one module hiding details from another may not be new to you. For example, your programs probably perform file I/O by calling a function or system service.

To use the file I/O service, you don't need to understand (or care) how the service works. Instead, you simply need to know which parameters pass to and from the service and the possible return values. In short, you treat the service as a black box, not caring what is inside. As a programmer opening a file, you can simply call a function or system service and rely upon the fact that your program will receive a file handle or a pointer to a file. Your program can use the file handle to read or write data. You don't worry about how data passes between your program and the hard disk. Nor do you think much about how the hard disk physically stores your data.

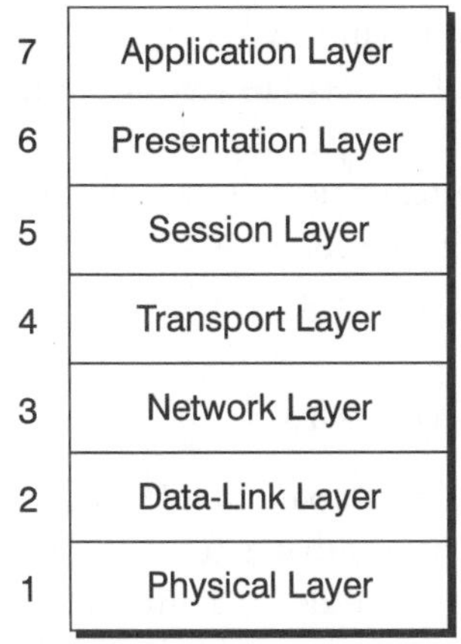

7	Application Layer
6	Presentation Layer
5	Session Layer
4	Transport Layer
3	Network Layer
2	Data-Link Layer
1	Physical Layer

Figure 2.1 Network layers in the ISO/OSI network model.

Each network layer provides a communication service to the layer above it. Network professionals design each network layer to hide, from the layer above it, all implementation details related to the layer's services. By building on each layer's services, network designers create functional modules with well-defined interfaces.

UNDERSTANDING NETWORK COMMUNICATIONS

As you learned in Chapter 1, networks consist of two basic components: applications and a network communications subsystem. Chapter 1's discussion of the communication subsystem focused primarily on the relationship between the communication subsystem and the network's physical elements. In this chapter, you will learn about the communication subsystem in a more abstract sense—a way that should make sense to you as a programmer.

As you have learned, eventually all computer-based communications translate into 1's and 0's. Since a network consists of interconnected computers, you can correctly say that networks communicate using the same binary language. However, as an applications programmer, you normally don't write programs in binary code. Instead, you use one or more computer programming languages to express your code. A programming language provides abstractions you use to develop computer programs. Within a network, protocols represent a similar type of abstraction you can use to design network communications.

WHAT IS A PROTOCOL?

A protocol is a set of rules and accepted conventions for communication. You might hear the term *protocol* in the context of diplomatic communications between countries. For example, government leaders might fire, or call home, a foreign diplomat for violating local protocols. Also, the nightly news may explain a foreign diplomat's strange behavior as a local protocol in the foreign country. In each case, protocol refers to the accepted (conventional) method or rules.

Protocols vary between countries and cultures. For example, in many cultures, a handshake is a form of greeting—it is the accepted protocol to communicate a greeting. In other cultures, men and women kiss each other as a form of greeting (the kiss is a communication protocol that says "hello"). Within a network, computers must follow established protocols that control communication. In other words, data communication protocols specify the rules programs must follow to transmit and receive data in an orderly fashion.

UNDERSTANDING NETWORK PROTOCOLS

As you have learned, networks use functional modules called layers. You have also learned that a protocol is a set of rules and conventions that a network layer uses for communication. In a layered network, each network layer uses well-defined protocols to communicate with its surrounding layers. Figure 2.2 shows a simple network based on the ISO/OSI network model. The figure represents the two network host computers as OSI layers. The arrows between each layer represent the communication paths between the layers.

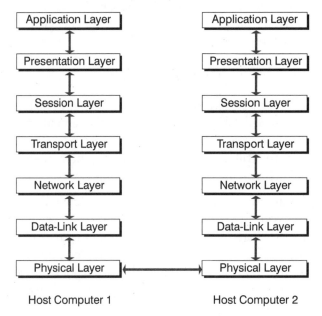

Figure 2.2 *A simple two-host network based on the ISO/OSI model.*

Within the ISO/OSI model, use the layer name to identify a layer's protocols. For example, refer to the transport-layer protocols as the transport protocols. Likewise, the network-layer protocols are the network protocols. You can refer to network communication between layers as *conversations*. For example, you can say the network layer carries on a conversation with the transport layer (or vice versa). Protocols define the rules for such conversations.

UNDERSTANDING PEER PROCESSES

Conceptually, when two host computers talk to each other, the corresponding layers within each host also carry on a conversation. You refer to corresponding layers in different network hosts as *peer processes*. For example, Figure 2.3 shows a two-node network model with a dotted line drawn between peer processes.

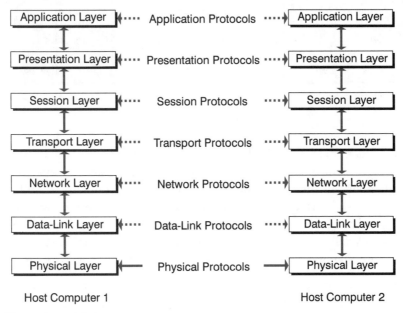

Figure 2.3 *Network model showing peer processes.*

Communication between peer processes is *virtual communication*. In reality, all communication between network hosts occurs in the bottom (physical) network layer, where the actual hardware (physical) connections exist. In short, it's at the physical layer where the electronic signals travel across wires between computers. You can refer to network communications that occur in the physical layer as *physical communication*.

UNDERSTANDING VIRTUAL COMMUNICATION

As briefly discussed, when two computers communicate, the different layers on each computer converse. In actuality, however, data sent from a host computer flows vertically downward to the bottom or physical layer in a network model. Within the physical layer, data flows horizontally (across actual network transmission lines—through the communication channel) to the destination host. At the destination host, data flows upward through the network layers. Figure 2.4 shows the physical path of data within a network model.

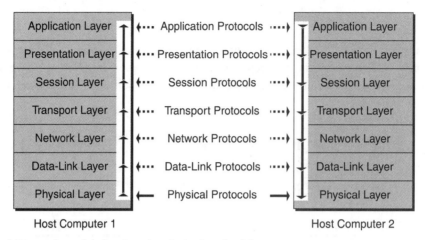

Figure 2.4 *Network model showing the physical path of data.*

As you can see, data from any layer in the sending host will eventually reach or pass through the corresponding layer in the destination host. Networks do not transfer data directly between peer processes. Rather, virtual communication occurs. With virtual communication between corresponding layers in two hosts, conversation appears to occur between the two layers. In reality, however, no such direct communication between peers exists. By using the virtual communication model, network designers (and Internet programmers) can ignore the details of layers beneath the two communicating peers. You can refer to such communication as a *virtual conversation.*

This concept of virtual conversations between peer processes may be new to you. However, you need to know this concept to understand much of the literature written about network communications and, more importantly, network programming. As you will learn, the concept of virtual conversations between peer processes simplifies network programming.

UNDERSTANDING COMMUNICATION SERVICES

Each layer in the ISO/OSI model provides specific communication services to the layer above it. In other words, each network layer performs a function upon which the layer above it depends. Likewise, with the exception of the bottom-level physical layer, each network layer builds upon the layer beneath it to add functionality. Each network layer performs one or more specific functions. Network designers refer to a layer's functionality in terms of services (or capabilities) the layer offers to the layer above it.

Each network layer follows specific rules (protocols) that define which services the layer offers. In short, a service defines a capability the layer provides to the layer above it, such as error detection. Protocols, in turn, are the rules the layer must follow to implement the service. You should understand that the ISO/OSI network model sharply distinguishes between a service and a protocol. Later sections in this chapter explain the specific services provided by each layer in the ISO/OSI model. For now, you simply need to understand the relationship between services and protocols.

SERVICES VERSUS PROTOCOLS

To understand the difference between a service and a protocol, consider what you know about the postal service. When you mail a letter to someone, you write the person's address on the outside of the envelope. The purpose or function of the address is to ensure that your letter reaches the intended recipient. In other words, the service or functionality provided by an address is correct mail delivery.

As you know, addresses on an envelope normally follow a standard format. The first line contains the recipient's name. The second line contains the recipient's street address. The last line usually contains a city, state, and zip code. Postal workers expect the sequence of information on each line to follow a specific format. For example, on the second line of the address, postal workers expect to see the street number before the street name. Likewise, on the last line, they expect to see a city, state, and zip code (in that order).

The address format on an envelope is based on a postal *protocol.* In the same way, a network service defines or describes a function and purpose, such as error detection. A network protocol defines or describes the format and structure of data packets that network software modules use to provide the service. In the case of the error detection service, a protocol would define which error conditions the service must detect.

In a similar way, a network layer requests services from the layers beneath it. The layer's protocols define the packet format and data structure to use for such service requests. Eventually, these service requests flow down to the physical layer, where they become data packets. As you examine each network layer, ask yourself, "What services does the layer provide?" As you will discover, when a network layer needs a specific service, the layer must use a specific packet format (protocol) to request the service.

In Section 2 of this book, you will write Internet programs. You will learn to use network services that are commonly available on TCP/IP networks. For example, in Section 2, you will write programs that use Windows-based services called the Winsock. Your programs will use the Winsock services to perform specific functions, such as looking up Internet addresses. You can picture your programs as layered on top of the Winsock services.

UNDERSTANDING MODES OF SERVICE

Networks can use several different methods to provide the same communication services between peer processes. You can refer to these different methods as *modes of service.* In short, a mode of service specifies how the layer performs an operation. One mode of service might check for errors while another may not. Network designers build modes of service into network protocols. In other words, when you want a service to perform an operation a specific way, you must specify a protocol that provides that mode of service.

Normally, your application's requirements will dictate that you use specific modes of service. For example, if your application requires error control, you will design your application around a protocol that has built-in error control. In other words, your application must use a protocol designed to provide error control as a mode of service. If an existing protocol does not offer all the modes of service your application requires, you must design your own protocol to implement all the required modes.

Your programs can request a communication service and ask the network to use a specific protocol to provide that service. If the communication service is available using that protocol, the network will provide the service. However, if the service is unavailable with the specified protocol, your program will receive an error message. If you don't specify a protocol, the network will provide the service using a default protocol. The mode of service that your application requires usually dictates your choice of protocol.

DEFINING CONNECTION-ORIENTED SERVICES

Chapter 1 introduced communication switching as a way to establish a communication path between two devices. As discussed, one form of communication switching is circuit switching. As you have learned, circuit switching creates an unbroken path, called a circuit, between two devices that want to communicate. Network professionals refer to this type of circuit (one with an unbroken path) as a point-to-point connection. In general, a network connection includes the path between two network devices, as well as the devices at each end of the path. A point-to-point connection is simply a circuit with an unbroken path between the devices.

Conceptually, a connection-oriented mode of service is the same as a point-to-point service. Connection-oriented services create a virtual circuit, which gives the illusion of a physical communication path. However, an actual circuit does not exist (that is, in reality, an unbroken communication path does not exist). Nonetheless, to an application using a connection-oriented service, the communication channel appears to be a solid, unbroken path for communication. In Chapter 3, you will learn how packet-switching networks provide virtual circuits. For now, you should understand that a connection-oriented service provides a service that appears to be a point-to-point connection.

DEFINING CONNECTIONLESS SERVICES

Whereas a connection-oriented service is similar to telephone communication, a connectionless mode of service provides communication in the form of a delivery service. For example, in a telephone conversation, you speak directly to the person with whom you want to communicate. In contrast, when you write a letter, you rely on someone else to deliver your message. In other words, a connectionless service does not establish a point-to-point connection.

Think of a connectionless service as a pony express mail delivery service. To deliver your letter, a pony express rider moves it from one stop to the next, where he hands the letter off to another rider. Your letter eventually reaches its recipient, but, based on weather conditions or other job hazards (rough terrain, bandits, and so on), the rider may encounter delays. If, instead of one letter, you send five large packages via pony express, each package may be so heavy that it requires its own rider and horse. Although all your packages eventually reach the recipient, weather conditions and other job hazards may slow down or temporarily stop several of the riders. As such, a connectionless service transmits your messages through the communication channel much like pony express riders deliver your letters and packages: your messages occasionally stop or encounter delays, but they eventually reach their destinations.

UNDERSTANDING SEQUENCING

For reasons you will learn in later chapters, a network may break a message into several units of data called packets. The sending host will transmit these packets in the same order as they occur in the original message. However, the packets may not arrive at their destination in the same order or sequence. *Sequencing* defines the order in which hosts receive data or messages. Some protocols guarantee delivery of data in the same order as the transmission sequence. Other protocols do not provide such guarantees. In either case, the receiver must eventually combine packets to build the original message. Most protocols that provide a connection-oriented mode of service will also guarantee proper sequencing. In other words, a connection-oriented protocol normally guarantees that the destination host will receive data transmitted through the communication channel in the same order as the transmission sequence. Normally, connectionless protocols do not guarantee sequencing.

UNDERSTANDING ERROR CONTROL

As messages travel electronically across networks, errors can occur. Such errors can result from electronic noise on the transmission wires or from attenuation (signal loss). An error-control mode of service guarantees that data will arrive at its destination uncorrupted. You may wonder how such a guarantee is at all possible. As with many network concepts, the error-control guarantee is a virtual rather than an actual guarantee. Corrupted data can still reach the destination host's network modules. However, when an error-control mode of service detects data corruption, it automatically requests that the sender re-transmit the data. As a result, corrupted data does not reach the destination application.

An error-control mode of service must detect and handle two forms of corruption: corrupted data and data loss. In other words, if data is modified during transit, error control must detect any data corruption that may result. Likewise, error control must detect any corruption in the communication channel that might cause data to become lost during transit. Generally speaking, protocols detect data corruption with checksums and cyclic redundancy checks (CRCs). Checksums and CRCs are values that programs use to check data transmissions for errors.

UNDERSTANDING CHECKSUMS

Cyclic redundancy checks (CRCs) require more intense computing than checksums. As such, CRCs are often hardware-based. On the other hand, checksums are relatively easy to implement, and most software-based integrity checks use checksums. The following paragraphs describe in general terms how to calculate a checksum.

To create a checksum, your program first divides your data into fixed lengths. (For example, the Internet checksum divides your data into 16-bit units.) Your program treats each data unit as an integer value. The program sums the binary value of each data unit in your entire data block and sends the summation value (called the checksum) with the data.

The receiving computer uses the same method to calculate a new checksum. The receiving computer then compares the new checksum to the transmitted checksum. A non-match indicates an error. Checksums can detect single-bit errors and some multiple-bit errors. In general, checksums are not as effective as the CRC method. However, checksums are easier to implement and thus more widely used. Hardware designs that incorporate data integrity checks (such as Ethernet network interface cards) use CRC values.

Networks can also use a system of acknowledgments to detect corruption in the communication channel. In such a system, both the sender and receiver must transmit acknowledgment messages that confirm the receipt of uncorrupted data. You can refer to this message exchange as a handshake. Figure 2.5 shows a communications handshake that consists of three exchanged messages.

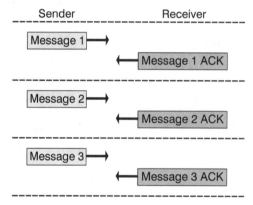

Figure 2.5 An example of a simple communications handshake.

For each message that the receiver sees, the receiver transmits an acknowledgment message (often referred to as an ACK message). Typically, the receiver is a passive player in the message exchange. In other words, the sender initiates all message exchanges, and the receiver simply responds to the sender's messages.

As shown in Figure 2.5, when the receiver sees MESSAGE 1, the receiver sends MESSAGE 1 ACK (an acknowledgment message). After the sender receives MESSAGE 1 ACK, the sender transmits MESSAGE 2. The sender will not transmit MESSAGE 3 until the sender receives MESSAGE 2 ACK. Typically, if the sender does not receive an ACK (acknowledgment) message after a predetermined time (called a time-out period), the sender will transmit the unacknowledged message again.

Suppose the messages shown in Figure 2.5 also contain checksums to further aid error detection. In addition, suppose the receiver sees MESSAGE 2 but the checksum the receiver calculates does not match the transmitted checksum (implying an error during transmission). The receiver can simply reject the corrupted message and wait for the sender to re-transmit the message. However, this method of handling corrupted data can cause unacceptable network communication delays.

Ideally, the receiver should acknowledge that it received the message. However, because of this error, the receiver cannot send a normal acknowledgment. If the receiver transmits MESSAGE 2 ACK, the sender will simply transmit the next message and remain unaware that the communications channel corrupted MESSAGE 2.

Many handshake protocols use a NAK (not acknowledged) message to acknowledge corrupted data. For example, when the receiver detects an invalid checksum in MESSAGE 2, the receiver sends a MESSAGE 2 NAK. When the sender receives MESSAGE 2 NAK, the sender knows that the communications channel corrupted MESSAGE 2. The sender can immediately re-transmit MESSAGE 2 rather than wait for the entire time-out period, and thus avoid unnecessary delays. In Chapter 4, you will learn how Internet protocols use all these methods (checksums, CRC values, and acknowledgment messages) to accomplish error control.

Note: *You can refer to protocols that provide error control and sequencing as **reliable** protocols.*

Understanding Flow Control

You can think of the messages that programs send across the network as a flow of data. To ensure the sender does not transmit data packets faster than the receiver can process the incoming messages, a mode of service must effectively control the data flow. You can refer to this mode of service as *flow control.* Flow control guarantees that the sender will not overrun or overflow the receiver's ability to process data. Flow control must manage data transfer speeds and respect the receiver's data buffer capacity.

Suppose a sender can transmit data at a rate of 1,000 bytes per second. Now, suppose the receiver can process data no faster than 100 bytes per second. Unless the receiving process allocates enough storage space to hold the vast amounts of incoming data, the receiver will lose the overflow data. A flow control mode of service guarantees that overflows will not cause data loss. In Chapter 4, you will learn how Internet protocols manage the flow of data and provide a flow control mode of service.

What Is a Byte-Stream Service?

A byte-stream mode of service treats data as a single, contiguous, serial stream of data. In other words, the service transfers your data without any type of record boundaries or divisions. On the Internet, protocols that provide a byte-stream service usually provide a connection-oriented service and are normally reliable—they provide error control and sequencing.

END-TO-END VERSUS HOP-BY-HOP SERVICES

Protocols can provide communication services, such as error control and flow control, on a hop-by-hop basis or an end-to-end basis. As you have learned, the Internet is a packet-switched network. Data flows from one packet switch to the next until it reaches its final destination. For example, packets of data might need to pass through a router to reach their destination. You can refer to each packet switch (or temporary stop) along the data's path as a *hop*.

A hop-by-hop service performs a function at each hop along the data's path. Suppose, for example, a data-link protocol calculates a checksum. Also, assume the data-link layer includes this checksum in the data transmitted through the communication channel. Assume each packet switch between the sending host and the destination host verifies this checksum. You would refer to an error control mode of service implemented in such a fashion as a hop-by-hop service. Each hop (or stop) performs the error control service.

An end-to-end service, on the other hand, ignores intermediate hops (and services found at those hops) between the sender and receiver. Suppose, for example, a network architect designs a transport protocol to include error control through the use of checksums. In this case, the transport layers in each host computer are responsible for handling the error control.

In other words, the sender calculates a checksum and includes it in the transmitted message. When the peer process in the destination host's transport layer receives the message, it verifies the checksum. Such a protocol provides error control as an end-to-end service. The corresponding layer at each end of the connection performs the error-control service.

UNDERSTANDING THE DESIGN ISSUES

As you have learned, networks consist of two basic conceptual components: applications and a communications subsystem. You have learned that network designers use layers to organize network communications into well-defined, functional modules. These network layers form a model of the network's communications subsystem. You have learned that the communications subsystem includes protocols that define rules and conventions for communications between each of the network layers. Finally, you have learned that protocols deliver various modes of service, such as error control and flow control.

Network professionals develop layers, subsystems, protocols, and modes of service to solve recurring problems encountered by network designers. The following paragraphs introduce you to many problems that network designers face. As you will discover, you have already met the solutions to several of these problems. Later chapters of *Internet Programming* will introduce the solutions that you do not meet in the following paragraphs.

MANAGING CONNECTIONS

Each layer in the network must be able to establish a connection with a peer process on another host. Since network computers invariably run multiple processes at the same time, process identification is important. To establish a connection, a process must identify the destination host and the destination process. In other words, addressing (hosts and processes) is an issue that network designers must resolve. As you will learn, most network messages include special identification numbers that uniquely identify each process on a host computer.

TRANSFERRING DATA

As programs execute, they transfer data—either to disk drives, to devices (such as a printer), or even to a remote network host. In the past, your programs may have transferred data between your application and a hard disk. If you program in a UNIX or Windows environment, your applications might transfer data between multiple processes, programs, or windows. Within a network, programs communicate by transferring data as network messages or packets. Network designers must decide how to exchange such information. Data transfer options include simplex, half-duplex, and full-duplex modes of transfer.

Network professionals usually design a network to include at least two communication channels per communication process. One channel handles normal data transfers. The second channel transfers control information, as well as something network designers call *urgent data*. An example of urgent data is an ESC (escape) or interrupt key that immediately terminates an application. Networks must transmit such urgent data in a separate communication channel that takes priority over the normal data transfer process. As you will learn, some Internet protocols provide data fields to store urgent data.

Note: *Network professionals often refer to urgent data transmitted through a separate, special communications channel as* **out-of-band** *data.*

HANDLING ERRORS

As you can imagine, error detection, correction, and recovery are critical in a network design. For example, consider the problem of detecting and responding to a communication error that involves the communication channel itself. Because the communication channel itself is corrupt, it may be impossible for the receiver to notify the sender of the error. Worse yet, lost data can include messages that report other lost data. As such, error handling rapidly becomes a vicious circle within a network. Luckily, some Internet protocols include error control as a mode of service.

PRESERVING SEQUENCE

When network designers build networks, they must make sure their networks can deliver data in the proper sequence. Network designers must either attempt to maintain data sequence or provide a means for software to recover and restore data to its proper sequence. As you will learn, Internet protocols that provide sequencing services include fields that help host computers sort data into the correct order.

MANAGING DATA FLOW

The problem of data overflow occurs at every level of the network model. Overflow problems can exist between peer processes or between layers in the same host. For example, multiple processes may use the same communications channel. As such, data from multiple processes can flow through a layer at the same time. Funneling such data through a layer can swamp the layer's ability to process data. When they build a network, network professionals must carefully design protocols to handle flow control. Luckily, in most cases, Internet protocols automatically handle flow control for your programs.

FRAGMENTING DATA

Even though network processes break large messages into smaller packets, there may be times when the packet size is still larger than some services can support. In such cases, the network must further divide the packets into smaller pieces. Network professionals refer to this division process as fragmenting data.

While fragmenting data is often necessary, the results can impact network performance and reliability. For example, as the network breaks a message into several smaller pieces, the probability that a piece may become lost increases. In many cases, the loss of a single piece of data causes the sender to re-transmit the entire message and thereby restart the fragmenting process.

Luckily, this is a problem that network designers must solve. In most cases, network protocols shield you and your programs from dealing with this problem. However, as you will learn, if you understand the fragmenting process, you can design programs that help the network protocols and thus improve the reliability of your data transmissions.

DEFINING NETWORK LAYERS

Before you examine the network layers in detail, it may be helpful to review how network designers decide which capabilities to assign to each layer. In other words, it may help to review the requirements for a network layer. As you have learned, network designers use the concept of layers to organize a network into well-defined, functional modules. In his book *Computer Networks*, Prentice Hall, 1981, Andrew S. Tanenbaum lists the five major principles used to develop the layers in the Open Systems Interconnection reference model:

1. Create a new network layer whenever the network software needs a different level of abstraction.

2. Each layer should perform a well-defined function.

3. Choose each layer's function with an eye toward defining internationally standardized protocols.

4. Choose layer boundaries to minimize the information flow across the interfaces.

5. The number of layers should be large enough so that the network designers don't need to place dissimilar functions in the same layer. However, the number of layers should not be so large that they become unwieldy.

Figure 2.6 shows the network layers that resulted from the application of these principles. As you have learned, these layers form a model called the Open Systems Interconnection reference model or ISO/OSI model. To give you a broad overview of the ISO/OSI model, the following paragraphs briefly describe each layer. Additionally, the sections that follow will describe each layer in more detail.

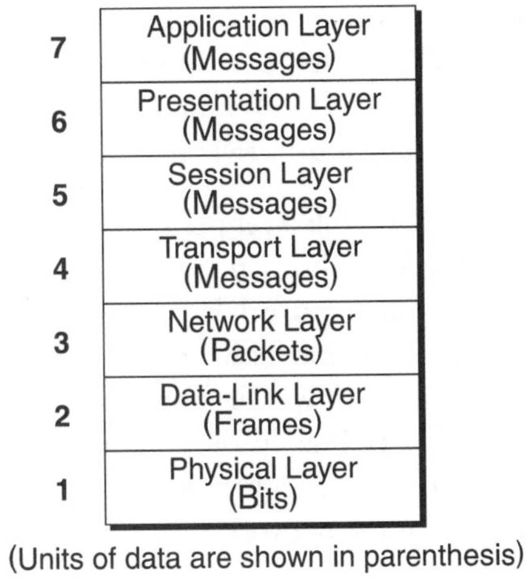

7	Application Layer (Messages)
6	Presentation Layer (Messages)
5	Session Layer (Messages)
4	Transport Layer (Messages)
3	Network Layer (Packets)
2	Data-Link Layer (Frames)
1	Physical Layer (Bits)

(Units of data are shown in parenthesis)

Figure 2.6 *Network layers in the ISO/OSI network model.*

You should note that each layer uses different units of data. For example, the application, presentation, session, and transport layers usually identify a unit of data as a message. The network layer identifies each unit of data as a packet. Within the data-link layer, the term *frame* refers to a unit of data. The physical layer sees all data as bits—binary data representing either a 1 or a 0.

Remember that the ISO/OSI model is a design guide—not a specification. As you will learn, the Internet consists of networks that network professionals describe in terms of the ISO/OSI model. As such, understanding the ISO/OSI model is important if you want to understand and learn to program the Internet.

DEFINING THE PHYSICAL LAYER

The physical layer transmits data through the network's communication channels. The physical layer includes the physical elements (hardware) needed to accomplish this function. As such, the network's transmission lines—the cables that connect all the computers on the network—are part of the physical layer. Data transmission methods, including control signals and timing, are also part of the physical layer. As such, the physical layer also includes network technologies (Ethernet, ARCNET, and token ring) that define parameters for data transmission.

DEFINING THE DATA-LINK LAYER

The data-link layer (or link layer) transfers raw data between the physical layer and the network layer. The network interface card represents the data-link layer in your computer. The data-link layer's primary function is to prevent data corruption within the physical layer. Network newcomers often find the link layer confusing because it seems to contradict what they know about the ISO/OSI model. They know every network layer has a link or interface to layers above and below itself (e.g., the transport layer has a link to the network layer and a link to the session layer). As such, they wonder why the link between the network layer and the physical layer deserves its own layer (the data-link layer) within the ISO/OSI model. You can answer this question by referring back to the five major principles used to derive the ISO/OSI model.

In accordance with principle 2, the data-link layer performs a well-defined function. To describe this function, you need a different level of abstraction (principle 1—the data-link layer's function is separate from those of the physical and network layers). Additionally, the data-link layer helps localize the definition of information flowing between the physical and network layers. In other words, the data-link layer minimizes the flow of information across the boundaries between the physical and network layers (principle 4). Finally, the data-link layer lets network designers locate these related functions within their own layer; otherwise, designers would need to arbitrarily place each function in either the physical or the network layer (principle 5).

DEFINING THE NETWORK LAYER

The network layer determines the route or path that data follows to reach its destination on the network. As such, the network layer must handle network traffic, congestion, and transfer rates (speed) across the transmission lines. The network layer must also handle data corruption within the communication channel. You can think of the network layer as the delivery system within a network. Chapter 4 discusses the Internet Protocol (IP). As you will learn, the Internet Protocol is synonymous with the network layer.

DEFINING THE TRANSPORT LAYER

Just as the network layer delivers data packets across the network, the transport layer delivers (or transports) data within a host computer. In other words, after the network layer delivers data to the correct host address, the transport layer delivers data to the correct application within the destination host. Figure 2.7 shows how data flows through the network and transport layers.

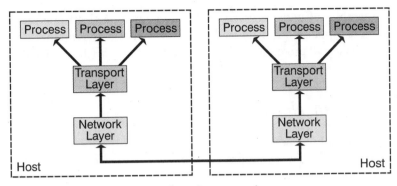

Figure 2.7 Data delivery within the network and transport layers.

DEFINING THE SESSION LAYER

As the user's interface to the network, the session layer negotiates connections between processes or applications on different host computers. As such, the session layer handles details such as account names, passwords, and user authorizations. For example, on many networks, you must login (enter your name or user identification and a password) before you can use any network services. In most cases, you must login each time you want to use the network. Network professionals refer to each login as a session. In many cases, you can login to the network more than once. In other words, you can create multiple login sessions on the network. Each time you want to use your computer to communicate with another computer on the network, the session layer handles the negotiations that must occur before the computers can establish a connection.

DEFINING THE PRESENTATION LAYER

The presentation layer consolidates common functions that networks must repeatedly use during network communications. The presentation layer handles details related to the network's interface to printers, video displays, and file formats. In short, the presentation layer defines how the network presents itself to your hardware and software. To understand the reasons for creating the presentation layer, you can again refer to the five major principles used to derive the OSI model. For example, even though every network application can independently perform all presentation-layer functions, you can also define all presentation-layer functions without reference to an application or any other network layer (principle 2). To do so, however, you must create a different level of abstraction and, thus, a new layer (principle 1). By locating all information related to printers, video displays, and file formats in the same layer, you minimize the flow of such interface information across other layer boundaries (principle 4).

DEFINING THE APPLICATION LAYER

The application layer contains details about network-wide applications. As an applications programmer or software developer, you will already be familiar with much of the application layer's functionality. Examples of network-wide applications include electronic mail (e-mail) and distributed databases. Applications that you develop for use across the Internet will be part of the application layer. In fact, all programs for network computer users (the network's end-users) are part of the network's application layer.

Understanding the Network Layers

In the following paragraphs, you will explore each of the OSI network layers in greater detail. As you do so, keep in mind the definitions presented in the previous sections. The layer definitions will help you keep the big picture in view.

Understanding the Physical Layer

As you have learned, the physical layer transmits data through the network's communication channels. As part of this function, the physical layer determines the mechanical and electrical properties of the network communications channel, as well as procedural details related to these characteristics. For example, the physical layer determines how many electrical pins or wires a network connection uses, what type of cable (coaxial or twisted pair) a transmission line uses, and what characteristics transmission lines have. In a similar fashion, the physical layer contains details about a network's topology. With such design details assigned exclusively to the physical layer, network designers can create the higher layers (data-link, network, session, transport, presentation, and application) without considering the network's topology.

Since network communications at the bit-level (binary data) occur in the physical layer, the physical layer also includes related design issues such as how hardware will represent 1's and 0's. For example, the physical layer determines what analog-signal frequency represents a 1 and what analog-signal frequency represents a 0. The physical layer will decide the point at which a changing frequency switches from a 1 to a 0 (and vice versa).

For example, assume that the physical layer uses voltage to represent binary data. The physical layer would determine at what point a changing voltage level toggles its logical state to represent the opposite binary number. The physical layer also ensures that the destination host receives each binary digit of data representing a 1 as a 1 and not as a 0. The physical layer also determines whether data transfers use simplex, half-duplex, or full-duplex modes of communication.

Understanding the Data-Link Layer

The physical layer manages raw data as bits (1's and 0's). The data-link layer formats or transforms raw binary data into something meaningful to the network layer—normally, frames of data. The data-link layer also accepts information from the network layer and translates the data into the correct binary format for the underlying physical layer (for example, FM signals or voltage levels). In all cases, the data-link layer ensures that binary transmissions between network hosts are free from errors.

IMPLEMENTING DATA-LINK LAYERS

Network professionals must design a different data-link layer for each different physical network design. For example, you have learned that the physical layer contains details about network technologies such as Ethernet, ARCNET, and token ring. To connect a computer to a network, you must plug a network-interface card into the computer.

Network-interface cards are peculiar to a specific network technology. The design of an Ethernet network-interface card is different from an ARCNET interface card. As such, you can think of the network-interface card within your computer as the data-link layer in most networks. In other words, as previously mentioned, the network card you place in your computer provides the data-link layer.

UNDERSTANDING DATA FRAMES

When the data-link layer formats raw bits, the units of data that result are generally called *frames*. Although the International Organization for Standardization calls these units *physical-layer-service-data-units*, most other network literature simply refers to such data as frames. As you might expect, a data frame's contents depend on the underlying network technology (the physical layer).

For example, assume you attach two personal computers, made by the same manufacturer, to an internetwork. However, suppose that one computer is on an Ethernet network and the other is on a token ring network. At the network layer level, data on these two computers will look identical. At the data-link and physical levels, however, the data format will be completely different. In other words, to package information, the data-link layer creates a very different frame for an Ethernet network than it does for a token ring network. The requirements of the underlying physical layer (network technology) determine the content of the data frame. For example, the physical layer doesn't care (the design is independent of) how (what format) the network layer transmits information to the data-link layer. At the same time, the network layer doesn't care (the design is independent of) how (what format) the data-link layer creates the frames (for the physical layer).

By design, data frames provide error-checking capabilities. You should understand that the primary purpose or function of the data-link layer is to prevent data corruption. People often assume that formatting data into frames is the primary purpose of the data-link layer. They miss the real goal of this formatting process. Data frames are simply a means to an end. As discussed next, the end goal is to prevent data corruption in the communication channel.

ENSURING DATA INTEGRITY

You should understand that networks use data frames to detect and correct data corruption in the network communication channel. Figure 2.8 shows the format of an Ethernet frame.

64 Bits	48 Bits	48 Bits	16 Bits	368-12,000 Bits	32 Bits
Preamble	Destination Address	Source Address	Frame Type	Frame Data	Cyclic Redundancy Check (CRC)

Figure 2.8 The contents of an Ethernet data frame.

To detect data corruption, the data-link layers of the sender and receiver use a cyclic redundancy check (CRC) value. The 32-bit CRC value is the result of a complex calculation performed on the data contained within the data frame. The sender calculates and then stores the CRC value at the end of the data frame. The receiver re-calculates the CRC then compares its CRC to the CRC value stored in the data frame. If the CRC value stored in the data frame matches the CRC value calculated by the receiver, the probability that the received data matches the originally transmitted data is extremely high. For all practical purposes, the CRCs guarantee the integrity of transmitted data.

The remainder of the data frame is important and necessary to properly identify and route the frame. For example, the Preamble field helps receiving hosts synchronize with the sender. In other words, the field identifies which piece of data the frame contains. As you will recall, networks can fragment data (break it into smaller pieces). Data frames must contain destination and source addresses for routing and error-reporting purposes. The receiver uses the Frame Type field to determine which protocol to use as the data passes upward through the network layers.

In short, a key data-link layer operation is to detect and prevent data corruption in the communication channel. As such, because the data-link layer needs an identifiable unit of data with which to calculate a CRC value, the layer formats or encapsulates data to create a finite entity (frame). The CRC value, in turn, ensures data integrity within the physical layer.

UNDERSTANDING THE NETWORK LAYER

As you have learned, the network layer is the primary delivery system within a network. In a packet-switched network, such as the Internet, the network layer delivers units of data as individual packets. As you might expect, each packet of information contains a destination and source address for routing purposes. As the network delivery system, the network layer defines the interface between host computers and all packet switches located between the source and destination addresses. As such, when network designers create the protocols for the network layer, they must define how much responsibility each network element will have for routing data. In other words, they must decide how to divide the responsibility for data delivery between the host computer and intervening packet switches. The network layer ensures that hosts receive the correct packets. According to the ISO/OSI reference model, the network layer is also responsible for ensuring proper sequencing. As you will learn, however, Internet networks design sequencing into the transport layer instead of the network layer.

ROUTING DATA

To route data, networks commonly use *routing tables*. A routing table is like a look-up database. Using a routing table, routers can look up the correct path (or best route) from a packet's current location to any destination on the network. Depending on the network's requirements, a designer can implement routing tables as static or dynamic. With a static routing table, the network administrator must update the table. Network software automatically updates dynamic routing tables.

A designer can use static routing tables if the network configuration rarely changes (in other words, when the workload to manually update the tables will be minimal). The designer stores routing information in a location that is accessible network-wide. When a network configuration change occurs, network administrators manually update the routing table information. As you might have guessed, network software that uses static routing tables is much easier to implement than network software that uses dynamic routing tables. With dynamic routing table designs, the network software must automatically update the routing tables each time a computer user starts a new network session (login) and possibly each time an application creates a new packet.

MANAGING TRAFFIC

As network administrators add more computers to a network or as computer users begin to use a network more frequently, network packet traffic increases. Just as increasing the number of cars on a freeway system can cause traffic congestion, increasing the number of packets on a network can cause network traffic congestion. As a network becomes congested, network packet traffic slows and users experience noticeable degradation in network performance. To reduce such network traffic congestion, the network layer must effectively manage packet routing.

As the network layer routes packets through the communication channel, the layer must avoid sending too many packets through the same packet switch. Otherwise, a traffic jam will occur. If the network layer cannot avoid an excessive flow of data, the layer must handle any resulting congestion. One way networks reduce congestion is to manage flow control. The network layer handles flow control problems while routing data. In other words, the network layer must handle problems such as a sender transmitting data faster than the receiver can accept data.

COUNTING NETWORK TRAFFIC

Networks can cross geopolitical boundaries. Many networks, such as the Internet, extend across the borders of two or more countries. In some cases, network professionals must design such networks to supply accounting information for cost and billing purposes. For example, network maintenance costs time, money, and effort. When the flow of data through a communications channel crosses national boundaries, countries may want to share these maintenance costs. For such networks, accounting information that tracks the quantity of data that moves through the network may be essential. The network may track such quantities in terms of numbers of packets, messages, characters, or bits.

Since the network layer has network-wide routing responsibilities, the function of tracking accounting information belongs in the network layer. As such, network professionals must design network layer software that reports accounting information, if required. This type of accounting information rapidly becomes complicated when different billing rates exist on both sides of a national border. Of course, such complications translate into complex network layer software. Fortunately, the Internet does not currently require such accounting information.

The network layer determines the route or path that data follows to reach its destination on the network. As such, the network layer must handle network traffic congestion and transfer rates (speed) within the communication channels. The physical, data-link, and network layers share responsibility for ensuring data integrity within the communication channel. You can think of the network layer as the network's delivery system. In short, the network layer delivers data between host computers and handles all traffic management problems related to routing and delivery.

UNDERSTANDING THE TRANSPORT LAYER

When two computers communicate across the network, two programs (or processes) actually exchange data. The network layer delivers data to a host computer and then hands the data off to the transport layer. Within the host computer, the transport layer delivers the data to the correct program or application.

As you have learned, peer processes can carry on virtual conversations. For example, given a connection between two host computers, the network layer in the source host carries on a virtual conversation with the network layer in the destination host. Likewise, the source transport layer carries on a virtual conversation with the destination transport layer.

UNDERSTANDING VIRTUAL CONVERSATIONS IN THE TRANSPORT LAYER

Figure 2.9 shows the network model that you saw previously. As you have learned, the dotted lines between the corresponding layers in each host indicate a virtual conversation between the layers.

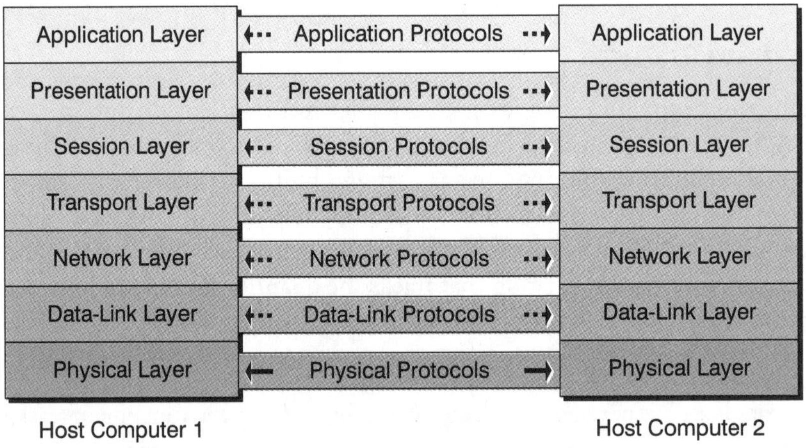

Application Layer	←·· Application Protocols ··→	Application Layer
Presentation Layer	←·· Presentation Protocols ··→	Presentation Layer
Session Layer	←·· Session Protocols ··→	Session Layer
Transport Layer	←·· Transport Protocols ··→	Transport Layer
Network Layer	←·· Network Protocols ··→	Network Layer
Data-Link Layer	←·· Data-Link Protocols ··→	Data-Link Layer
Physical Layer	← Physical Protocols →	Physical Layer

Host Computer 1   Host Computer 2

Figure 2.9 Network model showing peer processes.

In a packet-switched network, the network layer frequently must route data through packet switches to deliver data between host computers. Figure 2.10 modifies Figure 2.9 to show a more accurate picture of the peer-to-peer and virtual conversations that occur in a packet-switched network.

As you can see, a virtual conversation still occurs between the network, data-link, and physical layers. However, the conversations (which represent communication services) for these layers occur on a hop-by-hop basis instead of an end-to-end basis. On the other hand, the transport layer and the layers above it provide communication services on an end-to-end basis. As shown in Figure 2.10, you can refer to the intervening packet switches as a *communication subnet*. The communication subnet refers to the network or subnetwork elements that comprise the communication channel between the source and destination host computers.

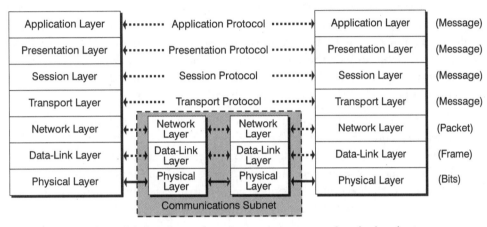

Figure 2.10 *Network model that shows virtual conversations on a hop-by-hop basis.*

UNDERSTANDING TRAFFIC MANAGEMENT IN THE TRANSPORT LAYER

As discussed, the network layer delivers data between host computers and handles all traffic management problems related to routing and delivery. In a packet-switched network, the transport layer must break or fragment data it receives from the session layer into the smaller pieces that the network layer requires. On the receiving end, the transport layer must reassemble the fragmented data. As such, the transport layer's design greatly impacts the quantity of packets that flow through the network. In other words, the transport layer produces the packet traffic that the network layer must manage.

Within a host computer, multiple programs (processes) may use the network at the same time, in different ways. The transport layer is responsible for getting data from, or sending data to, each network program. In this way, the transport layer must be able to interact with and manage the data for multiple programs at the same time.

INCREASING BANDWIDTH

Network professionals use the term *bandwidth* to describe the quantity of data that flows through a communications channel within a given time period. For example, consider the flow of water from a kitchen faucet. If you increase the amount of water flowing from the faucet, you can decrease the time it takes to fill one glass with water. Likewise, if you increase the flow of water, you can fill two or more glasses in the same amount of time that it formerly took you to fill one glass. Network bandwidth is like the quantity of water flowing from the kitchen faucet for a given period of time. Network designers can design transport layers to increase bandwidth—increase the number of packets that flow through the communications channel for a given time period.

To boost bandwidth (or throughput), transport layers can create multiple network connections for a single transport connection. When the transport layer uses a single transport connection for multiple network connections, it must multiplex and demultiplex transmitted data. The term *multiplex* refers to the process of combining multiple signals into a single communications channel. The term *demultiplex* refers to the reverse process. In this case, the transport layer of the sending host multiplexes (or merges) multiple messages on to the transport connection. The receiving transport layer, in turn, demultiplexes the data. Multiplexing and demultiplexing designs define how transport layers manage packet traffic in a network. Furthermore, these designs impact other areas of a network's performance, such as bandwidth and resource usage.

For example, consider transportation engineers (network designers) designing a road (communication channel) that connects two cities (host computers). The engineers could design a simple two-lane highway with one lane (network connection) going in each direction. They could also design and build a much more complex and costly freeway with six lanes (multiple network connections) running in each direction. The correct choice of roadway design depends on the expected quantity and priority of the traffic traveling between the two cities. If the designers decide that traffic delays are intolerable, they will design a multiple lane freeway. The number of lanes the designers choose to build will depend upon the expected quantity of traffic.

In the same way, network designers must determine the importance of throughput. If a transport layer establishes multiple network connections for a single transport, the layer must fragment or divide data as it transfers messages to the network layer. The transport layer must also reassemble the individual pieces of the transport message in the receiving host. As you might expect, the ability to divide and reassemble data adds complexity to the design of the transport layer and associated software. For a moment, consider the transport layer's task of managing multiple fragments for multiple processes, simultaneously. By hiding the implementation complexity within the transport layer, your network programs are unaware that other processes are using the transport layer and that fragmenting occurs.

In summary, while the network layer handles traffic management between multiple host computers, the transport layer manages traffic between multiple processes within a host computer. Both jobs are important, and yet they are completely different functions. According to the ISO's design principles, each layer should have a well-defined purpose. As such, network layers do not multiplex and demultiplex data like the transport layer.

Conserving Network Resources

In terms of network resources and complexity, the cost to create and maintain a network connection is significant. In some cases, a network's requirements may specify that cost control is more important than throughput (or bandwidth). In such cases, a network designer might design a transport layer that multiplexes several transports into a single network connection. In other words, if reducing costs is more important than increasing bandwidth, the network designer might build a single lane data highway versus a multiple lane data freeway—multiple transports on a single network connection.

Consider the problem of transportation engineers building a tunnel under a large body of water. The cost to build a single lane is extremely expensive. For example, the Sumner Tunnel in Boston, Massachusetts connects the city of Boston with Logan International Airport. The Sumner Tunnel runs underneath Boston Harbor. Because of its building costs, the Sumner Tunnel consists of only one lane of traffic traveling in each direction.

At each end of the Sumner Tunnel, traffic branches into three lanes. You can think of the roadway leading into the tunnel as multiplexing three lanes of traffic into one—a 3 to 1 multiplexer. As traffic exits the tunnel, the roadway demultiplexes traffic from one lane into three. The Sumner Tunnel carries heavy traffic between Logan International Airport and the city of Boston. As you might expect, merging traffic going into the tunnel creates frustrating traffic jams. Although travelers might disagree, transportation engineers (or at least the politicians who fund their projects) believe the congestion problem is less important than the cost to widen the tunnel.

Network designers face similar decisions when they design transport layers. When the importance of a network's throughput outweighs cost factors, designers will develop transports that create multiple network connections for each transport required. If cost control outweighs the importance of throughput, designers will multiplex several transports into a single network connection.

MANAGING DATA FLOW

As discussed, flow control is how software ensures that a sender does not send data packets faster than the receiver can process the incoming messages. Like the network layer, transport layers must also manage data flow. However, transport layers manage flow control on an end-to-end basis (from process to process) rather than a hop-by-hop basis (from computer to computer). In other words, the network layer handles flow control between end destinations represented by host computers. Likewise, the transport layer controls the data flow between peer processes or programs. Many transport layers, such as the transport layer on the Internet, manage flow control similar to error control. In other words, the transport layers exchange acknowledgment messages. The transport layers include flow control requests in the exchanged messages. For example, one transport layer can tell the other transport layer to either increase or decrease throughput.

UNDERSTANDING THE SESSION LAYER

As previously mentioned, on most networks, you must login (enter your name or user identification and a password) each time you want to use any network services. Network professionals refer to each login as a network session. In other words, each person that logs into a network creates a separate network session. Also, a single person can create multiple sessions by logging in multiple times. For each login (or network session), the session layer negotiates and establishes connections between processes or applications on different host computers. Network professionals refer to the process of setting up a session (a communication connection between two hosts) as binding.

MANAGING CONNECTIONS

Before you can establish a connection, both ends of the connection must negotiate options such as data transfer rates, error control, and the expected type of data transfer (simplex, half-duplex, or full-duplex). Either end of the connection can request changes to these options. The session layer must handle requests for a change to a negotiated option. Requests can occur at any time during the login session. The session layer must also authenticate both ends of a connection. In other words, the session layer requires each end of a connection to prove who they are. Both ends of a connection must also establish their authorization to use the specified connection or session.

COVERING FOR THE TRANSPORT LAYER

As discussed, either end of a connection can request changes to a login session. Session changes may also result from problems in the transport layer. For example, if transport layer connections are unreliable, the session layer must recover from broken transports. For example, assume you use a transaction-based, distributed database. Should transport layer errors occur, the session layer might need to rollback (undo) a partially completed transaction. In preparation for such crash recoveries, the session layer may group related messages and either deliver to an application (at one time) all related messages or none of them. By doing so, the session layer prevents an unreliable transport layer from aborting a transport message in the middle of a transaction. Also, when the transport layer does not provide sequencing services, the session layer must do so if an application requires sequencing.

ELIMINATING THE SESSION LAYER

When a network doesn't require application-to-application communication services, network designers may eliminate the session layer. As you will learn, the Internet networks eliminate the session layer completely. Although, in most cases, you must login to use the Internet, the software that verifies Internet user authorizations is not part of the network software design. Instead, such software on the Internet is a program running in the application layer. On the Internet, the transport layer protocols include many functions that the session layer normally handles.

REVIEWING THE SESSION LAYER

The session layer transforms data packaged for network transmissions into application data. Additionally, the session layer handles application requests for changes to data flow rates and error control. The session layer also verifies that a user or user process has the authority to use the requested connection or computer process on the network. As such, the session layer is the user's interface to a network. In short, the session layer establishes and manages connections between users and network applications. Network designers occasionally merge the session and transport layers. In most cases, the functionality required by a session layer does not disappear. Rather, other network software (either the transport layer or a custom application) assumes responsibility for session-layer functions.

UNDERSTANDING THE PRESENTATION LAYER

The presentation layer contains common functions that the network repeatedly uses during network communications. Common functions include the network's interface to printers, video displays, and file formats. In other words, the presentation layer determines how data appears to the user. As such, a presentation layer typically includes many data conversion routines.

Well-designed networks let you attach a wide variety of computers. The Internet is an excellent example. Computers on the Internet range from single-user personal computers to mini-computers and large mainframes. Within each of these groups of computers, an even wider variety of video display units and printers exist. Unrelated operating system software on these computers can result in incompatible file formats, as well as other incompatibilities. The presentation layer must integrate such diversity in a way that makes these differences transparent to network applications.

Unfortunately, Internet networks do not include a standard presentation layer. As such, application programs perform most presentation-layer functions. As an Internet programmer, you should follow the ISO/OSI design guidelines when you develop presentation-layer functions.

IMPLEMENTING THE PRESENTATION LAYER

Network professionals often implement the presentation layer in user-callable routines and libraries. As you will learn, the Windows Sockets Application Program Interface (API) forms a kind of session/presentation layer upon which you can build applications. In one way or another, the layers below the presentation layer perform functions required for correct network operations. The presentation layer provides useful but non-essential network services. The following paragraphs briefly describe some of the communication services that a presentation layer might provide.

ENCRYPTING DATA

The purpose of data encryption is security. On a network, encryption transforms intelligible data into something unintelligible prior to transmission. At the receiving end of the connection, the presentation layer must decipher the transmission and transform the data back into usable information. By encrypting data at the presentation level, programs can ensure data is encrypted before the data is visible to the other network layers. As such, data encryption belongs in the presentation layer.

COMPRESSING DATA AND INCREASING BANDWIDTH

Data compression also belongs in the presentation layer. Much like encryption, data compression involves the conversion of data. Also, data compression requires encoding similar to encryption. However, the goal of data compression is different from encryption. Whereas users encrypt data to hide its meaning, users compress data to reduce its size. The keys or methods of decoding compressed data are commonly available throughout the network.

By compressing data near the top network layer, the presentation layer reduces the amount of data that the network must transport. As such, efficient data compression in the presentation layer can significantly boost overall network performance. Network bandwidth refers to the amount of data that can flow through a communications channel within a given period of time. As you have learned, one way to increase bandwidth (or throughput) is to widen the communications channel—add more network connections for a single transport (more data freeway lanes). Another way to increase effective bandwidth is to reduce the size of the data that the network must transport.

All kinds of computer professionals use data compression to reduce the requirements for space on storage media such as hard disks. Network computers also have storage space problems. However, network computers often use data compression for another, and perhaps more important, purpose: to increase throughput or effective network bandwidth. For example, if your data compression routines let you hide three network messages in one, you can transport three network messages for the price of one. You have increased your throughput by a factor of three. Data compression also reduces network traffic. With a compression ratio of 3 to 1 (you reduced three messages into one), you can transmit one message instead of three. Fewer transmitted messages means less traffic. As such, data compression helps reduce network traffic congestion. Reducing network traffic congestion also helps boost network performance.

DISPLAYING DATA

Video displays present a special problem for the presentation layer. As an applications programmer, you may take a lot of video display characteristics for granted. However, well-designed network applications must handle problems caused by the following differences in video display characteristics. Different types of computers can use different values for all of these display characteristics. A well-designed presentation layer should handle such differences independent of the application itself:

- Differing interpretations of character sets
- Automatic echoing of typed characters
- Carriage-returns and line-feeds
- Tabs (both horizontal and vertical), Backspaces, and Form-feeds
- Cursor positioning

Various networks include *virtual terminal protocols* that make video and printer issues invisible to network applications. For example, in such a network, you can send data with a carriage-return line-feed to a virtual terminal that will correctly display your data. The protocols that handle such data translation reside in the network's presentation layer. In short, the presentation layer hides hardware differences that might affect how the network displays, prints, or interprets data for a user. Although Internet networks do not include an official presentation layer, the Internet includes the TELNET protocol. The TELNET protocol performs services similar to a virtual terminal protocol.

UNDERSTANDING THE APPLICATION LAYER

The application layer contains all details related to specific applications or computer programs designed for network users. As a network programmer, you are responsible for designing the application layer. In many cases, you will find that developing a network application is very similar to developing any other program. In other cases, you may develop a network application to take advantage of a network's special communication capabilities.

For example, networks offer tremendous opportunities for distributed data processing (storing data across multiple host computers). Using a network, you can also connect multiple computer processors and have them simultaneously attack a particular computing problem. However, to develop such programs, you will need to study and learn information that you may not have previously needed to know. You need to learn the basic differences between network applications and non-network applications. *Internet Programming's* ultimate goal is to help you understand such differences and help you learn to develop network programs for use on the Internet.

APPLICATION LAYER VERSUS PRESENTATION LAYER

The dividing line between the presentation layer and the application layer is important, especially since the Internet does not include an official presentation layer. As an Internet programmer, you should always ask the following question: *Is this programming issue a network problem or an application-specific problem?* You should design your programs so that separate software modules handle network-based problems versus application-specific problems.

For example, in the same program module, you can freely mix code to solve network-specific problems, such as video display issues, with code that solves application-specific problems, such as data structures. However, by doing so, you blur the application and presentation layers within the design of your application. In effect, you compromise software maintenance and portability. As you attach new computer hardware to your network, your application might require extensive and costly modifications.

DESIGNING YOUR SOFTWARE

The ISO/OSI network reference model is a proven model for network hardware and software design. Your network program designs will improve dramatically if you understand and adhere to the design principles defined by the ISO/OSI network reference model. Remember, as a network programmer, you design the applications layer in this model.

The reference model's layering ensures modularity in a network design. If you use this model as a design guide for creating your own Internet software modules, you will minimize present and future problems with your network applications. You will also enhance your reputation and skills as a software developer and network applications designer. In short, the network applications layer contains all design issues related to specific network applications. As a network programmer, your program design defines the design of the application layer.

UNDERSTANDING THE CLIENT/SERVER MODEL

The preceding sections described the ISO/OSI model for designing networks. As you have learned, this proven model uses the concept of layering to partition design issues and let network designers more easily resolve network problems. The applications layer within the ISO/OSI model contains design issues related to specific applications. In the next chapter, you will see Internet network designs explained in terms of the ISO/OSI model. However, before moving on to Chapter 3, you should become familiar with another model that programmers use to design software for network use—the client/server model.

DEFINING THE CLIENT/SERVER MODEL

Most network programmers use the client/server model to design programs for the network application layer. Network communication requires a network connection between two computers or programs that talk to each other. A network connection consists of both ends (or sides) of the communication process, as well as the path between them.

The client/server programming model divides a network application into two sides: the client side and the server side. By definition, the client side of a network connection requests information or services from the server side of the connection. The server side of a network connection responds to a client's requests. In other words, within the client/server program model, a network application performs two separate and well-defined functions: requesting information and responding to requests for information. The program that requests information functions as a client program. The program that responds to such requests functions as a server program.

In most cases, a network application consists of two separate programs—a client program and a server program. However, you can design a single program that performs both functions. In fact, as you will learn in Chapter 9, some server programs that cannot fulfill a service request will, in turn, act as a client program and request information from another server.

Note: Chapter 9 discusses the Internet's Domain Name System, which uses name-server programs to look up Internet addresses.

UNDERSTANDING THE PURPOSE

As you have learned, a network's principle purpose is to let applications on two computers communicate. A few feet may separate host computers located in the same room. However, geographic boundaries such as mountains and oceans may also separate host computers. Networks can consist of many different types of computers, as well as different types of network technologies. The ISO/OSI network reference model minimizes or hides such differences from network applications. The model lets network designers build networks composed of well-defined functional layers of software and hardware.

The client/server programming model is a design guide to help programmers create applications that smoothly integrate into the network communications environment. Like the ISO/OSI network reference model, the client/server programming model separates network software design issues into well-defined modules. In the case of networks, the ISO/OSI reference model divides design issues into network layers. For network programs, the client/server model divides application design into client issues and server issues.

DEFINING A VIRTUAL CIRCUIT

Network layers permit virtual conversations between (peer) layers on different host computers. A virtual conversation uses a virtual circuit (or connection). As you have learned, a virtual circuit gives the illusion of a physical communication path. However, an actual circuit (or unbroken communication path) does not exist. You can resolve many design issues surrounding network applications by treating virtual conversations as though a point-to-point connection truly exists. In other words, you can depend on the network software to handle network communication problems. The client/server program model treats virtual conversations as though a point-to-point connection exists.

IDENTIFYING CLIENTS AND SERVERS

As you will learn, you can refer to each end of a virtual circuit as a *socket*. Each socket (or end) of an established connection between two hosts typically performs a specific function. You can refer to the socket that requests a connection as the client side of the connection. Likewise, the software that requests the connection is the client application. You can refer to the socket that receives the request for a connection as the server side. The software on the server side of the connection is the server application.

UNDERSTANDING THE DIFFERENCES

At first, you may find it difficult to determine which side of a connection is the client and which side is the server. In many cases, both sides of a client/server connection can perform both client and server functions. The following paragraphs try to explain some typical differences between a client application and a server application.

A server application (or server process) usually initializes itself and then goes to sleep, spending much of its time simply waiting for a request from a client application. Server applications provide a specific service. Usually, this service is beneficial to all network users or at least to those in a specific industry, business, or group of network users. For example, a distributed database provides airline companies with reservation information. The airline reservation system uses a server process that provides access to the distributed database. This server process is useful across the network to the entire airline industry. Likewise, a corporate-wide e-mail system typically uses a server process. The e-mail server is accessible from any computer within the company's network. The e-mail server also provides any service that is available company-wide.

An interactive request from a network computer user usually activates a client application. Typically, a client process will transmit a request (across the network) for a connection to the server and then request some type of service through the connection. For example, a client application might request the time of day or request that a file be transferred. Likewise, Telnet client application transmits a request to login to a remote host computer. The Telnet client application transmits this request to a Telnet server application.

CLASSIFYING SERVER APPLICATIONS

You can divide server processes into two types: iterative servers and concurrent servers. The following paragraphs briefly describe each type.

DEFINING AN ITERATIVE SERVER

When a server process handles each request individually, you refer to the server as an iterative server. In other words, the server process manages requests one-at-a-time as they arrive. A time-of-day service is a good use for an iterative server. For example, when a time server receives a request for the time of day, the server program sends an immediate response. The time server does not handle any other service requests until it fulfills the current request. Iterative servers are relatively simple as compared to concurrent servers. However, for an iterative server to be effective, the service provided must be relatively short in duration. The time required to fulfill a service request is usually predictable in an iterative server. For example, since the time of day is immediately available to a computer, a time-of-day server can be iterative.

DEFINING A CONCURRENT SERVER

When the time required to fulfill a service request is unknown or unpredictable, server processes usually function as concurrent servers. A concurrent server creates a separate process to handle each request for service. In other words, the server manages multiple service requests concurrently or at the same time. For each client request, the server process spins-off a new process to fulfill the service request. Typically, the server itself goes back to sleep after starting each concurrent process and waits for the next request for service. A concurrent server requires an operating system that can manage multiple processes at the same time. In other words, a concurrent server requires a multi-tasking operating system. Concurrent servers usually handle most file-related communication services because the time required to fulfill the service request depends upon the size of the file. Since file sizes vary, the time to fulfill the service is unpredictable.

PUTTING IT ALL TOGETHER

In this chapter, you have completed *Internet Programming's* general introduction to networks. This chapter and Chapter 1 discussed networks in very general terms. In Chapter 3, you will move from the general to the specific (that is, you will begin to read about the Internet networks in particular). Before you move on to Chapter 3, make sure that you understand the following key concepts:

✓   Protocols define rules that network software use to send and receive data.

✓   The ISO/OSI network model describes networks as layers of functionality. Each layer in a network performs a well-defined function and uses one or more protocols to perform its functions.

✓   The physical layer transmits data through the network's communication channels and includes all hardware needed to accomplish this function.

✓   The data-link layer's primary function is to detect data corruption within the physical layer.

✓   The network layer delivers data between host computers on the network.

✓   The transport layer delivers data between applications on host computers.

✓   The session layer is the user's interface to the network.

✓   The presentation layer handles details related to the network's interface to printers, video displays, and file formats.

✓   The application layer contains details about all network-wide applications.

✓   The client/server model simplifies the development of network software by dividing the design process into client issues and server issues.

Chapter 3
An Introduction to TCP/IP

In Chapters 1 and 2, you learned about network fundamentals in general. In this chapter, you will learn the fundamentals of a particular type of network—one based upon the *TCP/IP protocol suite*. The Internet consists of thousands of networks that use the TCP/IP protocol suite. If you plan to program the Internet, you must understand TCP/IP network fundamentals. By the time you finish this chapter, you will understand the following key concepts:

- The definition and purpose of the TCP/IP protocol stack

- How data flows in a TCP/IP network

- How a TCP/IP network uses network technologies such as Ethernet

- A multihomed computer contains multiple network cards

- How a computer becomes a router

- The difference between connection-oriented and connectionless protocols

- The difference between a reliable and unreliable protocol

- The difference between a byte-stream and datagram delivery service

- The definition of a virtual circuit

UNDERSTANDING THE IMPORTANCE OF THE *TCP/IP* PROTOCOLS

For our purposes, protocols are rules which define how software must work. As an applications programmer, you know that computer operating systems use rules (protocols) to handle the flow of information that passes between users, your applications, and computers. Likewise, protocols manage the flow of information between network computers and your network programs.

If your network is the Internet, you will depend on a collection of protocols called the TCP/IP protocol suite, which manages all information that moves across the Internet. To be a successful network programmer, you need to understand how the TCP/IP protocol suite functions. The TCP/IP protocol suite consists of multiple protocols, each of which transfers data across the network in a different format and with different options (such as error checking). Depending on your program's requirements, you may need to use a specific protocol within the TCP/IP suite to transmit information across the Internet.

UNDERSTANDING *TCP/IP* TERMINOLOGY

TCP is an acronym for Transport Control Protocol. Likewise, IP stands for Internet Protocol. However, when you combine these two acronyms (TCP/IP), they represent more than just the two protocols. For this reason, the term *TCP/IP* often confuses TCP/IP newcomers.

DEFINING THE *TCP/IP* PROTOCOL SUITE

The Internet relies on a collection of protocols called the TCP/IP protocol suite. A *protocol suite* is a collection of complementary and cooperative protocols. The TCP/IP protocol suite includes the Transport Control Protocol and the Internet Protocol, as well as other protocols. All of these protocols work together to communicate information across the Internet. Table 3.1 lists the commonly used TCP/IP protocols.

Protocol	Purpose
IP	The Internet Protocol is a network-layer protocol that moves data between host computers.
TCP	The Transport Control Protocol is a transport-layer protocol that moves data between applications.
UDP	The User Datagram Protocol is another transport-layer protocol. UDP also moves data between applications; however, UDP is less complex (and less reliable) than TCP.
ICMP	The Internet Control Message Protocol carries network error messages and reports other conditions that require attention by network software.

Table 3.1 Commonly used TCP/IP protocols.

In RFC 1180, *A TCP/IP Tutorial,* Theodore Socolofsky and Claudia Kale state their belief that the term *internet technology* accurately describes the TCP/IP protocol suite and the applications that use it. They prefer to use the term *internet* to refer to any network that uses internet technology. You may also come across the term *Internet protocol suite.* This term is simply another name for the TCP/IP protocol suite.

At first, you may find the term *Internet protocol suite* less confusing and more comfortable than TCP/IP protocol suite. However, most writers, programmers, and Internet professionals commonly use the term *TCP/IP* to refer to the entire TCP/IP protocol suite. When writers, programmers, and Internet professionals need to refer to the individual protocols (such as TCP or IP), they refer to these protocols by their individual names or acronyms.

In other words, the term *TCP/IP* is shorthand for the collection of protocols generally referred to as the TCP/IP protocol suite, the Internet protocol suite, or internet technology. To keep with mainstream discussions of the Internet, *Internet Programming* will use the term *TCP/IP*. In this chapter, you will learn some of the differences between the Transport Control Protocol, the Internet Protocol, and the suite of protocols commonly referred to as TCP/IP. By the time you finish this chapter, you will understand how to use these terms like a professional.

DEFINING A PROTOCOL STACK

Chapter 2 introduced you to the ISO/OSI network model. As you have learned, this model divides networks into layers, each of which performs a very specific function. With each layer, the OSI model associates protocols that define the layer's functionality. For example, the network layer, which manages data delivery across the Internet, contains the Internet Protocol, which moves data between host computers.

As shown in Figure 3.1, the ISO/OSI model represents a network as a vertical stack of modules or layers. Since the model associates at least one protocol with each layer, you can say the model stacks protocols on top of each other. The term *protocol stack* comes from this concept of networks as vertical layers and stacked protocols.

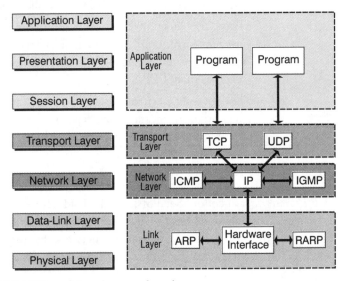

Figure 3.1 The ISO/OSI model and protocol stack.

The term *protocol stack* can refer to any combination of network layers and their associated protocols. The TCP/IP protocol stack is only one of many protocol stacks that support the ISO/OSI layered model. When someone uses the term *TCP/IP stack*, understand that they have identified a specific protocol stack. That is, they have simply told you which protocols their layered network uses—the TCP/IP protocols.

UNDERSTANDING THE DATA FLOW

As previously mentioned, the TCP/IP protocol suite moves information across the network. Since the TCP/IP protocol suite provides a collection of cooperating protocols, you can think of your data as flowing from one layer to another and from one protocol to the next. As you may recall from Figure 3.1, the top layer in the ISO/OSI model is the application layer. The bottom (physical) layer consists of the network transmission lines. As your data moves through the protocol stack, your data flows from the application layer down to the physical layer and across the network.

When your data arrives at its physical destination, your data flows up through the protocol stack toward the destination application. Figure 3.2 shows how data would flow across the network from a client application on one computer to a server application on another.

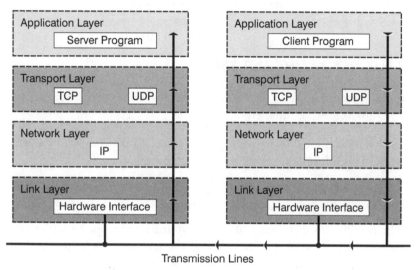

Figure 3.2 Information flowing through the protocol stack.

As your data flows through the protocol stack, the TCP/IP protocols may divide your data into smaller units (or pieces). As you will learn, TCP/IP often assigns each of these units a different name. However, even with such name changes, you can still trace your data through the network if you keep a clear picture of the TCP/IP data path.

UNDERSTANDING THE TCP/IP FRAMEWORK

When you program the Internet, you need a clear picture of how data flows through the layers of stacked protocols. Visualize a network as vertical layers (or levels) of functionality. The top layer represents the interface between your application and the network software. (Network software consists of the protocols that correspond to each layer in the ISO/OSI model.) The bottom layer represents the interface between the network software and the physical (hardware) network elements. To communicate with the network, your applications flow information down the protocol stack. The network, in turn, sends information up the protocol stack to communicate with your application. As such, when you program a TCP/IP network like the Internet, think of your application as sitting on top of the protocol stack. In other words, the TCP/IP protocol suite sits between your application and the hardware.

Think of the TCP/IP protocol suite as a team of personal assistants standing on a ladder. You live at the top of the ladder and your mailbox is at the bottom of the ladder. To send information across the network, you hand your data to the assistant that stands just beneath you, who then passes it to the assistant that stands beneath him, and so on. When your mail reaches the lowest level, the mailman (the network) carries your mail to its destination (a different ladder). The assistants at the bottom of the destination ladder then pass the mail up the ladder, one level at a time. Likewise, when you receive a message, your assistants hand the message up the ladder.

MOVING DATA ACROSS THE INTERNET

You can more easily understand TCP/IP if you separately examine the three essential steps required to move information across the Internet:

1. Information must flow between your application program and the network. This information flows through the protocol stack.

2. The network must determine where your information should go. More specifically, the network must resolve your data's destination address.

3. The network must transport and route your data to its physical destination on the Internet. At its physical destination, your data will flow through the protocol stack to the destination application.

Your network programs will spend a lot of time moving information through the protocol stack. For you to create such programs, it is essential that you understand the operation each layer performs.

EXPLORING THE *TCP/IP* PROTOCOL STACK

The ISO/OSI reference model defines seven functional layers for network designs. However, the ISO/OSI reference model is merely a guide—not a design in and of itself. For example, the TCP/IP network design only uses five of the ISO/OSI layers. Figure 3.3 shows a simple, five-layer network model with the TCP/IP protocols in their respective network layers. You will learn the purpose and function of each protocol module in the discussions that follow. For now, simply note that the network layers and their associated protocols form a model through which your data will flow as it moves between your application and the network hardware.

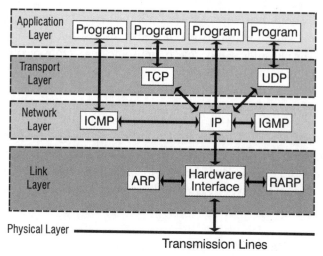

Figure 3.3 TCP/IP network model with associated protocols.

In Figure 3.3, the lines with arrows show possible avenues of communication between the various network software and hardware modules. For example, to communicate with the transport layer, your applications talk to the User Datagram Protocol (UDP) and Transport Control Protocol (TCP) modules. To communicate with the network layer, your applications talk to the Internet Control Message Protocol (ICMP) or Internet Protocol (IP) software modules. However, regardless of which route your data takes from the application layer to the network layer, your data must flow through the IP module to reach the network hardware.

In most cases, data flows sequentially from the top layer to the bottom layer. However, as shown in Figure 3.3, you can develop programs that bypass the transport layer and talk directly to the network layer. Although you will rarely need to create such programs, Chapter 14 will show you how to do so. As you will learn, bypassing the transport layer requires significantly more programming effort. In other words, you must develop a program that performs functions that the transport layer normally handles.

The following discussions use a bottom-up approach to show you how data moves through the protocol stack. In other words, you will start with the bottom layer (the physical layer) and work upward to the top layer (the application layer). As you can see from Figure 3.3, most of your network programming will take place in the middle layers. That is, your application must communicate with either the transport layer or the network layer.

Since you will spend most of your programming time in the top three layers, you might think a top-down approach is more logical. However, to understand the middle network layers, you must understand the bottom layers first. Much of what occurs in the middle network layers will not make any sense until you understand how the lower levels function. In the following sections, you will see how data moves up the protocol stack, from the network to your application. After you learn this process, you will easily understand how data flows from your application to the network. Furthermore, you will understand why you must include various pieces of information with all data that you transmit across the Internet.

UNDERSTANDING THE PHYSICAL LAYER

The physical layer in a TCP/IP network is identical to the ISO/OSI-model physical layer—it includes the transmission media that carries network data. This media is usually some type of twisted-pair or coaxial cable. Network designers and integrators must understand the transmission characteristics of such cables. However, as an applications programmer, you simply need to know that the cable attached to your computer is part of the network's physical layer.

UNDERSTANDING THE LINK LAYER

As you saw in Figure 3.3, the link layer includes a hardware interface and two protocol modules: the Address Resolution Protocol (ARP) and the Reverse Address Resolution Protocol (RARP). In Chapter 4, you will learn more about these protocols. For now, simply note that the link layer uses these two protocols to resolve addresses.

Note: ARP translates network layer addresses into link-layer addresses. In reverse fashion, RARP translates link-layer addresses into network addresses. The reasons why network software requires such translations will become clear in Chapter 4.

The link layer, which the ISO/OSI model calls the data-link, sits between the physical layer and the network layer. As its name implies, the link layer links the physical layer to the network layer. To fully understand the link layer, you must examine its interface to both the network layer and the physical layer—the layers above and below it, respectively. In Chapter 4, you will learn more details about the interface between the link and network layers. The following sections focus primarily on the link-layer's interface to the physical layer.

UNDERSTANDING THE PURPOSE OF THE LINK LAYER

As shown in Figure 3.4, the link layer handles the exchange of data between the physical layer and the network layer. More specifically, in the TCP/IP protocol suite, the link layer sends and receives data for the network layer's IP module.

Besides performing a specific function, each layer in a layered network hides network implementation details. As such, another purpose of the link layer is to hide the network's physical implementation from the network layer. When the link layer does its job, protocols in the network layer don't care whether the network uses Ethernet technology or IBM Token Ring technology. The network layer simply passes data to the link layer, which then handles all further data transmission.

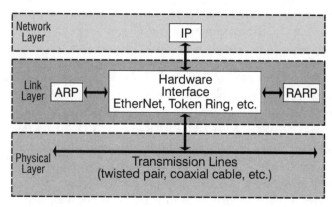

Figure 3.4 The link layer interface.

To develop Internet applications, you don't need a detailed understanding of network technologies such as Ethernet or IBM Token Ring. However, you do need to understand how information flows through the protocol stack. To understand how information moves through the link layer of the protocol stack, you need to have a general knowledge of at least one network technology.

An Ethernet Crash Course

Networks that use Ethernet technology are popular, widely used, and commonly understood. Many networks on the Internet use Ethernet technology. The following paragraphs present a simple overview of Ethernet technology. After you learn the basic elements of Ethernet technology, you will better understand the data flow between the physical and link layers in a TCP/IP network.

Computers on a network contain one or more network interface cards, which connect the computers to the network. Network interface cards are technology specific. In other words, if you use Ethernet, you need an Ethernet interface card. If you use IBM Token Ring, you need a token ring interface card and so on.

Why Computers Use Multiple Network Interface Cards

A networked computer must contain at least one network interface card. However, computers can also contain more than one such card. For example, a computer can contain multiple interface cards for the same network technology or for different network technologies.

A computer with multiple network interfaces is *multihomed*. If these multiple cards provide interfaces to multiple network technologies, the computer can also serve as a *router*. For example, if a computer has an Ethernet card and a token ring card, the computer can route data between the two types of networks—a token ring network and an Ethernet. If a computer

---

contains two Ethernet cards, the computer is *multihomed* but not a router. Such a computer can route data between two homogenous networks (the network technologies are the same).

In the past, network professionals also referred to routers as *gateways*. Today, however, the term *gateway* often refers to an application gateway. An application gateway is a program that connects two different types of protocol suites for a specific application, such as e-mail. For example, to send e-mail from your TCP/IP network to a network that does not use the TCP/IP protocol suite, your data must pass through an application gateway. Unfortunately, a lot of Internet literature uses the term *gateway* to refer to a router. Therefore, be careful when you see the term. Make sure you understand the term's usage in the proper context. A router, which Internet literature may refer to as an *IP router*, is always a router. However, the term *gateway* may refer to a router or an application gateway.

You connect computers to an Ethernet network by attaching their Ethernet interface cards to a cable. You must attach all computers on your Ethernet to the same cable. When your network application sends data across the network, your data flows from one network card to the next.

Every Ethernet interface card on a particular network has a unique address. As data moves across the network, Ethernet technology packages the data in a *frame*. An Ethernet frame contains a destination address, a source address, the actual data, and a field that identifies the type of data the frame includes. An Ethernet address is six bytes wide. Every Ethernet interface card on the network watches for its address in the Ethernet frames that pass by on the data bus. Ethernet cards also listen for a destination address of hex FF FF FF FF FF FF, which identifies the data as a broadcast message directed to all computers on the network.

While all interface cards can receive simultaneously, Ethernet technology lets only one device (interface card) transmit at a time. When two interface cards transmit at the same time, a data collision occurs. Ethernet technology detects such collisions and requires both devices to wait a short, but random, amount of time before they can transmit again. You can refer to Ethernet collision detection technology as *carrier sense multiple access with collision detection (CSMA/CD)*. For our purposes, the CSMA/CD implementation details are not important. However, should you desire more information, turn to RFC 1180, *A TCP/IP Tutorial*. In this RFC, T. Socolofsky and C. Kale provide an excellent analogy that describes how CSMA/CD works.

In their analogy, Socolofsky and Kale use a group of people talking in a dark room to represent Ethernet technology. Every person in the room can hear anyone that talks and everyone has an equal opportunity to talk (carrier sense multiple access). Everyone tries to follow the rules, which do not let anyone speak while another person talks. However, if two people accidentally speak at the same time, they both become immediately aware of the problem—they hear something they themselves have not said (collision detection). When this occurs, both people immediately stop talking and wait a moment before trying to speak again.

MODIFYING THE LINK LAYER

To connect your PC to an Ethernet network, you must first install a network interface card in your computer. The interface card must use Ethernet technology. Next, you attach a cable to the interface card. This cable connects the other computers on the network to your computer. The cable is the media across which data actually moves from one computer to the next. Your computer's network interface card connects your computer to the network cable. As such, in a layered network model, your network interface card represents the link layer—the link between the cable (the physical layer) and your network software.

As you will see when you explore the network layer, the protocols in the TCP/IP protocol suite work regardless of network technologies. You can attach your computer to a network that uses Ethernet, token ring, or any other network technology that includes a TCP/IP implementation. You can do this because the link layer (your network interface card) hides implementation details that are specific to each of these technologies. Consider what this means to you as a software developer. If you design your applications to use TCP/IP protocols, people can use your software regardless of whether their local network uses Ethernet or token ring technology. Also, people can change the technology they use for their local network and continue to use your software—without any modifications to your application.

Suppose you design and develop a client/server application that manages a custom medical database for doctors' offices. If you design the application around the TCP/IP protocol suite, you can sell your application to doctors that use either Ethernet or token ring network technologies. Assume you have developed applications for a hospital that decides to switch its network from token ring to Ethernet. The hospital will replace the existing network cards, re-route network cables, and maybe replace the network operating system. However, after the hospital drops the new network cards into the computers and brings the network back on-line, your application will run exactly as it did before. Neither you nor programmers at the hospital will have to make any modifications to your software. In each of these examples, the link layer (network card) is modified (actually replaced) without impacting any of the network layers above it. These examples demonstrate the power of the layered network model and protocol suites, such as TCP/IP.

EXPANDING YOUR TCP/IP VOCABULARY

You need to understand eight important terms to fully comprehend the TCP/IP protocol suite. These terms define the differences between the two TCP/IP transport protocols: the User Datagram Protocol (UDP) and the Transport Control Protocol (TCP). Furthermore, these terms describe protocol characteristics related to network connections, protocol reliability, and data services.

NETWORK CONNECTIONS

Network connections are either *connection-oriented* or *connectionless*. A connection-oriented protocol must establish a connection with another application before any communication can occur.

For example, when you use a telephone to communicate with someone, you dial a telephone number and wait for someone to answer. You cannot talk or communicate with anyone until someone picks up the telephone at the other end of your call. In the same way, a connection-oriented protocol cannot communicate or transport data until it establishes a connection. The Transport Control Protocol is a connection-oriented protocol.

A connectionless protocol does not establish a connection before transmitting messages. As a result, each message that uses a connectionless protocol must contain all delivery information. For example, when you mail a letter to someone, you must write a complete and accurate address on the envelope if you want the postal service to deliver your letter. However, you don't personally deliver the letter. You simply drop the letter into a mailbox and expect the postal service to deliver it. In the same way, each message transmitted by a connectionless protocol contains a complete and accurate address for delivery. A connectionless protocol passes the message to the next layer in the protocol stack and depends on the network for delivery. The User Datagram Protocol and Internet Protocol are connectionless protocols.

Protocol Reliability

Protocols are either *reliable* or *unreliable*. When your data passes through a reliable protocol, the protocol guarantees delivery of that data. Typically, reliable delivery includes several features. First, to ensure data delivery, the protocol exchanges acknowledgment messages between the communicating applications. In other words, each time a program sends a message, the program expects to receive a reply message that says, in effect, "Hey, I got your last message." If the sending program does not receive such an acknowledgment, the program automatically and repeatedly re-sends the message until it gets a reply message.

Second, to ensure delivery of valid data, a reliable protocol includes one or more checksums with each transmission. (As you learned in Chapter 2, computers create checksums by adding the binary value of each data-unit in a data block.) The receiving computer calculates a new checksum and compares it to the transmitted checksum. A non-match indicates an error.

If you are unfamiliar with checksums, don't worry. Later in this book, you will learn how to create a checksum. For now, simply understand that a checksum is a calculated value that ensures error-free data transmissions. The Transport Control Protocol is a reliable protocol that uses checksums, acknowledgment messages, and other techniques to help ensure reliable data delivery.

In contrast, an unreliable protocol does not ensure data delivery. The protocol will try to deliver the data but does not guarantee success. More significantly, an unreliable transport protocol does not notify the sending application when the delivery effort fails.

You can compare unreliable data delivery to a letter without a return address. If the delivery address is incorrect, you will never know that the letter was undelivered since the postal service cannot return the letter to you. Also, even when the delivery address is correct, there is no guarantee that the postal service won't lose your letter.

In the same way, a message that uses an unreliable protocol can simply become lost. An unreliable protocol does not guarantee delivery, nor does the protocol necessarily notify you when delivery was unsuccessful. However, in the same way that the postal service protects the contents of your letter, an unreliable protocol can protect data integrity by using one or more checksums.

For example, the Internet Protocol requires a checksum, but the checksum is optional in the User Datagram Protocol. Both the User Datagram Protocol and Internet Protocol are unreliable protocols. You may wonder why anyone would ever use an unreliable protocol. The answer is cost. An unreliable protocol is much simpler to design, implement, and use. Cost, in terms of complexity and network bandwidth, is significantly lower with an unreliable protocol.

Also, you should understand that an unreliable protocol can perform reliable data delivery. However, you must design the reliability features into your application and not depend on the protocol. For example, as you will learn, the Transport Control Protocol (a reliable protocol) uses the Internet Protocol (an unreliable protocol) for all data delivery. The protocol designers built reliability features into the Transport Control Protocol.

PROTOCOL DATA

Two basic types of data services exist within the TCP/IP protocol suite: a byte-stream service and a datagram service. A protocol that uses a byte stream transmits all information as a series of bytes. In other words, the protocol treats the data as a single serial stream of bytes, regardless of the data length and the number of transmissions required to send or receive all the data. For example, when using a byte-stream protocol, you might send five data segments (each consisting of ten bytes) and one data segment consisting of 50 bytes for a total transmission of 100 bytes. However, the receiving end of the connection might read your data in 20 byte increments (five reads). The Transport Control Protocol is a byte-stream protocol.

When you talk on the telephone, you don't worry about the size of your words or the length of your sentences. You know the person listening to you will hear your words in the same sequence that you speak them. Likewise, a byte-stream protocol doesn't care about the length of each data segment. When an application uses a byte-stream protocol to send data, the protocol guarantees the other end of the connection will receive the data in the same order as the transmission sequence.

In contrast, a protocol that uses datagrams transmits information as self-contained units of information. In other words, the protocol transmits each datagram independently—the datagram is not dependent upon any other datagram. Also, multiple datagrams that the protocol transmits to the same destination may not arrive in the same order as the transmission sequence. If the receiving application requires sequential data, the application must collate the data after it arrives. The User Datagram Protocol and Internet Protocol use datagrams to deliver data.

A datagram is like a letter. If you mailed two letters to the same person on the same day, you have no way of knowing which letter the person will open first. Likewise, if you mail letters to two people on two successive days, you cannot know which letter will reach its destination first. It's possible the letters could arrive in reverse order. In the same way, datagrams may arrive out of sequence. If the sequence in which your data arrives is unimportant, you might use a datagram service instead of a byte-stream to reduce the complexity of your program.

Virtual Circuits

A *virtual circuit* is a connection that appears to be a dedicated point-to-point link. For example, if you place a phone call from Los Angeles to New York, your connection is a virtual circuit. The link between your telephone and the telephone in New York appears to be a direct connection—as if there is a single wire that connects the two phones. In reality, the telephone company will route your call through many switches in several cities between Los Angeles and New York. In other words, you don't have a dedicated wire running directly from your telephone to the telephone in New York even though it seems that way when you talk.

In many cases, your programs will require a point-to-point connection or virtual circuit. For example, if you want to transfer a file from a remote host computer to your local system, you will probably want to establish a virtual circuit. You would not want to wait for a lot of individual datagrams to deliver the file a few bytes at a time—especially since the datagrams (and bytes) might arrive in the wrong order. Within the TCP/IP protocol suite, the Transport Control Protocol provides a virtual circuit for network communications; the User Datagram Protocol and Internet Protocol do not.

Octet

The term *octet* has absolutely nothing to do with the preceding terms. However, as you move further into the protocol stack, you will learn how protocols organize or structure data. If you read any literature that discusses Internet data structures, you will inevitably come across the term *octet*. In Section 1.6 of his book *TCP/IP Illustrated, Volume 1*, Addison-Wesley, 1994, W. Richard Stevens provides some background and amusing commentary on the term *octet*. He says, in part:

> "All Internet standards and most books on TCP/IP use the term octet instead of byte. The use of this cute, but baroque term is historical, since much of the early work on TCP/IP was done on systems such as the DEC-10, which did not use 8-bit bytes."

Stevens goes on to point out that most modern computer systems use 8-bit bytes. As such, in *TCP/IP Illustrated, Volume 1,* Stevens drops the term *octet* and uses the more familiar and commonly understood term, byte, to indicate an 8-bit unit of data. *Internet Programming* will follow Stevens' enlightened lead and use the term *byte* also.

Putting It All Together

As you learned in Chapters 1 and 2, network protocols deliver data and communicate messages across a network. In this chapter, you learned that the TCP/IP protocol suite is a collection of cooperative protocols; the protocols in the TCP/IP protocol suite coordinate their efforts to deliver data across the TCP/IP networks that comprise the Internet.

To program the Internet, you must understand how the TCP/IP protocols perform their assigned tasks. This chapter provided an introduction to the TCP/IP protocols and terminology. In the next two chapters, you will explore the Internet Protocol and the TCP/IP transport protocols. However, before you move on to Chapter 4, make sure you understand the following key concepts:

- ✓ The TCP/IP protocol suite is a collection of protocols that work together to communicate information across the Internet.

- ✓ A protocol stack refers to the vertical order in which protocols appear in a layered network.

- ✓ The TCP/IP protocol stack consists of all the protocols in the TCP/IP protocol suite.

- ✓ When your programs transmit data to a remote host on the Internet, your data flows down the protocol stack and across the network. At its destination, your data flows up the protocol stack to the destination program on the remote host computer.

- ✓ When a layered network uses Ethernet technology, the Ethernet network interface card represents the link layer.

- ✓ You can replace the link layer (the network interface card) with different network technologies and not affect existing TCP/IP applications.

- ✓ A multihomed computer contains multiple network interface cards, which let the computer communicate with multiple networks.

- ✓ A router delivers data between networks that use different network technologies, such as Ethernet and token ring.

- ✓ When a multihomed computer contains network interface cards for two or more different network technologies, the computer can serve as a router.

- ✓ Reliable protocols guarantee data delivery; unreliable protocols do not.

- ✓ A byte stream delivers data as a single, serial stream of data.

- ✓ A datagram delivers data as individual, self-contained units of data.

- ✓ A virtual circuit functions like a dedicated, point-to-point connection even though, in reality, it is not.

Chapter 4
Understanding the Internet Protocol

In every train yard, there is a conductor who decides how many engines, how many cars, and what kinds of cars each train should have. The conductor also decides, depending on the types of cargo each train will carry, the order in which these cars should be connected. If the conductor is competent, most trains will arrive safely at their destinations. However, if the conductor makes a bad decision, such as placing a caboose at the head of a train and an engine at the rear, the results can be disastrous. In such cases, the train may never arrive at its destination or, worse yet, may crash and lose all its cargo.

Much like a train conductor, the network layer decides how messages are packaged for transport across the TCP/IP network. The network layer uses the Internet Protocol (IP) to perform this task. As such, the network layer and the IP software module serve the same purpose. This chapter examines the Internet Protocol in detail. By the time you finish this chapter, you will understand the following key concepts:

- The purpose of the TCP/IP network layer
- How to decode IP addresses
- How IP address classes expand the number of Internet addresses
- The purpose of the Internet address protocols
- What information an IP datagram includes
- The purpose of the data fields in an IP datagram header
- How fragmentation occurs in a TCP/IP network
- How IP routes data and the purpose of routing tables

UNDERSTANDING THE NETWORK LAYER

The network layer is the heart of any network based on the TCP/IP protocol suite. As shown in Figure 4.1, the network layer includes the Internet Protocol (IP), the Internet Control Message Protocol (ICMP), and the Internet Group Management Protocol (IGMP). Within the network layer, IP performs most of the work. ICMP and IGMP are IP-support protocols that help the IP manage special network messages such as error and multicast messages (messages sent to two or more systems). Because of the close relationship between the Internet Protocol and the network layer, much Internet and TCP/IP literature refers to the network layer as the IP layer.

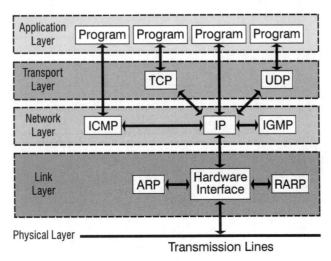

Figure 4.1 *The TCP/IP network layer includes the IP, ICMP, and IGMP software modules.*

DISSECTING THE INTERNET PROTOCOL

The Internet Protocol is the delivery system for the TCP/IP protocol suite. Even the other protocols in the TCP/IP protocol suite—such as TCP, UDP, and ICMP—use the Internet Protocol for data delivery. In a TCP/IP network, an Internet Protocol datagram encapsulates every protocol except the address resolution protocols. For more information on encapsulation, see the "Understanding Encapsulation" sidebar presented next.

UNDERSTANDING ENCAPSULATION

As you have learned, to transmit data across a layered network, you pass data from your application to a protocol on the protocol stack. After that protocol finishes with your data, it passes the data to the next protocol on the stack. As your data passes through each layer in the protocol stack, the network software (protocol modules) encapsulates the data for the next lower level in the stack. Encapsulation, therefore, is the process of storing your data in the format required by the next lower level protocol in the stack. As your data flows through the protocol stack, each layer builds on the previous layer's encapsulation. Figure 4.2 shows how the network software encapsulates your data when you use the Transport Control Protocol (TCP) on an Ethernet.

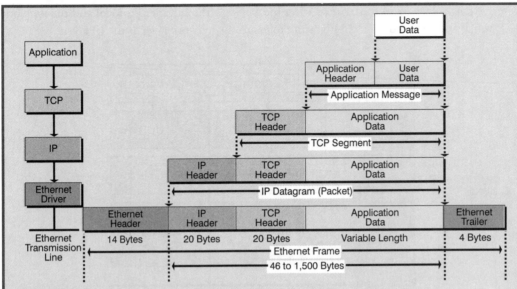

Figure 4.2 Data encapsulation using TCP on an Ethernet.

As you can see, the application module may encapsulate data from the user in an application message. A program's design determines whether a program uses an application message. In many cases, the program may format user data for use by a network protocol such as TCP. As shown in Figure 4.2, the TCP module formats application data into a TCP segment. The TCP segment includes the application data and the TCP header information required by the protocol. The application data includes an application header (if any) and the user data. As the data passes through the IP module in the network layer, the network software formats the TCP segment into an IP datagram (or packet). The Ethernet driver formats data from the IP module and places the data into an Ethernet frame.

Figure 4.2 is simply one example of the encapsulation process. As discussed, some programs may not use an application message. Also, a program that uses the User Datagram Protocol (UDP) instead of TCP will encapsulate application data within a UDP datagram. The important point to remember is that TCP/IP protocols encapsulate your data by formatting it to fit into a structure defined by the protocol. You will learn more about encapsulation as *Internet Programming* discusses each network layer.

As you may recall, the three-step process of moving information across the Internet includes flowing data through the protocol stack, determining the data's destination address, and transporting or routing the data to that destination. As you might expect, the Internet Protocol operates at the core of this process. You need to understand the relationship between the Internet Protocol and this three-step process of moving information across the Internet. As such, the following sections will discuss the Internet Protocol in three parts:

- First, you will learn how a TCP/IP network defines Internet addresses.

- Next, you will learn how the network creates IP datagrams within the protocol stack.

- Finally, you will learn how the Internet routes IP datagrams.

UNDERSTANDING INTERNET ADDRESSES

An Internet address is an IP address. Most users, and even much Internet literature, associate IP addresses with host computers. However, you should understand that a computer on the Internet does not really have an IP address. Chapter 3 presented an overview of Ethernet technology. As you have learned, Ethernet technology requires every network interface card on a particular network to have a unique Ethernet address. Like Ethernet interface cards, every interface on the Internet must also have a unique IP address.

Just as Ethernet associates Ethernet addresses with a network interface card, a TCP/IP network associates IP addresses with an interface card—not the host computer itself. Each network interface card attached to the Internet must have a unique IP address. However, as you have learned, one computer can contain several network interface cards. This means a single host computer on the Internet may have several valid IP addresses.

For simplicity, you can normally associate an IP address with a host computer. The only time this is a problem is when the computer has multiple network interface cards. Much Internet literature discusses IP addresses as though the host computer (rather than the network interface card) always owns the address. As such, *Internet Programming* will discuss IP addresses in the same way. However, as an applications programmer, you should understand and remember that the interface card (not the host computer) owns the IP address.

UNDERSTANDING DOTTED-DECIMAL NOTATION

An IP address is 32 bits or 4 bytes wide. If you use the C programming language, you can represent an IP address as a long integer. (In C, long integers are 32 bits or 4 bytes wide.) However, people normally write IP addresses in dotted-decimal notation. *Dotted-decimal notation* conveniently represents each IP address byte as a series of decimal numbers separated by periods (or dots). For example, the following numbers are equivalent representations of the same IP address:

IP Address as a binary number:	10000110 00011000 00001000 01000010
IP Address as a decimal number:	2,249,721,922 (or -2,045,245,374)
IP Address as a hexadecimal number:	0x86180842
IP Address in dotted-decimal notation:	134.24.8.66

Note: If you have not programmed in the C or C++ languages, the above arithmetic may not be obvious. You should understand that eight bits equal one byte and four bytes equal a long integer. You can use signed or unsigned long integers.

Table 4.1 may help clarify the numbers shown above. Table 4.1 shows the relationship between each byte of the IP address.

Decimal	Hex	Binary
134	0x86	10000110
24	0x18	00011000
8	0x08	00001000
66	0x42	01000010

Table 4.1 *The relationship between equivalent representations of an IP address.*

You should understand that the dotted-decimal notation is merely a convenient format to write IP addresses. That is, people read dotted-decimal notation much easier than binary, hex, or decimal representations of an IP address.

If you own a calculator that performs conversions between binary, hexadecimal, and decimal numbers, you can verify that the previous IP address representations are equivalent. If you use your calculator to convert the following numbers, you will see that they are also equivalent:

IP Address as a binary number:	11000000 01100110 11111001 00000011
IP Address as a decimal number:	3,227,973,891 (or -1,066,993,405)
IP Address as a hexadecimal number:	0xC066F903
IP Address in dotted-decimal notation:	192.102.249.3

DECODING IP ADDRESSES

The 32-bit IP address encodes (combines) a network number and a host number (actually an interface number). As you know, the Internet consists of thousands of interconnected networks. To distinguish one network from another, the *Internet Network Information Center (InterNIC)* ensures each network has a unique network identifier. As originally designed, the high-order byte in an IP address identified the network number and the lower three bytes identified the host computer (interface). For example, you could look at IP address 134.24.8.66 and know that the network ID number was decimal 134.

In general, Internet software interprets a field with all 1's as "all." An address field that contains all 1's represents a broadcast address (or, in other words, a message destined for all computers on the network). Normally, Internet software interprets a field with all 0's as "this." In other words, an address field with all 0's would represent "this" network and "this" host computer. The Internet reserves these two addresses (all 1's and all 0's) for these purposes only.

Note: In his book **Internetworking with TCP/IP, Volume 1**, *Prentice Hall, 1991, Douglas E. Comer states that an early release of Berkeley UNIX used all 0's for broadcast. As a result, some commercial systems derived from that release still use all 0's for broadcast.*

UNDERSTANDING ADDRESS CLASSES

As you know, the original address-encoding scheme used the high-order byte for a network ID number. As a result, users could interconnect only 255 networks. (Remember, the Internet reserves all 1's for broadcast messages.) To overcome this address-space limitation, Internet professionals devised a simple but effective encoding scheme. IP addresses no longer use the high-order byte for a network number. Instead, IP addresses use the high-order bits in the high-order byte to identify an *address class*. The address class specifies how many bytes the address uses for the network ID number. The class-encoding scheme sounds much more complicated than it really is. As you read the following paragraphs, refer to Table 4.2. This table will help you understand how the Internet's address-encoding scheme works.

Class	High-Order Bits	Bytes Available for a Network ID
A	0 - - - -	1
B	1 0 - - -	2
C	1 1 0 - -	3
D	1 1 1 0	(Used for multicasting)
E	1 1 1 1 0	(Reserved for future use)

Table 4.2 IP address classes.

As previously mentioned in the section entitled "Understanding Internet Addresses," a TCP/IP network requires every network interface on the same physical network to have the same network ID number but a unique host ID number. Later in this chapter, the section entitled "Understanding IP Routing" will explain the reason for this Internet rule. For now, you will take a closer look at each address class to help you understand the IP addresses that result from this encoding scheme. Also, you will learn how address classes expand the Internet address space, allowing the thousands of networks that exist today.

DEFINING A CLASS A ADDRESS

If you refer to Table 4.2, you can see that a Class A address uses a maximum of one byte for the class type and network ID. This leaves three bytes for host ID numbers:

Class A Address

In Table 4.2, you can also see that Class A addresses use one of the high-order bits for class encoding. As a result, only seven bits of the high-order byte are available for network ID numbers.

This means the Internet can interconnect only 127 networks with Class A addresses (seven bits can represent 128 unique values, but all 0's is a reserved address). However, because networks with a Class A address use 24 bits for host address space, each such network can theoretically attach 16,777,216 hosts. As such, only those few networks that need to attach more than 65,536 hosts use Class A addresses.

DEFINING A CLASS B ADDRESS

As shown in Table 4.2, Class B addresses use a maximum of two bytes for the class type and network ID. This leaves 16 bits for host ID numbers:

Class B Address

After you subtract the two high-order bits used for class encoding, you have 14 bits available for network ID numbers. As a result, the Internet can connect 16,384 networks with Class B addresses.Using 16 bits for the host identifier, each network with a Class B address can theoretically attach up to 65,536 hosts. Networks that need to attach more than 65,536 host computers require a Class A address. The InterNIC reserves Class B addresses for networks that expect to attach at least 256 host computers.

DEFINING A CLASS C ADDRESS

Class C addresses use a maximum of three bytes for the class and network ID, which leaves only eight bits for host ID numbers:

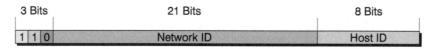

Class C Address

After you subtract the three high-order bits used for class encoding, you have 21 bits available for network ID numbers. As a result, the Internet can connect a staggering 2,097,152 individual networks that use Class C addresses. However, because Class C addresses have only eight bits available for host ID numbers, the Internet limits each of these networks to less than 256 host computers. In other words, small networks use Class C addresses.

DEFINING CLASS D AND E ADDRESSES

The InterNIC uses Class D for multicast addresses. A multicast address represents a group of Internet host computers. In other words, multicasting delivers messages to one or more host computers. The InterNIC reserves Class E addresses for future use. Although currently undefined,

Class E addresses will probably be assigned as broadcast and multicast addresses. It is unlikely that the InterNIC will assign Class E addresses to individual hosts. Before that were to happen, the Internet would probably adopt a new type of addressing or address-encoding scheme. Later in this chapter, you will learn more about multicast and broadcast addresses.

ADDING UP THE NUMBERS

If you have a calculator handy, you can appreciate what the class-encoding scheme did for the Internet's addressing capability. If you total the available network ID numbers, you will find that the Internet is theoretically capable of interconnecting over two million individual networks—not individual computers, but full-blown networks. If each host computer only contained one network interface and every network attached the maximum number of host computers, the Internet could conceivably consist of over 3.7 billion computers. If you find these numbers extraordinary, you might be astonished by the fact that many network designers are developing proposals to expand the Internet address space even further.

Compare the Internet address space with and without class encoding. With the original addressing scheme (using one byte for network IDs and three bytes for host identifiers), the Internet could connect over four billion computers. However, as previously mentioned, all these computers would be part of a mere 255 networks. Using the class-encoding scheme previously described, the Internet reduced the potential number of host computers by approximately ten percent. However, the class-encoding scheme increased the number of potential networks from 255 to more than two million. In other words, by using the class-encoding scheme, the Internet sacrificed a few individual host computer addresses to gain a tremendous number of individual network identifiers.

By expanding the number of network identifiers and generally reducing the number of computers attached to each network, the class-encoding scheme also simplifies network administration. For example, without class encoding, the Internet could use a simple 32-bit addressing scheme to represent over four billion computers. In this case, address administrators at InterNIC would have to track over four billion network addresses—an impossible task. Using the original encoding scheme in which the high-order byte defined a network, each network could contain over 16 million computer addresses. In addition to limiting the Internet to 255 networks, this encoding scheme would also require each network administrator to keep track of 16 million addresses!

With class encoding, only 127 network administrators (those responsible for Class A addresses) have to experience the 16-million-computer nightmare. Additionally, the class-encoding scheme significantly reduces the number of addresses that the other two-million-plus administrators (those responsible for networks with Class B and C addresses) must manage.

ASSIGNING IP ADDRESSES

As you have learned, the number of possible Internet addresses is staggering. Since each Internet address must be unique, you might wonder who is responsible for the mind-numbing task of ensuring the validity of 3.7 billion addresses. Fortunately, no one person or organization must guarantee address uniqueness. The Internet Network Information Center (InterNIC) assigns all network ID numbers and ensures their uniqueness. Within each network, the network's administrator assigns host (interface) ID numbers. As previously discussed, the InterNIC will assign large networks (over 65,536 hosts) a Class A address. Intermediate networks (between 256 and 65,536 hosts) receive a Class B address. Small networks (less than 256 hosts) receive a Class C address.

UNDERSTANDING SUBNET ADDRESSES

As noted above, the InterNIC assigns network ID numbers, and network administrators assign host ID numbers. As such, network administrators have significant flexibility when they set up their networks. Network administrators can use their networks' host address space any way they want so long as they identify each network interface with a unique address. A network administrator can subdivide his or her network's host address space to effectively create a local network of networks. For example, assume a network administrator is responsible for an Internet network that uses a Class B address. As just discussed, the network administrator has 16 bits available for host ID numbers. The network administrator can subdivide these 16 bits into two bytes, using one byte as a network ID number and one as a host ID number. By doing so, the network administrator creates a *subnet*.

*Note: A **subnet address** is any address derived from such a subnetting scheme. Such addressing schemes have meaning only within the network within which they are defined.*

Theoretically, this network administrator could create a subnet of 254 interconnected networks, each with 254 hosts (254 not 256 because the values containing all 1's and all 0's are reserved). Typically, network administrators use subnet addresses to let a single Internet address span more than one physical network. Systems attached to other networks send packets to the Internet address. Within subnetworks, however, internal routers will use the subnet addresses to route data to the correct physical address. In other words, networks use subnet addresses internally. Other networks use the normal Internet address.

UNDERSTANDING MULTICASTING

IP addresses fall into three categories: *unicast*, *broadcast*, and *multicast*. You can refer to the addresses in Classes A, B, and C as *unicast* addresses because they identify a single host. A *broadcast* address specifies that packet switches route data to all hosts on the network. In other words, broadcasting delivers messages to all computers on a particular network.

A *multicast* address identifies a group of specific host computers on the Internet. This host group can span multiple networks and include an unlimited number of computers. Furthermore, host group membership is dynamic, meaning that a host computer can join and leave a host group as it pleases. For applications such as interactive conferencing, you can use multicasting when you would want to deliver information to multiple recipients but not necessarily everyone on the network. Hosts and routers that support multicasting use the Internet Group Management Protocol (IGMP) module shown in Figure 4.1. If you have an interest in or need for multicasting, see RFC 1112, *Host extensions for IP multicasting*, S. Deering, 1989.

Examples of multicast addresses are 224.0.1.1, which is for NTP (Network Time Protocol); 224.0.0.9, which is for RIP-2 (Routing Information Protocol version 2); and 224.0.1.2, which is for Silicon Graphic's dogfight application (a game). The Internet Assigned Number Authority (IANA) assigns some multicast addresses as *well-known addresses*. A well-known address represents a permanent host group—permanent in terms of the address assigned, not the membership. You can find the current list of well-known multicast addresses in the latest version of the Request for Comments entitled "Assigned Numbers."

Note: Well-known addresses or permanent host groups are like the well-known TCP and UDP port numbers that you will learn about in Chapter 5.

UNDERSTANDING THE INTERNET ADDRESS PROTOCOLS

As previously shown in Figure 4.1, the link layer includes two address protocols: the Address Resolution Protocol (ARP) and the Reverse Address Resolution Protocol (RARP). In the preceding section, you examined IP addresses on the Internet. The previous section did not discuss the difference between an IP address and the address used by the link layer.

As you have learned, Ethernet addresses (at the physical level) are six bytes wide, as compared to four bytes for IP addresses. All data transmitted across a network using Ethernet technology must use Ethernet data frames. As you may recall, Ethernet interface cards watch the frames on the network looking for their own Ethernet address. The interface cards neither know nor care anything about IP addresses.

In other words, TCP/IP protocols only work with IP addresses and Ethernet frames only work with Ethernet addresses. These different address types present a network communication problem. The Address Resolution Protocol and the Reverse Address Resolution Protocol solve this problem by resolving addresses. That is, they translate an IP address into a link layer address and vice versa. Figure 4.3 shows the basic function of each protocol.

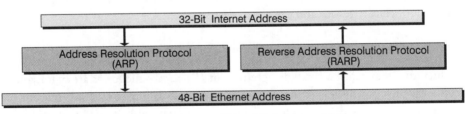

Figure 4.3 Address resolution protocols convert IP and link-layer addresses.

UNDERSTANDING THE ADDRESS RESOLUTION PROTOCOL

The Address Resolution Protocol (ARP) module maps addresses in the network layer (IP addresses) to the corresponding address in the link layer. The link-layer address is network technology specific.

For example, Ethernet addresses are six bytes wide. IBM Token Ring addresses are two or six bytes wide. And ARCNET addresses are one byte wide.

Network configurations can change as host computers join or leave the network. Luckily, ARP mapping is dynamic. In other words, ARP automatically re-maps addresses when the network configuration changes. The precise details of how ARP accomplishes this are unimportant. However, in general terms, ARP uses the link layer's broadcasting capability to query the network and identify computers that leave or join the network. The ARP module then caches (or saves) replies for later use.

UNDERSTANDING THE REVERSE ADDRESS RESOLUTION PROTOCOL

As its name implies, the Reverse Address Resolution Protocol (RARP) maps a link-layer address such as an Ethernet address into an IP address. As before, the actual conversion process depends on the link-layer technology (Ethernet, IBM Token Ring, ARCNET, and so on). As an interesting side note, TCP/IP developers designed RARP for use by computers without a disk drive. For example, a diskless workstation can read its link-layer address from its network interface card.

Using RARP, such a workstation can then broadcast a request that asks another host on the network to look up the link-layer address and report the diskless workstation's correct IP address. Using its IP address, the workstation can then broadcast a message asking another system to upload the workstation's operating system. As such, you can attach diskless workstations to the Internet and then boot the systems from remote sites across the network.

UNDERSTANDING THE IP DATAGRAM

As previously discussed, the Internet Protocol (IP) is the delivery system for the TCP/IP protocol suite and, thus, the entire Internet. The Internet Protocol uses unreliable, connectionless datagrams to deliver information across a TCP/IP network. You can refer to such datagrams as *IP datagrams*. TCP/IP networks transmit all application data across the Internet as IP datagrams. Each IP datagram includes an IP header and the actual data.

DEFINING AN IP PACKET

Internet literature may refer to an IP datagram as an *IP packet*—the terms are synonymous. This seemingly casual use of multiple names for the same unit of data may mislead you. For example, you have learned a precise definition for a datagram. You have also learned that multiple protocols such as IP and UDP use datagrams. However, you should also understand that an IP datagram and a UDP datagram are not the same.

As you have learned, a datagram is a self-contained unit of data. In contrast, a byte stream represents data as a continuous data flow (regardless of how many network messages actually deliver the data). The term *datagram* specifies a type of delivery service. That is, a protocol uses datagrams or a byte stream. A particular datagram type, such as an IP datagram, or a UDP datagram, specifies the datagram's format and contents.

The term *packet* is a generic term that refers to a unit of unidentified data. When you use the term *IP packet*, for example, you specify a unit of IP data. In other words, packet refers to the data. Datagram refers to the delivery service.

Tracking Your Data Through the Internet

As your data moves through the network layers, the name you use to refer to your data changes. In general, your data takes its name from the current module layer in the movement path. As your data moves from one layer to the next, the data name takes on the name of the new module. The following section describes the name changes your data incurs as it moves through the protocol stack and across the Internet.

Where Is It and What Is It Called?

You can refer to your data as an *application message* when it moves between the application layer and the transport layer. As you will learn in Chapter 5, the transport layer encapsulates your data using either the Transport Control Protocol (TCP) or User Datagram Protocol (UDP). TCP uses a byte-stream delivery service and UDP uses datagrams. As such, you will refer to your data as a *TCP segment* or a *UDP datagram* as your data moves from the transport layer into the network layer. Figure 4.4 shows how a TCP/IP network changes the name of a unit of data as it flows through the TCP/IP protocol stack.

Note: A TCP segment can be one of several related byte-stream transmissions.

Although not shown in Figure 4.4, you can also refer to a TCP segment as a *transport message*. When you first encounter the term *transport message*, you might think that it refers to either a TCP segment or a UDP datagram since TCP and UDP are both transport protocols. However, such an assumption is incorrect. Transport message always refers to a TCP segment—never a UDP datagram. A UDP datagram is only a UDP datagram—always.

Generally, across the Internet, the term *message* identifies data associated with a protocol or process that uses a virtual connection or byte stream. Internet literature rarely refers to datagrams as messages. Typically, if Internet literature refers to a datagram as anything other than a datagram, it will use the term "packet."

As shown in Figure 4.4, TCP segments and UDP datagrams both become IP packets as they move from the IP module into the link layer. A TCP/IP network encapsulates all TCP segments and UDP datagrams into an IP datagram when such data moves from the network layer into the link layer. As such, you should refer to your data as an IP datagram or IP packet when your data moves into the link layer.

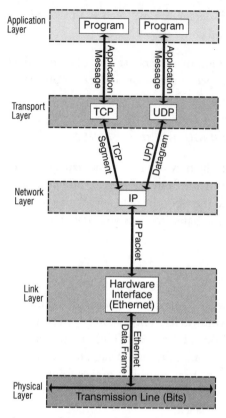

Figure 4.4 *How a unit of data's name changes as it flows through the TCP/IP protocol stack.*

If your network uses Ethernet technology, the network software will encapsulate your data into an Ethernet frame as the data moves from the link layer into the physical layer. As shown in Figure 4.4, when your data moves out of the link layer, you refer to the data as a *frame* of data or an Ethernet frame. After data reaches the physical layer, TCP/IP terminology becomes less precise and somewhat arbitrary. Section 1.3.3 of RFC 1122, *Requirements for Internet Hosts—Communication Layers*, provides some specific definitions. However, as you will discover, RFC 1122 uses the generic term "packet" to refer to a specific unit of Internet data. That is, RFC 1122 defines a packet as a unit of data passed between the internet (network) layer and the link layer.

AVOIDING THE CONFUSION

As you will discover, developing Internet programs is not much different from developing any other program. However, as you create Internet-based applications, you will inevitably refer to Internet specifications and documents such as RFCs. To correctly interpret such specifications and documents, you need a thorough understanding of the TCP/IP protocols, a clear picture of how data flows across the Internet, and a precise knowledge of commonly used TCP/IP and Internet terminology. Otherwise, official Internet documentation may confuse or mislead you—even when such documentation is technically accurate.

You can avoid confusion by understanding how data flows across the Internet. If you understand the flow of data across the Internet, you will more easily understand Internet documentation—even when such documentation uses Internet terms inconsistently or somewhat imprecisely. The following sections use a lot of official Internet terminology to identify data fields in the IP header. As you read about these fields, keep the Internet data flow in the back of your mind. Relate the function and purpose of the header fields to the data flow. In other words, remember that the purpose of the IP layer protocol is to move data across TCP/IP networks. The information in the IP header is the means by which the IP layer accomplishes this task. If you keep the big picture (Internet data flow) in view, the fields in the IP header will make much more sense.

UNDERSTANDING THE IP HEADER

As you have learned, a TCP/IP network encapsulates nearly all information that flows across the Internet within an IP datagram. The encapsulation creates an IP datagram that includes an IP header and data. The network software always creates an IP header in multiples of 32-bit words, even if it must pad (include additional zeros within) the IP header. The IP header includes all information necessary to deliver the data encapsulated within the IP datagram.

IDENTIFYING INFORMATION IN AN IP HEADER

As you might expect, since IP is the delivery system for the entire Internet, an IP header includes a lot of information. However, despite its importance and the amount of information it contains, an IP header only consumes 20 bytes of storage space. In fact, unless special IP header options are present, an IP header will always be 20 bytes wide. Figure 4.5 shows an IP datagram with the fields in the IP header identified.

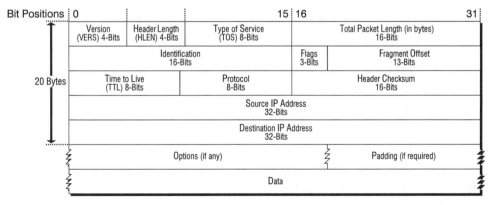

Figure 4.5 *The structure of an IP datagram showing the fields in the IP header.*

Although Figure 4.5 shows the header structure in layers, you should understand that the header is simply a serial stream of data at least 20 bytes wide. The following sections contain a brief description and explanation of each field in the IP header.

VERSION NUMBER (VERS)

Over time, the Internet Protocol has evolved. As such, you may encounter older programs written to support a different IP version. The first four bits in the IP header (otherwise known as the Version Number field) identify the version of the Internet Protocol used to create the datagram. TCP/IP requires all IP software to read this field. When IP data formats change, TCP/IP increments the IP version number stored in the Version Number field. By checking the Version Number field, IP software can reject incompatible versions of IP datagrams and thus avoid interpreting data using an outdated format. If the receiving software module does not support the IP version identified in this field, the software can report a problem. The Version Number field helps ensure network software will not misinterpret data within the IP datagram. At the time of this writing, the most recent version of the Internet Protocol was version 4.

HEADER LENGTH (HLEN)

The next four bits in the IP header (otherwise known as the Header Length field) specify the length of the IP header in 32-bit words. As previously mentioned, the length of an IP header is always a multiple of 32 bits. Without any special options (the following paragraphs will explain these options), an IP header is always 20 bytes wide. As such, the value of this field is normally 5 (five 32-bit words equal 20 bytes). More precisely, the value of this field is normally binary 0101.

Encapsulated data begins immediately after the IP header. By examining the Header Length field, Internet protocols and applications always know exactly where to find the encapsulated data. That is, you can design software to find and use the first byte of the encapsulated data using the following formula:

```
Start of encapsulated data = First byte of IP datagram + (HLEN x 4)
```

Note: *The number 4 in the above formula represents four bytes or 32 bits, which is the unit of measurement that HLEN uses to calculate the header length.*

TYPE OF SERVICE (TOS)

As a software developer, you must set priorities before you make design decisions. For example, sometimes you must decide whether performance is more important than memory conservation. Other times, you must determine if a feature is worth the time required to implement it. Just as you set priorities for the software you develop, the next eight bits in the IP header (known as the Type of Service field) define priorities for the IP packet. As you have learned, the network layer in a TCP/IP network manages data delivery through the Internet Protocol. The Type of Service field in the IP header lets the network layer make informed management decisions related to data delivery priorities. TCP/IP breaks the Type of Service field into the five subfields shown below:

Bits 0-2	3	4	5	6	7
Precedence	Delay	Throughput	Reliability	Cost	Unused

←————————————— 8 Bits —————————————→

The first three bits in the Type of Service field represent the Precedence subfield. Within this subfield, applications or protocols use a value ranging from 0 to 7 (three bits equal binary 000 to 111) to specify the importance of their data. As the number of Internet users continues to increase, data congestion may become a serious problem. Although rarely used today, the Precedence subfield provides a potential solution to such problems. Most hosts and routers ignore this field. However, as Douglas E. Comer points out in section 7.7.2 of his book, *Internetworking with TCP/IP, Volume 1*:

> *"...it is an important concept because it provides a mechanism that will eventually allow control information to have precedence over data."*

Comer notes that congestion control is one possible use of the Precedence subfield. He points out that if hosts and routers respected Precedence, you could design congestion control algorithms that would be unaffected by the congestion they try to control. Undoubtedly, concepts such as congestion control will become increasingly important as traffic on the Internet increases. For now, the Precedence subfield is like a data traffic cop that nobody on the information superhighway must obey.

The next four Type of Service subfields also define priorities that most hosts and routers ignore. However, as a programmer, you may find the priorities defined by these subfields quite interesting. While the Precedence subfield defines an overall priority for the IP packet, the other subfields define priorities that are application dependent.

For example, the Delay subfield indicates that you want to minimize delays. The Throughput subfield indicates you want to maximize throughput. When you set the Reliability bit to 1, you tell the network layer that you want to maximize reliability. Setting the Cost bit tells the network layer you want to minimize cost. As a programmer, you often must weigh such priorities as you develop software. These four Type of Service subfields let you communicate your design decisions to the network. Unfortunately, most hosts and routers may ignore your settings.

USING THE TYPE OF SERVICE SUBFIELDS

Today, Internet software does not widely support any of these Type of Service features. However, RFC 1340, *Assigned Numbers*, Reynolds and Postel, 1992, describes how standard Internet applications should set these bits. RFC 1349, *Type of Service in the Internet Protocol Suite*, Almquist, 1992, also discusses Type of Service features. To see how you might use the Type of Service bits, consider the following applications and protocols:

- Telnet is an interactive program that does not transfer much data. As such, a Telnet program would probably want to *minimize delay*. Most Telnet users don't like to wait for the network to echo their keystrokes on their computer screen.

- Unlike a Telnet program, an FTP application transfers massive amounts of data. As such, an FTP program would want to *maximize throughput*.

- Usenet manages massive amounts of information. However, Usenet data is not critical in terms of network operations or timeliness. As such, Usenet programs would probably want to *minimize cost*.

- As a network management protocol, Simple Network Management Protocol (SNMP) is critical to proper network operations. SNMP programs would probably want to *maximize reliability*.

As you develop Internet applications, you should keep in mind what priorities (speed, throughput, cost, and/or reliability) you want to emphasize when you transmit your data across the Internet. For example, if you want to save costs, you need to determine if you can sacrifice speed, throughput, and reliability without seriously handicapping your application. After you determine data delivery priorities for your programs, you can communicate your priorities to the network through the Type of Service subfields.

PACKET LENGTH

The next field in the IP header is the Packet Length field. The 16-bit Packet Length field specifies the length of the entire IP packet, including the IP header. TCP/IP specifies this length in bytes, not multiples of 32-bit words (like the Header Length field). Using Packet Length and Header Length, you can find the beginning and end of encapsulated data, and calculate the data's length:

```
Start of data = First byte of IP datagram + (HLEN x 4)
End of data = First byte of IP datagram + Packet Length
Length of data = Packet Length - Start of data
```

Since Packet Length is a 16-bit field, the theoretical maximum size of an IP datagram is 65,535 bytes. However, you need to remember that TCP/IP further encapsulates IP datagrams as they pass through the link layer. For example, if your local network uses Ethernet technology, the link layer will encapsulate your IP datagrams into Ethernet frames before transmitting your data. Each network technology specifies the maximum packet size it will accept. You can refer to this limitation as a network's *maximum transfer unit* or *MTU*. For example, the Ethernet specification limits transfers to 1,500 bytes. Maximum IBM Token Ring transfers are typically 4,464 bytes. Other network MTUs can be as small as 128 bytes or less.

If an application tries to transmit an IP packet larger than your underlying network's MTU, *fragmentation* occurs. Fragmentation breaks your data into smaller chunks for multiple transmissions. Your data can also become fragmented if it passes through a router with an MTU smaller than your local network. Unfortunately, fragmentation is an unavoidable fact of life on the Internet. Luckily, other than possible performance delays which result when the link layer breaks apart (fragments) the data and later repackages it, fragmentation is transparent to your application. Later in this chapter, you will learn more about fragmentation.

IDENTIFICATION

Because networks frequently break datagrams into smaller pieces, the TCP/IP designers include an Identification field in the IP header. Host computers use the 16-bit Identification field to uniquely identify each datagram they send. When a host computer receives datagrams, it uses the Identification field to determine which fragments belong to which datagram.

FLAGS AND FRAGMENT OFFSET

In general, host computers use the Identification, Flags, and Fragment Offset fields to reassemble fragmented IP packets. Later in this chapter, you will learn more about the Flags and Fragment Offset fields. For now, simply note that the Flags field consists of three bits and the Fragment Offset field is thirteen bits wide.

TIME-TO-LIVE (TTL)

The 8-bit Time-to-Live field specifies how long the packet can live out on the network. The purpose of this field is to prevent a packet from becoming "lost in Cyberspace." Without this field, it's possible an error could cause a packet to wander around the Internet—forever lost. The following paragraphs describe the process that prevents forever-wandering packets.

First, TCP/IP requires every router between the packet's source and destination to decrement the TTL field by one. Second, each router records the local time when an IP datagram arrives. When the router forwards the datagram, TCP/IP also decrements the TTL field by the number of seconds, if any, that the packet waited inside the router's buffer.

Note: According to Smoot Carl-Mitchell and John S. Quarterman in their book **Practical Internetworking with TCP/IP and UNIX**, *Addison-Wesley, 1993, most systems set the TTL field to 30.*

If the TTL field reaches zero before the packet reaches its destination, TCP/IP destroys the packet, no questions asked. When it destroys a packet, TCP/IP notifies the sending host with a message that uses the Internet Control Message Protocol (ICMP). Later in this book, you will learn more about ICMP when you develop an application that uses raw sockets.

PROTOCOL

As you have learned, the TCP/IP transport layer includes two protocols: the Transport Control Protocol and the User Datagram Protocol. Both protocols use IP for data delivery. The 8-bit Protocol field in the IP header indicates which protocol created the data encapsulated within the packet. For example, if the Protocol field contained the value 6 (binary 00000110), you would know that the network software formatted the packet's data area as a TCP segment. If the Protocol field contained the value 17 (binary 00010001), you would know that the network software formatted the data area as a UDP datagram.

The network layer uses the value in the Protocol field when it transfers data up the protocol stack into the transport layer. By examining the Protocol field, the network layer knows which transport module to contact. Table 4.3 shows Protocol field values for the TCP/IP protocols that use IP.

Protocol	Decimal	Binary
ICMP	1	00000001
IGMP	2	00000010
TCP	6	00000110
UDP	17	00010001

Table 4.3 *Protocol field values for the IP header.*

HEADER CHECKSUM

As you have learned, reliable and unreliable protocols use checksums to detect data transmission errors. For example, TCP uses a checksum to ensure that the data the destination host receives is the same as the data the sending host transmits. Although it is an unreliable protocol, the Internet Protocol also uses a checksum to detect such errors. The Header Checksum field in the IP header contains a 16-bit number that represents a checksum of the IP header fields only. The checksum does not include the data area of the packet. The protocols that create the information stored in the data area must calculate and evaluate checksums for the data.

To calculate the header checksum, network software treats the header as a sequence of 16-bit numbers. The network software uses 1's complement arithmetic to sum this sequence of 16-bit numbers. TCP/IP stores the 1's complement of this summation in the Header Checksum field. When the sending host calculates the checksum, the host treats the Header Checksum field as though it contains a 0. In other words, the host ignores the Header Checksum field in its calculations.

When the destination host receives the IP packet, the network layer recalculates the header checksum. However, the checksum calculated by the receiving host includes the checksum (stored in the Header Checksum field) calculated by the sending host. As such, if the communication channel transferred the header unmodified, the checksum calculated by the receiving host will be all 1's. If the receiving host detects a checksum error, TCP/IP throws away the IP datagram. The receiving host does not transmit an error message to the sender when this occurs.

Remember that IP is an unreliable protocol. As such, IP does not guarantee delivery. However, the header checksum used by IP does guarantee the validity of the datagram header. That is, IP detects and discards any corrupted packets. However, TCP/IP does not require IP to report the receipt of corrupted packets with any kind of an error message. Reliable protocols (such as TCP) do not depend on IP to report such errors. They use their own error detection mechanisms.

SOURCE AND DESTINATION IP ADDRESS

The 32-bit Source IP Address field contains the IP address of the sending host (interface). Regardless of how many routers the packet passes on the way to its destination, this field never changes. The Source IP Address field always contains the IP address of the original sender. Like the Source IP Address field, the Destination IP Address field contains a standard 32-bit IP address. Depending on the message type, the Destination IP Address field can contain a host IP address (unicast) or all 1's for a broadcast message.

IP OPTIONS

The 8-bit IP Options field provides features designed to let network professionals test and debug network applications. IP options control how the network fragments and routes IP packets. Because IP options are for testing and debugging purposes only, TCP/IP does not require network protocols to store any information in the IP Options field. For the same reason, not all hosts and routers support all IP options. However, this does not present a major problem since most network professionals use known hosts and routers when they test and debug network software anyway. Most network software rarely uses the IP options.

The following paragraphs provide a brief introduction to the IP Options field. If you plan to develop Internet applications, you might want to use some of these options when testing and debugging your applications. The IP Options field contains three subfields (Copy, Option Class, and Option Number), as shown in the following figure:

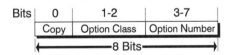

The Copy bit specifies how routers should handle the options if message fragmentation occurs. When you set the Copy bit to 1, routers must copy the options to each fragment. When you set the Copy bit to 0, the router copies the options to the first fragment only. The Option Class bits specify one of the classes shown in Table 4.4.

Option Class	Bit Pattern	Purpose of the Option
0	00	Datagram or network control
1	01	Reserved
2	10	Debugging and measurement
3	11	Reserved

Table 4.4 Classes of Options in the IP Options field of the IP header.

Within each class of options, the Option Number field selects a specific option. Table 4.5 shows the possible options including their corresponding class, number, length, and a brief description.

Class	Number	Length	Description
0	2	11	Security
0	7	Variable	Record route
0	3	Variable	Source Routing, Loose
0	9	Variable	Source Routing, Strict
2	4	Variable	Internet Timestamp

Table 4.5 Settings for the IP Options field of the IP header.

The security option designates security and handling restrictions for military applications. The record-route option tells the network software to record the route of the packet in the IP Options field. The source-routing options let you control the packet's routing. Loose routing lets you specify a list of IP addresses that the packet must traverse. Strict routing specifies that the packet can only traverse those addresses in the list. The Internet timestamp option requires each router to record its IP address and time as the packet passes through its control.

UNDERSTANDING FRAGMENTATION

As you have learned, network technologies such as Ethernet specify a maximum transfer unit (MTU). The MTU defines the maximum packet size that the network can transmit. When an application transmits a packet larger than the underlying network's MTU, the network software automatically breaks the packet into smaller chunks and transmits the data as multiple packets.

Fragmentation is the process of breaking a single packet into two or more smaller packets. As you have learned, fragmentation occurs when a packet's size exceeds the physical network's maximum transfer unit. Fragmentation also occurs when a packet passes through a router and the router's MTU is smaller than the MTU on the sender's local network. The previous section introduced you to the Identification, Flags, and Fragment Offset fields in the IP header. As you have learned, the Identification field uniquely identifies each packet transmitted by a particular host.

For fragmentation control, IP uses the first and last bits of the 3-bit Flags field. TCP/IP refers to the first bit in the Flag field as the "do not fragment" bit. Network software primarily uses this flag to test and debug other programs. In some applications, you might find a legitimate need to prevent fragmentation. However, in most cases, you should not set this bit or flag. If a program sets the "do not fragment" bit and IP determines fragmentation must occur, TCP/IP will discard your IP packet and return an error message to the sender.

TCP/IP refers to the last bit in the Flags field as the More Fragments flag. During the process of breaking a packet into smaller pieces, IP sets this flag for every fragment it creates except the last fragment. In other words, the More Fragments flag is true (IP sets the bit to 1) for every fragment except the last one. For the last fragment, the More Fragments flag is false (IP sets the bit to 0).

UNDERSTANDING IP ERROR MESSAGES

The Internet Protocol (IP) is an unreliable, connectionless protocol that uses datagrams for data delivery. You have also learned that such protocols do not guarantee data delivery, nor do they notify the sending host when delivery fails. Yet, despite these seemingly iron-clad rules, you have read about circumstances when IP does return an error message.

For example, you learned that TCP/IP returns an Internet Control Message Protocol (ICMP) error message to the sending host when the Time-to-Live value in an IP header reaches 0. Yet, you also learned that checksum errors cause TCP/IP to throw an IP datagram away without reporting any errors. You have just read that setting the "do not fragment" bit in the Flags field of an IP header can generate an error message. The key to understanding these apparent contradictions is to focus on the word "guarantee." The Internet Protocol does not guarantee reliable communication.

Within the TCP/IP protocol suite, the Internet Control Message Protocol (ICMP) communicates error messages and other conditions that require attention. Although ICMP is part of the same network layer as IP, ICMP functions like a higher level protocol. ICMP communicates directly with IP. Also, like most other TCP/IP protocols, ICMP relies on IP for delivery. As such, ICMP is also an unreliable, connectionless protocol.

If a protocol is unreliable, this does not imply that delivery is unlikely or that TCP/IP never sends an error message. An unreliable protocol simply does not *guarantee* delivery and error notification. You should understand that network professionals design unreliable protocols to succeed in their tasks. By defining a protocol as unreliable, developers simplify the protocol's design and implementation. As such, the developer delegates the responsibility and complexity of ensuring reliability to the higher level protocols.

As you have learned, IP does return error messages. TCP/IP uses ICMP to send such messages. However, you should note that ICMP relies upon IP for message deliveries. As such,

> TCP/IP does not guarantee the delivery of error messages—even when the network generates such messages. For this reason, you can and *should* check for error messages from the Internet Protocol and other unreliable protocols. However, you should never write an application that depends on an error message being returned from such protocols—IP does not guarantee delivery of error messages.

For efficiency and performance, IP tries to send the largest packets possible. However, there are times when avoiding fragmentation is impossible. To create each fragment, IP calculates a breaking point that results in a packet size equal to the underlying network's MTU. The *breaking point* is the packet byte location where IP actually divides the packet.

The breaking point represents the distance from the beginning of the datagram. IP stores each breaking point in the Fragment Offset field in the header of the newly created IP datagram. In other words, the header of the IP datagram that will deliver the data fragment contains the offset value for that fragment. Later, IP uses this break-point value on the receiving end to rebuild the packet.

Usually, the actual size of each fragment is slightly different from the MTU. IP calculates the breaking point for each fragment in multiples of eight bytes. Figure 4.6 shows the IP header diagram that you saw in the previous section. You should note that the Packet Length field is 16 bits wide and the Fragment Offset field is 13 bits wide.

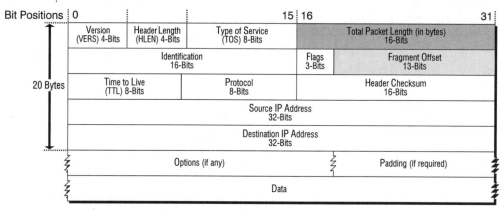

Figure 4.6 The Packet Length and Fragment Offset fields within the IP header.

As you have learned, a 16-bit Packet Length field means the maximum width of an IP packet is 65,535. The Fragment Offset field must be able to identify and point to an offset anywhere within an IP packet. This means that the Fragment Offset field must store values ranging from 1 to 65,535. However, as noted previously, the Fragment Offset field is only 13 bits wide. The largest number you can represent in 13 bits is 8,191. As such, if the value stored in the Fragment Offset field represents bytes, you can only point to the first 8,191 bytes of the data packet.

However, consider the results if you store your offsets as multiples of eight bytes. For example, assume that the value 1 represents an offset of eight bytes, the value 2 represents an offset of 16 bytes, and so on. Using all 13 bits of your Fragment Offset field means a fragment offset of 65,528 (8191 x 8). In effect, 65,528 points at the last eight bytes of the largest possible packet: byte number 65,528 plus 7 more bytes equals 65,535 (the maximum packet size).

SUMMARIZING THE FRAGMENTATION PROCESS

A network's maximum transfer unit (MTU) represents the largest packet size that a network can transfer. When the size of a packet exceeds the MTU, IP breaks the data portion of the packet into smaller pieces called fragments. The MTU determines the size of the fragments. That is, IP creates fragments using the maximum allowable transfer size.

IP calculates the starting point for each fragment from the beginning of the datagram. IP creates each fragment in multiples of eight bytes. IP stores this offset in the new IP datagram's Fragment Offset field. In the IP header of all but the last newly created fragment, IP sets the More Fragments flag to true. In the IP header of the datagram that contains the last fragment in the sequence, IP sets the More Fragments flag to false since no more fragments will follow.

REASSEMBLY OF THE FRAGMENTS

You have learned the reasons for fragmentation and how IP accomplishes the process. Now, you need to understand how IP reassembles the fragments. To reassemble fragmented packets, the receiving host examines the IP header fragmentation fields. You have already examined these fields: the Identification, Flags, and Fragment Offset fields.

When the destination host receives an IP packet with the More Fragments flag set, the host starts a *reassembly timer*. All fragments must arrive before the timer expires. If the reassembly timer expires before the host receives all fragments, the host discards all received fragments and does not process the datagram. As the host collects fragments in its reassembly buffer, the IP module uses the Source Address and Identification fields to determine which packets belong together. When the host receives a fragment with the More Fragments flag turned off, the IP module can calculate the length of the original datagram.

Remember, the Fragment Offset field specifies the fragment's starting point as measured from the beginning of the original packet. From the end fragment (the one with the More Fragments flag turned off), the IP module calculates the length of the original datagram by adding the values in the Fragment Offset and Packet Length fields.

After the IP module knows the length of the original datagram, IP can examine the Fragment Offset and Packet Length fields of all related fragments. By doing so, IP knows when the host has received all fragments. After the host receives all fragments, IP uses the Fragment Offset field to recombine the fragments into the proper sequence. In effect, IP reassembles the original datagram. After IP reassembles the datagram, the network layer handles the packet as though the network had never fragmented it.

UNDERSTANDING THE IMPLICATIONS

Both fragmentation and reassembly occur between the network and link layers of your network. From your viewpoint as an applications programmer, the entire process is transparent. That is, as you develop Internet applications, your programs do not need to accomplish any of this process—the network and link layers handle fragmentation and reassembly for you.

Although you don't have to design your applications to handle this process, you still need to understand the process. For example, you have learned that a single, missing fragment causes IP to discard the entire datagram. From this fact, you can deduce the following: *When fragmentation occurs, the probability that your datagram will fail to reach its destination increases.*

If the above statement is not obvious to you, consider what you know about datagrams. First, you have learned that a datagram is unreliable and thus the network does not guarantee delivery. Second, because delivery is unreliable, you know that protocols and applications that use datagrams should never depend on other datagrams being delivered—each datagram should stand alone in its functionality.

Now, consider the effects of fragmentation. First, your independent, stand-alone datagram has become multiple datagrams due to fragmentation. As such, each new datagram (or fragment) depends on *all* the fragments being delivered. If the network loses one fragment, the network layer throws away all fragments. Second, simple statistics tell you that the probability of losing a datagram rises as the number of fragments being sent increases.

As you can see, even seemingly inconsequential details about fragmentation are important to you as an applications programmer. If you want to successfully develop and deploy solid, Internet applications, you need a firm understanding of the TCP/IP protocol suite. Next, you need to apply this understanding to the design and development of your applications. As you learn more about TCP/IP, you should continually ask yourself the following questions:

- How does this information impact me and my applications?

- How does this new piece of information fit into the overall picture?

- How can I use this newfound knowledge to my advantage when I develop other programs for use on the Internet?

AVOIDING THE PROBLEM

By now, you may believe that fragmentation is an evil problem that you should avoid at all costs. Whether avoidance-at-all-costs is a cost-effective solution is something only you can decide. However, you should know that the Transport Control Protocol (TCP) uses a default MTU of 576 bytes when it sends data to hosts that exist several routers away. This value allows for 512 bytes of data and leaves room for the TCP and IP headers, as well as header options. Most link layer protocols support an MTU of 576 bytes and thus will not fragment your data prior to transmission.

Depending on the scope of your TCP/IP applications, you might analyze the potential routing paths that your data will take. Given such information, you may find that you can design your application to use a larger MTU—without the risk of fragmentation.

UNDERSTANDING IP ROUTING

Up to this point, each section of this chapter has progressively taken you deeper and deeper in your exploration of the TCP/IP protocol suite. In exploring the link layer, the network layer, Internet addresses, associated protocols, and datagrams, you have traveled to the heart of TCP/IP. You now have the essential knowledge you need to pull back and begin to view the big picture as you continue your tour of the TCP/IP protocol stack. You have learned that IP is the Internet delivery system. You have learned a lot of related information about the IP datagrams. You know that delivery of such datagrams is the means by which application data and protocol information move across the Internet. The key to delivering IP datagrams is the IP routing table.

An IP *routing table* stores addresses for selected destinations on the network. In other words, network software can search a routing table to find the best way to reach a specific destination. Routing protocols manage all routing table entries. These protocols are not part of TCP/IP. As such, *Internet Programming* will not discuss routing protocols.

Routing theory and design is an extremely complex subject that, today, is more art than science. As an applications programmer, you have little or no control over the routing of your data. However, you will probably make extensive use of IP addresses in your applications. IP addresses relate directly to the subject of IP routing. As such, the following paragraphs introduce a simplified concept of IP routing tables and Internet packet routing.

REVIEWING NETWORK ID NUMBERS

Before you delve into the details of IP routing tables, you should recall one important fact about IP addresses. Each network interface on the same physical network must have the same network ID number but a unique host ID number. IP must have some means of knowing how to route packets to any location on the Internet. IP uses a routing table for this purpose.

Routing tables rely on the rule that hosts on the same physical network use the same network ID. As you may recall, the Internet has the potential to connect over 3.7 billion host computers. Since you would not want to store every possible address in a routing table, IP uses a routing table to route packets between networks—not host computers. As such, routing tables use network ID numbers only.

UNDERSTANDING ROUTING TABLE ENTRIES

Each routing table entry includes the following three fields: Network, Gateway, and Flags. The first two fields contain network ID numbers. The Flags field identifies networks that directly connect to the owner of the routing table. The Network field contains a list of network ID numbers. The Gateway field is actually a router field. This Gateway (or Router) field identifies a router on a path that leads to the network identified in the Network field. However, the router may not directly connect to the destination network. In other words, routing tables only show the next hop in the path to a particular destination.

UNDERSTANDING DIRECT DELIVERY

When a host computer receives a packet, the IP module extracts the destination network number from the IP header. Next, the IP module consults a routing table. When IP finds an entry for the destination network number, it examines the Flags field. If the Flags field indicates a direct connection, this means the network can deliver the packet using a data frame for the underlying network technology (such as Ethernet or IBM Token Ring). The precise details of how this delivery would occur are technology dependent.

In general terms, direct delivery means the network can and will translate the destination IP address into a link layer address (such as an Ethernet address). This translation process can use the Address Resolution Protocol (ARP). The network will encapsulate the IP datagram into a data frame and transmit the data directly to its destination.

Note: For a datagram to reach its destination, the direct routing process must occur. Eventually, a datagram will reach a router directly connected to the destination network.

UNDERSTANDING INDIRECT DELIVERY

A routing table entry may indicate that the address is not connected directly to the destination network. This requires the network to indirectly deliver the packet. You need to understand that for a particular routing table, every gateway (router) entry directly connects to the host or router that owns the routing table. This means that the owner of the routing table can deliver the received packet to the designated router by using the direct delivery process previously described. Figure 4.7 shows a simple internet with four networks and three routers. Table 4.6 shows example routing table entries for Router B in Figure 4.7. In Table 4.6, you can see that if Router B receives a packet destined for network 100.0.0.0, the routing table identifies this network as directly connected. In this case, Router B can *directly deliver* the packet to its destination.

Network Destination	Route
100.0.0.0	Direct Delivery
200.0.0.0	Direct Delivery

Table 4.6 Router table entries for Router B in Figure 4.7. (continued on the next page)

Network Destination	Route
300.0.0.0	100.0.0.2
400.0.0.0	100.0.0.2

Table 4.6 *Router table entries for Router B in Figure 4.7. (continued from the previous page)*

If Router B receives a packet destined for network 400.0.0.0, the routing table specifies a routing destination of 100.0.0.2, even though network 100.0.0.0 does not directly connect to network 400.0.0.0. However, 100.0.0.2 is the next *hop* or direct connection along the path to 400.0.0.0. From packet switch 100.0.0.2, the packet will travel through Router A and then Router C to reach its destination on network 400.0.0.0. As such, Router B *indirectly delivered* the packet to its destination.

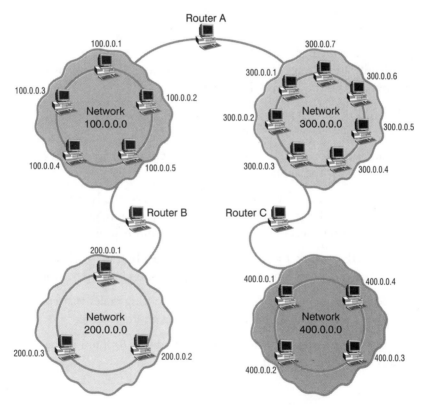

Figure 4.7 *A simple internet with four networks and three routers.*

PUTTING IT ALL TOGETHER

In this chapter, you learned that the TCP/IP network layer manages the delivery of all network data through the Internet Protocol. This chapter also discussed how IP performs this task. You have learned how the Internet Network Information Center (InterNIC) assigns IP identifiers and what those identifiers represent. In addition, you have seen how the Internet uses address classes to expand network address space on the Internet.

As you have learned, the network layer and the Internet Protocol deliver data between host computers on the Internet. In the next chapter, you will learn how, after data arrives at a host computer, the TCP/IP transport protocols deliver data to the correct application within that host computer. However, before you move on to Chapter 5, make sure you understand the following key concepts:

✓ The TCP/IP network layer manages data delivery between host computers on the network.

✓ A 32-bit IP address includes a unique network identifier; this address also includes a host identifier that is unique for each host computer attached to the network.

✓ TCP/IP uses the high-order bits in the high-order byte of an IP address to identify an address class; an address class defines how many bytes the address uses for the network identifier.

✓ The TCP/IP address protocols translate packet addresses between IP addresses and link-layer data-frame addresses.

✓ IP datagrams include an IP header, a transport protocol header (for either TCP or UDP), and application data.

✓ The IP datagram header includes fields that identify the IP version used to create the packet, the location of data in the packet, fragmentation information, error checking values, and routing information.

✓ In a TCP/IP network, fragmentation occurs when IP tries to deliver packets that exceed the maximum size (MTU) of the underlying network.

✓ To deliver data across the Internet, IP uses routing tables that contain destination information for selected addresses on the Internet.

✓ Routing tables identify the next destination address (or hop) in the path to any destination on the Internet.

Chapter 5
Understanding the Transport Protocols

Normally, to communicate with the Internet, your applications will exchange data with the TCP/IP transport layer. The transport layer includes two transport protocols: the Transport Control Protocol (TCP) and the User Datagram Protocol (UDP). As you develop Internet applications, you will normally build your application around one of these protocols.

Internet applications such as the Ftp program, which transfers files across the Internet, normally use TCP because it offers a reliable byte-stream service. Likewise, Internet e-mail applications normally use the TCP for the same reason. Applications with very simple requirements, such as programs based on the *Trivial File Transfer Protocol*, use UDP. Applications that use the Time Protocol to contact Internet Time servers can employ either transport protocol. By the time you finish this chapter, you will understand when you should use each transport protocol.

Keep in mind that the ultimate purpose of network communications is to transfer information between a client application and a server application. As such, to effectively design client/server programs, you need to understand the transport layer and transport protocols. By the time you finish this chapter, you will understand the following key concepts:

- How transport protocols use protocol ports to talk to applications
- The purpose of the data fields in a UDP header
- How TCP ensures data reliability
- How TCP uses a sliding window to increase network bandwidth
- How TCP modules establish and terminate TCP connections
- How TCP modules use acknowledgment messages
- The purpose of the data fields in a TCP header

UNDERSTANDING THE TRANSPORT LAYER

At first glance, the difference between IP, the Internet's delivery system, and the transport protocols may appear hazy. However, if you review what you know about the IP module, you will discover that IP delivers data between host computers. The transport layer and the transport protocols deliver data between applications.

In many ways, the transport protocols' responsibilities are similar to those of the IP module. As such, you may experience a sense of deja vu as you learn more about these protocols. Conceptually, much of what you learned about the IP datagram and the IP header also applies to the transport protocols. As you have learned, TCP/IP includes two transport protocols: the Transport Control Protocol (TCP) and the User Datagram Protocol (UDP). The Transport Control Protocol is a connection-oriented protocol that uses a reliable byte-stream to send and receive data. The Transport Control Protocol provides a virtual circuit for network communications. The User Datagram Protocol is an unreliable, connectionless protocol that uses datagrams to send and receive data.

UNDERSTANDING TRANSPORT-LAYER PORTS

In TCP/IP terminology, a *port* is like an IP address except that TCP/IP associates a port with a protocol rather than a host computer. In the same way that IP datagrams store source and destination IP addresses, transport protocols store source and destination port numbers. If the concept of transport-layer ports seems strange to you, consider what you know about hardware ports on your computer. You may have written programs that send data to a hardware port. If nothing else, in order to print, you've sent data to a parallel or serial port. If you have used a modem, the TCP/IP concept of ports should be even more familiar.

Personal computers name and number their ports. For example, you refer to your PC's parallel printer ports as LPT1 and LPT2. You refer to your serial ports as COM1 and COM2. On the Internet, networks simply number their protocol ports. On a PC, LPT1 refers to parallel printer port number 1. Thousands of personal computer applications understand and use this designation. For years, programmers have designed and developed PC programs with the assumption that LPT1 represents parallel printer port number 1. In the same way, programmers associate an Internet protocol port with a specific application and function.

UNDERSTANDING INTERNET PROTOCOL PORTS

As previously discussed, the Internet includes application protocols for commonly used applications such as Ftp, Telnet, and Mail. On the Internet, these common applications use something called a *well-known port assignment*. A well-known port assignment is a protocol port commonly used for a specific Internet application or function.

Just as PC programmers use printer port LPT1 to print, Internet programmers use a variety of protocol ports for specific Internet applications. For example, the well-known port assignment for the Trivial File Transfer Protocol is port number 69. The well-known port assignment for Telnet is port number 23. Table 5.1 lists well-known port assignments for commonly used Internet protocol ports:

Protocol	Port Number
Echo Protocol	7
Daytime Protocol	13
File Transfer Protocol	21
Telnet Protocol	23
Simple Mail Transfer Protocol	25
Time Protocol	37
Whois Protocol	43
Trivial File Transfer Protocol	69
Finger Protocol	79

Table 5.1 Commonly used protocol ports on the Internet.

UNDERSTANDING UDP PORT USAGE

You can compare protocols that use connectionless datagrams (such as IP and UDP) to a postal delivery system. If you don't remember this analogy, take a moment to re-read the section entitled *Expanding Your TCP/IP Vocabulary* in Chapter 3. If you slightly refine this postal delivery system analogy, you will easily see the relationship between UDP, ports, and applications. For this analogy, a post office is the host computer, P.O. boxes are ports, and the people who rent the P.O. boxes are the application protocols.

As you have learned, IP is the Internet delivery system. Previously, you may have thought of IP as a mail person. In reality, IP is more like a mail truck and the transport protocols are like mail-truck drivers or mail persons. Although the mail truck carries or delivers the mail to the correct addresses, it is the mail person who actually sorts and places letters in the mailbox.

Mail trucks (IP) deliver truck loads of mail (data) between post offices (host computers). At the post office, postal workers or mail persons (UDP) sort the mail by P.O. box numbers (ports). After they sort the mail, the mail persons (UDP) place the letters (data) in the correct P.O. boxes (ports). People (application protocols) who rent the P.O. boxes periodically check their boxes and pick up their mail. The mail persons (UDP) do not notify the recipients (applications protocols) that they have mail (data); they simply deposit the mail in the correct mailbox (port).

UNDERSTANDING TCP PORT USAGE

As you might expect, because TCP is a reliable, connection-oriented protocol, TCP uses ports differently than UDP. For example, as a connectionless protocol, UDP simply drops data off at the port. UDP does not maintain a connection between the sender and receiver. UDP data delivery focuses on the port. However, TCP is connection-oriented. TCP data delivery focuses on the connection—not the port itself. For example, applications that use TCP can open multiple connections to the same port and communicate without problems.

As you have learned, TCP is more like telephone communication than postal delivery. You can use a slightly refined version of the telephone communications analogy to explain the relationship between TCP, ports, and applications. In this refined analogy, a business office is the host computer, a telephone number is a port, and a telephone call is a connection. The employees that work in the office represent the application protocols, and their telephone conversations represent the exchange of data. As in the previous analogies, IP is the telephone company.

The employees (application protocols) that work in the business office (host computer) make sophisticated use of their telephone system (IP). The business office (host computer) assigns each employee (application protocol) their own telephone number (port). However, the business office leaves several telephone numbers (ports) free or unassigned. Any employee (application protocol) can use the unassigned telephone numbers. Every employee uses a multi-line telephone from which they can place calls (connections) using any telephone number (port) in the office (host computer).

When the telephone company (IP) routes a call into the office (host computer), a telephone rings. The telephone number (port) of the incoming call determines who answers the call (connection). Initially, the employee (application protocol) assigned to the number (port) always receives the incoming call (connection). If the employee and caller agree to talk to each other, a conversation (exchange of data) ensues.

The employees (application protocols) can handle incoming calls in several ways. For example, the employee (application protocol) can have another employee (application protocol) pick up the same telephone line (port) and share the caller's information (establish another connection using the same port). In some cases, the employee (application protocol) may not want to tie up one of the business' published telephone numbers (well-known port assignments). In such cases, the employee (application protocol) can transfer the call to a rarely used line (port) and continue the conversation (exchange of data) without interruption.

How Your Programs Use Port Numbers

The transport layer routes packets to and from application programs. As such, the transport layer needs a way to identify each application. That's where port numbers come in. Each application, regardless of whether it is a client or server, has a unique port number. When your program creates a session (connects to the network), your program is assigned a port number. If you are writing a client program, you normally won't care what port number your client uses. Your program doesn't need to know its port number—rather, the server does. Each time your client program sends a message, the transport layer automatically inserts the correct port number within the source port field. As you will learn in Chapter 19, when you create a server program, you can request that the network assign your program a specific port number. That's how, for example, server programs can support the commonly used protocol ports specified in Table 5.1.

UNDERSTANDING THE USER DATAGRAM PROTOCOL

UDP is very similar to IP in that both are unreliable, connectionless protocols that use datagrams for data delivery. IP delivers data to a host computer, however, only UDP can route data to multiple destinations (network programs) on a single host. Normally, the network associates such destinations with a protocol port. As you have learned, UDP uses datagrams for data delivery. In the same way that an IP datagram includes an IP header, a UDP datagram includes a UDP header. However, the structure of a UDP header is much simpler. Figure 5.1 shows the structure of a UDP datagram. As you can see, a UDP header includes four fields: Source Port, Destination Port, Message Length, and Checksum.

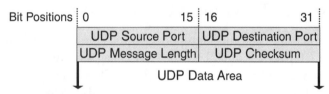

Figure 5.1 The structure of a UDP datagram.

The UDP header is only eight bytes wide. The port fields are 16-bit integer values that represent a protocol port. The Source Port field identifies the protocol-port number that sent the data. The Destination Port field identifies the port that will receive the data. The Message Length field specifies the length (in bytes) of the UDP datagram, including the UDP header. The UDP Checksum field, unlike the checksum in the IP header, includes the UDP data in its calculations. The data area immediately follows the UDP header.

*Note: Although the UDP checksum includes the UDP data, the protocol does not require that a checksum be calculated and included in the UDP header. This is contrary to the Internet Protocol and Transport Control Protocol. Both IP and TCP **require** a checksum in their respective headers.*

The UDP module accepts incoming datagrams and then sorts and distributes (demultiplexes) them based on destination port numbers. Figure 5.2 shows how data flows from the network layer, through the UDP module, and to the applications.

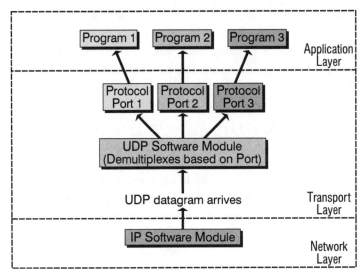

Figure 5.2 *Data flow through the UDP module.*

UNDERSTANDING THE TRANSPORT CONTROL PROTOCOL

Other than the Internet Protocol, the Transport Control Protocol is the most commonly used protocol in the TCP/IP protocol suite. Like the User Datagram Protocol, TCP transports data between the network and application layers. However, TCP is much more complex than UDP because it provides a reliable, byte-stream, connection-oriented data delivery service. In other words, TCP ensures that delivery occurs and that the destination application receives the data in the correct sequence. In contrast, UDP doesn't guarantee datagram delivery. Nor does UDP ensure that datagrams arrive in their proper sequence.

TCP also tries to optimize network bandwidth. In other words, TCP tries to maximize its throughput of data across the Internet. To optimize network throughput, TCP dynamically controls the flow of data between connections. As such, if the data buffer at the receiving end of the TCP connection starts to overflow, TCP will tell the sending end to reduce transmission speed.

Consider how the Transport Control Protocol uses IP for data delivery between host computers. As you do so, you may wonder how TCP could possibly use the delivery services of IP, an unreliable protocol, and still remain reliable. You may also be confused by the fact that TCP is connection-oriented and IP is connectionless. Finally, you may wonder how TCP can deliver data as a byte-stream when it's using IP datagrams for data delivery. The following paragraphs will answer all these questions and eliminate any confusion you may have. However, as you learn TCP's secrets, you should always remember that IP does deliver TCP data. As such, TCP must package its data into IP datagrams.

ENSURING RELIABILITY

To ensure reliability and byte-stream sequencing, TCP uses *acknowledgments*. As such, after the destination end of a TCP connection receives a transmission, the destination end transmits an acknowledgment message to the transmitting end. In short, to the sender, the acknowledgement says, "Yes, I got your message." Each time the transmitting end of a connection sends a message, TCP starts a timer. If the timer expires before the TCP module receives an acknowledgment, TCP automatically re-transmits the unacknowledged data. Figure 5.3 shows how this process could work.

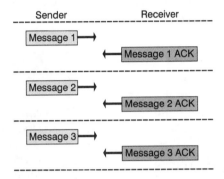

Figure 5.3 *Data transmission using simple acknowledgments.*

Unfortunately, the simple system of acknowledgments shown in Figure 5.3 is extremely inefficient. In this scheme, one end of the connection must always wait for data to arrive from the other end. As you will learn, TCP does not transmit or receive data and acknowledgments in a one-for-one exchange.

UNDERSTANDING A SLIDING WINDOW

To improve message throughput, TCP does not send a message and then wait until it receives an acknowledgment before transmitting another. Instead, TCP uses a concept called a *sliding window,* which lets TCP transmit several messages before it waits for an acknowledgment. Figure 5.4 illustrates the sliding window concept.

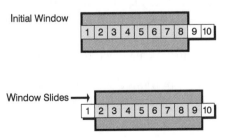

Figure 5.4 *A sliding window used by TCP.*

Conceptually, TCP places a window over the data stream and then transmits all data within the window. As TCP receives acknowledgments, TCP slides the window across the data stream and transmits the next message. By working with multiple messages in this way, TCP can pump a lot of information into the data stream at the same time. Because TCP transmits several messages beforeit waits for an acknowledgment, TCP greatly improves the efficiency and throughput of the transmit/acknowledgment cycle. Figure 5.5 illustrates the transmission and acknowledgment cycle usingTCP's approach. As you can see in Figure 5.5, the sender and the receiver use a sliding window that is three packets wide. As such, the sender sends three packets without waiting for any acknowledgment messages. After the sender receives the ACK 3 message in Figure 5.5, the sender can transmit another three messages.

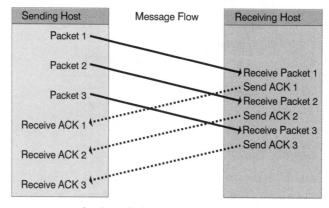

Figure 5.5 Data transmission and acknowledgments using a sliding window.

TCP also optimizes network bandwidth by negotiating data flow between TCP connections. TCP continues to negotiate the data flow rate throughout the entire life of a TCP connection. During these negotiations, TCP can expand and contract the width of the sliding window. When data traffic on the Internet is light and traffic congestion is minimal, TCP can expand the width of the sliding window. By doing so, TCP can pump more data into the channel at a faster rate. More data sent through the channel, in turn, increases throughput or network bandwidth.

When traffic congestion is high, TCP can reduce the width of the sliding window. For example, assume that the sliding window shown in Figure 5.4 covers eight units of data. If eight units represents the negotiated rate of flow on a day when Internet traffic is heavy, TCP might expand the window to cover ten or twenty units of data when traffic is light.

Understand that Figure 5.4 and the previous discussion is a simplified example—it illustrates the basic concept. TCP specifies window sizes in bytes. However, in actuality, the default window size may be several thousand bytes wide—not the eight, ten, or twenty bytes used in the previous example. In other words, TCP typically must transmit several segments before it saturates the window size advertised by the receiving TCP module. Many systems on the Internet use a default window size of 4,096 bytes. Other systems use 8,192 or 16,384 bytes as a default.

DEFINING A *TCP MESSAGE*

You can refer to each package, or unit of TCP data, as a TCP message or TCP segment. Both terms are correct and widely used in Internet literature. However, for reasons discussed in the following paragraphs, you might want to use the term *segment*. Remember, TCP treats data as a single, unbroken, serial stream of data. However, TCP must use IP datagrams for delivery. Luckily, your programs can treat TCP data as a continuous byte stream, ignoring IP datagrams.

Whenever you see the term *TCP message*, you may want to substitute the term *TCP segment*. By doing so, you will acknowledge the fact that each TCP message that an IP datagram delivers is really only one segment of the TCP byte stream. A TCP segment consists of a TCP header, TCP options, and the data that the segment transports. Figure 5.6 shows the structure of a TCP segment. Although Figure 5.6 shows the TCP header structure in layers, you should understand that the header is simply a serial stream of data that is at least 20 bytes wide. Table 5.2 briefly describes the purpose of each field in the TCP header.

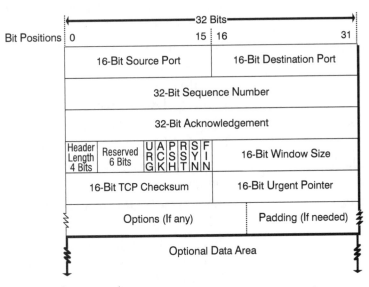

Figure 5.6 TCP segment (or message) structure.

Data Field	Purpose
Source Port	Identifies the protocol port of the sending application.
Destination Port	Identifies the protocol port of the receiving or destination application.
Sequence Number	Identifies the first byte of data in the data area of the TCP segment.
Acknowledgment Number	Identifies the next byte of data that the sender expects from the data stream.
Header Length	Specifies the length of the TCP header in 32-bit words.
URG Flag	Tells the receiving TCP module that the Urgent Pointer field points to urgent data.
ACK Flag	Tells the receiving TCP module that the Acknowledgment Number field contains a valid acknowledgment number.
PSH Flag	Tells the receiving TCP module to immediately send the data to the destination application.
RST Flag	Asks the receiving TCP module to *reset* the TCP connection.
SYN Flag	Tells the receiving TCP module to synchronize sequence numbers.
FIN Flag	Tells the receiving TCP module that the sender has finished sending data.
Window Size	Tells the receiving TCP module the number of bytes that the sender is willing to accept.
TCP Checksum	Helps the receiving TCP module detect data corruption.
Urgent Pointer	Points to the last byte of urgent data in the TCP data area.
Options	Usually used with the Maximum Segment Size option, which advertises the largest segment that the TCP module expects to receive.

Table 5.2 The purpose of the TCP header data fields

ESTABLISHING A TCP CONNECTION

To ensure data reliability and byte-stream ordering, TCP sends and receives acknowledgments. To accomplish these operations, TCP must have some method of identifying the transmitted data. Likewise, the network must somehow synchronize the receiving end of the TCP connection with the sending end. In other words, both ends of the TCP connection need to know when they can start transmitting data. They also need to know how to identify the sender's data. For example, suppose a TCP module receives a corrupted data packet. The receiving TCP module needs a way to tell the sending TCP module which packet to resend. To establish a TCP connection, both ends of the connection must negotiate and agree to use packet identification information that the other end understands.

Likewise, as part of this synchronization process, both ends of the TCP connection must establish some system for acknowledging messages. Otherwise, miscommunication may occur. The following paragraphs explain the header fields that TCP uses to accomplish these functions. To establish and terminate connections, as well as to send and receive acknowledgments, the TCP header uses the Sequence Number, Acknowledgment Number, and Flags fields. Each time your program wants to use TCP to transport data, your program transmits a request for a TCP connection to your host computer's transport layer. The TCP module in your host's transport layer, in turn, sends a TCP message with a Synchronization (SYN) flag to the remote port to which your program wants to connect.

The Synchronization flag tells the receiving (or server-side) TCP module that a client program wants to establish a TCP connection. Along with the Synchronization flag, the message also includes a 32-bit *sequence number* that the sending TCP module stores in the Sequence Number field. The server-side TCP module replies with a TCP segment that includes an Acknowledgment (ACK) flag and an *acknowledgment number*. To understand the entire TCP handshake that establishes a TCP connection, you must understand sequence and acknowledgment numbers. The following sections describe these numbers and the entire handshake process in greater detail.

UNDERSTANDING THE INITIAL SEQUENCE NUMBER

As noted, both ends of the TCP connection must be able to identify information in the data stream in order to send and receive acknowledgments. The sequence number is how TCP identifies data. Host computers can use a variety of methods for selecting the initial sequence number (for our purposes, which method a host computer uses is unimportant). In general, you can think of the initial sequence number as a random number.

The initial sequence number is simply a value that one end of a TCP connection sends to the other. The sending end of the TCP connection essentially tells the receiving end of the connection, "Hey! I want to establish a TCP connection and I'm going to start numbering (identifying) my data stream with this number." When the server side of this conversation receives the request for a connection, it replies with a message that includes its own initial sequence number. TCP generates the initial sequence number for the server-side completely independent of the initial sequence number for the client-side TCP module. In other words, to the client-side that requested the connection, the server-side says, "Hi! I got your request for a TCP connection and here's the number *I'm* going to use to identify my data."

TCP connections are full-duplex. In other words, data flows in both directions at the same time. As such, data flowing in one direction is independent of the data flowing in the other direction. Because of TCP's full-duplex capability, each end of a TCP connection must maintain two sequence numbers—one for each direction of data flow.

ACKNOWLEDGING DATA TRANSMISSIONS

In its initial reply message, the server-side TCP module sets two flags in the TCP header. The initial reply message sets the Synchronization (SYN) flag to tell the client-side TCP module to make a note of the server-side sequence number. The server-side TCP module also sets an Acknowledgment (ACK) flag that tells the client to examine the Acknowledgment Number field.

The server-side TCP module uses the sequence number received from the client-side TCP module to create an acknowledgment number. An acknowledgment number *always* specifies the *next sequence number* that the connection expects to receive. As such, in its initial reply message, the server-side TCP module stores the client-side sequence number plus one. For example, suppose the client-side TCP module that requested the TCP connection sent a sequence number of 1,000. In response, the server-side TCP module stores the number 1,001 in the Acknowledgment field of its initial reply message. In other words, to the client-side TCP module, the server-side TCP module says, "By the way, the next data element that I expect to receive is number 1,001."

OFFICIALLY ESTABLISHING A CONNECTION

Before it transfers any data, the client-side TCP module that requests the TCP connection must acknowledge the initial reply message from the server-side TCP module. As such, when the client-side TCP module receives the initial reply message, the client-side TCP module will send an acknowledgment of the acknowledgment. (Actually, the client-side is acknowledging the server-side's request for synchronization.)

The message sent by the client-side TCP module will also set the Acknowledgment flag. In the Acknowledgment Number field, the client-side TCP module will store the server-side TCP module's initial sequence number plus one. (The client-side TCP module will not set the Synchronization flag in this message since both sides have already synchronized with each other's initial sequence number.) In other words, a *three-way handshake* must occur before TCP establishes an official connection:

1. The client-side TCP module requests a TCP connection by sending a synchronization request and an initial sequence number.

2. The server-side TCP module acknowledges the request for a connection and, at the same time, requests that the client-side synchronize with the initial sequence number from server-side TCP module.

3. The client-side TCP module acknowledges the server-side request for synchronization.

After this three-way handshake, both sides of the TCP connection have all the information they need to identify data in the communications channel—sequence and acknowledgment numbers. In other words, both sides have synchronized their sequence numbers and acknowledged the synchronization.

UNDERSTANDING SEQUENCE NUMBERS

When two programs use TCP to send and receive data, they use a sequence number to keep track of what data has been sent and received. In short, the sequence number is like a bookmark that tracks the current location within the TCP data stream. The sequence number gives the sender and receiver a frame of reference. To begin, the sender might say "I'm sending you 300 bytes of data whose starting sequence number is 200. The receiver, in turn, may respond with, "I got them. I'm ready for data starting at 501 (200+300+1)." The sequence number works like a byte counter, tracking the number of bytes sent and received.

Sequence numbers can become a little confusing because they don't directly correspond to byte locations in the TCP data stream. That's because the starting sequence number is arbitrary—it's just a value the sender and receiver agree upon. They might, for example, start with sequence number *0, 100, 1,000*, or even *1,000,000*. The starting sequence number is not important as long as both sides agree to use the same number. In other words, a sender might say, "I'm sending you 1,000 bytes whose sequence numbers start at 5,000." The receiver, in turn, would respond with, "Okay, I got them. I'm waiting for byte 6,001 (1,000 + 5,000 + 1)."

The sequence number is a 32-bit number, which means it can reference values in the range 0 through 4,292,967,265. Over the course of a TCP connection, the sender and receiver may exchange millions of bytes. Should the sequence number exceed 4,292,967,265, it simply wraps back around past zero. Because the sequence number wraps for both the sender and receiver, the two processes remain in synch. The following example illustrates how a sender and receiver use the sequence number. Suppose your program uses TCP to transport 2,000 bytes of data from your client application to a server application. Assume that after TCP negotiates a connection and synchronizes sequence numbers, the next sequence number is 1,251. Also, assume your program needs to send the data in 500 byte segments. As such, the following sequence of events would occur:

1. The TCP module in your host computer's transport layer transmits a TCP segment that contains data bytes 1 through 500. The TCP module stores sequence number 1,251 in the Sequence Number field.

2. Next, the TCP module in your host computer transmits a TCP segment that includes data bytes 501 through 1,000. The transmitted sequence number is 1,751.

3. The next TCP segment from your host computer includes data bytes 1,001 through 1,500 and sequence number 2,251.

4. Finally, the TCP module in your host computer sends data bytes 1,501 through 2,000 and specifies a sequence number of 2,751.

In this example, the server-side TCP module would send acknowledgment numbers as shown below:

1. After receiving the first segment with data, the server-side TCP module sends an acknowledgment number of 1,751. By doing so, the server-side TCP module says, "Hey! I got some data and the next data I expect to receive is sequence number 1,751."

2. After receiving the second segment, the server-side TCP module sends an acknowledgment number of 2,251.

3. After receiving the third segment, the server-side TCP module sends an acknowledgment number of 2,751.

4. After receiving the fourth segment, the server-side TCP module sends an acknowledgment number of 3,251. (At this point, the client-side TCP module has not informed the server that it has finished transmitting data.)

USING FULL-DUPLEX SERVICES

As previously mentioned, TCP connections are *full-duplex*. As such, data flows in both directions at the same time. In other words, the data flowing in one direction is independent of the data flowing in the other direction. Because of TCP's full-duplex capability, each end of a TCP connection must maintain two sequence numbers—one for each direction of data flow.

If TCP's use of two identification numbers (sequence and acknowledgment numbers) doesn't make sense to you, consider the flow of data from one end of the connection. Assume you are looking at the data flow from the client end of the TCP connection. From the perspective of the client-side TCP module, the sequence number tracks or identifies the data that flows away from the client side of the TCP connection and toward the server side. Also, from the client-side point of view, the acknowledgment number (in the segments sent by the client-side TCP modules) identifies the data flowing from the server side of the TCP connection back to the client side. Figure 5.7 shows the flow of data and sequence numbers from the perspective of a client-side TCP module.

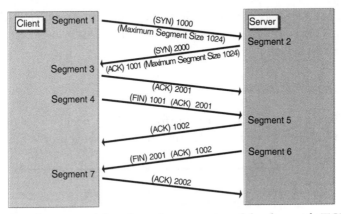

Figure 5.7 Data identification and flow from the perspective of the client-side TCP module.

Closing a TCP Connection

Programs close TCP connections using a *two-way handshake*. Either end of a TCP connection can initiate the close of the connection. To close a connection, one side of the connection sends a message with the Finished (FIN) flag set. However, because of TCP's full-duplex nature (data flowing in both directions), programs must shut down each direction of data flow independently. If you have programmed in the UNIX environment, the last statement may sound suspicious. As you may know, when you close a connection in UNIX, you can no longer communicate through that connection. TCP connections work differently. Even after one end of a TCP connection shuts down its flow of data (meaning it stops sending data), it can continue to receive data from the other end of the connection.

If the idea of being able to receive data on a closed connection seems strange to you, think of the Finished flag as a signal sent from one end of the connection to the other end—a signal that says the one end has finished *sending* data. The acknowledgment message from the other end of the TCP connection means that both ends have agreed to terminate data flow in one direction. At this point in the conversation, neither end of the TCP connection has made any comments about the data flowing in the other direction. Closing a TCP connection is a two-step process. One end performs an *active close* and the other end performs a *passive close*. The end that initiates the close by sending the first finished flag performs the active close. Normally, the end of a TCP connection that receives the Finished flag will initiate a passive close. A passive close simply means that the receiving end of the connection also sends a message with a Finished flag. In other words, the end of the connection that received the initial Finished flag essentially says, "Okay, if you have no more data to send me then I have no more data to send you." After both ends of the TCP connection have sent messages with Finished flags and received acknowledgments, the TCP connection officially ends.

Understanding a Half-Close

As you have learned, TCP's full-duplex capability lets you close or shut down data flowing in one direction but keep data flowing in the other direction. You can refer to closing the data flow in only one direction as a *half-close*. Very few TCP applications need or use a half-close. However, if you plan to develop custom Internet applications, the half-close is an interesting feature that you might be able to use someday.

UNDERSTANDING THE *TCP* HEADER

As you can see in Figure 5.8, the header structure for a TCP segment is much more complex than a UDP header. The following paragraphs describe the fields that comprise the TCP header.

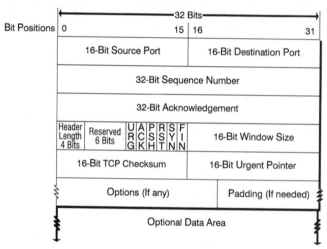

Figure 5.8 *TCP segment (or message) structure.*

SOURCE AND DESTINATION PORT

Both the 16-bit Source Port and Destination Port fields effectively identify the sending and receiving applications (or application protocols). The source and destination port numbers plus the source and destination IP addresses (in the IP header) combine to uniquely identify each TCP connection. You can refer to each end of a TCP connection as a *socket*.

SEQUENCE NUMBER

The 32-bit Sequence Number field identifies the first byte of data in the data area of the TCP segment. TCP identifies the byte by its relative offset from the beginning of the data stream. You can identify every byte in a data stream by a sequence number.

ACKNOWLEDGMENT NUMBER

The 32-bit Acknowledgment Number field identifies the next byte of data that the connection expects to receive from the data stream. For example, if the last byte received was sequence number 500, TCP will send an acknowledgment number of 501.

HEADER LENGTH

Like the IP header, the TCP Header Length field uses four bits to specify the length of the TCP header in 32-bit words. Also, like the IP header, a TCP header is normally 20 bytes wide. The data area begins immediately after the TCP header. By examining the Header Length field, receiving TCP modules can calculate the start of the data area as being header length times four bytes (32-bit words) from the beginning of the TCP segment.

FLAGS

The TCP header includes six one-bit flag fields. You have already met three of the flag fields: the Synchronization (SYN) flag, the Acknowledgment (ACK) flag, and the Finished (FIN) flag. The following paragraphs give a brief description of each flag.

URG   This flag tells the receiving TCP module that the Urgent Pointer field points to urgent data. (The TCP module must process urgent data before processing any other data.)

ACK   This flag tells the receiving TCP module that the Acknowledgment Number field contains a valid acknowledgment number. As you have learned, this flag helps TCP ensure data reliability.

PSH   This flag requests a *push*. In effect, this flag tells the receiving TCP module to immediately send the segment's data to the destination application. Normally, the TCP module buffers incoming data. As such, TCP does not send segment data to its destination application until the buffer reaches a specific threshold. The PSH flag tells the TCP module not to buffer the segment's data. For example, a Telnet application would normally set this flag. By doing so, Telnet forces TCP to immediately pass the user's keyboard inputs to the Telnet server. This helps eliminate delays in echoing the received character back to the sender—most Telnet users want to see what they are typing, as they type it.

RST   This flag requests that the receiving TCP module *reset* the connection. TCP will send a message with the RST flag when it detects a problem with a connection. Most applications simply terminate when they receive this flag. However, you could use the RST flag to design sophisticated programs that recover from hardware or software crashes.

SYN   This flag tells the receiving TCP module to synchronize sequence numbers. As you have learned, TCP uses this flag to tell the receiving TCP module that the sender is preparing to transmit a new stream of data.

FIN   This flag tells the receiving TCP module that the sender has finished transmitting data. The FIN flag only closes the data flow in the direction that it travels. The receiving TCP module must also send a message with a FIN flag in order to completely close the connection.

WINDOW SIZE

The 16-bit Window Size field tells the receiving TCP module the number of bytes that the sender is willing to accept. As you have learned, TCP uses a variable-length, sliding window to improve throughput and optimize network bandwidth. The value in this field specifies the width of the sliding window. Typically, the window size will be several thousand bytes.

TCP CHECKSUM

Like the UDP checksum, the 16-bit TCP Checksum field includes the TCP data in its calculations. TCP requires that senders calculate and include checksums in this field. Likewise, TCP requires receiving TCP modules to verify checksums when they receive data.

Note: Network software calculates the UDP and TCP checksums in a similar fashion. However, UDP does not require a checksum in its datagrams. A TCP checksum is mandatory for every TCP segment a sender transmits.

URGENT POINTER

The 16-bit Urgent Pointer field specifies a byte location in the TCP data area. The purpose of the URG flag and the urgent pointer is to notify the receiving TCP module that some kind of *urgent data* exists and to point the TCP module to that data. However, no one has adequately defined the term *urgent data.* Likewise, no one has defined the receiving TCP module's responsibility with regard to handling urgent data. Perhaps even more significant is the fact that what this byte location represents (or even its location) is the subject of much debate.

Douglas E. Comer, in the second edition of his classic book, *Internetworking with TCP/IP - Volume 1,* Prentice Hall, 1991, talks about the Urgent Pointer field in section 12.12 (*Out of Band Data*). However, W. Richard Stevens, in section 20.8 of an excellent book entitled *TCP/IP Illustrated - Volume 1,* Prentice Hall, 1994, comments:

> *"..many applications incorrectly call TCP's urgent mode out-of-band data."*

Obviously, Stevens believes many applications unacceptably blur the line between *urgent mode* and *out-of-band* data. He goes on to explain the reason he believes this has occurred:

> *"The confusion between TCP's urgent mode and out-of-band data is also because the predominant programming interface, the sockets API, maps TCP's urgent mode into what sockets call out-of-band data."*

With regard to the precise location of the urgent data, Stevens provides the following commentary:

> *"There is continuing debate about whether the urgent pointer points to the last byte of urgent data, or to the byte following the last byte of urgent data. The original TCP specification gave both interpretations but the Host Requirements RFC identifies which is correct: the pointer points to the last byte of urgent data."*

> *"The problem, however, is that most implementations (i.e. the Berkeley-derived implementations) continue to use the wrong interpretation. An implementation that follows the specification in the Host Requirements RFC might be compliant, but might not communicate correctly with most other hosts."*

Stevens and Comer agree that the urgent pointer points to the *last* byte of urgent data. Also, Stevens explicitly states that there is no way to identify the *start* of urgent data. After all of this, you may be curious about possible uses of urgent data. Practically everyone mentions Telnet as an example of an application that can use the TCP urgent mode. A Telnet application can use urgent data to process *escape* or *interrupt* characters. At the present time, you should probably limit your use of TCP's urgent mode. Unless you explicitly control the design of all programs that will use your application, other Internet programs may incorrectly interpret your urgent mode data.

OPTIONS

Like the IP header, the TCP header includes an optional Options field. During the initial negotiations between two ends of a TCP connection, TCP modules commonly use the Options field with the Maximum Segment Size option. TCP's maximum segment size is similar to the physical layer's maximum transfer unit (MTU)—it defines the largest message that the TCP module will accept. As you have learned, TCP optimizes network bandwidth by increasing throughput. The Maximum Segment Size option lets TCP modules advertise the largest segment or message that it expects to receive. TCP modules can only use the maximum segment size option in a message with the SYN flag set. However, the maximum segment size is not a negotiated option. One end of the TCP connection simply announces to the other end that it expects a maximum segment size of some value. If a TCP module does not transmit a maximum segment size, TCP assumes a default maximum segment size of 536 bytes.

UNDERSTANDING ENCAPSULATION

As previously mentioned, the software development process for Internet applications differs very little from any other kind of application. The layered network design and TCP/IP protocols help hide ugly details related to network software. The protocols perform the majority of the network-related work for you, and the layered design insulates you from much of the dirty work. The real sophistication of the Internet's data delivery system lies in its simplicity. You pass data from your application to a protocol on the protocol stack, and that protocol passes your data to the next protocol on the stack, and so on. As you have learned, understanding the entire process is important. However, as you develop Internet programs, you only need to concern yourself with the interface between your program and the protocol that transports your program's data.

This chapter and the last two chapters have introduced you to the different layers within a TCP/IP network. These chapters have also described the interfaces between the TCP/IP protocols and network layers. The process of flowing information through the protocol stack is really a process of encapsulating data. Encapsulation simply involves formatting data to fit within a particular protocol. As the data flows through the protocol stack, each layer builds on the previous layer's encapsulation. Figure 5.9 shows a bird's eye view of the entire process of flowing information through the protocol stack.

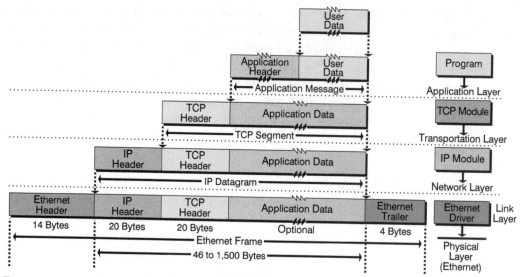

Figure 5.9 *Encapsulation of data as it flows through the protocol stack.*

You will design the basic functionality of your Internet programs just as you would any other application. When you need to transmit information across the Internet, you will encapsulate your data within a protocol that you select based upon your program's requirements. To select the correct protocol, you need to know which protocols are available and to understand their functions. To properly encapsulate data, you must know the format of the protocol's data structures. Hopefully, the last three chapters have helped you understand this process and many of the details necessary to accomplish these tasks.

UNDERSTANDING THE APPLICATION LAYER

You may already understand much of what occurs within the application layer. The application layer contains all the details about a specific application. In other words, as an Internet programmer, you design the application layer as you design your program.

By definition, if you are an application programmer, you have developed software applications. As you know, a program's design details depend on the program's purpose. For example, if you want to develop Internet applications, you obviously have information that you want to exchange with other applications on the Internet. As such, to successfully design your Internet programs, you must know how to send or receive information on Internet. As you design your Internet programs, you should ask yourself, "How do I communicate with the Internet?" You have already learned the basic answer: to communicate with the Internet, you simply send information *down* the *protocol stack*.

Your responsibility in the application layer is to communicate your information to the next appropriate layer in the protocol stack. Each successive layer in the protocol stack performs its respective function. The TCP/IP protocols all work together to properly address, route, and transport your data across the Internet. In order to communicate with protocols on the protocol stack, you must know which protocols exist. You must also know their locations in the stack and understand their functions. Normally, your programs will communicate with one of the transport protocols—TCP or UDP.

PUTTING IT ALL TOGETHER

In this chapter, you learned that TCP/IP transport protocols deliver data to network applications through a protocol port. You have learned that, in most cases, your applications will need to use TCP rather than UDP because TCP offers more reliable communication services. In addition, you have learned how a sliding window lets TCP increase network bandwidth and manage flow control.

In Chapter 6, you will read about two special purpose protocols: the Serial Line Internet Protocol (SLIP) and the Point-to-Point Protocol (PPP). You will learn how the Internet uses these two link-layer protocols to frame TCP data for transmission across serial links, such as modem connections to standard telephone lines. However, before you move on to Chapter 6, make sure you understand the following key concepts:

✓ A TCP/IP protocol port represents a network application address within a host computer.

✓ Transport protocols use protocol ports to talk to applications.

✓ TCP ensures data reliability by including checksums in TCP segments and exchanging acknowledgment messages between TCP modules.

✓ Sliding windows let TCP modules send multiple segments before waiting for an acknowledgment message.

✓ TCP uses a an adjustable window width to increase network bandwidth and manage flow control.

✓ TCP modules use a three-way handshake to establish TCP connections and a two-way handshake to terminate TCP connections.

✓ TCP uses full-duplex communication, which requires TCP modules to terminate data flow in both directions before closing a TCP connection.

✓ When TCP performs a half-close, TCP terminates data flow in one direction only.

Chapter 6
SLIP versus PPP

The fastest growing segment of Internet users are those who connect to the Internet through an Internet service provider. Such users connect their modems to standard telephone lines and then use serial communication to send and receive data. When these users want to connect to the Internet from Windows, they use one of two protocols that govern serial communications: SLIP and PPP. As such, before you can design effective Windows-based, network applications, you need to understand the key features of (and differences between) these two protocols. You also should have a basic understanding of Compressed SLIP, which is a derivative of SLIP. By the time you finish this chapter, you will understand the following key concepts:

- How SLIP encapsulates IP datagrams

- The SLIP deficiencies and why they exist

- How CSLIP improves network performance across a serial line

- How PPP encapsulates data

- How PPP negotiates and establishes TCP connections

- How PPP's Link Control Protocol manages a PPP connection

- What PPP options the Link Control Protocol can negotiate

- How PPP uses Network Control Protocols to configure network layers, such as the IP layer, in a TCP/IP network

REVIEWING SERIAL DATA COMMUNICATION PROTOCOLS

To create a SLIP connection, a pair of computers typically use modems and telephone lines to establish an asynchronous, serial link. The two computers then transmit data over the asynchronous link at arbitrary time intervals. Unfortunately, between these intervals, the transmission cable often collects electronic noise. As a result, devices that transmit across serial links use communication parameters to help them distinguish data bits from interval bits (or line noise).

When you use a modem and data communication software to exchange information with another computer, you must specify parameters such as the baud rate, data size, parity, and so on. To communicate using a serial connection (such as a modem phone connection), two systems must use the same data communication settings.

Users often express data communication settings as a baud rate, followed by the other settings in a format such as 8-N-1. If you have used a modem for data communication, you may have seen the communication parameters (which, in effect, define a protocol) specified as 8-N-1. The *8* means that the protocol uses eight bits for each data unit (like an 8-bit byte). When the devices communicate, they send or receive one data unit at a time.

UNDERSTANDING PARITY

Parity is a process that computers, modems, and other devices use to detect data corruption. The following paragraphs describe how your computer sets a parity bit, as well as how transmission devices use *parity bits* to detect data corruption. As you have learned, over a serial link, computers transmit data as a stream of 1's and 0's (bits). A pre-defined number of bits (usually eight) represent a unit of data. However, some serial protocols require the transmission device to add a bit, called a parity bit, to each unit (packet) of data. An odd parity protocol sets the parity bit's value so that the number of 1 bits in a packet is always odd. Likewise, an even parity protocol sets the parity bit's value so that the number of 1 bits in a packet is always even.

For example, suppose a modem uses odd parity and needs to transmit 10001010 as a byte of data. As you can see, 10001010 includes three (or an odd number of) 1's. In this case, the modem would use a parity bit of 0 since the byte already includes an odd number of 1's. However, suppose the next byte of data contains 10001011, which includes an even number of 1's (four). In this case, the modem would use a parity bit of 1 to make the total number of 1's an odd number (five).

To determine if any data corruption occurred during transmission, a receiving modem can count the number of 1's in each packet . For example, suppose the sending modem uses an odd parity protocol and the receiving modem counts an even number of 1's in the packet (which includes the parity bit). Because an even number of 1's bits disagrees with an odd-parity protocol, the receiving modem knows that the data is corrupt. With such knowledge, the receiving modem can discard the packet and, depending on the protocol requirements, request re-transmission. In an 8-N-1 set of communication parameters, the *N* represents *No parity*. When the parameters specify no parity, devices do not add a parity bit to each packet.

UNDERSTANDING START AND STOP BITS

As mentioned, modems transmit data packets over asynchronous, serial links at arbitrary intervals. As such, the receiving modem needs to know when a data packet begins and ends. Many communication protocols use a start and stop bit to help the modem correctly interpret the incoming data. A *start bit*, which is always a 1, signals to the receiving computer that the following bits constitute data. The *stop bit*, which is always a 0, signals the end of data.

To understand start and stop bits, think about how the receiving device knows data is present on the cable. Between data transmission intervals, the cable is not in use and has no signal present (a 0-bit status). Before the sending device transmits data, it places a wake up signal on the cable (the start bit). In short, the start bit tells the receiving device to "get ready, here comes my data." After the sender transmits its data, it sends a stop bit to reset the cable to its off (0 bit) state. A packet with an 8-N-1 set of communication parameters would include ten bits: one start bit, eight data bits, zero parity bits, and one stop bit.

Understanding Baud Rates

People commonly (and erroneously) believe *baud* represents data-bits per second. In other words, many people believe that 1200 baud means 1200 data-bits per second (bps). As you have learned, modems (and other transmission devices) typically send 8-bit units of data, which are sandwiched between one start bit and one stop bit and often include one parity bit. As such, each data packet contains ten or eleven bits. For example, a 1200-baud transmission line can transfer between 110 and 120 bytes-per-second. Likewise, a 9600-baud modem, on the other hand, can transfer between 850 and 960 bytes-per-second. By taking advantage of data compression techniques, newer modems can achieve very high data rates.

When you hear the term *baud*, you can loosely (imprecisely) substitute bits-per-second. However, as just discussed, because of the start, stop, and parity bits, you aren't really talking about data bits. Likewise, if the devices use data compression, the number of bits actually transferred may exceed the bits-per-second definition by 200 percent!

Understanding SLIP Connections

Serial Line Internet Protocol (SLIP) is one of the most popular methods used to link first-time PC and business computer users to the Internet. To use SLIP, you need software that manages a SLIP connection between your PC and the Internet. This management software (often called a TCP manager) is like a network device driver. However, you normally start (or load) the SLIP manager interactively, running the SLIP-manager software as you need it.

Note: *Many SLIP managers include a dialer program you can use to call your Internet provider.*

Establishing a SLIP Connection for Your PC

A SLIP connection is one of the easiest and most economical ways to link your computer to the Internet. If your local area network (LAN) does not have a direct connection to the Internet or if you plan to use a stand-alone PC, you may want to consider using a SLIP connection to the Internet. To establish a SLIP connection to the Internet, you must first find an Internet service provider that offers SLIP accounts. Because of SLIP's popularity, many commercial Internet service providers offer SLIP accounts.

Frequently, you can find an Internet service provider by looking in the yellow pages of your local phone book. If not, many books (such as *Success with Internet,* Allen Wyatt, Jamsa Press, 1994) contain appendices that list Internet service providers. To start, contact a provider

---

near you and ask if they offer SLIP accounts. In all probability, they will. Then, simply tell the provider you would like to establish a SLIP account. The Internet service provider, in turn, will give you a telephone number you can call to gain access to your account. The service provider should also give you instructions on how to start the SLIP server on the service provider's network. After you start the software on the provider computer, you can run a SLIP manager on your local PC. With your SLIP manager running, you can then run your Windows-based Internet programs.

Depending on the location of the Internet service provider's networked-computers, you may be able to call a local telephone number to gain access. Other times, the provider gives you a toll-free telephone number to call. As such, when you shop for an Internet service provider, be sure to factor phone charges into your cost estimates. Some services may seem inexpensive until you calculate the cost of long-distance phone bills. Typically, you will pay a monthly fee for the privilege of accessing your SLIP connection. However, in some cases, you may also pay an hourly rate for time spent on-line. As such, when you compare costs between Internet service providers, be sure to consider differences in monthly and hourly fees.

After you load your SLIP-manager software, you can run your TCP/IP-based programs, such as Windows-based Ftp. To run such programs, you need to have a local copy of the executable program on your PC. For example, if you want to do file transfers using the File Transfer Protocol, you need a local copy of an Ftp program. Likewise, if you want to read mail and network news across a SLIP connection, you need mail and newsreader software on your local computer. To understand why you need local copies of such Internet software, you need to understand what actually happens when you establish a SLIP connection to the Internet.

As you may know, with an Internet service provider, you can establish a basic (non-SLIP) account that lets your computer function as an Internet terminal. The service provider's computer, in turn, acts as your host computer on the Internet. For such connections, you normally access Internet services from a UNIX shell or from a menu program that the service provider makes available. For example, to start a Telnet (remote login) session on the Internet using a terminal-type connection, you either select a Telnet option from a menu or type **telnet** at a UNIX shell prompt.

When you start Telnet in this way, the Telnet client program that executes actually resides on the service provider's computer. In other words, the service provider's hard disk must contain any TCP/IP programs that you want to run. Remember, your computer acts like a terminal. In other words, your computer is not running the Internet program but, rather, simply displaying the program's results. When you instead establish a SLIP connection to the Internet, your computer becomes a node on the Internet. In other words, your computer becomes a host computer with its own IP address! As such, you can run TCP/IP programs from your PC! To do so, however, the executable program files must reside on your PC.

SLIP Means More Than Access

Initially, you will probably use your SLIP connection to run client programs, such as a Windows-based Telnet, Finger, or even Ftp. With a SLIP connection, the fact that you become a host computer with your own IP address presents some interesting possibilities. For example, as a host computer on the Internet, you can offer Internet services to other Internet users.

Suppose, for example, over a SLIP connection to the Internet, you run an Ftp server on your home or business PC. As such, other Internet users can transfer files from your PC to their own host computer. The host computer for such users can be a service provider's computer. However, if such users link to the Internet with a SLIP connection (as you did), your Ftp server can transmit files directly to their PCs. In effect, an Internet user in Australia can transfer files from my PC in the United States to their PC in Australia for the cost of a telephone call to their local Internet service provider!

Consider your cost to connect to the Internet. Using a SLIP connection, you become an Internet host computer. Of course, you need a home or business computer to do so. However, other than a computer and a modem, you have no other hardware costs. In other words, when you use a SLIP connection, your entry-level hardware costs to become a host computer on the Internet are minimal.

Normally, you will use an Internet service provider that provides you with a dedicated SLIP connection. In other words, the service provider assigns you a permanent IP address. Typically, such connections involve some set up fees, as well as monthly service charges. However, as you can see, the process is not complex. Beyond the initial cost of the computer and your monthly account fees, all you need is software. A wide variety of commercial Internet software is available to you. However, if you cannot buy what you need, Section 2 of *Internet Programming* will teach you the basic skills you need to develop your own Internet software.

Encapsulating Data in the Link Layer

As discussed in Chapter 4, each layer of the TCP/IP protocol stack encapsulates your data into formats that surrounding layers require. As your data flows through the protocol stack, each layer builds on the previous layer's encapsulation. To send IP datagrams for the network layer, the link layer translates data into data frames acceptable to the underlying network technology. The translation process encapsulates data into a structure defined by the network technology. For example, the link layer encapsulates IP datagrams into Ethernet frames for an Ethernet network. Likewise, the link layer encapsulates IP datagrams into token-ring frames for token-ring networks.

The Serial Line Internet Protocol (SLIP) and Compressed Serial Line Internet Protocol (CSLIP) simply define another level of encapsulation. SLIP and CSLIP encapsulation prepare your data for transmission across a serial (usually RS-232) link to the Internet. The Point-to-Point Protocol (PPP) also encapsulates data for the same purpose. However, as you will learn, PPP includes other features that provide a more sophisticated interface to the Internet, both across serial links and other point-to-point data links. The SLIP and PPP sit between your computer's serial port driver and the TCP/IP protocol stack within your PC.

UNDERSTANDING THE *SLIP* PROTOCOL

As you have learned, TCP/IP protocols run on top of a variety of network technologies. Most of these technologies have officially recognized encapsulation (or framing) requirements. The Institute of Electrical and Electronic Engineers (IEEE), founded in 1963, has over 300,000 members that help set standards for computers and communications, including standards used in local area networks (LANs). Like most standards-publishing organizations, IEEE numbers its standards documents. The IEEE 802 series standards cover LANs. For example, IEEE 802.1 covers network management. IEEE 802.3 and IEEE 802.5 define the physical layers for Ethernet and token-ring networks. IEEE 802.2 specifies the data link layer for both Ethernets and token rings, as well as a few other network technologies.

Request for Comments (RFC) 1055, *A Nonstandard for Transmission of IP Datagrams Over Serial Lines: SLIP*, Romkey, 1988, defines a standard for framing IP datagrams in preparation for transmission across a serial line. RFC 1055 is not an official Internet standard. However, RFC 1055 does define a de facto standard. In other words, although the Internet does not recognize or track RFC 1055 as an Internet standards document, the SLIP frame that RFC 1055 defines functions as a standard to which everyone's SLIP implementation conforms.

SLIP is a packet-framing protocol that defines how your computer encapsulates an IP datagram before transmitting it across a serial-data line. The protocol provides no addressing capability, packet-type identification, error detection or correction, or packet compression. In other words, SLIP is extremely simple. For these reasons, SLIP is easy to implement and tremendously popular. Although SLIP has tremendous popularity, companies and software vendors rarely adopt it as an official standard because SLIP is not an official Internet standard. Instead, most companies that adopt a standard for serial TCP/IP data communications use the Point-to-Point Protocol (PPP). The Point-to-Point Protocol is an official Internet standard that defines a protocol similar to SLIP for serial and point-to-point data communications.

UNDERSTANDING *SLIP* FRAMING

As you have learned, each protocol encapsulates or frames data; the SLIP protocol is no exception. SLIP uses a sequence of characters that frame or encapsulate each IP packet on the serial line. SLIP defines two characters for framing purposes: *End* and *Esc.* The End character is ASCII 192 (0xC0) and the Esc character is ASCII 219 (0xDB). A SLIP host transmits an End character at the end of each packet. SLIP uses the Esc character to mark data bytes within the packet that have the same value as End and Esc. The End value is not a magic number. Rather, it is simply a value SLIP developers chose for framing purposes. As such, it's very likely that this value may occur naturally within a user's data. When the value occurs, SLIP uses the Esc character to tell the receiver that the End value that follows is not the end of a frame. For example, if the data packet includes a byte with the value of 0xC0 (same as the End character), SLIP substitutes the two-byte escape sequence Esc 0xDC. If a byte within the packet has the same value as Esc, SLIP substitutes the two-byte escape sequence Esc 0xDD.

The SLIP implementation on the receiving end of a SLIP connection interprets the data in the opposite way. For example, when a SLIP host encounters the Esc character in a serial stream, SLIP immediately examines the next character and possibly substitutes Esc and the character as follows. When SLIP sees the two-byte escape sequence Esc 0xDC, SLIP substitutes a byte with the value of 0xC0 in place of the two bytes. If SLIP sees the two-byte escape sequence Esc 0xDD, SLIP replaces the two bytes with 0xDB. When SLIP sees the End character in the data stream, not preceded by Esc, SLIP knows it has reached the end of the frame. As such, SLIP passes all preceding data to the network layer as an IP packet. Suppose an IP packet includes two bytes, one with the value of Esc and one with the value of End. Figure 6.1 shows how SLIP would frame this packet. As you can see, SLIP substitutes the two-byte escape sequences described in the previous paragraph.

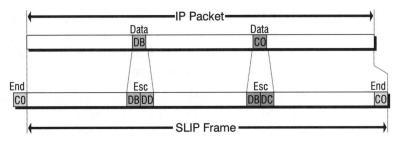

Figure 6.1 An IP packet with Esc and End characters in a SLIP frame.

Most SLIP implementations also place an End character at the beginning of an IP packet (though, strictly speaking, the SLIP protocol does not require it). In effect, by placing an End character at the beginning of a packet, SLIP flushes any erroneous bytes caused by noisy telephone or serial lines. A SLIP implementation that uses this technique can throw away the zero-length SLIP frame when it detects two back-to-back End characters. Figure 6.2 shows two IP packets framed by a SLIP implementation that uses a leading End character.

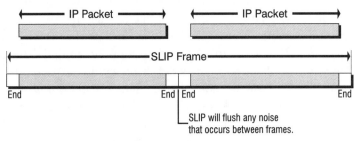

Figure 6.2 A SLIP implementation that uses a leading End character for framing.

UNDERSTANDING ERROR DETECTION WITH SLIP CONNECTIONS

As mentioned in the previous section, if you place an End character at the beginning of an IP packet, SLIP will flush any erroneous bytes that noisy transmission cables cause. However, SLIP does not provide any true error detection or correction. Instead, SLIP relies on the TCP/IP network and transport layers to detect and discard invalid packets and messages. For example, as you learned in Chapter 3, IP requires a checksum that covers the IP header. As such, on a SLIP connection, you don't have to worry about SLIP not detecting a corruption of IP header data. The IP layer will detect the error and reject the packet. Likewise, TCP connections use a checksum that detects errors in TCP headers and TCP segments. As such, TCP will detect any corruption to its data that occurs in the SLIP connection. Because SLIP can rely on the protocols above it to detect and handle errors, SLIP does not concern itself with error detection.

AVOID UDP AND SLIP

As you learned in the previous section, because IP and TCP both require checksums, you can rely on them to provide error detection for messages you send across a SLIP connection. In contrast, because UDP does not require a checksum, you have no guarantee that UDP datagrams you send on a SLIP connection will arrive uncorrupted. For example, assume you transmit a UDP datagram across a SLIP connection and noisy telephone lines corrupt the UDP data area. If the datagram does not include a UDP checksum, the receiving host will be unaware of the corruption. As such, when you write Internet programs that use a SLIP connection, do not use UDP datagrams to transmit critical data unless you include a UDP checksum. Otherwise, you invite disaster. Without a UDP checksum, your program might receive and process corrupted data.

UNDERSTANDING SLIP DEFICIENCIES

In addition to the lack of error detection noted above, SLIP lacks a few other features that most network professionals want or need. For example, SLIP is unable to address packets, identify different packet types, or to compress packet information. However, as noted in RFC 1055, the SLIP designers created the protocol when these features were not important.

ADDRESSING DEFICIENCIES

As previously discussed, each time you establish a SLIP connection, your PC becomes an Internet host with its own IP address. As a host, your computer can then provide services to other Internet users. However, because your provider normally assigns you an IP address from its pool of available addresses, you may get a different IP address with each SLIP connection. As such, other Internet hosts that want to access your server programs may have difficulty locating your computer.

Additionally, SLIP provides no method for the service provider to tell your SLIP software what your IP address is. As such, each time you establish a SLIP connection, you must manually tell your SLIP software what IP address to use. Likewise, SLIP offers no way for one host computer to inform another host of its IP address. As such, any time you establish a SLIP connection, you must manually transmit your IP address to the destination host computer. To correct some of SLIP's addressing deficiencies, you can establish a dedicated IP address (an address that does not change and belongs only to you) with an Internet service provider. However, dedicated IP address service is more expensive than using an IP address from an available pool of addresses.

Note: Some SLIP implementations automatically set the correct IP address for each SLIP connection. However, such implementations usually read the IP address from the text strings the service provider's computer transmits to your computer (which are destined for your screen display). This automated IP address assignment is implementation dependent—the SLIP protocol does nothing to facilitate this feature.

PACKET IDENTIFICATION DEFICIENCIES

Many computers can run more than one protocol family at the same time. For example, a Digital Equipment Corporation (DEC) computer might run TCP/IP and DECnet protocols. As such, to reduce cabling and hardware costs, you ideally want multiple protocols to share the same transmission lines (cables). With Ethernet packets, such cable sharing is possible. Ethernet frames include a "type" field that defines the packet's destination protocol. As such, Ethernet packets can share the same transmission line with other packets that have similar protocol-identification fields. Unfortunately, a SLIP frame does not include any fields that identify the packet's destination protocol. As such, you cannot mix SLIP, TCP/IP, and DECnet packets over the same serial line. SLIP encapsulates IP packets only. In other words, you cannot use SLIP encapsulation with more than one protocol.

COMPRESSION DEFICIENCIES

Ethernet networks can transmit up to 10 million bits-per-second. A SLIP connection might include high-speed modems that transmit data at 19,200 bits-per-second. In other words, Ethernet is over 500 times faster than a SLIP connection. To improve SLIP's relatively slow transmission speed, you can use *data compression*, which reduces the amount of data the network must transfer. By compressing data, you effectively send more information in less time. Assume, for example, you want to transfer a 100Kb (100 x 1,024 bytes) chapter of this book across a 1200-baud modem. As discussed, the 1200-baud modem can transmit about 120 bytes-per-second. To transmit the 100Kb chapter will require about 14 minutes:

> 100 x 1,024 = 102,400 bytes
>
> 102,400 bytes / 120 bytes-per-second = 853 seconds
>
> 853 seconds / 60 seconds-per-minute = 14 minutes

However, if you compress the book chapter, you may reduce the amount of data from 100Kb to 25Kb. As a result, you reduce your transmission time to less than four minutes. Many newer modems provide built-in compression techniques. Likewise, some software protocols include software support for data compression. For example, because IP and TCP headers include a lot of data that does not change between packets or segments, a protocol can include simple compression algorithms that transmit only the changed fields in these headers. The SLIP protocol, as defined by RFC 1055, does not include any type of data compression. However, as you will learn in the next section, Compressed SLIP compresses IP packet and TCP segment headers to improve performance.

Understanding Compressed *SLIP (CSLIP)*

RFC 1144, *Compressing TCP/IP Headers for Low-Speed Serial Links,* Jacobson, 1990, describes a compression method that improves TCP/IP performance over SLIP connections: the *compressed SLIP (CSLIP) algorithm.*

*Note: Some network literature refers to the Compressed SLIP (CSLIP) algorithm as **Van Jacobson CSLIP compression**, in recognition of the author who proposed the algorithm. The Point-to-Point Protocol refers to the algorithm as **Van Jacobson TCP/IP header compression**.*

CSLIP compresses header information only. CSLIP does not compress data. Specifically, CSLIP compresses only TCP headers and IP headers for TCP segments. CSLIP does not compress UDP headers nor IP headers for UDP datagrams. Since many reliable CSLIP implementations already exist, you probably won't develop your own CSLIP program. However, you may design and implement custom protocols that require you to transmit header information with each network message. CSLIP illustrates compression techniques you can build into these protocols. You can use these techniques for all network transmissions, not just for serial-line links.

Note: Most SLIP implementations support CSLIP. If your software (TCP Manager) supports CSLIP, you may want to enable CSLIP compression. In the worst case, the connection will not work. If you discover your serial link does not support CSLIP, you can disable CSLIP compression and reconnect with no harm done.

Understanding the Background for *CSLIP*

To understand why header compression is effective, you need to consider the typical Internet services you might want to access over a SLIP connection:

- Interactive terminal logins using the TELNET Protocol
- Interactive file transfers using the File Transfer Protocol (FTP)
- Electronic mail using the Simple Mail Transfer Protocol (SMTP)
- Usenet news using the Network News Transfer Protocol (NNTP)

Like any other network connection, a serial line connection like SLIP or CSLIP carries data packets that include a packet header and user data. To increase the amount of user data the connection transfers, you can use data compression to reduce the size of the packet header. You can divide network data transfer into two basic categories: interactive data and bulk transfer data. As you will learn, these two transfer categories have different line efficiencies.

FTP or NNTP-based programs are excellent examples of programs that perform bulk data transfers. Although you may manually initiate both processes, the majority of the data transfer does not occur interactively. For example, when you transfer a file from an FTP site, you specify the file to transfer and then start the transfer. The bulk of the data transferred is the data bytes that belong to the file. Likewise, with a network news program, you interactively select the newsgroup to transfer. However, the resulting data transfer (which constitutes the bulk of the data transferred during the session) requires no further action on your part—it is not interactive.

A Telnet-based application is a prime example of interactive data transfer. Typically, each keystroke in a Telnet program results in a data packet. Although Telnet provides a means of sending entire lines at a time, most implementations still send one packet per keystroke and the receiving host echoes each keystroke back across the net to your computer. As you have learned, TCP-based programs such as a Telnet program also require acknowledgment messages. In other words, an interactive program such as Telnet generates massive numbers of small data packets.

In Chapter 4, you learned that an IP header is normally 20 bytes wide. In Chapter 5, you learned that a TCP header is also normally 20 bytes wide. As such, a Telnet-based program generates large quantities of TCP segments that include 40 bytes worth of header information for each byte of data transmitted. To understand the CSLIP design methodology, you must understand two separate but interrelated concepts: line efficiency and interactive response. *Line efficiency* is simply the ratio of data to header-plus-data in a TCP/IP datagram. For example, you would calculate the line efficiency for an IP packet from a Telnet application as follows:

1. Assume the Telnet program transmits one packet per keystroke and that the data in the packet consists of only one byte—the typed character.

2. With a 20-byte IP header and a 20-byte TCP header, you have an IP packet size of 41 bytes—one byte of user data and 40 bytes of header data.

3. The packet-receiver must transmit an acknowledgement packet for each packet the Telnet program transmits. As such, the network must transport two 41-byte packets for each typed character—a 41-byte packet from the sender and a 41-byte acknowledgement packet from the receiver. (Remember, the acknowledgement packet will also include a 20-byte header for both the IP and TCP protocols, as well as the echo character to display on the user's screen.)

4. You can calculate the line efficiency for the packet exchange (which is less than three percent) as shown here:

```
Line Efficiency = Data / (Header Size + Data)
Line Efficiency = 1 Byte / (40 Bytes + 1 Byte)
Line Efficiency = 1 Byte / 41 Bytes
Line Efficiency = 0.0244
Line Efficiency = 2.44 Percent
```

Note: Remember, TCP is a full-duplex communication process—messages flow independently, in both directions at the same time. As such, you must calculate a separate line efficiency for each direction of communication. (In the previous example, line efficiency is the same in both directions.)

To boost line efficiency, you simply increase data per packet or decrease packet header size. As previously mentioned, the CSLIP design methodology also focuses on good interactive response from the TCP/IP internetwork. *Interactive response* refers to a computer user's perspective of the network operations in progress. For example, when a user presses a key on their keyboard, the user expects to see a letter appear on their computer monitor. If a network or computer operation causes a delay to occur before the letter appears, users will consider this delay as poor interactive response.

The term *human factors* refers to a computer user's perspective and a user's behavior with regard to computer operations. Human factors consider the personal side of computing rather than technical issues related to hardware and software. The CSLIP design takes human factors into consideration, as discussed in the following section.

CONSIDERING THE HUMAN FACTORS

In addition to considering line efficiencies for interactive programs, CSLIP addresses human factors issues. Human factors include intangible issues such as a computer user's perceptions. In his book, *Designing the User Interface: Strategies for Effective Human-Computer Interaction*, Addison-Wesley, 1987, Ben Shneiderman summarizes a lot of excellent information obtained from human factors studies. For example, in general, a user perceives an interactive response as bad if the feedback (such as a keyboard character echo) takes longer than 100 to 200 milliseconds (ms).

RFC 1144 identifies some ways in which protocol headers interact with such perceptions. For example, suppose each typed character results in a 41-byte packet transmission and a 41-byte echo response. To handle both packets within the 200ms window, the line speed must be at least 4,000 bits-per-second (bps). In other words, slow serial-line speed causes a user to perceive a program as slow, even though the program's performance may actually be quite fast.

Bulk data transfers can also impact an interactive program, even on a line that is fast enough to handle normal interactive responses. For example, to keep line efficiency above 90 percent for bulk data transfers, the maximum transfer unit (MTU) for bulk data transfers should be 500 to 1,000 bytes for a 40 byte TCP/IP header. Suppose your SLIP connection uses a 1,024-byte MTU over a 9600-bps line. As such, a single packet may take approximately one second to transfer one way (1,024 bytes times ten bits-per-byte divided by 9,600 bits-per-second). Unfortunately, any interactive data transfers must wait until an in-progress, bulk-data transfer completes.

CONSIDERING THE HARDWARE FACTORS

In addition to human factors, you must also consider hardware factors when you design custom protocols. For example, modem manufacturers use various schemes to improve effective bandwidth over normal telephone lines. As a programmer, you don't need to know specifically how they accomplish such improvements. However, you should be aware of some of the implications of these designs.

Note: Communications theory establishes actual (or real) bandwidth limits. Effective bandwidth is the result of implementation schemes that improve data transfer in a way that seems to exceed the theoretical or physical limits. For example, when you compress data, you boost effective bandwidth. In other words, compression results in more data transferred in the same amount of time. In some cases, your effective bandwidth exceeds the communication channel's theoretical limits.

In full-duplex data communication (which is common with a modem), data flows simultaneously in two directions. However, this data rarely flows at the same rate in both directions. For example, to improve effective bandwidth, one end of the modem connection often transfers more data than the other. To send more data, the faster modem steals transmission slots on the slower system's wire. In short, the faster system gets to use its own transmission cable and, at times, the slower system's transmission cable as well. The modems, in turn, manage when each system can use the cable and also sort out the data. Best of all, this wire sharing occurs transparently behind the scenes.

To determine which end of the connection receives the extra data transfer capability, modem manufacturers assume one end of the connection is human and thus needs high bandwidth. Based on this assumption, the manufacturers design the modems to guess which end of the connection has a human typing information. Manufacturers assume a demand of less than 300 bps indicates a human. Since most people have limited typing speed, 300 bps probably works in many cases. Unfortunately, TCP/IP packet exchanges with 40:1 header-to-data ratios often confuse such modems and cause them to *thrash*—constantly change the direction in which the most data flows. (A 41-byte IP packet represents 328 bits of data which the modem will not recognize as a character typed by a human being.) As you shop for modems, you should identify and understand the various compression and transmission capabilities each modem supports. If you buy the proper modem, you can significantly improve your transmission speeds. Before you purchase a modem, you may want to talk with your Internet provider to learn what types of modems they recommend and why.

IDENTIFYING THE DESIGN GOALS

With modern modem designs, you will want to limit the bandwidth demand of network traffic due to typing and acknowledgments to less than 300 bps. If you assume a ten-bit modem packet for each byte of data (one start and stop bit, plus eight bits of data), 300 bps means your CSLIP design goal is to limit bandwidth demand to 30 characters-per-second. Typically, a person's maximum typing speed is five characters-per-second. As such, you can use 25 (30 - 5) characters for headers and still achieve your bandwidth goal. In other words, to meet your design goal, you can use a five-byte header for each typed character. In addition, a five-byte header solves the human factors perception problem. In other words, you can easily transmit a six-byte packet (five-byte header plus one byte of data) and receive an acknowledgment in less than 200ms over a 4096-bps line.

In Figure 8 of RFC 1144, Jacobson plots effective throughput versus MTU. Jacobson's graphs (which also show lines for 2400-, 9600-, and 19,200-bps data transfers) show that increasing the MTU beyond 200 bytes yields very little increased throughput. For example, increasing the MTU from 200 to 576 bytes improves throughput by only three percent while it increases the average delay (as seen by the user) by 188 percent. In effect, Jacobson shows that optimum MTU is around 200 bytes. A 200-byte MTU solves interference problems that bulk data transfers cause. For example, with a 200-byte MTU on a 9600-bps line, you can transfer a single packet and receive an acknowledgment in less than 400ms. Once again, assume your interactive data must wait an average of half the MTU time for bulk data transfers to complete. As such, a 200-byte MTU keeps you within your target window of 200ms.

UNDERSTANDING THE IMPLEMENTATION

In RFC 1144, Jacobson describes a method that uses the design goals discussed in the previous section to reduce the 40-byte TCP/IP header to an average of 3 to 5 bytes. Jacobson shows that about one-half of the TCP/IP header information remains constant over the life of a TCP connection. As such, after the hosts establish the TCP connection, the CSLIP protocol requires the sending and receiving hosts to retain a copy of the last header received through the TCP connection. CSLIP substitutes a small connection identifier that the host computers use to identify each connection. The CSLIP protocol transmits changes as required and the host computer updates the locally stored header information.

As each CSLIP packet arrives, the network software examines the CSLIP connection identifier and restores the header information previously received. In other words, after establishing a connection, CSLIP does not transmit unchanging TCP/IP header information. This simple step reduces the TCP/IP header size by 20 bytes.

CSLIP also depends on the link-level framing protocol to tell the receiver the length of a received message. By doing so, CSLIP eliminates two more bytes from the TCP/IP header (the Total Length field in the IP header). However, after you eliminate the Total Length field, the IP-header checksum is the only essential part of the IP header that remains. As Jacobson points out, there is no reason to transmit a checksum for information that is not in the transmitted packet. CSLIP requires the receiver to test checksums for uncompressed packets. For compressed packets, CSLIP regenerates the checksum locally. This eliminates another two bytes from the TCP/IP header.

All of the above leaves 16 bytes of header information that can change during the life of a TCP connection. However, these 16 bytes do not change for each packet transmission. RFC 1144 notes that a data transfer that uses the File Transfer Protocol only changes the packet ID, sequence number, and checksum in the sender-to-receiver direction. The packet ID, acknowledgment message, checksum and (possibly) window, change in the receiver-to-sender direction. The CSLIP sender always retains a copy of the last packet sent. By doing so, the sender knows which fields must change in the current packet. If the sender only sent fields that changed, the compression scheme would reduce the average header size to around ten bytes. However, Jacobson analyzes how the fields actually change and shows how to further reduce the header size.

Jacobson notes that the packet ID typically comes from a counter that increments by one for each packet sent. This means the difference between the current and previous packet IDs is a small, positive integer, usually less than 256 (one byte); frequently, it will equal one. Also, from the sender side of a data transfer, the sequence number in the current packet will be the sequence number in the previous packet plus the amount of data in the previous packet. The maximum IP packet size is 64,000 bytes. This means the sequence number change must be less than two bytes. In other words, by sending the differences in the changed fields rather than the fields themselves, CSLIP saves another three or four bytes-per-packet.

All of the above reduces the 40-byte TCP/IP header to the five-byte header target. In Section 3.2 of RFC 1144, Jacobson describes *the ugly details* (his words) of how to accomplish the compression described above. He notes that if you identify and properly handle a couple of special cases related to interactive typing traffic and bulk data transfer, you can further reduce the header to an average of three bytes.

The implementation details in Section 3.2 are unimportant unless you want to develop your own CSLIP implementation. However, you can use the general CSLIP approach to reduce the size of any headers required by your custom application messages. In Jacobson's CSLIP compression algorithm, there is a key technique that you can use in your own applications. To begin, your sending and receiving program should store a copy of the application message header. Next, the sending program should only transmit those header fields whose values can change. By transmitting only changing header field data, your programs reduce network traffic. As header fields change, both the sender and receiver can update their copies of the message header accordingly.

*Note: The term for transmitting changes, instead of an entire field, is **differential coding**.*

UNDERSTANDING THE POINT-TO-POINT PROTOCOL

The Point-to-Point Protocol (PPP) resolves all the SLIP deficiencies (addressing, packet identification, and compression) identified in the previous sections. Additionally, PPP is an official Internet standard; SLIP is not. As such, software vendors and businesses that want to adopt an official standard for serial data links on the Internet should use the Point-to-Point Protocol which consists of three main components:

- An encapsulation method that lets network software use a single serial link for multiple protocols.

- A Link Control Protocol (LCP) that network software can use to establish, configure, and test the data-link connection. Both ends of the PPP connection use LCP to negotiate connection options.

- A family of Network Control Protocols (NCPs) that let PPP connections use different network-layer protocols.

Although there currently are more SLIP than PPP users, this will change. Because PPP offers significant advantages over SLIP, you can expect SLIP popularity to eventually decline and the number of PPP implementations to increase. As such, if you plan to create Internet programs that may use serial data links, you should have a general understanding of PPP. The following sections of *Internet Programming* provide a general overview of the Point-to-Point Protocol. If you want to study PPP in greater detail, you should read the following three RFCs:

- For general background information on PPP, read RFC 1547, *Requirements for an Internet Standard Point-to-Point Protocol*, Perkins, 1993.

- RFC 1661, *The Point-to-Point Protocol*, Simpson, 1994, defines the Point-to-Point Protocol and the PPP Link Control Protocol.

- RFC 1332, *The PPP Internet Protocol Control Protocol (IPCP)*, McGregor, 1992, defines the PPP Network Control Protocol for IP.

UNDERSTANDING PPP ENCAPSULATION

One design goal for a standard, Point-to-Point Protocol is an encapsulation method that lets network software use a single serial link for multiple protocols. RFC 1661, *The Point-to-Point Protocol*, Simpson, 1994, defines the Point-to-Point Protocol encapsulation. However, RFC 1661 does not discuss PPP framing. In other words, RFC 1661 defines PPP encapsulation but does not discuss the frame structure that the data-link layer uses to transmit the PPP packets.

DEFINING A PPP FRAME

To develop the Point-to-Point Protocol, PPP designers used an internationally accepted (ISO) frame structure. ISO International Standard 3309, *Data Communications—High-Level Data Link Control Procedures—Frame Structure*, 1979, defines a simple data-link layer protocol called *High-Level Data Link Control (HDLC)*. HDLC uses special flag characters to mark the beginning and end of frames, much like SLIP uses the End character. HDLC also uses a Cyclic Redundancy Check (CRC) field to detect errors in the frame. Figure 6.3 shows the format of a PPP frame.

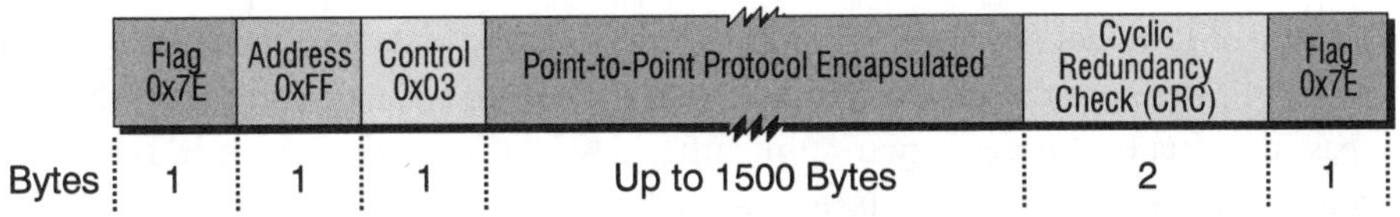

Flag 0x7E	Address 0xFF	Control 0x03	Point-to-Point Protocol Encapsulated	Cyclic Redundancy Check (CRC)	Flag 0x7E
Bytes 1	1	1	Up to 1500 Bytes	2	1

Figure 6.3 The format of a Point-to-Point Protocol frame.

Note: ISO refers to the CRC in HDLC as a Frame Check Sequence (FCS).

As you can see, each PPP frame begins and ends with a flag byte whose value is always 0x7E. The Address and Control fields use fixed values of 0xFF and 0x03, respectively. The PPP data-link layer uses 0x7D as an escape character within the PPP frame to mark data with a value of 0x7E (the flag byte) or 0x7D (the escape byte). The PPP data-link layer complements (toggles) the sixth bit of any byte that follows the escape character (0x7D).

For example, if the PPP data includes a byte with a value of 0x7E (the same value as the flag byte), the PPP data-link layer substitutes the two-byte escape sequence 0x7D, 0x5E. In other words, instead of transmitting a data byte of 0x7E, the PPP data-link layer transmits the escape character (0x7D) and the byte that results from complementing the sixth bit of 0x7E. Note that 0x7E equals binary 01111110 and 0x5E equals binary 01011110 (note the inversion of the sixth bit). Likewise, if the PPP data includes a byte with a value of 0x7D (the same value as the escape byte), the PPP data-link layer substitutes the two-byte escape sequence 0x7D, 0x5D. Note that 0x7D equals binary 01111101 and 0x5D equals binary 01011101 (again, note the inversion of the sixth bit).

Many modems use ASCII control characters (bytes with values less than 0x20) for special purposes. By default, the PPP data-link layer escapes any ASCII control characters in the PPP data in the same way described in the previous paragraph. By escaping ASCII control characters, the PPP data-link layer prevents modems and host serial communication drivers on either side of the PPP connection from misinterpreting the PPP data.

For example, many modems use ASCII 0x1B as their own escape character. In place of 0x1B, the PPP data-link layer substitutes the two-byte escape sequence 0x7D, 0x3B. Note that 0x1B equals binary 00011011 and 0x3B equals binary 00111011. As before, the PPP data-link layer inverts the sixth bit. In this case, however, the inversion toggles the sixth bit from a 0 to a 1. The previous inversions toggled the sixth bit from a 1 to a 0.

IDENTIFYING PPP DATA

Figure 6.4 shows the structure of the packet within the PPP frame. As you can see, the Protocol field is the key element of the PPP encapsulation. The first two bytes in the PPP encapsulation (the Protocol field) identify the type of data the remaining PPP information area contains. A Protocol-field value of 0x0021 tells the network software that the following data is an IP datagram. In other words, the PPP packet contains the kind of data that typically flows throughout a TCP/IP network.

Likewise, a Protocol-field value of 0xC021 identifies *link-control data.* As previously mentioned, the Link Control Protocol (LCP) establishes, configures, and tests the data-link connection. In other words, PPP will use the information in such packets to manage the data-link itself—PPP will not pass the data on for delivery to some other destination in the network. In a similar way, a Protocol-field value of 0x8021 identifies *network-control data.* PPP uses the Network Control Protocol information to choose and configure one or more network-layer protocols, such as IP.

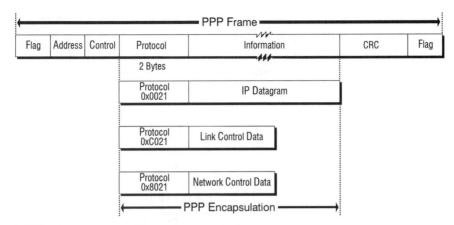

Figure 6.4 *The Point-to-Point Protocol encapsulation.*

COMPARING PPP ENCAPSULATION TO SLIP

As just discussed, the PPP Protocol field identifies an IP, link-control, or network-control packet. In actual practice, the PPP Protocol field can be one or two bytes wide. To eliminate one byte from every PPP frame (and thereby increase PPP throughput), PPP implementations frequently use the Link Control Protocol to negotiate a Protocol field size of one byte.

To reduce the frame size by another four bytes, PPP implementations can negotiate (using LCP) to eliminate the Flag, Address, and Control fields—all of which have fixed values. As such, PPP potentially adds only three bytes of overhead (one byte for the Protocol field and two bytes for the CRC field) compared to the SLIP encapsulation defined by RFC 1055. Also, TCP/IP implementations of PPP can use the Network Control Protocol to negotiate the use of Jacobson's CSLIP compression (RFC 1144). PPP provides the following advantages:

- PPP can support multiple protocols over a single serial link, using the Protocol field.

- Using the CRC in each PPP frame, PPP provides error checking.

- Using the Network Control Protocol, PPP can negotiate TCP/IP header compression. (Although not discussed previously in this book, the Network Control Protocol also lets PPP connections dynamically negotiate IP addresses.)

- PPP connections can negotiate new data-link options using the Link Control Protocol. (In other words, LCP lets vendors extend PPP—without redefining the protocol—as data-link technologies improve.)

UNDERSTANDING PPP LINK OPERATIONS

Before host computers can use PPP for normal network communications, the network software must configure and test the data link. Network software uses the Link Control Protocol to perform data-link tests. After the hosts configure and test the data link, they use the Network Control Protocol to choose and configure one or more network-layer protocols, such as IP. After the LCP and NCP negotiations are complete, the data-link remains active until either LCP or NCP negotiates to close the connection. Figure 6.5 shows the PPP link process. The following sections describe each phase in this process.

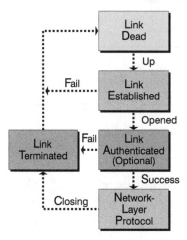

Figure 6.5 *The PPP link process.*

Note: *RFC 1661 includes a diagram similar to Figure 6.5. The RFC refers to the figure as a phase diagram. Figure 6.5 uses the phase names (within each block) specified by RFC 1661.*

UNDERSTANDING THE LINK DEAD PHASE

A PPP link always begins and ends with the Link Dead phase. In the Link Dead phase, the physical layer of the network is not ready for data communications. PPP moves from the Link Dead phase to the next phase (establishment) of the link process only after it receives some indication that the physical layer is ready for use. For example, over a dial-up connection, PPP would interpret the modem's carrier-detection signal as an indication that the physical layer is ready for use.

UNDERSTANDING THE LINK ESTABLISHMENT PHASE

After PPP receives an indication that the network's physical layer is ready for communication, PPP moves to the Link Establishment phase. During the Link Establishment phase, the PPP software module on each host computer uses the Link Control Protocol to establish and configure the data link. PPP assumes default values for all configuration options unless the host computers agree to alter an option during this phase. (Later sections in this chapter discuss the LCP configuration options in detail.) During the Link Establishment phase (which uses the Link Control Protocol), PPP also negotiates options that are independent of any particular network, such as options to eliminate non-changing flag bits from the PPP frame. PPP negotiates network-specific options during the Network-Layer Protocol Phase.

RFC 1661 requires PPP to *silently discard* all non-LCP packets (packets with a Protocol field that does not equal 0xC021) it receives during the Link Establishment phase. As defined by RFC 1661, the term *silently discard* means the PPP implementation must ignore the packet and perform no further processing of it. RFC 1661 recommends that PPP implementations provide a way to log silently discarded packets. The RFC also recommends that the implementation record the contents of the discarded packet, as well as the discard event in a statistics counter. However, RFC 1661 does not require PPP to log such errors, nor does the RFC define any specific requirements for the contents of error logs. As a result, error logging is PPP implementation dependent.

UNDERSTANDING THE LINK AUTHENTICATION PHASE

After PPP establishes the data link, it enters the Link Authentication phase. *Authentication* refers to the process that networks use to determine whether a host computer has sufficient privileges (authorization) to communicate with another host. In other words, a network may restrict communications between host computers or users on a host computer. Networks that routinely transport confidential information usually have a built-in authentication procedure. For example, suppose a company stores sensitive accounting information on a computer that runs a file server program. Although some employees in the company's accounting department may use this information, the company obviously doesn't want everybody to have access to it. As a result, the company asks its programmer to write an authentication protocol into the file server. Although some networks include an authentication protocol in the network layer, TCP/IP networks do not. For this reason, the Link Authentication phase is an optional part of the PPP link process.

UNDERSTANDING THE NETWORK-LAYER PROTOCOL PHASE

During the Network-Layer Protocol phase, PPP uses Network Control Protocols to configure one or more network-layer protocols, such as IP. After PPP configures the network-layer protocols, the PPP connection is ready for normal data communications and can carry packets for these network-layer protocols. As discussed, PPP supports more than one protocol over a single data link. As such, whenever the PPP data link is active, the Network Control Protocols can open and close specific protocol connections. For example, assume your network software module establishes a PPP connection and configures IP using the IP Network Control Protocol. Later, while the IP data link is still active, your network software module can use the same PPP connection to open a DECnet data link. Likewise, your network software module can shut down the DECnet data link without closing the IP data link.

In other words, during the Network-Layer Protocol phase, PPP uses Network Control Protocols to open, configure, and close network conversations that use multiple network-layer protocols. To configure each network-layer protocol, PPP uses a different Network Control Protocol. For example, the IP Network Control Protocol is different from the DECnet Network Control Protocol. Network professionals design each Network Control Protocol to handle the peculiar requirements of its corresponding network layer.

UNDERSTANDING THE LINK TERMINATION PHASE

During the Link Termination phase, PPP closes the connection. As shown in Figure 6.5, if PPP fails to authenticate the host computers, PPP enters the Link Termination phase. Also, the loss of a modem's carrier signal might cause PPP to enter the Link Termination phase. Normally, the Link Control Protocol negotiates a link's termination. PPP must notify the network-layer protocols (using the appropriate Network Control Protocol) whenever LCP begins to negotiate the close of a PPP data link. As discussed, PPP lets NCPs open and close protocol connections whenever the PPP data link is active. The implementation notes in RFC 1661 specifically state that closing all NCP connections is not sufficient reason to close the PPP link. In other words, the PPP implementation doesn't automatically close the link just because no data is flowing across the connection. Network software must specifically terminate a PPP link.

UNDERSTANDING THE LINK CONTROL PROTOCOL

PPP uses the Link Control Protocol (LCP) to negotiate an ever expanding list of configuration options in a variety of environments. As such, you can use PPP between host computers that network administrators have configured differently. LCP automatically negotiates the configuration options. For example, PPP uses LCP to negotiate encapsulation formats. In this case, LCP can automatically negotiate to eliminate fields within the PPP frame, reducing frame sizes and thus boosting PPP throughput. Through such negotiations, LCP can dynamically make configuration changes, based on the network's current state (traffic flow and so on), that are transparent to the user. In other words, regardless of the user's level of expertise, LCP can establish optimal configuration settings. The following paragraphs discuss LCP packet formats and then describe currently available LCP options.

IDENTIFYING LCP PACKETS

PPP defines three distinct classes of LCP packets: configuration, termination, and maintenance packets. PPP uses LCP configuration packets to establish and configure a PPP link. LCP termination packets end a PPP link. PPP uses LCP maintenance packets to manage and debug a PPP data link. As previously discussed, a Protocol-field value of 0xC021 identifies the data in a PPP frame as Link Control data. Figure 6.6 shows the general format of an LCP packet.

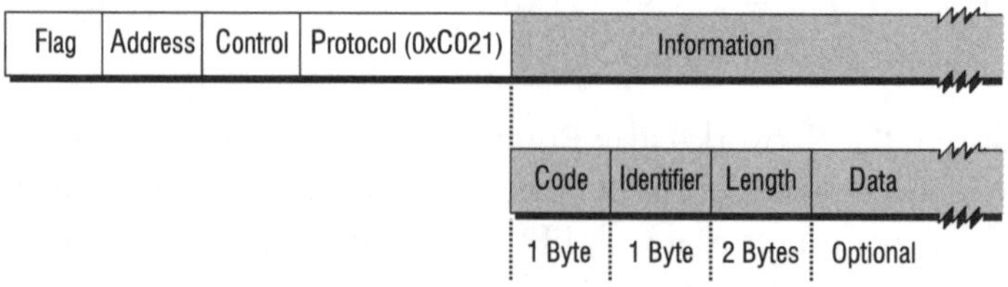

Figure 6.6 The Link Control Protocol packet format.

The one-byte Code field identifies the type of LCP packet that the PPP frame includes. PPP uses the one-byte LCP Identifier field to match requests and replies between network layers that use the PPP connection. The LCP Identifier field is similar to the Sequence Number field that the Transport Control Protocol uses. The LCP Length field is two-bytes wide and indicates the total length of the LCP packet, including the Code, Identifier, Length, and Data fields. The LCP Data field may be empty (zero bytes). The type of LCP packet, as identified by the Code field, determines the format and contents of the Data field. Table 6.1 shows the LCP codes defined as of July 1994.

LCP Code	Packet Name	Class
1	Configure-Request	Configuration
2	Configure-Ack	Configuration
3	Configure-Nak	Configuration
4	Configure-Reject	Configuration
5	Terminate-Request	Termination
6	Terminate-Ack	Termination
7	Code-Reject	Maintenance
8	Protocol-Reject	Maintenance
9	Echo-Request	Maintenance
10	Echo-Reply	Maintenance
11	Discard-Request	Maintenance

Table 6.1 Code field values for the PPP Link Control Protocol.

Note: As with any assigned numbers on the Internet, you can find the most recent list of LCP codes in the latest RFC entitled **Assigned Numbers**. This RFC constantly changes as new requirements arise.

DEFINING LCP CONFIGURATION PACKETS

As mentioned, PPP uses LCP configuration packets to establish and configure a PPP link. LCP includes four configuration packets: Configure-Request, Configure-Ack, Configure-Nak, and Configure-Reject. The Point-to-Point Protocol requires all PPP implementations to always transmit a Configure-Request packet to open a PPP connection. The Data field in an LCP Configure-Request packet contains a list of desired configuration options.

When a PPP host receives an LCP Configure-Request packet, it must transmit an appropriate response. If all configuration options listed in the LCP Data field are acceptable, the host transmits a Configure-Ack packet. The Data field in a Configure-Ack packet contains an exact copy of requested configuration options. In other words, the Configure-Ack packet says, "Okay, all the configuration options in the Data field are acceptable. Let's use them." You should note, however, the host that responds to a Configure-Request packet only sends a Configure-Ack if *all* configuration options in the Data field are acceptable.

If a host that receives a Configure-Request packet recognizes the requested configuration options but cannot currently support all of them, the host must transmit a Configure-Nak (configuration options not acknowledged) packet. The Data field in a Configure-Nak packet contains the unacceptable configuration options. In other words, when the host transmits a Configure-Nak packet, PPP filters out all acceptable configuration options. LCP also lets PPP implementations append configuration options to the Configure-Nak packet. In other words, the host that receives a Configure-Request packet can request additional configuration options when it transmits its Configure-Nak packet. When PPP receives a Configure-Nak packet, it must respond to any extra configuration options that the host requests in the Configure-Nak packet Data field.

PPP continues to send and receive Configure-Request and Configure-Nak packets until both ends of the PPP connection agree on the same configuration options. If the PPP module receives an LCP packet that contains unrecognized options, the PPP module must transmit an LCP Configure-Reject packet. The Configure-Reject packet's Data field contains only the rejected configuration options. The difference between the configuration options in a Configure-Nak packet and a Configure-Reject packet is that rejected options are not negotiable. In other words, a PPP module might choose to request the not-acknowledged options later during the life of the PPP connection. In contrast, the PPP module knows that the peer host will never negotiate any rejected options.

DEFINING LCP TERMINATION PACKETS

To negotiate a PPP link closure, PPP uses two LCP termination packets: Terminate-Request and Terminate-Ack. Neither packet uses the LCP Data field. PPP requires a host to transmit a Terminate-Ack packet whenever the host receives a Terminate-Request packet.

RFC 1661 states that an implementation that wants to close a connection *should* transmit a Terminate-Request packet. In other words, a Terminate-Request packet is not an absolute requirement for PPP implementations. As such, if you design software that uses PPP directly, you should not depend on PPP to transmit a Terminate-Request packet in all cases. RFC 1661 also states that a PPP implementation should continue to transmit Terminate-Request packets until one of three events occurs:

- The host receives a Terminate-Ack packet.

- The lower-network layer indicates that it is no longer available for communication (for example, the modem drops carrier detect).

- The host transmits enough unacknowledged Terminate-Request packets that the PPP implementation is reasonably certain that the peer host computer is down.

Note: *If a PPP module receives an unsolicited Terminate-Ack packet, the PPP module must re-negotiate the connection or assume the peer host computer is down.*

DEFINING LCP MAINTENANCE PACKETS

PPP uses the LCP maintenance packets to manage and debug PPP data links. PPP defines five LCP maintenance packets: Code-Reject, Protocol-Reject, Echo-Request, Echo-Reply, and Discard-Request. When a PPP module receives an LCP packet with an unrecognized value in the Code field, the module must transmit a Code-Reject packet. The Code-Reject packet's data area (which PPP calls the Rejected-Packet field) contains a copy of the rejected LCP packet. However, the Rejected-Packet field only includes the data in the PPP Information field. The Rejected-Packet field does not include data-link layer headers nor the CRC in the PPP frame. Figure 6.7 shows the format of a Code-Reject packet.

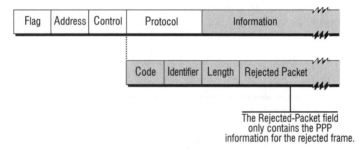

Figure 6.7 *The format of an LCP Code-Reject packet.*

In a similar way, PPP transmits the Protocol-Reject packet in response to an unrecognized value in the PPP Protocol field. As shown in Figure 6.8, the Protocol-Reject packet includes a two-byte Rejected-Protocol field, as well as a Rejected-Information field.

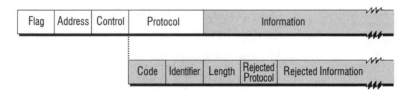

Figure 6.8 *The format of an LCP Protocol-Reject packet.*

The Rejected-Protocol field contains the unrecognized value that the PPP module received in the PPP Protocol field. Like the Rejected-Packet field in the Code-Reject packet, the Rejected-Information field only includes the data from the PPP Information field. Using the Echo-Request and Echo-Reply packets, a PPP implementation can exercise (or test) both directions of a PPP data link. When a PPP module receives an LCP Echo-Request, the module must transmit an Echo-

Reply packet. The Discard-Request packet lets a PPP module test the PPP data link in one direction only (from local to remote host). PPP modules must silently discard any Discard-Request packets that they receive.

In Echo-Request, Echo-Reply, and Discard-Request packets, the data area contains a Magic Number field. A Magic Number is a negotiable LCP option that detects looped-back data links. The next section discusses the Magic Number field, as well as the other LCP configuration options.

UNDERSTANDING *LCP* CONFIGURATION OPTIONS

LCP Configuration Options identify negotiable characteristics of a point-to-point link. Each Configuration Option has a default value. PPP uses the default value if a Configure-Request packet does not include the option during the Link Establishment phase of the PPP link process. The Configuration Option's default value lets PPP data links operate without negotiating the option. However, in some cases, the link's performance with a default value may be less than optimal. Figure 6.9 shows an LCP Configuration Option's general format.

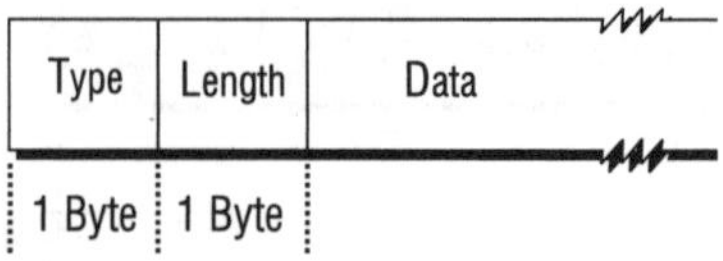

Figure 6.9 The general format for LCP Configuration Options.

An LCP Configuration Option's Length field (one-byte) specifies the length of the Configuration Option, including the Type, Length, and Data fields. The Data field's format and contents are specific to each Configuration Option. The one-byte Type field identifies the type of Configuration Option that the PPP implementation wants to negotiate. Table 6.2 shows Type field values, as of July 1994.

Type Field Value	Configuration Option Description
0	RESERVED
1	Maximum Receive Unit
3	Authentication Protocol
4	Quality Protocol
5	Magic Number
7	Protocol Field Compression
8	Address and Control Field Compression

Table 6.2 The Type field values for LCP Configuration Options.

CONFIGURING THE MAXIMUM RECEIVE UNIT

The Maximum Receive Unit (MRU) Configuration Option lets PPP modules negotiate the maximum size of a data packet. The default value is 1,500 bytes. PPP modules can negotiate packet sizes smaller or larger than the default value. For example, suppose a host computer wants to use a packet size of 2,048 bytes. If the peer host acknowledges the 2,048-byte MRU (in a Configure-Ack packet), the computers can transfer packets up to 2,048 bytes in size.

However, you should note that PPP implementations do not have to send packets that equal the MRU size. In other words, the MRU Configuration Option defines the maximum packet size but hosts do not have to pad packets to reach that size. PPP implementations can always send packets smaller than the maximum size. If, for some reason, a host computer prefers to use an MRU less than 1,500 bytes, the PPP module can use the MRU Configuration Option to request this size also. Figure 6.10 shows the format of the MRU Configuration Option.

Type	Length	Maximum Receive Unit
1 Byte	1 Byte	2 Bytes

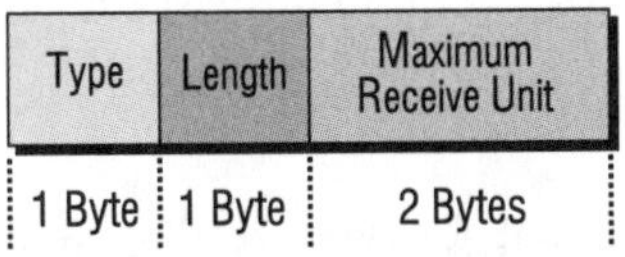

Figure 6.10 The format for the LCP Maximum Receive Unit Configuration Option.

The Length field for the MRU Configuration Option is always four. The two-byte Maximum Receive Unit field specifies the maximum number of bytes in the PPP Information field. In other words, the MRU size does not include the PPP Framing, Protocol, or CRC fields.

CONFIGURING THE AUTHENTICATION PROTOCOL

For networks that include network-layer authentication protocols, PPP modules can use the Authentication Protocol Configuration Option to negotiate the use of a specific authentication protocol. As discussed, since some networks do not include network-level authentication protocols, PPP (by default) does not require authentication. As you have learned, TCP/IP does not include a network-layer authentication protocol.

When a PPP module sends a Configure-Request packet that specifies the Authentication Protocol Configuration Option, the PPP module expects authentication from the peer computer. When a peer sends a Configure-Ack packet with the Authentication Protocol Configuration Option, the peer has agreed to authenticate the connection using the acknowledged authentication protocol.

As an interesting side note, PPP does not require full-duplex authentication. In other words, PPP does not require hosts to use the same authentication protocol in both directions. PPP modules can negotiate to use different protocols in each direction. The format of the Authentication Protocol Configuration Option is similar to the MRU Configuration Option shown in Figure 6.10. However, instead of the two-byte MRU field, the Authentication Protocol Configuration Option includes a two-byte Authentication Protocol field. Also, the Authentication Protocol Configuration Option includes a Data field that can contain any additional information that the specified authentication protocol requires.

CONFIGURING THE QUALITY PROTOCOL

PPP provides the ability to monitor the quality of a PPP connection. In general, to measure the quality of a data link, you examine the amount of data the link discards. In other words, you determine when and how often the link drops data. The Quality Protocol Configuration Option lets PPP modules negotiate the use of a specific protocol that monitors the amount of data the link drops. Like the Authentication Protocol Configuration Option, PPP does not require full-duplex quality monitoring. PPP modules can negotiate to use different quality protocols in each direction. The Quality Protocol Configuration Option is nearly identical to the Authentication Protocol Configuration Option. Both options rely on a two-byte field. Like Authentication Protocol Configuration Option, the Quality Protocol Configuration Option includes a Data field that can contain any additional information that the specified quality protocol requires.

UNDERSTANDING MAGIC NUMBERS

When your client programs send messages to servers, there may be times when the server program actually resides on your host computer. Rather than have messages routed on to and across the Internet and back to the server, PPP supports a loop-back data link. A looped-back data link lets client and server programs on the same computer communicate without actually transmitting data across the network. In other words, with a looped-back link, network software transmits packets to itself. Ideally, you want your network software to have the ability to test for looped-back link conditions, and then to use a looped-back link as required. PPP uses the Magic Number Configuration Option to detect looped-back links. In general, a PPP Magic Number is simply a unique number that PPP software modules use to detect looped-back links and other special data-link layer configurations. By default, PPP does not negotiate the Magic Number Configuration Option. Instead, PPP assigns a 0 to the Magic Number field.

Note: RFC 1661 contains a detailed discussion of the Magic Number Configuration Option.

The Magic Number Configuration Option scheme depends on the high probability that two host computers will not choose the same magic number. In fact, to increase the likelihood of unique magic numbers, the PPP specification encourages designers to select magic numbers as random numbers. In general, the scheme works as follows. First, when a PPP module receives a Configure-Request packet with the Magic Number Configuration Option, the module compares the received magic number with the magic number of the last Configure-Request packet sent to the peer computer. If the magic numbers are different, the PPP module knows that a looped-back link does not exist.

However, if the magic numbers are the same, it is possible that the data link is looped-back. In other words, the Configure-Request packet that the PPP module just received may be the same

Configure-Request packet that the PPP module previously transmitted. In other words, the PPP module is receiving its own transmissions (as indicated by the fact that the magic numbers are the same). When a PPP module receives a Configure-Request packet with a suspect magic number (a magic number that matches the receiver's last transmitted magic number), the PPP module must transmit a Configure-Nak packet with a new magic number. If the PPP module receives a Configure-Nak packet with a different magic number, the PPP module knows that a looped-back link does not exist. However, if the PPP module receives a Configure-Nak packet with the same magic number, the possibility of a looped-back link configuration increases.

When a looped-back link configuration exists, the process just described will repeat itself over and over again. While PPP provides a method to detect looped-back links, the protocol does not define a recovery procedure. In other words, all PPP implementations can detect looped-back links. However, the procedure that each implementation uses to recover from a looped-back link condition is PPP implementation-specific.

CONFIGURING PROTOCOL FIELD COMPRESSION

As previously discussed, in some cases, PPP can compress the normal two-byte Protocol field to one byte. The Protocol Field Compression (PFC) Configuration Option lets PPP modules negotiate to compress the PPP Protocol field. After a PPP module sends a Configure-Request packet with the PFC Configuration Option and receives a Configure-Ack packet, both PPP hosts can use one byte for the PPP Protocol field instead of two bytes. However, in all cases, the PPP implementation must always accept a two-byte Protocol field. PPP does not permit one-byte Protocol fields with an LCP packet. This means that LCP packets always contain an unambiguous Protocol field value. Also, note that when PPP uses a compressed Protocol field, PPP uses the compressed frame to calculate the PPP frame CRC.

CONFIGURING ADDRESS AND CONTROL FIELD COMPRESSION

Since, in a PPP frame, the data-link layer Address and Control fields are constant values, these fields are likely candidates for compression. The Address and Control Field Compression (ACFC) Configuration Option lets the PPP module negotiate data-link layer address and control compression. As discussed, eliminating these fields saves two bytes of overhead and boosts PPP throughput. As with the Protocol Field Compression Configuration Option, PPP does not permit compressed Address and Control fields in an LCP packet. As such, LCP packets always remain unambiguous. Also, when PPP uses compressed Address and Control fields, PPP uses the compressed frame to calculate the PPP frame CRC.

UNDERSTANDING THE IP NETWORK CONTROL PROTOCOL

As discussed, PPP includes a family of Network Control Protocols that let PPP connections use different network-layer protocols. RFC 1332, *The PPP Internet Protocol Control Protocol (IPCP)*, McGregor, 1992, defines the PPP Network Control Protocol for IP. In general, the Internet

Protocol Control Protocol (IPCP) configures, enables, and disables IP protocol modules for both ends of a point-to-point link.

COMPARING IPCP TO LCP

With only a few exceptions, the IP Control Protocol is very similar to the Link Control Protocol. However, PPP encapsulates only one IPCP packet in the Information field of a PPP frame. Also, the PPP Protocol field value for IPCP is 0x8021. IPCP uses only the first seven codes (Configure-Request, Configure-Ack, Configure-Nak, Configure-Reject, Terminate-Request, Terminate-Ack, and Code-Reject) that LCP defines. PPP requires IPCP to treat all other LCP Codes as unrecognized and thus transmit a Code-Reject packet. As you might expect, IPCP and LCP use completely different Configuration Options. The following paragraphs describe the IPCP Configuration Options.

UNDERSTANDING IPCP CONFIGURATION OPTIONS

The IP Control Protocol defines three configuration options. However, one of the options (named IP Addresses) is obsolete, and the current IPCP specification (RFC 1332) does not even discuss this option. Currently, the only valid IPCP options are IP Compression Protocol and IP Address.

Note: The obsolete option IP Addresses is plural—the replacement option IP Address is not.

CONFIGURING THE IP COMPRESSION PROTOCOL

As you have learned, Van Jacobson TCP/IP header compression can reduce the size of TCP/IP headers to three bytes. The IP Compression Protocol Configuration Option lets PPP modules negotiate to use a specific compression protocol, such as CSLIP. By default, PPP does not enable compression. The IP Compression Protocol Configuration Option includes a two-byte, IP Compression Protocol field. At this time, the only compression protocol identified for IP is the Van Jacobson TCP/IP header compression (CSLIP). The IP Compression Protocol field value for the Van Jacobson compression is 0x002D. PPP can also use this value (0x002D) in the PPP Protocol field when it initially configures a PPP link.

CONFIGURING THE IP ADDRESS

As you have learned, unless your service provider assigns you a permanent IP address, you must manually configure your computer's local IP address each time you establish a SLIP connection. As such, perhaps one of the most significant advantages that PPP (as compared to SLIP) offers to TCP/IP network users is the ability to negotiate IP addresses. The IP Address Configuration Option for the IP Control Protocol lets PPP modules negotiate IP addresses. A PPP module can request a specific IP address or ask the peer host to provide IP address information. Figure 6.11 shows the format of the IP Address Configuration Option.

As you can see, the IP Address field is four-bytes wide and can hold all 32 bits of an Internet address. The IP address negotiation process works as follows. First, to request a specific IP address, a PPP module transmits a Configure-Request packet with an IP Address Configuration Option. The IP Address Configuration Option's IP Address field contains the desired IP address.

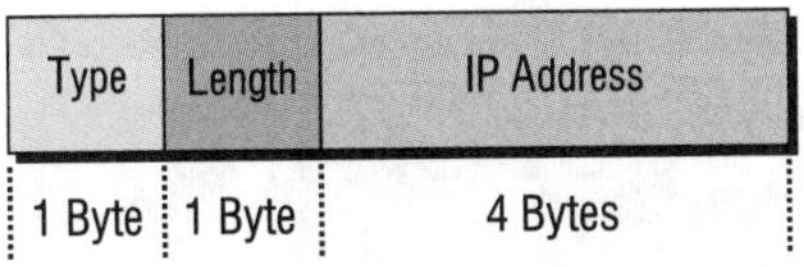

Type	Length	IP Address
1 Byte	1 Byte	4 Bytes

Figure 6.11 The format for the IP Address Configuration Option.

If the PPP module wants the peer host to provide an IP address, the PPP module also transmits a Configure-Request packet. However, in this case, PPP sets the IP Address Configuration Option's IP Address field to all 0's. To provide an IP address, the peer computer sends a Configure-Nak packet. The IP Address field of the Configure-Nak packet's IP Address Configuration Option includes a valid IP address. To acknowledge and accept a requested IP address, a PPP module simply transmits a Configure-Ack packet.

PUTTING IT ALL TOGETHER

In this chapter, you learned how a simple framing protocol, such as SLIP, provides an effective way to transmit IP datagrams across a serial data link. Furthermore, you examined how PPP resolves SLIP deficiencies related to packet type identification and IP addresses. Finally, you learned general details surrounding the IP Control Protocol—PPP's Network Control Protocol for TCP/IP networks.

In the next chapter, you will learn how the Berkeley sockets interface simplifies network programming on UNIX-based networks. After you read about Berkeley sockets in Chapter 7, you will explore Windows Sockets in Chapter 8. In Section 2, you will use the Windows Sockets API to create simple yet effective network programs for use on TCP/IP networks. However, before you move on to Chapter 7, make sure you understand the following key concepts:

✓ SLIP uses a special End character (0xC0) to encapsulate IP datagrams.

✓ CSLIP compresses IP header information to boost the transfer rate for serial connections.

✓ PPP retains CSLIP as a negotiable option to resolve SLIP's packet compression problem.

✓ PPP uses the Link Control Protocol to negotiate options such as the maximum size of a data packet and CSLIP compression.

✓ PPP uses a special Link Control Protocol to negotiate TCP connections across a PPP data-link.

✓ PPP uses a different Network Control Protocol for each type of network that uses PPP as a data-link.

Chapter 7
Understanding the Socket Interface

An *application program interface* (API) is simply a group of functions (a software interface) programmers use to develop application programs for a particular computer environment. For example, for software developers who want to create Windows applications, Microsoft provides an extensive collection of programming routines—the Windows API. In the 1980s, the U.S. government's Advanced Research Projects Agency (ARPA) provided funds to the University of California at Berkeley to implement TCP/IP protocols under the UNIX operating system. During this project, a group of Berkeley researchers developed an API for TCP/IP network communications. For reasons you will learn in this chapter, the designers called this API a *socket interface.*

Note: Because of Berkeley's involvement in the original development of the socket interface, people often refer to the socket interface as the Berkeley-socket interface or Berkeley sockets.

The socket interface is an API for TCP/IP networks. In other words, the socket interface defines a variety of software functions or routines that let programmers develop applications for use on TCP/IP networks. Today, the socket interface is one of the most popular APIs in use on TCP/IP networks. Therefore, if you want to develop programs for the TCP/IP networks that comprise the Internet, you need to understand the socket interface. By the time you finish this chapter, you will understand the following key concepts:

- How to create a socket
- How to configure a socket
- How to transmit data through a socket
- How to receive data from a socket
- How to use sockets with server programs

UNDERSTANDING SOCKET IMPLEMENTATIONS

The socket-interface designers originally built their interface into the UNIX operating system. However, as you will learn in Chapter 8, other operating systems or environments, such as Microsoft Windows, implement the socket interface as software libraries. In other words, in environments other than UNIX, you can call on a socket-library routine to perform TCP/IP network communications. However, regardless of the environment in which you program, your program code will look much the same. In your program code, you will always call a function to perform specific tasks. If you have developed socket-based programs for the UNIX operating system, you are probably already familiar with the documentation for socket function calls. If you are new to socket-based programming, however, and need more information about the Berkeley socket functions, you will need to obtain and review Section 2 of the *UNIX Programmer's Manual.*

NETWORK *I/O* VERSUS *FILE I/O*

You can more easily understand the Berkeley-socket interface if you have a general knowledge of UNIX system input/output (I/O). As mentioned, Berkeley designers developed the socket interface during a project to move TCP/IP to the UNIX operating system. As a result, the designers patterned the socket interface after existing UNIX system calls. In fact, they originally designed the socket interface to use the same function calls as the UNIX system. In other words, the designers built the original socket interface into the UNIX operating system. If you are not familiar with the UNIX operating system, the strategy of building the socket interface into the operating system software may seem strange to you. However, after you understand UNIX system I/O, you will see that the socket design is quite natural for UNIX.

In the UNIX operating system, system I/O calls take the form of an *open-read-write-close* process. To use a file, UNIX programmers first *open* the file. Next, they perform their *read* and *write* operations. Finally, they *close* the file. UNIX programmers follow these same steps to access hardware devices. In other words, under UNIX, you use the same system calls to access a printer, tape drive, and files. UNIX maps hardware devices and files into its file system. To open a file or to access a device (such as a tape drive), programmers call the same system function. In response to such calls, the function returns a pointer or handle, which UNIX calls a *file descriptor*, that points to a table entry (within UNIX) that describes the file or device. For a file, the file-descriptor table entry contains information such as the file name, file size, and file date. A UNIX file descriptor can point to a file, hardware device, or any other object that performs system I/O.

At the beginning stages of the socket design process, the Berkeley researchers tried to make network I/O function like any other type of UNIX system I/O. In other words, they wanted to design the socket interface to use the *open-read-write-close* process. As such, to communicate with a TCP/IP network, a program first opens a connection to the network. Next, the program reads and writes data through the connection. Finally, the program closes the connection. From a UNIX perspective, this design approach made network communications similar to all other UNIX system I/O—and thus easy to integrate into a UNIX operating system.

IDENTIFYING SOME OF THE PROBLEMS

As the Berkeley project progressed, the developers discovered that network I/O was much more complex than other types of I/O. To implement network I/O, the Berkeley researchers had to overcome obstacles unlike anything they'd encountered with file and device I/O. The following paragraphs briefly describe two network I/O problems that the socket-interface designers faced.

As you have learned, network program design typically follows the client/server model. As such, the socket-interface designers could easily modify the API for UNIX system I/O to let programmers create client programs that actively seek to make network connections. However, a network API must also let programmers create server programs that passively wait for contact from a client program. Since the normal UNIX system I/O doesn't incorporate much passive I/O capability, the socket designers had to create new system functions to handle passive I/O operations.

Likewise, the socket designers found that the communication functions of the UNIX system I/O weren't adequate to meet network needs. Typically, UNIX system I/O uses a fixed address to communicate with a file or device. In other words, the location (address) of the file or device on a stand-alone computer system does not change. Also, the connection (or data path) to the file or device is available throughout the entire read-write cycle—that is, until the program closes the connection to the file or device.

Fixed addresses work fine for connection-oriented network communication. However, for connectionless communications, fixed addresses present a problem. For example, when a network program transmits a datagram, the program specifies a destination address (the IP address of the host computer) but does not establish a point-to-point connection with the destination computer. The UNIX system I/O offered no provisions for this type of communication. In other words, when the Berkeley researchers started, the UNIX system I/O could only perform read-write operations on byte streams. Due to the problems previously described and other similar obstacles, the socket designers abandoned a pure UNIX system I/O approach. Instead of simply modifying the code for the existing API, the socket designers added new APIs (functions) to the UNIX operating system.

The socket interface that resulted from the Berkeley effort retains a common UNIX flavor. For example, the socket interface still refers to a socket handle as a file descriptor, and UNIX uses an entry in the file descriptor table to store the socket handle. As you learn more about the socket interface in this chapter and about the Windows Sockets API in the next chapter, remember that the socket interface originated as UNIX system code. Although many socket interface characteristics may initially seem strange to you, they will appear natural after you consider them in the light of their UNIX roots.

UNDERSTANDING THE SOCKET ABSTRACTION

Think of a socket as an endpoint for network communications. In other words, network communication involves two host computers or two processes that pass data between each other across a network. Network professionals refer to each end of this network conversation as an endpoint. When your programs use a socket interface for network communication, the socket is an abstract representation of the endpoint in the network communications process. For network communication to occur (through a socket interface), your program needs a socket at each end of the network conversation. The connection between the two sockets can be connection-oriented (a point-to-point connection) or connectionless. Although the socket-interface designers abandoned a pure (unmodified) UNIX approach, the socket interface still uses UNIX system I/O concepts for network communications. In other words, the socket-interface model for network communication still basically uses an open-read-write-close process.

To open or create a file in UNIX (and most other operating systems), you specify a description of the file (generally, the filename and how you want to use the file-read or write operations). Next, you ask the operating system to give you a handle that identifies the file. You can ask the operating system for a file handle (or descriptor) anytime you need one. You can also request handles to multiple files (one file at a time). In each case, the operating system returns a value (usually an integer number) that uniquely identifies the specified file. The socket interface works the same way. When you need a socket for network communication, you define the characteristics for a socket and then use an API to ask the network software for a handle (or descriptor) that identifies the specified socket. However, as explained in the following section, a socket handle differs from a file handle in a very subtle yet significant way.

COMPARING FILE AND SOCKET HANDLES

As you know, the steps you follow to obtain and use socket handles and file handles are very similar. However, the table entries to which these handles point vary significantly. Whereas a file handle points to a specific file (either an existing file or one that you create) or device, a socket handle does not represent a specific endpoint or destination address. The fact that a socket handle does not represent a specific endpoint is a subtle but significant departure from most file I/O systems. In most operating systems, a *valid* file handle must point to a specific file on a hard disk. However, as you will learn, socket-based programs create a socket and then, as a separate step, connect the socket to a destination endpoint. If file I/O had a comparable process, an application would obtain a valid file handle from the operating system and then, as a separate step, specify the hard disk location for the file.

Consider the requirements of a TCP/IP network program that transmits a datagram using connectionless protocols. The program will specify a destination address for the datagram but will not establish a direct connection with the destination host. Instead, the program transmits the datagram to the destination address. The network software (the IP layer, specifically) handles the delivery process. To integrate TCP/IP protocols into the UNIX operating system, the socket designers needed to add a new capability to the UNIX system I/O. The TCP/IP network API needed a way to obtain a valid I/O handle without creating a direct connection to the destination I/O address (the host computer on the network). Rather than try to modify the existing system I/O functions within UNIX, the socket designers created a new function called *socket*. As you will learn in the next section, the socket function lets a program obtain a socket handle without specifying a destination address.

CREATING A SOCKET

When you create TCP/IP programs, you need the ability to use connectionless and connection-oriented protocols. The socket interface lets your programs use both types of protocols through a socket connection. However, as discussed in the previous section, your network programs use separate steps to create a socket and to connect the socket to the destination host. To create a socket, your program calls the socket function. The socket function returns a handle that is similar to a file descriptor. In other words, the socket handle identifies a descriptor table entry that provides information about the socket. The following program statement shows an example of a socket function call:

```
socket_handle = socket(protocol_family, socket_type, protocol);
```

When you create a socket, you must specify three parameters: protocol family, socket type, and protocol. The protocol-family parameter identifies a family or collection of related protocols, such as the TCP/IP protocol suite. The socket-type parameter specifies whether your program will use the socket for datagram or byte-stream transmissions. The protcol parameter identifies the specific protocol that your program wants to use (TCP, for example). The following sections discuss the socket parameters in detail.

UNDERSTANDING THE SOCKET PARAMETERS

As the Berkeley researchers integrated TCP/IP protocols into the UNIX operating system, they also developed a general purpose API for multiple networks—not just TCP/IP networks running the UNIX operating system. Although the Berkeley researchers initially focused on creating a TCP/IP interface, they tried to design a socket interface that programmers could use on other networks. To accomplish this goal, the Berkeley researchers used the concept of protocol and address families.

USING PROTOCOL AND ADDRESS FAMILIES

As previously noted, the first parameter to the socket function (which creates a socket) identifies a family of protocols, such as the TCP/IP protocol suite. Because the socket function requires programmers to identify the protocols their programs will use, the socket interface can establish communications on multiple networks. In fact, in addition to the Internet's TCP/IP protocols, a Berkeley-style socket interface exists for UNIX internal protocols, and Xerox Network Services (XNS).

Note: XNS is a multilayer protocol system similar to TCP/IP. Although developed by Xerox's Palo Alto Research Center (PARC), XNS is the basis for many popular network architectures, including Novell's NetWare, Banyan's VINES, and 3Com's 3+.

The socket interface uses symbolic constants to identify the supported protocol families. For example, the symbolic constant PF_INET identifies the Internet protocol family (the TCP/IP protocol suite). Other protocol families use the PF_ prefix as well. PF_UNIX identifies the UNIX internal protocol family, and PF_NS identifies the Xerox Network Services protocol family.

Closely related to protocol families are *address families*. As you may know, the format of network addresses varies from network to network. The socket-interface designers recognized this fact and used the concept of address families to further generalize the socket interface for use on multiple networks. Address families use an AF_ prefix similar to the protocol family's PF_ prefix. For example, the symbolic constant for the Internet (TCP/IP) address family is AF_INET. In a similar way, AF_NS identifies the Xerox Network Services address family, and AF_UNIX identifies the UNIX file system.

Unfortunately, because of the close relationship between address and protocol families, many people aren't sure how to correctly use them. For example, the socket interface for TCP/IP networks defines PF_INET and AF_INET to be the same value. As a result, many otherwise excellent programming references tell the reader to use either symbolic constant since they represent the same value. However, as Comer and Stevens point out in *Internetworking with TCP/IP, Volume 3*, Prentice Hall, 1993, the distinction between protocol and address families lets programmers use network protocols that have multiple address representations within a single protocol family (or suite). In other words, the socket interface does not limit a protocol family to using one address format. Such flexibility is not valuable to Internet programmers since TCP/IP protocols use only one address format. However, the fact that this capability exists demonstrates the foresight and planning that went into the design of the socket interface.

Today, careless use of PF_INET and AF_INET will not cause problems for you—the symbolic constants represent equivalent values. However, you should plan for the future and observe the distinction between protocol and address families. As an Internet programmer, you should use PF_INET when it is appropriate to identify a protocol family and AF_INET when you need to specify an address family. Doing so will clarify your program code and make the code easier to port should the need arise.

SPECIFYING THE TYPE OF COMMUNICATION

As you have learned, TCP/IP lets your programs use connection-oriented or connectionless network communication. In connection-oriented network communication, data flows as a single, serial stream of bytes (or byte stream) without record or other types of boundaries. In connectionless network communication, data travels in separate, self-contained data packets called datagrams. As previously discussed, you can use sockets for connectionless communication (as with datagrams) or connection-oriented communications (like a byte stream). As such, the second parameter required by the socket function specifies which type of communication you want to use. The socket interface uses the symbolic constant SOCK_DGRAM for datagrams and SOCK_STREAM for byte streams.

The socket interface also defines a third type of communication called a *raw socket* (SOCK_RAW). A raw socket lets a program use the same low-level protocols that the network itself normally uses. For example, as you will see in Chapter 14, the Ping program creates a raw socket in order to use the Internet Control Message Protocol (ICMP). As you have learned, TCP/IP networks use ICMP for error messages.

Note: The socket interface also defines two other types of communication, but, as of this writing, no implementations that use them are available.

Normally, an application program does not use ICMP; instead, the program lets the network handle all errors. The TCP/IP transport protocols deliver any network error messages destined for your programs. However, as previous diagrams have shown, programs can bypass the transport layer and communicate directly with the IP and ICMP software modules. To bypass the transport layer and use low-level protocols such as IP or ICMP, your program must use a raw socket.

SELECTING A PROTOCOL

As you have learned, the TCP/IP protocol suite includes several protocols such as IP, ICMP, TCP, and UDP. Likewise, other protocol families provide multiple protocols that network programmers can use. The third parameter to the socket function lets you specify which protocol to use with the socket. As with the other socket parameters, you can use symbolic constants to specify protocols.

For TCP/IP networks, the symbolic constants for protocols begin with an IPPROTO_ prefix. For example, to specify the TCP protocol, you would use IPPROTO_TCP for the third socket parameter. The symbolic constant IPPROTO_UDP specifies the UDP protocol. The following program statement shows a typical call to the socket function:

```
socket_handle = socket(PF_INET, SOCK_STREAM, IPPROTO_TCP);
```

This statement tells the socket implementation that your program uses the Internet protocol family (PF_INET). The statement also says that your program will use the TCP protocol (IPPROTO_TCP) for byte-stream (SOCK_STREAM) communications through the requested socket.

UNDERSTANDING THE PROCESS

In the previous sections, you learned that a socket represents an endpoint for network communications. You also learned that a socket identifies an entry in a descriptor table similar to the way a file handle identifies an entry in a file descriptor table. Furthermore, you now understand that your programs call the socket function to create a socket.

SORTING THROUGH THE ADDRESSES

Addresses are a critical component in all network communications. In the last few chapters, you have read about buffer addresses, Internet addresses, and port addresses. To make sure you understand these addresses, the following paragraphs briefly discuss them in a side-by-side fashion. Buffer addresses are simply storage areas in a computer's random access memory (RAM). In some cases, network software (or perhaps an API such as the Berkeley sockets) will allocate memory for a data buffer. In other cases, your programs must allocate a buffer storage area for use by network software modules. In a C or C++ program, to access the data stored in a network buffer, you would assign the buffer address to a pointer variable.

As you have learned, an Internet (or IP) address identifies a host computer on a TCP/IP-based network. More precisely, an IP address identifies a network interface card installed in a host computer attached to the Internet. The IP layer in the TCP/IP protocol suite uses IP addresses to deliver data between host computers.

In Chapter 5, you learned that the TCP/IP transport layer uses protocol ports to deliver data to specific applications within a host computer. In effect, from a network perspective, a protocol port is an application or process address. In other words, a protocol port is like a task handle for network software. When a network software module, such as the TCP module in the transport layer, needs to communicate with a program (or process), the module uses a protocol port. A protocol port identifies a process on the host computer. A socket is an address in the same way that a file or task handle is an address. In other words, a socket identifies an entry in a descriptor table. The descriptor table's format and how the network software allocates space for the descriptor table is implementation dependent.

So far in this discussion, you have not seen a network address associated with the socket. In fact, previous sections of this chapter have explicitly made the point that you create a socket without specifying a network address. For example, the following socket function-call specifies a protocol family, a socket type, and a specific protocol—the call does not specify a network address:

```
socket_handle = socket(protocol_family, socket_type, protocol);
```

You may wonder how a socket can be an endpoint for network communication when the socket does not include an address. The following sections explain what actually occurs when you call the socket function and how the socket performs network I/O.

Understanding the Socket Descriptor

As you have learned, you do not specify an address when you create a socket. When you call the socket function, the socket implementation creates a socket and returns a socket handle (or descriptor) that actually identifies an entry in a descriptor table. The socket implementation manages the descriptor table for you. As an applications programmer, your only access to the descriptor table is through the socket descriptor. In actuality, "creating a socket" really means allocating storage space for a socket data structure.

Under the UNIX operating system, each process owns a single file-descriptor table. (Remember, the socket-interface designers used UNIX system I/O concepts for network I/O.) Under UNIX, the socket function obtains a descriptor from the file descriptor table. The descriptor is a pointer to an internal data structure. Figure 7.1 shows a simplified socket data structure.

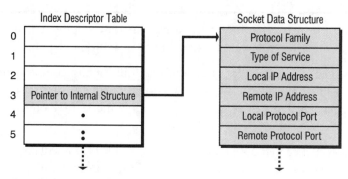

Figure 7.1 A simple socket data structure.

As you can see in Figure 7.1, the socket data structure includes elements to store values from the socket function parameters. However, the data structure also contains elements for four addresses: local IP, remote IP, local port, and remote port. Each time your program calls the socket function, the socket implementation allocates memory for a new data structure and fills in the address family, socket type, and protocol. In the file descriptor table, the socket implementation stores a pointer to the data structure. The handle your program receives from the socket function is an index into the descriptor table.

The socket interface does not specify how to manage the socket descriptors. UNIX handles sockets like file descriptors in the file descriptor table. However, other implementations are free to manage the socket descriptors in other ways. In other words, beyond the socket descriptor, details are implementation dependent. As an applications programmer, you don't need to concern yourself with details about the descriptor tables, internal data structures, and related memory allocation. The purpose of showing you these details is to explain how a socket stores network addresses. The socket function creates the socket data structure but leaves the address elements empty. To associate a socket with specific network addresses, you must call other functions within the socket API, as explained in the following sections.

Using the Socket Paradigm

As you have learned, the socket-interface paradigm (or model) for network communication refers to the communicating host computers or processes as endpoints. Every network conversation includes two endpoints—the local host and the remote (or destination) host. The socket interface refers to each endpoint in a network conversation as a socket. You have also learned that most network programs use the client/server model. Network communication in the client/server model also includes two endpoints. However, the client/server model makes a distinction between the two endpoints based on the function the endpoints perform. For example, the client/server model refers to the endpoint that initiates a request for network services as a client process or client program. The endpoint that responds to the client's request is the server process or program.

In Chapter 4, you learned that the IP layer uses an Internet address to identify host computers. As such, each host computer on the Internet requires a unique Internet address. Chapter 5 explained that the transport layer uses protocol ports to identify specific applications (processes) within each host computer. As such, every network-related process within a host computer uses a protocol port (which is like a task handle) as an address. Finally, you have learned that Internet programs must use a TCP/IP protocol to transfer data across the Internet. In summary, a network connection between two network programs includes five pieces of information:

- A local protocol port, which specifies where a program or process receives messages or datagrams

- A local host address, which identifies the host computer that will receive the data packets

- A remote protocol port, which identifies the destination program or process

- A remote host address, which identifies the destination host computer

- A protocol, which specifies how programs transfer data across the network

As previously shown in Figure 7.1, the socket data structure that corresponds to the socket handle (or descriptor) includes all five pieces of information. In other words, a socket is an abstract representation of an endpoint in the network communications process. The socket data structure includes all data elements required by one endpoint for network communication. A socket data structure greatly simplifies network communication. When one program wants to communicate with another, the sender program simply transmits information to the socket, and the socket API manages the interface to the TCP/IP protocol stack. However, before your program can send any information to a socket, your program must call the socket function to create the socket and then use other socket-interface functions to configure the socket. In the following sections, you will learn how to configure a socket using the socket API.

Defining Your Program's Socket Use

As you have learned, your program must configure a socket before using it for network communications. Most importantly, the socket's internal data structure must contain the correct addresses. The socket-data structure must contain the correct protocol port and IP address for both your program's local host and the remote host. As such, the term *socket addresses* refers not to the address of the socket itself, but rather to the protocol ports and host addresses stored in the internal socket-data structure. When you create a socket with the socket function, you do not specify protocol ports or host addresses. Instead, you use different API functions to store socket addresses and other configuration options, depending on how your program intends to use the socket. For example, if your program will use the socket as a server port, your program will call a function that specifies the local protocol port to use. Conversely, if your program will act as a network client, your program will probably let the socket implementation assign any port that is available for use when your program needs to actually use the socket. In other words, the socket function allocates storage space for a socket-data structure and returns a handle that your program can use to configure the socket. The parameters you specify when you create the socket will depend upon your program's purpose, as well as the type of delivery service (datagram or byte-stream) your program will use. The type of delivery service determines the protocol (TCP or UDP) that your program will specify. The API functions your program will use to store host addresses and protocol ports will depend on whether your program will use the socket for client or server operations.

CONFIGURING THE SOCKET

For each network program you write, you will first create a socket by calling the socket function. Next, you will use other functions to configure the socket based on your program's socket use. For example, to transfer data through a socket, you can use a byte stream or datagrams. Likewise, you can also use a socket to perform either server or client program functions. Table 7.1 lists socket API functions you use to configure a socket for network communications. As discussed, a network connection requires five pieces of information: a protocol, a local IP address, a remote IP address, a protocol port for the local process, and a protocol port for the remote process. The following section discusses how and when you use these functions to configure a socket.

Socket Use	Local Information	Remote Information
Connection-oriented client	One call to the connect function stores both local and remote information in the socket data structure.	
Connection-oriented server	bind	listen and accept
Connectionless client	bind	sendto
Connectionless server	bind	recvfrom

Table 7.1 Socket API functions used to configure a socket for network communications.

CONNECTING A SOCKET

Sockets provide an abstraction you can use to represent and program the two endpoints of a network conversation. As explained in previous chapters, a connection-oriented protocol establishes a virtual circuit between the connection endpoints. In other words, the link between the two endpoints appears to be a direct, point-to-point connection. In the TCP/IP transport layer, TCP (a connection-oriented protocol) maintains the virtual circuit (keeps the connection open) by exchanging acknowledgment messages between the two endpoints. As a result, a connection-oriented client program on a TCP/IP network does not care what local address the network software uses for data transfers. In other words, the client program can receive data at any protocol port. As such, in most cases, a connection-oriented client program does not specify a local protocol port.

A connection-oriented client program uses the connect function to configure a socket for network communication. In short, the connect function stores information in socket structures about the local and remote endpoints. The connect function requires you to specify a socket handle, an address structure that contains information about the remote host, and the length of the socket address structure. The following program statement shows a typical call to the connect function:

```
result = connect(socket_handle, remote_socket_address, address_length);
```

Notice that the connect function's first parameter, socket handle, is the socket descriptor value returned from the socket function. As stated, before your program can use the connect function to connect a socket, your program must call the socket function. The socket handle tells the socket implementation which descriptor table entry to use. In other words, the socket handle tells the socket implementation where to store the remote socket address information.

The connect function's second parameter, remote socket address, is a pointer to a special socket address structure. A socket address structure stores address information peculiar to a particular network. As a result, the structure's contents are network dependent. In other words, the structure's contents depend on the protocol family the program uses. In Section 2 of this book, you will learn more about the socket address structure. For now, simply note that, for a socket, the structure stores an address family, a protocol port, and a network host address. The connect function stores this information within the socket descriptor-table entry the socket handle (the connect function's first parameter) identifies.

Before your program calls the connect function, you must store address information for the remote host in the socket data structure. In other words, the connect function requires the remote host's IP address and protocol port. However, you don't have to store local IP addresses. The socket implementation automatically stores the local IP address for you and selects a local protocol port. In addition, the socket API makes sure your application receives data that the transport layer delivers to the local protocol port. In other words, the socket implementation selects the protocol port for your program and notifies your program when data arrives at the port—your program doesn't care which port the implementation uses.

The connect function's third parameter, address length, simply tells the socket implementation the size, in bytes, of the remote socket address data structure (the second parameter). As discussed, the contents and size of the remote host address structure are network dependent. The address-length parameter tells the connect function how large a data structure the remote host requires. In other words, when the socket implementation responds to the connect function, the implementation will retrieve the number of bytes specified by the address-length parameter from the data buffer pointed to by the remote-socket-address parameter.

SPECIFYING A LOCAL ADDRESS (PROTOCOL PORT)

The connect function initiates a direct connection with a remote host computer. The only time you ever connect a socket to a remote host computer is when your program uses the socket as connection-oriented client process. Remember, a connectionless protocol never establishes a direct connection. A connectionless protocol transmits datagrams across the network—such protocols never use byte streams. Likewise, a server program never initiates a connection. Although you may create a server program that uses a connection-oriented protocol, your program will passively listen at a protocol port for client requests. In other words, the client initiates the direct connection—not the server.

The key similarity to note between any program that uses a connectionless protocol and a server program that uses a connection-oriented protocol is that they all must listen to a protocol port. For example, both connectionless and connection-oriented server programs must listen for client requests at a protocol port. Likewise, since a connectionless client program does not establish a direct connection to a remote host, a connectionless client must also listen to a protocol port to receive a datagram reply to its requests for network services. The bind function in the socket API lets programs associate a local address (combination of host address and protocol port) with a socket. The following program line shows a typical call to the bind function:

```
result = bind(socket_handle, local_socket_address, address_length);
```

When you create a server program, you design your server to listen for client requests. As you have learned, the TCP/IP transport layer communicates with application programs (such as servers and clients) through a protocol port. In other words, to receive client requests, your server program must listen for the transport layer to deliver client requests at a specific protocol port. When you use the socket interface for a server program, your program uses the bind function to register a protocol port with the socket implementation. In other words, your program tells the socket implementation which protocol port to use for data delivery. The socket implementation, in turn, tells the transport layer that the specified protocol port is in use and to deliver all data received for that protocol port to the socket API.

As previously noted, a connectionless client must also listen to a protocol port. As you have learned, programs that use connectionless protocols do not establish a direct connection with a remote host. A connectionless client program transmits a network service request using a datagram, which does not establish a point-to-point connection. As such, the connectionless client must listen at a protocol port for a reply datagram.

Like server programs, connectionless client programs use the bind function to register protocol ports with the socket implementation. In other words, like a server program, your connectionless client tells the socket implementation which protocol port to use for data delivery. The socket implementation handles the interface between the client and the UDP software module in the transport layer. Later sections in this chapter discuss socket API functions (such as listen, accept, recvfrom, and recv) that your programs can use to retrieve data from a protocol port. For now, you should understand that to configure a socket to listen at a specific protocol port, your programs use the bind function.

TRANSMITTING DATA THROUGH THE SOCKET

After your program configures a socket, it can use the socket for network communication. The network communication process includes sending and receiving information. The socket interface includes several functions to perform both tasks. This section describes how a program sends or transmits data through a socket. Later sections discuss how your program receives data. The Berkeley-socket API provides five functions to transmit data through a socket. The socket interface divides the functions into two groups. Three functions require a destination address as a parameter. The other two functions do not. The primary difference between the two groups is whether the transmissions are connectionless or connection-oriented. Table 7.2 describes the five socket-API functions your programs can use for data transmissions.

Socket API Function	Description
send	Transmits data through a connected socket, can use special flags to control socket behavior
write	Transmits data through a connected socket, using a simple data buffer
writev	Transmits data through a connected socket, using non-contiguous memory as a data buffer
sendto	Transmits data through an unconnected socket, using a simple message buffer
sendmsg	Transmits data through an unconnected socket, using a flexible message structure as a message buffer

Table 7.2 Socket API functions your programs can use for data transmissions.

SENDING DATA THROUGH A CONNECTED SOCKET

Connection-oriented communications use virtual circuits—the link between the endpoints appears to be a point-to-point connection. In other words, after the network software establishes the connection, your program can exchange data with the remote host in a steady byte stream.

Socket-API functions that perform connection-oriented data transmissions do not require your programs to specify a destination address as a function parameter. As previously discussed, your program uses the connect function to configure a connection-oriented socket that contains the remote host's address information (protocol port and IP address). During the entire network conversation, the socket implementation maintains the address information and manages the interface to the transport layer for the connection-oriented socket. The send, write, and writev functions only work with connected sockets—they do not let your program specify a destination address. All three functions require your program to specify a socket handle as the first parameter in the function call. The following program statement shows a typical call to the write function:

```
result = write(socket_handle, message_buffer, buffer_length);
```

The write function's first parameter is the familiar socket handle that many socket-API functions require. As you have learned, the socket handle identifies a descriptor table entry that points to an internal socket data structure. The write function's second parameter points to a data buffer that contains the information your program transmits. Your program must allocate memory for this buffer, as well as fill the buffer with your data. The write function's third parameter simply specifies the size of the data buffer your program wants to transmit. The writev function call is very similar to write function call. However, the writev function does not require your data to occupy a contiguous block of memory; the write function does. In other words, writev lets your program specify an array of addresses that contain your data. The following statement illustrates the writev function call:

```
result = writev(socket_handle, io_vector, vector_length);
```

Like the write function, the writev function also requires a socket handle as its first parameter. The writev function's second parameter specifies the address of an array that contains a sequence of pointers. Assume that the data you want to transmit is stored in several different memory locations. In such cases, you would assign the address of each data buffer to the array of pointers. When the writev function transmits your data, it will send the data contained at each memory location specified by the pointer array. The writev function sends the data in the same order as the memory addresses appear in the array. The writev function's third parameter specifies the number of entries in the array of pointer values.

As previously mentioned, the writev function's second parameter specifies the address of an array that contains a sequence of pointers. These pointers indicate blocks of data that form the message your program will transmit. With each pointer in the array, the socket API associates a length value that specifies how many data bytes exist at the specified address. Figure 7.2 shows an example of the array of data pointers.

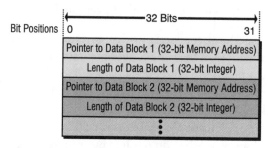

Figure 7.2 The array format pointed to by the writev function.

Because the write function forces your program to use a contiguous data buffer, the write function will perform faster than writev. However, writev, which lets you specify a sequence of address pointers, provides more flexibility for complex messages and for circumstances under which contiguous computer memory might be hard to obtain. The send function is the only other socket-API function that your programs can use with connected sockets. The following program statement shows a typical call to the send function:

```
result = send(socket_handle, message_buffer, buffer_length,
    special_flags);
```

The major advantage to the send function is that you can specify optional flags that control the transmission. For example, as you have learned, TCP/IP treats out-of-band or urgent data with a higher priority than other data. One of the optional flags you can use with the send function tells the receiving process that your transmission contains out-of-band data.

Note: Although the send function lets you transfer data as out-of-band, you should not do so unless you understand exactly how the receiver will respond to the data. Although, in theory, out-of-band data provides a powerful tool, its practical implementations are very complex and may differ greatly. TCP urgent data and urgent mode are among the least documented (and thus least understood) features in TCP. You can find what is probably one of the most enlightening discussions of this confusing subject in Chapter 16 of **Internetworking with TCP/IP, Volume II: Design, Implementation, and Internals,** *Douglas E. Comer and David L. Stevens, Prentice Hall, 1994.*

All three functions (write, writev, and send) return an integer result. If no errors occur, the functions return a value equivalent to the number of bytes transmitted through the socket. If an error occurs, the functions return the value -1. Berkeley sockets use the standard C language *errno* value to report additional information about such failures. However, be aware that not all PC-based C language implementations use the errno values used by UNIX. Also, as you will learn in the next chapter, Windows Sockets use a completely different error reporting and retrieval mechanism.

SENDING DATA THROUGH A CONNECTIONLESS SOCKET

Your programs can use the three functions discussed in the previous section to transmit data through a connected socket. However, as previously mentioned, those three functions do not let your programs specify a destination address. To send data through a connectionless socket (a socket configured to use a connectionless protocol), your programs must use one of two functions (sendto or sendmsg) that the socket API provides for that purpose. The sendto function requires six function parameters. The first four are identical to the send function. The sendto function's fifth parameter identifies the destination address. The sixth parameter specifies the width (or length) of the destination address in bytes. The following program statement shows a typical call to the sendto function:

```
result = sendto(socket_handle, message_buffer, buffer_length,
        special_flags, socket_address_structure,
        address_structure_length);
```

The sendmsg function lets your program use, for transmissions, a message structure instead of a simple data buffer. As shown in the following program statement, the sendmsg function requires a socket handle, a pointer to a message structure, and a flags parameter:

```
result = sendmsg(socket_handle, message_structure, special_flags);
```

The message structure lets your programs conveniently store long lists of message parameters in a single data structure. The sendmsg function is similar to the writev function in that your programs can format data into multiple blocks of memory. In other words, like the writev function, the message structure contains a pointer to an array of memory addresses. Figure 7.3 shows an example of the message structure format that sendmsg uses.

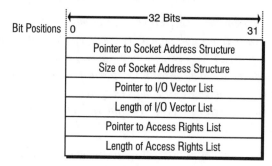

Figure 7.3 The message structure format used by the sendmsg function.

As you will learn in the next section, the socket API includes a function (recvmsg) that receives data into the same type of message structure that sendmsg function uses. You will also learn about other functions that your programs can use to receive data through a socket.

RECEIVING DATA THROUGH A SOCKET

The socket interface includes five functions (read, readv, recv, recvfrom, and recvmsg) that correspond to the five functions you use to transmit data. For example, the recv and send functions use similar parameters. You use the recv function to receive data and the send function to transmit data. Likewise, the writev and readv functions are similar. You use writev to transmit and readv to receive data. Both writev and readv let you specify an array of memory addresses for your data. The recvfrom and recvmsg functions correspond to the sendto and sendmsg functions, respectively. Table 7.3 lists the corresponding functions:

Transmit Function	Corresponding Receive Function
send	recv
write	read
writev	readv
sendto	recvfrom
sendmsg	recvmsg

Table 7.3 Corresponding transmit and receive functions in the socket API.

Although the socket interface includes corresponding transmit and receive functions, the socket interface does not require you to use corresponding functions. In other words, suppose a remote host uses the send function to transmit data to you. To retrieve the transmitted data, you do not have to use the recv function (the corresponding function). Keep in mind that once a function transmits to the socket, the data essentially becomes one byte stream. As such, you can read the data using either recv, read, or readv.

The socket interface lets you use whichever function best meets your requirements. For example, to eliminate any requirement for large blocks of contiguous computer memory, you can design all your programs to use readv function calls. However, other programmers may find your program code easier to read if you use corresponding functions (write/read, send/recv, and sendmsg/recvmsg).

REVIEWING THE PROCESS

Figure 7.4 shows the typical socket system calls your programs use with a connection-oriented protocol. The left side of the diagram shows the server function calls; the right side shows the client function calls. The lines and arrows between the server and client modules show the flow of network communication between the two programs. As you can see, a server program creates a socket with the socket function. More precisely, the server program asks the socket implementation to allocate a socket data structure and return a socket descriptor that the program can use in subsequent function calls. Next, the server binds the socket to a local protocol port.

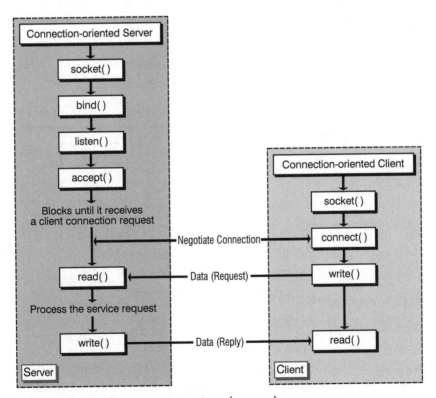

Figure 7.4 Using sockets with a connection-oriented protocol.

The next section will explain the listen and accept function calls. For now, you should understand that the listen function tells the socket to "listen" for incoming connections and to acknowledge connection requests. In other words, the listen function puts the socket into a passive listening mode. A listening socket will send each requester an acknowledgement message that tells the sender that the host received the connection request. However, a listening socket does not actually accept a connection request. To actually accept and establish a connection from an incoming connection request, your program must call the accept function.

As shown in Figure 7.4, the client program also creates a socket with the socket function. However, a client program that uses a connection-oriented protocol such as TCP does not care which local address the protocol uses. As such, the client program does not need to call the bind function. Instead, the connection-oriented, client program initiates the network conversation by calling the connect function. After the client and server establish the connection, further communication occurs through the write and read functions. However, the client and server programs could have just as easily used the send and recv functions or any other socket-API functions that work with connected sockets. Figure 7.5 illustrates the typical socket system calls used with a connectionless protocol.

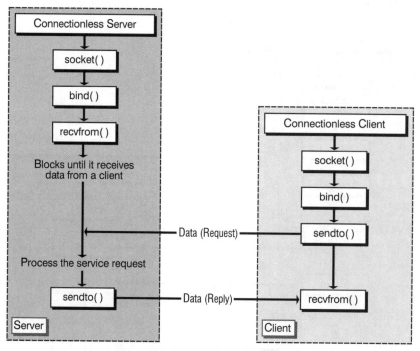

Figure 7.5 Using sockets with a connectionless protocol.

Much like a connection-oriented server, the connectionless server program in Figure 7.5 uses the socket and bind function calls to create and bind the socket. However, since the socket is connectionless, the client program uses the recvfrom function—rather than the recv or read functions—to retrieve data from the socket. Notice that the client program shown in Figure 7.5 calls the bind function but not the connect function. Remember, a connectionless protocol does not establish a point-to-point connection between both endpoints. Instead, as you have learned, the sendto function requires the program to specify a destination address as a parameter.

The recvfrom function also does not wait for a connection. Instead, the recvfrom function responds to any data that arrives at the bound protocol port. When the recvfrom function receives a datagram from the socket, it stores the network address of the process that transmitted the datagram, as well as the datagram itself. The programs (server and client) use the stored address to identify the sending (client) process. The server sends its reply datagrams (as required) to the address that the recvfrom function retrieves.

USING SOCKETS WITH SERVERS

As previously shown in Figure 7.4, a typical server program that uses a connection-oriented socket calls the listen and accept functions. As mentioned, the listen function places the server in a passive listening mode. The accept function, in turn, directs your program to establish a socket connection. The following paragraphs describe how and why servers use these two special purpose socket functions.

THREADS VERSUS PROCESSES

Most new operating systems are multi-threaded. A *thread* is a sequence of computing instructions that make up a program. In other words, think of threads as individual processes within a single application. A multi-threaded program (or process) can contain and independently execute multiple threads. If the multi-threaded program's host computer system uses multiple processors, the multi-threaded program can execute threads on each processor. Obviously, a multi-threaded program running on a computer with multiple processors will execute much faster than a single-threaded program running on a single processor machine.

Additionally, a multi-threaded program running on a single processor is usually faster than a single-threaded program. Also, a multi-threaded program typically executes more efficiently than multiple tasks on a single computer. A task switch in any multi-tasking operating system incurs significant overhead that a multi-threaded program does not. A concurrent server design requires the server program to create a separate process for each service request. If you design your concurrent server to be multi-threaded, you can enhance its performance. For example, instead of initiating a separate process or task for each service request, a multi-threaded concurrent server can initiate a separate thread that executes much faster. If your host computer uses multiple processors, your multi-threaded concurrent server will be able to execute multiple threads on multiple processors.

UNDERSTANDING THE LISTEN FUNCTION

As you learned in Chapter 2, you can classify server processes as either iterative or concurrent. A server process that handles each client request individually is an iterative server. In other words, an iterative server manages client requests, one at a time, as they arrive. However, as also discussed in Chapter 2, for an iterative server to be effective, the server must be able to provide the service during a relatively short duration of time. If a server responds to a variety of requests, the server process cannot know or predict the time it will require to fulfill the next service request. In such cases, a server process usually functions as a concurrent server. A concurrent server creates a separate process (or thread, if the operating system supports them) to handle each request for service. In other words, the server manages multiple service requests concurrently.

Now, consider what happens if multiple service requests arrive before the server can finish with the current request. In other words, suppose a client program tries to connect to an iterative server before the server finishes processing its most recent service request. Or, suppose a client program requests a connection from a concurrent server before the server finishes creating a separate process to handle the most recent service request.

In such cases, the server process can reject or ignore incoming requests for service. However, to better handle the problem, the server can use the listen function to place all incoming service requests in an incoming request queue (a waiting line) and handle the requests as fast as possible. The listen function not only puts the socket in a passive listening mode, but also tells the socket implementation to handle multiple, simultaneous requests for the socket. In other words, the listen function tells the socket implementation to create an incoming-data queue and store arriving service requests in the queue until the program can retrieve them.

The listen function requires two parameters: socket handle and queue length. The queue length specifies the maximum number of requests that can accumulate in the queue. The following program statement shows a typical call to the listen function:

```
result = listen(socket_handle, queue_length);
```

You can specify a maximum queue length of five messages when you invoke the listen function. If the incoming-data queue is full when a request arrives at the socket, the socket will refuse the connection and the client program will receive an error message.

With an iterative server, you can use the listen function as a backup measure. For example, you might expect your server program to handle all service requests in minimal time. However, the possibility always exists that multiple requests can arrive at the same time. To make sure your iterative server doesn't reject any client requests, you might want to use the listen function with a queue length of one or two.

UNDERSTANDING THE ACCEPT FUNCTION

As previously mentioned, the bind function lets you associate a network address and a local protocol port to a socket. Client programs initiate connections by binding their socket to a remote protocol port that resides on a remote host. The client program can specify these addresses because it knows which server it desires.

A server, on the other hand, has no idea which client programs will request services from it. As such, the server cannot specify the client host address or protocol port within its call to the bind function. Instead, a server program must call the bind function with a wildcard for the network address. In other words, a server program normally accepts a connection request from any client address.

Note: As you will learn in Chapter 19, the server specifies it's socket-address wildcard using the INADDR_ANY constant, which you can find in the header file winsock.h.

As its name implies, the accept function lets server programs accept connections from a client program. After it sets up an incoming-data queue, a server program calls the accept function, goes to sleep, and waits for a connection from a client program. To understand server operations that use a socket interface, you must know how the accept function works.

The accept function requires three parameters: socket handle, socket address, and address length. The socket-handle parameter identifies which socket the server must monitor. When a request arrives at the specified socket, the socket implementation fills the socket address structure (pointed to by the second parameter) with the address of the client that requested the connection.

The socket implementation also sets the address-length parameter to the length of the stored address. The following program statement shows a typical call to the accept function:

```
result = accept(socket_handle, socket_address, address_length);
```

After the socket implementation stores the client address information in the memory locations specified by your program's parameters, the socket implementation takes several steps that make server operations possible. First, as a result of receiving a connection request at the socket monitored by the accept function, the socket implementation creates a new socket. The socket implementation creates and binds the new socket with the address of the requesting process. Figure 7.6 shows the sequence of events that occur when two client programs connect to a concurrent server.

In summary, when a service request arrives at a socket monitored by the accept function, the socket implementation automatically creates a new socket and immediately connects the new socket with the client process. The original socket that received the service request remains open with its wildcard network address. As such, the original socket can continue to accept incoming requests.

Step 1: Client and server negotiate a connection.

Step 2: Concurrent server passes the connection to a child process.

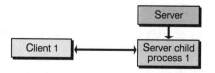

Step 3: If a second client process negotiates a connection, the concurrent server will pass the connection to a second child process.

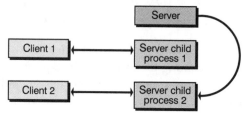

Figure 7.6 *Client programs connecting to a concurrent server.*

REVIEWING THE SERVER PROCESS

When a service request arrives at the socket that the accept function monitors, the accept function returns, to the calling server program, the socket descriptor of the newly created socket. What happens at this point depends on the server's design. As you have learned, you can design a server to handle requests in an iterative or concurrent fashion. Suppose you design an iterative server. When the accept function returns, your iterative server program would handle the service request and then close the new socket. After handling the service request, your iterative server would call the accept function again to retrieve and handle the next service request. If you have used the listen function, this accept call would retrieve the next service request, if any, from the incoming-data queue. If you did not use the listen function, your server would wait to receive the next service request directly from the socket.

In contrast, suppose you choose to design a concurrent server. After the accept function returns, a concurrent server program would create a new process to handle the service request. How your server creates the new process depends on your operating system. For example, under UNIX, you would *fork* a child process to handle the request. Regardless of how the master server creates the new process, the child or slave process receives a copy of the new socket and manages the service request. Then, the master server closes its copy of the socket and issues a new accept function call.

As you can see, you use practically the same process to create an iterative or concurrent server using the socket interface. The only difference is whether you choose to have your server program issue another accept function call before or after it finishes handling a service request. As an iterative server, your server program will handle each service request before it calls another accept function. As a concurrent server, your server program will spawn (or create) a child process that handles the service request and immediately calls the accept function again. Unless the service request is trivial (and hence consumes almost no time), the concurrent server will again call the accept function before the child process finishes the requested service. In other words, the server is capable of concurrently handling service requests.

UNDERSTANDING CONCURRENT SERVER DESIGNS

You may wonder how a concurrent server can use the same protocol port to simultaneously handle multiple service requests. Remember, sockets require two endpoints for network communications. These endpoints define the addresses that the communicating processes use. As long as each process connects to a different endpoint destination, multiple server processes can use the same protocol port without confusion. A concurrent server creates a new process for each service request. In other words, with a concurrent server, you have a single master server with a wildcard network address. Also, at any given time, you may have multiple child server processes, each with a network address that uniquely defines a client process.

For example, as you may recall, a TCP segment identifies itself with a unique address. When a concurrent server receives a TCP segment, the server sends the segment to the socket associated with the segment's address. If no such socket exists (which means this is a new service request), the server sends the segment to the socket with the wildcard address. Remember, the wildcard address directs the socket to accept a connection from any network address. At this point, the process begins all over again. In other words, the master-server socket (with the wildcard network address) spawns a new child process to handle the new service request.

You should also note that a socket with a wildcard address cannot have an open connection. Remember, to establish a point-to-point socket connection, you must define two endpoints, each with a specific address. Because the master-server socket always retains a wildcard as its destination network address, the socket can only accept new connections.

UNDERSTANDING THE SELECT FUNCTION

Although not shown in either Figure 7.4 or 7.5, another socket-interface function that servers commonly use is the select function. Sophisticated client programs can also use the select function. The select function lets a single process monitor or determine the status of multiple sockets. The select function requires five parameters. The first parameter, number of sockets, specifies the total number of sockets to monitor. The readable-sockets, writeable-sockets, and error-sockets parameters are bit masks that identify specific sockets. The following program statement shows a typical call to the select function:

```
result = select(number_of_sockets, readable_sockets,
    writeable_sockets, error_sockets, max_time);
```

A readable socket contains received data that your program can retrieve using socket functions such as recv or recvfrom. A writeable socket is one that has established a connection. Through a writeable socket, your program can transmit data using functions such as send or sendto. When an error occurs on a socket, the select function identifies the socket as having an exception (an error that the program must handle). In all cases, the select function only reports the status for sockets you identify in each bit mask. The socket interface uses a bit mask that specifies each set of sockets the select function is to check. When the select function returns to the calling program, it returns the number of sockets that are ready for I/O. The function also changes the bit masks for specified file descriptors.

In other words, you tell the select function which sockets to check and what kind of status you want from each socket. In turn, the select function tells you how many total sockets are ready for I/O (read, write, or error report). Additionally, the select function changes the bit masks so you can identify the individual sockets in each category. As such, before you call the select function, you must set bits which identify the sockets that you want to check. The select function will turn off the bits for any sockets not ready for the specified I/O. When the select function returns, your program can examine the bit masks. A socket with the identifier bit still set means that socket is ready for the specified I/O (read, write, or error report).

You can design your programs to take action based on results of the select function. For example, suppose you develop a program that creates three sockets. Suppose you have a single routine that handles read operations, a different routine that handles write operations, and one that handles exception errors. You can use the select function to simultaneously query the state of all three sockets. Suppose the select function reports that one socket is readable, one socket is writeable, and one socket contains an exception error. Your program could call the appropriate function to handle each operation. In each function call, you would specify the socket identified by the select function.

PUTTING IT ALL TOGETHER

In this chapter, you learned how the socket interface evolved from an effort to implement TCP/IP protocols under the UNIX operating system. The chapter explained how the socket abstraction represents an endpoint for network communications. You also learned how to create and configure sockets, as well as transmit and receive data through them.

In Chapter 8, you will read about the Windows Sockets (Winsock) API. The developers of the Winsock API derived it from the Berkeley-socket interface described in this chapter. To grasp

Winsock API concepts, you need a clear understanding of socket-interface fundamentals. Before you move on to Chapter 8, make sure you understand the following key concepts:

✓ A socket is an abstraction of an endpoint for network communication.

✓ The socket-interface designers developed the socket API for use on multiple networks—not just TCP/IP networks.

✓ The socket interface uses protocol and address families to support different types of networks.

✓ Your programs can use connection-oriented and connectionless protocols with the socket API, but each type of protocol requires different functions.

✓ You can develop client and server programs with the socket API, but each type of program requires different functions.

✓ Your programs must create a socket using the socket function before you can configure the socket for network communication.

✓ As a separate step from creating a socket, your programs use the connect function to connect a socket to a specific endpoint.

✓ The socket API contains a corresponding receive function for each transmit function.

Chapter 8
Understanding the Windows Sockets API

In recent years, the fastest growing programming environment is that of Microsoft Windows. With over 50 million users now running Windows—and with Windows 95 coming soon—the growth in the number of Windows programmers will not slow down anytime in the near future. Today, the fastest growing segment of Internet users are those who connect to the Internet from their Windows-based PCs. It makes sense, therefore, that the near future will bring a strong demand for Windows-based Internet programmers. Writing Windows-based Internet programs is what this chapter is all about. For many of you, this chapter alone is why you purchased this book.

In Chapter 7, you learned that you write Internet programs in terms of sockets which act as endpoints between two communicating computers. This chapter examines Windows-based sockets and special software called the Winsock that you use to access them. By the time you finish this chapter, you will understand the following key concepts:

- How Winsock fits into the Windows program environment

- The differences between Berkeley sockets and Winsock

- How Winsock handles blocking operations in Windows

- How to use key Windows-specific Winsock functions

UNDERSTANDING WINSOCK'S ORIGINS

As you have learned, in a network conversation, two processes on separate host computers exchange data. Network professionals refer to each end of this network conversation as an endpoint. A socket is an abstract representation of a network endpoint. During the 1980s, researchers at the University of California at Berkeley used this socket paradigm (or model) to develop an application program interface (API) for TCP/IP networks. (As you learned in Chapter 7, an API is a group of functions that programmers use to develop applications for a particular computer environment.) The Berkeley interface is only one (although, perhaps, the most popular) implementation of an API based on the socket model.

Windows Sockets (commonly referred to as Winsock) is also an API based on the socket paradigm. In fact, Winsock developers derived their API from the Berkeley-socket interface. However, whereas the Berkeley interface is an API that programmers can use with multiple operating systems, the

Winsock API specifically targets the Microsoft Windows family of operating systems, including Microsoft Windows, Windows NT, and Windows 95.

Winsock includes many of the Berkeley functions developed for UNIX (the operating system for which Berkeley researchers originally designed the socket interface), as well as Windows-specific extensions that let programmers take advantage of the Windows message-driven environment. This chapter discusses unique aspects of the Winsock API (as compared to Berkeley sockets) and Windows network programming in general. This chapter describes the API defined by version 1.1 of the Winsock specification.

Note: To understand the Winsock API, you need a clear picture of the socket-interface paradigm for network programming. The API depends heavily on concepts derived from the Berkeley sockets. As such, if you have not read Chapter 7, you should do so now. Your success in this chapter depends heavily on your clear understanding of basic socket-interface concepts.

FINDING MORE INFORMATION ON WINDOWS SOCKETS

If you want to develop Winsock-based programs, you should obtain a copy of the Windows Sockets specification. The University of North Carolina hosts an Ftp server site that contains a wide variety of Winsock-related information. Use an anonymous Ftp to log into SunSite.unc.edu and browse around in the subdirectory /pub/micro/pc-stuff/ms-windows/winsock. One of the server site's most useful files is the Winsock specification in a Windows Help file format (.HLP). You can find the Help file in ./winsock-1.1 subdirectory.

UNDERSTANDING THE WINSOCK IMPLEMENTATION

As you have learned, the Internet is a TCP/IP-based internetwork. As you probably know, Windows is one of the most popular operating-system environments in existence today. The Windows Sockets specification defines an accepted standard for Windows program development on TCP/IP networks. As such, the Windows Sockets API offers tremendous opportunities for programmers who want to write network applications. Microsoft Corporation, which owns and develops Windows, does not own Windows Sockets. In fact, the effort to define the Windows Sockets specification includes a large number of people from many different corporations. The goal of this effort is to define a single API that programmers and network software vendors can use as a standard to develop Windows-based network applications. Presently, Windows Sockets (version 1.1) only supports TCP/IP networks, though this may change in the future.

As discussed in Chapter 7, the socket-interface designers originally built the interface into the UNIX operating system. In other words, their implementation made the API part of the operating system. Windows Sockets implements the socket interface as a dynamic link library (DLL).

> ### UNDERSTANDING DYNAMIC LINK LIBRARIES
>
> In Windows, a *dynamic link library (DLL)* provides a standard way to add new functionality that Windows programs can use at run-time. A dynamic link library is an executable code module that Windows can load on demand (as programs need to use its functions). Windows can also unload the DLL when it and other programs no longer need the code modules the DLL stores. The design of most Windows DLLs lets multiple programs use the DLL at the same time.

THE WINSOCK LIBRARY: A QUICK RUN-DOWN

The Winsock API provides a collection (or library) of functions your programs can use to accomplish specific tasks. The Winsock specification organizes the API library into three groups:

- The Berkeley socket functions included in the Winsock API

- Database functions that let your programs retrieve Internet information about domain names, communication services, and protocols

- The Windows-specific extensions to the Berkeley socket routines

The following sections describe the functions in each of these groups. As you will find, *Internet Programming* identifies these functions as either *blocking* or *non-blocking*. A blocking function prevents your program from calling any other Winsock function until the blocking function completes its network operations. A non-blocking function will either immediately complete its operation or return with an error message. In other words, a non-blocking function does not "wait around" for an operation to complete.

Blocking is one of the most important issues you need to understand before you can write sophisticated Winsock programs. Because socket literature often uses (and rarely discusses) the term *blocking*, later sections in this chapter examine blocking in great detail. The following tables identify functions as blocking or non-blocking for your future reference.

SOCKET FUNCTIONS

As just discussed, a blocking operation prevents your programs from executing any other Winsock functions until that operation completes. Typically, blocking operations are Berkeley-style functions that perform network input/output (I/O). In other words, a blocking operation typically corresponds to a delay in sending or receiving information across the network. Table 8.1 shows the Berkeley-style socket routines that can block in the Winsock API.

Carefully examine the descriptions of the socket functions listed in Table 8.1. Notice that each function either performs some type of network I/O or waits for network I/O to occur before it can complete its operation. From these observations, you should note that any function that performs (or depends on) network I/O usually can block other Winsock functions.

Function	Description
accept	Acknowledges an incoming connection. Creates a new socket and connects it to the remote host that requested the connection. Returns the original socket to its listening state.
closesocket	Closes one end of a socket connection.
connect	Initiates a connection on the specified socket.
recv	Receives data from a connected socket.
recvfrom	Receives data from either a connected or unconnected socket.
select	Performs synchronous I/O multiplexing by monitoring the status of multiple sockets.
send	Sends data to a connected socket.
sendto	Sends data to a connected or unconnected socket.

Table 8.1 *The Berkeley-style functions that can block in the Winsock API.*

On the other hand, the functions shown in Table 8.2 do not require network I/O to complete their operations. These functions either use locally stored information (or routines), or they only work with your host computer's end of a socket connection. In other words, the functions perform no operations that require communication with a remote-host computer. As such, although the functions in Table 8.2 are also Berkeley-style socket routines, none of them will initiate a blocking operation.

Function	Description
bind	Assigns a local name to an unnamed socket.
getpeername	Retrieves the name of the peer connected to the specified socket. (As you will learn, Winsock stores this information in local data structures—the operation requires no network I/O.)
getsockname	Retrieves the local name for the specified socket.
getsockopt	Retrieves options associated with the specified socket.
htonl	Converts a 32-bit number from host byte-order to network byte-order.
htons	Converts a 16-bit number from host byte-order to network byte-order.

Table 8.2 *The Berkeley-style functions that will not block in the Winsock API. (continued on the next page)*

Function	Description
inet_addr	Converts a character string that represents an IP address in dotted-decimal notation to the 32-bit binary value (in network byte-order).
inet_ntoa	Converts an IP address to dotted-decimal notation.
ioctlsocket	Controls various parameters related to how the socket operates and handles network I/O.
listen	Tells a specific socket to listen for incoming connections. (This function places a socket into a listening mode. The function itself does not listen or otherwise perform any network I/O.)
ntohl	Converts a 32-bit number from network byte-order to host byte-order.
ntohs	Converts a 16-bit number from network byte-order to host byte-order.
setsockopt	Stores options associated with the specified socket.
shutdown	Shuts down part of a full-duplex connection (on the local host only).
socket	Creates an endpoint for communication and returns a socket handle (descriptor).

Table 8.2 The Berkeley-style functions that will not block in the Winsock API. (continued from the previous page)

DATABASE FUNCTIONS

Your Internet-based programs will work with different address types. For example, a user might specify a domain name, such as jamsa.com, or a dotted-decimal address, such as 168.158.20.102. However, before your Windows network programs can process such addresses, your programs must always convert the addresses into a socket-data structure that most Winsock functions understand. Likewise, when your programs need to display host address information to a user, they typically must convert the address information in the socket-data structure to a form that the user understands. Fortunately, the Winsock database functions shown in Table 8.3 can perform these address conversion tasks (as well as other operations) for your programs. The Winsock database functions let your programs retrieve Internet information about domain names, communication services, and protocols. To find such information, these functions can access a wide variety of database sources (both local and remote). The Winsock specification defines the interface, as well as the data that the database functions must return. However, the Winsock implementation determines where Winsock stores, and exactly how Winsock retrieves, the data.

Function	Description
gethostbyaddr	Retrieves the domain name(s) and IP address corresponding to a network address.
gethostbyname	Retrieves the domain name(s) and IP address corresponding to a host name.
gethostname	Retrieves the domain name of the local host.
getprotobyname	Retrieves a protocol by name (such as "TCP") and returns the official name and the number defined to represent the protocol. (Note that every protocol in the TCP/IP protocol suite is assigned an integer value that represents the protocol.)
getprotobynumber	Retrieves the protocol name and number represented by a specific number.
getservbyname	Retrieves a service name (such as "time") and a protocol port corresponding to the service name.
getservbyport	Retrieves the service name and port corresponding to a specific protocol port.

Table 8.3 The database functions in the Winsock API.

Several of the Winsock database functions return pointers to data or to data structures that are *volatile*. The Winsock implementation (WINSOCK.DLL) can reuse volatile data areas with each Winsock function call. As such, if your program needs any data a volatile-data area contains, your program needs to copy the data to a different memory location—one that your program allocates and maintains—before it calls another Winsock function. The volatile data that Winsock buffer areas contain is only valid until your program's next Winsock function call. The Winsock API includes asynchronous (Windows-specific) versions of all the database functions except the gethostname function. In later sections, *Internet Programming* discusses asynchronous Winsock functions in detail. For now, understand that the asynchronous functions are Windows-specific extensions to the Berkeley-socket interface. In other words, the Winsock developers designed the asynchronous functions to take advantage of the message-based capabilities inherent to Windows. Table 8.4 lists seven Berkeley-style functions and the equivalent asynchronous database functions included in the Winsock API.

Berkeley-Style Function	Equivalent Asynchronous Function
gethostbyaddr	WSAAsyncGetHostByAddr
gethostbyname	WSAAsyncGetHostByName
gethostname	(No equivalent)

Table 8.4 The asynchronous Winsock API database functions. (continued on the next page)

Berkeley-Style Function	Equivalent Asynchronous Function
getprotobyname	WSAAsyncGetProtoByName
getprotobynumber	WSAAsyncGetProtoByNumber
getservbyname	WSAAsyncGetServByName
getservbyport	WSAAsyncGetServByPort

Table 8.4 The asynchronous Winsock API database functions. (continued from the previous page)

MICROSOFT WINDOWS-SPECIFIC EXTENSION FUNCTIONS

As just mentioned, the Winsock developers designed special asynchronous versions of certain socket functions so that programmers could take advantage of message passing within Windows. As you learn to develop more sophisticated Windows-based network programs, you will use the asynchronous Winsock functions more frequently and effectively. Table 8.5 shows all the Microsoft Windows-specific extension functions included in the Winsock API, except for the asynchronous database functions. (See Table 8.4 for the asynchronous database functions.)

Function	Description
WSAAsyncSelect	Performs an asynchronous version of the select function.
WSACancelAsyncRequest	Cancels an outstanding instance of a WSAAsyncGetXByY function.
WSACancelBlockingCall	Cancels an outstanding blocking API call.
WSACleanup	Signs off from the underlying Windows Sockets DLL.
WSAGetLastError	Obtains details about the last Windows Sockets API error.
WSAIsBlocking	Determines whether the underlying Winsock DLL is blocking.
WSASetBlockingHook	Hooks the blocking method used by the underlying Winsock implementation. (Refer to the section that discusses blocking hooks for a better definition of this function.)
WSASetLastError	Sets the error return for the subsequent WSAGetLastError.
WSAStartup	Initializes the underlying Winsock DLL.
WSAUnhookBlockingHook	Restores the original blocking function.

Table 8.5 The Windows-specific extension functions, except the asynchronous database functions.

EXAMINING THE BIG PICTURE

To understand Windows-based Internet programming, you need to understand where Winsock fits into the big picture and what Winsock actually includes. Many software vendors that provide Winsock implementations include a variety of very useful features and utility programs. For someone who is unfamiliar with Winsock, it can be difficult to determine where the vendor's enhancements end and Winsock begins.

As discussed in Chapter 6, the Serial Line Internet Protocol (SLIP) and Point-to-Point Protocol (PPP) let you use a modem and standard telephone lines to establish a serial connection between your computer and the Internet. Many Winsock vendors include SLIP and PPP implementations with their products. Typically, these vendors also include a Windows-based dialer program that you can use to connect your computer to the Internet (using SLIP or PPP) through your modem. Frequently, vendors include a TCP/IP protocol stack as part of their Winsock products. Although you may find these products extremely useful (and even necessary) as you develop TCP/IP software, understand that they are not part of Winsock itself. Figure 8.1 shows where the Winsock interface fits into the overall scheme of TCP/IP program development in the Windows environment.

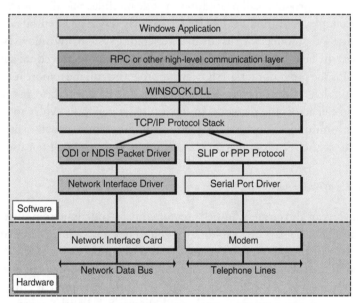

Figure 8.1 *Winsock's location within the Windows program environment.*

As you can see, the WINSOCK.DLL sits between the TCP/IP protocol stack and your applications. In other words, Winsock manages the interface to the TCP/IP protocols. Previous chapters of this book have discussed the TCP/IP protocol stack in detail, as well as the SLIP and PPP protocols. However, you may not be familiar with some of the other components shown in Figure 8.1. The following sections discuss the high-level communication layer and the other software driver modules shown in Figure 8.1.

UNDERSTANDING THE HIGH-LEVEL COMMUNICATION LAYER

Frequently, your Winsock vendor will supply the high-level communication layer shown in Figure 8.1. As you can see, this layer sits between your Windows program and the WINSOCK.DLL. The high-level communication layer can be a *Remote Procedure Call (RPC)* product or some other program that provides a similar service.

RPC is an interface that lets one program call a procedure that resides at a remote computer. As you know, programs make extensive use of functions and procedures. When your program calls a function, you usually pass parameters to the function. Normally, the function statements are contained within your program code or within a Windows DDL. In the case of a remote-procedure call, however, the function's code resides on a different computer. For example, suppose you develop programs on a local area network (LAN) that run TCP/IP protocols. Within your LAN, a remote computer may include a Winsock implementation. As your Internet-based programs run, they must call the procedures located in the WINSOCK.DLL. In this case, because the DLL resides on a remote computer, your program must perform a remote-procedure call.

An RPC interface lets a program call procedures in code modules that do not reside on your local computer—for example, code modules like DLLs that may reside on a central network computer. Microsoft includes RPC products with its advanced operating systems (Windows NT and Windows 95). In most cases, the fact that your program is invoking a remote procedure will be transparent to the user, as well as the programmer. In short, your programs call the remote function just as they would any function that resides on your local computer. The RPC interface, in turn, transparently maps the function call across the network. In the future, as networks evolve to play even a larger role in electronic communications than they do today, programmers will make extensive use of RPC. However, to create the programs presented in this book, you will not use RPCs.

USING SERIAL CONNECTIONS

Understand that you can also create Winsock programs on a stand-alone computer. In other words, your computer need not be part of a network for you to develop Winsock network applications. Obviously, to test your programs, you eventually need to connect to a TCP/IP network. However, as discussed in the following paragraphs, even then your computer can essentially remain a stand-alone PC. On a stand-alone computer, your Winsock development environment will not include the high-level communication layer shown in Figure 8.1. In other words, your stand-alone PC doesn't need the ability to call remote DLL procedures since all programs (and DLLs) reside on your local PC. However, you still need a way to connect to the Internet.

Suppose, like most of us, you own a stand-alone PC but want to develop Winsock network programs for the Internet. As discussed in Chapter 6, you can connect your PC to the Internet through a SLIP or PPP implementation that uses your modem and standard telephone lines. As discussed in Chapter 6, SLIP and PPP are link-layer framing protocols that encapsulate data packets prior to transmission across a point-to-point serial link. In other words, SLIP and PPP can encapsulate IP packets before your modem transmits them across telephone lines to another Internet host computer. As shown in Figure 8.1, the SLIP or PPP module sits between the TCP/IP protocol stack and a serial port driver. As you may know, a driver is simply a software module that provides an interface to a specific piece of hardware (in this case, your computer's communications port). Although you can buy replacement drivers, Windows includes a serial-port driver named COMM.DRV, which the Windows installation program automatically installs with Windows.

The COMM.DRV serial-port driver handles the low-level dirty work involved in transferring data between the Windows operating system and your computer hardware's communication serial ports (usually COM1 and COM2). In general, you don't have to understand anything about COMM.DRV other than the fact that it exists.

IMPROVING PERFORMANCE ON SERIAL LINKS TO THE INTERNET

If you develop Winsock programs and plan to use a serial link to the Internet, take advantage of hardware and software designed for high-speed serial communications. For example, buying a faster serial port driver (a replacement for COMM.DRV) can help improve performance. Obviously, a faster modem will also help. If you use an external modem, make sure your computer hardware's serial ports use an *advanced universal asynchronous receiver-transmitter chip (UART)*.

Note: Most internal modems have an advanced UART chip built-in. If you use an internal modem, you don't need to worry about the UART in your computer.

UART chips control a PC's serial ports. A UART converts incoming serial data (bits) into bytes that your computer's hardware normally uses. The UART also converts your computer's internal parallel data into serial data suitable for transmission across telephone lines. Most modern PCs use an advanced UART called a 16550, which is faster that the older 8250A and 16450 UARTs.

If you own a PC with an older UART, you can buy a serial port card that uses an advanced UART. Such cards replace your existing serial ports and are usually inexpensive. Note that chip manufacturers constantly produce newer and faster chips. By the time you read this book, a 16550 UART may not be an *advanced* UART. In other words, take a little time to investigate existing technologies for serial communications. You may find you can boost your computer's performance on the Internet for very little cost.

DEVELOPING WINSOCK PROGRAMS ON A NETWORK

If you develop Winsock programs on a network, your development environment will probably include one or more network drivers instead of a single serial port driver. As previously mentioned, a driver is simply a software interface to a specific piece of hardware. As shown in Figure 8.1, on a network, a packet driver and a network interface driver may sit between the TCP/IP protocol stack and the data bus. In most cases, to write network programs, you don't need to understand anything about these drivers other than the fact that they exist. The fact that these drivers exist is important because they sit between your Winsock programs and the bus that carries your network data. In other words, any problem with the packet or network drivers can adversely affect your programs' performance. Suppose you develop Winsock programs on a network, and you encounter program behavior that you can't explain. On such occasions, have the technical staff responsible for your network help you make sure your network's packet and interface card drivers are not the cause of the problem.

SUPPORTING MULTIPLE PROTOCOLS WITH ONE NETWORK CARD

Depending on your network, there may be times when one host runs two different protocols (such as TCP/IP and DECNet) over the same communication channel. To support multiple protocols, most network card manufacturers provide two different drivers for the same interface card. John Romkey at FTP Software in North Andover, Massachusetts, developed the packet driver specification that lets TCP/IP and other transport protocols share a common network interface card. The *Open Data-Link Interface (ODI)* developed by Novell and Apple also lets you run multiple protocols on the same network interface card. The *Network Driver Interface Specification (NDIS)* developed by Microsoft and 3Com provides a similar capability. However, the NDIS strategy is different. NDIS multiplexes protocols so that multiple protocol stacks can co-exist in the same host. In other words, network interface card vendors can develop network drivers that are NDIS compliant. Such drivers will be compatible with any other NDIS compliant driver.

CREATING WINSOCK PROGRAMS

As discussed in this chapter, Winsock programs require a dynamic link library (DLL) named WINSOCK.DLL, which incorporates the Winsock API. Your C/C++ language compiler will need a Winsock import library to build the Winsock programs described in Section 2. See your compiler reference manual for details. The *Internet Programming* companion disk includes a copy of a shareware WINSOCK.DLL developed by Peter Tattam from the University of Tasmania in Australia. For more information about Tattam's product, please see the READ.ME file located on the companion disk.

REVIEWING THE SOCKET PROGRAMMING PARADIGM

Chapter 7 discussed the socket as an abstract representation of a network endpoint. The chapter also discussed the Berkeley-socket interface built on the socket abstraction. Although it is a real API, the Berkeley-socket interface also represents a model or paradigm for network programming. As previously mentioned, the Winsock API depends very heavily on concepts derived from the Berkeley sockets.

The following sections provide a quick review of the socket-programming paradigm. If these sections do not explain a specific topic in sufficient detail for you, please refer to the discussions in Chapter 7 on the same subject. Later sections of this chapter discuss the Winsock API specifically within the context of the socket-programming paradigm. To use a socket interface for network communication, your programs follow a simple, four-step process:

1. First, your program creates a socket.

2. Second, your program configures the socket for use. In other words, your program either connects the socket to a remote host or binds the socket to a local protocol port.

3. Third, your program transmits or receives data through the socket as required by your application.

4. Finally, when finished, your program closes the socket.

CREATING A SOCKET

To use a socket for network communication, your program must first create a socket. To create a socket, your program calls the socket function. The following program statement shows a sample socket-function call:

```
socket_handle = socket(protocol_family, socket_type, protocol);
```

The handle that the Winsock-API socket function returns is different from the Berkeley-socket handle. (The section entitled *Using New Socket Descriptors*, found later in this chapter, explains in detail the new Winsock-API socket handles.) However, the Winsock-API socket function's parameters are identical to those of the Berkeley socket. In other words, the protocol-family parameter identifies a family or collection of related protocols, such as the TCP/IP protocol suite. The socket-type parameter specifies whether your program will use the socket for datagram or byte-stream transmissions. The protocol parameter identifies the specific protocol within the protocol family that your program wants to use, such as TCP or UDP.

As discussed in Chapter 7, the Berkeley socket-interface designers used the concept of protocol and address families to add a multi-network capability to the socket interface. In other words, since programmers must identify the protocols their programs use, vendors can implement the same interface for networks that use different protocol suites and address formats. Winsock uses the same symbolic constants as the Berkeley sockets to identify protocol and address families. For example, PF_INET identifies the Internet (TCP/IP) protocol family and AF_INET identifies the Internet address family. Your Winsock programs can use either connection-oriented or connectionless protocols. However, when your programs create a socket, they must specify which type of protocol they will use for the new socket. As you have learned, connection-oriented protocols use byte streams and connectionless protocols use datagrams. To specify a type of socket, your Winsock program uses, as the socket function's second parameter, the symbolic constant SOCK_DGRAM for datagrams or SOCK_STREAM for byte streams.

Note: Some Winsock implementations may also support a raw socket (SOCK_RAW). However, Winsock specification version 1.1 does not require raw-socket support. As such, the WINSOCK.DLL that you are using may not have raw-socket support. A raw socket provides access to low-level protocols, such as IP and ICMP.

The socket function's third parameter lets your program specify which protocol (such as TCP or UDP) to use with the socket. To specify a protocol, your program uses symbolic constants that begin with an IPPROTO_ prefix. For example, to specify the TCP protocol, your program would use IPPROTO_TCP for the third socket parameter. The symbolic constant IPPROTO_UDP specifies the UDP protocol. The following statement shows a typical call to the socket function:

```
socket_handle = socket(PF_INET, SOCK_STREAM, IPPROTO_TCP);
```

This socket will use the TCP protocol (IPPROTO_TCP) in the Internet protocol family (PF_INET) for byte-stream (SOCK_STREAM) communications. When your program calls the socket function to create a new socket, Winsock allocates memory for an internal data structure, which stores information about the socket.

Note: Winsock uses an internal data structure similar to Berkeley sockets. Chapter 7 describes in more detail the internal data structure used by the socket interface.

CONFIGURING A SOCKET

To configure a socket, your program will use different functions from the Winsock API. As discussed in Chapter 7, how your program configures a socket depends on the type of network connection your program establishes (connection-oriented or connectionless) and the purpose your program serves (client or server process). As explained in Chapter 7, each socket (or network endpoint) requires five pieces of information: IP addresses for the local and remote hosts, a protocol port for the local and remote processes, and a protocol to use over the connection. Table 8.6 shows the Winsock API functions your program will use to configure a socket for network communication.

Socket Use	Local Information	Remote Information
Connection-oriented client	One call to the connect function stores both local and remote information in the socket-data structure.	
Connection-oriented server	bind	listen and accept

Table 8.6 Socket API functions used to configure a socket for network communication. (continued on the next page)

Socket Use	Local Information	Remote Information
Connectionless client	bind	sendto
Connectionless server	bind	recvfrom

Table 8.6 Socket API functions used to configure a socket for network communication. (continued from the previous page)

As you will learn, your Winsock programs use the functions shown in Table 8.1 to supply IP address and protocol-port information about the local or remote host. The socket function supplies the fifth piece of information (the protocol to use) when you create the socket.

CONNECTING A SOCKET

As you have learned, a connection-oriented protocol establishes a virtual circuit between the connection endpoints. Connection-oriented protocols, such as TCP, keep the connection open by exchanging acknowledgment messages between the two endpoints. A connection-oriented client program does not care which local address (protocol port) the network software uses for data transfers. After establishing the connection, the client program can rely on the transport protocol (TCP) to deliver data to the client program. As such, a connection-oriented client program does not need to specify a local protocol port. In other words, the only address information a connection-oriented client program must supply to the socket is the remote host information—IP address and protocol port. Winsock automatically stores the local IP address and selects a local protocol port. The Winsock API makes sure that your client program receives all data the transport layer delivers to the local protocol port. In other words, Winsock selects the protocol port for your program and notifies your program when data arrives at the port—your program doesn't care which port Winsock uses.

A connection-oriented client program can use the connect function to configure a socket for network communication. The connect function requires three parameters: socket handle, remote socket address, and address length. The following program statement shows a typical call to the connect function:

```
result = connect(socket_handle, remote_socket_address, address_length);
```

The connect function's first parameter, socket handle, is the value returned from the socket function. As such, before your program can connect a socket (using the connect function), your program must create a socket by calling the socket function. The connect function's second parameter, remote socket address, is a pointer to a special socket-address structure. The address structure stores an address family, a protocol port, and a network host address for a socket. Before your program calls the connect function, you must store the remote host's IP address and protocol port in the structure.

Note: Chapter 9 will explain how your programs can retrieve a remote host's IP address and protocol port from the Internet.

When your program calls the connect function, Winsock stores the remote host's information (IP address and protocol port) in an internal data structure that the socket handle (the connect function's first parameter) identifies. In other words, after your program creates the socket and connects the socket to the remote host, all other functions in the Winsock API use the information stored in the internal data structure for the socket. After your programs call the socket and connect functions, the internal data structure contains all five pieces of information necessary for network communication:

- A protocol to use over the connection (your program uses the socket function to specify which protocol)

- An IP address for the local host (TCP extracts this address from the Winsock implementation)

- A protocol port for the local process (typically, TCP assigns this value for your program)

- An IP address for the remote host (your program uses the connect function to specify which host)

- A protocol port for the remote process (your program uses the connect function to specify which port)

The socket function stores the protocol (such as TCP) your program wants to use. Winsock automatically stores the local IP address and selects a protocol port for your program. Your program specifies the remote IP address and protocol port in the address structure pointed to by the connect function's second parameter. In all cases, Winsock stores the specified data in an internal data structure that the socket handle identifies.

LISTENING FOR INCOMING DATA OR CONNECTION REQUESTS

As discussed in Chapter 7, only connection-oriented client processes initiate a direct connection to a remote host's socket. Connectionless protocols never establish a direct connection. Instead, connectionless protocols transmit datagrams (not byte streams) across the network. Likewise, although a server program can use connection-oriented protocols, server programs never initiate a connection. A server listens passively at a protocol port for client requests. In other words, a connection-oriented client always initiates any direct connections. The server only responds to such requests.

As such, all connection-oriented servers and all connectionless programs (servers and clients) share a common characteristic: they all must listen to a protocol port. All server programs (connectionless and connection-oriented) listen for client requests at a protocol port. Likewise, a connectionless-client program must also listen to a protocol port for a response from the server. Remember, a connectionless protocol does not establish a direct connection to a remote host. As a result, a client program that uses a connectionless protocol must transmit a datagram with a service request and then wait for a reply. The reply will arrive in the form of a datagram from the remote host. In other words, a connectionless-client program must listen for server replies at a protocol port. The Winsock API's bind function lets programs associate the local IP address and a local protocol port with a socket. The following program statement shows a typical call to the bind function:

```
result = bind(socket_handle, local_socket_address, address_length);
```

As you have learned, a server program listens for service requests from client programs. The TCP/IP transport layer uses a protocol port to communicate with server and client programs. In other words, to receive client requests, a server listens at a specific protocol port for the transport layer to deliver client requests. The bind function lets your server programs register a protocol port with Winsock. In other words, your program tells Winsock which protocol port to monitor for data delivery. Winsock, in turn, tells the transport layer to deliver all data received at that protocol port to the Winsock API.

Connectionless client programs use the bind function in the same way. In other words, like a server program, a connectionless client tells Winsock which protocol port to monitor for data delivery. Winsock notifies the transport layer about the port's use and handles the interface between the client and the transport protocol (UDP). As you will see in later sections, when the client transmits a service request to a remote host, the client specifies which local protocol port the server should use for replies. When a server's reply datagram arrives at the specified protocol port, the transport layer notifies Winsock. Later sections explain how your programs can use the Winsock API to retrieve data from a protocol port. For now, simply note that the bind function configures a socket to listen for datagrams or connection requests at a specific protocol port.

USING A SOCKET

Your programs can use the Winsock API to transmit and receive data through a properly configured socket. The Berkeley-socket interface uses UNIX system input/output (I/O) functions for network I/O. Since Winsock implementations are not an integral part of the Windows operating system, Winsock network I/O is slightly different from Berkeley sockets. Berkeley sockets include five functions to transmit data and five functions to receive data through a socket. Winsock includes four functions: two for data transmission and two for data reception. Table 8.7 lists, and provides a brief description of, those functions.

Winsock API Function	Description
send	Transmits data through a connected socket, using special flags to control socket behavior.
sendto	Transmits data to a host address specified in a socket address structure, using a simple message buffer.

Table 8.7 Winsock API functions used for network I/O. (continued on the next page)

Winsock API Function	Description
recv	Receives data from a connected socket, using special flags to control socket behavior.
recvfrom	Receives data from a socket and optionally records the network address of the sending host, using a simple message buffer.

Table 8.7 Winsock API functions used for network I/O. (continued from the previous page)

The key difference between the functions in Table 8.7 is that your programs can use the send and recv functions only on connected sockets. The sendto and recvfrom functions can specify network addresses. In other words, your programs can use the sendto and recvfrom functions on unconnected sockets. Additionally, your programs can use the sendto and recvfrom functions on connected sockets—Winsock simply ignores the address parameters included with sendto and recvfrom. As a rule, however, if your programs use only connected sockets, they should call the send and recv functions. In this way, other programmers who examine your code can tell easily that you are using connected sockets.

There may be times, however, when you create a generic function that can perform connection-oriented or connectionless data-transfer operations. In such cases, your function should use the sendto and recvfrom API functions. In this way, you can use the function to send or receive data regardless of the socket type that programs pass to the function.

USING A CONNECTED SOCKET

The following program statement is a typical call to the send function:

```
result = send(socket_handle, message_buffer, buffer_length,
    special_flags);
```

Since the send function provides no way to specify a destination address, your program can only use the send function with a connected socket. In other words, before your program can use the send function, your program must create a socket (using the socket function) and then connect the socket (using the connect function).

As discussed, the connect function stores remote host address information in Winsock's internal socket-data structure. When your programs call the send function, Winsock retrieves the destination information (IP address and protocol port) from the internal socket-data structure that the socket handle (the send function's first parameter) identifies. Then, the send function transmits the data in the message buffer (the send function's second parameter). The destination of this data is the network address specified in Winsock's internal socket-data structure. The recv function is the companion to the send function. The following program statement shows a typical call to the recv function:

```
result = recv(socket_handle, message_buffer, buffer_length,
   special_flags);
```

The recv function retrieves data from a local protocol port and stores the data in the message buffer (the recv function's second parameter). When your programs call the recv function, Winsock uses its internal data structure (as identified by the recv function's first parameter, socket handle) to tell the recv function which protocol port to access. Although Winsock and the transport layer manage an incoming-data queue for the protocol port, your programs cannot use this buffer for data storage. (Remember, the transport layer may be servicing multiple programs.) As such, before your programs can receive data from a protocol port, they must use the recv function's second parameter, message buffer, to specify an alternate storage location. The recv function copies data from the incoming-data queue to your program's message buffer. The buffer-length parameter tells Winsock the maximum number of bytes the message buffer can store.

Winsock provides two special flags your programs can use for the recv function's last parameter. Using the symbolic constant MSG_OOB as a flag value, your programs can request out-of-band data from the protocol port. (Remember, out-of-band data is urgent data that your program should immediately process.) If you call the recv function using the MSG_OOB flag and out-of-band data exists, recv immediately returns the "urgent" data to your program. If no out-of-band data is present, recv returns the constant error value EINVAL.

Using the symbolic constant MSG_PEEK as a flag value, your programs can analyze the data in the transport layer's incoming-data queue. Normally, after a program copies data from the incoming-data queue (using recv), the transport layer discards all the data in the buffer. However, when your programs specify the MSG_PEEK flag in the recv function, the transport layer does not remove copied data from the incoming-data queue. As such, MSG_PEEK lets your programs analyze incoming data before they decide how to process it. Your programs can then decide to retrieve all, or only a portion of, the data at one time. The FTP program examples in Section 3 of *Internet Programming* demonstrate how your programs can use the MSG_PEEK flag.

However, be aware that your programs do not have to use either MSG_PEEK or MSG_OOB. Instead, your programs can specify zero (0) as the special flags parameter. In response, the recv function will simply copy data from the transport layer's incoming-data queue to your program's message buffer. As previously mentioned, your programs can also use the sendto and recvfrom functions on connected sockets. On a connected socket, the sendto and recvfrom functions operate the same as the send and recv functions. However, your programs normally use the sendto and recvfrom functions on unconnected sockets.

USING AN UNCONNECTED SOCKET

As shown in the previous section, the send and recv functions do not provide any way to specify a remote host address. In other words, your programs must connect the socket to a remote host before it can call the send or recv functions. In contrast, your programs can use the sendto and recvfrom functions on unconnected sockets. Like the sendto function in Berkeley sockets, the Winsock sendto function requires six parameters. The first four parameters are identical to those the send function uses. The fifth parameter, socket address structure, identifies the destination address. The sixth parameter, address structure length, specifies the destination address' width (or length) in bytes. The following program statement shows a typical call to the sendto function:

```
result = sendto(socket_handle, message_buffer, buffer_length,
    special_flags, socket_address_structure, address_structure_length);
```

As previously discussed, your programs use the bind function to store local-address information (IP address and protocol port) for sockets configured to use connectionless protocols. As previously shown in Table 8.7, the sendto function stores remote-host information in the Winsock's internal data structure. Before your programs call the sendto function, they must store remote host information in a socket-data structure. Your programs pass a pointer to this address structure as the fifth parameter to the sendto function. When Winsock contacts the transport layer to transmit the data in the sendto message buffer, Winsock passes the information stored in its internal data structure to the transport layer. The transport layer uses the information in the data structure to format a UDP datagram header and transmit the data across the network.

Note: *When your programs use the sendto function on a connected socket, Winsock ignores the socket-address-structure and address-structure-length parameters. Also, the transport layer will format the data in the message buffer as a TCP segment—not a UDP datagram.*

Just as the send function has recv as its companion, the sendto function has recvfrom. The following program statement shows a typical call to the recvfrom function:

```
result = recvfrom (socket_handle, message_buffer, buffer_length,
    special_flags, socket_address_structure, address_structure_length);
```

The recvfrom function retrieves data from a protocol port in the same fashion as the recv function. However, on an unconnected socket (SOCK_DGRAM), the recvfrom function can also extract from a datagram header the network address of the host that sent the datagram.

A server program that uses the recvfrom function would always extract the sender's address. In other words, the server program always needs to know where to send the requested information. In the case of a client program that uses recvfrom, however, the client might extract the sender's address if the client needs to continue an ongoing network conversation. Also, the client might extract the sender's address to verify that the data came from the expected host. However, in many (and perhaps most) cases, a client program does not need to know the sender's address.

In other words, from the datagram header, the recvfrom function copies the network address of the host that sent the datagram into the socket-address structure pointed to by recvfrom's fifth argument. The recvfrom function only extracts the sender's address if the socket-address-structure field contains a valid pointer (the parameter is not NULL). If the socket-address-structure field is NULL, the recvfrom function does not copy or otherwise extract the sender's address from the datagram header.

BERKELEY SOCKETS VERSUS WINDOWS SOCKETS

The Winsock-programming model described in the previous sections closely parallels the Berkeley model described in Chapter 7. As previously mentioned, the Winsock developers derived the Winsock API from the Berkeley-sockets interface. The Berkeley-sockets model virtually rules TCP/IP software development in the UNIX world. As you have learned, the socket paradigm provides programmers with a readily understandable model for network-software development. As discussed in Chapter 7, the socket interface developed by the Berkeley researchers provides a variety of functions that help you create sophisticated server operations, as well as develop robust client programs. As such, one of the stated goals of the Winsock specification is:

> ". . . to provide a high degree of familiarity for programmers who are used to programming with sockets in UNIX and other environments, and to simplify the task of porting existing sockets-based source code."

The specification achieves the first part of this goal quite effectively. If you have used the Berkeley sockets API to develop network programs, Windows Sockets will feel very comfortable to you. However, the second part of the specification's goal, "to simplify the task of porting existing sockets-based source code," is tougher to achieve. Although Windows Sockets simplifies the porting process, porting existing sockets-based source code to Windows is not simple. If you are familiar with Berkeley sockets and plan to develop Windows-based TCP/IP programs from scratch, you are already well on your way to success. However, if your job is to port programs from Berkeley sockets to Windows Sockets, you have your work cut out for you. As such, you may initially want to avoid using the Windows-specific extensions and make your programs work with the Windows Sockets functions derived from the Berkeley-socket interface.

Over time, you can begin to phase in the Windows-specific functions. However, you should be aware that, due to the differences between UNIX and Windows, you eventually may have to completely rewrite the program to port it to Windows Sockets. This rewrite may be necessary before your program can take advantage of the Windows-specific extensions in the Winsock specification. Regardless of whether you plan to port existing programs or create programs from scratch, the following summary of differences between Berkeley sockets and Windows Sockets will aid you in your development efforts. Of course, this summary assumes you are already familiar with Berkeley sockets as described in Chapter 7.

ADDING A NEW HEADER FILE

In a UNIX environment, your network programs must include a variety of header files. In contrast, network programs you write for a Windows environment need only a single header file named *winsock.h.* If your application uses any socket definitions or calls any Winsock functions, you need to include the winsock.h header file (#include <winsock.h>) in your program code. Most Windows programs you write must include the Windows header file, *windows.h.* However, if you've already placed the winsock.h header file into your code, you don't need to also include windows.h. Since the winsock.h header file depends on several definitions in windows.h, the winsock.h header file includes windows.h for you.

MANAGING YOUR DATA

As you develop Windows programs, always remember that Winsock requires you to ensure any memory objects, such as data buffers or variables, remain available to the WINSOCK.DLL during all Winsock operations. In the multi-threaded versions of Windows, your program must also coordinate access to memory objects. The Winsock specification specifically relieves all Winsock implementations (WINSOCK.DLL) from this responsibility.

IDENTIFYING REQUIRED FUNCTION CALLS

Windows Sockets requires two Windows-specific functions, WSAStartup and WSACleanup, for all Winsock programs. You must call the WSAStartup function before you call any other Winsock functions. For each call to the WSAStartup function, your program should later include a corresponding call to the WSACleanup function. The following sections explain these two key functions.

USING THE WSASTARTUP FUNCTION

The WSAStartup function lets your program specify which version of the Windows Sockets API it requires. The function also retrieves details about the Winsock implementation your program uses. In effect, when your program calls WSAStartup, a negotiation between your program and the WINSOCK.DLL occurs. Windows Sockets uses this negotiation process to provide support for future Winsock implementations. In other words, your program specifies the minimum version of Winsock it requires. The WINSOCK.DLL, in turn, reports the highest version it supports. Then, your program acts according to what the WINSOCK.DLL reports. The Winsock specification includes a chart that describes how the WSAStartup negotiation works with different versions of DLLs.

USING THE WSACLEANUP FUNCTION

Your programs may call the WSAStartup function several times during their execution. For example, suppose different functions within your program need to know implementation details about the WINSOCK.DLL. Rather than using global variables to store the Winsock data, Winsock lets your program freely call the WSAStartup function each time your program needs implementation details. The WSACleanup function is the companion function to WSAStartup. For each call your program makes to the WSAStartup function, your program must make a corresponding call to the WSACleanup function. To track how many times your program calls these functions,

Winsock maintains an internal counter. Each time your program calls the WSAStartup function, Winsock increments the counter. Conversely, each time your program calls the WSACleanup function, Winsock decrements the counter. The final WSACleanup function (which sets the internal counter to zero) tells the WINSOCK.DLL to perform cleanup operations.

Typically, Winsock implementations (WINSOCK.DLL) allocate resources that each program can use. For example, most Winsock implementations use and reuse static data-storage buffers. Although each Winsock program gets its own set of buffers, your program can only access these buffers through the Winsock API. In other words, the buffers are internal to Winsock like the socket-data structure previously discussed. When Winsock performs cleanup operations, Winsock frees all internally allocated data buffers, as well as any other resources it allocated on your program's behalf. In effect, the final WSACleanup function call tells Winsock that your program no longer requires Winsock to manage any resources on its behalf. Just as the WSAStartup function initializes the WINSOCK.DLL for use by your program, the WSACleanup function terminates your program's use of the WINSOCK.DLL.

When your program calls the WSACleanup function for the last time, Winsock disconnects any remaining byte-stream sockets. However, Winsock will transmit pending data from a closed socket after you call WSACleanup. For example, suppose your program issues a send command just before it closes a socket. Even though the network software may not have transmitted your program's data when your program called the WSACleanup function (the data may be in an outgoing data queue), Winsock will still send the pending data.

As discussed, your programs should always clean-up by calling the WSACleanup function. Depending on the Winsock implementation and the functions your program invokes, the Winsock may, for example, allocate memory on your program's behalf. By calling the WSACleanup function, you inform Winsock that your program no longer requires its services or memory it may have allocated. Winsock, in turn, can release any allocated memory for use by the programs.

However, most WINSOCK.DLLs can recover when a program terminates without calling WSACleanup for the final cleanup. The Winsock specification tells Winsock suppliers to expect and prepare for such occurrences. However, Winsock does not require WINSOCK.DLLs to take specific action for such occurrences. In other words, if a program terminates without calling the WSACleanup function for the final clean-up, what occurs next depends on the particular Winsock implementation. As such, you should provide sufficient error-checking in your Winsock programs to ensure final clean-up. In this way, should your program encounter a critical error, your program can end in a controlled manner, cleaning up after itself so the error does not affect the Winsock implementation or Winsock-based programs.

Note: If you develop Winsock programs for multi-threaded environments, such as Windows NT or Windows 95, be aware that the WSACleanup function terminates Winsock operations for all program threads. In other words, many Winsock functions only affect a specific thread within a program or process. The WSACleanup function is not one of them—the WSACleanup function terminates Winsock operations for all threads associated with the program that calls the function.

USING NEW SOCKET DESCRIPTORS

As you learned in Chapter 7, Berkeley sockets base their socket handle on a file descriptor. Winsock defines a new data type, named SOCKET, which Winsock uses as a socket handle (or descriptor). Under UNIX, socket handles (like all handles) are small, positive integers. In fact, many Berkeley sockets-based programs assume that a socket handle is positive. However, Winsock does not restrict socket handles to positive values.

The Winsock specification conveniently defines SOCKET as an unsigned data type. Winsock uses the constant INVALID_SOCKET to identify invalid sockets. The specification defines INVALID_SOCKET as (SOCKET)(~0)—a negative one (-1) cast as an unsigned data type. The Winsock specification also states that a valid socket handle can be any value in the range of zero to INVALID_SOCKET-1. As such, the only integer value that identifies an invalid socket is the largest possible unsigned integer, 0xFFFF. As you have learned in Chapter 7, programs that use the socket interface must use socket handles quite extensively. If you must port Berkeley sockets-based programs, remember that, under Windows Sockets, any program code that assumes a negative socket handle indicates an invalid socket may incorrectly report failure.

SOCKET DESCRIPTORS VERSUS FILE DESCRIPTORS

As discussed in Chapter 7, the Berkeley-socket handles (descriptors) are equivalent to UNIX file handles. When UNIX-based programs want to use file I/O functions to perform network I/O, they simply pass such functions a socket handle. However, a Winsock socket handle is not the same as a file handle—you cannot perform file I/O functions using Winsock sockets.

Note: Although Winsock does not use a file descriptor table for socket handles, the internal socket-data structure Winsock uses is similar to the simple socket-data structure described in Chapter 7.

If you must port Berkeley-socket programs to Windows Sockets, you will need to carefully restructure UNIX code that uses functions such as *read* and *write*. Winsock does not include these functions. To port such code, you will need to replace the read and write function calls with recv and send function calls. Also, in Winsock, you must use the closesocket function instead of the close function, as well as the ioctlsocket function instead of the ioctl function. Table 8.8 summarizes these changes.

Berkeley Function	Winsock Replacement Function
read	recv
write	send
close	closesocket
ioctl	ioctlsocket

Table 8.8 Berkeley functions you must change when porting programs to Winsock.

Note that the functions Table 8.8 identifies are the most common and easiest Berkeley function calls to port. There is no easy way to port other UNIX-based Berkeley functions such as readv, writev, recvmsg, and sendmsg. In most cases, Berkeley-socket program code that uses these functions will require a complete re-write.

USING WINSOCK ERROR-HANDLING FUNCTIONS

In the event of a socket error, the Berkeley-sockets interface sets the C run-time library *errno* variable. Winsock does not use *errno*. Instead, Winsock defines a new constant, SOCKET_ERROR (which Winsock defines to be -1), as the value that identifies socket errors. As such, when a socket error occurs, Winsock functions normally return the SOCKET_ERROR constant. In response, your program must call the new Windows-specific WSAGetLastError function to identify the specific error condition that caused the error.

For 16-bit Windows such as version 3.1, the WSAGetLastError function retrieves the last network error that occurred for a specific Winsock program. As such, your program needs to call the WSAGetLastError function immediately after it detects an error. If your program calls another Winsock function before it calls WSAGetLastError, the second Winsock function call may also fail, changing the error condition reported by WSAGetLastError. In a multi-threaded environment, such as Windows NT and Windows 95, the WSAGetLastError function calls the Win32 GetLastError function. The GetLastError function returns the error status for all Win32 functions on a thread-by-thread basis.

To help you port existing Berkeley-sockets-based programs, Winsock supports most Berkeley-error constants. However, as you develop new Winsock programs or port existing socket programs to Windows Sockets, you should use the new Winsock constants. To make your transition from Berkeley-error constants to Winsock constants easier, Winsock prefixes the Berkeley constants with WSA (which stands for Windows Sockets API). For example, Winsock transforms the Berkeley-error constant ENETDOWN, which the Berkeley API uses to indicate a failure in the underlying network, into WSAENETDOWN.

USING SELECT WITH WINSOCK

As you learned in Chapter 7, the Berkeley API's select function lets a single process monitor or determine the status of multiple sockets. Winsock's select function performs the same job. In other words, you use the select function to tell Winsock to report status changes for a specific set of sockets. For example, your program might have data ready to send to a remote host. However, before your program can transmit the data, your program may need to receive a response from the remote host. Your program can use the select function to tell Winsock to check for responses from the remote host. When Winsock reports a response, your program can then transmit its previously prepared data.

As discussed in Chapter 7, the Berkeley-sockets API lets your program determine the read, write, and error status of multiple sockets. To do so, your program examines the bits in a single, socket-handle bit mask that your program sets prior to calling the select function. In contrast, your Winsock programs do not use bit masks. Instead, your Winsock programs use an array of socket handles for select operations. Note that Winsock continues to use the Berkeley-socket term *set*. You should understand that a *set* is a specific list of sockets that Winsock will monitor for status changes. To manipulate the array of socket handles (the set or list of sockets), Winsock requires your programs to use the macros listed in Table 8.9. (You can find the definitions for these macros in the winsock.h header file.)

Macro Name	Function
FD_CLR	Removes a socket handle from a set.
FD_ISSET	Returns a non-zero value (true) if the socket handle is set and zero (false) if the socket handle is not set.
FD_SET	Adds a socket handle to a set.
FD_ZERO	Initializes a set of socket handles.

Table 8.9 Macros that manipulate sets of socket handles for the select function.

Note: *Although you can continue to use the select function in Windows Sockets, one of the Windows-specific extensions to Winsock is an asynchronous version of select named WSAAsyncSelect.*

Beware of Mixed Memory Models

Memory usage under UNIX differs quite dramatically from Windows memory usage on a PC. As you may know, all 16-bit versions of Windows, such as Windows 3.1 (and any other 16-bit programs on an Intel-based PC), distinguish between near (16-bit) pointers and far (32-bit segment, offset) pointers. On Intel-based PCs, a near pointer stores a memory address as a 16-bit memory offset. The offset address points to a specific memory location within a 64KB segment, such as the code, data, stack, or extra-segment. A far pointer stores memory addresses as a 16-bit segment address and a 16-bit memory offset. The 32-bit versions of Windows, such as Windows NT, use a flat memory model where memory addresses are all 32-bit offsets.

On a PC, you create programs that use near or far pointers, by default, when you compile program modules that use different memory models. For example, a small memory-model program assumes all pointers are near pointers unless you use the FAR type modifier (char FAR *address) to specify otherwise. On the other hand, a large memory-model program assumes all pointers are far pointers unless you use the NEAR type modifier (char NEAR *address) to specify otherwise. Table 8.10 summarizes the difference between the four main memory models on a PC.

Memory Model	Code Segments	Data Segments
Small	1	1
Medium	many	1

Table 8.10 Primary memory models on an Intel-based PC. (continued on the next page)

Memory Model	Code Segments	Data Segments
Compact	1	many
Large	many	many

Table 8.10 *Primary memory models on an Intel-based PC. (continued from the previous page)*

Note: *Intel-based PCs can also use the huge memory model. The huge memory model is identical to the large memory model except that, in a huge memory model, a single data item can extend across more than one data segment. In all the memory models listed in Table 8.10, a single data item must fit within a single data segment.*

Normally, using the smaller 16-bit near pointers will boost program performance. However, unless you are very careful, mixing program modules that use different memory models can produce unexpected results and, potentially, create some very nasty debugging problems. In addition, near and far pointer mixing makes your programs more difficult for others to understand.

Of course, in a UNIX operating system environment, the memory model concept does not apply. Like Windows NT, UNIX uses a flat address space. As such, if you come from a UNIX background and are not familiar with the Intel memory models, you initially may want to build only large memory-model programs. That way, you can temporarily avoid this nasty legacy from 16-bit DOS programming. Eventually, you will want to move to Windows NT or Windows 95—where this problem disappears. Unfortunately, the large memory model (as well as the compact memory model) eventually present other programming problems under Windows. A detailed discussion of these problems is beyond the scope of *Internet Programming*. If you are new to Windows programming, you should read about Windows memory management in Charles Petzold's classic book, *Programming Windows 3.1, Third Edition*, Microsoft Press, 1992.

BEWARE OF CALLING CONVENTIONS

As you switch from Berkeley sockets in UNIX to Windows Sockets on a PC, you need to pay attention to function-calling conventions. As you may know, you always declare Windows functions as FAR PASCAL. The FAR keyword tells the compiler the functions may reside in a different code segment than your program's code. The PASCAL keyword tells the compiler to use the Pascal function-calling convention instead of the normal C-calling convention. By default, a C compiler generates code that pushes function parameters on the memory stack from right to left, beginning with the last parameter. Also, the code that calls the function must adjust the stack pointer after the function returns. This is the normal function calling sequence for the C programming language. When you specify a Pascal-calling convention, the compiler generates code to push function parameters on to the stack from left to right, and the called function cleans up the stack. Again, calling conventions may be unfamiliar to you if you have only a UNIX background. Your C compiler will warn you of inconsistent function use as long as you include the function prototypes defined in *winsock.h*. (Your C++ compiler will warn you if you forget to include a function prototype.)

Understanding Blocking

Because Windows is a programming environment in which multiple tasks appear to execute at the same time, you must understand how blocking affects program execution in order to write sophisticated Winsock programs. A blocking function will not let your program call another operation until after the function completes its assigned task. For example, if your program executes a function call that performs a disk read, your program will not execute the next program statement until the function finishes reading the disk. In effect, the call to the disk read function blocks the execution of any other program statements within that module. In socket terminology, you refer to the function's action as blocking.

In contrast, a non-blocking operation is one that completes immediately. For example, assume you write a program that draws graphical images on the screen until the user presses a keyboard key. If your program used a blocking function to read the keyboard, the function would stop the program's execution until the user presses the key. In other words, even the display of graphics would be on hold. A better solution would be to use a non-blocking function that quickly checks the keyboard for a keypress. If a keypress was present, this function would read it. If not, the function would return a value that indicates no key press so the program could continue.

Reviewing Program Execution Scenarios

Under DOS, each computer program statement must complete its task before the next program statement can execute. A single function call may cause a series of cascading events to occur in your computer. However, from a program perspective, only one program statement at a time executes. In a multi-tasking environment such as UNIX, multiple programs (tasks) can execute at the same time. As such, multiple tasks may seem to occur at the same time within your computer under UNIX. However, once again, within each executing program, only one program statement at a time executes. A similar process occurs within the cooperative multi-tasking environment of Windows 3.1.

Preemptive versus Cooperative Multi-tasking

On the surface, multi-tasking operating systems, such as Windows and UNIX, appear to manage simultaneous activity within your computer. However, as you may know, this is an illusion—the activity only appears to occur simultaneously. In reality, a multi-tasking operating system lets the computer's central processing unit (CPU) quickly move from one executing task to another. For example, Windows 3.1 lets a program execute one or more program statements, then lets a second program execute one or more program statements, and so on. Similarly, on a single-processor computer, most UNIX systems let multiple programs share a computer's CPU. However, Windows and UNIX do not achieve processor-sharing in the same way. Windows expects (and requires) cooperation from programs sharing the computer's CPU. UNIX, in contrast, preempts or interrupts a program to gain control of the CPU.

In other words, Windows 3.1 depends on each program to relinquish control of the CPU back to the operating system. Although Windows permits multiple tasks to execute, Windows expects each program to cooperate with the operating system and let other programs share the CPU. If a Windows program refuses to give up the computer's CPU, Windows is helpless (and locked up). Because Windows requires cooperation from programs, computer professionals call Windows a cooperative multi-tasking operating system.

To understand preemption and cooperation, think of the last time you had your favorite television show preempted by a news report. The UNIX operating system can do the same thing to your UNIX-based programs. UNIX does not need a program to cooperate with the operating system. When the operating system needs the CPU, UNIX can cause a program to temporarily stop executing. Within the Windows family of operating systems, Windows NT and Windows 95 are also preemptive operating systems. As you will learn in the following sections, preemptive and cooperative multi-tasking operating systems handle blocking operations quite differently.

BLOCKING THREADS OF EXECUTION

In a multi-threaded environment such as Windows NT, a single program can contain multiple threads of execution (scaled-down internal processes) that appear to execute at the same time. However, even in a multi-threaded environment, each program statement in a thread must finish its operation before the thread's next program statement can execute. Regardless of your operating system environment, every thread of execution for an application occurs one program statement at a time. Under DOS, only one program or thread of execution exists in the entire computer at any given instance. Under many UNIX systems, multiple threads of execution exist but only one thread per program. A multi-threaded environment, such as Windows NT, lets multiple threads of execution occur within the same program. However, in all cases, each thread executes one program statement at a time.

The purpose of driving this point home is to make clear that every operating system must contend with the problem of blocking. That is, within every operating system, a program or program thread can execute a statement that does not immediately complete its assigned task. In other words, the statement's operation causes the thread to block. For example, under DOS, a blocking operation causes all other computer activity to stop. Under many UNIX systems or Windows 3.1, a blocking operation causes all other activity to stop within the task that initiated the operation. Within Windows NT or Windows 95, a blocking operation stops all other activity for the thread that caused the blocking operation.

In a Winsock program, a call to a function that performs network I/O usually initiates a blocking operation. (As explained in the following section, your programs can prevent a blocking operation, but, by default, the functions discussed here will block.) For example, the connect function, which initiates a direct connection with a remote host, will block until the transport layer establishes the connection and notifies Winsock that the connection is ready for use. Likewise, when your program calls the recv function and no data exists in the incoming-data queue, the recv function blocks further program execution until data arrives at the socket's protocol port. Refer to Tables 8.2 and 8.4 for a list of other Winsock functions that can initiate blocking operations.

USING NON-BLOCKING FUNCTION CALLS

Both the Berkeley and Winsock APIs let your program execute function calls that do not perform blocking operations. To do so, however, your program must designate the socket it uses with the function as a non-blocking socket. Neither the Berkeley nor the Winsock APIs define separate functions for blocking and non-blocking operations. Whether a function blocks or not depends on the characteristics of the socket your program uses for the function call.

Suppose you want to call the recv function to retrieve data from a socket, but you can't afford to let the function block. (For example, your program may need to maintain a TCP connection with a remote host.) Furthermore, assume both your program and the remote host use the same connection to transmit messages to each other. However, suppose that the messages are not a one-for-one exchange. In other words, your program may transmit several messages to the remote host before it expects a reply. Under this scenario, if your program calls the recv function and the function blocks, the blocking operation will prevent your program from transmitting any more messages to the remote host. Quite possibly, the remote host may never respond until it receives another message from your program. In such cases, calling the recv function on a blocking socket will effectively hang your program—your program will wait forever for data from the remote host while the remote host waits forever for a message from your program.

Note: *You will see an example of this scenario in the FTP program examples in Section 3 of* **Internet Programming**.

To create a non-blocking socket, your program first creates and connects a socket using the socket and connect functions. Next, your program calls a Winsock function that changes the socket from blocking to non-blocking. (By default, both Berkeley and Winsock APIs create blocking sockets.) After you designate a socket as non-blocking, both Berkeley and Winsock APIs guarantee that no function that uses that socket—including the recv function—will cause a blocking operation.

What much socket literature does not make clear to many first-time users of a socket API is how a non-blocking socket works. There is no magical way to make a function not block. All the program statement execution scenarios previously described are still in play. In other words, within any thread of execution, the operating system still executes one program statement at a time. For example, suppose your program designates a socket as non-blocking. Also, suppose your program calls the recv function and finds that no data has arrived at the socket. If the recv function must wait for data to arrive at the socket, the recv function will block all other activity for that thread until data arrives. There is no way to force the recv function to wait and yet avoid a blocking operation. As such, you may wonder what happens when you use the recv function with a non-blocking socket that contains no data.

The answer is simple—nothing happens. When you use a non-blocking socket with a function call that would cause a blocking operation, the function returns an error. When you designate a socket as non-blocking, the socket implementation (UNIX kernel or WINSOCK.DLL) always checks to see if it can immediately complete any requested operations with that socket before it actually initiates the operation. If the socket implementation cannot immediately complete the function (that is, it cannot avoid a blocking operation), the socket implementation returns an error. If the requested function does not cause a blocking operation, the function completes normally.

The major problem with a lot of Winsock literature (and even the Winsock specification) is that it implies you can avoid many problems by using non-blocking sockets. While this is true, much of the literature treats a non-blocking socket as a magic bullet. In other words, the literature tells you that non-blocking sockets exist and that they are the solution to your problems, but the literature never gets around to telling you how to use them. As you have learned, a function call to a non-blocking socket returns an error if the function would cause a blocking operation. At first, given such results, you may wonder why you would want to use a non-blocking socket. You might also wonder how you get data out of a non-blocking socket.

NON-BLOCKING VERSUS ASYNCHRONOUS FUNCTIONS

Many first time Winsock users assume the asynchronous, Windows-specific functions in the Winsock API are the only non-blocking functions available. The Winsock specification helps foster this incorrect assumption by using non-blocking and asynchronous as synonymous terms. The specification also seems to imply that you can initiate a non-blocking operation only by using the asynchronous, Windows-specific functions in the Winsock API. This implication, as well as the specification's use (or misuse) of the terms *non-blocking* and *asynchronous*, is extremely misleading, especially if you are not familiar with Berkeley sockets.

As you have learned, after your program designates a socket as non-blocking, your program can use any Berkeley or Winsock function with that socket without initiating a blocking operation. In other words, Winsock does not restrict you to the asynchronous, Windows-specific functions for non-blocking operations. In fact, the Berkeley socket interface does not include any asynchronous functions. Yet, as you have learned, you can designate a Berkeley socket as non-blocking. There is an excellent reason why the Berkeley socket interface does not include any asynchronous functions—I/O in UNIX, where the sockets interface originated, is not asynchronous.

SYNCHRONOUS VERSUS ASYNCHRONOUS

UNIX I/O is synchronous, meaning that UNIX I/O operations occur at the same time as function calls. For example, in UNIX, a read or write function call will not return until the operation finishes. (As you have learned, in socket terminology, you refer to this action as blocking.) In asynchronous operations (including I/O), a program initiates an operation by calling a function that immediately returns. Although asynchronous operations are very much like non-blocking socket operations, there is a significant difference. An operation on a non-blocking socket that cannot immediately complete does nothing except return an error message. When your program makes an asynchronous function call, the fact that the operation cannot immediately complete does not cause an error.

An asynchronous function call is responsible only for initiating the operation—it does not wait around for the operation to complete. Instead, the operating system monitors the completion of the operation. Most operating systems that use asynchronous functions send a message to report success or failure of the asynchronous operation. Windows is an asynchronous operating system. Practically every event within Windows occurs asynchronously. When an event occurs or an asynchronous task completes, Windows sends a message to the object (usually a window) that your program specified when it initiated the asynchronous operation. In many cases, you can specify the message you want Windows to send.

Windows is not the only operating system that uses asynchronous functions. Even DOS performs asynchronous operations. For example, under DOS, if you press CTRL-C, an interrupt occurs. This interrupt is essentially an asynchronous message or signal to the operating system that says you want to interrupt or break out of the executing program. Most operating systems include a mechanism that handles certain types of asynchronous events. However, what distinguishes Windows from most other operating systems is that the entire operating system is primarily asynchronous. In other words, the foundation of the Windows operating system is an extensive collection of asynchronous messages that Windows sends in response to system events and application requests.

When you develop programs for the Windows environment, you use this message-based model (or paradigm). Typically, your program will generate its own asynchronous messages and corresponding actions, as well as handle asynchronous messages from the Windows operating system. In other words, to develop a sophisticated Windows program, you create sophisticated message handling routines. Likewise, to develop sophisticated Winsock programs, you create non-blocking operations with the asynchronous functions that the Winsock API provides. You should remember the following important points. An asynchronous operation is non-blocking. However, in the Winsock API, your programs don't need to use asynchronous functions to perform non-blocking socket operations.

REVISITING THE SELECT FUNCTION

As you have learned, the select function lets a single process monitor or determine the status of multiple sockets. As discussed, the select function lets you determine the read, write, and error status of multiple sockets. Winsock provides an asynchronous version of *select* named *WSAAsyncSelect*. The WSAAsyncSelect function is your key to non-blocking socket operations in Windows Sockets.

UNDERSTANDING THE *WSAAsyncSelect* FUNCTION

In the blocking socket scenario (with recv) discussed previously, your program can call the WSAAsyncSelect function to change the socket operation from blocking to non-blocking. The

WSAAsyncSelect function is the only asynchronous, Windows-specific function in the Winsock specification that uses a socket handle (descriptor) as a parameter. Other than being asynchronous, the major difference between the select and WSAAsyncSelect functions is that the select function monitors multiple sockets. Although your program can use the WSAAsyncSelect function to monitor multiple sockets, your program must issue a WSAAsyncSelect function call for each socket your program wants to monitor. In other words, WSAAsyncSelect only accepts one socket handle at a time as a parameter. The following program statement shows the Winsock prototype for the WSAAsyncSelect function:

```
int PASCAL FAR WSAAsyncSelect(SOCKET s, HWND hWnd, unsigned int wMsg,
     long lEvent);
```

As the WSAAsyncSelect's first parameter, your program specifies the handle of the socket you want it to monitor. The WSAAsyncSelect's fourth (and final) parameter is a bit mask that specifies which combination of network events you want your program to monitor. You can use the constants shown in Table 8.11 as lEvent parameter values for WSAAsyncSelect.

Constant	Meaning
FD_READ	Requests notification of readiness for reading.
FD_WRITE	Requests notification of readiness for writing.
FD_OOB	Requests notification of the arrival of out-of-band data.
FD_ACCEPT	Requests notification of incoming connections.
FD_CONNECT	Requests notification of completed connections.
FD_CLOSE	Requests notification of socket closure.

Table 8.11 Constants the WSAAsyncSelect function uses to request notification of network events.

To have your program monitor a socket for more than one event, you can combine the values shown in Table 8.11 using a bit-wise OR operation. For example, suppose you want Windows to send your program a message when a socket is ready to send data or when incoming data arrives. To do so, you would OR the FD_READ and FD_WRITE constants (FD_READ | FD_WRITE). When the status for the specified socket becomes true (for example, a socket contains data to read after a FD_READ request), Windows sends a message to your main Windows procedure (the same procedure that handles Windows messages such as WM_COMMAND). The WSAAsyncSelect function's second and third parameters are common parameters in Windows program functions. The third parameter, wMsg, defines the message you want Windows to send when the specified network event(s) occurs. The second parameter, hWnd, specifies the handle of the window to receive the message.

When one of the network events specified in your program's WSAAsyncSelect function call occurs, Windows sends a message in the standard Windows format. As you may know, the standard

Windows message includes a window handle, a message identifier, and two message parameters (a 16-bit parameter and a 32-bit parameter). The 16-bit message parameter Windows sends as a result of WSAAsyncSelect identifies the socket (by socket handle) on which the event occurred. The low 16 bits in the 32-bit parameter identifies the network event that occurred. The high 16 bits contains any error codes. If you consider the asynchronous, message-based nature of Windows, the fact that you must call the WSAAsyncSelect function for each socket you want to monitor makes sense. For example, at any given time, you may want your program to monitor several sockets for different network events. Likewise, a server may monitor several sockets for connection requests. Additionally, when a server negotiates a TCP connection with a client, the server may need to monitor one or more sockets for data arrival.

USING THE WSAASYNCSELECT FUNCTION

When you call the WSAAsyncSelect function, Winsock designates the socket your program specifies as non-blocking. Returning to the example in the previous section, suppose you want your program to use the recv function but do not want to risk a blocking operation. To do so, your program first uses the socket and connect functions to create and connect the socket. Then, your program calls the WSAAsyncSelect function (instead of the recv function). The WSAAsyncSelect has the following four parameters:

- Your socket handle

- The window you want to receive the message

- The message identifier to send

- The network event to report (which, in this case, is FD_READ)

In other words, the WSAAsyncSelect function tells Windows to notify your program when the socket is ready to read. When your socket receives data, Windows will send the corresponding message identifier to the window the WSAAsyncSelect function specifies. When the message handling procedure for this window receives the message, your program can execute code that calls the recv function. Since Windows only sends this message after data arrives at the socket, the recv function can probably retrieve the newly arrived data immediately, without risk of blocking. As you will learn, even under the circumstances just described, your Windows Sockets programs must handle other problems that blocking operations cause. However, using the WSAAsyncSelect function, your programs can avoid initiating a blocking operation with the recv function.

BLOCKING PROBLEMS UNDER WINDOWS 3.1

As you have learned, every operating system must contend with the problem of blocking function calls. Under a preemptive, multi-tasking operating system such as UNIX, a blocking operation that one function causes does not affect other computer processes. In effect, the process that causes the blocking operation goes to sleep until the blocking operation completes. All other processes continue to execute as normal. However, under Windows 3.1, a blocking operation causes serious problems. A blocking operation will cause *all* other processes under Windows to stop. All other processes stop because, under Windows, each program must voluntarily relinquish control before Windows can let another program continue to execute. Figure 8.2 shows the general program flow for a connection-oriented socket in Windows Sockets. The flow is practically the same as shown in Chapter 7 for the Berkeley sockets. The only difference is that Winsock uses the recv and send functions instead of the read and write functions.

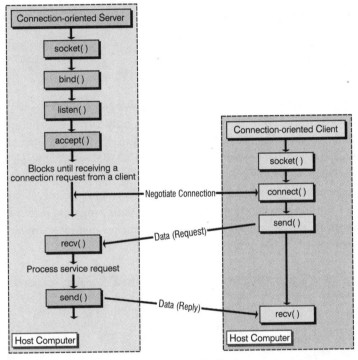

Figure 8.2 A connection-oriented socket in Windows Sockets.

In Figure 8.2, you need to focus on the point where the server blocks after it calls the accept function. As mentioned, due to the cooperative multi-tasking nature of Windows, a blocking operation in Windows will cause all other processes under Windows to stop. To prevent the occurrence of this problem, Winsock never permits a blocking operation to occur within Windows.

BLOCKING IN WINDOWS SOCKETS

The Winsock specification contains detailed technical discussions about blocking issues. However, the specification assumes a clear understanding of Windows operations that many programmers rarely need to consider. The following paragraphs provide a quick review of message handling processes in Windows.

Note: In the Winsock specification, see Section 3.1.1, **Blocking/Non blocking & Data Volatility,** and Section 3.3.3, **Hooking Blocking Methods,** for discussions of blocking.

WINDOWS MESSAGE HANDLING: A QUICK REVIEW

As you may know, Windows usually handles messages in a program loop that looks similar to the following program statements:

```
MSG msg;
while(GetMessage(&msg, NULL, 0, 0))
  {
    TranslateMessage(&msg);
    DispatchMessage(&msg);
  }
```

The previous *while* loop should be familiar to all Windows programmers—virtually every Windows program uses a similar loop to retrieve, process, and dispatch program messages. The GetMessage function receives a message from Windows itself. The TranslateMessage function, in turn, translates keystroke messages (such as WM_KEYDOWN or WM_SYSKEYDOWN) into character messages (such as WM_CHAR). Lastly, the DispatchMessage function sends all Windows messages to the window identified by the message. As you may know, Windows expects you to create a message-handling procedure for each window your program creates. For example, you typically will create one or more message-handling procedures that look similar to the following program statements:

```
long FAR PASCAL _export WndProc(HWND hwnd, UINT iMessage, UINT wParam,
    LONG lParam)
{
  LRESULT lResult;

  switch (iMessage)
    {
      case WM_PAINT:
        // Paint the window
        lResult = 0;
        break;

      case WM_COMMAND:
        // Respond to a command
        lResult = 0;
        break;

      case WM_DESTROY:
        // Exit the program
        PostQuitMessage(0);
        lResult = 0;
```

```
        break;

    default:
        lResult = DefWindowProc(hwnd, iMessage, wParam, lParam);
        break;
    }

    return(lResult);
}
```

Windows is responsible for sending all messages. However, many different events can cause Windows to create or generate a message. In some cases, a system event (such as an internal timer) can prompt Windows to generate a message. In other cases, a user action (such as re-sizing or closing a window) causes Windows to generate a message. A user can also select a menu option that causes Windows to generate a message. As such, you should design your Windows program to respond to messages that system events and user actions generate, as well as to activity that your program initiates. For example, suppose you design a menu that includes an option to send e-mail across the Internet. Windows will send a message when the user selects the send e-mail option. When your message-handling procedure receives this message, it will execute whatever program statements you defined for the *send e-mail* message.

In response to a user's request to send e-mail, your program will probably establish a network connection. Your program will probably also include function calls that cause Windows to send messages announcing the completion of certain steps in the connection process. For example, you might use the WSAAsyncSelect function to tell Windows to notify you when the connection is in place and ready for data transmission. In general, all Windows programs operate as described in the previous paragraphs. In other words, Windows programs perform their functions in response to asynchronous, message-based activity. UNIX programs are quite different. Although multi-tasking, UNIX is essentially a synchronous operating system. The challenge for Winsock developers was to design an asynchronous API derived from an API developed for a synchronous environment. To meet this challenge, Winsock developers created some clever work-around solutions to seemingly incompatible differences. The method Winsock uses to handle blocking function calls is a prime example of such solutions.

UNDERSTANDING THE BLOCKING HOOK

As previously mentioned, Winsock never permits a blocking operation to occur within Windows. Instead, when a program calls a function that would cause a blocking operation, Winsock enters a loop and repeatedly calls a *blocking handler* or *hook* routine. The purpose of the blocking handler is to intercept function calls that would cause a blocking operation. The standard Winsock blocking handler includes code that looks similar to the following program statements:

```
if (PeekMessage(&msg, NULL, 0, 0, PM_REMOVE))
```

```
{
    TranslateMessage(&msg);
    DispatchMessage(&msg);
}
```

The PeekMessage function checks the application's message queue for a message. If the PeekMessage finds a message, it places the message in a Windows MSG structure and returns a non-zero value. As you can see, this lets the TranslateMessage and DispatchMessage functions handle the message. Unlike GetMessage (the normal Windows message-handling function), PeekMessage doesn't wait for a message to arrive in the message queue. In effect, the blocking hook lets other Windows tasks continue to run. At the same time, the blocking hook processes messages for the current task, which would otherwise cause a blocking operation.

UNDERSTANDING THE PROBLEM

The blocking hook prevents Windows from "locking up" due to a blocking operation. However, the blocking hook presents another problem that the Winsock designers had to solve. When the blocking hook runs, it is possible that a Windows message may arrive for the current task, and that the arriving message might cause the program to call another Winsock function. With regard to this situation, Section 3.1.1 of the Winsock specification states, "Because of the difficulty of managing this condition safely, the Windows Sockets specification does not support such application behavior." In other words, anytime a Winsock blocking operation is in progress, your program cannot call any other Winsock functions. This restriction applies for blocking and non-blocking operations. As such, while Winsock keeps Windows from locking up due to a blocking operation, you, as a Winsock programmer, still face the same problem that Berkeley-socket API users face. When a blocking operation occurs, your program must wait for the operation to complete before your program can call any other Winsock functions.

MANAGING THE PROBLEM

Winsock provides two functions to help you detect and manage blocking operations: WSAIsBlocking and WSACancelBlockingCall. You can use these functions to determine if a blocking operation is occurring and, if so, to cancel the operation. The following program statements show the Winsock prototypes for both functions:

```
BOOL PASCAL FAR WSAIsBlocking(void);
int PASCAL FAR WSACancelBlockingCall(void);
```

As you can see, neither function accepts any parameters. You call the WSAIsBlocking function to determine whether a blocking operation is in progress. The WSAIsBlocking function returns the Boolean value True if a blocking operation is in progress and the Boolean value False if not. Depending on your program's requirements, you may choose to call the WSACancelBlockingCall function to cancel the blocking operation in progress. WSACancelBlockingCall will cause the blocking operation to fail. The function call that initiated the blocking operation, in turn, will return with the error value WSAEINTR. If you call any Winsock function other than WSAIsBlocking or WSACancelBlockingCall during a blocking operation, Winsock causes the function to return with the error WSAINPROGRESS.

CREATING YOUR OWN SOLUTION

A sophisticated program may require more complex message handling for blocking operations than the default Winsock procedures provide. For such programs, the Winsock API includes two functions that an advanced programmer can use to manage blocking operations: WSASetBlockingHook and WSAUnhookBlockingHook. The WSASetBlockingHook function lets you define and use your own blocking hook routine. The WSAUnhookBlockingHook function restores the default blocking hook. If you find it necessary to create your own blocking hook routine, you will want to study Section 4.3.13, *WSASetBlockingHook(),* in the Winsock specification very carefully. This section describes the WSASetBlockingHook function in detail. Section 4.3.13 also includes pseudo-code for the loop a Winsock implementation (WINSOCK.DLL) enters when a program initiates a blocking operation. This section also shows example code for the default blocking hook Winsock uses.

Note: You must address reentrancy issues when designing your own blocking hook routine. Before you implement your own blocking hook, be sure you have a clear understanding of the problems that reentrant code can introduce and how to avoid those problems. Reentrancy issues are beyond the scope of this book.

BLOCKING UNDER WINDOWS NT AND WINDOWS 95

As discussed, blocking operations can occur under any operating system. For multi-tasking, multi-threading operating systems such as Windows NT and Windows 95, blocking occurs on a thread-by-thread basis. Because the multi-threaded versions of Window are preemptive multi-taskers, blocking operations within a thread do not affect other threads or tasks within the Windows environment.

Winsock does not include a blocking hook for multi-threaded versions of Windows. When a blocking operation occurs in the multi-threaded versions of Windows, all further activity in the thread stops until the blocking operation completes. However, Winsock lets you use the WSASetBlockingHook function within Windows NT and Windows 95. As such, you can implement your own blocking hook on a thread-by-thread basis under these versions of Windows.

By permitting you to implement your own blocking hook on a thread-by-thread basis, Winsock lets you more easily port 16-bit (Windows 3.1) applications to the 32-bit versions of Windows (Windows NT and Windows 95). For example, suppose you develop a Winsock program that requires a custom blocking hook. Also, suppose that you later decide to port your program to

Windows NT. Remember, by default, Windows NT blocks just like a UNIX program when a blocking operation occurs within a thread of execution. Since you designed your program to use a custom blocking hook, the default behavior of Windows NT for blocking operations might cause a problem. However, since Winsock lets you use custom blocking hooks (by calling WSASetBlockingHook on a thread-by-thread basis), you can overcome any problems by porting your custom blocking hook also.

PUTTING IT ALL TOGETHER

In this chapter, you learned that Winsock, which manages the interface between your Windows programs and the TCP/IP protocol stack, resides where you might expect: between your Windows programs and the TCP/IP protocols. In general, you found that using sockets in Windows is very similar to performing operations with Berkeley sockets. You also learned how Windows uses a blocking hook function to simulate the UNIX blocking operations that occur in Berkeley sockets.

This chapter discussed the differences between Berkeley sockets and Winsock, such as the new Winsock header file, the new Winsock socket descriptors, and Winsock's method of handling socket errors. This chapter also explained how to use the new Windows-specific socket functions to perform asynchronous Winsock operations and manage blocking sockets. In the next chapter, which starts section 2 of this book, you will begin to develop Internet programs built on the TCP/IP protocols. To do so, you will use the Winsock API described in this chapter. Before you move on to Chapter 9, make sure you understand the following key concepts:

- ✓ Winsock implements the socket API as a DLL named WINSOCK.DLL.

- ✓ Winsock functions fall into one of three categories: socket functions, Internet database functions, or Windows-specific asynchronous functions.

- ✓ Winsock manages the interface between your Windows applications and the TCP/IP protocols.

- ✓ You can develop Winsock-based network programs on a network or on a stand-alone PC attached to the Internet through a serial connection.

- ✓ Winsock simulates a blocking operation by passing blocking function calls to a blocking hook function that lets normal Windows processes continue.

- ✓ Winsock does not define blocking and non-blocking functions—Winsock programs designate sockets (not functions) as blocking or non-blocking.

Chapter 9
Understanding the Domain Name System

In Chapter 4, you learned that an Internet address is a 32-bit number. Normally, users (as well as programmers) use dotted-decimal notation to specify an Internet or IP address. However, as shown here, it's possible for you to express an IP address using binary, decimal, hexadecimal, and dotted-decimal notation:

IP Address as a binary number:	10000110 00011000 00001000 01000010
IP Address as a decimal number:	2,249,721,922
IP Address as a hexadecimal number:	0x86180842
IP Address in dotted-decimal notation:	134.24.8.66

By far, dotted-decimal notation is the easiest for people to read and remember. However, using dotted-decimal notation for IP addresses is still little like trying to remember all your friends by their social security numbers instead of their names. Most people find names easier to use and remember. For this reason, network designers developed Internet's Domain Name System (DNS). The Domain Name System lets Internet users refer to host computers by names, such as cerfnet.com, instead of IP addresses, such as 192.102.249.3. By the time you finish this chapter, you will understand the following key concepts:

- How the Internet uses a distributed database to store domain names

- How the Domain Name System lets users refer to host computers by names rather than dotted-decimal or 32-bit binary addresses

- How the Internet uses name servers to translate (resolve) domain names into 32-bit or dotted-decimal addresses (and vice-versa)

- How to create a client program that translates domain names to 32-bit or dotted-decimal IP addresses (and vice-versa)

As you write Internet programs, you will need to use Internet addresses. In many cases, your programs will ask the user to enter an Internet address. People that use your programs will usually want to specify an address using a host-computer name, such as cerfnet.com, rather than a dotted-decimal IP address, such as 192.102.249.3. Likewise, if your program displays the address of a host computer, most users will expect the program to display the address as a name. Other times, the user may want to know the name and dotted-decimal address of a host computer. Internally, however, your programs will work in terms of 32-bit Internet addresses. As such, most of your Internet programs will convert between host-computer names and 32-bit IP addresses. The point to remember is that each address technique represents the same Internet address.

USING DNS AS AN EXAMPLE

The Internet Domain Name System lets your programs use a domain name, such as *jamsa.com*, to refer to a host computer. As you will learn, the Windows Sockets API hides most of the details that surround the Internet's Domain Name System. In fact, you could probably develop a wide variety of successful Internet programs without understanding any DNS details. However, it is to your advantage to understand the details. The more you learn about the Internet's Domain Name System, the better you'll be able to design practical network applications. For example, more and more businesses connect to the Internet every day. Big and small companies alike are rushing to take advantage of the Internet's distributed database capabilities. As such, the more you understand about distributed databases, the more attractive your services as a network programmer will be to the corporate world. Fortunately for you, the Internet's Domain Name System (the subject of this chapter) is an excellent example of a distributed database system.

A *distributed database* physically stores data on two or more computer systems. To programs that use the data, the geographic location of the computers is irrelevant. In other words, the "database" might include files stored on computers located in California and New York. The distributed-database software manages and controls the entire collection of data as a single database. Although you may never design a Domain Name System, you can apply the Internet's DNS design principles to distributed databases in general. The Internet's Domain Name System provides a good case study of how you might implement a distributed database on the Internet. As you learn about the Internet's DNS, you should understand that the DNS illustrates how to implement a large-scale, distributed database system using the client/server program paradigm.

FLAT NAME-SPACE VERSUS HIERARCHICAL NAMES

Originally, the Internet used a flat name-space for interconnected computers and networks. In other words, the Internet designers did not structure computer names to represent relationships between the interconnected computers and networks. For example, on a smaller scale, a business might use names such as *payroll, accounting, timekeeping, production*, and *research* to identify computers in a flat name-space model. The computers named *payroll, accounting*, and *timekeeping* might all belong to the company's Accounting and Finance division. However, the computer names themselves do not indicate any such relationship.

In contrast, a hierarchical-naming system is similar to the organization chart that exists within most large companies. For example, at the top of an organization chart, you usually have the President, CEO, or Chairman of the Board. The next lower level in the organization chart might have division managers. The company might further break each division into departments. The organization chart reflects the structural make-up of the company. A hierarchical-naming system represents host-computer names in a structure similar to a company organization chart. At the top of the hierarchical-naming structure is a single entity that has overall responsibility for decisions. The top-level entity then delegates responsibility to lower-level portions of the organization.

INTERNET USES A HIERARCHICAL-NAMING SCHEME

As you have learned, every Internet host computer must have a unique address. In the early days of the Internet, a flat name-space was not a problem—the Internet only interconnected a few dozen networks. Assigning unique addresses to each computer was easy. However, as the Internet's size grew, the work required to maintain the list of addresses also grew. Today, over 20,000 computer networks (each containing multiple computers) connect to the Internet. Each of these millions of computers requires a unique address. Because the task of assigning unique addresses for all these systems would far exceed the ability of any single organization, the Internet's original flat-address space naming system evolved into a hierarchical scheme. A hierarchical-naming system decentralizes authority and responsibility for assigning names. In other words, many different organizations are responsible for assigning unique addresses at different levels of the hierarchy. In this way, no single organization carries the burden for the entire Internet.

Telephone numbers represent an example of a hierarchical-naming scheme. In the United States, a ten-digit telephone number consists of a three-digit area code, a three-digit prefix or exchange, and a four-digit number that represents a specific telephone connection. The area code represents a specific geographic region of the country. The prefix represents a smaller area within that region. This hierarchical-naming scheme simplifies the routing of phone calls through the telephone networks. As you can imagine, assigning millions of phone numbers is a huge task. Fortunately, no single organization assigns phone numbers for the entire country. First, government and commercial organizations divide the country into area codes. Within each area code, telephone service organizations assign prefixes. Then, the local telephone company assigns the unique four-digit numbers. In other words, the entire system is decentralized and somewhat hierarchical.

Like the US telecommunications system, the Internet uses a hierarchical-naming scheme. However, the Internet does not orient host computer names geographically or physically. In other words, the Internet's naming system does not assign names based on a computer's physical location. As such, two computer networks that exist in the same city or state will not necessarily share similar names. Likewise, the Internet's naming system also avoids using a computer's physical network connections to derive a name. As such, two computers you connect to the same physical network may not necessarily share similar names.

UNDERSTANDING A DOMAIN NAMING SYSTEM

The Internet's DNS uses names like *ftp.microsoft.com* to identify a specific computer. You refer to each element of the name as a *label*. For example, ftp.microsoft.com consists of three labels: *ftp*, *microsoft,* and *com.* You separate Internet name labels with a period that you read as the word *dot.* In other words, you would say the name *ftp.microsoft.com* as f-t-p dot Microsoft dot com.

One definition of *domain* is *a sphere of activity, concern, or function.* This definition describes how the Internet assigns computer names. For example, consider the computer name *ftp.microsoft.com.* The label ftp indicates that the computer is an ftp site, which describes the computer's function (to support file transfer operations). The label *microsoft* describes the organization or entity that owns the computer—Microsoft Corporation. The label *com* tells you that the organization uses the computer for commercial enterprises. In other words, each label in the computer name *ftp.microsoft.com* is a domain that describes a sphere of activity, concern, or function.

Defining the Structure of the Internet's DNS

View the Internet's DNS like a corporate organization chart. At the top of the chart is an unnamed starting point you can call the root. The DNS root is like the root directory on your computer's disk—neither root has a name. However, like directories on your computer, each domain has a name. Just as you can further divide each directory on your computer into subdirectories, the Internet DNS further divides each domain into sub-domains. Figure 9.1 shows the hierarchical structure of the Internet's DNS.

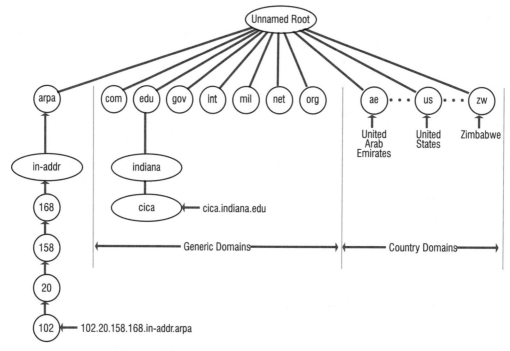

Figure 9.1 *The hierarchical structure of the Internet's Domain Name System.*

The level immediately below the root of the Internet DNS consists of three top-level domains:

1. *Arpa* is a special Internet domain that maps dotted-decimal IP addresses to domain names rather than domain names to dotted-decimal addresses.

2. The generic or organizational group consists of three-character domain labels such as *com, edu,* and *gov.*

3. The country or geographical group consists of domain labels that represent two-character country codes that the International Standards Organization defines in the document ISO 3166.

If you've surfed Internet sites in the past, you may be most familiar with the generic or organizational domains. The Internet normally divides this group of domains into seven basic categories. Table 9.1 identifies the seven basic classifications of the organizational domains.

Domain	Description
com	Commercial organizations, such as businesses
edu	Educational organizations, such as universities
gov	US government organizations
int	International organizations
mil	US military organizations
net	A network that doesn't fit into one of the other organizational domain categories
org	An organization that doesn't fit into one of the other organizational domain categories

Table 9.1 The normal three-character generic or organizational domains.

Contrary to popular opinion, the Internet does not restrict the use of three-character organizational domains to the United States. Only the gov and mil domains strictly represent US government and US military organizations. All the other generic or organizational domains include many non-US organizations. Likewise, many organizations in the US use the two-character country code for the United States (*us*) rather than a three-character organizational domain.

ASSIGNING RESPONSIBILITIES

As previously mentioned, the major problem with a flat name-space is the workload it generates for the organization that has to assign names. The hierarchical-naming system delegates responsibility for assigning names at different levels of the hierarchy. The Internet Network Information Center (InterNIC) manages the top-level domain names. The InterNIC delegates responsibility for assigning names to different organizations. Each organization is responsible for a specific portion of the DNS tree structure. Internet professionals refer to these areas of responsibility as *zones*. In other words, the InterNIC delegates responsibility for assigning names within a specific zone (portion of the DNS tree structure) to specific organizations. The organization responsible for a specific zone can further subdivide the zone and delegate responsibility for assigning names. For example, a business might divide itself into zones based on divisions, and each division might partition itself into zones based on departments. This subdivision normally continues until one person can manage the responsibility for name assignments within a well-defined zone. You refer to such an individual as a DNS administrator. A DNS administrator must set up name servers for his or her zone.

Understanding the Name Server Concept

As discussed, network-computer users generally prefer to use domain names instead of dotted-decimal addresses. However, internally, when they call socket functions, your programs need to use 32-bit IP addresses. As such, to ensure successful internetwork communications between your programs and users, you need a fast, reliable method of translating between address schemes. For this reason, network designers developed name-server software. A *name server* is a program that translates domain names into IP addresses. Across the Internet, thousands of computers contain special name-server software. When your programs need to connect to a particular host, they typically first contact a name-server program and request a DNS lookup service. Such DNS queries usually store data in a data structure that contains the host's name, dotted-decimal address, and 32-bit binary address.

In many cases, an organization may dedicate a computer to run the name-server program. In such cases, you can refer to the computer itself as a name server. DNS lookup services are critical operations. Unless an Internet program can translate domain names into binary IP addresses, no internetwork communication can occur. As you will learn, each zone in the Domain Name System includes one primary name server and at least one or more secondary (backup) name servers. One important point to note, however, is that name servers are hierarchical. In other words, no particular name server knows every address on the Internet. As previously mentioned, DNS is a (client/server-based) distributed database system—the DNS distributes specific address details among various name servers. However, by talking to each other (server to server), name servers can resolve any address on the Internet. Figure 9.2 shows the conceptual layout of the Internet's name servers.

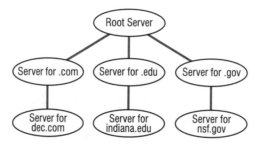

Figure 9.2 A conceptual arrangement of name servers on the Internet.

Conceptually, the root (top-level) server knows which name server can resolve names for each top level domain. The second-level servers can identify the correct name server for each sub-domain and so on. DNS uses the client/server paradigm. You refer to the client software used with DNS as a *name resolver* or just resolver. The general concept is that your programs (through a name resolver) ask a name server to resolve a DNS address query.

In theory, a resolver contacts the root server with a request to translate a name into an IP address. The root server, in turn, hands the resolver's request to the appropriate second-level name server, which then passes the request down the hierarchical tree. Eventually, the resolver's query reaches a name server that can do the translation. At that point, the name server returns, to the requesting resolver, the IP address that corresponds to the computer name in the resolver's request.

UNDERSTANDING THE REALITY

In reality, a single name server can contain large portions of the name-server tree. In other words, the name-server tree is broad and shallow with very few levels. As a result, the server doesn't have to pass a name query to very many name servers before the Internet DNS can resolve the name. Figure 9.3 shows a more realistic layout of name servers on the Internet.

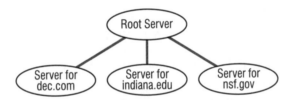

Figure 9.3 *A realistic arrangement of name servers on the Internet.*

Each name server is responsible for one or more zones in the DNS tree. As discussed, a DNS administrator must set up name servers for their zones of responsibility. The Internet requires each zone to have a primary name-server and one or more secondary name-servers. In general, secondary servers provide a backup mechanism should the primary server fail (or become overloaded with queries).

A primary name-server stores DNS information locally. In other words, a primary name-server loads DNS information from files stored on the name-server computer system. A secondary name-server collects information from the primary name-server in the zone. You refer to the process of a secondary name-server obtaining information from a primary name-server as a *zone transfer*. Typically, a secondary name-server will query the primary name-server every few hours.

The primary and secondary name-servers do not depend on each other. In fact, they contain redundant information. The purpose of using multiple name-servers for the same zone is to increase DNS reliability. By using more than one name-server for each zone, the failure of a single system in a zone cannot cripple the Internet DNS.

RESOLVING NAMES INTO IP ADDRESSES

The actual process of using DNS to resolve names significantly differs from the conceptual process. In reality, a client (resolver) contacts the name server for a zone. The server examines the query to determine if it has authority for the specified domain. If so, the server translates the name into an IP address, using the local name-server database, and sends the answer to the client.

When the contacted server in the zone cannot resolve the name, the server's response depends on the type of query sent by the resolver. Resolvers can request a domain name translation in one of two ways. First, the resolver can ask the server to perform the complete translation. The official terminology to describe this type of query is *recursive resolution*. If the client requests recursive resolution and the server cannot resolve the name, the server will contact a domain-name server that can resolve the name and then return the answer to the client.

Resolvers can also request *iterative resolution* of domain names. A request for iterative resolution tells the server to either resolve the name or tell the client which server to contact next. In other words, when a server receives a request for iterative resolution and cannot resolve the domain name, the server will tell the client which server to contact next. The server does not handle the complete resolution for the client.

UNDERSTANDING NAME SERVER COMMUNICATIONS

A name server does not have to know the name or IP address of every other name server in the Domain Name System. Instead, every name server in the DNS must know how to contact the root name servers. The configuration files for each primary name server contain the IP address of each root name server. The root servers must know the name and IP address of every second-level domain name server. Table 9.2 shows the DNS root name servers, as of May 1994.

HOSTNAME	NET ADDRESSES	SERVER PROGRAM
NS.NIC.DDN.MIL	192.112.36.4	bind (UNIX)
AOS.BRL.MIL	128.63.4.82	bind (UNIX)
	26.3.0.29	
	192.5.25.82	
C.NYSER.NET	192.33.4.12	bind (UNIX)
TERP.UMD.EDU	128.8.10.90	bind (UNIX)
NS.NASA.GOV	192.52.195.10	bind (UNIX)
	128.102.16.10	

Table 9.2 Internet root domain name servers as of May 1994. (continued on the next page)

HOSTNAME	NET ADDRESSES	SERVER PROGRAM
NIC.NORDU.NET	192.36.148.17	bind (UNIX)
NS1.ISI.EDU	128.9.0.107	bind (UNIX)
NS.ISC.ORG	192.5.5.241	bind (UNIX)
NS.INTERNIC.NET	198.41.0.4	bind (UNIX)

Table 9.2 Internet root domain name servers as of May 1994. (continued from the previous page)

Note: The file **netinfo/root-servers.txt** on **nic.ddn.mil** always contains the current list of root name servers. You can retrieve this file using anonymous ftp.

UNDERSTANDING THE RESOLVER

You refer to special client-side functions within the DNS client/server software as the "resolver" or "name resolver." The Windows Sockets API provides two resolver functions: gethostbyaddr and gethostbyname. As their names imply, both functions get or retrieve host-computer information. Your programs (through the gethostbyaddr or gethostbyname functions) use the name-resolver process to resolve IP and domain name addresses. In both cases, the resolver functions contact one or more name servers to return the requested information. In other words, your programs call a resolver function to resolve an address. The resolver function, in turn, opens up a communication channel to a domain server to query the server about your address. When the resolver function has the address information, it ends its communication with the server and returns the result to your program.

The following program, QLookup (Quick Lookup), illustrates the basic steps required to access a domain name server. QLookup strips away everything except the bare essentials so you can focus on the gethostbyaddr and gethostbyname functions. By "hard coding" values and using message boxes, the program avoids the overhead associated with a Windows user interface and window message handling. You can find QLOOKUP.CPP on the companion disk included with *Internet Programming*. The following section discusses QLookup in detail. Shown here is the complete program listing for QLookup:

```
#include "..\winsock.h"

#define PROG_NAME "Simple DNS Lookup"

#define HOST_NAME "CERFNET.COM"      // This can be any valid host name
#define WINSOCK_VERSION 0x0101       // Program requires Winsock version 1.1
#define AF_INET_LENGTH 4             // Address length for Internet protocol
                                     // family is always 4 bytes
#define HOST_ADDR "129.79.26.27" // winftp.cica.indiana.edu
```

```
int PASCAL WinMain(HANDLE hInstance, HANDLE hPrevInstance,
    LPSTR lpszCmdParam, int nCmdShow)
{
  WSADATA wsaData;            // Winsock implementation details
  LPHOSTENT lpHostEnt;        // Internet host information structure
  DWORD dwIPAddr;             // IP address as an unsigned long
  LPSTR szIPAddr;             // IP address as a dotted decimal string

  if (WSAStartup(WINSOCK_VERSION, &wsaData))
    MessageBox(NULL, "Could not load Windows Sockets DLL.", PROG_NAME,
        MB_OK|MB_ICONSTOP);

  else// Resolve the host name
    {
      lpHostEnt = gethostbyname(HOST_NAME);

      if (!lpHostEnt)
        MessageBox(NULL, "Could not get IP address!", HOST_NAME,
            MB_OK|MB_ICONSTOP);

      else // Convert the IP address into a dotted-decimal string
        {
          szIPAddr = inet_ntoa(*(LPIN_ADDR)*(lpHostEnt->h_addr_list));

          MessageBox(NULL, szIPAddr, lpHostEnt->h_name,
              MB_OK|MB_ICONINFORMATION);
        }

      // Convert a dotted-decimal string into a 32-bit IP address
      dwIPAddr = inet_addr(HOST_ADDR);

      if (dwIPAddr == INADDR_NONE)
        MessageBox(NULL, "Invalid Internet address!", HOST_ADDR,
            MB_OK|MB_ICONSTOP);

      else// Resolve the IP address
        {
          lpHostEnt = gethostbyaddr((LPSTR) &dwIPAddr, AF_INET_LENGTH,
              AF_INET);

          if (!lpHostEnt)
            MessageBox(NULL, "Could not get host name!", HOST_ADDR,
                MB_OK|MB_ICONSTOP);
          else
            MessageBox(NULL, lpHostEnt->h_name, HOST_ADDR,
                MB_OK|MB_ICONINFORMATION);
        }
    }
}
```

```
    WSACleanup(); // Free all allocated program resources and exit
    return(NULL);
}
```

CREATING THE QUICK LOOKUP PROGRAM

The first line of QLookup includes the Windows Sockets header file, winsock.h:

```
#include "..\winsock.h"
```

As you have learned, you should include this header file in every program file that uses the Windows Sockets API. The winsock.h header file defines commonly used Windows Sockets constants and declares function prototypes for the entire Windows Sockets API.

USING "..\WINSOCK.H"

As you review the program examples contained on the *Internet Programming* companion disk, you will repeatedly encounter *include* statements similar to the one shown here:

```
#include "..\winsock.h"
```

As you probably know, the two dots in front of the back-slash ("..\") indicate that the winsock.h file resides in the directory immediately above the current subdirectory. Every Winsock program should include the winsock.h header file. This header file contains useful symbolic constants, as well as function prototypes for the functions in the WINSOCK.DLL.

If you are primarily a Winsock developer, you will probably want to copy this header file to your compiler's include directory (with all your compiler's other header files). If, for whatever reason, you prefer not to mix winsock.h with your compiler's other header files, one option is to copy the header file to the subdirectory where all your other project files reside. For example, if you are a new Winsock programmer, you may want to keep the winsock.h header file in an easily accessible location so you can refer to it when you have questions.

Rather than arbitrarily make such decisions for you, the *Internet Programming* setup program copies the winsock.h header file to a single directory—the parent directory for all the other *Internet Programming* example programs. Feel free to copy the winsock.h header file to the subdirectory containing your compiler's other header files and change the include statements in the example programs to this:

```
#include <winsock.h>
```

> Or, if you prefer, you can copy the header file to the current working directory for your project and change the include statement to this:
>
> ```
> #include "winsock.h"
> ```
>
> The include statements in example programs assume you will try to compile the programs from their installed directories. As such, if you decide to copy the program examples to a directory other than the original installation directories, be sure to change the include statements as appropriate. Otherwise, your compiler will protest that it cannot find the winsock.h header file.

As you may know, most Windows programs require you to include the windows.h header file. Near the top or beginning of winsock.h, you can find the following program statements:

```
#ifndef _INC_WINDOWS
#include <windows.h>
#endif
```

These three lines, in effect, automatically include windows.h for you if you haven't already included it. The windows.h header file includes the following program statements that help prevent programs from including the header file more than once:

```
#ifndef _INC_WINDOWS
#define _INC_WINDOWS // #defined if windows.h has been included
```

DEFINING CONSTANT VALUES

Following the winsock.h include statement, QLookup uses the following five statements to define constant values the program requires:

```
#define PROG_NAME "Simple DNS Lookup"
#define HOST_NAME "CERFNET.COM"    // This can be any valid host name
#define WINSOCK_VERSION 0x0101     // Program requires Winsock version 1.1
#define AF_INET_LENGTH 4           // Address length for Internet protocol
                                   // family is always 4 bytes
#define HOST_ADDR "129.79.26.27"   // winftp.cica.indiana.edu
```

WINSOCK_VERSION defines the version of the Windows Sockets API the program requires (version 1.1). AF_INET_LENGTH defines the length (in bytes) of the address the gethostbyaddr function uses. You will use these two constants in many of the Internet programs included in *Internet Programming*.

PROG_NAME simply defines the name or a description of this program. You can use this constant throughout the program. As you will discover, most of the programs require the same initial steps. If you reuse the initial setup code, you can change all references to a program's name by simply changing the value of PROG_NAME.

HOST_NAME and HOST_ADDR specify the name and address of a host computer on the Internet. You can change these values to any valid host name and IP address. For QLookup, the host name and IP address do not need to specify the same host computer. For example, 129.79.26.27 is the IP address for winftp.cica.indiana.edu—not cerfnet.com.

DECLARING VARIABLES

The next several lines in QLookup begin the definition of the WinMain function (which every Windows program requires) and declare three local variables: dwIPAddr, wsaData, and lpHostEnt.

```
int PASCAL WinMain(HANDLE hInstance, HANDLE hPrevInstance,
    LPSTR lpszCmdParam, int nCmdShow)
{
  WSADATA wsaData;              // Winsock implementation details
  LPHOSTENT lpHostEnt;          // Internet host information structure
  DWORD dwIPAddr;               // IP address as an unsigned long
  LPSTR szIPAddr;               // IP address as a dotted decimal string
```

As you learned in Chapter 3, an IP address is a 32-bit value. The variable dwIPAddr is an unsigned long (double word or DWORD) that QLookup uses to store a binary (32-bit) representation of an IP address. As you have learned, WSADATA defines a data structure that contains version, description, status, and socket information about a Windows Sockets DLL. QLookup uses wsaData to store details about the Windows Sockets implementation. As discussed, you use the gethostbyaddr and gethostbyname functions to access a DNS name resolver. Both functions return information about the host computer. Windows Sockets stores host computer information in a special host-entry data structure. The data type LPHOSTENT declares a pointer variable that points to a host-entry data structure. You can find the host-entry data structure shown next in winsock.h:

```
struct hostent
{
  charFAR * h_name;
  charFAR * FAR * h_aliases;
  short h_addrtype;
  short h_length;
  char FAR * FAR * h_addr_list;
#define h_addr h_addr_list[0]   // Address, for backward compatibility
};
```

Table 9.3 describes each element in the data structure.

Element	Usage
h_name	Official name of the host
h_aliases	A NULL-terminated array of alternate names
h_addrtype	The type of address being returned; for Windows Sockets, this is always AF_INET.
h_length	The length, in bytes, of each address. For AF_INET, this value is always 4. (*Internet Programming* uses the constant AF_INET_LENGTH for this value throughout the sample programs.)
h_addr_list	A NULL-terminated list of addresses for the host. Windows Sockets returns these addresses in network byte-order.

Table 9.3 *Elements in the Windows Sockets host-entry data structure.*

QLookup uses LPHOSTENT to declare the variable lpHostEnt. QLookup will use lpHostEnt to store host computer information the gethostbyname and gethostbyaddr functions return.

INITIALIZING THE WINSOCK DLL

As you have learned, the Windows Sockets API requires you to call the WSAStartup function before you can use any other Windows Sockets function. The next few lines in QLookup simply initialize the Windows Sockets DLL by calling WSAStartup. QLookup then checks the value WSAStartup returns. (WSAStartup returns a zero, if successful, and an error code if not successful.) WSAStartup uses the standard Windows MessageBox function to display an error message if the function fails:

```
if (WSAStartup(WINSOCK_VERSION, &wsaData))
    MessageBox(NULL, "Could not load Windows Sockets DLL.", PROG_NAME,
        MB_OK|MB_ICONSTOP);
else
{
    // Continue with the program
}

WSACleanup();  // Free all allocated program resources and exit
return(NULL);
```

As shown in the above code fragment, the QLookup program will exit if the WSAStartup function fails. As you have learned, the WSACleanup function deregisters the calling program from the Winsock DLL. You should always call WSACleanup before exiting a Windows Sockets application. Doing so lets the Winsock DLL free any resources allocated on behalf of your program. QLookup always returns NULL when it exits.

GETTING HOST INFORMATION USING A COMPUTER NAME

As you have learned, the Windows Sockets API includes seven database functions that retrieve information about host computers, protocols, and communication services. The gethostbyname function, for example, returns host information corresponding to a hostname. The following program statement shows the function prototype for gethostbyname:

```
struct hostent FAR * PASCAL FAR gethostbyname(const char FAR * name);
```

To use gethostbyname, you pass it a single parameter that is a pointer to a host computer name, such as cerfnet.com. The following statement in QLookup calls the gethostbyname function:

```
lpHostEnt = gethostbyname(HOST_NAME);
```

In this case, QLookup uses the constant HOST_NAME to pass to gethostbyname the host-computer name *cerfnet.com*. The gethostbyname function, in turn, resolves the address and returns a pointer to a host-entry structure. Within this structure, QLookup uses the LPHOSTENT variable lpHostEnt to store this pointer value.

UNDERSTANDING THE GETHOSTBYNAME FUNCTION

The pointer returned by the gethostbyname function points to a host-entry structure that the Windows Sockets library allocates. Windows Sockets only keeps one copy of this structure. As such, the data area pointed to by gethostbyname's return value is volatile (not constant) on a per-program basis. The Windows Sockets specification guarantees the validity of this data only until your program's next Winsock API function call.

In other words, the Windows Sockets specification lets Winsock DLL implementations reuse this data area with each call to a Winsock API function. As such, after you call gethostbyname and before you call any other Windows Sockets function, you must copy any values that you need from the host-entry structure pointed to by gethostbyname into variables that you allocate and control.

USING WINDOWS SOCKETS POINTER VALUES

Like gethostbyname, most Windows Sockets API functions that return pointer variables use volatile data areas. As you develop Internet applications using the Windows Sockets API, you should habitually follow these steps:

> 1. Call the desired Windows Sockets API function.
>
> 2. If the function returns a pointer, you should immediately use the pointer value or copy any values that you want to use later into variables that you allocate and control.
>
> 3. Call additional Windows Sockets API functions as required.
>
> Many Windows Sockets API functions return pointer values that point to volatile data areas. If you neglect to copy data pointed to by these variables into your own variables, you risk using invalid data.

As shown in the following program statements, the next several lines in QLookup test the return value from gethostbyname and display the results:

```
lpHostEnt = gethostbyname(HOST_NAME);

if (!lpHostEnt)
   MessageBox(NULL, "Could not get IP address!", HOST_NAME,
       MB_OK|MB_ICONSTOP);

else // Convert the IP address into a dotted-decimal string
{
   szIPAddr = inet_ntoa(*(LPIN_ADDR)*(lpHostEnt->h_addr_list));

   MessageBox(NULL, szIPAddr, lpHostEnt->h_name,
       MB_OK|MB_ICONINFORMATION);
}
```

If gethostbyname cannot resolve the host name pointed to by your parameter, it will return a NULL pointer. If lpHostEnt is not NULL, QLookup uses the Windows MessageBox function to display the host IP address in dotted-decimal format.

Understanding the inet_ntoa Function

As you have learned, the host-entry element, h_addr_list, points to a list of IP addresses that belong to the host computer. Remember, a single host computer can contain multiple network interface cards and thus multiple IP addresses. QLookup uses the inet_ntoa function to convert the first address pointed to by h_addr_list into a character string formatted as a dotted-decimal address. The following program statement shows the function prototype for inet_ntoa:

```
char FAR * PASCAL FAR inet_ntoa(struct in_addr in);
```

As you can see, the inet_ntoa function requires you to pass, as a parameter, an in_addr structure. The in_addr structure uses a union to conveniently store a 32-bit IP address three ways: as four bytes, two 16-bit values, or as a single 32-bit number. Within the winsock.h header file, you will find the in_addr structure definition shown here:

```
struct in_addr
{
  union
    {
      struct          // IP address in bytes
        {
          u_char      // (Four 8-bit byte values)
            s_b1,     // Byte 1 (the high order byte)
            s_b2,     // Byte 2
            s_b3,     // Byte 3
            s_b4;     // Byte 4 (the low order byte)
        } S_un_b;
      struct          // IP address as two 16 bit values
        {
          u_short
            s_w1,     // 1st 16 bits (high order)
            s_w2;     // 2nd 16 bits (low order)
        } S_un_w;
      u_long S_addr;  // IP address as a 32-bit value
    } S_un;
}
```

Note: As you can see, the in_addr structure conveniently stores IP addresses in every possible format that your programs might need. As such, this address structure helps you avoid errors that local address translation routines cause.

The inet_ntoa function returns a pointer to a string that represents the Internet address found in the in_addr structure in dotted-decimal notation. To specify the text the message box is to display, QLookup uses the return value from inet_ntoa as the second parameter to the Windows MessageBox function. For example, if gethostbyname returns a valid pointer to a host-entry structure and you use "cerfnet.com" as the parameter to gethostbyname, QLookup will display the message box shown in Figure 9.4.

Figure 9.4 QLookup message box after successfully getting the IP address for cerfnet.com.

As you can see in Figure 9.4, the text in the message box is the IP address 192.102.249.3—the IP address for cerfnet.com. As you have learned, h_name field in a host-entry structure is a pointer to the official name of the host. QLookup uses this element (lpHostEnt->h_name) in the message box title bar.

If the pointer (lpHostEnt) is NULL, QLookup uses the MessageBox function to display the message, "Could not get IP address." Within the message-box title bar, QLookup displays the parameter (which it could not resolve) that you passed to gethostbyname. For example, Figure 9.5 shows the QLookup message box that would result if the gethostbyname function could not resolve the host name *cerfnet.com*.

Figure 9.5 *QLookup message box showing gethostbyname failure.*

Understanding the inet_addr Function

Regardless of whether QLookup successfully gets host information using the computer's name, QLookup next tries to get host information using an IP address. To do so, QLookup converts the dotted-decimal address to a 32-bit IP address. The Windows Sockets library includes the inet_addr function. The inet_addr function does not access the Internet (or TCP/IP network) in any way. The purpose of inet_addr is to convert a string containing an IP address in dotted-decimal notation into a binary representation of that address. The following program statement shows the function prototype for inet_addr:

```
unsigned long PASCAL FAR inet_addr(const char FAR * cp);
```

As you can see, inet_addr returns an unsigned-long value, which is a 32-bit number—the same as an IP address. QLookup uses the inet_addr function to convert the constant value in HOST_ADDR into an unsigned-long (dword) value, saving the result in the variable dwIPAddr:

```
dwIPAddr = inet_addr(HOST_ADDR);
```

If the inet_addr function cannot convert the string parameter passed to it, inet_addr returns the value INADDR_NONE. QLookup tests inet_addr's return value (stored in dwIPAddr) to determine if the conversion was successful:

```
if (dwIPAddr == INADDR_NONE)
   MessageBox(NULL, "Invalid Internet address!", HOST_ADDR,
       MB_OK|MB_ICONSTOP);
```

If inet_addr returns the value INADDR_NONE, QLookup uses a message box to display the message "Invalid Internet address."

UNDERSTANDING THE GETHOSTBYADDR FUNCTION

If dwIPAddr contains a valid 32-bit IP address, QLookup tries to retrieve host information using the IP address. To do so, QLookup uses the gethostbyaddr function. The following program statement shows the function prototype for gethostbyaddr:

```
struct hostent FAR * PASCAL FAR gethostbyaddr(const char FAR * addr,
    int len, int type);
```

The gethostbyaddr function requires three parameters: a pointer to an IP address (in network byte-order as returned by inet_addr), the length of the address (which is always four bytes for Internet addresses), and the type of address (which is always AF_INET). QLookup uses the value returned from inet_addr (and stored in dwIPAddr) for the first parameter. For the other two parameters, QLookup uses the symbolic constants AF_INET_LENGTH and AF_INET. QLookup defines AF_INET_LENGTH to be four bytes. The winsock.h header file defines the constant AF_INET. As shown next, QLookup reuses the host-entry pointer variable, lpHostEnt, to store the return value from gethostbyaddr:

```
lpHostEnt = gethostbyaddr((LPSTR) &dwIPAddr, AF_INET_LENGTH,
```

Like gethostbyname, the gethostbyaddr function returns a pointer to a host-entry structure. As shown next, QLookup once again tests the returned pointer (which QLookup stored in the variable lpHostEnt):

```
if (!lpHostEnt)
   MessageBox(NULL, "Could not get host name!", HOST_ADDR,
       MB_OK|MB_ICONSTOP);
else
   MessageBox(NULL, lpHostEnt->h_name, HOST_ADDR,
       MB_OK|MB_ICONINFORMATION);
```

Also, like gethostbyname, the gethostbyaddr function returns a NULL pointer if an error occurs. If the return value is not NULL, QLookup displays the h_name (host name) field of the host-entry structure (lpHostEnt->h_name) in a message box. QLookup displays the constant HOST_ADDR in the message box title bar. (Remember, HOST_ADDR contains the value passed, as the first parameter, to inet_addr.) For example, if you define HOST_ADDR to be 129.79.26.27, QLookup will display the message box shown in Figure 9.6.

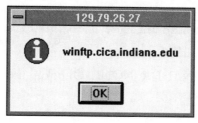

Figure 9.6 QLookup showing the host name for IP address 129.79.26.27.

If lpHostEnt is NULL, QLookup displays a message box with the text "Could not get host name," as shown in Figure 9.7.

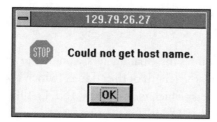

Figure 9.7 QLookup message box showing gethostbyaddr failure.

PUTTING IT ALL TOGETHER

In this chapter, you have learned that the Internet's Domain Name System represents an excellent example of a large-scale distributed database system. By establishing a hierarchical (decentralized authority) system for naming host computers, the DNS easily manages the millions of computer names associated with Internet host computers.

In the next chapter, you will use the programming techniques learned in this chapter to resolve a domain name into an IP address. You will also learn how to send a query to that IP address and request user information using the Finger user-information protocol. However, before you move on to Chapter 10, make sure you understand the following key concepts:

✓   The Internet Domain Name System lets Internet users refer to a host computer by a name, such as jamsa.com, instead of an IP address, such as 168.158.20.102.

✓   The Internet's Domain Name System maps host computer names into their correct dotted-decimal and 32-bit binary addresses.

✓   The Internet uses a distributed database for storing domain names.

✓   Internet name servers communicate with each other to translate any domain name into a 32-bit IP address.

Chapter 10
The Finger User-Information Protocol

In Chapter 9, you learned how to use the Windows Sockets API to look up host-computer names and IP addresses. Specifically, you used the Windows Sockets database functions to access entries in the Internet's Domain Name System (DNS). You can view the DNS lookup program (QLookup) that you created in Chapter 9 as an essential utility program for users or as an essential function for programs. Without the ability to look up Internet addresses, you (or your programs) cannot use the Windows Sockets API to access anything on the Internet.

In this chapter, however, you will move beyond simply retrieving general information about a host computer. The Finger program you will create in this chapter lets you retrieve the names of everyone logged on to a host computer (such as *jamsa.com*). Also, Finger lets you obtain public information about a specific user (such as *kcope@jamsa.com*). As you develop the Finger program, you will learn how to use the *Finger user-information protocol* to retrieve specific information from a host computer. In doing so, you will define a socket connection on your computer and then connect that socket to a remote host computer. After you have established both ends of the connection, you will communicate with the remote host to retrieve user information.

After you learn how to use the Finger service, you will understand the basic procedure for accessing most communication services on the Internet. Although the protocols, services, and message formats will vary, the basic steps you follow to access communication services are the same. After you understand how to access existing services, you'll be only a small step away from creating your own Internet services. By the time you finish this chapter, you will understand the following key concepts:

- How a virtual terminal hides differences between operating systems
- How to retrieve information from the network services database
- How to send Finger queries and receive replies
- How to find and understand important information in Internet Request for Comments (RFC) documents

REVISITING THE PRESENTATION LAYER

As you have learned, not all computer systems interpret character sets and other commonly used display operations (such as carriage-returns, line-feeds, tabs, and backspaces) in the same way. For example, some operating systems such as UNIX require a line of text to end with a carriage-return (CR). Other systems may require a line-feed (LF) character. Still other systems require both a carriage-return and a line-feed to designate the end of a line of text. Likewise, most computer systems let users interrupt a program by pressing an interrupt key (such as Esc) or key-combination (such as Ctrl-C). However, not all systems use the same key or keyboard combination to initiate an interrupt function.

The key point to understand is that all computers (more specifically, operating systems) perform operations such as those described in the last two paragraphs. As you run your programs on the Internet, system incompatibilities may arise because not all computers accomplish these tasks (and many others) in the same way. A well-designed network must resolve incompatibilities in a way that minimizes the workload on network programs.

In many networks, the presentation layer resolves incompatibilities between host computers. In addition, many network programs use *virtual-terminal protocols* that perform presentation-layer functions. Like the presentation layer, such protocols make video and printer differences disappear from the perspective of a network program. For example, suppose your application uses a virtual-terminal protocol to send data across the Internet. Using the characters the virtual-terminal protocol specifies, your application encodes the end of a line of text. The virtual-terminal protocol, for example, may specify that you mark each line of text with a carriage-return line-feed. The receiving computer, in turn, decodes the end-of-line characters as the virtual-terminal protocol specifies. The receiving computer then translates the end-of-line characters, as required for proper text display or storage on the receiving system.

The TCP/IP protocol suite does not include a separate presentation layer. Instead, the TCP/IP application layer includes the basic functionality of the ISO/OSI model's application, presentation, and session layers. However, TCP/IP does include a protocol similar to a virtual terminal protocol.

UNDERSTANDING THE NETWORK VIRTUAL TERMINAL

The TCP/IP protocol suite includes the TELNET protocol. Although you may be familiar with Telnet programs that let you login to remote computer systems, you may not have known that such applications use a specially designed protocol. RFC 854, *Telnet Protocol Specification*, Postal and Reynolds, 1983, defines the TELNET Protocol. One of the principle ideas underlying this protocol is the concept of a *Network Virtual Terminal (NVT)*. Many Internet protocols and programs, such as Finger, use the NVT concept. The TELNET-protocol specification describes the Network Virtual Terminal as an imaginary device that provides a standard interface to terminal or video display units. In effect, this imaginary device, the Network Virtual Terminal, embodies all the characteristics you normally find in a computer monitor or dumb terminal, such as a VT100.

The NVT concept that the TELNET-protocol specification describes is essentially a virtual-terminal protocol. However, the TELNET protocol itself is not simply a virtual-terminal protocol.

In Chapter 16, you will learn more details about the TELNET protocol. Before you develop any other Internet programs, it's important that you understand the Network Virtual Terminal concept that the TELNET specification defines. As you have learned, all computer terminals perform similar operations when they display information for users. For example, when a program fills the screen with text, most terminals will scroll text off the top of the screen to make room for new text to appear at the bottom of the screen. Likewise, most terminals let users erase characters typed on the screen. In fact, many terminals let a user erase entire lines at a time.

Every terminal also includes a concept based on the old typewriter carriage-return. Older type-writers used a device called a *carriage*, which held the typist's paper. When the typist pressed the Return key, the carriage would return to the far right. This return placed the paper on the carriage in a position where the typist could start typing at the left margin of the page. On a computer, users perform a similar function by pressing the RETURN or ENTER key, which causes the video cursor to return to the left side of the computer screen. We still refer to this function as a *carriage-return (CR)*. The Network Virtual Terminal specification defines how you send data and transmit commands, such as those that erase characters, create new lines, and perform carriage-returns across the Internet. By defining a common standard for such functions, the NVT hides differences between computers attached to the Internet's networks. Figure 10.1 shows how the NVT fits into network communications on the Internet.

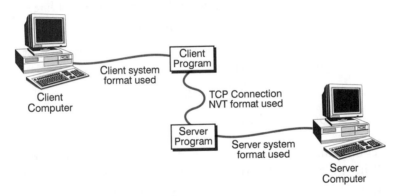

Figure 10.1 The Network Virtual Terminal concept.

Before they transmit data and commands across the Internet, both client and server programs translate such information into a format specified by the Network Virtual Terminal. When programs receive such transmissions, they can use the NVT definitions to decode or translate data and commands into the format the local computer uses.

DEFINING THE NVT FORMAT

The NVT format defined by the TELNET-protocol specification is fairly simple. As you have learned, a byte (eight bits) is the smallest amount of data that modern computers transmit. NVT uses the United States-American Standard Code for Information Interchange (US-ASCII) to represent data for network transmissions. In contrast, standard ASCII (not extended ASCII) uses seven bits to represent data. NVT uses the eighth or high-order bit for command sequences.

Note: The 7-bit US-ASCII can represent 128 characters total. Binary 1111111 (seven bits) equals decimal 127. When you include zero or the absence of all bits, you have a total of 128 possible character representations using seven bits of data.

As you may know, the US-ASCII character set includes 95 printable characters and 33 control codes. The printable characters include letters, digits or numbers, punctuation marks, and a few other symbols. Some of the 33 ASCII control codes also have standard interpretations. For example, most programs interpret ASCII 7 as the BEL command that causes the computer to make an audible sound. NVT uses several of the 33 ASCII control codes, as shown in Table 10.1.

Control Code	Hex Value	Assigned Meaning
NUL	0x00	No operation or effect
BEL	0x07	Create an audible (bell) or visible signal
BS	0x08	Move left (backspace) one character position
HT	0x09	Move right to the next horizontal tab stop
LF	0x0A	Move down (line-feed) to the next line
VT	0x0B	Move down to the next vertical tab stop
FF	0x0C	Move to the top of the next page (formfeed)
CR	0x0D	Move to the left margin of the current line (carriage-return)

Table 10.1 NVT use of ASCII control codes.

NVT also defines the standard-line termination as the two-character carriage-return (CR) and a line-feed (LF). When a user presses ENTER or RETURN, programs that use the NVT standard must translate that keystroke into a CRLF combination prior to transmission across the network. You can refer to the NVT definitions previously described as NVT ASCII. Many Internet programs and protocols use NVT ASCII as defined by the TELNET-protocol specification.

Note: NVT defines other command sequences that use the eighth or high-order bit. However, those command sequences provide functions that few programs, aside from Telnet applications, use.

REVIEWING THE NETWORK VIRTUAL TERMINAL

Internet RFC 854, *Telnet Protocol Specification*, Postal and Reynolds, 1983, defines a Network Virtual Terminal (NVT) as part of the TELNET-protocol specification. NVT provides a standard network interface that is similar to a network virtual protocol, which hides computer differences related to line-feeds, form-feeds, carriage-returns, end-of-line markers, and other such characteristics. The NVT format uses standard 7-bit ASCII encoding for letters, digits, and punctuation marks. Of the 33 control codes included in 7-bit ASCII, NVT uses standard interpretation for eight of the control codes and ignores the others. (See Table 10.1 for NVT use of ASCII control codes.) NVT uses a *carriage-return and line-feed combination (CRLF)* to represent the end of a line. Internet professionals commonly refer to NVT's use of 7-bit ASCII as NVT ASCII. Many Internet programs and protocols use NVT ASCII encoding when they transmit data across the Internet.

CREATING A QUICK FINGER PROGRAM

Conceptually, a program that uses the Finger user-information protocol is quite simple. Finger has a well-known port assignment of 79. As you may recall, a port (or protocol port) identifies a specific program to the TCP/IP transport-layer protocols. To access a Finger-server program, you establish a TCP connection to port 79 of the host computer that you want to send a Finger query. All Finger queries use NVT ASCII. You transmit a blank line to ask the Finger server for a list of all users currently logged on. To request information about a specific user, you transmit the user's login ID or real name. You must end each query with an end-of-line command (as defined by TELNET NVT)—a carriage-return line-feed (CRLF).

In this section, you will create a quick Finger program named QFinger. Like the QLookup program in the previous chapter, QFinger highlights a few key Internet programming concepts by eliminating everything except the bare essentials. QFinger hard codes values that a user would normally enter and uses message boxes to avoid the overhead associated with a Windows user interface and window message handling.

You can find QFINGER.CPP on the floppy disk included with *Internet Programming*. The section that follows discusses QFinger in detail. The program statements shown next are the complete program listing for QFINGER.CPP:

```
#include "..\winsock.h"

#define PROG_NAME "Simple Finger Query"

#define HOST_NAME "cerfnet.com"        // This can be any valid host name
#define WINSOCK_VERSION 0x0101         // Program requires Winsock version 1.1

#define FINGER_QUERY "lonetech"        // This can be a login or real name
#define DEFAULT_PROTOCOL 0             // No protocol specified, use default
#define SEND_FLAGS 0                   // No send() flags specified
```

```
#define RECV_FLAGS 0                    // No recv() flags specified

int PASCAL WinMain(HANDLE hInstance, HANDLE hPrevInstance,
    LPSTR lpszCmdParam, int nCmdShow)
{
  WSADATA wsaData;                 // Winsock implementation details
  LPHOSTENT lpHostEnt;             // Internet host information structure
  SOCKET nSocket;                  // Socket number used by this program
  SOCKADDR_IN sockAddr;            // Socket address structure
  LPSERVENT lpServEnt;             // Service information structure
  short iFingerPort;               // Well-known port assignment is 79
  char szFingerInfo[5000];         // Buffer to hold Finger information
  char szFingerQuery[100];         // Buffer to hold Finger query
  int nCharSent;                   // Number of characters transmitted
  int nCharRecv;                   // Number of characters received
  int nConnect;                    // Socket connection results

  if (WSAStartup(WINSOCK_VERSION, &wsaData))
    MessageBox(NULL, "Could not load Windows Sockets DLL.",
         PROG_NAME, MB_OK|MB_ICONSTOP);

  else// Resolve the host name
    {
      lpHostEnt = gethostbyname(HOST_NAME);

      if (!lpHostEnt)
        MessageBox(NULL, "Could not get IP address!", HOST_NAME,
            MB_OK|MB_ICONSTOP);

      else// Create the socket
        {
          nSocket = socket(PF_INET, SOCK_STREAM, DEFAULT_PROTOCOL);

          if (nSocket == INVALID_SOCKET)
            MessageBox(NULL, "Invalid socket!!", PROG_NAME,
                MB_OK|MB_ICONSTOP);

          else  // Configure the socket
            {
              // Get the Finger service information
              lpServEnt = getservbyname("Finger", NULL);

              if (lpServEnt == NULL)
                iFingerPort = IPPORT_FINGER; // Use the well-known port
              else
                iFingerPort = lpServEnt->s_port;

              // Define the socket address
              sockAddr.sin_family = AF_INET; // Internet address family
              sockAddr.sin_port = iFingerPort;
```

```
            sockAddr.sin_addr = *((LPIN_ADDR)*lpHostEnt->h_addr_list);

            // Connect the socket
            nConnect = connect(nSocket, (LPSOCKADDR) &sockAddr,
                    sizeof(sockAddr));

            if (nConnect)
              MessageBox(NULL, "Error connecting socket!!", PROG_NAME,
                    MB_OK|MB_ICONSTOP);

            else// Format and send the Finger query
              {
                 wsprintf(szFingerQuery,"%s\n", FINGER_QUERY);

                 nCharSent = send(nSocket, szFingerQuery,
                       lstrlen(szFingerQuery), SEND_FLAGS);

                 if (nCharSent == SOCKET_ERROR)
                   MessageBox(NULL, "Error occurred during send()!",
                         PROG_NAME, MB_OK|MB_ICONSTOP);

                 else   // Get the Finger information from the host
                   {
                     do {
                         nCharRecv = recv(nSocket,
                                 (LPSTR)&szFingerInfo[nConnect],
                                 sizeof(szFingerInfo) - nConnect,
                                 RECV_FLAGS);
                         nConnect+=nCharRecv;
                     } while (nCharRecv > 0);

                     if (nCharRecv == SOCKET_ERROR)
                       MessageBox(NULL, "Error occurred during recv!",
                             PROG_NAME, MB_OK|MB_ICONSTOP);
                     else   // Display the Finger information
                       {
                         wsprintf(szFingerQuery,"%s@%s", FINGER_QUERY,
                               HOST_NAME);
                         MessageBox(NULL, szFingerInfo, szFingerQuery,
                               MB_OK|MB_ICONINFORMATION);
                       }
                   }
              }
          }
       }
    }
  }
WSACleanup(); // Free all allocated program resources and exit
return NULL;
}
```

Defining Constant Values

Like all Internet programs that use the Windows Sockets API, QFinger includes the winsock.h header file. After the winsock.h include statement, QLookup defines several constants the program requires:

```
#include "..\winsock.h"

#define PROG_NAME "Simple Finger Query"

#define HOST_NAME "cerfnet.com"      // This can be any valid host name
#define WINSOCK_VERSION 0x0101       // Program requires Winsock version 1.1

#define FINGER_QUERY "lonetech"      // This can be a login or real name
#define DEFAULT_PROTOCOL 0           // No protocol specified, use default
#define SEND_FLAGS 0                 // No send() flags specified
#define RECV_FLAGS 0                 // No recv() flags specified
```

QFinger uses the constants PROG_NAME, HOST_NAME, and WINSOCK_VERSION in the same way as QLookup. You can define HOST_NAME to be any valid host computer name on the Internet. To the server program on the remote host that HOST_NAME defines, QFinger transmits the constant definition of FINGER_QUERY.

In this case, the HOST_NAME constant corresponds to the host *cerfnet.com*. Likewise, the FINGER_QUERY constant references the user ID *lonetech*. You can substitute any valid user name or login ID recognized by the remote host computer. As you have learned, network designers designate a default protocol for use by all network communication services. QFinger uses the constant DEFAULT_PROTOCOL to tell the Windows Sockets functions to use the default protocol specified for the Finger service.

As you will learn, you can control how some Winsock functions perform tasks by including special flags in the function calls. QFinger does not use any special flags so QFinger defines both SEND_FLAGS and RECV_FLAGS as zero.

Declaring Variables

The next several lines in QFINGER.CPP define the WinMain function and declare the program's local variables:

```
int PASCAL WinMain(HANDLE hInstance, HANDLE hPrevInstance,
    LPSTR lpszCmdParam, int nCmdShow)
{
  WSADATA wsaData;                  // Winsock implementation details
```

```
LPHOSTENT lpHostEnt;          // Internet host information structure
SOCKET nSocket;               // Socket handle used by this program
SOCKADDR_IN sockAddr;         // Socket address structure
LPSERVENT lpServEnt;          // Service information structure
short iFingerPort;            // Well-known port assignment is 79
char szFingerInfo[5000];      // Buffer to hold Finger information
char szFingerQuery[100];      // Buffer to hold Finger query
int nCharSent;                // Number of characters transmitted
int nCharRecv;                // Number of characters received
int nConnect;                 // Socket connection results
```

Like the Quick Lookup program, QFinger uses the wsaData variable to store details about the Windows Sockets implementation returned by the WSAStartup function. QFinger also uses the variable lpHostEnt to point to the host computer information returned by the gethostbyname function. As you may recall, the gethostbyname function returns a pointer to information about the host computer you specify.

In Chapter 9, Table 9.3 describes the elements in Windows Socket's host-entry structure. Before you can transmit and receive Finger information, you will need to use the IP address stored in the host-entry structure to create a communication socket.

QFinger declares and uses a SOCKET variable named nSocket. The winsock.h header file defines a SOCKET to be an unsigned integer. A SOCKET variable is like a file handle. A single Windows Sockets program can create multiple sockets just as a DOS or Windows program can open multiple files at the same time. You use a SOCKET variable to specify which socket is to receive your program's network commands. The iFingerPort variable temporarily stores the well-known port for the Finger service. QFinger uses szFingerInfo as a buffer to store Finger information received from the remote host.

The program uses the szFingerQuery buffer to format a Finger query as required by the Finger server. The integer variables, nCharSent and nCharRecv, track the number of characters that QFinger sends and receives through the communications socket.

The nConnect variable stores the results from the socket connection. In this case, QFinger simply examines the value of nConnect to verify the connection was successful. The following sections describe the sockAddr and lpServEnt variables and their purpose in detail.

GETTING STARTED

As shown here, the first few program statements in QFINGER.CPP are identical to the Quick Lookup program that you saw in Chapter 9:

```
if (WSAStartup(WINSOCK_VERSION, &wsaData))
  MessageBox(NULL, "Could not load Windows Sockets DLL.", PROG_NAME,
      MB_OK|MB_ICONSTOP);

else // Resolve the host name
{
  lpHostEnt = gethostbyname(HOST_NAME);

  if (!lpHostEnt)
    MessageBox(NULL, "Could not get IP address!", HOST_NAME,
        MB_OK|MB_ICONSTOP);
  else
    {
      // Continue with the Quick Finger program
    }
}
WSACleanup();  // Free all allocated program resources and exit
return NULL;
```

As you can see, QFinger first calls WSAStartup to initialize the Windows Sockets DLL. Next, the program retrieves host information from the Internet's Domain Name System (DNS) by calling the gethostbyname function. The gethostbyname function accepts a host name as parameter and returns a pointer to a Windows Sockets host-entry structure. Finally, QFinger evaluates the pointer to the host-entry structure (lpHostEnt) to ensure the function was successful. If the pointer to the host-entry structure is NULL (invalid), the program displays a message box that tells you that the program's attempt to resolve the host name failed. Since the remainder of the program falls within else braces ({}), if the gethostbyname function fails, the program will call WSACleanup and exit. As you have learned, WSACleanup function deregisters the calling program from the Winsock DLL. You should always call the WSACleanup function before exiting a Windows Sockets application. Doing so lets the Winsock DLL free resources it allocated on behalf of your program.

CREATING THE SOCKET

As shown next, if the host entry pointer variable, lpHostEnt, is valid (not NULL), QFinger calls the socket function to create a network-communications socket:

```
if (!lpHostEnt)
  MessageBox(NULL, "Could not get IP address!", HOST_NAME,
      MB_OK|MB_ICONSTOP);

else // Create the socket
{
  nSocket = socket(PF_INET, SOCK_STREAM, DEFAULT_PROTOCOL);

  if (nSocket == INVALID_SOCKET)
    MessageBox(NULL, "Invalid socket!!", PROG_NAME, MB_OK|MB_ICONSTOP);
```

The socket function returns a socket descriptor. As previously shown, QFinger stores the socket descriptor in a SOCKET variable named nSocket. The next program statement evaluates nSocket to ensure a valid socket is available. If nSocket is invalid, QFinger displays a message box that tells you so and then exits. The Windows Sockets specification prototypes the *socket* function as shown:

```
SOCKET PASCAL FAR socket (int af, int type, int protocol);
```

The socket function requires three parameters. The first parameter specifies an address format. As of version 1.1 of the Windows Sockets specification, the only address format that Windows Sockets supports is the Internet address or protocol family, which winsock.h defines as AF_INET and PF_INET. The second parameter to the socket function specifies the type of data service (byte stream or datagram) you want to use with this socket. Windows Sockets version 1.1 supports two data types, which the winsock.h header defines as SOCK_STREAM and SOCK_DGRAM.

Note: As you will learn in Chapter 14, some implementations of Windows Sockets support a third data type called a raw socket, which winsock.h defines as SOCK_RAW. However, Windows Sockets version 1.1 does not require raw socket support. As such, not all implementations support this type of data service.

The SOCK_STREAM data service provides a sequenced, reliable, two-way, connection-based byte stream. This data service uses TCP as the transport protocol. The SOCK_DGRAM data service uses datagrams and the UDP transport protocol. The QFinger program uses a constant named DEFAULT_PROTOCOL for the third parameter to the socket function. The third parameter lets you specify a particular protocol to use with the socket. You can use zero as the third parameter if you do not want to specify a protocol. In fact, QFinger defines DEFAULT_PROTOCOL to be zero.

After QFinger validates the socket descriptor, the program begins to configure a socket address for use by the remote host. The first step in this process is to obtain information about the desired communication service from the network services database. In QFinger's case, the desired communication service is the Finger service.

Understanding the Network Services Database

The network services database stores information for Internet services such as Finger, Ftp, Mail, Telnet, and so on. For each service, the database identifies the associated port, available protocols, and aliases (other names for the same service). Typically, on a personal computer, a network services database exists as a simple ASCII file named SERVICES. You can usually find the SERVICES file located in the same directory as your WINSOCK.DLL. As shown next, QFinger declares a variable named lpServEnt, which is a pointer to a service-entry structure:

```
LPSERVENT lpServEnt;        // Service information structure
```

The header file winsock.h defines the LPSERVENT service-entry structure as shown here:

```
typedef struct servent FAR *LPSERVENT; // Windows Extended data type

struct servent
{
  char FAR * s_name;
  char FAR * FAR * s_aliases;
  short s_port;
  char FAR * s_proto;
};
```

Typically, you will use the getservbyname function to fill the elements in a service-entry structure. Shown next is the Windows Sockets prototype for the getservbyname function:

```
struct servent FAR * PASCAL FAR getservbyname(const char FAR * name,
       const char FAR * proto);
```

Table 10.2 briefly describes each element in the service-entry structure.

Element	Usage
s_name	The official service name, such as Finger.
s_aliases	A list of alias or alternative service names.
s_port	The protocol-port number to use for this service, such as 79 for Finger.
s_proto	The name of the protocol to use for this service, such as TCP or UDP.

Table 10.2 Elements in the Windows Sockets service-entry structure.

The getservbyname function takes two pointers as parameters—a pointer to a service name and a pointer to a protocol name. The function returns a pointer to a servent data structure. The getservbyname function requires you to specify a protocol name. However, you can use a NULL pointer as the protocol name parameter, and the getservbyname function will return the first entry that matches the specified service name. In the case of QFinger, the program uses the service name "finger" and NULL for the protocol name. (A NULL for the protocol name tells Winsock that the program will use the default protocol.)

The getservbyname function performs its task by examining a network services database. Typically, on a personal computer, this database exists as a simple ASCII file named SERVICES. You can usually find the SERVICES file located in the same directory as your WINSOCK.DLL. Shown next is part of a network services database. As you can see, the file consists of three columns. The first column identifies the network services. The second column specifies corresponding ports and protocols. And the third column specifies corresponding aliases:

```
# Network services, Internet style
#
#name port/protocol aliases
#
echo          7/tcp
echo          7/udp
discard       9/tcp         sink null
discard       9/udp         sink null
systat       11/tcp         users
daytime      13/tcp
daytime      13/udp
netstat      15/tcp
qotd1         7/tcp         quote
chargen      19/tcp         ttytst source
chargen      19/udp         ttytst source
ftp          21/tcp
telnet       23/tcp
smtp         25/tcp         mail
time         37/tcp         timserver
time         37/udp         timserver
rlp          39/udp         resource      # resource location
nameserver   42/tcp         name          # IEN 116
whois        43/tcp         nicname
domain       53/tcp         nameserver    # name-domain server
domain       53/udp         nameserver
mtp          57/tcp                       # deprecated
tftp         69/udp
rje          77/tcp         netrjs
Finger       79/tcp
link         87/tcp         ttylink
supdup       95/tcp
hostnames   101/tcp         hostname      # usually from sri-nic
ns          105/tcp                       # ph name server
pop2        109/tcp         postoffice2
pop3        110/tcp         postoffice
sunrpc      111/tcp         portmapper
sunrpc      111/udp         portmapper
auth        113/tcp         authentication
sftp        115/tcp
uucp-path   117/tcp
nntp        119/tcp         readnews untp # USENET News Transfer Protocol
```

Note: The Windows Sockets specification does not dictate implementation requirements for the network services database. However, on a PC, Winsock vendors typically implement the network services database as an ASCII file named SERVICES. You can expect to find the SERVICES file in the same directory with your WINSOCK.DLL.

Examine the first two network service entries in the previous listing. As you can see, the echo service has a well-known port number of 7 and is available using the Transport Control Protocol

(TCP) or User Datagram Protocol (UDP). An echo service or server simply returns or echoes anything that it receives back to the sender. Suppose you called the getservbyname function with the parameters shown next:

```
getservbyname("echo", NULL);
```

Using the network services database shown in the previous listing, the getservbyname function will fill a service-entry structure with the first echo entry that it finds (the one that uses the TCP protocol). For example, the getservbyname function call shown previously will result in the service-entry structure contents shown here:

```
s_name[] = "echo";
s_aliases = NULL;
s_port = 7;
s_proto[] = "tcp";
```

If you want to use an echo service with the UDP protocol, you must specify UDP as your second parameter as shown here:

```
getservbyname("echo", "UDP");
```

In this case, the getservbyname function will fill a service-entry structure with the echo entry that uses the UDP protocol. Shown next is an example of the results you would see from such a function call:

```
s_name[] = "echo";
s_aliases = NULL;
s_port = 7;
s_proto[] = "udp";
```

As you can see from the sample network services database, not all services are available to programs using more than one protocol. For example, FTP (File Transfer Protocol) is available with the TCP protocol only. Likewise, TFTP (Trivial FTP) service is available with the UDP protocol only.

If you carefully examine the network services database, you will discover that the TCP protocol normally occurs first, even when a service is available using UDP. Unless you specifically need to use the UDP protocol, you can use a NULL pointer as your second parameter in getservbyname. The getservbyname function will always return the host entry that uses TCP—assuming TCP is available for the specified service.

Shown next are examples of aliases (other equivalent names) in the network services database. As you can see, the SMTP (Simple Mail Transfer Protocol) service has an alias of mail. Likewise, timserver is an alias for the time service, and whois has an alias of nicname:

```
#name  port/protocol aliases
#
smtp   25/tcpmail
time   37/tcptimserver
time   37/udptimserver
whois  43/tcpnicname
```

In such cases, you use the service name or its alias, interchangeably. As such, both of the following function calls will return a pointer to the same service entry:

```
getservbyname("smtp", NULL);
getservbyname("mail", NULL);
```

Shown next are the service entries that would result from either of the previous function calls:

```
s_name[] = "smtp";
s_aliases[] = "mail";
s_port = 25;
s_proto[] = "tcp";
```

Likewise, the following function calls are equivalent:

```
lpServEnt = getservbyname("whois", NULL);
lpServEnt = getservbyname("nicname", NULL);
```

Both would result in the service entries shown here:

```
s_name[] = "whois";
s_aliases[] = "nicname";
s_port = 43;
s_proto[] = "tcp";
```

REVIEWING THE NETWORK SERVICES DATABASE

The network services database contains a list of common network services, such as Ftp, Telnet, and Finger. For each service, the database identifies the well-known port assignment and the service protocol. There are many services available that can use more than one protocol (such as TCP and UDP). In such cases, the database contains a separate entry for each available protocol. The database also identifies any alias names associated with the service.

Typically, on a PC, you can find the network services database in the same directory as your Windows Sockets library, WINSOCK.DLL. The network services database is usually a simple ASCII file named SERVICES. You can use the getservbyname function to obtain information about a service from the network service database.

Getting Network Service Information

As shown next, QFinger evaluates the pointer variable lpHostEnt, which points to host-entry structure. If the pointer is valid, the program continues and tries to retrieve the Finger service information from the network services database. The program uses the getservbyname function to obtain a pointer to a service-entry structure for the Finger service. In lpServEnt, QFinger stores the pointer returned by the getservbyname function. Then, QFinger evaluates the lpServEnt pointer:

```
if (!lpHostEnt)
  MessageBox(NULL, "Could not get IP address!", HOST_NAME,
     MB_OK|MB_ICONSTOP);

else // Get the Finger service information
{
  lpServEnt = getservbyname("Finger", NULL);

  if (lpServEnt == NULL)
    iFingerPort = IPPORT_FINGER;   // Use the well-known port
  else
    iFingerPort = lpServEnt->s_port;
```

As you can see, if lpServEnt is valid (not NULL), the program uses the iFingerPort variable to store the protocol port identified in the service-entry structure (lpServEnt->s_port). If lpServEnt is invalid (NULL), the program uses the constant defined by IPPORT_FINGER.

As shown next, winsock.h defines port values for many of the network services you saw in the example network services database. Among these definitions is IPPORT_FINGER, which winsock.h defines to be 79—the well-known port for the Finger service:

```
// Well-known port assignments for common network services
#define IPPORT_ECHO            7
#define IPPORT_DISCARD         9
#define IPPORT_SYSTAT          11
#define IPPORT_DAYTIME         13
#define IPPORT_NETSTAT         15
#define IPPORT_FTP             21
#define IPPORT_TELNET          23
#define IPPORT_SMTP            25
#define IPPORT_TIMESERVER      37
#define IPPORT_NAMESERVER      42
#define IPPORT_WHOIS           43
#define IPPORT_MTP             57
#define IPPORT_TFTP            69
#define IPPORT_RJE             77
#define IPPORT_FINGER          79
#define IPPORT_TTYLINK         87
#define IPPORT_SUPDUP  95
```

In other words, in the following code fragment, QFinger uses the getservbyname function to access the network services database. If the effort fails and lpServEnt is NULL, the program uses a default protocol port as defined by winsock.h for the Finger service:

```
lpServEnt = getservbyname("Finger", NULL);
if (lpServEnt == NULL)
   iFingerPort = IPPORT_FINGER;   // Use the well-known port
else
 iFingerPort = lpServEnt->s_port;
```

For the QFinger program, a failure by the getservbyname function is not critical. However, in other cases, the Winsock header file may not include a definition for a default port. For example, winsock.h does not define a port value for the network news transfer protocol (nntp) or the USENET news transfer protocol (untp). Also, in some cases, you may not know what protocols are available for a specific service. In both of these cases, you need valid service entries before you can continue. Otherwise, if the getservbyname function fails, you might have to abort program execution.

Understanding the Internet Socket-Address Structure

As you saw previously, QFinger declares a SOCKADDR_IN variable named sockAddr, as shown:

```
SOCKADDR_IN sockAddr;        // Socket address structure
```

The winsock.h header file defines SOCKADDR_IN to be an Internet socket-address structure, as shown here:

```
typedef struct sockaddr_in SOCKADDR_IN; // MS Windows Extended data type
struct sockaddr_in
 {
   short sin_family;
   u_short sin_port;
   struct in_addr sin_addr;
   char sin_zero[8];
 };
```

Table 10.3 briefly describes each element in the socket-address structure.

Element	Usage
sin_family	The type of socket address, which for Internet TCP/IP networks is always the Internet address family defined as AF_INET
sin_port	The protocol port number

Table 10.3 Elements in the Winsock socket-address structure. (continued on the next page)

Element	Usage
sin_addr	The IP address of a host computer stored in a Windows Sockets in_addr structure
sin_zero	Currently unused and set to zero

Table 10.3 Elements in the Winsock socket-address structure. (continued from the previous page)

The sockaddr_in address structure stores socket information the Windows Sockets libraries require. As discussed, most Internet programs require a valid host address before you can obtain any data from an Internet host computer. All programs that use the Windows Sockets API to create a network communications socket require a valid IP address. Winsock programs store the IP address in the sin_addr element of the socket-address structure.

The sin_addr element is actually an in_addr structure. As you may recall from Chapter 9, the in_addr structure uses a union to conveniently store a 32-bit IP address in three ways: as four 8-bit values, two 16-bit values, and as a single 32-bit number. The sin_port element is simply a protocol port. As you learned in Chapter 5, a TCP/IP port is like an IP address. However, TCP/IP associates a port with a protocol instead of a host computer. Many protocols have well-known port assignments. As discussed, the well-known port for the Finger user-information protocol is port 79. Before calling the connect function, QFinger assigns the Finger-service port number to the sin_port field within the sockaddr_in structure.

UNDERSTANDING ADDRESS AND PROTOCOL FAMILIES

The sin_family element in the socket-address structure, shown in the previous section, identifies the type of address a socket uses. As noted in Table 10.3, for Internet TCP/IP networks, sin_family is always the Internet address family (AF_INET). Network protocols can use different representations of network addresses. The concept of address or protocol families lets software manipulate addresses without knowing implementation details. For example, using the concept of an address or protocol family, you can write a routine that accepts a network address and performs different actions depending on the type of address or protocol family specified.

In other words, like the Berkeley socket API, developers can implement Windows Sockets for networks other than TCP/IP. The parameters in the Winsock functions let a programmer specify which network will host the program. Likewise, in many cases, the design will simplify porting Windows Sockets programs from one network to another. In some cases, the programmer may only need to change the protocol and address family constants to move a program from one network to another.

Note: At the time of this writing, Windows Sockets implementations were available only for TCP/IP networks. However, by supporting address and protocol families, the function designs make other implementations possible without redesigning the basic Windows Sockets API.

The Windows Sockets gethostbyaddr function is a good example of a routine designed to work with multiple protocol or address families. As you have learned in Chapter 9, the Windows Sockets specification prototypes the gethostbyaddr function as shown here:

```
struct hostent FAR * PASCAL FAR gethostbyaddr(const char FAR * addr,
    int len, int type);
```

As you may recall, the first parameter to the gethostbyaddr function must point to a valid IP address. The address must be in a binary format (network byte-order) suitable for use on the Internet. However, you may not have noticed the variable type declared for the first parameter. Remember, an IP address is a 32-bit number. As you can see, the prototype declares a pointer to a variable of type *char*—not an unsigned long (32 bit number) as you might have expected.

Windows Sockets designed the gethostbyaddr function to work with different protocol families. Along with passing it a valid address, the function requires you to tell it the length of your network address and to identify the type of address or protocol family. Consider what this means to you as an applications developer. Assume you develop an Internet application that uses the Windows Sockets API. Suppose that, a couple of years later, you want to move this application to a new network that also supports Windows Sockets. Among other changes, you will need to modify your program's use of the gethostbyaddr function.

In the gethostbyaddr function, you will need to specify the new protocol family (the third parameter) and maybe change the address length (the second parameter). The Windows Sockets library on the new network will examine the length and protocol-family parameters and take the correct action to fill a host-entry structure defined by the new network. Suppose the Windows Sockets specification simply defined the gethostbyaddr function to accept a 32-bit IP address. Assume your new network used a 64-bit address. Under this scenario, you could no longer use the gethostbyaddr function to fill a host-entry structure. The Windows Sockets specification would need to specify a different function for every network that used a different address size.

Also, suppose another network used a 32-bit address but did not use the Internet's network byte-order. As such, the Windows Sockets specification would need to specify a unique function for each unique combination of network address size and byte-order. Windows Sockets avoids these complications by specifying functions that accept address and protocol-family parameters.

You will see the constants AF_INET and PF_INET in most programs that use the Windows Sockets API. AF_INET represents the Internet (INET) address family (AF) and PF_INET represents the Internet protocol family (PF). At this time, the Windows Sockets specification (version 1.1) defines protocol families to be the same as address families. In other words, the Winsock header file defines PF_INET to be equivalent to AF_INET, as shown here:

```
#define PF_INET    AF_INET
```

DEFINING THE SOCKET ADDRESS

As discussed, QFinger uses a SOCKADDR_IN structure named sockAddr. As you have learned, SOCKADDR_IN is an Internet socket-address structure defined by the Windows Sockets specification.

The next several program statements in QFINGER.CPP store information in the sockAddr variable that the program needs to connect the socket to a remote host:

```
// Define the socket address
sockAddr.sin_family = AF_INET;    // Internet address family
sockAddr.sin_port = iFingerPort;
sockAddr.sin_addr = *((LPIN_ADDR)*lpHostEnt->h_addr_list);
```

First, QFinger stores the definition for the Internet address family (AF_INET) in the sin_family field of the socket-address structure. Next, the program assigns the port number to the sin_port field. (Remember, iFingerPort contains either the default port, IPPORT_FINGER, or the port found in the service-entry structure filled by getservbyname.) Finally, QFinger assigns the IP address in the host-entry structure to the sin_addr element of the socket-address structure.

CONNECTING THE SOCKET

After you have defined a socket address, you are ready to connect the socket to the remote host. You use the Windows Sockets connect function to do so. Shown next is the prototype for the connect function:

```
int PASCAL FAR connect(SOCKET s, const struct sockaddr FAR * name,
        int namelen);
```

You have already met the connect function's parameters. The first parameter is the socket descriptor, returned by the socket function. The connect function's second parameter is a pointer to a valid socket-address structure. Earlier in this chapter, the section entitled *Understanding the Internet Socket Address Structure* discussed socket-address structures in detail. Likewise, the section entitled *Defining the Socket Address* showed you the values QFinger assigns to the socket-address structure named sockAddr. In this case, QFinger passes the sockAddr variable to the connect function.

The third parameter is simply the length of the socket-address structure. QFinger uses the C/C++ *sizeof* operator to obtain the length of sockAddr and passes the results directly to the connect function. Shown next are the program statements used in QFINGER.CPP to connect the socket:

```
nConnect = connect(nSocket, (LPSOCKADDR) &sockAddr, sizeof(sockAddr));

if (nConnect)
  MessageBox(NULL, "Error connecting socket!!", PROG_NAME,
      MB_OK|MB_ICONSTOP);
```

If no errors occur, the connect function will return a zero. As you can see, QFinger stores the connect function's return value in the integer variable nConnect and then examines the value. If nConnect indicates an error occurred, QFinger displays a message box to that effect and exits. As you have learned, when you create a socket using the socket function, you must specify a data service. You can request a sequenced, reliable, two-way, connection-based byte stream by using the constant SOCK_STREAM. To create a datagram service, you use SOCK_DGRAM as a parameter to the socket function. The socket function, in turn, returns a socket descriptor.

The connect function examines its first parameter (the socket descriptor) to determine which data service you specified. For a byte-stream data service (specified by SOCK_STREAM), the connect function creates an active connection with the remote host. For a datagram socket (specified by SOCK_DGRAM), the connect function sets a default destination for use by subsequent transmissions through the socket. If the connect function returns without errors, you are ready to transmit data through the socket to the remote host computer.

REVIEWING SOCKET CONNECTIONS

As previously discussed, to access most communication services on the Internet using the Windows Sockets API, you follow the same basic steps. After you learn this process, you will also understand many of the steps you need to perform to create custom network services.

Perhaps the best way to view the steps required to create a communications socket for an existing network service is to start with the socket and work your way backwards. In other words, to create a socket connection, the socket requires you to provide certain information. You can understand the process easier if you first examine the socket's information requirements and then trace the steps required to provide that information. Shown next are steps your program must perform to create a communications socket. The steps are in reverse order. In other words, they start with the socket creation and work backwards.

1. To create a socket connection, you use the connect function. The connect function requires a valid socket descriptor and socket address.

2. To obtain a socket descriptor, you use the socket function. The socket function requires you to specify a data service—either a byte-stream or datagram. You can also specify a protocol or accept a default protocol.

3. To create a socket address, you store data in a socket-address structure. The socket-address structure requires you to specify a protocol port and a valid IP address in the form of an Internet-address structure.

4. To obtain a protocol port, you can use the getservbyname function. The getservbyname function requires you to specify a network service. You can also specify a protocol or accept a default protocol.

> 5. To obtain a valid IP address in an Internet-address structure, you can use one of the Windows Sockets database functions, such as gethostbyname or gethostbyaddr.

SENDING THE FINGER QUERY

As discussed, after you establish a socket connection, you can transmit data to the remote host computer through the socket. Typically, you will use the Windows Sockets send function to transmit data to a remote host. Shown next is the prototype for the send function:

```
int PASCAL FAR send(SOCKET s, const char FAR * buf, int len, int flags);
```

As you might expect, the send function requires you to specify the socket through which you want to transmit. You tell send which socket to use by specifying a socket descriptor. The send function requires a socket descriptor as its first parameter. The remaining parameters are peculiar to your application. The second parameter must be a pointer to a buffer containing your application data. The third parameter specifies the length of the data your buffer contains. You can use the fourth parameter to specify special flags that influence the behavior of the socket transmission. Version 1.1 of the Windows Sockets specification only identifies two flags for use by the send function: MSG_DONTROUTE and MSG_OOB.

The MSG_DONTROUTE flag tells the send function that the transmitted message should not be subject to routing. In other words, the transmitted message should bypass the normal routing process the underlying protocol follows. As such, the send function transmits the message directly to the network address specified by the socket address. Windows Sockets specification version 1.1 lets Windows Sockets developers ignore this flag. As such, you will not want to use this flag except possibly for testing purposes.

The MSG_OOB flag tells the send function (as well as the receiver) to treat the transmitted message as out-of-band data. As you have learned in Chapter 5, out-of-band or urgent data is a great concept. However, since there is much confusion about how to use out-of-band data for practical purposes, you probably will want (at least for the present) to avoid using it. Also, the MSG_OOB option is only valid for sockets configured for byte-stream data delivery. If you specify the MSG_OOB option with a datagram socket, the send function will return an error.

If you examine the send function call within QFinger, you will find that the function passes the constant SEND_FLAGS as the third parameter. QFinger defines the SEND_FLAGS constant as zero. As discussed, the Finger server program at port 79 expects to see NVT ASCII data. You can transmit a blank line to ask the Finger server for a list of all users currently logged on. To request information about a specific user, you transmit the user's login ID or real name. You must end each query with an end-of-line command as defined by Telnet NVT—a carriage-return line-feed (CRLF).

QFinger uses the constant FINGER_QUERY to define the Finger query. You can define this value to be any username or login ID that is valid on the host computer you specified with the constant HOST_NAME. If the return value from the connect function indicates a successful connection, QFinger uses the Windows wsprintf function to format the szFingerQuery buffer by adding carriage-return line-feed (CRLF or \n) to FINGER_QUERY. As shown next, the program passes the socket descriptor nSocket to the send function, a pointer to the szFingerQuery buffer, the length of the buffer (using the Windows lstrlen function), and the flags defined by SEND_FLAGS:

```
if (nConnect)
  MessageBox(NULL, "Error connecting socket!!", PROG_NAME,
     MB_OK|MB_ICONSTOP);

else // Format and send the Finger query
{
  wsprintf(szFingerQuery,"%s\n", FINGER_QUERY);

  nCharSent = send(nSocket, szFingerQuery, lstrlen(szFingerQuery),
     SEND_FLAGS);

  if (nCharSent == SOCKET_ERROR)
    MessageBox(NULL, "Error occurred during send()!", PROG_NAME,
       MB_OK|MB_ICONSTOP);
```

If no errors occur, the send function returns the number of characters transmitted. Otherwise, the send function indicates an error by returning the value SOCKET_ERROR. QFinger stores the return from the send function in the integer variable nCharSent and then tests the value. If the send function returned SOCKET_ERROR, the program displays a message box with an error message and exits the program.

Note: Successful completion of the send function only means that the function successfully transmitted the data. It does not mean that the network successfully delivered the data.

RECEIVING FINGER INFORMATION

After the send function successfully transmits your data, QFinger enters a do-while loop that uses the recv function to receive data from the socket. Shown next is the prototype for the recv function, as defined in the winsock.h header file:

```
int PASCAL FAR recv(int s, char FAR * buf, int len, int flags);
```

The recv function returns the number of bytes received from a socket. The first parameter the recv function requires is a socket descriptor. The specification should actually declare this parameter as a SOCKET variable. However, since winsock.h defines a SOCKET as an unsigned int, the prototype is technically correct. As usual, QFinger uses the nSocket variable for the socket descriptor parameter. As its second parameter, the recv function requires a pointer to an incoming-data queue. The recv function stores incoming data in this buffer. The third parameter tells the recv function the size of the buffer. If the socket uses a byte-stream data service, the recv function collects data up to the size of the buffer. If the socket uses a datagram service and the size of the incoming data exceeds the incoming-data queue's size, the recv function will lose the excess data and return an error message.

Version 1.1 of the Windows Sockets specification identifies two flags that you can use as the fourth parameter to the recv function: MSG_OOB, which you have already met, and MSG_PEEK. The MSG_PEEK flag tells the recv function to copy data from the socket's incoming-data queue into the program's message buffer, just like normal. However, when you use the MSG_PEEK flag, the recv function does not remove the data from the socket's incoming-data queue. In other words, the MSG_PEEK flag lets you sneak a peek at the data but leaves the data in the queue. Normally, the socket discards incoming data after a function copies it out of the incoming-data queue.

If you examine the recv function within QFinger, you will find that QFinger passes the RECV_FLAGS constant, which QFinger has defined as zero (or none), to the function. The following program statements illustrate how QFinger receives data from the socket:

```
if (nCharSent == SOCKET_ERROR)
   MessageBox(NULL, "Error occurred during send()!", PROG_NAME,
       MB_OK|MB_ICONSTOP);

else // Get the Finger information from the host
 {
   do
     {
       nCharRecv = recv(nSocket, (LPSTR)&szFingerInfo[nConnect],
             sizeof(szFingerInfo) - nConnect, RECV_FLAGS);
       nConnect+=nCharRecv;
     }
   while (nCharRecv > 0);
```

You should note one very important point regarding the size of the incoming-data queue. Since the Finger service uses TCP (a byte-stream protocol), the program must use a do-while loop to collect all the incoming data. Even if you define a buffer large enough to hold all incoming data, the remote host may not transmit all the data at the same time. For example, suppose you modify the Finger query to include a carriage-return line-feed only. In other words, you want to request a list of all users currently logged on to the remote host. Suppose the remote host had a large number of users logged on. Also, suppose the information about these users required a data buffer size that exceeded the maximum transfer unit (MTU) of the remote host's network.

As you have learned, to avoid fragmentation, TCP transmits such data in multiple message segments. As such, your byte-stream socket would receive multiple message segments before the remote Finger server finished sending data. A Finger server automatically closes a connection after it sends all requested data. The recv function, in turn, detects the closure and thus returns a zero. In other words, the do-while loop uses the recv function to receive data from the socket. The program stores the received data in the szFingerInfo buffer. For each call to the recv function, the program records the number of characters received in the integer variable nCharRecv:

```
do
{
  nCharRecv = recv(nSocket, (LPSTR)&szFingerInfo[nConnect],
        sizeof(szFingerInfo) - nConnect, RECV_FLAGS);
  nConnect+=nCharRecv;
}
while (nCharRecv > 0);
```

The QFinger program uses the nConnect variable to record the total number of characters received during the do-while loop. It does so by summing the number of characters received from each call to the recv function, as shown next:

```
nConnect+=nCharRecv;
```

The do-while loop continues until nRecvChar is equal to or less than zero. A value of zero (returned by recv) indicates that the Finger server closed the connection. A value of less than zero indicates a socket error. (winsock.h defines SOCKET_ERROR to be -1.) When the program exits the do-while loop, QFinger tests the last value stored in nCharRecv. As shown next, if nCharRecv indicates an error occurred (SOCKET_ERROR), the program informs you with a message box containing an error message:

```
if (nCharRecv == SOCKET_ERROR)
  MessageBox(NULL, "Error occurred during recv()!", PROG_NAME,
      MB_OK|MB_ICONSTOP);

else    // Display the Finger information
{
  wsprintf(szFingerQuery,"%s@%s", FINGER_QUERY, HOST_NAME);
  MessageBox(NULL, szFingerInfo, szFingerQuery,
        MB_OK|MB_ICONINFORMATION);
}
```

If no errors occur, the program reformats the szFingerQuery buffer to contain the user ID and host name used to obtain the Finger results. The program formats this value in the commonly used *username@hostname* syntax. QFinger uses the new szFingerQuery value in the title bar of the message box that displays the Finger results. Figure 10.2 shows the message box the QFinger program displays.

Figure 10.2 *Message box with results from the Quick Finger program, QFinger.*

Understanding the Finger User-Information Protocol

A Finger server requires very little information. When a Finger server receives a carriage-return line-feed (blank line), the server transmits a list of users currently logged into the server's host computer. If the Finger server receives anything other than a blank line, the server assumes the text identifies a specific user. In such cases, the server will return all publicly-available information about all users that have a matching name or login ID. To create a Finger client program, the most difficult thing you need to know is how to create and connect a socket to a remote host. The Finger information (and its format) that you transmit and receive is simple. As you have learned in Section 1, not all protocols are this easy to use. Many protocols require a lot of information in a very structured format. As previously discussed, sometimes the best way to understand something is to start at the end and work backwards to the beginning. Now that you understand how a Finger program works, you can understand the underlying protocol more easily.

Putting It All Together

In the previous chapter, you learned how to perform DNS lookups to retrieve address information about an Internet host. As discussed in this chapter, for most Winsock programs, a successful DNS query must occur before any other network operations will succeed. The quick Finger program illustrates how you can use the results from a DNS query.

In this chapter, you learned how to use the Finger user-information protocol to retrieve user information from a host computer. As you will learn throughout the remainder of this book, most application protocols, such as Finger, are very similar. Although the format of these application protocols (as well as the information they return) will change, the steps for using these protocols will be much the same. In other words, you probably won't need to create many Finger programs. However, when you start to develop your own network applications, you can use the network I/O procedures you learned while creating the quick Finger program. Before you move on to Chapter 11, make sure you understand the following key concepts:

✓ The Telnet Network Virtual Terminal (NVT) uses seven-bit ASCII encoding for data and carriage-return line-feeds as end-of-line markers.

✓ Many application protocols, such as Finger, use Telnet's NVT data format to send and receive information.

✓ On a PC, the network services database is a simple ASCII file (named SERVICES) that contains information about communication services such as Finger, Mail, Ftp, Telnet, and so on.

✓ The network services database contains the well-known port assignment and the service protocol for each communication service in the database.

✓ The Finger user-information protocol tells you everyone logged on to a host computer or public information about a specific user.

✓ To send a Finger query to a network host, you connect a socket to protocol port 79 (the well-known port for Finger) and send an NVT ASCII character string terminated by a CRLF.

✓ To ask a Finger server to report all users logged on to a host computer, you send the server an empty string (terminated by a CRLF).

✓ To ask a Finger server for information about a specific user on a host computer, you send the server the user's name (terminated by a CRLF).

Chapter 11
Asynchronous Windows Sockets

In Chapter 9, you learned how to resolve host-computer names and IP addresses. In Chapter 10, you learned how to communicate with a remote host computer through a communications socket. In both chapters, the programs you developed used Winsock API functions to perform these operations from within Windows. However, in each case, your programs did not use any Microsoft Windows-specific extensions, which Windows Sockets includes to help you create software that conforms to the Windows programming model.

In this chapter, you will learn how the Windows programming model uses messages between windows and tasks (running programs). Furthermore, you will discover how the Winsock-extended APIs, which contain the Microsoft Windows-specific extensions, let you use Windows messages to manage network-related events.

Microsoft Windows messages are asynchronous—they do not occur in a pre-defined sequence or at specific time intervals. Within a Windows-based program, you can initiate a task and tell Windows to inform you with a message when the task completes. While the task is in progress, your program can continue to perform other tasks in cooperation with the Windows operating system.

In this chapter, you will learn how to use Winsock's asynchronous functions to develop Windows-based Internet programs. By the time you finish this chapter, you will understand the following key concepts:

♦ The parameters a typical asynchronous Winsock function requires

♦ How to create an asynchronous DNS lookup function

♦ How to use task handles to identify Windows messages from asynchronous Winsock tasks

♦ How to extract Winsock error messages from Windows messages

As you have learned, the Berkeley Sockets API uses only synchronous functions. In other words, each function in the Berkeley Sockets API must complete its task before the next program statement executes. The Windows Sockets specification includes most of the functions from the Berkeley Sockets API. However, because of the asynchronous nature of Windows messages and functions, the Winsock specification also includes Microsoft Windows extensions that are asynchronous.

CREATING THE SOCKMAN TEMPLATE

Appendix B describes the Sockman program template you will use throughout Section 2 of *Internet Programming*. If you have not already done so, you should review Appendix B at this time. The program's basic template performs no network-related tasks. Instead, the template simply provides a shell that performs most of the general Windows tasks for you. As you may already know, Windows programs require a significant amount of programming overhead to perform even simple tasks. For example, even an operation as simple as displaying and processing a dialog box can require considerable programming. Part of the reason *Internet Programming* didn't discuss the asynchronous Winsock functions in the previous two chapters was to avoid this overhead.

In this chapter, you will begin to modify the Sockman template described in Appendix B. Specifically, you will add, to the Sockman Program, the ability to resolve host names and dotted-decimal addresses into 32-bit IP addresses. As you change the program, you will learn the basic steps necessary to use the asynchronous functions in the Windows Sockets API. This chapter will not discuss the Sockman functions that Appendix B describes. The following sections only present the new and modified functions in the Sockman template—specifically, those functions related to resolving host names and dotted-decimal addresses into 32-bit IP addresses.

REVIEWING WINDOW CLASSES AND INSTANCES

The Windows operating system revolves around an object called a window. In most cases, a *window* is simply a frame (or container) within which your programs can display data. The Windows operating system sends messages to a window object based on system events or messages that other tasks (such as your Windows-based programs) generate.

Each window your program displays must be a specific window-class type. A window *class* lets you specify characteristics—such as size, color, and menu use—you want to apply to one or more windows. In addition, for each window-class type, there is a corresponding procedure (or function) that processes messages for windows of that window-class type.

The relationship between a window class and a window procedure is simple. Anytime Windows sees or generates a message for a particular window object, it sends the message to the window-class procedure associated with the window object. Windows-based programs can create multiple windows based on the same window class. Windows refers to each occurrence of a window class as an *instance*. In other words, for a particular window class, multiple instances may exist within the Windows environment.

When multiple instances of a window class exist, the corresponding window procedure must be able to identify which instance should receive the message's action. To identify each instance of a class, Windows assigns a unique instance handle to each occurrence of a particular window class. When Windows sends a message to a window procedure, Windows always includes, as one of the message's parameters, the instance handle of the corresponding window. If you want to successfully develop Windows-based programs, you must understand the relationship between window classes, procedures, and instance handles. Many *Internet Programming* program examples, such as those found in this chapter, assume you are familiar with basic Windows programming concepts.

ADDING A LOOKUP CAPABILITY TO SOCKMAN

The companion disk that accompanies *Internet Programming* includes the source code for (and an executable version of) the Sockman application named Sockman2, which incorporates host-name and Internet-address lookup capabilities into the Sockman template. A usable host-lookup capability lets users specify host names and addresses.

To provide this capability, Sockman2 adds an IDD_TEXT dialog box. As shown in Figure 11.1, the IDD_TEXT dialog box is a simple, general purpose dialog box that lets a user type information into a single text box.

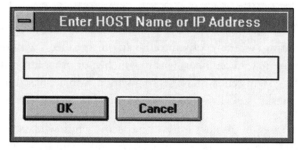

Figure 11.1 *The IDD_TEXT dialog box used for Sockman's host-lookup menu option.*

Sockman2 provides users with the ability to perform a blocking or a non-blocking lookup of host names and dotted-decimal addresses. Sockman2 performs these lookup operations using two different functions. Using synchronous functions on a blocking socket, LookupHostBlocking resolves either a host name or 32-bit IP address. On the other hand, the LookupHostAsynch function uses asynchronous functions to perform the same tasks.

As discussed in Appendix B, three functions (WndProc, WinMain, and DoMenuCommand) handle the majority of the Windows messages for the Sockman program. The main Sockman window passes messages on to WinMain, which, in turn, passes them on to WndProc (the main message-handling function). The WndProc function then passes all WM_COMMAND messages to DoMenuCommand. The DoMenuCommand function handles all WM_COMMAND messages that are not Winsock-related, such as the Help and File menu options. By default, DoMenuCommand passes any message that it does not handle to the DoWinsockProgram function. Figure 11.2 shows the main flow of messages within the Sockman application.

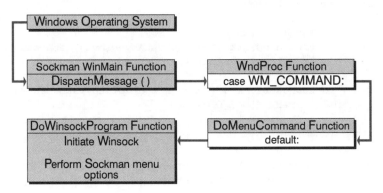

Figure 11.2 *Primary message path within the Sockman application.*

As shown in Appendix B, the original Winsock template "stubbed out" each Winsock task with programming statements that display a Windows message box. The message box, in turn, informs you that the program (or utility) is not currently implemented. As you add functionality to the Sockman program, you will replace the message-box stubs with statements that perform the corresponding operation. As you can see in Figure 11.2, the DoWinsockProgram function initiates all Winsock-related processing. As such, each time you add a new Winsock program (or utility) to Sockman, you will need to modify the DoWinsockProgram function.

Modifying the DoWinsockProgram Function

When a user selects the Utility menu Lookup option and chooses Async Lookup or Blocking Lookup, Windows sends a WM_COMMAND message to the Sockman window. WndProc passes this message to the DoMenuCommand function which, in turn, calls DoWinsockProgram.

Note: You will always find the DoWinsockProgram function in the SOCKMAN.CPP source code file. For example, in Sockman version 2, the DoWinsockProgram function resides in SOCKMAN2.CPP. In Sockman version 3, the DoWinsockProgram function resides in SOCKMAN3.CPP and so on.

The following program fragment shows how the DoWinsockProgram function processes both Lookup submenu options (Async Lookup and Blocking Lookup):

```
long DoWinsockProgram(HWND hwnd, UINT wParam, LONG lParam)
{
```

```
switch (wParam)
  {
    case IDM_LOOKUP_ASYNC:
    case IDM_LOOKUP_BLOCKING:
      if (LookupHostDialog())
        {
          if (wParam == IDM_LOOKUP_ASYNC)
            hAsyncLookupTask = LookupHostAsync(hwnd, szLookupText,
                   szLookupBuffer, (LPDWORD)&dwLookupAddr);
          else
            LookupHostBlocking(hwnd, szLookupText, szLookupBuffer,
                   TASK_BLOCK_LOOKUP);
        }
      return(TRUE);
```

When a user selects the Utility menu Lookup option and chooses Async Lookup, the wParam variable will be equal to IDM_LOOKUP_ASYNC. When a user selects the Utility menu Lookup Host option and chooses Blocking Lookup, the wParam parameter contains the value IDM_LOOKUP_BLOCKING.

In either case, the DoWinsockProgram function will call the LookupHostDialog function. The LookupHostDialog function displays the IDD_TEXT dialog box that you saw in Figure 11.1. Using the user's dialog-box entries, the program will perform the host-lookup operation.

UNDERSTANDING THE DIALOG BOX

Sockman constructs the IDD_TEXT dialog box from the following resource statements, which you can find in the SOCKMAN2.RC file:

```
IDD_TEXT DIALOG DISCARDABLE  0, 0, 161, 65
STYLE DS_MODALFRAME | WS_POPUP | WS_VISIBLE | WS_CAPTION | WS_SYSMENU
CAPTION "Enter Value"
FONT 8, "MS Sans Serif"
BEGIN
EDITTEXT IDC_TEXTBOX,5,15,150,15,ES_AUTOHSCROLL
DEFPUSHBUTTON "OK",IDOK,5,40,50,15
PUSHBUTTON "Cancel",IDCANCEL,60,40,50,15
END
```

The IDD_TEXT dialog box includes the WS_SYSMENU style (which adds the Control menu) and buttons for OK and Cancel. A user can exit the IDD_TEXT dialog box using the Control menu Close option or by clicking their mouse on either the Cancel or OK button. If the user selects the default OK button, the IDD_TEXT dialog box returns the constant value IDOK. If the user instead selects the Cancel button, IDD_TEXT returns IDCANCEL.

UNDERSTANDING THE DIALOG FUNCTION

As discussed, when the DoWinsockProgram function calls LookupHostDialog, the LookupHostDialog function creates and displays the IDD_TEXT dialog box. You can find the source code for the LookupHostDialog function in the LOOKUP2.CPP file. The following statements implement the LookupHostDialog box function:

```
LPSTR LookupHostDialog(VOID)
{
    // The dialog procedure uses the global static buffer szLookupText
    // to store the user's entry from the text box. Callers should copy
    // this value to their own locally allocated buffer since buffer
    // szLookupText can be immediately reused by another program
    // doing a host lookup.

    DLGPROC lpfnDialogProc;
    BOOL    bOkay;

    // Create a dialog box for the user's entry
    lpfnDialogProc = MakeProcInstance((DLGPROC)LookupHostDialogProc,
          hInstanceSockman);
    bOkay = DialogBox(hInstanceSockman,"IDD_TEXT", hwndSockman,
          lpfnDialogProc);
    FreeProcInstance(lpfnDialogProc);

    return(bOkay ? szLookupText : (LPSTR) NULL);
}
```

LookupHostDialog uses a common Windows-programming technique to create and display a generic dialog box. First, LookupHostDialog calls the Windows MakeProcInstance function and specifies a call-back function named LookupHostDialogProc. As you may already know, the return value from MakeProcInstance is the prolog (startup) code for the specified procedure—in this case, LookupHostDialogProc. When Windows later needs to process messages for the dialog box, Windows will send the messages to the function that corresponds to the prolog code.

UNDERSTANDING CALL-BACK FUNCTIONS

As you have learned, each window class must have a corresponding function to which Windows can send all messages destined for that window class type. Within the window-class structure, you assign the name of this special "call back" function. Call-back functions are so named because Windows uses them to "call back" or notify your program about messages it has received for the corresponding window type. In short, Windows passes the messages to the call-back function, and the function, in turn, handles the message based on its program statements.

You must create and specify a call-back function for every window class your program uses. Normally, because the window class and call-back function both reside in your program, assigning the call-back function to the window class is easy. The difficulty occurs when you need to use a window class that's defined outside of your program, such as a window class that the Windows-API DialogBox function uses. For example, assume you want Windows to pass messages to your function from the generic dialog-box window class. To do so, Windows must call (invoke) your function. Because your call-back function resides within your program's address space and the generic dialog-box class does not, Windows must first perform several housekeeping operations before it can call your function. These housekeeping steps require that the compiler include special instructions, called *prolog statements*, immediately before your function.

When Windows needs to call back your function (to process a message), Windows first executes the function's prolog statements. However, if your program calls the function, your program ignores the prolog statements. After your call-back function ends, Windows executes additional housekeeping instructions called *epilog statements*. As before, should your program call the function, your program ignores the epilog statements.

To direct the compiler to include the prolog and epilog instructions, you must precede your function name with the CALLBACK macro that the windows.h header file defines. In addition, you must include special command-line switches that direct the compiler to create the special prolog and epilog code. Normally, when you define and register your own window class, you don't need to worry about prolog and epilog code statements. The only time call-back functions require such statements is when the function resides in an address space that differs from that of the window class.

The LookupHostDialog function stores the prolog-code address (returned by MakeProcInstance) in the local variable, lpfnDialogProc. Next, LookupHostDialog calls the Windows DialogBox function. In the DialogBox function call, LookupHostDialog specifies the task instance for Sockman. (The instance handle represents this particular copy of the executing Sockman program. As you know, it's possible to run the same program two or more times, at the same time.) LookupHostDialog also specifies the IDD_TEXT dialog box, the Sockman window handle (which tells Windows where to send Sockman messages), and lpfnDialogProc (which holds the address of the LookupHostDialogProc prolog code). In other words, the DialogBox function call creates the IDD_TEXT dialog box and tells Windows to send all messages from the dialog box to the LookupHostDialogProc call-back function.

UNDERSTANDING PROLOG AND EPILOG CODE

As you have learned, when the call-back function for a window resides in different address space than the window class, you must direct the compiler to generate special prolog and epilog code which precedes and follows the call-back function's statements. When the window class and call-back function reside in different address locations, they use different code segments and data segments. When you include the CALLBACK macro with the call-back function's declaration, the compiler treats the function as a far call. As such, the compiler automatically eliminates any significant differences between the code segments. However, to resolve the differences between data segments, the compiler needs a way to set the data segment register to the call-back function's address space for each function call. That's where the prolog and epilog statements come in.

Before the call-back function begins, the prolog statements set the data-segment (DS) register to the function's address space. To assign the address space, the prolog statements assign the contents of the AX register to the DS register. As it turns out, Windows helps out behind the scenes (using special code that Windows programmers refer to as a *thunk*) by pre-assigning the AX register with the call-back function's data-segment address.

Before the function returns, the epilog statements restore the DS-register contents by popping the previous DS-register contents from the stack. Once again, because you used the CALLBACK macro (as well as necessary compiler switches), the compiler knew the call-back function used prolog and epilog code, so it pushed the DS-register contents on to the stack before calling the function.

When the user closes or exits the IDD_TEXT dialog box, the DialogBox function returns to the calling function, LookupHostDialog. The LookupHostDialog function, in turn, frees the procedure-instance address for LookupHostDialogProc. If the user clicks the OK button in the IDD_TEXT dialog box, LookupHostDialog returns a pointer to the global variable szLookupText, which will contain the user's input. Otherwise, LookupHostDialog returns a NULL.

UNDERSTANDING THE DIALOG PROCEDURE

LookupHostDialogProc is a call-back function that processes all Windows messages from the IDD_TEXT dialog box. The following statements implement LookupHostDialogProc:

```
BOOL _export CALLBACK LookupHostDialogProc(HWND hwndDlg, UINT iMessage,
    WPARAM wParam, LPARAM lParam)
{
  switch (iMessage)
    {
      case WM_INITDIALOG:                      // Initialize the dialog box
        SetDlgItemText(hwndDlg, IDC_TEXTBOX, (LPSTR)szLookupText );
        SetWindowText(hwndDlg, "Enter HOST Name or IP Address");
        CenterWindow(hwndDlg);
        return(TRUE);
```

```
      case WM_CLOSE:                        // Handle the same as Cancel
        PostMessage(hwndDlg, WM_COMMAND, IDCANCEL, 0L);
        return(TRUE);

      case WM_COMMAND:
        switch (wParam)
          {
            case IDOK:                      // Handle the OK button
              GetDlgItemText(hwndDlg, IDC_TEXTBOX, (LPSTR)szLookupText,
                  MAX_HOST_NAME);
              EndDialog(hwndDlg, TRUE);
              return(TRUE);

            case IDCANCEL:                  // Handle the Cancel button
              EndDialog(hwndDlg, FALSE);
              return(TRUE);

            default:
              return(TRUE);
          }
      }
   return(FALSE);
}
```

As you can see, the LookupHostDialogProc function processes three Windows messages from the IDD_TEXT dialog box: WM_INITDIALOG, WM_CLOSE, and WM_COMMAND. Windows sends the WM_INITDIALOG message to the dialog-box call-back function before it displays the dialog box. LookupHostDialogProc uses this message to initialize the dialog box.

UNDERSTANDING OUR USE OF MULTIPLE RETURNS AND GOTO STATEMENTS

At first glance, many software engineers that examine the LookupHostDialog function definition may choke on the multiple return statements that appear within the function. In general, we would find their reaction both understandable and justified. Because multiple return statements (as well as goto statements) often lead to poorly designed programs, programmers are taught to avoid using such statements. Since we've had numerous opportunities to debug and correct such errant code, we fully support the following statements:

> *"Avoid the use of the goto statement at all cost. Likewise, your functions should only have one entry point and one exit point (one return statement). Follow these rules in all cases—except when violating the rules makes your program easier to maintain and understand."*

The primary objective of the program examples in *Internet Programming* is to present the information you need to understand various protocols and to create Internet programs. To let you focus on Internet programming concepts, we may occasionally violate otherwise sound programming practices to make important information more clear. The use of multiple return statements within the example programs is one such case.

As you will find, *Internet Programming* will dissect many of the example functions and examine their different parts, one piece at a time. In other words, we spend considerable time discussing code fragments. Using multiple return statements, we can better present each fragment's processing. In many cases, we found that when we eliminated the multiple returns using nested *if* statements, our result was structured-code. However, this structured code made it more difficult for us to explain the key Internet programming concepts—our primary goal.

INITIALIZING THE DIALOG BOX

When the LookupHostDialogProc function receives the WM_INITDIALOG message, the function initializes the IDC_TEXTBOX text-box control with any text the Sockman user previously entered. LookupHostDialogProc obtains this text from the szLookupText global variable, which Sockman uses to store any lookup text the user enters. LookupHostDialogProc uses szLookupText as the default value that appears in the IDD_TEXT dialog box. To assign the default setting, the LookupHostDialogProc dialog box procedure uses Windows SetDlgItemText function to set the IDC_TEXTBOX text-box control equal to szLookupText. Also, during the dialog box initialization, LookupHostDialogProc sets the dialog-box title bar text to the prompt, "Enter HOST Name or IP Address." Finally, LookupHostDialogProc calls the CenterWindow function found in the source-code file COMMON2.CPP. The CenterWindow function centers the dialog box on top of the main Sockman window. After successfully completing the dialog box initialization, the CenterWindow function returns a True value to Windows.

PROCESSING COMMANDS FROM THE DIALOG BOX

As discussed, users can close the IDD_TEXT dialog box using the Control menu Close option or by clicking their mouse on either the Cancel or OK button. Windows generates a WM_CLOSE message when the user exits using the Control menu and a WM_COMMAND message for either command button. When a user clicks their mouse on the Cancel button, Windows generates a WM_COMMAND with IDCANCEL as a parameter. When the LookupHostDialogProc function, in turn, receives a WM_COMMAND with an IDCANCEL parameter, it calls the EndDialog function with a False parameter. As you may already know, calling the EndDialog function causes Windows to destroy the dialog box. However, the destruction occurs only after the DialogBox function returns. After the EndDialog function completes, the LookupHostDialogProc returns a True value to Windows, as shown in the following program statements:

```
case WM_COMMAND:
switch (wParam)
  {
    case IDCANCEL:
      EndDialog(hwndDlg, FALSE);
      return(TRUE);
```

The following steps show the entire host-lookup dialog process:

1. The LookupHostDialog function calls the DialogBox function to create the IDD_TEXT dialog box. Within the DialogBox function call, LookupHostDialog specifies the LookupHostDialogProc function as the dialog box's callback procedure.

2. Windows sends all messages from the IDD_TEXT dialog box to LookupHostDialogProc.

3. When the user closes the IDD_TEXT dialog box, LookupHostDialogProc calls the EndDialog function with a value that the DialogBox function will return to the LookupHostDialog function.

4. When LookupHostDialogProc receives a WM_COMMAND message with an IDOK parameter, LookupHostDialogProc passes the EndDialog function a parameter of True. When the LookupHostDialogProc function receives a WM_COMMAND message with an IDCANCEL parameter, LookupHostDialogProc passes the EndDialog function a parameter of False. In other words, EndDialog will report which button the user selected.

5. The DialogBox function returns the value passed by the function LookupHostDialogProc in the call to EndDialog (either True or False).

6. Windows destroys the IDD_TEXT dialog box.

If the user closes the dialog box using the Control menu, the LookupHostDialogProc function receives a WM_CLOSE message. LookupHostDialogProc handles a WM_CLOSE message as though the user clicked the Cancel button. To do this, LookupHostDialogProc simply uses the Windows PostMessage function to send a WM_COMMAND with an IDCANCEL parameter to itself:

```
case WM_CLOSE:
    PostMessage(hwndDlg, WM_COMMAND, IDCANCEL, 0L);
    return(TRUE);
```

In this case, the PostMessage function call causes Windows to send the IDD_TEXT dialog box a WM_COMMAND with an IDCANCEL parameter. Windows sends the message to the

LookupHostDialogProc function, which handles the message as just described. In other words, LookupHostDialogProc generates a message to itself that is identical to the message Windows sends when the user clicks their mouse on the Cancel button. When the user clicks their mouse on the OK button, Windows generates a WM_COMMAND message with an IDOK parameter, as previously shown in the resource statements in the file SOCKMAN2.RC. When the function LookupHostDialogProc receives this message, it uses Windows GetDlgItemText function to retrieve the user's text input from the IDC_TEXTBOX control. The LookupHostDialogProc function then stores this text in the szLookupText global variable:

```
case WM_COMMAND:
switch (wParam)
  {
    case IDOK:
      GetDlgItemText(hwndDlg, IDC_TEXTBOX, (LPSTR)szLookupText,
          MAX_HOST_NAME);
      EndDialog(hwndDlg, TRUE);
      return(TRUE);
```

After storing the user's text, LookupHostDialogProc calls Windows EndDialog function with a True value and then returns. As discussed, calling EndDialog with a True value causes the DialogBox function to return a True value to LookupHostDialog. Windows, in turn, will destroy the dialog box after the DialogBox function returns.

RETURNING TO DOWINSOCKPROGRAM

As you have learned, when the user closes the IDD_TEXT dialog box, the LookupHostDialog function will return either a NULL value or a pointer to the user's input (which Sockman stores in szLookupText). As shown next, if the return value from LookupHostDialog is not NULL, the program tests the message parameter that wParam stores to determine if the user wants to perform an asynchronous or blocking operation:

```
if (LookupHostDialog())
{
  if (wParam == IDM_LOOKUP_ASYNC)
    hAsyncLookupTask = LookupHostAsync(szLookupText, szLookupBuffer,
        (LPDWORD)&wLookupAddr);
  else
    LookupHostBlocking(szLookupText, szLookupBuffer, TASK_BLOCK_LOOKUP);
}
```

When Windows sends a message in response to a user's Sockman menu selection, Windows stores the menu option value in the wParam parameter. The value in wParam comes from the resource file that defines the menu. For example, Sockman2.rc defines the host-lookup options for the Sockman menu as shown:

```
POPUP "&Lookup Host..."
BEGIN
MENUITEM "&Async Lookup",    IDM_LOOKUP_ASYNC
MENUITEM "&Blocking Lookup", IDM_LOOKUP_BLOCKING
END
```

As such, when the user selects the Async Lookup submenu option, Windows generates a WM_COMMAND message with a wParam equal to IDM_LOOKUP_ASYNC. Likewise, if the user selects the Blocking Lookup submenu option, Windows will generate a WM_COMMAND message with a wParam equal to IDM_LOOKUP_BLOCKING. When the DoWinsockProgram function receives a WM_COMMAND message with wParam equal to the symbolic constant IDM_LOOKUP_BLOCKING and LookupHostDialog does not return a NULL value, the program will call the LookupHostBlocking function to perform a blocking operation as shown:

```
LookupHostBlocking(szLookupText, szLookupBuffer, TASK_BLOCK_LOOKUP);
```

PERFORMING A BLOCKING LOOKUP

The LookupHostBlocking function is practically the same as the QLookup program you saw in Chapter 9. However, instead of using pre-defined values for host names and IP addresses, the LookupHostBlocking function uses values the user enters. The following program statements show the complete function definition for the LookupHostBlocking function:

```
LPHOSTENT LookupHostBlocking(LPSTR szUserEntry, LPSTR szHostEntryBuffer,
    HTASK hTask)
{
  LPARAM lParam;         // Message parameter for error reporting
  DWORD dwIPAddr;        // IP address as an unsigned long
  LPHOSTENT lpHostEntry; // Pointer to an Internet host data structure

  lpHostEntry = NULL;

  // Assume a dotted-decimal address and try to convert
  if ((dwIPAddr = inet_addr(szUserEntry)) == INADDR_NONE)
    {
      // If it wasn't a dotted-decimal address, assume it's a host name
      if ((lpHostEntry = gethostbyname(szUserEntry)) == NULL)
        {
          MessageBeep(0);
          MessageBox(NULL, "Could not get host name.", szUserEntry,
              MB_OK|MB_ICONSTOP);
        }
    }
```

```
  else  // Resolve the IP address
    {
      if ((lpHostEntry = gethostbyaddr((LPCSTR) &dwIPAddr,
          AF_INET_LENGTH, AF_INET)) == NULL)
        {
          MessageBeep(0);
          MessageBox(NULL, "Could not get IP address.", szUserEntry,
              MB_OK|MB_ICONSTOP);
        }
    }

// If the host entry is valid, copy it to the program's global
// host entry variable, szHostEntryBuffer, before calling any
// other Winsock functions
if (lpHostEntry)
  {
    memcpy(szHostEntryBuffer, (LPSTR)lpHostEntry, sizeof(HOSTENT));
    // Set lParam to zero, to indicate no errors
    lParam = 0L;
  }
else
  // Get the error value and store it in the hi-word of lParam
  lParam = MAKELONG(0, WSAGetLastError());

// Have Windows send a message indicating the blocking lookup is done
SendMessage(hwndSockman, WM_BLOCK_LOOKUP_DONE, hTask, lParam);

// If valid, return a pointer to the host entry, otherwise return NULL
return((lpHostEntry ? (LPHOSTENT)szHostEntryBuffer :
    (LPHOSTENT)NULL));
}
```

As you can see, the LookupHostBlocking function uses three parameters. The first parameter is a pointer to the user's entry from the IDD_TEXT dialog box. The second parameter is a pointer to a global variable that stores data from the host entry structure. The last parameter is a task handle that LookupHostBlocking will use to identify itself in the message from Windows generated by a call to the Windows function SendMessage.

The following steps describe how the LookupHostBlocking function resolves dotted-decimal addresses and host names:

1. LookupHostBlocking assumes the first parameter is a dotted-decimal address and tries to convert it into an IP address using inet_addr.

2. If the conversion fails, LookupHostBlocking assumes the parameter is a host name and tries to resolve it using the gethostbyname function.

3. If the first parameter was a dotted-decimal address and the inet_addr conversion succeeds, LookupHostBlocking tries to resolve it using the gethostbyaddr function.

4. LookupHostBlocking uses the pointer (lpHostEntry) to store the address the DNS resolver (either gethostbyname or gethostbyaddr) returns. Then, LookupHostBlocking tests the pointer's value.

5. If the host-entry pointer (lpHostEntry) is valid, LookupHostBlocking copies the host-entry data into a global variable pointed to by LookupHostBlocking's second parameter (in this case, szLookupBuffer).

6. Upon success or failure of a host-lookup operation, LookupHostBlocking generates a Windows message indicating completion. The function uses the lParam to pass any error codes to the Windows message handler.

7. If LookupHostBlocking successfully resolves the IP address, the function returns a pointer to a buffer that contains the host-entry data. If LookupHostBlocking fails to resolve the IP address, the function returns a NULL pointer.

Although the LookupHostBlocking function does not use asynchronous Winsock functions, we've designed LookupHostBlocking to use the Windows programming model anyway. In other words, the Windows operating system initiates most function calls as a result of a Windows message. In most cases, when a called function completes its assigned task, the function generates another Windows message that signals its completion. Other program modules in the application can use the Windows message procedures to receive and respond to such signals.

Other than using values from the user, the network processing is very similar to the procedure the QLookup program (in Chapter 9) uses. The only significant difference occurs toward the end of the function. As you will learn, many asynchronous Winsock functions return task handles. As discussed, task handles uniquely identify asynchronous tasks initiated by a function. You use task handles to identify and process Windows messages generated by the asynchronous functions.

The LookupHostBlocking function does not use an asynchronous task to resolve IP addresses. As a result, LookupHostBlocking does not generate a real task handle. However, LookupHostBlocking uses the Windows SendMessage function to generate a message that simulates the results of an asynchronous lookup. LookupHostBlocking uses the hTask variable to simulate the task handle that a real asynchronous Winsock function would return.

BUILDING REDUNDANCY INTO YOUR PROGRAMS

You may wonder why the LookupHostBlocking function simulates an asynchronous message or why Sockman implements both an asynchronous and blocking version of the host-lookup functions. Unlike the QLookup program, the LookupHostBlocking function must interface with other functions. As you have learned, nearly every Internet program requires you to resolve IP addresses. As such, if you design your functions correctly, you can use the lookup functions within other programs and utilities in the Sockman application. To simplify the design of these other programs, the LookupHostBlocking function behaves in the same way as the asynchronous lookup function, LookupHostAsync. Although their internal statements are drastically different, both functions produce the same results. Any Sockman application can use either LookupHostBlocking or LookupHostAsync in the exact same way.

As a rule, you should use asynchronous Winsock functions whenever possible. You will find the asynchronous Winsock functions integrate more neatly into the message-based environment of Windows. However, some implementations of the Windows Sockets DLL are notoriously poor at resolving IP addresses asynchronously. By implementing both blocking and asynchronous lookup functions (that provide the same results), you essentially create a backup system that also resolves IP addresses. In other words, when your program needs to resolve an IP address, your program module can call the asynchronous lookup function LookupHostAsync. If the function fails, your program module can then call the blocking version of the lookup function, LookupHostBlocking. By designing the functions to produce the same result, you can use the same program functions to retrieve the host data in either case. Ensuring that you can always resolve a valid IP address is the first step toward building solid Internet applications.

Creating such redundancy may be overkill for many programs. However, if you develop Internet-based business applications that serve company-critical purposes, you may want to consider building redundant functionality into your programs. Remember, nothing can happen within your Internet programs until you can first obtain a valid IP address.

Performing an Asynchronous Lookup

As you have learned, when a user selects the Async Lookup submenu option, Windows generates a WM_COMMAND message with a wParam parameter equal to IDM_LOOKUP_ASYNC. When the DoWinsockProgram function receives such a message and the LookupHostDialog function does not return a NULL value, the program will call the LookupHostAsync function, as shown in the following program lines:

```
if (LookupHostDialog())
{
  if (wParam == IDM_LOOKUP_ASYNC)
    hAsyncLookupTask = LookupHostAsync(szLookupText, szLookupBuffer,
        (LPDWORD)&dwLookupAddr);
  else
    LookupHostBlocking(szLookupText, szLookupBuffer, TASK_BLOCK_LOOKUP);
}
```

As you can see, the first two parameters the LookupHostAsync function uses are the same as those the LookupHostBlocking uses. The first parameter, szLookupText, is a pointer to the global variable that contains the user's inputs from the IDD_TEXT dialog box. The second parameter, szLookupBuffer, is a pointer to a global variable where the lookup will store host-entry information. The third parameter, dwLookupAddr, is a global variable that stores a binary IP address. The following program statements implement the LookupHostAsync function:

```
HTASK LookupHostAsync(LPSTR szUserEntry, LPSTR szHostEntryBuffer,
    LPDWORD lpdwAddr)
{
  HTASK hTask;                              // Asynchronous task handle

  //Assume a dotted-decimal address and try to convert
  if ((*lpdwAddr = inet_addr(szUserEntry)) == INADDR_NONE)
    {
      lstrcpy(szHostName, szUserEntry);  // Store the host name
      hTask = WSAAsyncGetHostByName(hwndSockman, WM_ASYNC_LOOKUP_DONE,
            szUserEntry, szHostEntryBuffer, MAXGETHOSTSTRUCT);
    }
  else
    {
      lstrcpy(szIPAddress, szUserEntry); // Store the host address
      hTask = WSAAsyncGetHostByAddr(hwndSockman, WM_ASYNC_LOOKUP_DONE,
            (LPCSTR)&lpdwAddr, AF_INET_LENGTH, AF_INET,
            szHostEntryBuffer, MAXGETHOSTSTRUCT);
    }
  return(hTask);                           // Return the task handle
}
```

Like the LookupHostBlocking function, LookupHostAsync assumes its first argument is a dotted-decimal address and tries to convert it using the inet_addr function. If the conversion fails, LookupHostAsync tries to resolve the argument as a host name. In either case, LookupHostAsync copies the value stored in szUserEntry into a global variable.

If the user enters a host name, Sockman stores it in szHostName. If the user enters a dotted-decimal address, Sockman stores it in szIPAddress. Sockman then uses these values as default values for other Sockman program modules. For example, when a user chooses the Finger menu option, Sockman can use these values to offer the last resolved host computer as the default Finger host.

As shown in the previous function definition, LookupHostAsync uses two new (asynchronous) Winsock functions to resolve host names and addresses. Instead of using gethostbyname like the LookupHostBlocking function, LookupHostAsync uses the WSAAsyncGetHostByName function. Also, instead of using the gethostbyaddr function, LookupHostAsync uses the WSAAsyncGetHostByAddr function.

UNDERSTANDING ASYNCHRONOUS WINSOCK FUNCTIONS

The following statement provides the prototype for the WSAAsyncGetHostByAddr function. At first glance, this function may seem much more complicated than the corresponding Berkeley-style gethostbyaddr function:

```
HANDLE PASCAL FAR WSAAsyncGetHostByAddr(HWND hWnd, unsigned int wMsg,
    const char FAR * addr, int len, int type, char FAR * buf, int buflen);
```

The WSAAsyncGetHostByAddr function requires seven parameters, four more than gethostbyaddr. However, if you examine the WSAAsyncGetHostByAddr parameters carefully, you will discover that three of the seven parameters are identical to the gethostbyaddr function. The following program statement shows the function prototype for gethostbyaddr:

```
struct hostent FAR * PASCAL FAR gethostbyaddr(const char FAR * addr,
    int len, int type);
```

As you can see, both functions require the following three parameters:

```
const char FAR * addr  // Pointer to an IP address in network byte order
int len                // The address length, which is 4 for the Internet
int type               // The type of address—AF_INET for the Internet
```

The most important difference between the gethostbyaddr and WSAAsyncGetHostByAddr functions is the return values. The gethostbyaddr function returns a pointer to a host-entry structure. WSAAsyncGetHostByAddr returns a task handle. The key to understanding the asynchronous Winsock functions is understanding how to use the task handle such functions return.

UNDERSTANDING ASYNCHRONOUS TASK HANDLES

In addition to the normal parameters that a Berkeley-style version of a Winsock function requires, asynchronous versions of a Winsock function usually require two special parameters. The first parameter is the handle of the window you want Windows to notify when the asynchronous task completes. The second parameter is the message you want Windows to send to this window. When the asynchronous function completes its operation, Windows sends the specified message to the window. For example, the LookupHostAsync function calls WSAAsyncGetHostByName, as shown in the following program statement:

```
hTask = WSAAsyncGetHostByName(hwndSockman, WM_ASYNC_LOOKUP_DONE,
    szUserEntry, szHostEntryBuffer, MAXGETHOSTSTRUCT);
```

The WSAAsyncGetHostByName function initiates a task that tries to resolve an IP address using the value that the szUserEntry parameter contains. The WSAAsyncGetHostByName function immediately returns control to the caller after initiating the task. WSAAsyncGetHostByName does not wait until the resolver is complete before returning, as the gethostbyname function does. Since the WSAAsyncGetHostByName function does not immediately resolve the IP address, WSAAsyncGetHostByName cannot return a pointer to valid host entry structure (as does the gethostbyname function). Instead, WSAAsyncGetHostByName returns a Windows task handle that uniquely identifies the resolver task. As you can see, the program stores this task handle in the variable hTask.

After the resolver task completes its operation, it tells Windows to generate a message. Windows sends this message to the window that the hwndSockman handle identifies. The message identifier will be WM_ASYNC_LOOKUP_DONE. In other words, the resolver task uses the first two parameters in the WSAAsyncGetHostByName function call to tell Windows what message to send and where to send it. Asynchronous Winsock functions initiate an operation and then immediately return to the calling function. Most asynchronous functions return an asynchronous task handle. This task handle uniquely identifies the asynchronous task that the function initiates. You use this task handle to later identify messages that the asynchronous task generates.

Understanding Asynchronous Message Parameters

As you may know, Windows sends messages using a well-defined format that includes four variables: the handle of the window that is to receive the message, a message identifier, a 16-bit message parameter, and a 32-bit message parameter. Windows programmers commonly refer to the first message parameter as the wParam argument, which represents a word (16-bit) parameter. They commonly refer to the second parameter as the lParam argument, which represents a long (32-bit) parameter.

Many Windows messages do not use the wParam and lParam arguments to store useful information. However, the Winsock functions do. The wParam argument of a Winsock message contains the asynchronous task handle returned by the function that initiated the asynchronous operation. The high 16 bits of lParam contain any error codes the asynchronous operation (a zero indicates no errors) causes. The following section describes how Winsock messages use the low 16 bits of lParam.

Understanding Asynchronous Winsock Errors

Most asynchronous Winsock functions that retrieve Internet data require you to pass a pointer to a data buffer, as well as a parameter that specifies the size of your buffer. These parameters are usually the last two parameters to an asynchronous function. Windows Sockets developers cleverly designed asynchronous Winsock functions to report errors caused by data buffers that are too small to store the requested data. Windows Sockets use the low 16 bits of the lParam for this purpose. Suppose the data an asynchronous Winsock function retrieves is too large to fit into the storage buffer that you specified when you called the function. Rather than overwrite the end of your buffer or simply fail the operation, the Winsock function tells Windows to send a message with an error code of WSANOBUFS. As just discussed, Windows places the WSANOBUFS error status in the high 16 bits of the 1Param message parameter. The WSANOBUFS error code indicates that you either did not allocate a buffer or that the allocated buffer is too small to hold the retrieved data.

When an WSANOBUFS error condition occurs, the Winsock function also uses the low 16 bits. When the data buffer specified in a call to an asynchronous Winsock function is too small, the Winsock function tells Windows to store the required buffer size in the low 16 bits of the message's 1Param. In other words, asynchronous Winsock functions not only tell you when your data buffer is too small, they also tell you the buffer size your program needs to store all of the requested data.

Dynamically Allocating Data Storage Buffers

When your program specifies a data buffer that is too small to hold the requested data, the function returns the WSANOBUFS error value in the high-order two bytes of the 1Param message parameter and the needed buffer size in the low-order two bytes. Consider the implications of the Windows Sockets error-reporting features. If your Winsock programs must run under tight memory constraints, you can use the error-reporting features just described to perform dynamic memory allocation. For example, you can call an asynchronous Winsock function and specify a data buffer size of zero. As you've learned, the function will return a WSANOBUFS error code.

When you receive the message with the WSANOBUFS error code, you can examine the low 16 bits of the lParam to determine exactly how much memory you need to allocate for the data buffer. After your program dynamically allocates the exact amount of memory it requires, you can call the asynchronous Winsock function again and specify the correct buffer size. By doing so, you always use the minimum amount of memory required by the function. Like many software development decisions, the previous scenario involves a design trade-off. In the situation just described, you sacrifice performance (two function calls versus one) for memory conservation (minimum dynamic allocation versus maximum worst-case static allocation).

Windows Sockets conveniently provides two macros you can use to extract error codes and buffer size information from the lParam parameter in a Winsock message. The Winsock macro WSAGETASYNCERROR returns the error code that the high 16 bits of the message's lParam stores. The macro WSAGETASYNCBUFLEN returns the required buffer size that lParam's low 16 bits stores. You can use these macros as shown here:

```
UINT nErrorNumber = WSAGETASYNCERROR(lParam);
UINT nRequiredBuf = WSAGETASYNCBUFLEN(lParam);
```

RETURNING TO DOWINSOCKPROGRAM

As you will recall, the LookupHostAsync function returns the task handle of the asynchronous resolver task (WSAAsyncGetHostByName or WSAAsyncGetHostByAddr). As shown here, the DoWinsockProgram function stores the return value from LookupHostAsync in the hAsyncLookupTask global variable:

```
if (wParam == IDM_LOOKUP_ASYNC)
hAsyncLookupTask = LookupHostAsync(szLookupText, szLookupBuffer,
     (LPDWORD)&wLookupAddr);
```

At this point, the next move belongs to Windows. In other words, in response to a user's selection of the Async Lookup submenu option, Sockman has performed all the required steps to initiate an asynchronous lookup. The following list summarizes these steps:

1. Sockman displays a dialog box that lets the user enter a host name or dotted-decimal address.

2. Sockman passes the user's entry to the LookupHostAsync function.

3. The LookupHostAsync function initiates an asynchronous task to resolve the user's entry.

4. Sockman stores the task handle for the resolver task in the global variable hAsyncLookupTask. (By storing the task handle in a global variable, other procedures can easily identify messages from the asynchronous lookup task.)

As you have learned, Windows will send a message when the asynchronous resolver operation finishes. The following program lines show the asynchronous Winsock function calls that the LookupHostAsync performs:

```
hTask = WSAAsyncGetHostByName(hwndSockman, WM_ASYNC_LOOKUP_DONE,
    szUserEntry, szHostEntryBuffer, MAXGETHOSTSTRUCT);

hTask = WSAAsyncGetHostByAddr(hwndSockman, WM_ASYNC_LOOKUP_DONE,
    (LPCSTR)&lpdwAddr, AF_INET_LENGTH, AF_INET, szHostEntryBuffer,
    MAXGETHOSTSTRUCT);
```

Notice that both functions (WSAAsyncGetHostByName and WSAAsyncGetHostByAddr) use the same window handle and message identifier. In other words, they both specify window handle hwndSockman and message identifier WM_ASYNC_LOOKUP_DONE. The hwndSockman handle identifies the Sockman window. Windows will send the WM_ASYNC_LOOKUP_DONE message to the main Sockman window when the asynchronous resolver task finishes. In turn, the main message-handling procedure for Sockman, WndProc, will receive this message.

MODIFYING THE WNDPROC FUNCTION

As you have learned, both the LookupHostAsync and LookupHostBlocking functions initiate a DNS resolver task and later direct Windows to send a message when the resolver finishes. The resolver task sends this message to the WndProc function, which handles all messages for the main window in the Sockman application.

When the resolver task initiated by LookupHostAsync finishes, Windows will send a WM_ASYNC_LOOKUP_DONE message to the WndProc function. When the resolver in LookupHostBlocking finishes, Windows sends the WM_BLOCK_LOOKUP_DONE message to WndProc. To handle these messages, you need to add the case statements shown in the following program statements to the WndProc function in SOCKMAN2.CPP:

```
long FAR PASCAL _export WndProc(HWND hwnd, UINT iMessage, UINT wParam,
    LONG lParam)
{
  switch (iMessage)
    {
      case WM_ASYNC_LOOKUP_DONE:
      case WM_BLOCK_LOOKUP_DONE:
        DisplayHostEntry(hwnd, iMessage, wParam, lParam);
        return(0);                                      // Finished
```

As you can see, both messages cause WndProc to call the DisplayHostEntry function. As you will learn, when you add other functions that need to resolve IP addresses, you will need to modify these case statements. After the resolver task finishes, WndProc calls DisplayHostEntry, which, as its name implies, displays the results from the resolver.

UNDERSTANDING THE DISPLAYHOSTENTRY FUNCTION

The DisplayHostEntry function displays the results from a DNS resolver task that a user initiates from the Sockman menu. As shown next, the DisplayHostEntry function uses the Windows Sockets macro, WSAGETASYNCERROR, to check for asynchronous error messages.

Note: Remember, the LookupHostBlocking function also simulates an asynchronous error message. LookupHostBlocking calls the SendMessage function and stores any error codes in the lParam argument of the generated message. As such, the DisplayHostEntry function processes error messages from either the asynchronous or blocking lookup functions in Sockman.

```
VOID DisplayHostEntry(HWND hwnd, UINT iMessage, UINT wParam, LONG lParam)
{
  int nErrCode;                        // Error code from the DNS resolver

  if (nErrCode = WSAGETASYNCERROR(lParam))
    {
      wsprintf(szScratchBuffer, "%s LOOKUP caused Winsock ERROR No. %d",
          szLookupText, nErrCode);
      MessageBeep(0);
      MessageBox(NULL, szScratchBuffer, szLookupText,
          MB_OK|MB_ICONSTOP);
      //  Set the lookup buffer to NULL when an error occurs.
      szLookupBuffer[0] = '\0';
    }
  else
    {
      PHOSTENT pHostEntry;

      pHostEntry = (PHOSTENT) szLookupBuffer;
      lstrcpy(szHostName, pHostEntry->h_name);
      lstrcpy(szIPAddress,
          inet_ntoa(*(PIN_ADDR)*(pHostEntry->h_addr_list)));
      wsprintf(szScratchBuffer,
          "%s\tLOOKUP RESULTS\nHost Name:\t%s\nIP Address:\t%s",
          szLookupText,szHostName, szIPAddress);
    }
  PaintWindow(szScratchBuffer);
  return;
}
```

If the lParam tested by WSAGETASYNCERROR indicates an error, the DisplayHostEntry function displays an error message and sets the global data buffer, szLookupBuffer, length to zero. If no errors have occurred, DisplayHostEntry uses the host-entry data that the szLookupBuffer stores to display the results from the resolver. To display the resolver results, the DisplayHostEntry function first casts the szLookupBuffer address to a PHOSTENT (pointer to a host-entry structure) variable. Next, DisplayHostEntry copies the h_name field from the host-entry structure into a global variable (szHostName) that stores the last resolved host name. Doing so lets Sockman use this host name as the default value for other function dialog boxes that require a host name.

The DisplayHostEntry function uses inet_ntoa to convert the h_addr_list element from the host-entry structure into an ASCII string. DisplayHostEntry then copies the string into a global variable (szIPAddress) that stores the last resolved IP address. Once again, doing so lets Sockman use this address as the default value for other function dialog boxes. After storing the host name and address, the DisplayHostEntry function uses wsprintf to create a result string in the global scratch buffer, szScratchBuffer. The DisplayHostEntry function passes a pointer to this buffer to the PaintWindow function, which displays the resolver results in the main Sockman window.

PUTTING IT ALL TOGETHER

In this chapter, you learned how to integrate into a full-scale Windows program the same simple DNS lookup procedure that you developed in Chapter 9. You also learned how to create an equivalent asynchronous version of the same procedure. In addition, you found that, unlike Berkeley-style synchronous functions (which return data or a pointer to data), most asynchronous Winsock functions that perform network I/O return a task handle. In other words, asynchronous Winsock functions typically initiate a network operation and then immediately return a task handle to the calling function. The Winsock task handle uniquely identifies the asynchronous task that the function initiates. You can use this task handle to later identify messages that the asynchronous task generates.

In the next chapter, you will learn how to integrate the simple Finger query that you developed in Chapter 10 into a full-scale Windows program. In addition, you will also learn how to develop an asynchronous version of the same routine. However, before you move on to Chapter 12, make sure you understand the following key concepts:

- ✓ Asynchronous Winsock functions that retrieve data typically require a pointer to a data buffer and a parameter that specifies the size of the buffer.

- ✓ Asynchronous Winsock functions that perform network I/O typically return a task handle that uniquely identifies the asynchronous task.

- ✓ Windows messages from asynchronous Winsock tasks include the task's handle in the 16-bit message parameter (wParam).

- ✓ Windows messages from asynchronous Winsock tasks include any error messages in the high 16 bits of the 32-bit message parameter (lParam).

- ✓ When a data-storage buffer for an asynchronous Winsock task is too small to store the requested data, the Windows message from the task will include the WSANOBUFS error message in high 16 bits of the 32-bit message parameter from Windows.

- ✓ When a function receives a WSANOBUFS error message (buffer size too small), your programs can use the WSAGETASYNCBUFLEN macro to extract the required buffer size from the low 16 bits of the 32-bit message parameter (lParam).

Chapter 12
Using Winsock Task Handles

In Chapter 11, you learned how to use the asynchronous Winsock database functions to resolve Internet addresses. In this chapter, you will learn how to better manage the asynchronous database functions. To better understand these functions, you must understand how Winsock uses task handles. As you have learned, a handle is a value that uniquely identifies a specific object. For example, Winsock uses socket handles to identify sockets. Likewise, programs that perform file I/O operations rely on file handles. As a multitasking environment within which multiple programs (tasks) execute simultaneously, Windows uses task handles to uniquely identify each program.

In Chapter 11, you developed the Sockman program, which you can use to resolve Internet addresses. In this chapter, you will add a functional program-module to the Sockman template, modifying the template so that it responds to the Utilities menu Finger option. Specifically, you will provide Sockman users with the ability to perform asynchronous or blocking Finger operations. By the time you finish this chapter, you will understand the following key concepts:

- How to initiate synchronous and asynchronous Finger operations from within a full-scale Windows program

- How to use asynchronous Winsock task handles to monitor the progress of an asynchronous operation

This chapter assumes you have read Chapter 11, which describes how to perform DNS lookup operations in a full-scale Windows program. As such, if you have not already read Chapter 11, do so before you continue with this chapter. As previously discussed, DNS lookup services are critical to most network operations—without a valid host address, your programs will have nowhere to go on the Internet.

ADDING FINGER TO SOCKMAN

The companion disk that accompanies *Internet Programming* includes the source code for, and an executable version of, the Sockman application named Sockman3, which incorporates the Finger utility into the Sockman template. You can use the Sockman3 program as is or modify the template described in Appendix B. (If you plan to modify the original Sockman template, be sure to include the Chapter 11 modifications as well—Sockman3 depends on functions discussed in Chapter 11.)

To create a Finger utility, you should first add a dialog box, just as you did when you added the host-lookup capability to Sockman. In this dialog box, users will specify host names and user IDs. The resource file SOCKMAN3.RC defines a Finger dialog box called IDD_FINGER. You can either use SOCKMAN3.RC or add, to your own resource file, the IDD_FINGER definition shown here:

```
IDD_FINGER DIALOG DISCARDABLE 0, 0, 185, 73
STYLE DS_MODALFRAME | WS_POPUP | WS_VISIBLE | WS_CAPTION | WS_SYSMENU
CAPTION "FINGER"
FONT 8, "MS Sans Serif"
BEGIN
    EDITTEXT        IDC_FINGER_HOST,31,10,140,15,ES_AUTOHSCROLL
    EDITTEXT        IDC_FINGER_USER,31,29,140,14,ES_AUTOHSCROLL
    DEFPUSHBUTTON   "OK",IDOK,31,50,50,14
    PUSHBUTTON      "Cancel",IDCANCEL,91,50,50,14
    RTEXT           "Host:",IDC_STATIC,11,14,20,13
    RTEXT           "User:",IDC_STATIC,5,33,25,9
END
```

Users access the Finger program from the Sockman Utilities menu. When the user selects, from the Finger submenu, either the Async Finger option or the Blocking Finger option, SOCKMAN3 will display the IDD_FINGER dialog box shown in Figure 12.1. As you can see, the dialog box lets users enter an Internet host name and a user name or ID.

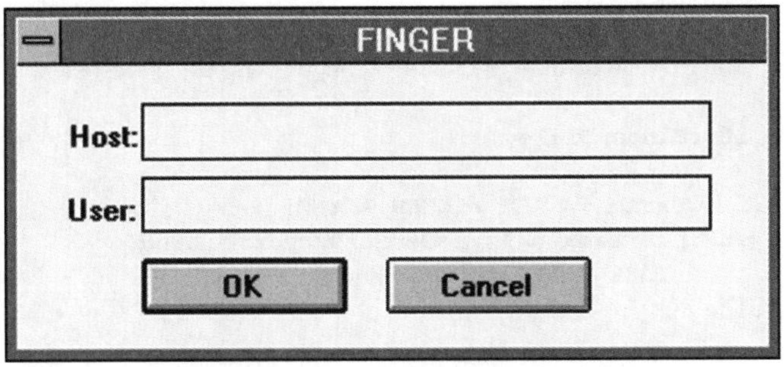

Figure 12.1 *The IDD_FINGER dialog box used for Sockman's Finger utility.*

As you saw in Chapter 11, Figure 11.2, the DoWinsockProgram function eventually handles all Windows messages that initiate Winsock programs. After you add the IDD_FINGER definition to your resource file, you need to modify the DoWinsockProgram function, which resides in the SOCKMAN.CPP file. (Note that the SOCKMAN3.CPP source-file provided on this book's companion disk already contains the modifications described in the following sections).

MODIFYING DOWINSOCKPROGRAM FOR FINGER

When a user selects the Utility menu Lookup option and chooses Async Finger or Blocking Finger, behind the scenes, Windows sends a WM_COMMAND message to the WndProc function. WndProc then passes this message to the DoMenuCommand function, which, in turn, calls DoWinsockProgram. If the user selects the Utility menu Lookup option and chooses Async Finger, the wParam variable will equal IDM_FINGER_ASYNC. If the user user selects the Utility menu Lookup option and chooses Blocking Finger, the wParam variable will equal IDM_FINGER_BLOCKING. As such, if you are building a Sockman program from scratch, you need to add the following program statements for the Finger case statement in the DoWinsockProgram function.

*Note: You can find the following DoWinsockProgram function definition in the FINGER3.CPP source file on the **Internet Programming** companion disk.*

```
long DoWinsockProgram(HWND hwnd, UINT wParam, LONG lParam)
{
  switch (wParam)
    {
      case IDM_FINGER_ASYNC:
      case IDM_FINGER_BLOCKING:
        if (hFingerTask)              // Sockman only allows 1 Finger call
          {                           // at a time
            MessageBeep(0);
            MessageBox(hwnd,
                "Finger utility is already in use. Please wait...",
                "SockMan - FINGER", MB_ICONSTOP | MB_OK);
          }
        else if (FingerDialog())
          {
            if (wParam == IDM_FINGER_ASYNC)
              hFingerTask = AsyncGetServiceInfo(hwnd,
                  TASK_ASYNC_FINGER);
            else
              {
                hFingerTask = TASK_BLOCK_FINGER;
                FingerHostBlocking();
                hFingerTask = 0;
              }
          }
        break;
```

To support multiple (simultaneous) finger operations, Sockman would need to manage a separate data buffer for each operation. As such, to simplify data storage, Sockman lets the user initiate only one Finger operation at a time. To prevent more than one Finger operation at a time, DoWinsockProgram tests the global Finger task handle, hFingerTask. If hFingerTask contains a value greater than zero, a Finger operation is already in progress. As shown next, if a Finger operation is in progress (hFingerTask is a value other than zero), DoWinsockProgram displays a message box that so informs the user and does not execute any other Finger program statements:

```
case IDM_FINGER_ASYNC:
case IDM_FINGER_BLOCKING:
if (hFingerTask) // Sockman only allows 1 Finger call at a time
  {
    MessageBeep(0);
    MessageBox(hwnd,
          "Finger utility is already in use. Please wait...",
          "SockMan - FINGER", MB_ICONSTOP | MB_OK);
    break;
  }
```

If no Finger operations are in progress, DoWinsockProgram calls the FingerDialog function, which displays the IDD_FINGER dialog box.

UNDERSTANDING THE FINGER DIALOG BOX

As previously shown in Figure 12.1, the Finger dialog box lets the user specify the host or user about which they desire information. The following statements implement the FingerDialog function. As you can see, the function is practically identical to the function LookupHostDialog you saw in LOOKUP2.CPP:

```
BOOL FingerDialog(VOID)
 {
   DLGPROC lpfnDialogProc;
   BOOL bOkay;

   //Create a dialog-box for the user's entry
   lpfnDialogProc = MakeProcInstance((DLGPROC)FingerDialogProc,
          hInstanceSockman);
   bOkay = DialogBox(hInstanceSockman,"IDD_FINGER", hwndSockman,
          lpfnDialogProc);
   FreeProcInstance(lpfnDialogProc);

   return(bOkay);
 }
```

There are only three differences between the FingerDialog function and the LookupHostDialog function. First, the FingerDialog function uses a callback function named FingerDialogProc. Second, the DialogBox function in FingerDialog specifies the IDD_FINGER dialog box instead of the IDD_TEXT that LookupHostDialog uses. Third, the FingerDialog function returns a Boolean True-or-False value (BOOL) instead of a long pointer to char (LPSTR). As you can see,

FingerDialog and LookupHostDialog use the same Windows-API functions to create and display the dialog box.

UNDERSTANDING THE FINGER DIALOG PROCEDURE

The Finger dialog box callback function, FingerDialogProc, (also called a dialog procedure) is similar to the callback function the Lookup dialog box uses. Just as the LookupHostDialog function processes all messages for the IDD_TEXT dialog box in the Lookup module, the FingerDialogProc function processes all messages for the IDD_FINGER dialog box in the Finger program module. The following statements implement the FingerDialogProc function:

```
BOOL _export CALLBACK FingerDialogProc(HWND hwndDlg, UINT iMessage,
    WPARAM wParam, LPARAM lParam)
{
  switch(iMessage)
    {
      case WM_INITDIALOG:              // Initialize the dialog box
        LPSTR pHost;

        pHost = lstrlen(szFingerHost) ? szFingerHost : szHostName;
        SetDlgItemText(hwndDlg, IDC_FINGER_HOST, pHost);
        SetDlgItemText(hwndDlg, IDC_FINGER_USER, szFingerUser);
        CenterWindow(hwndDlg);
        return(TRUE);

      case WM_CLOSE:                   // Handle same as the Cancel button
        PostMessage(hwndDlg, WM_COMMAND, IDCANCEL, 0L);
        return(TRUE);

      case WM_COMMAND:
        switch(wParam)
          {
            case IDOK:                 // Handle the OK button
              GetDlgItemText(hwndDlg, IDC_FINGER_HOST,
                      (LPSTR)szFingerHost, MAX_HOST_NAME);
              GetDlgItemText(hwndDlg, IDC_FINGER_USER,
                      (LPSTR)szFingerUser, MAX_USER_NAME);
              lstrcpy(szLookupText, szFingerHost);
              EndDialog(hwndDlg, TRUE);
              return(TRUE);

            case IDCANCEL:             // Handle the Cancel button
              EndDialog(hwndDlg, FALSE);
              return(TRUE);
          }
    }
  return(FALSE);                       // Return false for unhandled messages
}
```

Like LookupHostDialogProc, the FingerDialogProc function processes the WM_INITDIALOG, WM_CLOSE, and WM_COMMAND Windows messages.

INITIALIZING THE FINGER DIALOG BOX

As you have learned, Windows sends the WM_INITDIALOG message to initialize a dialog box before Windows displays it on your screen. When the FingerDialogProc function receives the WM_INITDIALOG message, the function initializes the two text-box controls in the dialog box and then centers the dialog box on the user's screen. The IDD_FINGER dialog box uses two text-box controls: IDC_FINGER_HOST and IDC_FINGER_USER. IDC_FINGER_HOST contains a Finger host, such as *jamsa.com,* and IDC_FINGER_USER contains a Finger query, which typically is a user ID such as *kcope*. During dialog-box initialization, the FingerDialogProc function sets the IDC_FINGER_USER text-box to the value the szFingerUser global variable stores. In the szFingerUser variable, the program always stores the user ID last used by a Finger operation. Doing so lets Sockman offer the last user-ID as a default value in the text-box.

To begin, the FingerDialogProc function first tests the length of the szFingerHost global variable. The szFingerHost variable stores the last host-name used by a Finger operation. If the length of szFingerHost is zero, the user has not performed a previous Finger operation during this Sockman session. In such cases, the FingerDialogProc function sets the IDC_FINGER_USER text-box equal to the last host name (if any) used by the Lookup program module. The Lookup program module stores the last resolved host name in the szHostName global variable. In other words, Sockman tracks the values the user enters in the various Sockman utility dialog boxes. To minimize the amount of typing the user must perform, Sockman offers (whenever possible) the last entered value as a default.

For example, a user might perform a host lookup to verify that they have a valid domain name for a host computer. Next, the user might Ping the host to see if the host is on-line (Chapter 14 demonstrates how to create a Ping program). Finally, the user might Finger the host system to see who is on-line. Because Sockman tracks the most recent user entries, the user would need to enter the host name or dotted-decimal address only one time. After the FingerDialogProc function initializes both text-box controls and centers the IDD_FINGER dialog box, the function returns a True value to tell Windows that it has handled the message.

PROCESSING COMMANDS FROM THE DIALOG BOX

To close the IDD_FINGER dialog box, users can select the Control menu Close option or click their mouse on either the Cancel or OK button. As you have learned, Windows generates a WM_CLOSE message when the user selects the Control menu Close option to exit. Windows generates a WM_COMMAND message when the user clicks on either command button (Cancel or OK) to exit. When the user selects the Control menu Close option to close the dialog box, the FingerDialogProc function calls the PostMessage function, which causes Windows to send a

WM_COMMAND with an IDCANCEL parameter. When the FingerDialogProc function receives the message with the IDCANCEL parameter (or a WM_COMMAND message from the Cancel button), FingerDialogProc calls the EndDialog function, which causes Windows to destroy the dialog box.

In a similar fashion, when the user clicks their mouse on the OK button, the FingerDialogProc function receives a WM_COMMAND with an IDOK parameter. When FingerDialogProc receives this message, it uses the Windows GetDlgItemText function to retrieve the user's entries from the IDC_FINGER_HOST and IDC_FINGER_USER text-box controls. Next, the FingerDialogProc function updates the szLookupText global variable by calling Windows lstrcpy function, as shown here:

```
lstrcpy(szLookupText, szFingerHost);
```

Note: *Remember, to simplify user operations, Sockman uses the most recently entered value as a default value in program dialog boxes. By updating the variable szLookupText, Sockman ensures that the user's next lookup operation will use the Finger host as a default value.*

After storing the user's text, the FingerDialogProc function calls Windows EndDialog function with a True value and then returns. As you have learned, the EndDialog function causes the DialogBox function to return, which, in turn, causes Windows to destroy the dialog box.

RETURNING TO DOWINSOCKPROGRAM

After the DialogBox function call from FingerDialog returns, the FingerDialog function returns control to the DoWinsockProgram function. In doing so, the FingerDialog function returns the Boolean value specified by the Finger dialog procedure, FingerDialogProc. This True or False value tells the DoWinsockProgram function how the user closed the dialog box. A True value indicates the user clicked their mouse on the OK button. If the user clicked their mouse on the Cancel button or used the Control menu Close option, the FingerDialog function returns a False value. If FingerDialog returns False, the user has canceled the Finger operation and, in response, the DoWinsockProgram function takes no further action. However, if the user clicks their mouse on the OK button and the FingerDialog function returns a True value, DoWinsockProgram tests the message's wParam value. The value contained in wParam tells DoWinsockProgram whether the user wants to perform an asynchronous or blocking Finger operation. If the user selects the Utility menu Finger option and chooses Async Finger, wParam parameter will equal IDM_FINGER_ASYNC. In such cases, DoWinsockProgram calls the AsyncGetServiceInfo function:

```
if (wParam == IDM_FINGER_ASYNC)
  hFingerTask = AsyncGetServiceInfo(hwnd, TASK_ASYNC_FINGER);
else
 {
```

```
    hFingerTask = TASK_BLOCK_FINGER;
    FingerHostBlocking();
    hFingerTask = 0;
}
```

UNDERSTANDING THE ASYNCGETSERVICEINFO FUNCTION

As you have learned, the network-services database contains the names of commonly used network services, such as Ftp, Telnet, SMTP, and Finger. The database also identifies port numbers,
protocols, and alias names for each listed service. The AsyncGetServiceInfo function simply initiates an asynchronous process that retrieves service information from the network-services database.
The following program statements define the AsyncGetServiceInfo function:

```
HTASK AsyncGetServiceInfo(HWND hwnd, HTASK hService)
{
  // Store the task handle from WSAAsyncGetServByName
  HTASK hTask = WSAAsyncGetServByName(hwnd,WM_GOT_SERVICE,
        (LPSTR)IPSERVICE_FINGER, NULL, (LPSTR)szFingerBuffer,
        sizeof(szFingerBuffer));

  if (!hTask)
    {
      LPARAMlParam;

      hTask = hService;                         // Return the service ID
      lParam = MAKELONG(0, WSAGetLastError()); // Log the error code
      PostMessage(hwnd, WM_GOT_SERVICE, hService, lParam);
    }
  return(hTask);
}
```

As you can see, Sockman builds the AsyncGetServiceInfo function around the Windows Sockets
function WSAAsyncGetServByName. However, as discussed next, you could actually use
WSAAsyncGetServByName instead of AsyncGetServiceInfo. The AsyncGetServiceInfo function
provides a "wrapper" for WSAAsyncGetServByName. One advantage of using a wrapper function is you can locate the error-checking code in one function. In this way, you don't need to
replicate the error-checking code each time you need to call WSAAsyncGetServByName. Instead,
you can call the AsyncGetServiceInfo function and it will execute the same error checks for each
WSAAsyncGetServByName function call. By restricting such error checks to one function, you
remove a large number of replicated statements from your programs. As a result, your programs
contain much less clutter, which makes them easier to read, understand, and modify.

UNDERSTANDING THE WSAASYNCGETSERVBYNAME FUNCTION

The WSAAsyncGetServByName function is similar to the AsyncGetServiceInfo function you met
earlier in this chapter. However, rather than retrieving a host name from the database,

WSAAsyncGetServByName retrieves a protocol and port number. The following program statement defines the WSAAsyncGetServByName prototype:

```
HANDLE PASCAL FAR WSAAsyncGetServByName(HWND hWnd, unsigned int wMsg,
    const char FAR * name, const char FAR * proto, char FAR * buf,
    int buflen);
```

As you can see, the WSAAsyncGetServByName function requires several parameters. Like many asynchronous Winsock functions, WSAAsyncGetServByName requires a window handle and a message identifier for its first two parameters. As you have learned, when an asynchronous Winsock function completes its operation, Windows usually sends a message to your window's message-handling procedure. This message from the asynchronous function indicates that its operation finished. The message that Windows sends is the identifier in the second parameter (wMsg). Windows sends wMsg to the window that the handle in the first parameter (hWnd) identifies.

WSAAsyncGetServByName is an asynchronous version of the getservbyname function that you met in the QFinger program. As you may recall, the getservbyname function retrieves a protocol and port for the named service from the network services database. Compare the WSAAsyncGetServByName prototype with the prototype for the getservbyname function, shown next:

```
struct servent FAR * PASCAL FAR getservbyname(const char FAR * name,
    const char FAR * proto );
```

As you can see, two of the getservbyname function parameters (name and proto) are identical to the parameters the WSAAsyncGetServByName function requires. The name parameter points to a service name and the proto parameter points to a protocol name. Like getservbyname, the WSAAsyncGetServByName function lets you use a default protocol by specifying a NULL value for the proto parameter. Like most asynchronous Winsock functions that retrieve data, WSAAsyncGetServByName requires your programs to allocate a data buffer and pass to the function a pointer to (the address of) the buffer. In the WSAAsyncGetServByName function prototype, the data-buffer address corresponds to the buf parameter. Also, WSAAsyncGetServByName requires the size of your data buffer. When WSAAsyncGetServByName finishes, it copies the service information into the buffer specified by the buf parameter, and then returns a task handle.

UNDERSTANDING THE ASYNCGETSERVICEINFO MESSAGE PARAMETERS

The WSAAsyncGetServByName function parameters dictate the AsyncGetServiceInfo function parameters. In other words, because it uses the WSAAsyncGetServByName function to retrieve service information, the AsyncGetServiceInfo function needs most of the same parameters as WSAAsyncGetServByName. The AsyncGetServiceInfo function design does not assume you want all messages sent to the main Sockman window. As such, you must pass AsyncGetServiceInfo a window handle. The other AsyncGetServiceInfo parameter identifies the requested service by a task identifier (in this case, TASK_ASYNC_FINGER).

UNDERSTANDING THE ASYNCGETSERVICEINFO ERROR CHECKING

The following program statements show the error checks that the AsyncGetServiceInfo function performs for the WSAAsyncGetServByName function:

```
HTASK hTask = WSAAsyncGetServByName(hwnd,WM_GOT_SERVICE, (LPSTR)
    IPSERVICE_FINGER, NULL, (LPSTR)szFingerBuffer,
    sizeof(szFingerBuffer));

if (!hTask)
{
  LPARAM lParam;

  hTask = hService;                          // Return the service ID
  lParam = MAKELONG(0, WSAGetLastError());   // Log the error code
  PostMessage(hwnd, WM_GOT_SERVICE, hService, lParam);
}
```

To begin, the AsyncGetServiceInfo function tests the task handle (hTask) it receives from the WSAAsyncGetServByName function. If the task handle is NULL, the AsyncGetServiceInfo function uses the MAKELONG macro to create an error message. When AsyncGetServiceInfo uses the MAKELONG macro, MAKELONG stores, in the high 16 bits of the local lParam variable, the error code that the WSAGetLastError function returns. (The function uses the local lParam variable in a simulated error message similar to the kind that many Winsock asynchronous functions return). Finally, AsyncGetServiceInfo uses the Windows PostMessage function to send the message that contains the error code to the main Sockman window (as identified by the window handle hwndSockman). Of course, if no errors occur, AsyncGetServiceInfo returns the task handle for the asynchronous process to the calling function.

RETURNING TO DOWINSOCKPROGRAM

When the AsyncGetServiceInfo function returns control to DoWinsockProgram, the DoWinsockProgram function stores the task handle for the asynchronous service retrieval in the hFingerTask global variable, as shown here:

```
if (wParam == IDM_FINGER_ASYNC)
  hFingerTask = AsyncGetServiceInfo(hwnd, TASK_ASYNC_FINGER);
else
{
  // The user selected a blocking finger IDM_FINGER_BLOCKING
  hFingerTask = TASK_BLOCK_FINGER;
  FingerHostBlocking();

  // Since the Finger operation has finished, reset the global Finger
  // task handle to zero so the user can initiate another one.
  hFingerTask = 0;
}
```

The DoWinsockProgram function does not test the hFingerTask variable, which now either contains a NULL value (if the AsyncGetServiceInfo function could not initiate the asynchronous operation) or the task handle for the asynchronous service-retrieval operation. If the task handle is NULL, the DoWinsockProgram function does not need to change the value of hFingerTask—a null value already indicates that no Finger operation is in progress.

At first, you might wonder why the DoWinsockProgram function stores the constant TASK_FINGER_BLOCK in the hFingerTask variable. If hFingerTask is null (or zero), it indicates that no Finger operation is in progress. However, as discussed next, for Finger port numbers, you can use an alternative to the network services database. As you may recall from the QFinger program, the only value QFinger extracts from the service-entry structure is the protocol port for Finger. As you may also recall, Windows Sockets defines constants for the well-known ports for many network services, including Finger.

As such, for the Finger utility, you do not need to terminate the Finger operation just because Winsock could not resolve the service entry. Instead, you can continue and use the well-known port defined for use by the winsock.h header file. Sockman's use of the hFingerTask variable and the TASK_BLOCK-FINGER identifier will become more clear to you in the following sections. As you will learn, the WndProc function uses hFingerTask and TASK_BLOCK_FINGER to identify the Finger task and continue the Finger operation.

MODIFYING THE WNDPROC FUNCTION

As you have learned, asynchronous Winsock functions, such as WSAAsyncGetServByName, cause Windows to send a notification message when the asynchronous operation completes. (WSAAsyncGetServByName sends the notification to the window specified by its first parameter). In the Sockman application, Windows sends all such messages to the WndProc function. Take another look at the WSAAsyncGetServByName function call, shown here, which occurs in the AsyncGetServiceInfo function:

```
hTask = WSAAsyncGetServByName(hwnd,WM_GOT_SERVICE, (LPSTR)
    IPSERVICE_FINGER,NULL,(LPSTR)szFingerBuffer,sizeof(szFingerBuffer));
```

As discussed, AsyncGetServiceInfo is a wrapper for the WSAAsyncGetServByName function. As such, AsyncGetServiceInfo passes its first parameter directly to the WSAAsyncGetServByName function. WSAAsyncGetServByName uses the first parameter passed to AsyncGetServiceInfo as its window handle.

In this case, the previously shown AsyncGetServiceInfo function call will result in a Windows message to the WndProc function that contains the WM_GOT_SERVICE identifier. Windows will send this message when the WSAAsyncGetServByName operation completes. In other words, as soon as WSAAsyncGetServByName retrieves the service-entry data for Finger, Windows will send a WM_GOT_SERVICE message to the WndProc function. To handle this message, you need to add (to the WndProc function in SOCKMAN3.CPP), the program statements for the WM_GOT_SERVICE case, as shown here:

```
long FAR PASCAL _export WndProc(HWND hwnd, UINT iMessage, UINT wParam,
    LONG lParam)
{
  switch (iMessage)
    {
      case WM_GOT_SERVICE:
        if (wParam == hFingerTask)
          LookupFingerHost(lParam);
        return(0);
```

As you can see, when the WndProc function receives a WM_GOT_SERVICE message, the function tests the wParam value, which contains the task handle for an asynchronous Winsock operation. In the code just shown, the WndProc function tests wParam to see if it is equal to the global variable that stores the Finger task handle. If wParam matches the Finger task handle, the WndProc function calls the LookupFingerHost function, which tries to resolve the host name or dotted-decimal address the user enters.

Note: Later in this chapter, you will learn why you usually want to identify which asynchronous Winsock operation triggered a Windows message.

UNDERSTANDING THE LOOKUPFINGERHOST FUNCTION

The primary purpose of the LookupFingerHost function is to initiate an asynchronous lookup of the host name or address that the Sockman user enters. The following program statements define the LookupFingerHost function:

```
VOID LookupFingerHost(LPARAM lError)
{
  // Sockman uses WSAAsyncGetServByName to fill szFingerBuffer with
  // the service entry information. The function extracts the finger
  // service port from szFingerBuffer before reusing the buffer to
  // store the host entry information.
  if (WSAGETASYNCERROR(lError))              // If an error occurs, use the
    nFingerPort = htons(IPPORT_FINGER);  // well-known protocol port
  else
    nFingerPort = ((LPSERVENT)szFingerBuffer)->s_port;

  hFingerTask = LookupHostAsync(hwndSockman, szFingerHost,
        szFingerBuffer, (LPDWORD)&dwFingerAddr);

  if (!hFingerTask)
```

```
        {
          wsprintf(szFingerBuffer,"Lookup failed: %s", (LPSTR)szFingerHost);
          MessageBeep(0);
          MessageBox(hwndSockman, szFingerBuffer, "SockMan - FINGER",
                MB_OK|MB_ICONSTOP);
        }
     return;
   }
```

The LookupFingerHost function uses the szFingerBuffer global variable to store the host data the asynchronous operation returns. As you may have noticed, the AsyncGetServiceInfo function also uses the szFingerBuffer variable. (AsyncGetServiceInfo stores network service information in szFingerBuffer.) As a result, before the LookupFingerHost function can reuse szFingerBuffer to store host data, the function must store any required network service information elsewhere. The only data element Finger needs from the service-entry structure is the protocol port for the Finger. The LookupFingerHost function uses the WSAGETASYNCERROR macro to test the lError parameter for any Winsock errors. The lError parameter will contain the error code for any errors that occurred when Sockman accessed the network-services database. If LookupFingerHost detects an error, the function stores the default port, IPPORT_FINGER, in the global Finger port variable, nFingerPort. If no errors have occurred, the LookupFingerHost function uses the s_port element of the service structure.

After storing the Finger protocol-port in nFingerPort, the LookupFingerHost function uses the LookupHostAsync function to initiate an asynchronous host lookup. The LookupHostAsync function returns a task handle for an asynchronous resolver function. The LookupFingerHost function stores this task handle in the hFingerTask global variable, which tracks the current asynchronous task handle for the on-going Finger operation. If the task handle that the LookupHostAsync function returns is NULL, the LookupFingerHost function displays a message box that warns the user that the DNS lookup operation failed. Once again, after the program initiates an asynchronous operation (the LookupFingerHost function calls the LookupHostAsync function), Sockman must wait for a message from Windows before the program can continue. As you have learned, the LookupHostAsync function will cause Windows to generate a WM_ASYNC_LOOKUP_DONE message when the function completes the asynchronous resolver operation. As such, your next change to the Sockman code is to add program statements to the WndProc function that handles the WM_ASYNC_LOOKUP_DONE message for the Finger lookup operation.

MODIFYING THE WNDPROC FUNCTION (AGAIN)

As you have learned, the LookupHostAsync function will cause Windows to generate a WM_ASYNC_LOOKUP_DONE message when the function completes the asynchronous resolver operation. In the Sockman2 version of Sockman, the WndProc function handled both the

WM_ASYNC_LOOKUP_DONE and WM_BLOCK_LOOKUP_DONE messages by calling the DisplayHostEntry function:

```
case WM_ASYNC_LOOKUP_DONE:
case WM_BLOCK_LOOKUP_DONE:
   DisplayHostEntry(lParam);
   return(0);
```

However, when the LookupHostAsync function performs the asynchronous lookup for a Finger operation, you don't want your monitor to display the results, as was the case in the QLookup program. Instead, your program needs to pass the IP address to other functions that use it to complete the Finger operation. When you first begin to use the asynchronous Winsock functions, it may not be obvious how to accomplish such an operation. The key to understanding the asynchronous database functions in the Winsock API is understanding how Winsock uses task handles.

Solving a Problem

Consider the problem you face with Sockman as it currently exists. You have used the LookupHostAsync function to asynchronously resolve Internet addresses for two different menu selections. First, Sockman calls the LookupHostAsync function when the user chooses to perform an asynchronous lookup by selecting Async Lookup from the Utilities menu Lookup option.

Second, as you have just seen, the program also calls the LookupHostAsync function to resolve an Internet address for the Finger modules. In both cases, the LookupHostAsync function will cause Windows to generate the same message, WM_ASYNC_LOOKUP_DONE.

However, you want to execute different program statements for each case. As such, you need to know which asynchronous operation triggered the WM_ASYNC_LOOKUP_DONE message. To obtain this information, you look to the message's wParam.

As you have learned, many asynchronous Winsock functions require you specify a message identifier in the function call. Windows sends a message with this identifier when the asynchronous operation completes. Any asynchronous Winsock function that requires you to specify a message identifier will return a task handle. When the function tells Windows to generate the specified message, the function also tells Windows to store the task handle in the message's wParam. By examining a message's wParam, you can identify the asynchronous Winsock operation that triggered the message. Previously, Sockman called the DisplayHostEntry function for both the WM_ASYNC_LOOKUP_DONE and the WM_BLOCK_LOOKUP_DONE messages.

As such, to add Finger operations to Sockman, you need to modify the program statements for the WM_ASYNC_LOOKUP_DONE and WM_BLOCK_LOOKUP_DONE cases in the WndProc function:

```
long FAR PASCAL _export WndProc(HWND hwnd, UINT iMessage, UINT wParam,
    LONG lParam)
{
  switch (iMessage)
    {
      case WM_ASYNC_LOOKUP_DONE:
        if (wParam == hAsyncLookupTask)
          DisplayHostEntry(lParam);

        if (wParam == hFingerTask)
          {
            PaintWindow("Asynchronous lookup for Finger completed.");
            FingerHostAsync(lParam);
            hFingerTask = 0;
          }
        return(0);

      case WM_BLOCK_LOOKUP_DONE:
        if (wParam == TASK_BLOCK_LOOKUP)
          DisplayHostEntry(lParam);

        if (wParam == TASK_BLOCK_FINGER)
          PaintWindow("Blocking lookup for Finger completed.");
        return(0);
```

As you can see, Sockman no longer uses a single DisplayHostEntry function call for both messages. Instead, Sockman encapsulates two DisplayHostEntry function calls within two *if* constructs that test the value of the message's wParam for each message identifier. In other words, these modifications let the WndProc function in Sockman determine which asynchronous Winsock operation triggered the Windows message.

Performing an Asynchronous Finger

As you have learned, Sockman stores the current asynchronous task handle for the Finger operation in the hFingerTask global variable. As you saw in the DoWinsockProgram function, Sockman also uses the constant TASK_BLOCK_FINGER to identify asynchronous Finger operations. As shown next, when the WndProc function receives a WM_ASYNC_LOOKUP_DONE message from Windows, the function tests wParam to determine whether the task handle belongs to a Finger operation. If wParam contains TASK_BLOCK_FINGER or the same value as the Finger task handle (hFingerTask), WndProc calls the FingerHostAsync function:

```
if (wParam == hFingerTask)
{
  PaintWindow("Asynchronous lookup for Finger completed.");
  FingerHostAsync(lParam);
  hFingerTask = 0;
}
```

The FingerHostAsync function is the last stop in Sockman's asynchronous Finger operations. As such, when the FingerHostAsync function returns, WndProc sets hFingerTask to zero to indicate that a Finger operation is no longer in progress. (Remember, Sockman only allows one Finger operation at a time.)

UNDERSTANDING THE FINGERHOSTASYNC FUNCTION

As you have learned, SOCKMAN3 provides users with the ability to perform either an asynchronous or blocking Finger operation. A WM_ASYNC_LOOKUP_DONE message from an asynchronous Finger operation causes the WndProc function to call the FingerHostAsync function. As you will learn, the actual socket operations for an asynchronous and blocking Finger operation are identical. The name of the function that performs the actual Finger operation is DoFingerOperation. Both asynchronous and blocking Finger operations call the function DoFingerOperation. However, the asynchronous and blocking Finger operations perform different steps before they call DoFingerOperation.

The DoFingerOperation front-end for asynchronous Finger operations is the FingerHostAsync function. The DoFingerOperation front-end for blocking Finger operations is the FingerHostBlocking function. In an asynchronous Finger operation, Sockman resolves the IP address for the user's host computer just before it calls the FingerHostAsync function. If any errors occur, Windows stores the error code in the WM_ASYNC_LOOKUP_DONE message that triggers the FingerHostAsync function call. (Within the message, Windows stores the code in the high 16 bits of lParam.) The FingerHostAsync function, in turn, tests the lParam value, which the function names lError:

```
BOOL FingerHostAsync(LPARAM lError)
{
   int nErr;                         // Error code from asynchronous lookup

   if (nErr = WSAGETASYNCERROR(lError))
     {
       MessageBeep(0);
       PaintWindow("Async lookup failed! Trying a blocking finger.");
       hFingerTask = TASK_BLOCK_FINGER;
       FingerHostBlocking();
       hFingerTask = 0;
       return(FALSE);
     }

   // All data required to perform the Finger query is available so do it.
   return(DoFingerOperation());
}
```

As shown in the previous example, if the asynchronous resolver process fails, Sockman displays a message that notifies the user of the failure. Sockman then proceeds to try a blocking resolution of the address. Only after the blocking resolver fails does Sockman quit trying to perform the Finger operation. If Sockman successfully resolves the IP address, either asynchronously or with a blocking function, the FingerHostAsync function calls the DoFingerOperation function. At this point, the asynchronous Finger modules have collected all the information they need to perform the actual Finger operation. Now it's almost time to examine the actual Finger operation. However, before you do so, the following section will return you to the DoWinsockProgram and so that you can quickly review the steps a blocking Finger operation performs.

PERFORMING A BLOCKING FINGER OPERATION

As you have learned, the DoWinsockProgram function tests the wParam argument from a Finger message to determine whether the user selected an asynchronous or blocking Finger operation. If wParam is equal to IDM_FINGER_ASYNC, the user selected an asynchronous Finger operation. Otherwise, the DoWinsockProgram function assumes the user selected a blocking Finger. For a blocking Finger, the DoWinsockProgram function executes the program statements within the *else* construct:

```
if (wParam == IDM_FINGER_ASYNC)
hFingerTask = AsyncGetServiceInfo(hwnd, TASK_ASYNC_FINGER);

else
{
   // The user selected a blocking finger IDM_FINGER_BLOCKING
   hFingerTask = TASK_BLOCK_FINGER;
   FingerHostBlocking();

   // Since the Finger operation has finished, reset the global Finger
   // task handle to zero so the user can initiate another one.
   hFingerTask = 0;
}
```

First, the DoWinsockProgram function sets the Finger task-handle variable (hFingerTask) to TASK_BLOCK_FINGER to indicate that a Finger operation is in progress. As discussed, setting this variable (flag) prevents the user from initiating more than one Finger operation at a time. Next, the DoWinsockProgram function calls the FingerHostBlocking function which is similar to the FingerHostAsync function in that both functions are front-ends to the DoFingerOperation function, which performs the actual Finger operation across the network.) When the function FingerHostBlocking returns, the DoWinsockProgram function resets the Finger task-handle variable (hFingerTask) to 0 to indicate that the Finger operation is no longer in progress.

UNDERSTANDING THE FINGERHOSTBLOCKING FUNCTION

As you have learned, both asynchronous Finger functions and blocking Finger functions call the DoFingerOperation function to perform Finger-based socket communications across the network. As such, asynchronous and blocking Finger-program modules must collect the same information—a valid IP address and a protocol port number for the Finger service—before they call the DoFingerOperation function. To obtain this information, a blocking Finger operation uses blocking functions. As shown in the following block of code, the FingerHostBlocking function first resolves the IP address by calling LookupHostBlocking. Next, the FingerHostBlocking function uses getservbyname, a synchronous Winsock function, to obtain a pointer to a service entry from the network services database. Finally, if the getservbyname function succeeds, FingerHostBlocking stores the Finger port number in the nFingerPort global variable. If the getservbyname function fails, FingerHostBlocking uses the well-known port defined by the winsock.h header file (IPPORT_FINGER):

```
BOOL FingerHostBlocking(VOID)
{
  LPSERVENT lpServiceEntry;        // Service information structure

  if (!LookupHostBlocking(hwndSockman, szFingerHost,
        (LPSTR)&szFingerBuffer, TASK_BLOCK_FINGER))
    return(FALSE);                 // Failed to resolve the host address

  if ((lpServiceEntry = getservbyname("finger", NULL)) == NULL)
    nFingerPort = htons(IPPORT_FINGER);
  else
    nFingerPort = lpServiceEntry->s_port;

  return(DoFingerOperation());
}
```

At this point, if all is well, FingerHostBlocking calls DoFingerOperation.

UNDERSTANDING THE DOFINGEROPERATION FUNCTION

The following program statements define the DoFingerOperation function. As you can see, the DoFingerOperation function is very similar to the QFinger program you saw in Chapter 10:

```
BOOL DoFingerOperation(VOID)
{
  LPHOSTENT lpHostEntry;           // Internet host information structure
  SOCKET nSocket;                  // Socket number used by this program
  SOCKADDR_IN sockAddr;            // Socket address structure
  int nErr;                        // Error code
```

```
int nCharSent;                  // Number of characters received
int nCharRecv;                  // Number of characters transmitted
BOOL bOkay = FALSE;             // Status code for the Finger operation
int nLength = 0;                // Length of returned Finger information

// Data buffers
char szUser[MAX_HOST_NAME+MAX_USER_NAME+3];  // Finger query buffer
char szFingerInfo[MAX_PRINT_BUFFER+1];       // Finger results buffer

if ((nSocket = socket(PF_INET, SOCK_STREAM, DEFAULT_PROTOCOL)) !=
      INVALID_SOCKET)
  {
    lpHostEntry = (LPHOSTENT)szFingerBuffer;
    sockAddr.sin_family = AF_INET;            // Internet Address family
    sockAddr.sin_port = nFingerPort;
    sockAddr.sin_addr = *((LPIN_ADDR)*lpHostEntry->h_addr_list);

    if (!connect(nSocket, (SOCKADDR *)&sockAddr, sizeof(sockAddr)))
      {
        wsprintf(szUser, "%s\r\n", (LPSTR)szFingerUser);

        if ((nCharSent = send(nSocket, szUser, lstrlen(szUser),
            NO_FLAGS)) != SOCKET_ERROR)
          {
            do {
                nCharRecv = recv(nSocket,
                        (LPSTR)&szFingerInfo[nLength],
                        sizeof(szFingerInfo) - nLength, NO_FLAGS);
                nLength+=nCharRecv;
            } while (nCharRecv > 0);

            closesocket(nSocket);

            if (nCharRecv != SOCKET_ERROR)
              {
                // Null terminate the Finger buffer
                szFingerInfo[nLength] = '\0';
                // Set the Scratch buffer to zero length
                szScratchBuffer[0] = '\0';

                wsprintf(szScratchBuffer, "FINGER:\t%s@%s\n\n",
                        (LPSTR)szFingerUser, (LPSTR)szFingerHost);
                lstrcat(szScratchBuffer, szFingerInfo);
                PaintWindow(szScratchBuffer);
                MessageBeep(0);
                bOkay = TRUE;
              }
          }
      }
  }
```

```
      if (!bOkay)
      {
        nErr = WSAGetLastError();
        closesocket(nSocket);
        wsprintf(szFingerInfo, "Error number %d", nErr);
        MessageBeep(MB_ICONSTOP);
        MessageBox(hwndSockman, szFingerInfo, "Finger Operation",
              MB_OK|MB_ICONSTOP);
      }
    return(bOkay);
}
```

Rather than repeat the same discussion that appeared in Chapter 10, the following paragraphs briefly describe the steps followed by the DoFingerOperation function. For a more detailed description of these steps, refer to the appropriate sections in Chapter 10:

1. Sockman requests a socket descriptor from Windows Sockets by calling the Winsock socket function.

2. To define a socket address, Sockman uses the protocol port nFingerPort stores and the Internet address szFingerBuffer stores.

3. Sockman calls the Winsock connect function to connect the socket (nSocket) to the remote host.

4. Sockman uses the szUser and szFingerUser variables to format a Finger query. Sockman then uses the Winsock send function to send the query to the remote host.

5. Sockman uses the recv function within a do-while loop to retrieve the Finger information that the remote host transmits through the socket.

6. Sockman closes the socket and displays the results.

Sockman's Finger operations effectively end when the DoFingerOperation function returns. If the user initiates an asynchronous Finger operation, DoFingerOperation will return to the FingerHostAsync function that called DoFingerOperation. If the user initiates a blocking Finger operation, DoFingerOperation will return to the FingerHostBlocking function.

LOOKING AT THE BIG PICTURE

It's time to step back and review how Sockman manages task handles for Finger operations. As you have learned, Sockman uses the hFingerTask global variable in several different functions that comprise the Finger program modules. As previously mentioned, to understand the asynchronous database functions, you must understand how Winsock uses task handles.

REVIEWING THE FINGER PROCESS

Shown next is a brief outline of the steps SOCKMAN3 follows to perform an asynchronous Finger operation. As you review this process, note how Sockman uses the Finger task-handle variable, hFingerTask:

1. Sockman tests the Finger task-handle variable, hFingerTask, to ensure only one Finger operation at a time occurs.

2. Sockman calls the FingerDialog function to obtain a host and remote-user-ID from the user.

3. Sockman calls the AsyncGetServiceInfo function to obtain the Finger protocol port from the network services database and stores the task handle for this asynchronous operation in the Finger task-handle variable, hFingerTask.

4. Sockman waits for the message WM_GOT_SERVICE, which signals the completion of the asynchronous service operation.

5. As soon as Sockman receives WM_GOT_SERVICE, Sockman tests the 16-bit message parameter, which contains the task handle of the process that generated WM_GOT_SERVICE. If the task handle matches the Finger task-handle variable, hFingerTask, Sockman calls the function LookupFingerHost.

6. Sockman extracts the Finger protocol port from the data buffer AsyncGetServiceInfo fills. Sockman then calls the LookupHostAsync function to asynchronously resolve the address for the host computer that the user specifies. Sockman stores the task handle for this asynchronous operation in hFingerTask.

7. Sockman waits for the message WM_ASYNC_LOOKUP_DONE, which signals the completion of the asynchronous DNS operation.

8. As soon as Sockman receives WM_ASYNC_LOOKUP_DONE, Sockman tests the 16-bit message parameter, which contains the task handle of the process that generated WM_ASYNC_LOOKUP_DONE. If the task handle matches the Finger task-handle variable, hFingerTask, Sockman calls the FingerHostAsync function.

9. To ensure no errors occurred during the asynchronous lookup, Sockman tests the high 16-bits in WM_ASYNC_LOOKUP_DONE's 32-bit message parameter. If no errors occurred, Sockman calls the function DoFingerOperation.

10. Sockman performs the Finger operation using synchronous Winsock functions on a blocking socket.

PUTTING IT ALL TOGETHER

As you have learned, the asynchronous database functions that retrieve information from the Internet send messages when they complete their operations. The asynchronous database functions include their task handle in the 16-bit message parameter of the message they send. Sockman tests the 16-bit message parameter to identify the asynchronous database operations. By tracking the task handle, you can take different actions for the same message identifier. Because Sockman restricts the Finger operations to one at a time, the Windows message traffic is not very heavy. However, in a more complex program, you may have several asynchronous Winsock database operations in progress at the same time. You might want or need all these operations to send messages with the same identifier. However, you can use the task handles for these operations to sort through the message traffic and take the appropriate action for each operation.

As you develop more sophisticated Internet programs, remember how Winsock uses the task handles from the asynchronous database functions. You may decide to implement a similar concept within your own programs. In other words, you can use task handles to identify your own custom Winsock operations. Before you move on to Chapter 13, make sure you understand the following key concepts:

- ✓ Most asynchronous Winsock functions return a task handle.

- ✓ Your programs can use the Winsock task handles to identify Windows messages that asynchronous Winsock functions trigger.

- ✓ Your programs can use the WSAGETASYNCERROR Winsock macro to extract error codes from Windows messages that asynchronous Winsock functions trigger.

Chapter 13
Time and the Network Byte-Order

When you create programs for use on a specific computer (such as a PC), you normally pay little attention to how the computer internally represents your data. However, when you create network-based programs, you must pay attention not only to how the local computer represents numeric values, but also to how remote computers do as well. For example, suppose that you lose a one dollar bet to a Macintosh user named Larry. To let Larry know that you intend to honor the bet, you use your PC and your new Internet-programming skills to create a program that sends Larry the following message:

> *Larry,*
> *I owe you $1.*
> *Ken*

Imagine your surprise when Larry calls you on the telephone and says, in an excited tone of voice, that his Mac screen displays the following message:

> *Larry,*
> *I owe you $512.*
> *Ken*

The message you sent differs from the message Larry received because Mac and PC represent numeric values differently. As such, when you create Internet-based programs, you need to remember that computers use different methods of storing numeric data. Although all computers use one or more bytes to represent numeric values, not all use the same byte sequence for numeric data. (You refer to the sequence of numeric data in a computer's memory as the computer's *byte-order* or *byte-ordering*.)

In this chapter, you will use one of the simplest Internet protocols, the Time Protocol, to learn more about byte-ordering. By the time you finish this chapter, you will understand the following key concepts:

- ◆ How a big-endian byte-order differs from a little-endian byte-order
- ◆ How to convert between network and host (PC) byte-orders
- ◆ How careless type casting of Internet data can cause problems
- ◆ How careless use of signed and unsigned variables causes confusion

UNDERSTANDING NETWORK BYTE-ORDER

Because the Internet connects a wide range of computers, the Internet establishes a standard sequence for storing numeric data. Internet professionals refer to this sequence as the *network byte-order*. This standard network byte-order helps minimize data misinterpretation between host computers that store and represent data differently. To distinguish between network byte-order and the computer's normal byte-order, Internet professionals refer to a computer's byte-order as the *host byte-order*. On a PC, the host byte-order is different from the network byte-order. As such, before your PC programs transfer a numeric value to an Internet software module, your programs must convert the value from host to network byte-order. Likewise, when your programs receive a numeric value from the Internet, your programs must convert the value from network to host byte-order.

Note: Your programs do not need to perform byte-order conversions on numbers embedded as text in a datagram or message. In other words, byte-order conversions are only necessary when you want the network software to treat data as a numeric value.

Sooner or later (usually sooner), every business application uses numbers. Business programs on the Internet are no different. If they don't deal with money, they eventually deal with quantities—order quantities, sales quantities, inventory quantities, and so on. If your programs transmit numeric data across the Internet, you need to understand byte-ordering. Acquiring a conceptual understanding of byte-ordering is easy. Solving problems related to byte-ordering is also quite simple. However, at first, you may find the practical aspects of byte-ordering a little confusing.

IDENTIFYING THE INTERNET TIME PROTOCOLS

Internet professionals design time protocols for two different purposes. On the Internet, time protocols either provide a point of reference for network computers or a point of reference for people. Today, you will find four different time protocols in use on the Internet, the Time Protocol, the Daytime Protocol, the Network Time Protocol (NTP), and the Simple Network Time Protocol (SNTP). You can use the Daytime and Time Protocols to obtain the current time from the Internet. As discussed next, the Network Time Protocol and the Simple Network Time Protocol provide completely different services.

Request For Comments (RFC) 1305, *Network Time Protocol (Version 3) Specification*, Mills, 1992, defines the Network Time Protocol, which accurately synchronizes the time between host computers. In other words, the protocol helps set the internal clocks on two or more computers to the same time. RFC 1305 describes the sophisticated algorithms that NTP uses to provide accurate time synchronization to within 1 to 50 milliseconds of an official time standard. As discussed in RFC 1361, *Simple Network Time Protocol (SNTP)*, Mills, 1992, the Simple Network Time Protocol is a scaled-down version of the Network Time Protocol. Although, in practice, SNTP provides accuracy similar to that of the Network Time Protocol, SNTP does not *guarantee* such accuracy. Systems that do not require the guaranteed performance that NTP provides can choose to implement the Simple Network Time Protocol. In contrast to NTP and SNTP, the Daytime and Time protocols are very simple network protocols. These protocols, as described in RFC 867, *Daytime Protocol*, Postel, 1983, and RFC 868, *Time Protocol*, Postel and Harrenstien, 1983, provide the current time-of-day to within an accuracy of one second. The Time Protocol returns a 32-bit number that represents elapsed time (in seconds) since 1 January 1900. The Daytime Protocol returns a text string formatted for people to read. The Daytime Protocol does not specify a format for the text string; however, in general, the string will look something like the following ("\r\n" represents a carriage-return line-feed):

```
Thu Jan 19 15:54:25 1995\r\n
```

As you might expect, the difference between the two groups of time protocols is significant. Whereas RFC 1305 takes over 100 pages to describe the algorithms that the Network Time Protocol uses, RFCs 867 and 868 are each only two pages long. The difference in the length of the RFCs indicates how the two protocol groups differ in sophistication. This chapter uses the Time Protocol described in RFC 868 to explain network byte-ordering. *Internet Programming* does not discuss the other time protocols.

UNDERSTANDING THE TIME PROTOCOL

If you have used personal computers for several years, you may remember when PCs did not contain internal clocks. In the early PC days, you had to manually enter the current date-and-time every time you turned on your PC and booted the operating system. People who remember those days will probably also remember the problems caused by not setting the computer's clock at boot time. For example, when you had multiple files with the same names in different directories, you could not use the file date-and-time stamp to tell which file was the latest version.

Today, not setting an accurate date-and-time on your PC can cause even more serious problems. For example, most PC programs expect a computer's clock to report an accurate date-and-time. Many such programs use the computer's date-and-time within their processing. If the date-and-time is wrong, so too may be your program's result.

If multiple computers run the same program and share data, computers may need to have a synchronized date-and-time. To synchronize their system clocks, the computers can access a network host that runs a time server. Time-server programs, which use the Time Protocol defined by RFC 868, report the current date-and-time (within an accuracy of one second) to client programs. The Time Protocol can use either of the transport protocols within the TCP/IP protocol suite. In other words, to deliver data between server and client programs that use the Time Protocol, you can use either the Transport Control Protocol (TCP) or the User Datagram Protocol (UDP). The well-known protocol port for the Time Protocol is 37. A time-server program listens for TCP connections and UDP datagrams on port 37. Both TCP and UDP use the same port. (The protocol association on port 37 is between the port and the Time Protocol—not TCP or UDP.)

Using the Time Server

When a time server hears a TCP connection on port 37, the server returns a 32-bit number that represents the current date-and-time. The server then initiates an active close of the TCP connection. If the time server cannot determine the current time on its own host computer, the protocol requires the server to either refuse the connection or close the connection without returning anything. When a time server uses TCP, the following sequence of events occurs:

1. The time server listens on port 37.

2. A time client connects to port 37.

3. The time server sends a 32-bit binary number that represents the current date-and-time.

4. The time client receives the date-and-time, as represented in the 32-bit binary number.

5. The time server initiates an active close.

6. The time client initiates a passive close.

If a time server hears a datagram arrive on port 37, the server returns a datagram with a 32-bit time value. If the time server cannot determine the current time on its own host computer, the protocol requires the server to discard the received datagram and send no reply. When a time program uses the User Datagram Protocol, the following sequence of events occurs:

1. The time server listens on port 37.

2. A time client sends an empty datagram to port 37.

3. The time server receives the empty datagram.

4. The time server sends a datagram that contains a 32-bit number that represents the current date-and-time.

5. The time client receives the datagram.

Note that the sequence of events for a UDP time service does not include an active or passive close. Remember, UDP is a connectionless protocol. As such, there is no direct connection between the protocol ports of the time server program and the time client program. In other words, with a UDP time service, there is no connection to close.

DECODING THE TIME

The Time Protocol uses a 32-bit number to represent the current date-and-time. This 32-bit number represents time as the number of seconds since 00:00 (midnight) 1 January 1900. In other words, a Time-Protocol value of 1 would represent 12:00:01 am on 1 January 1900. Table 13.1 lists the numbers that the Time Protocol specification (RFC 868) uses as examples.

Unsigned	Signed	Hex	Date - Midnight GMT
2,208,988,800	-2,085,978,496	0x83AA7E80	1 Jan 1970 GMT
2,398,291,200	-1,896,676,096	0x8EF30500	1 Jan 1976 GMT
2,524,521,600	-1,770,445,696	0x96792480	1 Jan 1980 GMT
2,629,584,000	-1,665,383,296	0x9CBC4480	1 May 1983 GMT
2,997,239,296	-1,297,728,000	0xB2A63E00	17 Nov 1858 GMT

Table 13.1 Examples of 32-bit date-and-time stamp numbers from the Time Protocol specification.

As you can see from Table 13.1, the decimal values for the Time Protocol dates vary depending on whether you use signed or unsigned storage locations. As such, when you develop and test Internet programs that use numbers, you need to be especially careful when you use decimal numbers to view your data. (Since using decimal numbers to evaluate your data can be highly problematic, you may want to use binary numbers or hexadecimal values instead.)

UNDERSTANDING BYTE-ORDERS

As you have learned, a byte is the smallest unit of data that a computer can manipulate. All modern computers treat eight bits of data as a single byte. As such, when you use a single byte of data, it is unlikely you will encounter any unusual problems. However, you will not always work with single-byte units of data. For example, C/C++ programmers commonly use integer variables to store numbers. Integer variables come in two sizes: short integers and long integers. A short integer uses 16 bits or two bytes to store data. A long integer uses 32 bits or four bytes to store data. Typically, you refer to a variable's storage size as its width.

In other words, you can say a long integer is 32 bits wide and a short integer is 16 bits wide. When you work with a multi-byte unit of data, you can encounter incompatibilities between computers—especially on an internetwork such as the Internet. The Internet interconnects many different types of computers. All these computers do not store multi-byte units of data in the same way. Over the years, many people have argued about the proper way to store numeric data in a computer. As a result, computer manufacturers have built computers that store numeric data in a variety of ways. The following paragraphs outline the basic differences between the two most common data-storage sequences.

BIG ENDIAN VERSUS LITTLE ENDIAN

The English-speaking world reads from left to right. In the case of numbers (decimal, hex, or binary), you start at the most significant (leftmost) digit and read toward the least significant (rightmost) digit—left to right. Computer professionals treat memory addresses in a computer as numbers. Frequently, they view these memory locations vertically rather than horizontally. When you view text vertically, it is more natural to read from top to bottom. However, with numbers, you can read from bottom to top almost as easily as from top to bottom.

Unfortunately, when you begin with a view of memory addresses in the horizontal position, you face a problem. Figure 13.1 is a simple diagram that shows two views of the same memory locations in a computer. The left half of the diagram shows the memory addresses running from top to bottom—the lowest memory address is on top. The right half of the diagram shows the same addresses running from left to right—the lowest memory address is on the left. As you can see, the diagram labels the address locations from 1001 to 1008.

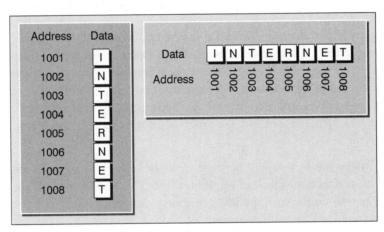

Figure 13.1 Two views of memory locations within a computer.

Each memory location in Figure 13.1 represents a byte of data. As you can see, the diagram shows the word INTERNET stored in the eight memory locations—one letter per byte of memory. You can read the data in Figure 13.1 quite naturally. In other words, you can read the left half of the diagram from top to bottom and the right half of the diagram from left to right. However, you should note that the memory addresses running from left to right begin with least significant memory address and end with the most significant address. This is contrary to your customary view of numbers, which is left-to-right, most significant to least significant.

Now, let's complicate the situation. First, assume you want to store numeric data in the memory locations shown in Figure 13.1. To keep things as simple as possible, you use hexadecimal values to represent the numeric data. (As you have learned, you can represent any byte of data as a two-digit hexadecimal number.) Next, assume you want to store two 32-bit numbers (eight bytes total) in memory locations 1001 through 1008. Also assume the two numbers are 0x12345678 (decimal 305,419,896) and 0x12ABCDEF (decimal 313,249,263). Every two-digit hex combination represents a byte of data. As discussed, you normally read numbers from left to right—most significant digit to least significant digit. The byte-order controversy revolves around whether you view your numeric data or your memory addresses from left to right (most significant digit to least significant digit). Figure 13.2 shows the two example numbers instead of the word, INTERNET, in the computer memory locations.

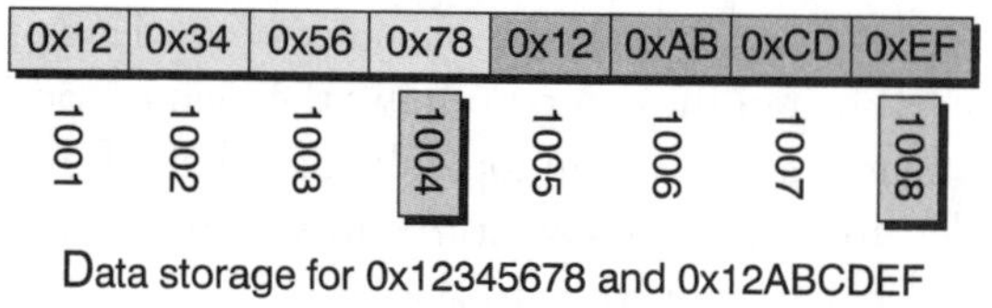

0x12	0x34	0x56	0x78	0x12	0xAB	0xCD	0xEF
1001	1002	1003	1004	1005	1006	1007	1008

Data storage for 0x12345678 and 0x12ABCDEF

Figure 13.2 *Memory locations containing two 32-bit numbers in big-endian byte-order.*

As shown in Figure 13.2, you can still read the numbers quite naturally—from left to right. Computer professionals refer to this byte-order as *big endian*. In other words, the most significant (big) byte occurs at the end you encounter first. Using the big-endian byte-order, you store your most significant byte of data in the lowest or least significant memory address. In other words, as you read from left to right, the significance of your data decreases and the significance of your memory address increases. As such, the sequence (or order) of your memory addresses and your data run in opposite directions.

In contrast, in *little-endian* byte-order, the sequence (or order) of your memory addresses and your data run in the same direction. The least significant (little) byte occurs first. As the significance of your data increases, so do the corresponding memory addresses. Figure 13.3 shows the two example numbers stored in little-endian byte-order.

0x12	0xAB	0xCD	0xEF	0x12	0x34	0x56	0x78
1008	1007	1006	1005	1004	1003	1002	1001

Data storage for 0x12345678 and 0x12ABCDEF

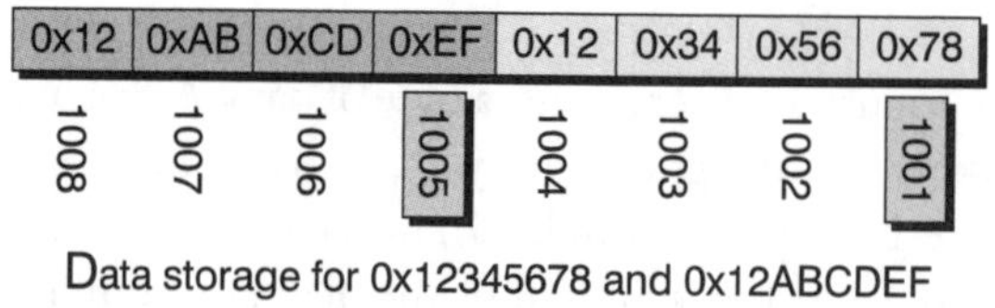

Figure 13.3 *Memory locations containing two 32-bit numbers in little-endian byte-order.*

Compare the position of the memory addresses in Figure 13.3 with those in Figure 13.2. As you can see, Figure 13.3 reversed the memory-address sequence to show you the sample numbers in the order you normally read them. Figure 13.2 numbers the memory addresses from left to right starting at address 1001. In contrast, Figure 13.3 numbers the memory addresses from right to left with address 1008 being on the leftmost side of the figure.

Figure 13.4 shows both byte-orders: big and little endian. As you can see, Figure 13.4 numbers the memory addresses like Figure 13.2—from left to right starting at address 1001. When you view the byte-orders next to each other, as shown in Figure 13.4, the differences become more apparent.

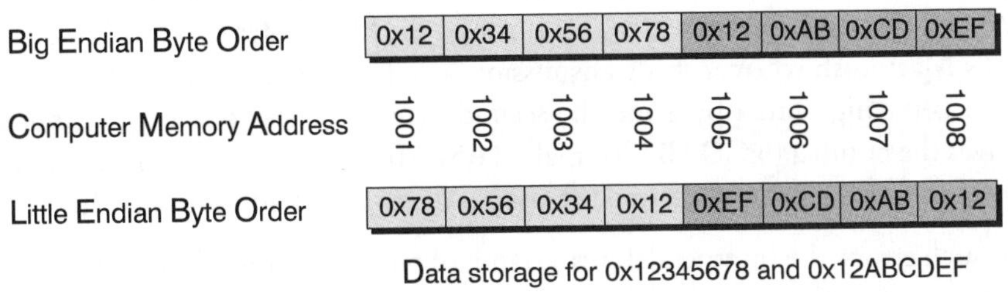

Figure 13.4 *A comparison between big-endian and little-endian byte-orders.*

The principle argument for using the little-endian byte-order is that a lower address implies a low-order byte. However, the little-endian byte-order requires some mental gymnastics if you want to read text and data within the same data segment. If you position the little-endian memory locations so your text reads naturally (left to right—lower to higher), you must read your numbers in reverse. In contrast, the big-endian byte-order lets you read text and numbers naturally. Normally, you don't need to be concerned about big endian versus little endian byte-order. Your computer automatically decides which byte-order it will use, and the arguments about which byte-order is superior are rather academic. However, as soon as you start to connect computers together, you have to consider byte-order issues carefully. If two computers use the same byte-order, it doesn't matter whether the byte-order is big endian or little endian—the two computers will transfer and interpret numeric values correctly. However, if the computers have different byte-orders, the computers must agree on how to interpret numeric data. The simplest solution is to adopt a particular byte-order as the network standard. As explained in the following sections, this is precisely what network professionals on the Internet decided to do.

DEFINING THE NETWORK STANDARD BYTE-ORDER

A computer's byte-order is dependent upon its microprocessor—in other words, the hardware design defines the byte-order. Table 13.2 identifies the byte-order that several popular computer systems use. As you write Internet-based programs, you may encounter each of these computers.

Computer System	Big Endian	Little Endian
Intel 80x86 (PC)		X
DEC VAX and PDP		X
Motorola 68000	X	
IBM 370	X	
Pyramid	X	

Table 13.2 *Byte-orders for various computer systems.*

As you have learned, to move data from one computer to the next, a network's physical layer transmits a serial stream of data bits across the network transmission lines. As such, the physical layer does not modify the bit sequence of the data it transmits. When you transmit the number 0xABCD (decimal 43,981) from your PC to your friend's Macintosh, your PC (using a little-endian byte-order) transmits the low-order byte (0xCD) first and the high-order byte (0xAB) second. When your friend's Macintosh receives this transmission, it interprets (using a big-endian byte-order) the first byte as the high-order byte and the second byte as the low-order byte. As a result, your friend receives the number 0xCDAB (decimal 52,651). In other words, in this example, the byte-order difference causes an 8,670 difference between the transmitted value and the received value.

To prevent such errors, the Internet defines a standard network byte-order—the big-endian byte-order. In other words, the Internet dictates that you store all integer values with the high-order byte before the low-order byte. As you view bytes of data that represent integer values in an Internet packet, the most significant (high-order) byte will occur first—toward the beginning of the packet. The least significant (low-order) byte will occur last—toward the end of the packet.

Note: Within the user data area of a packet, you are free to store data in any format that you choose— big endian, little endian, or any other way. However, understand that the program that receives your data must, in turn, convert the data to the byte-order that its host computer uses.

You must translate all integer values into network byte-order prior to transmission. Also, you need to remember to convert integer data you receive from the Internet into the byte-order your host computer requires. Fortunately, the Windows Sockets (Winsock) specification provides utility functions that perform this service for you. As shown in Table 13.3, the Winsock API includes four functions that perform byte-ordering operations.

Winsock Function	Purpose
htonl	Converts a 32-bit quantity from host byte-order to network byte-order.
htons	Converts a 16-bit quantity from host byte-order to network byte-order.
ntohl	Converts a 32-bit quantity from network byte-order to host byte-order.
ntohs	Converts a 16-bit quantity from network byte-order to host byte-order.

Table 13.3 Winsock functions that perform byte-ordering operations.

USING THE TIME PROTOCOL

As discussed, the Time Protocol is one of the simplest protocols on the Internet. As defined by RFC 867, the Time Protocol returns the current time-of-day to within an accuracy of one second from an Internet time-server program. The Time Protocol uses a 32-bit number to represent the current date-and-time as the number of seconds since 00:00 (midnight) 1 January 1900. PCs also use a specific point of reference for date-and-time functions. Unfortunately, a PC's reference point is not the same as the Internet's Time Protocol. Timers on personal computers represent the current date-and-time as the number of elapsed seconds since midnight (00:00), 1 January 1970 GMT. As previously shown in Table 13.1, midnight, January 1, 1970 GMT occurred 2,208,988,800 (0x83AA7E80) seconds after 1 January 1900. As such, to use your PC's date-and-time functions to interpret Internet date-and-time values, you need to subtract 2,208,988,800 (the 70-year difference) from any 32-bit number you receive from the Internet.

CREATING A QUICK TIME PROGRAM

As you have learned, communication between time server and time client programs is simple. The well-known port for time servers is protocol port 37. You can use TCP to connect to port 37, or you can send an empty UDP datagram to port 37. In either case, the time server will return a 32-bit number that represents the current date-and-time as the number of seconds elapsed since midnight, 1 January 1900. In this section, you will create a simple program (QTime) that uses a TCP connection to retrieve the current date-and-time from the Internet. The QTime program will follow the pattern of the previous *quick* programs that you have created in *Internet Programming*. In other words, to highlight a few key Internet programming concepts, QTime eliminates everything except the bare essentials. QTime "hard codes" values and uses message boxes to avoid the overhead associated with a Windows user interface and window message handling. You can find the QTIME.CPP source file on the companion disk included with *Internet Programming*. Shown next is the complete program listing for QTIME.CPP. The following section discusses QTime in detail.

Note: As written, QTime connects to a time server on the host computer **cerfnet.com**. Many computers on the Internet run time-server programs, and QTime will work with any of them. If you encounter problems connecting to **cerfnet.com**, you can modify QTime to use another host computer.

```
#include <stdlib.h>
#include <time.h>
#include "..\winsock.h"


#define PROG_NAME "Simple Timeserver Query"


#define HOST_NAME "cerfnet.com"        // This can be any valid host name
#define WINSOCK_VERSION 0x0101         // Program requires Winsock version 1.1
#define DEFAULT_PROTOCOL 0             // No protocol specified, use default
#define NO_FLAGS 0                     // No special flags specified
#define PC_REF_TIME 2208988800L        // Reference point for PC date and time


SOCKET ConnectTimeServerSocket(VOID)
{
```

```
WSADATA wsaData;                    // Winsock implementation details
LPHOSTENT lpHostEnt;                // Internet host information structure
SOCKADDR_IN sockAddr;               // Socket address structure
LPSERVENT pServEnt;                 // Service information structure
short iTimePort;                    // Well-known port assignment is 37
int nConnect;                       // Socket connection results

SOCKET nTimeserverSocket = INVALID_SOCKET; // Default socket number

if (WSAStartup(WINSOCK_VERSION, &wsaData))
  MessageBox(NULL, "Could not load Windows Sockets DLL.",
        PROG_NAME, MB_OK|MB_ICONSTOP);

else// Resolve the host name
  {
    lpHostEnt = gethostbyname(HOST_NAME);

    if (!lpHostEnt)
      MessageBox(NULL, "Could not get IP address!", HOST_NAME,
          MB_OK|MB_ICONSTOP);

    else  // Create the socket
      {
        nTimeserverSocket = socket(PF_INET, SOCK_STREAM,
            DEFAULT_PROTOCOL);

        if (nTimeserverSocket == INVALID_SOCKET)
          MessageBox(NULL, "Invalid socket!!", PROG_NAME,
              MB_OK|MB_ICONSTOP);

        else  // Configure the socket
          {
            // Get the time service information
            pServEnt = getservbyname("time", "tcp");

            if (pServEnt == NULL)
              iTimePort = htons(IPPORT_TIMESERVER);// Well-known port
            else
              iTimePort = pServEnt->s_port;

            // Define the socket address using Internet address family
            sockAddr.sin_family = AF_INET;
            sockAddr.sin_port = iTimePort;
            sockAddr.sin_addr = *((LPIN_ADDR)*lpHostEnt->h_addr_list);

            // Connect the socket
            nConnect = connect(nTimeserverSocket,
                (PSOCKADDR)&sockAddr,
                  sizeof(sockAddr));
```

```
                if( nConnect)
                  {
                      MessageBox(NULL, "Error connecting socket!!",
                          PROG_NAME, MB_OK|MB_ICONSTOP);
                      nTimeserverSocket = INVALID_SOCKET;
                  }
              }
          }
      }
    return(nTimeserverSocket);
}

int PASCAL WinMain(HANDLE hInstance, HANDLE hPrevInstance,
    LPSTR lpszCmdParam, int nCmdShow)
{
    SOCKET nSocket;                 // Socket number for the timeserver
    int nCharSent;                  // Number of characters transmitted
    int nCharRecv;                  // Number of characters received
    DWORD dwNetTime;                // Internet time value as an unsigned long
    LONG lNetTime;                  // Internet time value as a signed long
    LONG lPCTime;                   // PC time value as a signed long
    char szHostOrder[33];           // Hex time value in host byte order
    char szNetOrder[33];            // Hex time value in network byte order
    char szUnsignedValue[33];       // Internet time value as an unsigned long
    char szSignedValue[33];         // Internet time value as a signed long
    char szMsg[100];                // General purpose buffer for messages

    nSocket = ConnectTimeServerSocket();

    if (nSocket != INVALID_SOCKET)
      {
        // Ask the server for the current time by sending a CRLF
        nCharSent = send(nSocket, "\n", lstrlen("\n"), NO_FLAGS);

        if (nCharSent == SOCKET_ERROR)
          MessageBox(NULL, "Error occurred during send()!", PROG_NAME,
              MB_OK|MB_ICONSTOP);

        else  // Get the current time from the timeserver
          {
            nCharRecv = recv(nSocket, (LPSTR)&lNetTime, sizeof(lNetTime),
                NO_FLAGS);

            if (nCharRecv == SOCKET_ERROR)
              MessageBox(NULL, "Error occurred during recv()!", PROG_NAME,
                  MB_OK|MB_ICONSTOP);

            else  // Convert the results from network to host byte-order
              {
```

```
            lPCTime = ntohl(lNetTime);

            // Convert numbers to ASCII values for message box use
            _ltoa(lPCTime, szHostOrder, 16); // Use hexadecimal (16)
            _ltoa(lNetTime, szNetOrder, 16); // Use hexadecimal (16)

            lPCTime = lPCTime - PC_REF_TIME; // Subtract PC reference

            wsprintf(szMsg,
                    "%s\n\nBYTE-ORDER\n\nNetwork:\t%s\nHost PC:\t%s",
                    (LPSTR)ctime(&lPCTime), (LPSTR)szNetOrder,
                    (LPSTR)szHostOrder);
            MessageBox(NULL, szMsg, PROG_NAME,
                    MB_OK|MB_ICONINFORMATION);

            // Assign the network time to an unsigned variable
            dwNetTime = lNetTime;

            // Format the 32-bit network time as an unsigned long
            _ultoa(dwNetTime, szUnsignedValue, 10);

            // Format the 32-bit network time as a signed long
            _ltoa(lNetTime, szSignedValue, 10);

            // Display the 32-bit number from the network.
            wsprintf(szMsg, "Unsigned:\t%s\nSigned:\t\t%s",
                    (LPSTR)szUnsignedValue, (LPSTR)szSignedValue);
            MessageBox(NULL, szMsg, PROG_NAME,
                    MB_OK|MB_ICONINFORMATION);
        }
    }
  }

  WSACleanup(); // Free all allocated program resources and exit
  return(NULL);
}
```

What Is New?

As discussed, the QTime program follows the same pattern, and uses many of the same program statements, as QLookup and QFinger. The following sections discuss how QTime changes program statements you saw in the earlier *quick* programs.

How QTime Queries The Time Server

As you review the following program statement, notice the "data" QTime sends to the time server on the remote host. At first glance, it may appear that QTime sends no data. However, if you examine the statement closely, you will see that QTime uses the send function to send a blank line (nothing but a newline character):

```
nCharSent = send(nSocket, "\n", lstrlen("\n"), NO_FLAGS);
```

In fact, the newline character is the data QTime sends to the time server. A newline or a carriage-return line-feed tells the time server that a connection exists.

DEFINING CONSTANT VALUES

QTime uses several of the constant definitions you saw in the QLookup and QFinger programs. PC_REF_TIME (shown in the following program statement) is the only new definition:

```
#define PC_REF_TIME 2208988800L   // Reference point for PC date and time
```

As previously discussed, PCs use midnight, 1 January 1970 as a reference point for date-and-time functions. The Internet Time Protocol uses midnight, 1 January 1900 as a point of reference. The Time-Protocol value for midnight, 1 January 1970 is 2,208,988,800. As such, to interpret date-and-time values your PC receives from the Internet, you can subtract 2,208,988,800 from the 32-bit, Time-Protocol number and use the PC's date-and-time functions.

USING MORE THAN ONE FUNCTION

To reduce program complexity, the previous *quick* programs placed all program statements into one function—WinMain. In contrast, the QTime program uses more than one function. In the other *quick* programs, the initial program statements were practically identical. *Internet Programming* includes the first two *quick* programs to help familiarize you with those initial startup steps. In this chapter, QTime locates those initial startup steps in a separate function named ConnectTimeServerSocket. The following program statement shows the prototype for the ConnectTimeServerSocket function.

```
SOCKET ConnectTimeServerSocket(VOID);
```

As you can see, the ConnectTimeServerSocket function requires no parameters and returns a SOCKET value. As its name implies, the purpose of the ConnectTimeServerSocket function is to connect a socket to a time server on the Internet and then return the socket's handle to the caller.

REVIEWING THE CONNECTTIMESERVERSOCKET FUNCTION

In the ConnectTimeServerSocket function, the program statements, and even the variable names, are practically the same as those you saw in QLookup and QFinger. The following steps explain the ConnectTimeServerSocket function in detail. If you want to review more details about any of these steps, refer to the appropriate sections in Chapters 9 and 10.

1. ConnectTimeServerSocket calls the WSAStartup function to initialize the Winsock DLL.

2. ConnectTimeServerSocket calls the gethostbyname function to resolve the IP address for the string that the constant HOST_NAME defines.

3. ConnectTimeServerSocket creates a communication socket and calls the socket function to obtain a socket descriptor.

4. ConnectTimeServerSocket calls the getservbyname function to retrieve an entry for a time service (from the network services database) that uses TCP.

5. To define a socket address, ConnectTimeServerSocket assigns values to a Winsock socket-address structure (defined by SOCKADDR_IN). ConnectTimeServerSocket specifies an address family, protocol port, and host address for the socket.

6. ConnectTimeServerSocket calls the Winsock connect function to connect the socket to the remote host.

7. If ConnectTimeServerSocket successfully connects the communications socket, it returns the socket descriptor. Otherwise, it returns the constant INVALID_SOCKET.

Understanding the WinMain Function

The first few lines in QTime's WinMain function declare the program's local variables. You have already encountered several of these variables in the previous *quick* programs. Shown next are the new variables the QTime program uses:

```
DWORD dwNetTime              // Internet time value as an unsigned long
LONG lNetTime;               // Internet time value as a signed long
LONG lPCTime;                // PC time value as a signed long
char szHostOrder[33];        // Hex time value in host byte order
char szNetOrder[33];         // Hex time value in network byte order
char szUnsignedVal[33];      // Internet time value as an unsigned long
char szSignedVal[33];        // Internet time value as a signed long
char szMsg[100];             // General purpose buffer for messages
```

As you have learned, the Time Protocol returns a 32-bit number that represents the current date-and-time. As you may know, a long integer is 32 bits wide. QTime uses two long-integer variables, dwNetTime and lNetTime, to store the value it receives from the Time Protocol. As indicated by their Hungarian prefixes, lNetTime stores the Time-Protocol value as signed-long integer and dwNetTime stores the value as an unsigned-long integer. QTime only needs one of the long integers for the Time-Protocol number. However, as you have learned, the same binary data can represent two different decimal values: one signed and the other unsigned. To illustrate this point, QTime displays the 32-bit, Time-Protocol number as both a signed and unsigned value.

QTime uses the third long integer, lPCTime, to store the 32-bit, Time-Protocol number in a format suitable for use by the PC's date-and-time functions. To generate the Time-Protocol number, QTime first subtracts the Internet's date-and-time reference point (1 January 1900) from your PC's corresponding reference point (1 January 1970). Then, QTime subtracts the difference between the reference points from the current Internet time. Because QTime stores the Time-Protocol number in 1PCTime, you can manipulate the Internet-time value with the date-and-time functions in your compiler's run-time library. QTime uses the remaining character-array variables to store various interpretations of the 32-bit date-and-time value. The szHostOrder and szNetOrder variables display the different byte-orders between your PC and the Internet. The szUnsignedVal and szSignedVal variables display signed and unsigned versions of the 32-bit date-and-time value. The szMsg variable is a general-purpose array that QTime uses to format text strings for it's message boxes.

GETTING STARTED

After the WinMain function declares its local variables, it calls the ConnectTimeServerSocket function, which creates a communication socket and establishes a connection with a time server on a remote host. If the ConnectTimeServerSocket function fails to establish a valid circuit, the function returns the value INVALID_SOCKET. The following program statements show a general outline of WinMain's structure:

```
nSocket = ConnectTimeServerSocket();

if (nSocket != INVALID_SOCKET)
{
   // Execute program statements to retrieve and display the current
   // date and time from the Internet.
}

WSACleanup();  // Free all allocated program resources and exit
return(NULL);
```

As you can see, if ConnectTimeServerSocket fails, QTime calls the WSACleanup function and exits. As you have learned, the WSACleanup function deregisters the calling program from the Winsock DLL and frees any resources allocated on behalf of your program.

COMMUNICATING WITH THE TIME SERVER

The following program statements are not much different from what you have seen in the previous *quick* programs. The time server does not require any special messages. As soon as the time server hears a TCP connection, the server transmits a 32-bit date-and-time value. QTime uses the send function to transmit a carriage-return line-feed that signals the success of its socket connection. If no errors occur, QTime uses the recv function to collect the time server's response:

```
if (nSocket != INVALID_SOCKET)
{
  // Ask the server for the current time by sending a CRLF
  nCharSent = send(nSocket, "\n", lstrlen("\n"), NO_FLAGS);

  if (nCharSent == SOCKET_ERROR)
    MessageBox(NULL, "Error occurred during send()!", PROG_NAME,
         MB_OK|MB_ICONSTOP);

  else  // Get the current time from the timeserver
    {

      nCharRecv = recv(nSocket, (LPSTR)&lNetTime, sizeof(lNetTime),
           NO_FLAGS);

      if (nCharRecv == SOCKET_ERROR)
        MessageBox(NULL, "Error occurred during recv()!", PROG_NAME,
             MB_OK|MB_ICONSTOP);
```

Regarding the previous program statements, one point is worth noting here. As you have learned, the Winsock prototype for the recv function is:

```
int PASCAL FAR recv(int s, char FAR * buf, int len, int flags);
```

As you can see, the second recv parameter is a far pointer to a character-string buffer (char), where recv will store incoming data. To let you use Winsock library functions on multiple networks and with a wide variety of data, Winsock's recv function uses this pointer to char for the message buffer. If the receive function didn't contain this pointer, your network programs would have to contain a different recv function for every possible type of data that a network might transmit. Because it is byte-aligned, a pointer to char can point to any type of data. For example, suppose the incoming data is a long integer (32 bits wide). To store this data, your program must allocate at least four bytes of storage space. However, Winsock doesn't care how you allocate the storage space. Your program can declare a long integer (which would reserve four bytes) or declare a character array with four elements. In either case, all the Winsock recv function needs is a pointer to the address of the first byte of storage space.

When your Winsock-based program uses the recv function, your program must allocate storage space for a message buffer. However, your program can use any type or size of buffer. To use the buffer with recv, your program simply casts the address of your buffer to a LPSTR (which is defined as char FAR *). Your compiler, in turn, will compile the program statement without complaint (warning messages about parameter types). Since the Time Protocol returns a 32-bit value, QTime uses a long integer (which is 32 bits wide) as its message buffer. QTime could just as easily have used a character array for the message buffer. However, doing so would require the program to type cast the contents of the character array to a long integer. A good Winsock programming practice to adopt is the use of correct data types for your message buffers.

TYPE CASTING WINSOCK VALUES

As a rule, C/C++ programmers should avoid type casts if at all possible. Type casts defeat the error-checking capabilities built into most modern C/C++ compilers that trap variable type errors. In other words, every time you perform a type cast, you circumvent the compiler's ability to warn you that you have used a variable type in a way that is potentially wrong. You cannot avoid all type casts. They serve a legitimate and useful purpose. In fact, without the ability to perform type casts, function libraries such as the Windows Sockets API would be much more complex and cumbersome to use. Unfortunately, C/C++ programmers can easily misuse type casts. Due to the flexible design of the Winsock function-library, type casts are an inescapable part of Internet programming with Winsock. The key point to remember is that you should type cast the variables you pass as parameters in your Winsock function calls. Do not design your programs so that you must type cast your data-storage buffers to manipulate received data. In other words, declare your message buffers to be the data type you expect to receive from the Internet. Following this principle will let your compiler continue to perform a lot of valuable error checking for you.

CONVERTING THE BYTE-ORDER

If the recv function returns no errors, QTime must convert, from network byte-order to host byte-order, the network-time value that the message buffer stores. As shown in the following program statements, QTime does so by calling the Winsock ntohl function:

```
if (nCharRecv == SOCKET_ERROR)
MessageBox(NULL, "Error occurred during recv()!", PROG_NAME,
    MB_OK|MB_ICONSTOP);

else // Convert the results from network to host byte order
{
  lPCTime = ntohl(lNetTime);
```

Note: Since QTime uses a long-integer variable (lNetTime) as the message buffer, the call to ntohl requires no type casts.

The ntohl function simply takes, as a parameter, a long value in network byte-order and returns a long value in host byte-order. The following program statement shows the function prototype for ntohl:

```
u_long PASCAL FAR ntohl(u_long netlong);
```

As previously mentioned, the Winsock API includes four functions that perform operations similar to ntohl. Two functions change byte-orders for 16-bit integers (shorts) and two functions change byte-orders for 32-bit integers (longs). As you have learned, you need to remember to transmit integer values across the Internet in network byte-order. Otherwise, computers that receive your integer values may misinterpret them. After QTime converts the byte-order, the program stores

ASCII representations of the 32-bit, Time-Protocol value in hex. As shown in the following code statements, QTime uses the C function _ltoa to perform this conversion:

```
lPCTime = ntohl(lNetTime);

// Convert numbers to ASCII values for message box use
_ltoa(lPCTime, szHostOrder, 16); // Use hexadecimal (16)
_ltoa(lNetTime, szNetOrder, 16); // Use hexadecimal (16)
```

When you execute the program, QTime displays the Time-Protocol value in network and host byte-orders. For example, as you can see in Figure 13.5, a time server on the Internet reported the value 0xC6F7F2B2 on February 20, 1995 at 03:13:10.

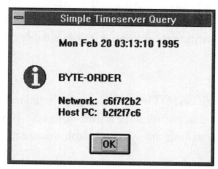

Figure 13.5 Time-Protocol values for February 20, 1995 obtained by QTime.

As you can see, the value that QTime displays for the network byte-order is 0xC6F7F2B2; the same value in host byte-order is 0xB2F2F7C6. Remember, every two-digit hexadecimal value represents one byte. In other words, these eight-digit, hex numbers represent four bytes (or 32 bits) of data. Note that the least-significant byte in the network byte-order, 0xB2, becomes the most-significant (leftmost) byte in the host byte-order. Likewise, the most-significant byte in the network byte-order, 0xC6, becomes the least-significant (rightmost) byte in the host byte-order. If you view each number as four, two-digit, hex values, you will see that these two numbers reverse each other's byte-order. In other words, the four bytes in the network value,

```
0xC6  0xF7  0xF2  0xB2
```

are the same four bytes in the host value, except that they occur in reverse order:

```
0xB2  0xF2  0xF7  0xC6
```

ADJUSTING FOR THE PC'S REFERENCE TIME

The Internet uses 1 January 1900 as a date-and-time reference point while PCs use 1 January 1970. According to the Time-Protocol specification (RFC 868), the Time-Protocol value for 1 January

1970 is 2,208,988,800. As shown in the following program statement, QTime uses the constant PC_REF_TIME to define this value:

```
#define PC_REF_TIME 2208988800L   // Reference point for PC date and time
```

Next, QTime converts the byte-order of the 32-bit, time-server value and stores the new time value in lPCTime. Finally, QTime subtracts PC_REF_TIME from the new time value. As shown in the following program statement, QTime continues to use lPCTime to store the time value, which is now in host byte-order:

```
lPCTime = lPCTime - PC_REF_TIME; // Subtract PC reference
```

Displaying Time from the Internet

After you convert the byte-order and adjust the date-and-time value received from the Internet, you can use the date-and-time functions in your C/C++ compiler's run-time library to manipulate the data. As shown in the following code statements, QTime uses the ctime function to convert the time value for display in a Windows message box:

```
lPCTime = lPCTime - PC_REF_TIME; // Subtract PC reference

wsprintf(szMsg, "%s\n\nBYTE ORDER\n\nNetwork:\t%s\nHost PC:\t%s",
    ctime(&lPCTime), szNetOrder, szHostOrder);
MessageBox(NULL, szMsg, PROG_NAME, MB_OK|MB_ICONINFORMATION);
```

As you may know, the ctime function converts a PC time value to a string. As you saw in Figure 13.5, QTime displays this character string above the byte-order values.

Viewing Your data as Signed and Unsigned Values

The last several program statements in the WinMain function simply show the network-time value as signed- and unsigned-decimal values. As shown in the following program statements, QTime assigns the signed value, lNetTime, to the unsigned-long integer, dwNetTime, before converting the decimal value to ASCII with the _ultoa function:

```
// Assign the network time value to an unsigned variable
dwNetTime = lNetTime;

// Format the 32-bit network time value as an unsigned long
_ultoa(dwNetTime, szUnsignedValue, 10);
```

The _ultoa function converts unsigned-long values to their ASCII equivalents. However, if you pass a signed value to the _ultoa function, many run-time libraries will out smart you. The function will assume that you really meant to use the _ltoa function (which converts signed longs) and will convert your value to an ASCII representation of a signed long. To avoid this problem, QTime assigns the network-time value in lNetTime to a variable declared as an unsigned long (dwNetTime) and then uses the unsigned variable in the function call. As you saw in Figure 13.5, QTime displays the network-time value as a hex number in QTime's first message box. Hex values make byte-order differences obvious. However, in the second message box, QTime displays the network-time value as both signed and unsigned decimal numbers. By doing so, you can readily see that the same binary data appears to be two different values when you use signed and unsigned variables for storage. The following program statements convert the network-time value to an ASCII representation of a signed-long integer. In a Windows message box, QTime displays this value and the ASCII representation of the unsigned long:

```
// Format the 32-bit network time value as a signed long
_ltoa(lNetTime, szSignedValue, 10);

// Display the 32-bit number from the network.
wsprintf(szMsg, "Unsigned:\t%s\nSigned:\t%s", szUnsignedValue,
    szSignedValue);
MessageBox(NULL, szMsg, PROG_NAME, MB_OK|MB_ICONINFORMATION);
```

Note: The second parameter passed to the _ltoa and _ultoa functions determines the base-numbering system used for the ASCII conversions. For example, the function call shown in the previous code block uses 10 to request a decimal-numbering system. The earlier call to _ltoa used 16 to request the hexa-decimal-numbering system.

ADDING A TIME SERVER QUERY TO SOCKMAN

You probably have an internal clock on your computer. However, if you're like most people, you don't worry about the accuracy of that internal clock. For example, if your computer has the right date, you probably don't pay close attention to the actual time. However, depending on the programs you run, it may be critical that your system's internal date-and-time be accurate. As such, you may need to periodically reset the clock's date-and-time values. On most computers, setting the correct date-and-time on the system clock is a trivial process. However, to obtain the precise time, you do typically have to place a phone call and listen to a recording. Fortunately, if you connect to the Internet, you don't need to place a separate time-of-day call. Instead, with a couple of mouse clicks, you can use the Sockman time-server utility to set your computer's system clock to the correct time. The following sections show you how to incorporate a time client into the Sockman template.

VIEWING THE BIG PICTURE

The Sockman time-server utility follows the user-interface pattern established in Chapters 11 and 12. In other words, you use a menu option to launch a dialog box, which, in turn, starts the utility program with the options you specify. Like all Windows programs, the WinMain function processes all Windows messages by sending them to the master callback function (which is WndProc in Sockman). As shown in Figure 13.6, the Sockman design uses the WndProc, DoMenuCommand, and DoWinsockProgram functions to break the program into manageable pieces. The WndProc function handles the general-purpose Windows messages and passes all command-related messages (WM_COMMAND) to the DoMenuCommand function. In turn, DoMenuCommand handles all messages that Sockman's menus generate except for those that actually initiate a Winsock process. Sockman initiates all Winsock processes from the DoWinsockProgram function.

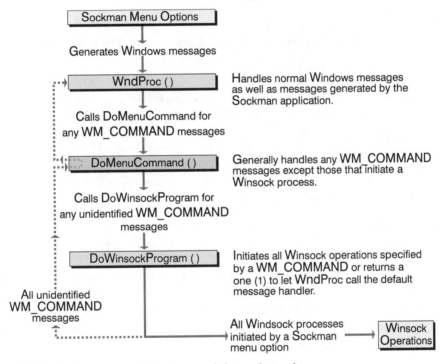

Figure 13.6 The Sockman control functions and their relationships.

As you have learned, the time-server utility, like all of the programs in Sockman, can generate Windows messages that the WndProc and DoMenuCommand functions handle. However, each network process starts from the DoWinsockProgram function.

STARTING THE TIME SERVER UTILITY

When a Sockman user clicks their mouse on the Utilities menu Time Server option, Windows sends the WndProc function a WM_COMMAND message with a wParam argument that equals IDM_TIME_UTIL. The WndProc function passes the message to DoMenuCommand, which, in turn, calls the DoWinsockProgram function. As the following program statements show, DoWinsockProgram tests the hTimeServerTask global variable to make sure a time-server operation is not already in progress. If a time-server task is in progress, Winsock displays a message box that tells the user to "please wait":

```
long DoWinsockProgram(HWND hwnd, UINT wParam, LONG lParam)
{
  switch (wParam)
    {
      // ...other case statements

      case IDM_TIME_UTIL:
        if (hTimeServerTask) // Only 1 time server query at a time
          {
            MessageBeep(0);
            MessageBox(hwnd,
                "Timeserver utility is already in use. Please wait...",
                "SockMan - TIME SERVER", MB_ICONSTOP | MB_OK);
          }
        else
          TimeServerDialog();
        return(TRUE);

      // ...other case statements
    }
  return(FALSE);
}
```

As you can see, if no time-server operations are in progress, DoWinsockProgram calls the TimeServerDialog function, which creates a dialog box that Sockman users can use to query a time server. In contrast to the Lookup and Finger utilities, which keep the dialog box open only long enough to launch their processes, Sockman doesn't close the Time Server dialog box until communications with the network time server complete.

USING THE TIME SERVER DIALOG BOX

The Time Server dialog box is open during all time-server operations. As such, the dialog box's function, TimeServerDialogProc, handles all Windows messages during time-server operations. As shown in Figure 13.7, the Time Server dialog box includes three text boxes (fields) and three command buttons. Of the three fields, only the Server Host field is editable. To specify a time-server host, you must type an IP address or DNS name into this field. As you can see, the Your Time field displays your computer current time. When you click your mouse on the Query button, Sockman performs a time-server query (just like the one you saw in QTime) against the specified host. Sockman displays the query results in the Server Time field.

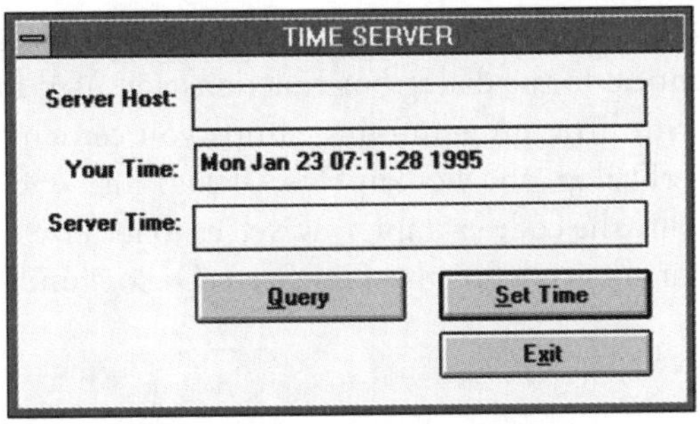

Figure 13.7 Sockman's dialog box for the time-server utility.

Note: Most Internet service providers run a Time server at protocol port 37.

The Set Time button performs a time-server query that is identical to the one the Query button initiates. However, the Set Time button also sets your computer's system clock to the date-and-time value that the time server returns. Before you decide to change your system clock, you can use the Query button to see the difference between your computer's time and the time on the specified host. Sockman does not require you to query the time server before you decide to change your system clock. In other words, you can simply click on the Set Time button and Sockman, in one step, will perform the query and change the time. The Exit button closes the dialog box.

CREATING THE DIALOG BOX

The Sockman resource file, SOCKMAN4.RC, contains the resource definition for the Time Server dialog box. As shown in the following program statements, there is nothing special about the Time Server dialog box. IDD_TIMESERVER defines the dialog box shown in Figure 13.7.

```
IDD_TIMESERVER DIALOG DISCARDABLE 0, 0, 206, 113
STYLE DS_MODALFRAME | WS_POPUP | WS_VISIBLE | WS_CAPTION | WS_SYSMENU
CAPTION "TIME SERVER"
FONT 8, "MS Sans Serif"
BEGIN
    EDITTEXT        IDC_TIMESERVER,54,9,140,15,ES_AUTOHSCROLL
    DEFPUSHBUTTON   "&Query",IDOK,55,70,65,16
    DEFPUSHBUTTON   "&Set Time",IDSETTIME,130,70,65,16,NOT WS_TABSTOP
    PUSHBUTTON      "E&xit",IDCANCEL,130,90,65,15
    RTEXT           "Server Host:",IDC_STATIC,5,9,45,13
    RTEXT           "Your Time:",IDC_STATIC,4,32,47,11
    EDITTEXT        IDC_LOCAL_TIME,55,28,140,15,ES_AUTOHSCROLL |
                        ES_READONLY | WS_DISABLED | NOT WS_TABSTOP
    RTEXT           "Server Time:",IDC_STATIC,5,49,46,10
    EDITTEXT        IDC_SERVER_TIME,54,48,140,15,ES_AUTOHSCROLL |
                        ES_READONLY | WS_DISABLED | NOT WS_TABSTOP
END
```

As discussed, the DoWinsockProgram function calls TimeServerDialog. The TimeServerDialog function is practically identical to the dialog box functions you used for the Lookup and Finger menu options. In fact, with little programming effort, you can combine all three functions (TimeServerDialog, FingerDialog, and LookupHostDialog) into one. Sockman keeps all three functions separate to simplify the code examples, as well as to localize related program functions. The following program statements define the TimeServerDialog function:

```
BOOL TimeServerDialog(VOID)
{
  DLGPROC lpfnDialogProc;
  BOOL bOkay;

  // Create a dialog box for the user's entry
  lpfnDialogProc = MakeProcInstance((DLGPROC)TimeServerDialogProc,
      hInstanceSockman);
  bOkay = DialogBox(hInstanceSockman, "IDD_TIMESERVER",  hwndSockman,
      lpfnDialogProc);
  FreeProcInstance(lpfnDialogProc);

  if (bOkay == -1)
    {
      wsprintf(szScratchBuffer, "Unable to create dialog box!");
      MessageBeep(0);
      MessageBox(hwndSockman, szScratchBuffer,
          "SockMan-TIME SERVER QUERY", MB_OK|MB_ICONINFORMATION);
      bOkay = FALSE;
    }

  return(bOkay);
}
```

As you can see, TimeServerDialog uses the Windows MakeProcInstance function to obtain a handle for IDD_TIMESERVER's dialog procedure, TimeServerDialogProc.

Next, TimeServerDialog calls the DialogBox function to create IDD_TIMESERVER. The TimeServerDialogProc function manages the Windows messages for the dialog box and controls the logic behind Sockman's time-server operations. When you exit the Time Server dialog box, the TimeServerDialog function frees the dialog-box instance handle and returns to the DoWinsockProgram function.

MANAGING THE TIME SERVER DIALOG BOX

The following program statements show the basic structure of the TimeServerDialogProc function. As you can see, TimeServerDialogProc handles five messages, some of which you have seen before. For example, Windows sends the WM_INITDIALOG message before displaying the dialog box. When you click your mouse on the Control menu Close option, you generate a WM_CLOSE message. Later sections discuss WM_GOT_SERVICE and WM_ASYNC_LOOKUP_DONE, which are application specific messages (defined in SOCKMAN4.H):

```
BOOL _export CALLBACK TimeServerDialogProc(HWND hwndDlg, UINT iMessage,
    WPARAM wParam, LPARAM lParam)
{
  static BOOL bSetTime;          // Flag to set the PC time clock
  time_t lPCTime;                // PC time
  time_t lNetTime;               // Network time
  NPSTR npTime;                  // Temporary pointer for time values

  switch (iMessage)
    {
      case WM_INITDIALOG:
        // Initialize the dialog box
        return(TRUE);

      case WM_CLOSE:
        PostMessage(hwndDlg, WM_COMMAND, IDCANCEL, 0L);
        return(TRUE);

      case WM_GOT_SERVICE:
        LookupTimeServer(hwndDlg, lParam);
        return(TRUE);

      case WM_COMMAND:
        // Process dialog box commands
        break;

      case WM_ASYNC_LOOKUP_DONE:
        // Perform the time server query and manage the results
        return(TRUE);
    }

  return(FALSE);
}
```

The WM_COMMAND messages result from your mouse clicks on the dialog-box command buttons. As shown in the following program statements, the case statement for WM_COMMAND includes another (nested) switch-case construct. TimeServerDialogProc's WM_COMMAND message includes a separate case statement for each command button in the dialog box:

```
case WM_COMMAND:
 switch (wParam)
   {
     case IDSETTIME:
       bSetTime = TRUE;
       // Perform IDOK functions.
```

```
    case IDOK:
      GetDlgItemText(hwndDlg, IDC_TIMESERVER,
            (LPSTR)szTimeServer, MAX_HOST_NAME);
      if (lstrlen(szTimeServer) > 0)
        hTimeServerTask = AsyncGetServiceInfo(hwndDlg, TASK_TIMESERVER);
      else
        {
          bSetTime = FALSE;
          wsprintf(szScratchBuffer, "Please enter a host name.");
          MessageBeep(0);
          MessageBox(hwndDlg, szScratchBuffer,
                "SockMan-TIME SERVER QUERY",
                MB_OK|MB_ICONINFORMATION);
        }
      return(TRUE);

    case IDCANCEL:
      PostMessage(hwndSockman, WM_COMMAND, IDM_FILE_CLEAR, 0L);
      EndDialog(hwndDlg, FALSE);
      return(TRUE);

  }
break;
```

When you click your mouse on the Set Time button, Windows generates a WM_COMMAND message with a wParam option equal to IDSETTIME. If the user selects the Query button, wParam equals IDOK. Likewise, a user selection of the Exit button results in wParam equal to IDCANCEL. When you click your mouse on the Exit button, the TimeServerDialogProc function posts the WM_COMMAND/IDM_FILE_CLEAR message to the main Sockman window. This message causes Sockman to clear the window display. In other words, when you exit the Time Server dialog box, Sockman erases any time-server messages that Sockman's main window displays.

The Set Time and Query command buttons work together. As shown in the previous code fragment, the IDSETTIME case sets the Boolean variable bSetTime to True and then falls through to perform the same steps as IDOK. In other words, just like the Query button, the Set Time button causes Sockman to perform another time-server query. The only difference is that IDSETTIME sets a flag that tells Sockman to change the system clock to the date-and-time that the time-server returns.

To initiate the time-server operation when it receives IDOK, TimeServerDialogProc uses the GetDlgItemText function to copy the host server entry from the IDC_TIMESERVER text box into the szTimeServer global string array. TimeServerDialogProc tests the string length of szTimeServer to make sure an entry exists. If the user failed to specify a host server, TimeServerDialogProc displays a message box with instructions to do so. If a host-server entry exists, TimeServerDialogProc calls the AsyncGetServiceInfo function.

RETRIEVING INTERNET INFORMATION FOR THE QUERY

As you have learned from the *quick* programs, your program must retrieve information such as protocol ports and IP addresses before it can establish a connection to a remote host-server program. The network-services database lists Internet protocols and well-known port assignments. As discussed in previous chapters, the AsyncGetServiceInfo function initiates an asynchronous retrieval from the network-services database. The AsyncGetServiceInfo program statements (shown in the following code statements) for the time-server task are identical to the Finger-program statements except for the service name (IPSERVICE_TIME):

```
HTASK AsyncGetServiceInfo(HWND hwnd, HTASK hService)
{
  HTASK hTask;              // Task handle for asynchronnous service
  LPSTR lpServiceName;      // The service name to resolve
  LPSTR lpBuffer;           // Pointer to the data-storage buffer
  int nLength;              // The length of the data-storage buffer

  switch (hService)
    {
      case TASK_ASYNC_FINGER:
        // ...Finger service information
        break;

      case TASK_TIMESERVER:
        lpServiceName = (LPSTR)IPSERVICE_TIME;
        lpBuffer = (LPSTR)szTimeServerBuffer;
        nLength = sizeof(szTimeServerBuffer);
        break;

      default:
        // ...Warn the caller that the service was unanticipated.
        return(0);
    }

  hTask = WSAAsyncGetServByName(hwnd, WM_GOT_SERVICE, lpServiceName,
        NULL, lpBuffer, nLength);

  if (!hTask)
    // ...Post an error message

  return(hTask);
}
```

The AsyncGetServiceInfo function calls Winsock's WSAAsyncGetServByName function to retrieve the time-service entry from the network-services database. WSAAsyncGetServByName, in turn, causes Windows to send a WM_GOT_SERVICE message to the specified window:

```
hTask = WSAAsyncGetServByName(hwnd, WM_GOT_SERVICE, lpServiceName, NULL,
    lpBuffer, nLength);
```

In the case of the time-server task, the dialog procedure TimeServerDialogProc will receive the WM_GOT_SERVICE. As previously shown, the statements for the WM_GOT_SERVICE case in the TimeServerDialogProc function call LookupTimeServer using the parameters shown here:

```
LookupTimeServer(hwndDlg, lParam);
```

The hwndDlg parameter identifies the dialog-box window, and the lParam parameter contains any error conditions that the asynchronous lookup of the time-service entry causes. As shown in the following program statements, the LookupTimeServer function first tests for an error from the asynchronous time-service lookup. If the WSAGETASYNCERROR macro detects an error, LookupTimeServer uses the default protocol port (IPPORT_TIMESERVER) that winsock.h defines. Otherwise, LookupTimeServer extracts the protocol port from the service entry that WSAAsyncGetServByName retrieves and szTimeServerBuffer stores. LookupTimeServer stores the time-service protocol port in the nTimeServerPort global variable and then calls LookupHostAsync:

```
VOID LookupTimeServer(HWND hwnd, LPARAM lError)
{
  if (WSAGETASYNCERROR(lError))
    nTimeServerPort = htons(IPPORT_TIMESERVER);
  else
    nTimeServerPort = ((LPSERVENT)szTimeServerBuffer)->s_port;

  hTimeServerTask = LookupHostAsync(hwnd, szTimeServer,
        szTimeServerBuffer,
        (LPDWORD)&dwTimeServerAddr);

  if (!hTimeServerTask)
    {
      wsprintf(szTimeServerBuffer, "Unable to lookup: %s",
            (LPSTR)szTimeServer);
      MessageBeep(0);
      MessageBox(hwnd, szTimeServerBuffer,
            "SockMan-TIME SERVER QUERY", MB_OK|MB_ICONINFORMATION);
      PaintWindow(szTimeServerBuffer);
    }
  return;
}
```

Although not shown in the previous code statements, LookupHostAsync can use Winsock's WSAAsyncGetHostByName or WSAAsyncGetHostByAddr functions to asynchronously resolve either a DNS host name or dotted-decimal IP address. As called by the LookupHostAsync functions, both WSAAsyncGetHostByName and WSAAsyncGetHostByAddr cause Windows to send a WM_ASYNC_LOOKUP_DONE message after they resolve the host address. In other words, when LookupHostAsync finishes resolving the host address szTimeServer specifies, the Time Server dialog box will receive a WM_ASYNC_LOOKUP_DONE message.

STARTING THE TIME SERVER QUERY

After Sockman retrieves the protocol port from the network-services database (using AsyncGetServiceInfo) and resolves the server host's Internet address (using LookupHostAsync), Sockman has all the information it needs to initiate the time-server query. When the time-server dialog-box procedure, TimeServerDialogProc, receives the WM_ASYNC_LOOKUP_DONE message, TimeServerDialogProc calls the PaintWindow function with a message that notifies the user that the asynchronous address lookup for the time-server operation has completed.

As shown in the following code statements, after informing the user of the address resolution, TimeServerDialogProc calls the TimeServerQuery function, which actually performs the time-server query. After TimeServerQuery returns, TimeServerDialogProc sets the time-server task variable, hTimeServerTask, to zero to indicate that a time server operation is no longer in progress:

```
case WM_ASYNC_LOOKUP_DONE:
  PaintWindow("Asynchronous lookup for Time Server completed.");
  lNetTime = TimeServerQuery(hwndDlg, lParam);
  hTimeServerTask = 0;

if (lNetTime != SOCKET_ERROR)
  // Process the results
else
  SetDlgItemText(hwndDlg, IDC_SERVER_TIME, "");

MessageBeep(0);
return(TRUE);
```

The TimeServerQuery function returns a time value suitable for use with the PC's date-and-time functions. In other words, TimeServerQuery returns the current date-and-time as a value that represents the number of seconds since midnight, 1 January 1970. If the query fails, TimeServerQuery returns the Winsock constant SOCKET_ERROR and TimeServerDialogProc sets the dialog-box IDC_SERVER_TIME text-box to a zero-length string. In other words, when an error occurs, TimeServerDialogProc erases any previous time and dates Sockman displays.

If no errors occur (that is, TimeServerQuery does not return SOCKET_ERROR), TimeServerDialogProc processes the results of the time-server query. Regardless of whether an error occurs, TimeServerDialogProc uses the Windows MessageBeep function to notify you when the time-server operation finishes.

As previously discussed, when you click your mouse on the Set Time button in the Time Server dialog box, the TimeServerDialogProc function sets the Boolean-flag variable bSetTime to True. When the TimeServerQuery function returns a valid value for lNetTime and bSetTime is True, TimeServerDialogProc changes your computer's system clock to the value that lNetTime stores. After changing the system clock (if necessary), TimeServerDialogProc calls the ctime function to convert the network time and PC time (stored in lNetTime and lPCTime respectively) to a string value. TimeServerDialogProc then calls the Windows SetDlgItemText function to store the string values in the dialog-box text boxes IDC_SERVER_TIME and IDC_LOCAL_TIME. TimeServerDialogProc also calls PaintWindow to paint the current PC time in Sockman's main window.

As shown in the following code statements, TimeServerDialogProc uses standard DOS functions and structures to change your PC's system clock. TimeServerDialogProc uses dostime_t and dosdate_t structures, as well as a pointer to the DOS tm structure. To convert the lNetTime value from TimeServerQuery to a DOS tm structure, TimeServerDialogProc calls localtime, a C run-time library function:

```
if (bSetTime)
{
  struct tm *npTMStruct;
  struct dostime_t dosTimeStruct;
  struct dosdate_t dosDateStruct;

  npTMStruct = localtime(&lNetTime);

  dosTimeStruct.hour = (BYTE)(npTMStruct->tm_hour);
  dosTimeStruct.minute = (BYTE)(npTMStruct->tm_min);
  dosTimeStruct.second = (BYTE)(npTMStruct->tm_sec);
  dosTimeStruct.hsecond = (BYTE)0;
  _dos_settime(&dosTimeStruct);

  dosDateStruct.year = npTMStruct->tm_year + 1900;
  dosDateStruct.month = (BYTE)(npTMStruct->tm_mon +1);
  dosDateStruct.day = (BYTE)(npTMStruct->tm_mday);
  _dos_setdate(&dosDateStruct);

  bSetTime = FALSE;
}
```

The localtime function returns a pointer to an internal-static buffer with the tm values. TimeServerDialogProc uses the tm values to store the time-server's date-and-time in the dostime_t and dosdate_t structures. After storing the appropriate values in the dostime_t and dosdate_t structures, TimeServerDialogProc calls the _dos_settime and _dos_setdate functions to change your system's date-and-time. Before exiting the *if* construct, TimeServerDialogProc resets the bSetTime flag variable to False.

UNDERSTANDING THE TIME SERVER QUERY

As previously shown, TimeServerDialogProc calls the TimeServerQuery function to initiate the time-server query:

```
lNetTime = TimeServerQuery(hwndDlg, lParam);
```

The TimeServerQuery function performs the time-server query in practically the same way as the QTime program previously reviewed in this chapter. The companion disk contains the complete source code for TimeServerQuery. However, rather than reexamine the QTime program statements, review the following pseudo-code that shows the general procedure that TimeServerQuery follows:

```
LONG TimeServerQuery(HWND hwnd, LPARAM lError)
{
  // First, declare local variables.

  // Next, test for an error value in lError
  if (WSAGETASYNCERROR(lError))
  // If an error exists, display a message box and return SOCKET_ERROR.

  // Otherwise obtain a pointer to the host entry structure
  // and store values in a socket address structure.

  // Create the socket.
  if ((hSocket = socket(AF_INET, SOCK_STREAM, DEFAULT_PROTOOCOL)) ==
        INVALID_SOCKET)
  // If an error exists, display a message box and return SOCKET_ERROR.

  // Otherwise, connect the socket to the remote host.
  if (connect(hSocket, (PSOCKADDR)&socketAddr, sizeof(socketAddr)))
  // If an error exists, display a message box and return SOCKET_ERROR.

  // Send a CR/LF to the time server.
  send(hSocket, "\n", sizeof("\n"), NO_FLAGS);

  // Get the value returned by the time server and close the socket.
  nLength = recv(hSocket, (LPSTR)&lNetTime, sizeof(lNetTime), 0);
  closesocket(hSocket);

  // Test recv's return for any socket errors.
  if(nLength == SOCKET_ERROR)
  // If an error exists, display a message box and return SOCKET_ERROR.
```

```
// Otherwise, convert lNetTime's byte order from network to host byte
// order and then adjust the network time to PC time. Remember, the
// Internet uses 1 January 1900 as a point of reference while PC run-
// time functions use 1 January 1970.
lPCTime = ntohl(lNetTime);
lPCTime -= PC_REF_TIME;

// Finally, return the network time as a PC time value.
return(lPCTime);
}
```

Putting It All Together

In this chapter, you have learned how to use the Internet's Time Protocol to retrieve the current date-and-time from a time-server program on an Internet host. In the process, you have discovered that PCs often store numeric data differently than other Internet computers. For example, you have seen how the PC and the Internet use opposite byte-orders for storing numeric data. You have learned to convert byte-orders and examined some of the problems that can occur when you forget to do so. You also learned how careless use of signed and unsigned variables can cause you additional confusion when you trouble-shoot programs that transmit numeric data across the Internet. In the next chapter, you will learn how to create a raw socket, which lets your programs access low-level Internet protocols such as the Internet Control Message Protocol (ICMP). Before you move ahead to raw sockets and the Ping utility in Chapter 14, make sure you understand the following key concepts:

- ✓ Big-endian byte-order stores the most-significant digit of a numeric value in the first (lowest) memory address of a message buffer.

- ✓ Little-endian byte-order stores the least-significant digit of a numeric value in the first (lowest) memory address of a message buffer.

- ✓ PCs use a little-endian byte-order for numeric values.

- ✓ The Internet requires a big-endian byte-order for numeric values.

- ✓ The Winsock API provides four functions that convert byte-orders—two convert 16-bit numbers and two convert 32-bit numbers.

- ✓ Binary data can appear to represent two different values depending on whether you use signed or unsigned variables.

Chapter 14
Understanding Raw Sockets

As you have learned, the Internet relies upon an unreliable (yet effective) datagram delivery service—the Internet Protocol (IP). IP doesn't guarantee delivery of network packets, nor does it guarantee notification of failure when the communication channel loses or corrupts data packets. However, under certain conditions, the TCP/IP network software does generate error messages. This chapter takes a closer look at those error messages, the conditions under which they occur, and the protocol that delivers the error messages—the Internet Control Message Protocol (ICMP).

In this chapter, you will also learn how to use the Windows Sockets (Winsock) API to generate your own ICMP messages. To do so, your programs must create and use a *raw socket*. As previously mentioned, a raw socket provides your programs with access to low-level protocols, such as ICMP. By the time you finish this chapter, you will understand the following key concepts:

- How the TCP/IP network design limits error reporting

- What kind of errors ICMP reports and how

- How ICMP query messages help network professionals

- How to create and communicate through a raw socket

Depending on the WINSOCK.DLL your programs use, they may not be able to use raw sockets. (Version 1.1 of the Winsock specification does not require support for raw sockets.) Likewise, if your programs use raw sockets, your programs may not run on all local area TCP/IP networks (depending on the WINSOCK.DLL the network uses). This chapter shows you a simple error check you can perform to determine whether the Winsock implementation your program uses supports raw sockets.

*Note: The Trumpet WINSOCK.DLL (included on the **Internet Programming** companion disk) supports raw sockets. As such, even if your local area network doesn't support raw sockets, you can use the Trumpet WINSOCK.DLL to develop raw socket-based programs on a stand-alone PC.*

UNDERSTANDING ICMP

The Internet Control Message Protocol (ICMP) carries network error messages and reports other conditions that require the attention of network software. In those rare instances when your programs need to bypass the TCP/IP transport layer and communicate directly with the TCP/IP network layer, they typically use ICMP. (Request for Comments (RFC) 792, *Internet Control Message Protocol*, Postel, 1981 defines ICMP.) To use a low-level protocol such as ICMP, your programs must use a raw socket. However, you should understand that creating a raw socket involves considerable programming effort. For example, to use ICMP on a raw socket, your programs must create and fill data structures that represent ICMP headers.

Understanding the Big Picture

As previously shown in Chapter 4, the TCP/IP network layer includes the IP module and two other protocol modules: ICMP and the Internet Group Message Protocol (IGMP). As with other protocols (such as TCP and UDP) in the TCP/IP protocol suite, ICMP uses the Internet Protocol for data delivery. Figure 14.1 shows the position of ICMP within the TCP/IP protocol stack.

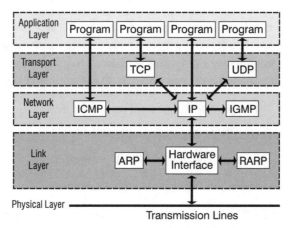

Figure 14.1 *The TCP/IP network layer showing the IP, ICMP, and IGMP software modules.*

Like IP, ICMP is part of the network layer. In relation to IP, however, ICMP acts as though it is a higher-level protocol than IP. In other words, ICMP communicates with (relies upon) IP as part of the network layer within a host computer. However, ICMP also relies on IP to deliver messages to other host computers on the network in much the same way as TCP and UDP rely on IP for data delivery. As you have learned, IP delivers data through a network of packet switches or gateways. Although, in most cases, the system works quite well, IP does not include any method to notify a packet switch (or a gateway) that a data-delivery problem exists. (To simplify the IP design, the protocol designers eliminated error notification.) As such, an efficient network needs some method to handle errors that impact network data-delivery services. As you will learn, ICMP adds this capability to the network layer in TCP/IP networks. As discussed, unless your programs use a reliable protocol, they cannot depend on TCP/IP network software to report error conditions. In general, the TCP/IP network design limits network-generated error messages to the network and transport layers. In other words, typically, only the network or transport layer see low-level TCP/IP error messages.

UNDERSTANDING REPORTABLE ERROR CONDITIONS

When host computers work properly and all host computers agree on how to route network data, a TCP/IP network delivers data quite efficiently. Obviously, computer failure and transmission-line problems can impact data delivery. However, such hardware-based problems are not peculiar to any one type of network, such as TCP/IP. When a local malfunction occurs, most network hardware generates some type of error message. Network professionals that maintain TCP/IP-based local area networks have a variety of hardware and software tools they can use to analyze network hardware problems. On the other hand, when a remote malfunction occurs, a network technician must first determine where the problem occurred. Next, the technician must understand the configuration details of the communications subnet—the combination of packet switches, routers, and host computers included in the error path. On an internetwork, collecting such information may be impossible or impractical.

With an internetwork (TCP/IP-based or any other kind), a host computer cannot always tell whether a problem resulted from a local or remote malfunction. The typical tools that network professionals use to analyze a LAN usually don't help debug remote malfunctions. For example, network debugging tools (hardware- and software-based) typically assume that the network professional knows the hardware configuration of the network under test. Obviously, in many cases, a network professional will not know specific configuration details about remote networks. Because IP doesn't include a mechanism to help network professionals debug remote network problems, network professionals designed and added ICMP to the TCP/IP protocol suite. As such, every IP implementation must include ICMP. Although ICMP and IP are separate protocols, think them as Siamese twins—permanently attached. The following sections discuss the ICMP design and its operation within the TCP/IP protocol suite.

DEFINING THE PURPOSE OF *ICMP*

The original purpose of ICMP was to let gateways (routers) report the cause of delivery errors to the transmitting host's network layer, which, in turn, would decide how to respond to the errors. However, the protocol design does not limit the use of ICMP to network routers—any TCP/IP host can use ICMP to transmit network error, control, and information messages to another host on the network (or TCP/IP internetwork). TCP/IP networks encapsulate ICMP messages in IP datagrams. In other words, an ICMP message travels across a TCP/IP network in the data area of an IP datagram. However, the destination of an ICMP message is always a network-layer software module—never a specific user or network application. The ICMP module in the destination IP layer determines whether to forward the message to any higher-level software modules, such as a transport-layer or application-layer module. As discussed in the following sections, TCP/IP restricts the use of some ICMP messages.

UNDERSTANDING *ICMP* ERROR REPORTING

As discussed, ICMP only provides error-reporting services. In other words, ICMP doesn't provide any error-correction services. Furthermore, ICMP doesn't specify any action for network-layer software modules to take in response to the errors it reports.

Understanding ICMP Limitations

When an error occurs, ICMP reports the problem to the source host only. In other words, ICMP notifies only the host that sent the packet that caused the error. Since most errors originate with the sending host, this source-only notification usually is not a significant limitation. However, because ICMP doesn't notify intermediate packet switches of such errors, sending hosts can't always correct routing problems. For example, suppose a packet switch incorrectly routes a data packet to the wrong computer. Using ICMP, the computer that receives the mis-routed packet can only report the error back to the sending host. As a result, the sending host may not be able to determine which router caused the problem, much less take action to correct the problem.

To understand why ICMP has limited capabilities, you must review what you know about the TCP/IP protocol suite design. Specifically, you must recall what you have learned about how TCP/IP networks route IP datagrams. Remember that an IP datagram header contains only the source and destination IP addresses, which don't change as the datagram travels across the network. As a datagram passes through a packet switch, the packet switch examines the destination IP address and then consults its routing table. Based on the destination address and the information in its routing table, the packet switch then chooses the next intermediate destination for the packet. Eventually, the datagram reaches a packet switch directly connected to the destination host, and that packet switch transmits the datagram directly to the destination host computer.

Remember that TCP/IP networks dynamically configure the routing tables that packet switches use. In other words, no single packet switch knows the master routing map for the entire internetwork. (To simplify network software design, TCP/IP hides routing details from network software, including the protocol suite itself.) As a result, when a datagram arrives at a destination host, neither the datagram nor the destination host has any idea (nor way of finding out) which path the datagram took to reach its destination. Nor can either of them know what packet switches the datagram might pass through on a return trip to the source host. In other words, as a result of the TCP/IP network design, ICMP can report network errors or other network information to the source host only. For ICMP designers to create an error-reporting mechanism that provided more options, someone would have to redesign the TCP/IP protocol suite. As you will learn, despite its limitations, ICMP adds significant power and capability to the TCP/IP protocol suite.

Understanding the Problems

As discussed, ICMP uses IP for data delivery. As a result, an ICMP message is no more reliable, nor does it have any higher priority, than any other IP packet. The network may lose or discard an ICMP message like any other packet on the network. In addition, an ICMP message can cause additional data-delivery problems. For example, if network congestion generates an ICMP error message, the ICMP message itself will compound the congestion and related problems. Likewise, if a packet that contains an ICMP error message were allowed to generate another error message, that message might, in turn, generate still another error message, and so on. Network professionals have established several rules that prevent the occurrence of unnecessary ICMP error messages.

However, before you review these rules, you need to understand that ICMP defines two types of ICMP messages: a *query message* and an *error message*. Later in this chapter, you will use an ICMP query message to measure a data packet's round-trip travel time between two hosts. ICMP query messages either request or provide network information.

ICMP Error Messages versus ICMP Query Messages

In general, ICMP error messages result from packet-delivery problems. As such, an ICMP error message is always associated with a specific IP datagram. As you will learn, an ICMP error message always includes the IP header and the first 64 bits (eight bytes) of data from the datagram that causes the error. On the other hand, an ICMP query message does not report problems. An ICMP query message reports network- or host-related information. Typically, network professionals design programs to use query messages as troubleshooting tools.

Understanding the ICMP Error-Reporting Rules

TCP/IP defines strict rules for when network hosts can transmit ICMP messages. For example, ICMP query messages can cause an ICMP error message. However, to ensure that one error message doesn't generate a string of others (and thus flood the communication channel), TCP/IP network software never generates an ICMP error message for a datagram that carries an ICMP error message. Likewise, network software never generates ICMP error messages for datagrams with an IP broadcast or multicast address. As you have learned, a broadcast or multicast address specifies multiple computers as a destination. By prohibiting error-message generation from packets that contain multiple destination (or source) addresses, ICMP prevents TCP/IP *broadcast storms*.

To understand the term *broadcast storm*, consider what would happen if a broadcast datagram encountered a problem and did generate an ICMP error message. Since a broadcast datagram's destination includes every computer on the network, the IP layer in every host computer that receives the datagram would generate an ICMP error message, creating a storm of network messages (a broadcast storm). To a lesser degree, a multicast address would cause the same problem. Likewise, since ICMP sends error messages to source hosts, an indeterminate source address causes a problem also. As you have learned, when a datagram is too large for a network's underlying physical layer, TCP/IP fragments the datagram for transport across the network. As such, if the network discards the datagram for any reason, the source host will receive an ICMP error message. However, because the source host only needs one error message to know it must retransmit the entire datagram, TCP/IP network software reports only the first discarded fragment. As a result, ICMP doesn't flood the network with multiple error messages about the same fragmented datagram.

Defining ICMP Messages

As discussed, ICMP delivers error and query messages. TCP/IP encapsulates each ICMP message in an IP datagram. Network software identifies each ICMP message by two values: an 8-bit Type value and an 8-bit Code value. As shown in Figure 14.2, these two values comprise the first two fields in the ICMP message header.

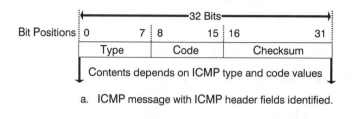

a. ICMP message with ICMP header fields identified.

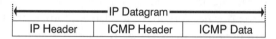

b. ICMP Encapsulation.

Figure 14.2 The ICMP message format and encapsulation.

Immediately following the type and code bytes, ICMP includes a 16-bit Checksum field. As you have learned, a checksum helps the peer network module detect packet data corruption. Later in this chapter, you will see the C/C++ language source code to generate this checksum. The checksum covers the entire ICMP message, not just the ICMP header.

The header information that follows the first three fields (Type, Code, and Checksum) depends on the specific ICMP message. Also, as previously mentioned, ICMP messages that report errors include the IP header and the first 64 bits (eight bytes) of data from the datagram that triggered the error. In addition to classifying ICMP messages as either error or query messages, the ICMP protocol defines 15 specific ICMP message types. As shown in Table 14.1, these 15 message types include a mix of ICMP query and error messages.

Type	Query/Error	Description
0	QUERY	Echo reply
3	ERROR	Destination unreachable
4	ERROR	Source quench
5	ERROR	Redirect
8	QUERY	Echo request
9	QUERY	Router advertisement
10	QUERY	Router solicitation
11	ERROR	Time exceeded
12	ERROR	Parameter problem

Table 14.1 ICMP message type values. (continued on the next page)

Type	Query/Error	Description
13	QUERY	Timestamp request
14	QUERY	Timestamp reply
15	QUERY	Information request (obsolete)
16	QUERY	Information reply (obsolete)
17	QUERY	Address Mask request
18	QUERY	Address Mask reply

Table 14.1 ICMP message type values. (continued from the previous page)

UNDERSTANDING ICMP ERROR MESSAGES

As shown in Table 14.1, ICMP defines a wide variety of messages, including five different types of error messages. The following sections discuss each specific type of ICMP error message. Some of these message types are broad categories of error messages. For example, the destination-unreachable error messages (type 3) include 16 different destination unreachable codes.

REPORTING DESTINATION UNREACHABLE ERRORS

As discussed, protocol designers originally added ICMP to the TCP/IP protocol suite so network routers could report packet-delivery problems. Whenever a router cannot deliver a packet, the router sends a destination-unreachable (type 3) error message to the source host. Since reporting these types of errors was the original purpose of ICMP, the destination-unreachable type messages include more error codes than any other ICMP-error message type. As shown in Table 14.2, ICMP includes 16 (0-15) destination-unreachable error codes.

Code	Description
0	Network unreachable
1	Host unreachable
2	Protocol unreachable
3	Port unreachable
4	Fragmentation needed but *don't fragment* bit is set
5	Source route failed
6	Destination network unknown
7	Destination host unknown

Table 14.2 ICMP destination-unreachable error codes for type 3 ICMP messages.(continued on the next page)

Code	Description
8	Source host isolated (obsolete)
9	Destination network administratively prohibited
10	Destination host administratively prohibited
11	Network unreachable for type-of-service (TOS)
12	Host unreachable for type-of-service (TOS)
13	Communication administratively prohibited by filtering
14	Host precedence violation
15	Precedence cutoff in effect

Table 14.2 ICMP destination-unreachable error codes for type 3 ICMP messages.(continued from the previous page)

As you have learned, IP cannot guarantee data delivery. However, IP should still successfully deliver most datagrams. If IP fails to deliver a datagram, the cause may be a delivery problem or a routing problem. If you study the descriptions in Table 14.2, you will learn that most of the destination-unreachable error codes specify a failure related to either a host or a network. Typically, an host-unreachable error code indicates a delivery problem. A network-unreachable error code indicates a routing problem. Figure 14.3 shows the ICMP message format for a destination-unreachable error message. As you can see, the message format is the same as the general message format shown in Figure 14.2. For a destination-unreachable error message, the Type field is always 3 and the Code field will be an 8-bit integer value ranging from 0 to 15. As previously discussed, an ICMP error message also includes the IP header and first 64 bits (eight bytes) of data from the datagram that triggered the error message.

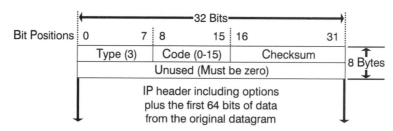

Figure 14.3 The ICMP message format for a destination-unreachable error message.

A destination may be unreachable if the IP header contains an incorrect destination address. Likewise, off-line hardware (temporarily out of service) might prevent a packet from reaching its destination. Although unlikely, it is also possible that a packet switch's routing table may not include a path to the destination network. All routers must report packet-delivery failures to the packet's sender. However, as you have learned, the network may lose or discard such error messages. The possible loss of error-message notifications makes the ICMP error-reporting mechanism unreliable. (Remember, ICMP relies on an unreliable protocol—IP.)

REPORTING REDIRECT ERRORS

As discussed in Chapter 4, TCP/IP packet switches use routing tables to send data packets to their correct destination. As you have learned, TCP/IP routing relies on the network ID in the host address to correctly route data. In other words, a TCP/IP routing table includes entries to reach any network in the internetwork. However, each router only knows the next stop along the route. In many cases, a router may know more than one route to a destination network. Routers periodically exchange routing information with each other to help keep routing information current. However, in general, routing table entries do not frequently change. Typically, host computers initialize their routing tables from locally stored configuration files. Their configuration file contains minimal routing information—typically, the address of a single router or gateway. A host computer depends on network routers to update the host's routing table. As explained in the following paragraphs, the ICMP redirect messages are one method used to accomplish this task.

Suppose your host computer sends a datagram to your friend's host computer, which (as shown in Figure 14.4) resides on a different physical network. To send the datagram, your host computer must use a router. Assume your host computer sends the datagram to Router #2. Based on its routing tables, Router #2 knows that Router #1 is the next hop on the path to your friend's network and, as such, it forwards the packet to Router #1.

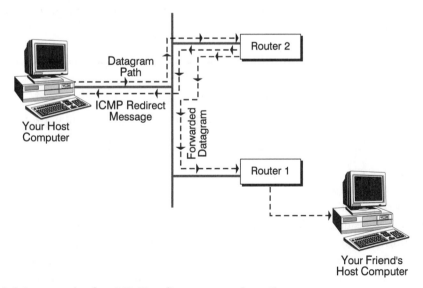

Figure 14.4 An example of an ICMP redirect message (type 5).

However, Router #2 also knows (from the information in the packet and its routing tables) that your computer resides on the same physical network as Router #1. In other words, your computer can send packets directly to Router #1—a more direct (or optimal) path to your friend's host computer. When a router determines that a host computer is using a non-optimal route, the router sends the host an ICMP redirect message that tells the host to use the more direct route. Figure 14.5 shows the format of an ICMP redirect message.

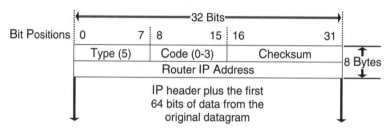

Figure 14.5 The ICMP message format for an ICMP redirect message (type 5).

The Router IP Address in the ICMP redirect message header tells the receiving host computer which router to use in the future. In other words, when a host ICMP module receives an ICMP redirect message, the module must examine the message's IP header (in the data area) and Router IP Address (the second 32-bit word in the ICMP message header). The IP header tells the host which packet (and destination address) used a non-optimal route. The Router IP Address tells the host which router address to use in the future. The ICMP module can use this information to update the host's routing table. Table 14.3 lists the four codes defined for ICMP redirect error messages (type 5). For the example shown in Figure 14.4, the router would send a type 5 message with a 1 in the code field (Redirect for host).

Code	Description
0	Redirect for network
1	Redirect for host
2	Redirect for Type of Service (TOS) and network
3	Redirect for Type of Service (TOS) and host

Table 14.3 ICMP redirect error messages (type 5).

Routers can also generate a redirect message as a result of Type of Service values in the transmitted datagram's IP header. As discussed in Chapter 4, the IP header Type of Service field defines datagram priorities. Although network software rarely uses this field, the Type of Service field may become important in the future. If so, the ICMP design already includes redirect messages to help hosts update their routing tables for specific Type of Service values. The ICMP protocol specifies several rules that limit the use of ICMP redirect error messages. For example, technically, any host computer can act as a router. However, only systems specifically configured as routers can send ICMP redirect messages. As such, TCP/IP prohibits a host computer from generating an ICMP redirect message. Also, routers do not update their routing tables when they receive a redirect message. Instead, as discussed in Chapter 4, routers use special routing protocols to maintain their information.

REPORTING TIME EXCEEDED ERRORS

As you have learned, routers only calculate the next hop in a packet's data path. Errors in routing tables can result in an infinite routing loop (or *routing cycle*). A routing cycle occurs when two or more routers continuously exchange a particular packet, with each router expecting the other to forward the packet to its destination. As you learned in Chapter 4, IP datagram headers include a Time-to-Live (TTL) field that limits the life of a packet. Each router that receives and forwards an IP packet decrements the value in the TTL field. Routers also decrement the TTL field for each second the packet spends in their data queues.

When the TTL field in an IP datagram reaches zero, the network software discards the packet and sends an ICMP time-exceeded message (type 11) to the packet's sender. The format of ICMP type 11 messages is the same as the destination-unreachable message shown in Figure 14.3. The only difference is that the Type field will be 11 instead of 3. As shown in Table 14.4, ICMP time-exceeded error messages can be one of two kinds. A code 0 indicates that the TTL field reached zero during transit (possibly due to a routing cycle, as previously described). A code 1 indicates that the host's fragment-reassembly timer expired before all fragments arrived.

Code	Description
0	Time-to-Live (TTL) equals 0 during transit
1	Fragment reassembly time exceeded

Table 14.4 ICMP time exceeded error messages (type 11).

As discussed in Chapter 4, when a destination host receives an IP packet with the More Fragments flag set, the host starts a *reassembly timer*. All fragments must arrive before the timer expires. If the reassembly timer expires before the host receives all fragments, the host discards all received fragments and does not process the datagram. In such cases, the host also generates an ICMP type 11 error message with the Code field set to 1.

REPORTING PARAMETER PROBLEMS

Hosts or routers send the parameter-problem error message when a routing or delivery failure occurs and the computer cannot identify the cause of the problem. As shown in Table 14.5, ICMP parameter-problem error messages can be one of two kinds.

Code	Description
0	IP header bad (a catchall error)
1	Required option missing

Table 14.5 ICMP parameter-problem error messages (type 12).

When a datagram doesn't contain all the information the TCP/IP software module requires for network transmission, ICMP transmits the required-option-missing error message (code 1). For example, assume you have built a protocol for secure communications into a corporate or government application. If a client program tries to transmit a request to this application but doesn't send a key security option with the request message, your protocol might dictate that the server application transmit a required-option-missing error message. IP header bad (code 0) is a catchall message for all unknown error conditions. Figure 14.6 shows the format for ICMP parameter-problem messages. The Pointer field identifies the byte in the original datagram that triggered the error message. For required-option-missing messages, the Pointer field is zero.

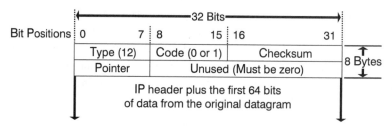

Figure 14.6 The ICMP message format for an ICMP parameter problem message (type 12).

SENDING SOURCE QUENCH MESSAGES

As discussed in Chapter 2, flow control ensures that a sending host does not transmit data packets faster than the receiver can process the incoming messages. In other words, flow control guarantees that the sender will not overrun or overflow the receiver's incoming-data queue. As you learned in Chapter 5, the Transport Control Protocol includes flow control as a communication service. Unfortunately, the flow control discussed in Chapters 2 and 5 only works with connection-oriented protocols. In other words, a protocol (such as IP) that uses connectionless datagrams cannot implement flow control like TCP. Because routers work with IP datagrams, it is possible for incoming packets to swamp or overwhelm a router's capacity to handle data.

Network traffic congestion occurs when a router cannot handle all incoming data packets. When congestion occurs, routers begin to discard incoming packets and send ICMP source-quench error messages (type 4) to the hosts that transmitted the packets. The source-quench error message signals a traffic congestion condition and tells the transmitting host to "reduce speed." In effect, the ICMP source-quench message helps IP perform a kind of flow control. Typically, a router sends a source-quench message for each discarded packet. When a host computer receives a source-quench message, the host begins to decrease the rate at which it transmits datagrams to the router.

If the router continues to send source-quench messages, the host continues to lower the transmission rate. When the host stops receiving source-quench messages, it can start to increase the transmission rate again. This process of increasing and decreasing transmission rates continues until the host reaches full transmission capacity. The ICMP source-quench message format is identical to the destination-unreachable format shown in Figure 14.3. However, for source-quench messages, the Type field is 4. The source-quench message is the only message of its type. In other words, the Code field in an ICMP header for a source-quench message is always zero—there are no other source-quench codes.

Understanding *ICMP* Query Messages

As previously discussed, in addition to error messages, the ICMP protocol defines query messages that provide network information related to routing, packet delivery, network performance, and subnet addresses. Network professionals use this information to solve TCP/IP internetwork debugging problems. The following sections discuss each type of ICMP query.

Understanding Router Queries

As you have learned, host computers typically initialize their routing tables from locally stored configuration files. However, using the ICMP router-query messages, host computers can dynamically initialize their routing tables rather than depend on static (and possibly outdated) initialization files.

To understand how ICMP router-query messages dynamically initialize routing tables, first note that ICMP defines two router queries: a router-solicitation message (type 10) and a router-advertisement message (type 9). Each time a host computer starts, it transmits a router-solicitation message. In response, one or more routers transmit a router-advertisement message. The router-advertisement message contains information that the host can use to initialize its routing tables.

RFC 1256, *ICMP Router Discovery Messages*, Deering, 1991, defines the format for the router-query messages. Figure 14.7 shows the format for both query messages. As you can see, the format for the router-solicitation message is similar to the destination-unreachable format shown in Figure 14.3. However, the router-solicitation message does not include any datagram information the ICMP message's data area.

As shown in Figure 14.7, routers can advertise multiple addresses in a single ICMP message. (Remember, each network interface card in a host computer or router has its own IP address.) The Number of Addresses field in the ICMP message header tells the receiving host how many addresses the message contains.

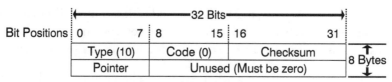

a. Format of the ICMP router-solicitation message (type 10).

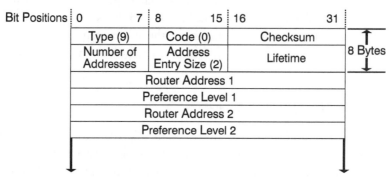

b. Format of the ICMP router-advertisement message (type 9).

Figure 14.7 *The ICMP message format for router query messages (types 9 and 10).*

The Address Entry Size field specifies the length of each address in terms of 32-bit words. As currently defined, the Address Entry Size field always has the value 2. In other words, the address length is eight bytes (a 32-bit Router Address and a 32-bit Preference Level). The Lifetime field specifies the number of seconds that the advertised addresses are valid. The lifetime is usually 30 minutes (1800 seconds). An ICMP router-advertisement message can contain one or more Router Address and corresponding Preference Level fields. Remember, IP addresses represent a network interface card—not a host computer. As such, multiple IP addresses can reference the same host computer. Preference Level fields are signed 32-bit integers that tell the receiving host which address to use first or most frequently. The higher the Preference Level field value, the more the router prefers the corresponding address as a default router address.

Routers broadcast ICMP router-advertisement messages at random intervals. Typically, the interval ranges between 450 and 600 seconds. As mentioned, the default value for the Lifetime field is 30 minutes. Routers can also use the Lifetime field to notify network hosts that the router is going off-line. In other words, to tell network hosts that the addresses in the ICMP message data area are no longer available, the router can broadcast an ICMP router-advertisement message with a Lifetime field value of zero. Typically, a host transmits three router-solicitation query messages, three seconds apart, at boot time. The host stops transmitting router-solicitation messages as soon as it receives a router-advertisement message. Although ICMP router-query messages represent a more sophisticated and reliable way to initialize host routing tables, the messages are relatively new and not all systems support them.

UNDERSTANDING TIMESTAMP QUERIES

The ICMP timestamp queries (message types 13 and 14) let network professionals estimate packet transit-time between host computers. Figure 14.8 shows the message format (which is identical) for both types of messages—timestamp request and timestamp reply.

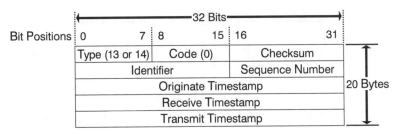

Figure 14.8 The ICMP format for timestamp request and reply messages (types 13 and 14).

The sender uses the ICMP header's Identifier and Sequence Number fields to distinguish between multiple timestamp requests. The sender can use these fields however seems most appropriate. In other words, ICMP does not care what values these fields contain. The three Timestamp fields represent the number of seconds past midnight. Just before it transmits the datagram, the sending host fills the Originate Timestamp field with the current time. The receiver fills the Receive Timestamp field as soon as the datagram arrives. Additionally, the receiver fills the Transmit Timestamp field just before transmitting its reply. As a network programmer, you should understand that the practical value of timestamps is questionable. Because the round-trip travel time for a single packet can fluctuate widely over short time periods, it is very difficult to accurately measure round-trip travel times for data packets. Even if network professionals send multiple queries and perform statistical analysis on the results, packet losses on the network can severely bias the results.

Note: Most hosts set the Receive Timestamp and Transmit Timestamp fields to the same value.

UNDERSTANDING ADDRESS MASK QUERIES

As discussed in Chapter 4, the Internet Network Information Center (InterNIC) assigns network ID numbers and network system administrators assign host ID numbers. As such, by manipulating host ID numbers, system administrators can divide their host's address space to effectively create their own local network of networks (or subnet). In other words, system administrators use a portion of their host ID number space as a network address and the remainder as host IDs. Network professionals refer to the exact partitioning of this address space as a subnet mask. As also discussed in Chapter 4, the Reverse Address Resolution Protocol (RARP) maps a link-layer address, such as an Ethernet address, into an IP address. Using RARP, a diskless workstation can ask other hosts to look up its correct IP address. When the diskless workstation receives a reply to its request, the diskless workstation can then broadcast a request for a host to download the workstation's operating system. In a similar way, diskless workstations can also use the ICMP address-mask queries to obtain their subnet mask. However, to use such a query, the workstations need to know which part of their 32-bit IP address to use as a subnet network ID and which part represents a host ID. Figure 14.9 shows the message format for ICMP address-mask request and reply messages.

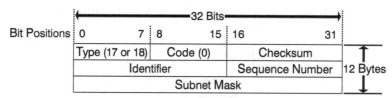

Figure 14.9 The ICMP format for address-mask request and reply messages (types 17 and 18).

The Identifier and Sequence Number fields in the address-mask messages are identical to the same fields in the timestamp messages. In other words, the sender can use these fields however seems most appropriate—ICMP does not care what values these fields contain. The ICMP address-mask-reply message contains the subnet mask for the host that sent the request. To use the ICMP address-mask-request message, the diskless workstation at boot time can simply broadcast the query. One or more hosts on the network will respond with an ICMP address-mask-reply message that contains the workstation's subnet mask.

Understanding the Echo request and Reply

In many cases, protocol designers build, into protocols, capabilities that let network managers or network users troubleshoot problems. The ICMP echo-request and echo-reply messages are a prime example of such capability. When an ICMP software module on a host computer receives an echo request, the ICMP module transmits an echo-reply packet that is identical to the echo request. The reply packet tells the echo-request sender that the host computer that received the echo request is on-line and responding to network messages.

The ICMP echo-request and echo-reply messages are among the more popular ICMP messages that programs, such as Ping (Packet **IN**ternet **G**roper), use behind the scenes. Typically, the Ping program transmits an echo request and then measures the round-trip travel time. Network managers and users use the Ping program to determine whether a remote host is currently available and accessible on the network. Figure 14.10 shows the message format for ICMP echo-request and echo-reply messages.

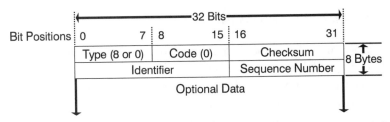

Figure 14.10 The ICMP format for echo-request and echo-reply messages (types 8 and 0).

The ICMP echo messages use the Identifier and Sequence Number fields to associate replies with requests. However, like the timestamp and address-mask messages, the ICMP echo messages can store in these fields whatever information seems most appropriate. Likewise, the sender can store any information (or nothing) in the Optional Data area. A host computer that receives an ICMP echo request acts like an echo server—the host simply echoes or returns, as an ICMP echo-reply message, whatever it receives.

Using Raw Sockets

Now that you have a solid understanding of ICMP, you should have no trouble understanding raw-socket operations that use ICMP. A raw socket lets your programs bypass the TCP/IP transport layer and access low-level protocols, such as ICMP. As such, your programs must perform normal transport-layer functions, such as data encapsulation, for the IP layer. In general, raw socket operations occur as follows. First, your program uses the Winsock socket function to create a raw socket. However, instead of specifying SOCK_STREAM or SOCK_DGRAM for the type of communication, your program specifies SOCK_RAW. Additionally, your program must also specify one particular protocol (ICMP, for example). Thereafter, the Winsock implementation pre-pends an IP header to any data written to the socket. In the Protocol field of the pre-pended IP header, the Winsock implementation stores the protocol value your program specified when it created the socket.

Whenever the Winsock implementation receives any data for the specified protocol, Winsock passes a copy of the data (including the datagram's IP header) to all processes that create a raw socket for that protocol. For example, if your program creates a raw socket for the ICMP protocol, your program will receive a copy of all arriving ICMP data packets. Your program examines each of these copies it receives to determine which packets belong to it. Normally, the transport layer would carry out this operation. However, because your program uses a raw socket to bypass the transport layer, the transport layer is no longer available to associate incoming data with particular sockets or protocol ports. The following sections show you how to create and use a raw socket. You will also learn how to generate Internet checksums. In later sections of this chapter, you will incorporate most of this code (unchanged) into the Sockman template.

REVIEWING THE QUICK PING PROGRAM

The quick Ping program (QPing) described in this section is a simplified version of the Ping program commonly found on the Internet. Like the other quick programs discussed in *Internet Programming*, QPing uses hard-coded values and Windows message boxes. As a result, QPing is a fully functional Winsock program that demonstrates key programming concepts yet avoids the normal overhead associated with a Windows program. The following program statements show the basic outline of QPing. To start, you should note that the program defines three functions: InternetChksum, DoPingOperation, and WinMain. The InternetChksum and DoPingOperation functions (shown below) show pseudo-code rather than actual program statements. The WinMain function definition is, in fact, complete:

```c
#include <time.h>
#include <stdlib.h>
#include "..\winsock.h"

// Define symbolic constants

// Declare IP and ICMP data structures
char szPingBuffer[100];            // General purpose buffer for messages

WORD InternetChksum(LPWORD lpwIcmpData, WORD wDataLength)
{
  // Create an Internet checksum
  return(wAnswer);
}


BOOL DoPingOperation(HANDLE hInstance)
{
  // Declare local variables
  // Resolve the IP address for the target host
  // Assign address family and host address to a socket structure
  // Retrieve the value for ICMP from the network services database
  // Create a "raw" socket and specify ICMP as the protocol
  // Assign values to the ICMP data structure
  // Put the tick count in the optional data area
  // Create the Internet checksum for the ICMP message
  // Send the datagram with the ICMP echo request through the raw socket
  // Wait for a reply
  // Close the socket after receiving data
  // Calculate the round-trip travel time
  // Verify the received data is an ICMP message
  // Verify the message is an ICMP "echo reply"
  // Verify that this program sent the packet
  // Note the IP address and host name of the sender
  return(TRUE);
}
```

```
int PASCAL WinMain(HANDLE hInstance, HANDLE hPrevInstance,
    LPSTR lpszCmdParam, int nCmdShow)
{
  WSADATA wsaData;                    // Winsock implementation details

  // Start the program here
  WSAStartup(WINSOCK_VERSION, &wsaData);

  DoPingOperation(hInstance);
  MessageBox(NULL, szPingBuffer, PROG_NAME, MB_OK|MB_ICONSTOP);

  WSACleanup();
  return(NULL);
}
```

As you can see, WinMain first calls WSAStartup to initialize the WINSOCK.DLL. Next, WinMain calls DoPingOperation, which sends and receives the ICMP echo messages. When DoPingOperation returns, WinMain displays the DoPingOperation results stored in the szPingBuffer global variable. Finally, the program exits. As shown in the previous program outline, before the QPing actually enters any function definitions, QPing defines symbolic constants and declares data structures for the IP header and ICMP messages. Like the previous quick programs, QPing uses the PROG_NAME constant to define the program project. The HOST_NAME constant can contain any valid Internet host computer. The WINSOCK_VERSION and NO_FLAGS constants are also identical to previous quick programs. WINSOCK_VERSION defines the WINSOCK.DLL support that the program requires, and NO_FLAGS defines the Winsock value for no special flags as an argument to Winsock functions.

Although ICMP_ECHO, ICMP_ECHOREPLY, and ICMP_HEADERSIZE are new, their values should be familiar to you from the previous discussions in this chapter. All three constants take their values from RFC 792. (As previously mentioned, RFC 792 defines the ICMP protocol.) ICMP_ECHO defines the ICMP message Type value for ICMP echo request messages. Likewise, ICMP_ECHOREPLY defines the ICMP message Type value for ICMP echo-reply messages. ICMP_HEADERSIZE defines the ICMP header length for ICMP echo messages, which (as shown in Figure 14.10) is eight bytes:

```
#define PROG_NAME "A Simple Ping Program"

#define HOST_NAME "cerfnet.com"    // This can be any valid host name
#define WINSOCK_VERSION 0x0101     // Program requires Winsock version 1.1
#define NO_FLAGS 0                 // No special flags specified
                                   // RFC 792 defines ICMP message values
#define ICMP_ECHO 8                // An ICMP echo message
#define ICMP_ECHOREPLY 0           // An ICMP echo reply message
#define ICMP_HEADERSIZE 8          // ICMP header size for "echo messages"
```

UNDERSTANDING THE QPING DATA STRUCTURES

Immediately following the symbolic constant definitions, QPing defines two data structures: struct ip and struct icmp. Both struct ip and struct icmp definitions are new. However, if you examine these structures closely, you will discover that they simply define IP and ICMP headers. If you compare the fields of the ip structure to Chapter 4's discussion of an IP datagram's header, you will find that you can easily match the structure field names with the IP header fields. Likewise, if you compare the ICMP header discussed earlier in this chapter with the structure field names in icmp, you will find the field names in each structure match. If you carefully examine the structure data types, you will also discover that the structure elements and header fields are the same width. The following program statements show the struct ip and struct icmp definitions:

```
struct ip                        // Structure for IP datagram header
{
  BYTE ip_verlen;                // Version and header length
  BYTE ip_tos;                   // Type of service
  WORD ip_len;                   // Total packet length
  UINT ip_id;                    // Datagram identification
  WORD ip_fragoff;               // Fragment offset
  BYTE ip_ttl;                   // Time to live
  BYTE ip_proto;                 // Protocol
  UINT ip_chksum;                // Checksum
  IN_ADDR ip_src_addr;           // Source address
  IN_ADDR ip_dst_addr;           // Destination address
  BYTE ip_data[1];               // Variable length data area
};

struct icmp                      // Structure for an ICMP header
{
  BYTE icmp_type;                // Type of message
  BYTE icmp_code;                // Type "sub code" (zero for echos)
  WORD icmp_cksum;               // 1's complement checksum
  WORD icmp_id;                  // Unique ID (our instance handle)
  WORD icmp_seq;                 // Track multiple pings
  BYTE icmp_data[1];             // Start of optional data
};
```

To create a raw socket, you must perform significantly more programming than when you create standard sockets. To begin, you must define your own data structures to store datagram-header information, as well as fill the structures with the correct values. To accurately create the required data structures, you must completely understand the underlying protocol and its packet structure. In other words, if you omit fields, store the wrong values in a field, or define a field to be the wrong size (width), your raw-socket-based program will fail. On the other hand, after you understand a protocol's operation and associated data, you can use a raw socket without much difficulty. Due to the structure definitions and assignment statements that a raw socket requires, you will have to write more lines of code than you would for a standard socket. But actually composing lines for a raw socket is no more difficult than for a standard socket. However, you will need to pay close attention to detail. In other words, you will need to make sure you define the data structures according to the protocol's specification and verify you store the correct values in the structure.

UNDERSTANDING THE INTERNET CHECKSUM

As you have learned, protocols use checksums and cyclic redundancy checks (CRCs) to detect data corruption. As discussed in Chapter 2, computers create checksums by adding the binary value of each alphanumeric character in a data block. To check for data corruption, the receiving computer calculates a new checksum and compares it to the checksum the sender transmitted with the message. A non-match indicates an error. Before reviewing DoPingOperation, you should review the InternetChksum function, which calculates the Internet checksum for the ICMP message. The basic algorithm is relatively simple. Your program combines adjacent bytes of data to form 16-bit integer values. Your program sums these 16-bit values and then calculates a 1's complement of the sum. The 1's complement of the sum is your Internet checksum, which your program can store in the protocol's Checksum field. The following program statements show the Internet checksum implementation that both QPing and Sockman's Ping utility use:

```
WORD InternetChksum(LPWORD lpwIcmpData, WORD wDataLength)
{
   long lSum;           // Store summation
   WORD wOddByte;       // Left over byte from summation
   WORD wAnswer;        // 1's complement checksum

   lSum = 0L;

   while (wDataLength > 1)
     {
       lSum += *lpwIcmpData++;
       wDataLength -= 2;
     }

   // Handle the odd byte if necessary and make sure the top half is zero
   if (wDataLength == 1)
     {
       wOddByte = 0;
       *((LPBYTE) &wOddByte) = *(LPBYTE)lpwIcmpData;  // One byte only
       lSum += wOddByte;
     }

   // Add back the carry outs from the 16 bits to the low 16 bits
   lSum = (lSum >> 16) + (lSum & 0xffff); // Add high-16 to low-16
   lSum += (lSum >> 16);                  // Add carry
   wAnswer = (WORD)~lSum;                 // 1's complement, then
                                          // truncate to 16 bits

   return(wAnswer);
}
```

RFC 1071, *Computing the Internet Checksum*, Braden, Borman, Partridge, 1988, discusses the Internet checksum in detail. As the authors point out, an efficient checksum implementation is critical to good network performance. As such, Internet programmers should implement the Internet checksum algorithm in ways that let them take advantage of their host computer's specific hardware characteristics and squeeze every ounce of performance from the implementation. For example, one programming technique, not in the InternetChksum function in QPing, is to declare the lSum and wAnswer variables as the storage class *register*. The register keyword tells the compiler to store the variable in one of your computer's hardware registers (instead of memory), if possible. Doing so may improve the function's speed. If you plan to use raw sockets, you should study RFC 1071, as well as the other sources of information listed in RFC 1071. First, make sure you understand the basic Internet checksum algorithm. Then, consider the authors suggestions for handcrafting an Internet checksum implementation.

UNDERSTANDING THE PING OPERATION

The DoPingOperation function sends the ICMP echo request and retrieves the ICMP echo reply. DoPingOperation consists of several more lines of code than the previous quick program functions. However, most of the extra lines of code are variable declarations, simple assignment statements, and other non-Internet related program statements. When you eliminate error checking and strip DoPingOperation down to only the program statements that include Winsock API function calls, the function definition looks like this:

```
BOOL DoPingOperation(HANDLE hInstance)
{
  // ...Declare local variables

  // Resolve the IP address for the target host
  if ((lpHostEntry = gethostbyname(HOST_NAME)) == NULL)
    return(FALSE);

  // ...Assign correct values to the socket address structure

  // With a raw socket, the program must specify a protocol
  if ((lpProtocolEntry = getprotobyname("icmp")) == NULL)
    nProtocol = IPPROTO_ICMP;
  else
    nProtocol = lpProtocolEntry->p_proto;

  // Create a "raw" socket and specify ICMP as the protocol
  if ((hSocket = socket(PF_INET, SOCK_RAW, nProtocol)) ==
      INVALID_SOCKET)
    return(FALSE);

  // ...Assign values to the structure for the ICMP message header
  // ...Put tick count in the optional data area
```

```
    // ...Calculate the Internet checksum for the ICMP message

    if (pIcmpHeader->icmp_cksum !=0 )
      {
        // Send the ICMP echo request message
        iSentBytes = sendto(hSocket, (LPSTR) IcmpSendPacket, iPacketSize,
                NO_FLAGS, (LPSOCKADDR) &sockAddrLocal,
                sizeof(sockAddrLocal));

        // Receive the ICMP echo reply message
        iReceivedBytes = recvfrom(hSocket, (LPSTR) IcmpRecvPacket,
                sizeof(IcmpRecvPacket), NO_FLAGS, (LPSOCKADDR)
                &sockAddrHost, &iHostAddrLength);
      }

    // Close the socket
    closesocket(hSocket);

    // ...Calculate the round-trip time and verify the reception of a
    // ...valid ICMP echo reply that, in fact, was sent by this program.

    return(TRUE);
}
```

As you can see, QPing includes very little Winsock code that you have not seen before. In fact, QPing uses only three new Winsock functions: getprotobyname, sendto, and recvfro. The Winsock getprotobyname function requires one parameter—a pointer to a protocol name. First, from your network services database, getprotobyname retrieves information for the protocol its one parameter specifies. Then, the function returns a pointer to the Winsock protocol-entry structure shown next:

```
struct protoent
{
  char FAR *p_name;               // Official name
  char FAR * FAR *p_aliases;      // Alternate names
  short p_proto;                  // Protocol number, in host byte order
};
```

The p_name field identifies the official name of the protocol and the p_aliases field identifies a NULL-terminated array of alternate names for the protocol. For the QPing program, the only element of interest is the p_proto field, which identifies the protocol number (in host byte-order). The previous quick programs (QLookup, QFinger, and QTime) used TCP (a connection-oriented protocol) on a byte-stream socket. As such, those programs used Winsock's send and recv functions to transmit and receive data. With a raw socket, your programs use connectionless protocols that deliver data with datagrams. As such, because send and recv functions only work on connected sockets, the QPing program must use the sendto and recvfrom functions. The difference between the two pairs of functions is that sendto and recvfrom let your programs specify a specific destination address—send and recv do not. The send and recv functions only work on sockets that your program has already connected to a destination host. The following program statement shows the Winsock prototype for the sendto function:

```
int PASCAL FAR sendto(SOCKET s, const char FAR * buf, int len,
        int flags, const struct sockaddr FAR * to, int tolen );
```

The first sendto parameter identifies the socket to use. The second parameter points to the buffer that contains the data your program wants to send. The third parameter tells Winsock the length of the data in your send buffer. For the fourth sendto parameter, your programs can use the same two flags previously described for the send function—MSG_DONTROUTE and MSG_OOB. If you don't want your data subject to routing, you need to use the MSG_DONTROUTE flag. If your program needs to send out-of-band data, your program should use the MSG_OOB flag. In most cases, the example programs in *Internet Programming* use no flags.

The fifth sendto parameter points to a socket-address structure that contains the destination address for your data. The last parameter specifies the length of the socket address. The Winsock prototype for the recvfrom function, shown next, is very similar to the sendto function:

```
int PASCAL FAR recvfrom(int s, char FAR * buf, int len, int flags,
        struct sockaddr FAR * from, int FAR * fromlen );
```

The only real difference between the sendto and recvfrom function parameters is that the fifth and sixth recvfrom parameters are optional. If your program uses a non-zero value for the *from* parameter, Winsock copies the peer address for received datagrams into the memory address pointed to by the *from* parameter. For example, if your program wants to know the address of any host that sends a datagram to the specified socket, your program must first allocate a buffer for a socket-address structure and then pass recvfrom (as its fifth parameter) a pointer to the socket-address buffer. Then, when the recvfrom function retrieves a datagram, Winsock will store the address of the peer host that sent the datagram in your socket-address buffer. Furthermore, Winsock will store the length of the peer address in the memory location pointed to by the fromlen parameter. If your program does not need to know the sending host's address, your program should set recvfrom's fifth parameter to zero.

The only other function with which you may not be familiar is the Windows GetTickCount function. GetTickCount retrieves the number of milliseconds that have elapsed since Windows started. QPing uses the value GetTickCount returns to calculate the round-trip travel time in milliseconds for the ICMP echo request (the ping). Shown next is the complete source code listing for the DoPingOperation function:

```
BOOL DoPingOperation(HANDLE hInstance)
 {
```

```
                              // Local variables
int iPacketSize;              // ICMP packet size
int iHostAddrLength;          // Host address length
int iIPHeadLength;            // IP datagram header length
int iReceivedBytes;           // Number of bytes received
int iSentBytes;               // Number of bytes sent
int nProtocol;                // ICMP protocol number
int iSocketError;             // Stores any error codes
PDWORD pdwTimeStamp;          // Tick count at transmission
DWORD dwReturnTime;           // Tick count upon receipt of echo reply
DWORD dwRoundTrip;            // Tick count for the round-trip
                              // Structures defined in WINSOCK.H
SOCKADDR_IN sockAddrLocal;    // Local host socket address structure
SOCKADDR_IN sockAddrHost;     // Remote host socket address structure
SOCKET hSocket;               // Socket handle (or descriptor)
LPHOSTENT lpHostEntry;        // Internet host data structure
LPPROTOENT lpProtocolEntry;   // Internet protocol data structure

BYTE IcmpSendPacket[1024];    // Buffer space for data to send
BYTE IcmpRecvPacket[4096];    // Buffer space for received data

struct icmp *pIcmpHeader;     // A pointer to the ICMP structure
struct ip *pIpHeader;         // A pointer to the IP header structure
LPSTR lpszHostName;           // A pointer to the time server host

lpszHostName = HOST_NAME;

if ((lpHostEntry = gethostbyname(HOST_NAME)) == NULL)
  {
    wsprintf(szPingBuffer, "Could not get %s IP address.",
          (LPSTR)lpszHostName);
    return(FALSE);
  }

sockAddrLocal.sin_family = AF_INET;
sockAddrLocal.sin_addr = *((LPIN_ADDR) *lpHostEntry->h_addr_list);

// With a raw socket, the program must specify a protocol
if ((lpProtocolEntry = getprotobyname("icmp")) == NULL)
  nProtocol = IPPROTO_ICMP;
else
  nProtocol = lpProtocolEntry->p_proto;

// Create a "raw" socket and specify ICMP as the protocol to use
if ((hSocket = socket(PF_INET, SOCK_RAW, nProtocol)) ==
      INVALID_SOCKET)
  {
    wsprintf(szPingBuffer, "Could not create a RAW socket.");
    return(FALSE);
```

```
    }

pIcmpHeader = (struct icmp *)IcmpSendPacket; // Point at the data area
pIcmpHeader->icmp_type = ICMP_ECHO;           // and fill in the data.
pIcmpHeader->icmp_code = 0;                    // Use the instance
pIcmpHeader->icmp_id = hInstance;              // handle as a unique ID.
pIcmpHeader->icmp_seq = 0;                     // Remember to reset
pIcmpHeader->icmp_cksum = 0;                   // the checksum to zero.

//Put tick count in the optional data area
pdwTimeStamp = (PDWORD)&IcmpSendPacket[ICMP_HEADERSIZE];
*pdwTimeStamp = GetTickCount();
iPacketSize = ICMP_HEADERSIZE + sizeof(DWORD);
pIcmpHeader->icmp_cksum = InternetChksum((LPWORD)pIcmpHeader,
      iPacketSize);

if (pIcmpHeader->icmp_cksum !=0 )
  {
    iSentBytes = sendto(hSocket, (LPSTR) IcmpSendPacket, iPacketSize,
         NO_FLAGS, (LPSOCKADDR) &sockAddrLocal,
         sizeof(sockAddrLocal));

    if (iSentBytes == SOCKET_ERROR)
      {
        closesocket(hSocket);
        wsprintf(szPingBuffer,
             "The sendto() function returned a socket error.");
        return(FALSE);
      }

    if (iSentBytes != iPacketSize)
      {
        closesocket(hSocket);
        wsprintf(szPingBuffer,
             "Wrong number of bytes sent: %d", iSentBytes);
        return(FALSE);
      }

    iHostAddrLength = sizeof(sockAddrHost);

    iReceivedBytes = recvfrom(hSocket, (LPSTR) IcmpRecvPacket,
         sizeof(IcmpRecvPacket), NO_FLAGS, (LPSOCKADDR)&sockAddrHost,
         &iHostAddrLength);
  }
else
  {
    closesocket(hSocket);
    wsprintf(szPingBuffer,
         "Checksum computation error! Result was zero!");
```

```
        return(FALSE);
    }

closesocket(hSocket);

if (iReceivedBytes == SOCKET_ERROR)
  {
    iSocketError = WSAGetLastError();
    if (iSocketError == 10004)
      {
        wsprintf(szPingBuffer,
              "Ping operation for %s was cancelled.",
              (LPSTR)lpszHostName);
        dwRoundTrip = 0;
        return(TRUE);
      }
    else
      {
        wsprintf(szPingBuffer,
              "Socket Error from recvfrom(): %d", iSocketError);
        return(FALSE);
      }
  }

dwReturnTime = GetTickCount();
dwRoundTrip = dwReturnTime - *pdwTimeStamp;

// Point to the IP Header in the received packet
pIpHeader = (struct ip *)IcmpRecvPacket;

// Extract bits 4-7 and convert the number of 32-bit words to bytes
iIPHeadLength = (pIpHeader->ip_verlen >> 4) << 2;

// Test the length to make sure an ICMP header was received
if (iReceivedBytes < iIPHeadLength + ICMP_HEADERSIZE)
  {
    wsprintf(szPingBuffer, "Received packet was too short.");
    return(FALSE);
  }

// Point to the ICMP message which immediately follows the IP header
pIcmpHeader = (struct icmp *) (IcmpRecvPacket + iIPHeadLength);

// Make sure this is an ICMP "echo reply"
if (pIcmpHeader->icmp_type != ICMP_ECHOREPLY)
  {
    wsprintf(szPingBuffer,
          "Received packet was not an echo reply to your ping.");
    return(FALSE);
  }
```

```
   // Make sure this program sent the packet
   if (pIcmpHeader->icmp_id != (WORD)hInstance)
     {
       wsprintf(szPingBuffer,
             "Received packet was not sent by this program.");
       return(FALSE);
     }

   // This appears to be a matching reply. Note the IP address and
   // host name that sent the ICMP echo reply message.
   lstrcpy(lpszHostName, (LPSTR)lpHostEntry->h_name);
   wsprintf(szPingBuffer,
         "Round-trip travel time to %s [%s] was %d milliseconds.",
         (LPSTR)lpszHostName, (LPSTR)inet_ntoa(sockAddrHost.sin_addr),
         dwRoundTrip);

   return(TRUE);
}
```

ADDING THE PING UTILITY TO SOCKMAN

The Sockman5 source-code files on the *Internet Programming* companion disk contain the complete source code for a Sockman template that includes a Ping utility. The Sockman5 Ping utility uses a dialog box in a way similar to Sockman4's time-server utility. To incorporate Ping into an existing version of Sockman, you will need to add the PING5.CPP source-code file to your project file list or makefile. PING5.CPP also uses a header file named sockraw.h that includes the data structures you saw in QPing for the IP and ICMP headers. The Sockman5 source files implement the Ping utility using synchronous, blocking sockets only. In other words, the Sockman5 Ping utility does not use any asynchronous, Windows-specific, Winsock functions. To call the Ping dialog box, you only need to add a few global variables the Ping functions use and modify the DoWinsockProgram function. The PING5.CPP source-code file contains the rest of the Ping utility. The Ping functions use the global variables shown here:

```
HTASK hPingTask;                      // Ping task handle
char szPingHost[MAX_HOST_NAME+1];     // The name of the host to ping
char szPingBuffer[MAXGETHOSTSTRUCT]; // Ping-only data buffer
```

Sockman5.h includes the function prototypes for Ping shown here:

```
// Function prototypes for PING.CPP

BOOL PingDialog(VOID);
BOOL _export CALLBACK PingDialogProc(HWND, UINT, WPARAM, LPARAM);
BOOL DoPingOperation(HWND, LPSTR, PDWORD);
WORD InternetChksum(LPWORD, WORD);
```

PingDialog and PingDialogProc are similar to the other dialog procedures you created in previous versions of Sockman. PingDialog creates the dialog box and PingDialogProc handles messages for the dialog box. Shown next is the Ping dialog-box definition in Sockman5.RC:

```
IDD_PING DIALOG DISCARDABLE  0, 0, 221, 98
STYLE DS_MODALFRAME | WS_POPUP | WS_VISIBLE | WS_CAPTION | WS_SYSMENU
CAPTION "PING"
FONT 8, "MS Sans Serif"
BEGIN
    EDITTEXT        IDC_PING_HOST,30,10,140,15,ES_AUTOHSCROLL
    PUSHBUTTON      "&Ping",IDOK,30,50,59,16
    PUSHBUTTON      "&Cancel",IDCANCEL,110,50,59,16
    PUSHBUTTON      "E&xit",IDEXIT,110,75,59,16
    RTEXT           "Host:",IDC_STATIC,10,10,20,13
    RTEXT           "Round-trip Travel Time:",IDC_STATIC,25,30,82,10
    EDITTEXT        IDC_PING_TIME,110,30,60,15,ES_AUTOHSCROLL |
                        ES_READONLY | WS_DISABLED | NOT WS_TABSTOP
    LTEXT           "milliseconds",IDC_STATIC,175,30,40,11
END
```

When you select the Ping option from the Sockman Utilities menu, Sockman creates a dialog box from the IDD_PING definition in the resource file and displays the Ping dialog box shown in Figure 14.11.

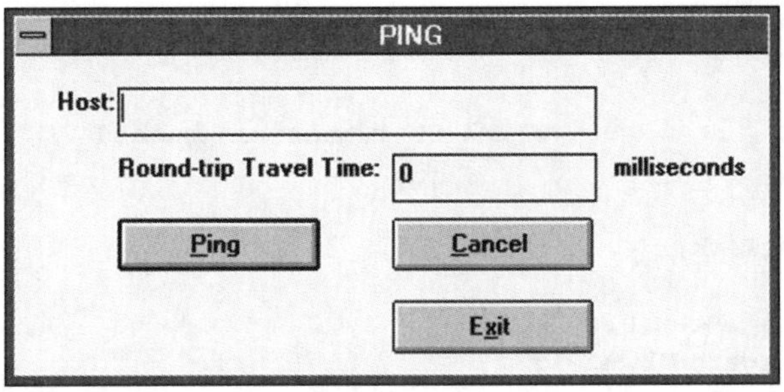

Figure 14.11 *The Sockman Ping dialog box.*

The DNS host name or IP address that you type into the Host text-box (or field) tells Sockman which host to ping. When you click your mouse on the Ping button, Sockman initiates a Ping operation that essentially performs the same steps you saw in the QPing version of DoPingOperation. The Cancel button cancels any Ping operations already in progress. The Exit button cancels any ongoing Ping operations and closes the Ping dialog box. As shown in the following program statement, the Sockman version of DoPingOperation requires different parameters than the QPing version:

```
BOOL DoPingOperation(HWND hwnd, LPSTR lpszHostName, PDWORD dwRoundTrip);
```

The Sockman DoPingOperation function requires a window handle, a pointer to the name of an Internet host, and a pointer to a storage buffer for the round-trip travel time. However, other than parameter differences, the QPing and Sockman versions of DoPingOperation are identical. Both DoPingOperation versions call the same InternetChksum function. To call the PingDialog function (which creates and displays the IDD_PING dialog-box), you need to change the IDM_PING case statement in DoWinsockProgram, as shown here:

```
case IDM_PING:
   PingDialog();
   break;
```

Note: *The DoWinsockProgram function definition is in Sockman5.CPP.*

UNDERSTANDING THE PING UTILITY LOGIC

The WM_COMMAND case statement in PingDialogProc contains the control logic behind the Ping dialog-box buttons. As shown next, PingDialogProc's WM_COMMAND case statement includes a nested-switch construct that handles the messages that the three dialog-box buttons create. The Ping button generates a WM_COMMAND message with wParam equal to IDOK. The Cancel button sends WM_COMMAND with wParam equal to IDCANCEL. The Exit button results in a WM_COMMAND with wParam equal to IDEXIT:

```
case WM_COMMAND:               // Handle the command buttons
switch (wParam)
  {
    case IDOK:                 // The OK button was pushed
      dwTravelTime = 0;

      if (hPingTask)
        {
          MessageBeep(0);
          MessageBox(hwndDlg,
                "Ping operation is already in progress use.",
                "SockMan-PING", MB_ICONSTOP | MB_OK);
          return(TRUE);
        }
      hPingTask = TASK_PING;

      SetDlgItemInt(hwndDlg, IDC_PING_TIME, (UINT)dwTravelTime, TRUE);
      GetDlgItemText(hwndDlg, IDC_PING_HOST, (LPSTR)szPingHost,
          MAX_HOST_NAME);
      if (lstrlen(szPingHost) > 0)
        {
          if (WSAIsBlocking())
            WSACancelBlockingCall();
          bPingOkay = DoPingOperation(hwndDlg, szPingHost,
```

```
                      &dwTravelTime);
            }
        else
            {
            wsprintf(szScratchBuffer, "Please enter a host name.");
            MessageBeep(0);
            MessageBox(hwndDlg, szScratchBuffer, "SockMan-PING",
                MB_OK|MB_ICONINFORMATION);
            }

        if(!bPingOkay)
            {
            // If Ping failed, the ping buffer contains the error.
            MessageBox(NULL, szPingBuffer, "SockMan-PING",
                MB_OK|MB_ICONSTOP);
            dwTravelTime = 0;
            }

        MessageBeep(0);
        SetDlgItemInt(hwndDlg, IDC_PING_TIME, (UINT)dwTravelTime, TRUE);
        PaintWindow(szPingBuffer);
        hPingTask = 0;
        return(TRUE);

    case IDCANCEL:          // The Cancel button was pushed
        if (WSAIsBlocking())
            WSACancelBlockingCall();
        return(TRUE);

    case IDEXIT:            // The Exit button was pushed
        if (WSAIsBlocking())
            WSACancelBlockingCall();
        PostMessage(hwndSockman, WM_COMMAND, IDM_FILE_CLEAR, OL);
        EndDialog(hwndDlg, FALSE);
        return(TRUE);
    }
break;
```

If a blocking-function call is in progress when the user clicks the Cancel button (IDCANCEL), PingDialogProc calls WSACancelBlockingCall, which causes Winsock to cancel any Winsock blocking operations already in progress. The Exit button (IDEXIT) causes a similar action to occur. However, after the Winsock cancels the blocking operation (if any) for an exit operation, PingDialogProc posts a message to the main Sockman window that clears the window and then closes the dialog box. The Ping button (which results in IDOK) causes most of the action in PingDialogProc. First, PingDialogProc sets the dwTravelTime variable to zero. The dwTravelTime variable stores the round-trip travel time that the DoPingOperation function calculates. (PingDialogProc passes DoPingOperation a pointer to dwTravelTime.)

If a Ping operation is already in progress (hPingTask is true), Sockman notifies the user. The user can choose to wait or click the Cancel button to cancel the operation. If no Ping operations are in progress, PingDialogProc sets hPingTask equal to the symbolic constant TASK_PING (defined in sockman5.h) to indicate the start of a Ping operation. Next, PingDialogProc stores dwTravelTime in the IDC_PING_TIME text-box (the round-trip travel time). In effect, this resets any previous round-trip travel times displayed in the text-box to zero. Immediately after PingDialogProc resets the IDC_PING_TIME text-box, PingDialogProc retrieves the Ping host name from the IDC_PING_HOST text-box.

After the PingDialogProc function retrieves the Ping host name, the function verifies that a IDC_PING_HOST text-box entry exists (using the lstrlen function). If so, PingDialogProc calls the DoPingOperation function, which sends and receives the ICMP echo messages as previously discussed. When DoPingOperation returns, PingDialogProc reports the results and stores the new dwTravelTime value the IDC_PING_TIME text-box. PingDialogProc also paints the main Sockman window with the results and beeps the computer's speaker to notify the user that the Ping operation finished.

ADDING OTHER APPLICATIONS TO SOCKMAN

The Sockman template described in this chapter is the last version that *Internet Programming* will discuss. You should now have a general idea of how to use the Winsock API within the Windows environment. Rather than continue to add functionality to Sockman, the remaining *Internet Programming* chapters will focus on stand-alone applications. However, the program statements shown next demonstrate how to add stand-alone applications to the Sockman program shell. As you have learned, DoWinsockProgram manages all Windows messages that initiate Winsock operations from a Sockman menu option. As shown next, DoWinsockProgram tests the wParam value to determine whether the user selected the Mail or Ftp Application menu options. Sockman uses the Windows ShellExecute function to launch the selected program. In this case, Sockman will execute the SockMail or SockFTP programs based on the user's menu selection. As you create other Internet-based programs, you can replace these two executable program names with the name of the file that corresponds to the program you want Sockman to run.

```
long DoWinsockProgram(HWND hwnd, UINT wParam, LONG lParam)
{
  HINSTANCE hInstance;
  LPSTR lpstr;

  switch (wParam)
    {
      case IDM_APP_MAIL:
      case IDM_APP_FTP:
        if (wParam == IDM_APP_MAIL)
          lpstr = "SOCKMAIL.EXE";
```

```
        else
          lpstr = "SOCKFTP.EXE";

        hInstance = ShellExecute(hwnd, (LPCSTR)"open", lpstr, NULL,
              NULL, SW_SHOWNORMAL);
        if (hInstance <= 32)
          {
            wsprintf(szScratchBuffer,
                  "Could not run %s.\n\nShellExecute() Error# %d",
                  (LPSTR)lpstr, hInstance);
            MessageBeep(0);
            MessageBox(NULL, szScratchBuffer, "SockMan - Application",
                  MB_OK|MB_ICONSTOP);
          }
        else
          wsprintf(szScratchBuffer, "Launched %s!",(LPSTR)lpstr);

        PaintWindow(szScratchBuffer);
        return(TRUE);

    // ...Additional program statements
```

In summary, you can continue to modify the Sockman shell to suit your own personal tastes. Or, you can use the Sockman program shell as a launch-pad to develop stand-alone programs.

PUTTING IT ALL TOGETHER

In this chapter, you discovered that the Internet Control Message Protocol provides a wide-array of error-reporting messages. You learned that ICMP error messages report packet delivery and routing problems and that ICMP query messages provide network professionals with the information they need to solve network and internetwork problems. Likewise, you have learned how your programs can use raw sockets to access low-level protocols, such as ICMP. Before you move on to with Chapter 17 and the Simple Mail Transfer Protocol, make sure you understand the following key concepts:

- ✓ ICMP error messages report packet delivery errors and routing problems.

- ✓ ICMP query messages report information that can help network professionals debug internetwork problems.

- ✓ Raw sockets require your programs to perform transport layer functions, such as data encapsulation.

- ✓ Raw sockets require your programs to create and fill data structures that represent network protocol data-structures, such as IP and ICMP headers.

Chapter 15
Understanding Internet E-Mail

On most networks, electronic mail (e-mail) is the most widely used application. In fact, of all TCP connections that Internet users establish, about one-half are for sending and receiving e-mail messages. As such, to be an effective network programmer, you need to understand Internet e-mail concepts. This chapter discusses the backbone of Internet e-mail, the Simple Mail Transfer Protocol (SMTP), as well as other e-mail-related protocols and extensions.

Even though you may never need to write your own Internet e-mail application, studying e-mail concepts is not a waste of your time. Internet e-mail concepts provide you with an excellent example of how to implement a simple yet effective Internet service. As you read through this chapter, you may find that Internet e-mail concepts help you generate ideas for custom protocol designs that you can use to implement your own Internet services. Or, better still, you may discover that Internet e-mail enhancements let you provide custom services without implementing your own custom protocols. As you will learn, extensions to Internet e-mail (already in-place) let you mail binary data such as graphic images, audio files, and video files. By the time you finish this chapter, you will understand the following key concepts:

- How e-mail moves messages across the Internet

- How to send and receive e-mail messages

- How to encode and decode binary data in e-mail messages

*Note: For more information on the number of Internet e-mail connections, see Caceres, R., Danzig, P., Jamin, S., and Mitzel, D.J. "Characteristics of Wide-Area TCP/IP Conversations," **Computer Communication Review**, vol. 21, no. 4, pp. 101-112 (Sept. 1991) Also see Paxson, V. "Empirically-Derived Analytic Models of Wide-Area TCP Connections: Extended Report," LBL-34086, Lawrence Berkeley Laboratory and EECS Division, University of California, Berkeley (June 1993).*

REVIEWING THE BIG PICTURE

Because of e-mail's widespread popularity, many Internet documents discuss Internet e-mail concepts. Rather than attempt to examine all these documents, this section explains only key concepts and terms. If, after you finish this chapter, you need more information about Internet e-mail concepts, you can refer to and (as a result of reading this section) understand the applicable Request for Comments (RFCs).

UNDERSTANDING THE CONCEPTUAL COMPONENTS

Figure 15.1 shows the basic elements that a network e-mail system includes. As you can see, each e-mail message has a sender and a receiver, both of which have a user-interface into the network's electronic-mail system.

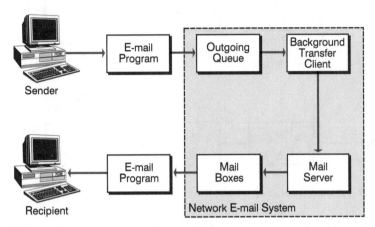

Figure 15.1 *The basic elements in a network e-mail system.*

The network e-mail system consists of an outgoing queue (collection of messages), a client process, a server process, and mailboxes for incoming mail. Although the user-interface (the e-mail application program) is often an integral part of the e-mail system, it doesn't have to be. In other words, the user-interface can be a separate client program that uses a client/server model to interact with the e-mail system. A *mailbox* can refer to a user address (user identification and host name—username@name.domain) or a *container file* that stores e-mail data. Think of a container file as a branch office of the postal service. When you send a letter (an e-mail message) to your friend Larry's PO box (user address), you physically send the letter to a postal service branch office (e-mail container file). The branch office (container file) then holds your letter (incoming mail) until Larry picks it up.

UNDERSTANDING THE INTERNET E-MAIL COMPONENTS

The Internet e-mail system incorporates the same concepts discussed in the previous section. However, Figure 15.2 shows the real components that the Internet e-mail system uses in place of the conceptual components shown in Figure 15.1. Note the use of the terms *user agent (UA)* and *message transfer agent (MTA)*. As you can see, the user agent replaces the e-mail program and the message transfer agent replaces the client and server processes.

Internet documentation frequently uses the term *agent* to refer to special purpose software that performs a task for a person or another program. Most Internet e-mail specifications refer to an e-mail program as a *user agent (UA)*. Likewise, a *message transfer agent (MTA)* is a client or server program that performs e-mail-related services, such as sending or receiving mail for a host computer.

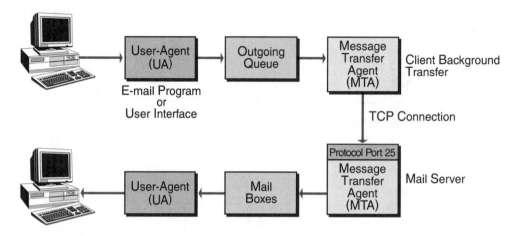

Figure 15.2 *The essential components in the Internet e-mail system.*

You interact with a user-agent program, which, in turn, interacts with an e-mail container (or possibly an MTA program) on your behalf. At the same time, the MTA program acts as an agent on behalf of a host computer. The user agent shields you from interacting with a wide variety of different e-mail hosts. Likewise, the MTA shields the host from a wide variety of user agents or other MTAs.

Conceptually, the user agent (user-interface) to an e-mail system is separate from the message transfer agent. Although you can implement both the user agent and the message transfer agent in a single program, you should isolate the design of each agent in separate modules. Although closely related, the two agents perform very different functions. Many long-time Internet users (UNIX-based) are familiar with Internet e-mail programs, such as MH, Berkeley Mail, Elm, Mush, and Pine. However, Windows-based Internet users may be more familiar with products such as the PC Eudora e-mail program. Each of these programs is a user agent. Each provides an Internet user with an interface to the Internet e-mail system. The purpose of an e-mail program (user agent) is to put a friendly front-end on a network's e-mail system.

On the Internet, the message transfer agents (client and server programs) represent the Internet's e-mail system. Before you can understand the user-agent interface into the Internet e-mail system, you need to understand a little more about message transfer agents. As explained in the following section, Internet MTAs that establish TCP connections to communicate with other MTAs typically use the Simple Mail Transfer Protocol (SMTP). The following section provides a basic introduction to SMTP. For complete details, see RFC 821, *Simple Mail Transfer Protocol,* Postel, 1982.

UNDERSTANDING THE SIMPLE MAIL TRANSFER PROTOCOL

The core of the Internet's e-mail system is the message transfer agent. As previously mentioned, the message transfer agent represents the e-mail system to a host computer. Although Internet e-mail users rarely work with a message transfer agent (message transfer agents are not exactly user-friendly), MTAs play a crucial role in all e-mail transmissions. For example, after the user-agent software sends an e-mail message to a message queue (which you can view as a container file), the message transfer agent retrieves the message and transmits it to another MTA. This process of passing the message from one MTA to another continues until the message reaches its destination address. To communicate with another MTA across a TCP connection, most Internet message transfer agents use the Simple Mail Transfer Protocol (SMTP). Normally, such MTA communication on the Internet uses Network Virtual Terminal (NVT) ASCII. As you may recall from Chapter 10, NVT is similar to a network virtual protocol, which hides computer differences related to line-feeds, form-feeds, carriage-returns, end-of-line markers, and other terminal characteristics. NVT uses standard, 7-bit ASCII encoding for all data, including letters, digits, and punctuation marks. Internet professionals commonly refer to NVT's use of 7-bit ASCII as NVT ASCII. If you want more details about NVT ASCII, re-read the appropriate sections in Chapter 10.

DEFINING THE SMTP COMMANDS

The Simple Mail Transfer Protocol provides for a two-way communication between the client (local) and server (remote) MTAs. The client MTA sends commands to the server MTA, which, in turn, sends replies back to the client MTA. In other words, SMTP commands require replies (described later in this chapter) from the SMTP receiver-module. SMTP refers to the exchange of SMTP commands and replies between two hosts (MTAs) as a *mail transaction*. As discussed, SMTP uses NVT ASCII for data. However, the Simple Mail Transfer Protocol also uses NVT ASCII for SMTP commands. SMTP defines keywords (not specially coded characters) as commands to perform its mail transfer operations. Table 15.1 provides a brief description of the SMTP commands (keywords) that the SMTP specification (RFC 821) defines.

Command	Required	Description
HELO	X	Identifies the sender-SMTP to the receiver-SMTP— a *hello* command.
MAIL	X	Initiates a *mail* transaction that eventually transfers mail data to one or more mailboxes.
RCPT	X	Identifies an individual *recipient* of mail data.

Table 15.1 Commands included in the Simple Mail Transfer Protocol (SMTP) (continued on the next page).

Command	Required	Description
DATA	X	The receiver-SMTP treats lines that follow the DATA command as mail *data*. For SMTP, the CRLF period CRLF character string identifies the end of mail data.
RSET	X	Aborts (*resets*) the current mail transaction.
NOOP	X	Requires the receiver-SMTP to perform no action (*no operation*) other than return an OK reply. (Used for client/server testing purposes.)
QUIT	X	Requires the receiver-SMTP to return an OK reply and close the transmission channel.
VRFY	*	Asks the receiver-SMTP to confirm or *verify* that the argument identifies a user. (See note.)
SEND		Initiates a mail transaction that delivers data to one or more terminals. (Note that SEND delivers data to a terminal rather than a mailbox)
SOML		Initiates a SEND or MAIL transaction that delivers mail data to one or more terminals or mailboxes.
SAML		Initiates a SEND and MAIL transaction that delivers mail data to one or more terminals and mailboxes.
EXPN		Asks the receiver-SMTP to confirm that the argument identifies a mailing list and, if so, to return (*expand*) the membership of the list.
HELP		Asks the receiver-SMTP to send helpful information to the sender-SMTP.
TURN		Requires the receiver-SMTP either to send an OK reply and take on the role of sender-SMTP or return a refusal reply and retain the role of receiver-SMTP.

Table 15.1 Commands included in the Simple Mail Transfer Protocol (SMTP) (continued from the previous page).

*Note: RFC 821 does not require the VRFY command as a minimal implementation. However, RFC 1123, **Requirements for Internet Hosts—Application and Support**, Braden, 1989, lists the VRFY command as mandatory for SMTP implementations on the Internet.*

According to the specification, a minimal SMTP implementation must include the commands marked required (X) in Table 15.1. The other SMTP commands are optional. Each SMTP command either ends with a space (if arguments follow) or a carriage-return line-feed (CRLF). Notice that the descriptions in Table 15.1 use the term *mail data* rather than mail message. As you will learn, SMTP extensions permit MTAs to transfer image, audio, and video files using SMTP. In other words, the SMTP protocol and associated commands can transfer more than just text-based e-mail messages. As such, when you read SMTP-related articles, do not restrict the term *message* to text-based data.

UNDERSTANDING TERMINAL MAIL

As you may know, many operating systems provide broadcast services that let a system manager send a message to all users in one step. For example, to inform users of a system shutdown, a system manager can simultaneously transmit the same warning message to every system terminal. However, users don't have to receive the message. Most host computers let the user establish a default configuration that either accepts or rejects such messages.

For many hosts, the implementation that sends messages to a terminal is similar to the mail implementation. SMTP includes commands that permit both types of mail delivery. In SMTP terms, *mailing* is mail delivery to a user's mailbox, and *sending* is mail delivery to a terminal (hence the MAIL and SEND commands). SMTP's minimal implementation requires the MAIL command—the SEND command is optional.

UNDERSTANDING THE SMTP COMMAND SEQUENCE

As previously mentioned, SMTP provides for two-way communication between client and server MTAs. Clients send commands to servers, and servers send replies to clients. However, SMTP restricts the sequence (or order) in which SMTP commands occur. The easiest way to understand the SMTP command sequence is to see an example of a mail transaction. The following example (similar to the one found in RFC 821) shows a typical SMTP mail transaction scenario. This example shows mail that Smith (at host *usc.edu*) sends to Jones, Green, and Brown (at host *mit.edu*). The message transfer agent on mit.edu accepts mail data for Jones and Brown; however, Green does not have a mailbox at host mit.edu.

For discussion purposes, each line includes a line number and identifies whether the transmission is from the receiver or sender MTA. On each line, the text to the right of "RECEIVER:" or "SENDER:" is the actual data transmission—the line numbers to the left simplify the discussion. The three-digit numeric codes in the data transmissions are SMTP replies (explained in the following section). As you will learn, an SMTP reply is similar to an acknowledgment message. The reply tells the sender how the receiver interpreted the previous command.

```
1. RECEIVER:  220 mit.edu Simple Mail Transfer Service Ready

2. SENDER:    HELO usc.edu

3. RECEIVER:  250 mit.edu
```

```
 4. SENDER:    MAIL FROM:<Smith@usc.edu>

 5. RECEIVER: 250 OK

 6. SENDER:    RCPT TO:<Jones@mit.edu>

 7. RECEIVER: 250 OK

 8. SENDER:    RCPT TO:<Green@mit.edu>

 9. RECEIVER: 550 No such user here

10. SENDER:    RCPT TO:<Brown@mit.edu>

11. RECEIVER: 250 OK

12. SENDER:    DATA

13. RECEIVER: 354 Start mail input; end with <CRLF>.<CRLF>

14. SENDER:    Blah blah blah...

15. SENDER:    ...etc. etc. etc.

16. SENDER:    .

17. RECEIVER: 250 OK

18. SENDER:    QUIT

19. RECEIVER: 221 mit.edu Service closing transmission channel
```

As shown in line 1, when a (SMTP-based) client MTA establishes a TCP connection to protocol port 25, the (SMTP-based) server MTA responds with a 220 reply code, which means that SMTP mail services are ready:

```
1. RECEIVER: 220 mit.edu Simple Mail Transfer Service Ready
```

After the MTAs at mit.edu and usc.edu establish the TCP connection and the server MTA (receiver) sends the 220 reply code, SMTP requires the client MTA (sender) to transmit the HELO command as its first command. As shown in line 2, the client MTA transmits the HELO command with the client's host as an argument. In other words, the client MTA says, "Hello, I'm usc.edu." The SMTP HELO command requires the client-host argument as shown here:

```
2. SENDER:    HELO usc.edu
```

As shown in line 3, the receiver (server) transmits a 250 reply code in response to the HELO command. The 250 reply code tells the SENDER that the requested action is okay and completed:

```
3. RECEIVER: 250 mit.edu
```

After the client MTA establishes the TCP connection, identifies itself to the server MTA (using HELO), and receives a reply from the server, the client MTA starts the mail transaction. To start the transaction, the client MTA transmits one of the following commands: MAIL, SEND, SOML, or SAML. As shown next, the client MTA in this example uses the MAIL command to initiate the mail transaction:

```
4. SENDER:    MAIL FROM:<Smith@usc.edu>
```

All four commands—MAIL, SEND, SOML, and SAML—use the syntax shown here:

```
MAIL <space> FROM:<reverse-path> <carriage-return line-feed>
```

Note: The SEND, SOML, and SAML are optional commands and, in actuality, rarely implemented.

The reverse-path argument tells the server MTA how to send error messages back to the original e-mail sender. Later in this chapter, you will learn more about the reverse-path argument. For now, simply note that the reverse-path includes the mailbox address of the sender (in this example, Smith@usc.edu). After the server MTA transmits another 250 reply code to indicate that the sender's mailbox address is acceptable (see line 5), the client MTA must identify the recipient(s) of the mail data. To do so, the client MTA can transmit the RCPT command (which identifies an individual recipient of mail data) once for a single recipient or several times to identify multiple recipients of the same mail data. As shown in lines 6, 8, and 10, the client MTA in this example transmits three RCPT commands. The RCPT command uses syntax similar to MAIL, as shown:

```
RCPT <space> TO:<forward-path> <carriage-return line-feed>
```

In contrast to the SMTP MAIL command, RCPT uses the word "TO:" instead of "FROM:", and the argument includes a forward-path instead of a reverse-path. Later in this chapter, you will learn more about the forward-path argument. For now, simply note that the forward-path includes the mailbox address of the recipient. For each RCPT command, the client MTA expects to receive a 250 reply code . However, in response to line 8,

```
8. SENDER:    RCPT TO:<Green@mit.edu>
```

the server MTA transmits a 550 reply code, as shown here:

```
9. RECEIVER: 550 No such user here
```

An SMTP 550 reply code means the server MTA cannot fulfill the client's request—the mailbox is unavailable. As stated at the beginning of this example, the user *Green* does not have a mailbox at host mit.edu. To inform the client MTA that the mailbox *Green@mit.edu* does not exist, the server MTA transmits a 550 reply code. The SMTP requires the server MTA to notify the client when a mailbox specified as a recipient does not exist. However, SMTP does not dictate that the client MTA act on this information.

After the client MTA uses the RCPT command to identify all recipients, the client must transmit a DATA command to tell the server that the subsequent transmissions represent the mail data.

Line 12 shows the client MTA (sender) DATA command and line 13 shows the server MTA (receiver) response—a 354 reply code. This reply code (shown next) tells the client MTA to start the mail-data transfer and to signal the end of the data with a CRLF-period-CRLF-character sequence (a new line with nothing but a period).

```
12. SENDER:   DATA
13. RECEIVER: 354 Start mail input; end with <CRLF>.<CRLF>
```

After the client MTA receives the 354 reply code, it can transmit the mail data. The server MTA stores the mail data in an incoming-data queue. The server MTA sends no other messages until the client transmits the CRLF-period-CRLF-character sequence, which signals the end of data. As shown in lines 16 and 17, after the client MTA (sender) transmits a period on a line by itself, the server MTA (receiver) responds with a 250 reply code. As previously discussed, the 250 reply code indicates that the requested mail action completed okay:

```
16. SENDER:   .
17. RECEIVER: 250 OK
```

To end the mail transaction, SMTP requires the client MTA to transmit a QUIT command. As shown next, after the client MTA transmits the QUIT command, the server MTA responds with a 221 reply code. The 221 reply code acknowledges the request to close the transmission channel:

```
18. SENDER:   QUIT
19. RECEIVER: 221 mit.edu Service closing transmission channel
```

At any time during a mail transaction, the client MTA can use NOOP, HELP, EXPN, and VRFY commands. These commands return information to the client MTA. Although the client MTA may choose a specific course of action based on this information, SMTP does not require the client MTA to do so. For example, a client MTA might transmit a VRFY command to confirm that a username is valid. If the server MTA reports that the username is invalid, the client MTA can choose not to transmit the mail data to the specified user. However, SMTP does not require this action or any other in response to a VRFY command. The client MTA can choose to use or ignore the results from the VRFY command (as well as NOOP, HELP, and EXPN). The client MTA's designer determines how it will respond to the these commands.

DEFINING SMTP REPLIES

As you have learned, SMTP requires server MTAs to acknowledge every command that they receive from a client MTA. As discussed, server MTAs respond to each SMTP command with a three-digit reply code followed by helpful text information. Each SMTP command can result in only one reply code. However, a single reply code may include several lines of text (as explained later in this section).

Note:Normally, only the EXPN and HELP commands will result in multiline replies. However, SMTP permits multiline replies for any SMTP command.

Each digit in the SMTP reply codes has special significance. The first digit indicates whether the command result was good (2), bad (5), or incomplete (3). As discussed in Appendix E of RFC 821, an unsophisticated (SMTP-based) client MTA can simply examine the first digit of the reply code to determine its next action. The second and third digits of the reply code continue to refine the reply code explanation. If you model a custom protocol after SMTP, be sure to study the design of SMTP reply codes. SMTP's technique of assigning special significance to specific reply code digits is an excellent example to follow. Table 15.2 lists the SMTP reply codes that RFC 821 defines.

Reply Code	Description
211	System status or system help reply
214	Help message
220	<domain> Service ready
221	<domain> Service closing transmission channel
250	Requested mail action okay, completed
251	user not local; will forward to <forward-path>
354	Start mail input; end with <CRLF>.<CRLF>
421	<domain> Service not available, closing transmission channel
450	Requested mail action not taken: mailbox unavailable
451	Requested action aborted: local error in processing
452	Requested action not taken: insufficient system storage
500	Syntax error, command unrecognized
501	Syntax error in parameters or arguments
502	Command not implemented
503	Bad sequence of commands
504	Command parameter not implemented
550	Requested action not taken: mailbox unavailable
551	User not local; please try <forward-path>
552	Requested mail action aborted: exceeded storage allocation
553	Requested action not taken: mailbox name not allowed
554	Transaction failed

Table 15.2 The SMTP reply codes with descriptions

INTERPRETING THE FIRST DIGIT OF THE SMTP REPLY CODE

SMTP defines five values for the first digit of the reply code. A 1 indicates the server MTA accepted the command but that the requested action requires the client MTA to confirm the reply information. The sender MTA should send another command that specifies whether to continue or abort the action. As you can see in Table 15.1, SMTP does not include any reply codes with a 1 as the first digit. This is an excellent example of protocol designers planning ahead. At this time, SMTP does not include commands that allow this type of reply. In other words, SMTP currently doesn't define any commands that require subsequent confirmation of specific reply information. However, from the beginning, SMTP protocol designers anticipated such a possibility and reserved reply codes, beginning with 1, for possible future commands that do require a continue or abort confirmation.

A reply code with a 2 as the first digit indicates that the server MTA successfully completed the requested action and that the client MTA can initiate a new request. A reply code with a 3 as the first digit indicates the server MTA accepts the command but requires further information to perform the requested action. For example, to tell the client MTA to start mail input, the server MTA sends a 354 reply code. The server MTA then waits for the client to respond with mail data. A reply code with a 4 as the first digit indicates that the server MTA did not accept the command and the requested action did not occur. However, the 400-series reply codes indicate that the error condition is temporary and encourage the client MTA to try again. The 500-series reply codes also indicate that the server did not accept the command and the requested action did not occur. However, these reply codes do not encourage the sender to repeat the same request (at least not in the same sequence).

INTERPRETING THE SECOND DIGIT OF THE SMTP REPLY CODE

The second digit in the SMTP reply codes specifies error categories. For example, a reply code with a 0 as the second digit identifies syntax errors. A syntax-error reply code might indicate a command that's too long, an invalid command argument, or an unimplemented command.

Examine the messages for reply codes 211 and 214 in Table 15.2. Notice that both reply codes have a 1 as their second digit and both are information replies. Likewise, notice how reply codes 220, 221, and 421, all of which have a 2 as their second digit, refer to the transmission or communication channel. A reply code with a 5 as the second digit identifies replies related to the mail system itself (see reply codes 250, 450 and 550 in Table 15.2). Currently, SMTP does not specify any definitions for reply codes with a 3 or a 4 in the second digit position.

INTERPRETING THE THIRD DIGIT OF THE SMTP REPLY CODE

The SMTP specification defines a different third digit for each descriptive text string in a particular series of reply codes. For example, examine the messages for reply codes 500-504. All five messages are syntax-error messages. However, the text string (which describes the specific type of syntax error) is different for each message. For these reply codes, SMTP recommends specific text strings (which are similar to the descriptions in Table 15.2) but does not mandate their use.

UNDERSTANDING MULTILINE REPLIES

As previously mentioned, reply text can exceed a single line. However, SMTP defines a specific format for multiple lines of text. For multiline replies, each line of text (except the last line) must begin with a reply code, followed by a hyphen (-), followed by text and a carriage-return line-feed (CRLF). The last line must begin with a reply code, followed by a space:

```
123-First line of a multiline message
123-Note the message number 123 does not change
123-1 thing to note-lines can begin with numbers
123 The last line uses a space, not a hyphen
```

Note that a hyphen follows the reply code on all but the last line of the multiline reply. After a client MTA begins to receive a multiline reply from a server MTA, the client looks for the reply code without the trailing hyphen to identify the last line.

DEFINING SIZE LIMITATIONS FOR SMTP

In general, SMTP states that implementations should not impose length limits on objects (perhaps, for future expandability). However, SMTP currently defines the size limits listed in Table 15.3.

SMTP Object	Size Limitation
User	The maximum length of a username is 64 characters.
Domain	The maximum length of a domain name or number is 64 characters.
Path	The maximum length of a reverse-path or forward-path, including the punctuation and element separators, is 256 Characters.
Command line	The maximum length of a command line, including the command word and the <CRLF>, is 512 characters.
Reply line	The maximum length of a reply line, including the reply code and the <CRLF>, is 512 characters.
Text line	The maximum length of a text line, including the <CRLF>, is 1,000 characters.
Recipients buffer	The maximum number of buffered recipients is 100.

Table 15.3 Object size limitations currently imposed by SMTP.

According to the SMTP specification (RFC 821), if a client MTA's request exceeds the limits listed in Table 15.3, a server MTA may transmit any of the following reply codes:

```
500 Line too long.
501 Path too long.
552 Too many recipients.
552 Too much mail data.
```

UNDERSTANDING RELAY AGENTS

SMTP uses the term *forward-path* to distinguish between a mailbox address (which is absolute) and the route (which is variable) that the mail data follows to reach a mailbox. For example, assume you want to send two messages to the same destination host. As you know, both these messages will have the same mailbox address. However, both messages do not have to use the same forward-path (sequence of routers) to reach that mailbox. Likewise, should the message recipient send a response back to the sender for each message, the two response messages may not follow the same *reverse-path* (another sequence of routers) to return to the sender. Often, system administrators will want e-mail to follow a very specific path to reach the e-mail recipient. As such, to direct the flow of an e-mail message, a system administrator uses the forward- and reverse-path arguments to specify one or more relay agents. A *relay agent* is an MTA configured as a mail hub. To transmit a message, each user agent transfers mail data to a local MTA, which, in turn, transfers mail data to the relay MTA (or relay agent). In the following example, Smith@usc.edu represents a mailbox address. HOST1, HOST2, and HOST3 represent relay agents:

```
MAIL FROM:<@HOST1, @HOST2, @HOST3:Smith@usc.edu>
```

Today, most network e-mail systems on the Internet use relay agents. Figure 15.3 shows a typical Internet e-mail configuration that uses relay agents.

To simplify its e-mail configuration, an organization may have all its network's host computers send mail directly to a *relay host*, which is a relay agent (a single computer) that handles the network's communications across the Internet. Additionally, to prevent computer hackers (renegade computer users) from illegally penetrating the network through the e-mail system, an organization may use the relay host to hide all other network computers. By restricting the e-mail entry point to a single host (the relay host), a system localizes the problem. In other words, a system administrator needs to deploy e-mail penetration counter-measures only on the relay host. SMTP can send mail data directly from the sending user's host to the receiving user's host when the two hosts connect to the same mail transport service. Unfortunately, across the network, this is seldom the case. Instead, SMTP often transports data through one or more relay hosts when the source and destination hosts do not connect to the same mail transport service. To provide the relay capability, the client SMTP must include the name of the ultimate destination host as well as the destination mailbox name.

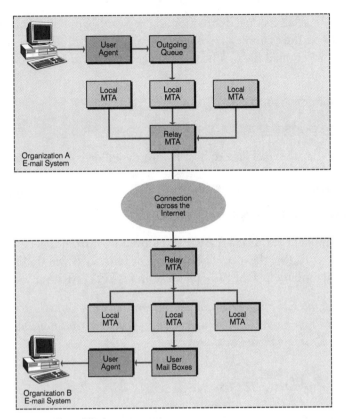

Figure 15.3 Internet e-mail with relay agents.

The argument to the MAIL command is a reverse-path, which identifies who sent the mail (including relay hosts). The argument to the RCPT command is a forward-path, which identifies the intended recipient of the mail. The forward-path is a destination route, while the reverse-path is a return route. SMTP uses the reverse-path to return a message to the sender when an error occurs with a relayed message. As you will learn, as a message crosses the Internet, these forward- and reverse-paths change at each hop. System administrators must properly configure the local MTAs to send mail data to the designated relay host. Likewise, they must configure the relay host to transfer received mail to the correct local MTA. Configuring the relay host is a major task. However, if, after properly configuring the local MTAs, the system administrator changes the relay host, the only local MTA change required is a DNS name change. Otherwise, the local MTA configurations do not change. In other words, once again, by using an e-mail relay setup, the system administrator restricts the major headache (MTA configuration for Internet communications) to a single system—the relay host.

In general, for relay configurations, the SMTP e-mail transaction process works as follows. Before a host transfers mail data to the next host specified in the "TO:" header, the host removes itself from the beginning of the forward-path and puts itself at the beginning of the reverse path.

When the mail data reaches its final destination, the forward-path only contains the destination mailbox. RFC 821 uses the example shown next to explain the path changes that occur when relay agents process SMTP mail data. When relay agent A receives mail data with the following arguments:

```
FROM:<USERX@HOSTY.ARPA>

TO:<@HOSTA.ARPA,@HOSTB.ARPA:USERC@HOSTD.ARPA>
```

the relay agent will relay the mail data to host B with the following arguments:

```
FROM:<@HOSTA.ARPA:USERX@HOSTY.ARPA>

TO:<@HOSTB.ARPA:USERC@HOSTD.ARPA>.
```

As you can see, relay agent A (HOSTA.ARPA) removed itself from the "TO:" header and prepended itself to the "FROM:" header. The relay agent for host B will do likewise and the next stop for the mail data should be USERC's mailbox on HOSTD.ARPA.

Note: In other words, the SMTP MTAs build the forward- and reverse-paths as mail data passes from one MTA to the next. If the receiver-SMTP does not implement the relay function, it may use the same reply code as the one for an unknown local user.

DEFINING THE E-MAIL PIECES

Internet professionals commonly describe electronic mail as consisting of three components: an *envelope* that the message transfer agents (MTAs) use, *headers* that your e-mail program (user agent) uses, and the e-mail *body* which contains the message or data the recipient uses. The envelope information consists of the delivery information in the "FROM:" and "TO:" fields previously shown in connection with SMTP's SEND and RCPT commands. In other words, the SMTP specification (RFC 821) defines the envelope information—the information that e-mail requires to deliver data from one host computer to another.

RFC 822, *Standard for the Format of ARPA Internet Text Messages*, Crocker, 1982, defines the criteria for the other two e-mail components: headers and body. (Certain segments of the Internet community, such as e-mail experts, refer to the text format that RFC 822 defines as simply "822." For example, they might say that a protocol uses "822 text.") To illustrate a rather complex header construction, RFC 822 uses the following header fields: Date, From, Subject, Reply-To, cc, Comment, In-Reply-To, X-Special-Action, and Message-ID. As you can see, the general header format is a fieldname followed by a colon, followed by text that represents the field value:

```
Date       : 27 Aug 76 0932 PDT

From       : Ken Davis <KDavis@This-Host.This-net>
```

```
Subject    : Re: The Syntax in the RFC

Sender     : KSecy@Other-Host

Reply-To   : Sam.Irving@Reg.Organization

To         : George Jones <Group@Some-Reg.An-Org>,
             Al.Neuman@MAD.Publisher

cc         : Important folk:
               Tom Softwood <Balsa@Tree.Root>,
               "Sam Irving"@Other-Host;,
             Standard Distribution:
               /main/davis/people/standard@Other-Host,
               "<Jones>standard.dist.3"@Tops-20-Host>;

Comment    : Sam is away on business. He asked me to handle his mail
             for him.  He'll be able to provide a more accurate
             explanation when he returns next week.

In-Reply-To: <some.string@DBM.Group>, George's message

X-Special-action: This is a sample of user-defined field-names.
             There could also be a field-name "Special-action", but
             its name might later be preempted

Message-ID: <4231.629.XYzi-What@Other-Host>
```

As previously mentioned, the e-mail body includes the primary information the user sending the message wants the recipient to receive. Typically, the body of Internet e-mail messages uses NVT ASCII. In addition, a blank line usually separates the e-mail headers from e-mail message body.

During a mail transaction, the user enters the e-mail data (the body) within the user-agent software (the e-mail program). Next, the user agent adds the header fields (with header-field contents the user specifies) and then transfers the body and header to an MTA. The MTA, in turn, adds the network delivery (envelope) information and then transfers the entire mail-data package to another MTA—either a destination MTA or perhaps a relay agent.

IMPROVING THE PIECES

Current efforts to improve Internet e-mail focus on all three components of an e-mail message: the delivery (or envelope information), the headers, and the message body. This section provides a brief introduction to some of the existing enhancements to Internet e-mail. Probably the most interesting enhancements include changes to the e-mail message body. These changes let Internet users mail multimedia data—such as image, audio, and video files—to other users. In this section, you will learn how to encode such data for transmission across the Internet e-mail system.

EXTENDING SMTP

Perhaps the most important document related to SMTP enhancements is RFC 1425, *SMTP Service Extensions*, Klensin et al, 1993. In addition to improving SMTP, RFC 1425 establishes a well-thought-out framework for all future enhancements. Internet professionals generally refer to an SMTP implementation that uses the RFC 1425 framework as *extended SMTP* or *ESMTP*. Although extended SMTP operates much the same as the non-extended protocol, ESMTP uses the EHLO (extended hello) command instead of HELO. To determine whether the server MTA supports extended SMTP, a client MTA transmits the EHLO command. If the server MTA supports ESMTP, the server will respond with a 250 reply code. If not, the server will send an error-reply code. In response to this error-reply code, the client MTA can transmit the older HELO command to obtain non-extended SMTP services. If the server MTA supports ESMTP, the 250 reply usually will be multiline (formatted as previously discussed). Each line after the initial 250 reply code identifies an extended SMTP option the server supports. For example, a server might respond to an EHLO command with the following reply code lines:

```
250-mail.server.com

250-EXPN

250-HELP

250 TURN
```

The second, third, and fourth 250 reply code lines identify the extended options this ESMTP server supports. As shown, this server supports the SMTP optional commands Table 15.1 identifies. In fact, the only extensions RFC 1425 identifies are the optional SMTP commands. In other words, as the first six extensions to ESMTP, RFC 1425 added EXPN, HELP, TURN, SEND, SOML, and SAML. RFC 1427, *SMTP Service Extension for Message Size Declaration*, Klensin et al, 1993, defines the SIZE extension, which lets (SMTP-based) client and server MTAs advertise a message size. If a server MTA's response to EHLO includes the SIZE keyword, the server supports the SIZE extension. As you may know, (SMTP-based) server MTAs have fixed upper limits on the size message they will accept. If a client MTA tries to transfer a message larger than the server's upper limit, the transfer will fail. Likewise, servers often have limited disk-storage space to store incoming messages. As such, message transfers may fail in the present due to a lack of disk space (and may succeed in the future if more storage space becomes free).

Unfortunately, a client MTA that doesn't use ESMTP has no way of knowing, prior to transmission, how much data is too much data. For example, suppose you develop an e-mail program (and MTA) that uses SMTP to transport large multimedia documents. Your client MTA might transmit a message containing megabytes of multimedia only to discover (after the fact) that the server MTA does not accept messages of that size. If you plan to mail multimedia documents (such as image, audio, and video files) through the Internet e-mail system, you will appreciate the SIZE extension (technically, the extension name is *Message Size Declaration service extension*). The SIZE extension advertises a maximum message size by including an optional size argument after the 250 reply code and SIZE keyword. For example, the following server response declares a 100-Megabyte (MB) maximum message size:

```
250 SIZE 100000000
```

A client MTA can evaluate the reply line with the SIZE keyword to detect the maximum message size the server supports and take action as necessary. In addition, server MTAs that support the Message Size Declaration service extension let a client declare a message size as an argument in the MAIL command. For example, the following ESMTP command from a client MTA declares the size of the message to be 500 KB:

```
MAIL FROM:<happy@jamsa.com> SIZE=500000
```

A server MTA that supports the Message Size Declaration service extension will evaluate the SIZE argument and, in most cases, report an error before the client initiates the message transfer. (RFC 1427 defines a few conditions for which an error may occur after the transfer begins.) Other extensions to SMTP follow the same basic pattern as the SIZE option. In other words, the extension defines a keyword that an (ESMTP-based) server MTA will report in response to the EHLO command. Your programs can use the extension as defined by the extension specification. In some cases, the extension keyword simply advertises a capability. In other cases, the extension may define new parameter options to one or more existing SMTP commands (such as the SIZE argument to the MAIL command).

UNDERSTANDING LOCAL EXTENSIONS

By definition, any field, command, or option name that begins with the letter *X* is a *local (or user-defined) extension*. For example, a previous section of this chapter that discussed RFC 822 field names mentioned the following X-Special-action header field:

```
X-Special-action: This is a sample of user-defined field-names.
            There could also be a field-name "Special-action", but
            its name might later be preempted
```

As the initial X indicates, X-Special-action is a user-defined field name. Although users can define local extensions any way they want, any extension or option name that does not begin with the letter *X* could, in the future, identify a standard Internet extension. If a local extension and an Internet standard share the same name but not the same function, any network system that uses the local extension may be incompatible with other Internet implementations. As such, when programmers design (and system administers deploy) SMTP implementations that utilize local extensions, the extension name should always begin with the letter *X*. For example, if an organization implements a local extension that performs special decoding of selected messages, the system administrator should name the extension XDECODE rather than simply DECODE. The organization's (SMTP-based) server MTA should report the local extension with the following 250 reply code:

```
250 XDECODE
```

UNDERSTANDING *MIME*

RFC 1521, *MIME (Multipurpose Internet Mail Extensions)*, Borenstein and Bellcore, 1993, describes MIME, which provides some of the more exciting extensions to Internet e-mail. MIME requires no changes to existing MTAs. Two user agents that understand MIME can use the existing Internet e-mail system to exchange MIME messages. MIME simply adds five new header fields (in accordance with RFC 822) to Internet e-mail messages:

- MIME-Version
- Content-Type
- Content-Transfer-Encoding
- Content-ID
- Content-Description

As MIME evolves, so too will its version numbers. The MIME-Version field specifies the MIME version an agent supports. By identifying the MIME version used to generate the message, the MIME-Version field prevents user agents from misinterpreting MIME messages using incompatible versions of MIME. Following is an example of the Mime-Version and Content-Type fields:

```
Mime-Version:     1.0

Content-Type:     TEXT/PLAIN; charset=US-ASCII
```

In the previous example, MIME version 1.0 creates the message. The content type is TEXT, and the subtype is PLAIN with a US-ASCII character set. Table 15.4 shows the existing MIME content types and subtypes.

Content Type	Subtype	Description
Text	Plain	Unformatted text
	Richtext	Text with simple formatting, such as bold italic, underline, and so on
	Enriched	A clarification, simplification, and refinement of richtext
Multipart	Mixed	Multiple body parts—process sequentially
	Parallel	Multiple body parts—process in parallel

Table 15.4 MIME content types and subtypes. (continued on the next page)

Content Type	Subtype	Description
	Digest	An electronic mail digest
	Alternative	Multiple body parts—all with identical semantic content
Message	RFC822	Another RFC822 mail message
	Partial	A fragment of a mail message
	External-Body	A pointer to the actual message (not included in the e-mail message)
Application	Octet-Stream	Arbitrary binary data
	Postscript	A Postscript program
Image	JPEG	ISO 10918 format
	GIF	CompuServe's Graphic Interchange Format
Audio	Basic	Encoded using 8-bit ISDN mu-law format
Video	MPEG	ISO 11172 format

Table 15.4 MIME content types and subtypes. (continued from the previous page)

The Content-ID and Content-Description header fields are optional. User agents can use the Content-ID value to identify MIME entities. Content-Description lets a user add descriptive information about a message body's contents. For example, if the message body is an encoded image, the sender might include a description of the image in the Content-Description header field. Table 15.5 lists the Content-Transfer-Encoding formats currently available with MIME.

Content-Transfer-Encoding	Description
7bit	NVT ASCII—the default for Internet e-mail
Quoted-printable	Useful when a small fraction of characters use their eighth bit
Base64	Encodes three data bytes as four six-bit values
8bit	Contains lines of characters with some non-ASCII characters (Some characters have their eighth bit is set)
Binary	Eight-bit data typically without line breaks

Table 15.5 MIME Content-Transfer-Encoding values.

As you have learned, NVT ASCII is the default format for Internet e-mail messages. Although eight-bit mail transports are practically non-existent, if they become available, the popularity of 8-bit and binary encoding will probably soar. However, until then, users will probably use quoted-printable and base-64 encoding to transfer 8-bit data through the Internet's 7-bit e-mail system. The following section discusses these two encoding schemes in detail.

UNDERSTANDING *MIME* ENCODING SCHEMES

Quoted-printable Content-Transfer-Encoding provides a simple yet effective method for encoding small amounts of 8-bit data for transmission as 7-bit NVT ASCII. To use quoted-printable encoding, you transmit any character with its eighth bit set as a three-character sequence. The three-character sequence always begins with an equal sign (=). Immediately following the equal sign is a two-digit hexadecimal code (represented as two ASCII characters) that represents the ASCII value for the encoded character. Although the characters in the words JAMSA PRESS do not have their eighth bit set, you can use these characters to understand quoted-printable encoding. For example, you would encode JAMSA PRESS as shown here:

```
=4A=41=4D=53=41=20=50=52=45=53=53
```

In other words, for *J*, the hexadecimal value for the ASCII code is 0x4A. The ASCII hexadecimal value for *A* is 0x41, and so on. Note that quoted-printable encoding transfers the ASCII character codes for each character. In the case of the letter *J* (ASCII 0x4A), for example, the encoding scheme transmits three bytes: one for the equal sign (ASCII 0x3D), one for the digit *4* (ASCII 0x34), and one for the letter *A* (ASCII 0x41). Although simple to use, quoted-printable encoding triples the size of your data. As such, quoted-printable encoding is only good for small amounts of 8-bit data embedded in otherwise 7-bit data.

As described in Table 15.5, quoted-printable encoding is useful when a small fraction of the characters in a mail message use their eighth bit. For example, if your name is Shöenburg, you might prefer to send e-mail messages that include the correct spelling of your name. To do so, you could use quoted-printable encoding to encode the letter ö as =94. In other words, you might conclude your e-mail messages as shown here:

```
Regards,

H. Sh=94enburg
```

A recipient user agent that understands MIME extensions (quotable-printable encoding, in particular) would decode and display the e-mail text as shown here:

```
Regards,

H. Shöenburg
```

Note: RFC 1522, MIME (Multipurpose Internet Mail Extensions) Part Two: Message Header Extensions for Non-ASCII Text, Moore, 1993, defines an encoding scheme that lets you include 8-bit data in message headers also.

In contrast to quoted-printable encoding, base-64 encoding increases message sizes by only about one third. To use base-64 encoding, you represent each consecutive three-byte (24-bit) combination of data as four six-bit values (again, 24 bits total). Your programs transmit each 6-bit value as one of the NVT ASCII characters shown in Table 15.6.

6-bit	ASCII	6-bit	ASCII	6-bit	ASCII	6-bit	ASCII
0	A	16	Q	32	g	48	w
1	B	17	R	33	h	49	x
2	C	18	S	34	i	50	y
3	D	19	T	35	j	51	z
4	E	20	U	36	k	52	0
5	F	21	V	37	l	53	1
6	G	22	W	38	m	54	2
7	H	23	X	39	n	55	3
8	I	24	Y	40	o	56	4
9	J	25	Z	41	p	57	5
10	K	26	a	42	q	58	6
11	L	27	b	43	r	59	7
12	M	28	c	44	s	60	8
13	N	29	d	45	t	61	9
14	O	30	e	46	u	62	+
15	P	31	f	47	v	63	/

Table 15.6 Base-64 encoding table.

*Note: The base-64 encoding MIME uses is virtually identical to the scheme used in Privacy Enhanced Mail (PEM) applications, as defined by RFC 1421, **Privacy Enhancement for Internet Electronic Mail: Part I: Message Encryption and Authentication Procedures**, Linn, 1993.*

When your data does not consist of an even multiple of three-byte data blocks, the encoding scheme uses an equal sign to pad your data. Figure 15.4 shows three examples of base-64 encoding. The name *KEN* is an even multiple of three bytes and requires no characters for padding. The name *COPE* has one extra byte and thus requires two equal signs as padding. The name *JAMSA* has two extra bytes, so it only requires one equal sign as a padding character. In other words, in all cases of base-64 encoding, you transmit your data as multiples of three-byte units.

A. KEN is "S0VO" in Base-64 encoding (no padding required).

Letter:	K	E	N
Hex:	0x4B	0x45	0x4E
Binary:	01 00 10 11	01 00 01 01	01 00 11 10

6 Bits:	01 00 10	11 01 00	01 01 01	00 11 10
Decimal:	18	52	21	14
Base-64:	S	0	V	O

B. COPE is "Q09QRQ==" in Base-64 encoding (two padding characters required).

Letter:	C	O	P	E	=	=
Hex:	0x43	0x4F	0x50	0x45		
Binary:	01 00 00 11	01 00 11 11	01 01 00 00	01 00 01 01	Fill 6 Bits with zeros as required.	

6 Bits:	01 00 00	11 01 00	11 11 01	01 00 00	01 00 01	01 00 00
Decimal:	16	52	61	16	17	16
Base-64:	Q	0	9	Q	R	Q

(with trailing `=  =`)

C. JAMSA is "SkFNU0E=" in Base-64 encoding (one padding character required).

Letter:	J	A	M	S	A	=
Hex:	0x4A	0x41	0x4D	0x53	0x41	
Binary:	01 00 10 10	01 00 00 01	01 00 11 01	01 01 00 11	01 00 00 01	Fill with zeros

6 Bits:	01 00 10	10 01 00	00 01 01	00 11 01	01 01 00	11 01 00	00 01 00
Decimal:	18	36	5	13	20	52	4
Base-64:	S	k	F	N	U	0	E

(with trailing `=`)

Figure 15.4 Base-64 encoding examples that show padding.

IMPLEMENTING BASE-64 ENCODING

If you rarely work with data as individual bits, you may wonder how difficult base-64 encoding is to implement. As it turns out, if you are familiar with the bitwise AND, bitwise OR, and binary-shift operators in the C/C++ language, base-64 encoding is quite simple to implement. As you may know, the binary-shift operators shift bits to the left or right by the number of places your program statement specifies. The bitwise AND operator provides a convenient way to mask out bits that you don't want to use. Likewise, the bitwise OR operator lets you combine bits from two different bytes of data.

Figure 15.5 shows the process of encoding the name *KEN* in base-64. The left side of the figure illustrates the bit movements while the right side of the diagram shows the program statements that accomplish the bit operations. Refer to the circled numbers in the center of the diagram to find the points of discussion in the following paragraphs. The top-left corner in Figure 15.5 shows the characters *K*, *E*, and *N* with their associated hex and binary ASCII values. The up arrows inside the box show the break points for the six-bit, base-64 values. The top-right corner of the figure shows the declarations for the variables that the program statements use.

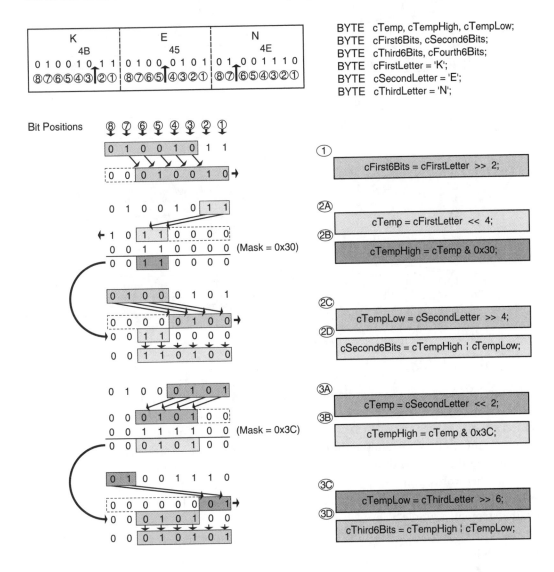

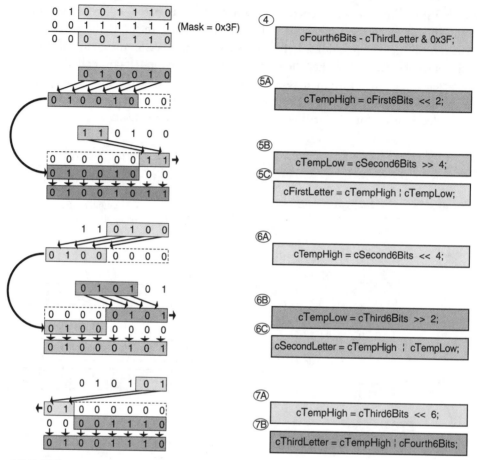

Figure 15.5 C/C++ program statements to implement base-64 encoding.

ENCODING DATA IN BASE-*64*

Your first six-bit value uses the high six-bits in the letter *K.* To start, step 1 performs a binary-right operation on the cFirstLetter variable (which stores the character *K*). The right-shift-by-two operation actually creates a new byte that stores the first six bits of your data. As such, the step 1 program statement stores the result in the cFirst6Bits variable. Next, to create your second six-bit value, you need the two low-order bits from the letter *K* and the four high-order bits from the letter *E.* In other words, you first need to move bits 1 and 2 in the letter *K* to positions 5 and 6—these two bits should be the two high-order bits in your next 6-bit value. As shown in the step 2A program statement, a simple binary-left-shift-by-four operation moves these bits into the desired positions. Step 2A stores the result of the left-shift-by-four operation in the temporary storage variable cTemp.

While the left shift in step 2A clears bit positions 1 through 4, bits 3 and 4 from the letter *K* now reside in positions 7 and 8. You need to ensure bit positions 7 and 8 are clear since you only want to use the first six bits of your new byte. To clear bit positions 7 and 8, you can perform a bitwise AND, as shown in step 2B. As shown in step 2B, the binary mask 00110000 (0x30) clears all bits except bit positions 5 and 6 (which hold your data of interest). Since the bits now in positions 5 and 6 will be the two high-order bits in your next base-64 value, the program statement in step 2B stores the result of the bitwise AND in temporary storage variable cTempHigh.

After step 2B, you have the correct bits in positions 5 and 6. Bit positions 1 through 4 of your new byte need to come from the four high bits in the second letter. To move the four high bits in the second letter into the correct position for your second six bits of data, you can perform a right-shift-by-four operation, as shown in step 2C. As shown in step 2C stores the results from the right-shift-by-four operation in the temporary storage variable cTempLow. Now, cTempLow holds the low four bits and cTempHigh holds the high two bits of your next 6-bit value. To combine these two values and create your second 6-bit, base-64 value, perform a bitwise OR, as shown in step 2D. This step stores the results from the bitwise OR in variable cSecond6Bits.

Your third six-bit value uses the low four bits in the letter *E* and the two high-order bits in the letter *N*. As such, you need to move bits 1 through 4 in the letter *E* to positions 3 through 6. To do so, you can perform a left-shift-by-two operation, as shown in step 3A. Step 3A stores the results from the left shift in temporary storage variable cTemp. The left shift clears bit positions 1 and 2 for you. However, you need to ensure that bit positions 7 and 8 are clear also. In other words, the only bits that you want to keep are now in bit positions 3 through 6. To clear bit positions 7 and 8 but retain the bits in positions 3 through 6, you can perform a bitwise AND, as shown in step 3B, with the binary bit mask 00111100 (0x3C). Step 3B stores the results from the bitwise AND in temporary storage variable cTempHigh.

Next, you need to move the two high-order bits in the letter *N* into bit positions 1 and 2. The right-shift-by-six operation shown in step 3C accomplishes this for you. Step 3C stores the results of the right shift in temporary storage variable cTempLow. Now, you have the low four bits from the letter *E* in cTempHigh and the two high-order bits from the letter *N* in cTempLow. To combine these bits to create your third six-bit value, you perform the bitwise OR shown in step 3D. Step 3D stores your third six-bit value in cThird6Bits. Obtaining your fourth six-bit value is easy—the desired six-bits are already in position. Your fourth six-bit value consists of the low six bits in the letter *N*. If you mask off bit positions 7 and 8, you will have the six-bit value you need. You can do so by performing a bitwise AND, using the bit mask 00111111 (0x3F), as shown in step 4. Step 4 stores the results of the bitwise AND in cFourth6Bits.

DECODING DATA IN BASE-64

After performing steps 1 through 4 shown in Figure 15.5, you have four six-bit values stored in cFirst6Bits, cSecond6Bits, cThird6Bits, and cFourth6Bits. Steps 5A through 7B use this data to show you how to decode base-64 data. The base-64 decoding process is even more straightforward than the encoding process. To extract each encoded byte (except for the third one), you perform a left shift, a right shift, and a bitwise OR. (The third byte does not require a right shift—only a left shift and a bitwise OR.) The key is knowing how many bits to shift in each direction.

The six bits in your first base-64 character represent the high six bits in your first data byte. You need to move these bits from positions 1 through 6 into positions 3 through 8. To do so, perform the left-shift-by-two operation shown in step 5A. Since these bits represent the high-order bits in your first data byte, step 5A stores the results of the left-shift-by-two operation in cTempHigh. You now need the bits from positions 5 and 6 in your second six-bit value. These bit positions store the two low-order bits for your first byte of data. To move these bits into the correct position, perform the right-shift-by-four operation shown in step 5B. Step 5B stores the results in cTempLow. You now have the first six bits of your first byte in cTempHigh and the low two bits in cTempLow. To combine these values and obtain your first byte of data, perform the bitwise OR shown in step 5C.

To obtain your second data byte, you perform practically the same steps. However, instead of shifting left by two and right by four, you shift left by four and right by two, as shown in steps 6A and 6B. As shown in step 6C, your perform a bitwise OR on the results from steps 6A and 6B to contain your second byte of data. For your third byte of data, bit positions 1 through 6 in your fourth six-bit character already hold the desired values. However, bit positions 1 and 2 in the third six-bit value hold bits 7 and 8 of your third data byte. To move these bits into the correct position, perform a left-shift-by-six operation, as shown in step 7A. Finally, you can extract your third byte of base-64 encoded data by performing the bitwise OR shown in step 7B.

Reviewing the Implementation

As you have learned, base-64 encoding operates on 24-bit units of data. The two algorithms (to encode and decode data) shown in the previous sections also operate on 24-bit units of data. In other words, although the previous sections did not show complete function definitions, these algorithms expect you to pass them 24 bits of data. The encoding algorithm only uses ten lines of code (and very fast bitwise operations) to turn three data bytes into four, six-bit, base-64 values. Likewise, the decoding algorithm expects four, six-bit, base 64 values and uses eight lines of equally fast bitwise operations to turn these values into three 8-bit data bytes.

Considering the Implications

The 18 lines of code discussed in the previous sections let you encode and decode binary data. If you must send image, audio, or video files on the Internet, you now know how to encode that data for e-mail transport. In fact, you can use base-64 encoding to transport any type of binary file across the Internet. For example, if you develop software for a living—either independently or as an employee—you can deliver program updates by Internet e-mail. In fact, if your customer base or employer makes heavy use of Internet e-mail, you can probably find a lot of ways to use Internet e-mail to your (and their) advantage.

UNDERSTANDING THE POST OFFICE PROTOCOL (POP)

In the previous sections of this chapter, you learned about Internet's e-mail delivery system. In this section, you will learn how to use the Post Office Protocol (POP) to retrieve e-mail from an Internet mailbox. As you will discover, previous sections in this chapter have already introduced and explained the basic concepts, principles, and operational techniques POP uses. (POP looks, feels, and functions very much like SMTP.) Other than a few differences in the protocol commands that clients transmit, POP operations are practically identical to SMTP. Figure 15.6 shows a typical POP client/server arrangement. As you can see, the POP server sets between the user agent and the e-mail mailboxes.

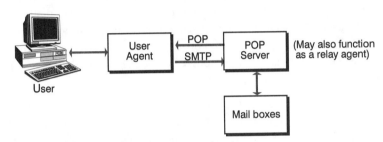

Figure 15.6 A Post Office Protocol client/server configuration.

Currently, two versions of POP exist: POP2 and POP3. Both protocols offer similar capabilities, but they are not compatible. In fact, POP2 and POP3 use different protocol ports. In other words, POP2 and POP3 do not share a relationship like SMTP and ESMTP. POP3 is not an extension or revision of POP2—it is a completely different protocol. RFC 937, *Post Office Protocol-Version 2*, Butler, et al, 1985, defines POP2. RFC 1225, *Post Office Protocol-Version 3*, Rose, 1991, defines POP3. The following sections rapidly cover POP in general and POP3 in particular. *Internet Programming* does not discuss POP2. However, if you understand SMTP, you will have no trouble understanding the POP2 specification. POP2 is more closely related to SMTP than is POP3. The POP2 commands and their structure closely parallel SMTP commands and structure. In contrast, the POP3 designer specifically addresses remote, PC-based e-mail problems and related operations.

DEFINING THE PROBLEM

In the past, on many networks, the e-mail system delivered mail messages to a destination workstation. Unfortunately, that mode of operation presents problems if a user frequently changes workstations or perhaps shares a workstation with other users. Today, most e-mail systems deposit mail in mailboxes located on some type of e-mail server system. Many e-mail systems still require a user to login to a network before they can read their mail. In other words, the user needs an account on the server system to use it for e-mail purposes. Unfortunately, remote logins to such systems sometimes confuse novice users. Also, because system administrators frequently disable remote login capabilities for security reasons, users must use the server system's e-mail software (user agent) to retrieve their messages. The Post Office Protocol provides an alternative solution to such e-mail access and remote login problems.

REVIEWING POP3

The POP design lets a user login to a POP server and retrieve mail from a remote system rather than login to the network itself. The user can access the POP server from any system on the Internet and run any user agent (front-end) that understands and speaks the Post Office Protocol. The model underlying POP3 is a remote PC-based workstation that acts strictly as a client to the message transport system. In this model, the PC does not provide delivery or authentication services for others. Also, while the PC uses POP for retrieval, it uses SMTP to send mail. In other words, conceptually, the PC uses two user agents to interface with the mail transport system—SMTP (for sending) and POP3 (for retrieving). The POP3 protocol designer refers to this model as *split-UA*. The POP3 specification briefly discusses the split-UA (user agent) model for which the protocol designer developed POP3.

POP3 defines three states (or stages) through which a typical POP3 session passes: authorization, transaction, and update. After the POP3 client and server establish a connection, the session enters the authorization state. In the authorization state, the client identifies itself to the server. If authorization is successful, the server opens the client's mailbox and the session enters the transaction state. In the transaction state, the client requests the POP3 server provide information (such as a mail listing) or perform an action (such as retrieve a specific mail message). Next, the session enters the update state, in which the connection terminates. Table 15.7 lists the POP3 commands that a minimal POP3 implementation on the Internet requires.

Command	Description
USER	Requires a name that identifies the user.
PASS	Requires a password for the user/server.
QUIT	Closes the TCP connection.
STAT	The server returns the number of messages in the mailbox plus the total size of the messages.
LIST	Returns message IDs and sizes—a scan-line listing. (Permits an optional message ID as a parameter.)
RETR	Retrieves a message from a mailbox. (Requires a message ID as a parameter.)
DELE	Marks a message for deletion. (Requires a message ID as a parameter.)
NOOP	The server returns a positive response but takes no action.
LAST	The server returns the highest message number accessed.
RSET	Unmarks all messages marked for deletion.

Table 15.7 Post Office Protocol Version 3 commands (required by minimal implementation).

Although POP3 defines several commands (as shown in Table 15.7), POP3 only defines two replies. The text *+OK* is a positive success indicator similar to an ACK message. The text *-ERR* is a negative success indicator similar to a NAK message. Both replies indicate success insofar as the POP server received and responded to the command. Typically, descriptive text strings will follow the server replies. RFC 1225 includes several example POP3 sessions. The following sections contain some specification examples that should give you a general idea about the flow of commands during a POP3 session.

AUTHORIZING A USER

After your program establishes a TCP connection to the POP3 protocol port (well-known port 110), POP3 requires a USER command with a name parameter as the first transmission. If the server returns a positive reply (+OK), the next command must be PASS with a password parameter:

```
CLIENT:     USER kcope
SERVER:     +OK
CLIENT:     PASS secret
SERVER:     +OK kcope's maildrop has 2 messages (320 octets) ...
```

REVIEWING POP3 TRANSACTIONS

After the server authenticates the user, the POP3 conversation enters the transaction stage. The following examples illustrate the use of POP3 commands that return information during the transaction stage. The STAT command returns the number of messages and the number of bytes in the messages:

```
CLIENT:     STAT
SERVER:     +OK 2 320
```

The LIST command (without a parameter) lists the file identifier and message size of each message in the mailbox:

```
CLIENT:     LIST
SERVER:     +OK 2 messages (320 octets)
SERVER:     1 120
SERVER:     2 200
SERVER:     . ...
```

The LIST command, with an argument, lists information about the specified message:

```
CLIENT:     LIST 2
SERVER:     +OK 2 200 ...

CLIENT:     LIST 3
SERVER:     -ERR no such message, only 2 messages in maildrop
```

The TOP command lists the headers of the message, a blank line, and the first ten lines of the message:

```
CLIENT:    TOP 10
SERVER:    +OK
SERVER:    <the POP3 server sends the headers of the message, a blank
line, and the first 10 lines of the message body>
SERVER:    . ...

CLIENT:    TOP 100
SERVER:    -ERR no such message
```

Technically, the NOOP (no operation) command doesn't really return any information except a positive reply from the server. However, the positive reply tells the client that the server is on-line and receiving service requests:

```
CLIENT:    NOOP
SERVER:    +OK
```

The following examples initiate action on the POP3 server. For example, the RETR command retrieves the specified message into a local buffer allocated by the UA:

```
CLIENT:    RETR 1
SERVER:    +OK 120 octets
SERVER:    <the POP3 server sends the entire message here>
SERVER:    .
```

Likewise, the DELE command marks messages for deletion:

```
CLIENT:    DELE 1
SERVER:    +OK message 1 deleted ...
CLIENT:    DELE 2
SERVER:    -ERR message 2 already deleted
```

The RSET command unmarks all messages marked for deletion:

```
CLIENT:    RSET
SERVER:    +OK maildrop has 2 messages (320 octets)
```

Of course, the QUIT command ends the TCP connection:

```
CLIENT:    QUIT
SERVER:    +OK dewey POP3 server signing off
CLIENT:    QUIT
SERVER:    +OK dewey POP3 server signing off (maildrop empty) ...
CLIENT:    QUIT
SERVER:    +OK dewey POP3 server signing off (2 messages left) ...
```

Note that the server does not actually destroy messages marked for deletion until the POP3 session enters the update state (which occurs when the client transmits the QUIT command). At any time during the transaction state, the client can transmit the RSET command and unmark all messages previously marked for deletion.

PUTTING IT ALL TO USE

Despite all the information covered in this chapter, there are very few new programming techniques for you to implement in the quick programs that demonstrate SMTP and POP3. In fact, there is absolutely nothing new from a Winsock perspective. However, a little explanation is in order regarding the technique the quick programs use to send the protocol command strings. SMTP and POP3 are *lock-step* protocols. In other words, after your SMTP- or POP3-based client program establishes a connection, it sends a command and waits for the server to respond. The communication process then advances one step at a time, with your program and the server moving in concert (or lock-step) together. As you have learned, your programs can use SMTP to *transfer* mail messages across the Internet and POP3 to *retrieve* mail from the Internet. To keep the SMTP and POP3 quick programs as simple as possible, *Internet Programming* uses two separate programs: QSMTP for sending mail and QPOP3 for retrieving mail.

The key to using SMTP and POP3 is knowing which commands to use and when to use them. The quick programs QSMTP and QPOP3 use an array of character strings to make it easy for you to experiment with both protocols. Each program defines its own command strings. The technique works as follows. First, the program declares and defines an array. The following command string array is from the QSMTP program. As you can see, each array element contains an SMTP command (with arguments as required):

```
char *MailMessage[] =
    {
      "HELO your.host\r\n",
      "MAIL FROM:<userid@yourhost.domain>\r\n",
      "RCPT TO:<recipient@computer.host>\r\n",
      "DATA\r\n",
      "This is my message to someone.\r\n\r\n.\r\n",
      "QUIT\r\n",
      NULL
    };
```

The next group of code statements shows the command string array from the QPOP3 program. As you can see, the only significant difference these code statements and the QSMTP's command string array is that QPOP3 contains POP3 commands instead of SMTP commands.

```
char *POPMessage[] =
    {
      "USER your_mailbox_id\r\n",
```

```
        "PASS your_password\r\n",
        "STAT\r\n",
        "LIST\r\n",
        "RETR 1\r\n",
        "DELE 1\r\n",
        "QUIT\r\n",
        NULL
    };
```

Note that the last element in both POPMessage[] and MailMessage[] is NULL. This is intentional. As shown next, the quick programs use a do-while construct that loops until it finds a NULL message pointer. In other words, if you use the QSMTP and QPOP3 programs to experiment with the protocols, make sure you don't inadvertently replace the last element with a valid pointer. The last element must remain NULL for the do-while message-processing loop to work correctly. The following code statements show an abbreviated version of the message-processing loop (the following code fragment doesn't include any error checks):

```
int iLength;
int iMsg = 0;
int iEnd = 0;
BYTE sReceiveBuffer[4096];

do
  {
    send(hSocket, (LPSTR)POPMessage[iMsg], strlen(POPMessage[iMsg]),
        NO_FLAGS);

    iLength = recv(hSocket, (LPSTR)sReceiveBuffer+iEnd,
        sizeof(sReceiveBuffer)-iEnd, NO_FLAGS);

    iEnd += iLength;
    sReceiveBuffer[iEnd] = '\0';

    MessageBox(NULL, (LPSTR)sReceiveBuffer, (LPSTR)POPMessage[iMsg],
        MB_OK|MB_ICONSTOP);

    iMsg++;
  }
while (POPMessage[iMsg]);
```

As shown in the code fragment, the program uses the send function to transmit the POPMessage string. Then, the program calls the recv function and waits for the server's response. When the program receives data, it terminates the receive buffer with a NULL and then displays the results in a Windows message box. The program uses the iEnd and iLength variables to keep track of the data in the receive buffer. In other words, the program appends each new message from the server to the old data in the receive buffer. As previously mentioned, the do-while construct loops until the POPMessage array element becomes NULL (indicating the last element in the command string array). The do-while construct for QSMTP is identical to QPOP3 except that QSMTP transmits the contents of the MailMessage array instead of the POPMessage array. The technique just described requires you to recompile the programs each time you change the command strings for a new experiment. Obviously, you can build a simple user-interface (perhaps using pieces from the Sockman template) to make the experimentation process more flexible. However, to do so, you must manage Windows messages and the associated overhead of a normal Windows program. As usual, the quick programs for this chapter are bare-bones programs that narrowly focus on the network communication process (in this case, the process associated with Internet e-mail).

As discussed, other than the command strings and the do-while loop that processes the command strings, QSMTP and QPOP3 are practically identical to the quick programs described in previous chapters. Each program defines three functions: WinMain, a function that connects a socket to the server (similar to the ConnectTimerServerSocket function shown in Chapter 13), and a function that sends and receives network data through the connected socket. QPOP3 uses a function named GetMail to retrieve e-mail messages using the POP3 protocol. QSMTP uses a function named SendMail to send e-mail messages using SMTP. The *Internet Programming* companion disk contains the complete source code for both QSMTP.CPP and QPOP3.CPP.

PUTTING IT ALL TOGETHER

In this chapter, you learned much about electronic mail in general and the Internet's e-mail system in particular. Specifically, you learned how message transfer agents (MTAs) use the Simple Mail Transfer Protocol, as well as how system administrators can configure MTAs to act as relay agents for Internet e-mail. Additionally, you saw how two separate protocols use similar command and reply methods to perform their respective functions. As you will learn in the next chapter, the File Transfer Protocol (FTP) uses similar concepts as SMTP and POP3, except with a few special twists. If you understand SMTP, ESMTP, and POP3, you will have no trouble understanding and using FTP. As such, before you move ahead to the File Transfer Protocol in Chapter 16, make sure you understand the following key concepts:

- ✓ The Internet e-mail system primarily consists of user agents, message transfer agents, and mailboxes.

- ✓ User agents make the human interface to e-mail user-friendly.

- ✓ Message transfer agents (MTAs) transfer mail between host computers.

- ✓ A relay agent is a message transfer agent configured to receive mail data from several local MTAs and then transfer the mail across the Internet.

- ✓ Your programs can use base-64 encoding to transfer 8-bit binary data through the Internet's 7-bit mail transport system.

- ✓ A Post Office Protocol (POP) server lets users retrieve mail from anywhere on the Internet using any user agent that understands the protocol.

Chapter 16
Understanding the File Transfer Protocols

Although electronic mail is probably the most widely used application on the Internet, the File Transfer Protocol (FTP) carries the most data. As you may know, Ftp programs transfer files from one host computer to another. On many computer systems, you must first log into the system before you can access the files its disks store. To make it easier for users to access files, many systems let users log in using the login name *anonymous*. With *anonymous FTP*, a user can log into an FTP server system and download or transfer files without having an account on the server system. In other words, anonymous FTP lets people freely collect data files that include every type of information in existence on the Internet. Such anonymous FTP operations make Ftp one of the most popular programs on the Internet.

FTP controls most file-transfer operations across the Internet. This chapter discusses FTP's design and operation. As you will learn, FTP requires two TCP connections to perform file-transfer operations—unlike other protocols previously discussed in Internet Programming, that require only one TCP connection. FTP uses the first TCP connection to transfer commands and replies similar to those SMTP and POP3 use. FTP uses the second TCP connection for data-transfer operations. By the time you finish this chapter, you will understand the following key concepts:

- What commands FTP uses to perform file transfer operations
- How FTP uses two TCP connections to manage file transfers
- How TELNET and FTP manage TCP urgent-data messages
- How FTP uses the TELNET protocol to cancel file-transfer operations

LAYING AN FTP FOUNDATION

As a programmer, you should find the File Transfer Protocol interesting for several reasons. First, its sheer popularity and widespread use on the Internet should give you incentive to understand it. An accomplished Internet programmer should know how to use FTP and how to develop programs that perform similar operations. Second, FTP is similar to SMTP and POP3 (the e-mail protocols) in that it uses NVT ASCII command strings and reply codes. In other words, if you have read Chapter 15, the FTP protocol should feel familiar. Like SMTP and POP3, FTP uses a lock-step protocol approach (send a command and wait for a reply before sending the next command) for file-transfer operations. However, unlike the e-mail protocols, FTP uses two TCP connections for such operations—one connection for commands and one connection for data transfers. To be a successful Internet programmer, you should understand how to implement and simultaneously use multiple TCP connections. As you will learn, a program that uses multiple TCP connections can efficiently perform some very sophisticated network operations.

AN INTERACTIVE FTP SESSION

The Internet attracts many users, in part, because it offers them the ability to retrieve information, programs, various types of documentation, and other resources. To retrieve files that Internet host computers store, network users primarily use FTP-based programs. Of the many types of FTP-based client programs, the command-line FTP client is the most popular. You will encounter command-line FTP client programs on most UNIX operating systems (as well as other systems).

An FTP session with a command-line FTP program can help you understand the File Transfer Protocol, especially if you have never used FTP-based programs. If you are not familiar with FTP, you may find it useful to log into your Internet host, gain access to a command-line prompt, and work your way through the interactive FTP session described in the following paragraphs. Most UNIX-based Internet service providers provide access to a command line through a UNIX shell such as csh. On most Internet hosts, to start an FTP client, you simply type **ftp** from the command-line prompt. To indicate that you have started an FTP session, the host computer will typically change your command-line prompt to include the letters *ftp*, as shown here:

```
ftp>
```

From the FTP prompt, you can type commands that tell the client program exactly what service you want it to perform. For example, to transfer files from an Internet host, you must first establish a connection to the host. To tell the FTP client program to establish a TCP connection for FTP operations, you usually type the open command followed by the name of the Internet host with which you want to establish a connection, as shown here:

```
ftp>  open  nic.ddn.mil  <ENTER>
```

From the FTP prompt on your Internet host, type the open command shown and press ENTER. The FTP client, in turn, will try to establish a TCP connection to the DOD Network Information Center host nic.ddn.mil. (As an Internet programmer, you might find this FTP server site interesting because it contains an on-line archive of most Request for Comments (RFC) documents to which you might need to refer.) In response to an FTP connection request, most FTP servers respond with a reply message that tells you how to log into the system. For example, if you type **open nic.ddn.mil** from the FTP prompt, (assuming the connection is successful) you should see a response similar to the one shown here:

```
Connected to nic.ddn.mil.
220-*****Welcome to the DOD Network Information Center*****
     *****Login with username "anonymous" and password "guest"
     *****You may change directories to the following:
        ddn-news            - DDN Management Bulletins
        domain              - Root Zone Files
        gosip               - DOD GOSIP Registration and Information
        internet-drafts     - Internet Drafts
        netinfo             - NIC Information Files
        rfc                 - RFC Repository
        scc                 - DDN Security Bulletins
        std                 - Internet Protocol Standards
220 And more!
Name (nic.ddn.mil:happy):
```

As you can see, the server, in response to your connection request, transmits a message that tells you to login using the username *anonymous* and the password *guest*. The server host also presents you with a username login prompt. As directed, type the word **anonymous** at the username prompt and press ENTER. In response, the server host will probably transmit another message similar to the one shown here:

```
331 Guest login ok, send "guest" as password.
Password:
```

In other words, in response to your username, the server host transmits another information message that includes a reminder to use the word *guest* as a password. Type the word **guest** and press ENTER. If the login is successful, the server host will transmit another message, which should look something like this:

```
230 Guest login ok, access restrictions apply.
ftp>
```

After receiving the "login ok" message, the client will present you with your FTP prompt again. This pattern of a client command followed by a server response represents the general flow of client/server communications throughout all FTP sessions. After you login, you can tell the client to transmit messages that cause the server host to change working directories, list directories, and transfer files. For example, to tell the server host to change the working directory to **rfc** (where all the RFCs reside), type the cd command, as shown here:

```
ftp> cd rfc <ENTER>
```

The server host will change its working directory to rfc. To tell your FTP client to retrieve the latest For Your Information (FYI) index, type the get command, as shown here:

```
ftp> get fyi-index.txt <ENTER>
200 PORT command successful.
```

```
150 Opening ASCII mode connection for fyi-index.txt (8584 bytes).
226 Transfer complete.
local: fyi-index.txt remote: fyi-index.txt
8765 bytes received in 0.77 seconds (11 Kbytes/s)
```

The FTP client and server will negotiate the file transfer and use the reply messages shown to keep you informed of their progress. After the file transfer completes, you can close the TCP connection by typing the **close** command (the server will typically respond with a "Goodbye" message) and then terminate the FTP session by typing **quit** as shown:

```
ftp> close <ENTER>
221 Goodbye.
ftp> quit <ENTER>
```

IDENTIFYING THE FILE TRANSFER PROTOCOLS

Although FTP is the most widely known and used file-transfer protocol on the Internet, you should be aware that others exist. In fact, three file-transfer protocols (and one file transfer program) are worthy of note. Request for Comments (RFC) 959, *File Transfer Protocol (FTP)*, Reynolds, 1985, defines the protocol that most people use and on which this chapter will focus. The following sections briefly describe the others.

CONSIDERING THE TRIVIAL FILE TRANSFER PROTOCOL

RFC 783, *The TFTP Protocol (Revision 2)*, Sollins, 1981, defines the Trivial File Transfer Protocol (TFTP). TFTP intentionally omits most of FTP's capabilities and instead narrowly focuses on performing two file-transfer operations: reading a file and writing a file. To perform these operations, TFTP uses the User Datagram Protocol (UDP). Unlike the FTP protocol, TFTP does not list directories or authenticate users. TFTP uses a system of acknowledgments to ensure data delivery between the TFTP server and the TFTP client. A TFTP operation begins with a UDP datagram that requests a file transfer. If the server accepts the request, the server will send the requested file in 512-byte fixed-length blocks. The server waits for the client to acknowledge each data block before it transmits the next. (Note that doing so guarantees correct sequencing for the transmitted file.)

To signal the completion of the transfer, the TFTP server sends a UDP datagram of less than 512 bytes. In other words, the final UDP datagram will contain the last few bytes of data for the file. A TFTP client initiates a file-transfer operation and then simply loops, receiving the file from the server 512 bytes at a time. When the server sends a UDP datagram that contains less than 512 bytes, the client knows it has received the end of the file. Although not very fast or robust in terms of capability, the TFTP protocol is very small and easy to implement—two of the design criteria stated in the specification (RFC 783). Like the Simple Mail Transfer Protocol, TFTP seems forgettable due to its simplicity and obvious limitations. However, in 1984, Ross Finlayson of Stanford University proposed an interesting use for TFTP. In RFC 906, *Bootstrap Loading using TFTP*,

Finlayson, 1984, he proposed to use TFTP to transfer bootstrap loaders from across the network. A *bootstrap loader* is a mini-program that executes each time a user turns on a computer. A bootstrap loader loads essential parts of the operating system into the computer's memory so the computer can complete the boot up process.

For example, a diskless workstation must load one or more code files from across a network in order to boot up. Different computer manufacturers use different methods to boot diskless workstations. In most cases, the diskless workstation starts using ROM-based instructions that direct the workstation to send out requests across the network for a server to download the workstation's operating system. Finlayson and others encountered the problem that each different computer manufacturer's solution to copying the bootstrap loader from the network required a different network server due to the varying implementations for bootstrapping. In RFC 906, Finlayson proposed to establish TFTP as an Internet standard for performing the task of copying bootstrap loaders across the network for diskless workstations. It should come as no surprise to you that Finlayson was also one of the authors of RFC 903, *Reverse Address Resolution Protocol*, Finlayson et al, 1984. As you may recall from Chapter 4, the Reverse Address Resolution Protocol (RARP) also addressed problems for diskless workstations. RARP maps a link-layer address, such as an Ethernet address, into an IP address. Diskless workstations can read their link-layer address from their network interface cards. Then, using RARP, workstations can broadcast a request that asks another host on the network to look up the link-layer address and report the diskless workstation's correct IP address.

REVIEWING THE SIMPLE FILE TRANSFER PROTOCOL

As previously mentioned, FTP uses two TCP connections to accomplish file transfer operations—one connection for commands and one connection for data transfers. On the other hand, TFTP uses UDP datagrams to transfer files. The Simple File Transfer Protocol (SFTP), as described in RFC 913, *Simple File Transfer Protocol*, Lottor, 1984, is an attempt to find a happy medium between the FTP and the TFTP. SFTP supports user validation (access control), file transfers, directory listings, directory changing, file renaming, and file deleting. Like FTP, SFTP uses TCP. However, unlike FTP, SFTP uses only one TCP connection. The commands, reply codes, and general operational features of SFTP look a lot like FTP. In fact, SFTP performs very similar to FTP. Unfortunately, we weren't able to implement a *quick* program based on SFTP because we could not find an Internet host running an SFTP server. The Simple File Transfer Protocol never achieved the popularity of its simple cousin, the Simple Mail Transfer Protocol. While SMTP servers dominate e-mail systems on the Internet, FTP dominates the file-transfer sites located on the Internet. As such, *Internet Programming* will use FTP for all file-transfer program examples.

UNDERSTANDING THE FTP MODEL

As previously mentioned, the File Transfer Protocol is similar to SMTP and POP3 in that it uses NVT ASCII command strings and reply codes. However, unlike any previous protocols discussed in *Internet Programming*, FTP uses two TCP connections to accomplish its file-transfer operations. FTP identifies its two TCP connections as a *control* connection and a *data* connection. The control connection is similar to the other TCP connections you have created in previous chapters. In other words, the control connection is a typical client/server setup. The FTP server performs a passive open on a well-known port (protocol port 21) and waits for client connections. The FTP client, in turn, contacts the FTP server at the well-known protocol port, and the programs negotiate a typical TCP connection (as discussed in Chapter 5). The control connection remains active throughout the entire FTP transaction. The client and server exchange NVT ASCII command strings and reply codes across the control connection. FTP creates a separate data connection for each file-transfer operation (and at other times as well). Figure 16.1 shows a typical configuration for FTP operations.

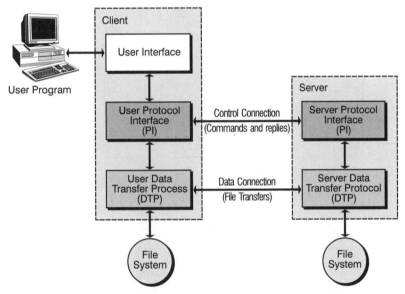

Figure 16.1 A typical configuration for FTP operations.

At the core of the operation are the protocol interpreters (PIs) and the data transfer processes (DTPs). As you can see, the client and server each have their own protocol interpreter and data transfer process. The data transfer processes establish and manage the data connection. The protocol interpreters interpret FTP commands and communicate through the control connection, which the client-PI establishes at the beginning of the FTP session.

The user-interface shields the user from the FTP commands and replies. Ftp programs generally come in two varieties—either full screen (menu-driven) or command-line driven. Many UNIX-based Ftp programs are command-line driven. In other words, the UNIX user executes the Ftp program (typically named Ftp) and then types commands at an FTP prompt similar to the DOS prompt on a PC. However, in most cases, the typed commands in a command-line-driven version of the program are not actual FTP commands. Instead, a user-interface program parses the user's command line and translates the user's requests into FTP commands. For example, a user might type "get" instead of "RETR" and "put" instead of "STOR." Most Windows-based Ftp programs are menu and dialog-box driven. In many cases, the user-interface in a Windows-based Ftp program will be a dialog box with command buttons, list boxes, and scroll bars, as shown in Figure 16.2.

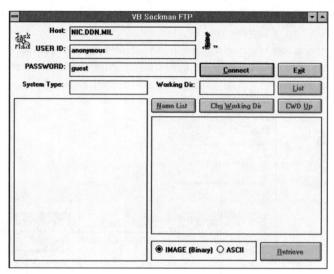

Figure 16.2 A Windows-based Ftp session.

Managing the Data

From the beginning, FTP protocol designers developed the protocol to work with different host computers using different operating systems, files structures, and character sets. As a result, FTP requires users to choose from a wide variety of options for file-transfer operations. FTP options fall into four categories: file types, file formats, file structures, and transmission modes. The following sections describe each of these options.

Understanding FTP File Types

FTP can manage four different *file types*: local, image (or binary), EBCDIC, and ASCII. The local file-type supports file transfers between hosts that use different byte sizes. As you may recall from the discussion about the term *octet* in Chapter 3, much of the early TCP/IP development occurred on computer systems that did not use 8-bit bytes. The local file-type is a holdover from those days. In other words, the local file-type lets a user transfer data from a host that uses eight-bits-per-byte to a host that uses a different number of bits-per-byte (7 or 10, for example). For a system that uses 8-bit bytes, the local file-type is identical to the image file-type. Since most modern computers use 8-bit bytes, there is little use for a local file-type FTP transfer today.

The image (or binary) file-type transfer treats file data as a contiguous data stream. In other words, an image file transfer does not include (or identify) any type of boundaries in the internal data structure of a file (such as a carriage-return for the end of a line). Typically, FTP users transfer most files as image files. As you have learned, most computers use ASCII codes to represent textual data. However, some systems, such as IBM mainframes and minicomputers, use EBCDIC instead. EBCDIC (pronounced Eb-si-dick) stands for Extended Binary Coded Decimal Interchange Code. Although EBCDIC and ASCII both use eight bits to represent characters, their respective codes are very different. As such, a computer that understands EBCDIC will not understand ASCII (although many programs exist that will translate between the two schemes).

FTP's EBCDIC file-type transfer is an alternative file transfer method for two computers that use EBCDIC encoding. In other words, if the hosts on each end of the FTP connection use EBCDIC, they can use FTP's EBCDIC file-type transfer to simplify the transfer of text-based files. ASCII file-type transfers are the default for FTP file transfers. To use the ASCII file-type transfer, the sending host must convert the local text file into NVT ASCII (7-bit ASCII). The receiving host must then translate NVT ASCII into the local convention for text storage.

The primary problem with ASCII file-type transfers are the end-of-line markers. As you have learned, the end-of-line marker that various computers use differs from the NVT ASCII convention of a carriage-return line-feed (CRLF) character pair. As such, host receivers that use end-of-line identifiers other than CRLF must scan each byte of incoming data to identify the end of each line of text. Obviously, such a requirement adds significant data-processing overhead to the receiver program. In other words, a receiver that uses CRLF end-of-line markers (the same as those FTP's ASCII file-type transfers use) can simply read data from the incoming-data queue and write the data to a local file. On the other hand, a receiver that uses a different convention must examine every byte pair in the incoming-data queue to determine when the program needs to substitute its own end-of-line marker (typically, a single line-feed character).

UNDERSTANDING FTP FILE FORMATS

As discussed in the previous section, FTP users can choose to transfer files as ASCII or EBCDIC. When a user specifies ASCII or EBCDIC as the file-type transfer, the user must also specify a *format control.* FTP defines three types of format controls: nonprint, Telnet format control, and FORTRAN carriage control. For text files, FTP's default format control is nonprint, which means the file contains no vertical format information, such as vertical tabs, that a printer might use to position text on paper. The Telnet format control, on the other hand, uses vertical format controls for printers. Telnet vertical format controls are embedded-character sequences that tell a printer how to print the surrounding text. FORTRAN (a computer-programming language) also uses specially embedded characters. FORTRAN carriage control means the first character of each line is a FORTRAN control character, which, in turn, specifies that line's formatting. The Telnet format control and FORTRAN carriage control are holdovers from the early days of the Internet. Today, most FTP implementations (especially on UNIX-based systems) restrict the format control to nonprint only.

Understanding FTP Transmission Modes

The final FTP file-transfer characteristic that a user must define is the *transmission mode*. The transmission mode specifies how FTP transmits the file across the TCP data connection. FTP defines three transmission modes: block mode, compressed mode, and stream mode. The block mode transfers a file as a series of blocks where each block includes one or more header bytes. FTP sends the data blocks for a file in the same sequence in which they occur in the file. The block header in each data block specifies the size of the data block (which can vary) as well as descriptor codes, which identify the end of the file or the end of a record (if any). In compressed mode, a simple run-length encoding algorithm compresses consecutive occurrences of the same byte. Run-length encoding uses a special symbol followed by a count. For example, suppose the file you want to transfer is a heavily commented source-code file. Suppose you have delimited each function definition with an entire line of forward slashes. In other words, at the beginning and end of each function, your file includes a series of 70 forward slashes (C++ comment designators):

```
//////////////////////////////////////////////////////////////////////
void main(void)
 {
   return(0)
 }
//////////////////////////////////////////////////////////////////////
```

Run-length encoding would replace the consecutive slashes with a sequence of three characters: a {} symbol, a number, and a forward slash. For example, in {}70/, the symbol {} marks the beginning of the run, the number 70 specifies the number of characters in the run, and the forward slash specifies which character the file used in the run. Although actual implementations of run-length encoding are different, this example describes the basic idea. Typically, run-length encoding would compress spaces in a text file and strings of zero bytes in a binary file. Most FTP users rarely use compressed mode, and many implementations do not support it. Most users prefer to use compression algorithms, which, in general, perform far better than run-length encoding algorithms.

In stream mode, FTP transfers a file as a stream of data bytes. If the FTP structure-type is a record structure, FTP uses a special two-byte character sequence to mark the end of a record and the end of a file. When FTP transfers a "file structure," FTP signals the end of a file by closing the TCP data connection. In other words, after FTP transfers the last byte from the file, FTP closes the connection. The receiver understands that the closure means that the last transmission contained the last few bytes of data for the transferred file.

SUMMARIZING THE CHOICES

In general, most FTP implementations only support nonprint format control, file structures, and stream transmission modes. In other words, the only choice a user typically must make is whether to use ASCII or image file-types for the file-transfer operation.

UNDERSTANDING THE *FTP/TELNET* RELATIONSHIP

Like several other application protocols (such as SMTP and POP3), the FTP protocol depends on the TELNET protocol definition for some of its operations. In addition to using NVT ASCII text strings to define commands (as did SMTP and POP3), FTP uses TELNET control codes to signal the existence of urgent data. For example, whenever an FTP client wants to interrupt a file transfer, the FTP client transmits the TELNET Synch signal to tell the server to stop the file transfer. In other words, FTP uses the TELNET protocol on the control connection to manage file-transfer operations. As mentioned, FTP defines its own NVT ASCII command strings (like those SMTP and POP3 use). Although FTP follows the TELNET protocol, it only uses a small subset of the TELNET commands. To understand certain operations (such as canceling a file transfer) in FTP, you need a general understanding of the TELNET protocol. In fact, the FTP specification (RFC 959) explicitly states that it assumes knowledge of the Transport Control Protocol and the TELNET protocol. You will understand why you need to understand the TELNET protocol after you read the following sections, which provide a general overview of the TELNET protocol and then discuss the TELNET Synch signal in detail.

USING *TELNET* TO PREVIEW OTHER PROTOCOLS

As you may know, you can use TELNET client programs to log into a remote host as though your computer is a terminal attached directly to the remote host's network. To use a TELNET client, you tell the client the name (address) of the remote host to which you want to connect. The client, in turn, will establish a TCP connection to port 23 (the well-known port for TELNET). Then, the remote host will present you with a login prompt at which you can type a username. Depending on the TELNET server you contact, you may also have to enter a password. Thousands of special TELNET servers exist throughout the Internet. These special servers provide easy access to information about everything from agriculture to weather. Many special TELNET servers advertise a username and password that you can use for TELNET logins. In other words, like sites that authorize anonymous FTP logins, many Internet hosts provide publicly accessible TELNET servers. The difference is that TELNET servers do not have a standard guest name and password to use.

You can use a TELNET client (that lets you specify a port) to establish a TCP connection to any protocol port on practically any host on the Internet. As a programmer, you can use

---

this capability with a TELNET client to test other protocols. As discussed elsewhere in *Internet Programming*, most application protocols use TELNET's NVT ASCII for data transfers. As you have learned, most application protocols, such as SMTP and POP3, also use NVT ASCII for commands. For example, you can use a TELNET client to connect to port 79 of an Internet host and test the Finger User-Information Protocol. As a more sophisticated exercise, you can send Internet e-mail by using a TELNET client to connect to port 25—the well-known port for SMTP. If you do so, you will discover that you can manually type SMTP commands and see the reply codes from the SMTP server. Likewise, you can actually retrieve your Internet e-mail using a TELNET client to connect to port 110— the well-known port for POP3. Of course, in all cases, you must know which protocol commands to type and what syntax the commands use. However, you can use a TELNET client to test your understanding of how a protocol operates before you ever write a program built on the protocol.

Internet Programming discusses most TELNET programming concepts in the context of other application protocols that use TELNET principles or definitions. For example, as mentioned, one essential component of a remote login protocol is a universally understood data format for all network transmissions. You have already encountered and frequently used this format in previous chapters of this book—the data format is NVT ASCII. As previously discussed, the TELNET protocol defines NVT ASCII. Regardless of a computer's (or terminal's) type, each must perform such screen operations as erasing a character, line, or even the entire screen. Likewise, most support a special key (such as Esc) or keyboard combination (such as Ctrl-C) that signals the operating system to end or interrupt the current program. As discussed, the TELNET protocol uses the virtual-terminal protocol to make such differences between terminals transparent to the end user. TELNET also provides this capability by defining escape sequences for such operations. Other TELNET-based programs can interpret and translate these escape sequences into the appropriate commands the program's host computer requires.

Understanding *TELNET* Commands

RFC 854, *TELNET Protocol Specification*, Postel and Reynolds, 1983, defines the TELNET protocol, including the control codes that TELNET-based programs (and protocols that depend on TELNET commands) use and understand. The basic TELNET commands are not too difficult to understand or remember. However, an important feature of the TELNET protocol is that it permits TELNET clients and servers to negotiate a wide variety of options. Without TELNET's option negotiation features, the protocol is actually quite simple. Unfortunately, the option negotiations add a significant amount of complexity (as well as power) to the protocol. As a result, writing a Telnet client can be a challenging task. As you will learn in the following paragraphs, several TELNET commands focus on option negations.

Note: A series of RFCs (RFC 855 through 861, as well as others) define negotiable options for the TELNET protocol.

As you have learned, many Internet protocols (in fact, most application protocols) use a synchronous exchange of commands and replies to perform their network operations. For example, SMTP and POP3 clients send NVT ASCII character strings that represent protocol commands and then wait for a server reply. TELNET uses a similar approach. However, at any time, either side of a TELNET connection can (and does) transmit TELNET commands. In other words, in the application protocols previously discussed, the flow of protocol commands was essentially one-way—from client to server. TELNET lets commands flow in both directions. Also, TELNET does not use NVT ASCII character strings to represent TELNET commands. Instead, TELNET transmits commands as specially defined *escape sequences*.

An escape sequence uses a reserved character (often referred to as an escape character) to identify the beginning of a command. The character (or characters) that follow the reserved (or escape) character identify the command. For example, on a PC, the most commonly used escape character is ASCII decimal code 27 (0x1B). In fact, the *name* for ASCII 27 is ESC, which stands for escape. The TELNET protocol refers to its reserved escape character as IAC, which stands for *interpret as command*. An important feature of TELNET command codes is that they have their eighth bit set. As you may recall, one of the problems with NVT ASCII is that it is a 7-bit data encoding scheme (whereas today, most computers use all eight bits to encode data). The reason TELNET limits NVT ASCII to 7-bits is that the protocol normally reserves bytes that use the eighth bit for use as TELNET commands. RFC 856, *TELNET Binary Transmissions*, Postel and Reynolds, 1983, defines an option that permits TELNET to transmit 8-bit data rather than the normal 7-bit data. However, the creators of this option designed it for transmission of binary data—not text. As previously discussed, TELNET uses NVT ASCII (7-bit codes) to transmit textual data.

The ASCII decimal code for TELNET's IAC escape character is 255 (binary 11111111). Each TELNET escape (or command) sequence must begin with IAC. Table 16.1 lists TELNET commands that IAC identifies. In other words, the commands Table 16.1 lists only have significance if the IAC character precedes them. An example escape sequence is "IAC GA" (0xFF 0xF9), which tells the receiver to *go ahead*. TELNET treats a data byte with the value of 0xF9 as ordinary data unless IAC (0xFF) precedes it.

NAME	CODE	MEANING
EOF	236 (0xEF)	End of file
SUSP	237 (0xED)	Suspend current process
ABORT	238 (0xEE)	Abort process
EOR	239 (0xEF)	End of record
SE	240 (0xF0)	End of sub-negotiation parameters
NOP	241 (0xF1)	No operation

Table 16.1 TELNET commands the IAC (interpret as command) escape character identifies.
(continued on the next page)

NAME	CODE	MEANING
DATA MARK or DM	242 (0xF2)	The data stream portion of a Synch (TCP urgent notification should always accompany DM.)
BRK	243 (0xF3)	NVT break character
IP	244 (0xF4)	Interrupt Process function
AO	245 (0xF5)	Abort Output function
AYT	246 (0xF6)	Are You There function
EC	247 (0xF7)	Erase character function
EL	248 (0xF8)	Erase Line function
GA	249 (0xF9)	Go ahead signal
SB	250 (0xFA)	Indicates that what follows is sub-negotiation of the indicated option.
WILL (option code)	251 (0xFB)	Indicates the desire to begin, or confirmation that you are now performing, the indicated option.
WON'T (option code)	252 (0xFC)	Indicates the refusal to perform, or continue performing, the indicated option.
DO (option code)	253 (0xFD)	Indicates the request that the other party perform, or confirmation that you are expecting the other party to perform, the indicated option.
DON'T (option code)	254 (0xFE)	Indicates the demand that the other party stop performing, or confirmation that you are no longer expecting the other party to perform.
IAC	255 (0xFF)	Data Byte 255 (In other words, the escape sequence IAC represents a data byte with a value of 255—0xFF.)

Table 16.1 TELNET commands the IAC (interpret as command) escape character identifies.
(continued from the previous page)

TELNET uses the WILL, WON'T, DO, and DON'T commands with an option parameter to negotiate TELNET options. The WILL command says the sender wants to enable the option for itself. The WON'T command says the sender wants to disable the option for itself. Likewise, the DO command says the sender wants the receiver to enable the option, and the DON'T command says the sender wants the receiver to disable the option. TELNET protocol rules let either side of the connection accept or reject a request to enable an option. However, the rules also require both sides to honor any request to disable an option. As such, TELNET option negotiations can only follow one of the six scenarios shown in Table 16.2.

Sender Request	Receiver Response	Description
WILL	DO	The sender wants to enable the option, and the receiver says OK.
WILL	DON'T	The sender wants to enable the option, and the receiver says NO.
DO	WILL	The sender wants the receiver to enable the option, and the receiver says OK.
DO	WON'T	The sender wants the receiver to enable the option, and the receiver says NO.
WON'T	DON'T	The sender wants to disable the option, and the receiver MUST say OK.
DON'T	WON'T	The sender wants the receiver to disable the option, and the receiver MUST say OK.

Table 16.2 TELNET option negotiation scenarios.

TELNET option negotiations require three bytes: the IAC escape character, the command byte (WILL, WON'T, DO, or DON'T), and the option code. TELNET includes over 40 negotiable options. *Internet Programming* will not discuss the TELNET options. To find the latest list of TELNET options and the RFCs that define them, you should consult the latest version of the Internet's Assigned Numbers RFC, as defined by the Internet Assigned Numbers Authority (IANA).

UNDERSTANDING THE *TELNET* SYNCH SIGNAL

As you may recall from Chapter 5, the 16-bit Urgent Pointer field in the TCP header specifies a byte location in the TCP data area that contains urgent data. The purpose of the TCP URG flag and the urgent pointer is to notify the receiving TCP module that some kind of *urgent data* exists and to point the TCP module to it. As explained in Chapter 5, despite some controversy, Internet professionals generally agree that the urgent pointer points to the *last* byte of urgent data. As also discussed, practically everyone mentions TELNET as an example of an application that needs to use TCP urgent mode data.

Note: TCP urgent data and urgent mode are among the least documented (and thus least understood) features in TCP. You can find what is probably one of the most enlightening discussions of this confusing subject in Chapter 16 of **Internetworking with TCP/IP, Volume II: Design, Implementation, and Internals**, *Douglas E. Comer and David L. Stevens, Prentice Hall, 1994.*

Most computer systems provide some way to let a user terminate a runaway process (such as a "buggy" program caught in an infinite loop). TELNET includes the Interrupt Process (IP) and Abort Output (AO) functions for this purpose. On a stand-alone computer, most operating systems recognize some type of interrupt or break signal that tells the operating system to halt a program or process. For example, DOS recognizes the **CTRL-C** keyboard combination. Windows recognizes the **CTRL-ALT-DEL** keyboard combination. Both sets of keystrokes send an interrupt signal to the operating system.

On networked computers, the network's flow-control mechanisms may buffer an interrupt signal. For example, an interrupt signal transmitted to another host may get stuck in an outgoing-data buffer due to network traffic congestion. As you have learned, TCP uses a full-duplex communication mode. As such, while the user's interrupt signal may be stuck in traffic, the other side of the network highway (data flowing toward the user) may continue to arrive. To counter this problem, TELNET defines a *Synch* mechanism. A TELNET Synch signal consists of a TCP urgent notification and TELNET's DATA MARK command. As you have learned, TCP urgent notification is not subject to flow control. As such, TELNET can use TCP urgent notification to bypass flow control and require the receiver TCP module to immediately process the urgent data in the communication channel. The following paragraphs describe how TELNET processes urgent data.

When a TCP segment with the URG flag arrives, the URG flag signals the fact that the segment contains urgent data. The TCP receiver must immediately notify the receiver application. In other words, TCP does not wait for the application to process data that has already arrived. Instead, TCP places the application in *urgent mode*, which means it tells the application that urgent data has arrived. Typically, when an application is in urgent mode, it reads data from the TCP connection until it reaches the end of urgent data (as identified by the urgent pointer in the TCP segment header). After the application reads the last byte of urgent data, TCP notifies the application that it has processed the last byte of urgent data.

INTERPRETING TCP URGENT DATA

As you may recall from Chapter 5, the TCP urgent pointer should point to the last byte of urgent data. However, many existing implementations erroneously point to the byte past the last byte of urgent data. As you will learn, TELNET's urgent-mode handling of DATA MARK makes this inconsistency irrelevant. As you may recall, the TCP specification does not define urgent data, nor does it specify how an application should handle urgent data. Currently, two schools of thought exist with regard to urgent-data processing. Some Internet professionals prefer to treat urgent data as out-of-band data. Today, the treatment of urgent data as out-of-band data is not popular. As such, *Internet Programming* will not discuss the out-of-band interpretation of TCP urgent data.

Note: The out-of-band interpretation says that protocols should deliver urgent data separate from normal data rather than in-line with normal data.

Today, most applications pattern their treatment of urgent data after TELNET's Synch signal mechanism, which uses the DATA MARK command-byte. This school of thought, called the DATA MARK interpretation, views urgent data as discussed in the following paragraphs. In effect, when in TCP urgent mode, an application can read and either discard or buffer incoming data up to the end of the urgent pointer. How an application behaves and processes the incoming urgent data is application dependent. For example, when in urgent mode, TELNET immediately begins to scan the incoming data stream for TELNET commands and simply discards any intervening data.

To send the TELNET Synch signal, an application sends a TCP segment with the Urgent (URG) flag set and DATA MARK as the last (or only) data byte. The TELNET DATA MARK is the synchronizing mark in the data stream that tells the receiver application when it can resume normal processing of the data stream. In other words, when the receiver is in urgent mode, DATA MARK signals the end of the urgent processing. When in normal mode, the receiver treats a DATA MARK as a no operation command—in other words, in normal mode, the receiver does nothing. If TCP signals the end of urgent data before the receiver finds a DATA MARK, the TELNET specification requires the receiver to continue special handling of the data stream until it finds a DATA MARK. In other words, after TCP places the receiver in urgent mode, the receiver continues to read and discard data until it finds a DATA MARK.

The TELNET specification also lets a receiver merge multiple urgent notifications. For example, suppose the receiver finds a DATA MARK but TCP signals that more urgent data exists. (In other words, TCP does not notify the receiver that it has reached the end of urgent data). This can only mean that TCP received another Synch signal. In such cases, the receiver application should continue the special handling of the data stream (reading and discarding data) until it finds another DATA MARK. In effect, the TELNET Synch signal clears the communication channel (between the TELNET sender and receiver) of all data except TELNET commands. The TELNET specification describes how other protocols can use the Synch signal for similar purposes. For example, as you will learn, FTP defines an abort command (ABOR) designed to cancel a file-transfer operation. According to the TELNET specification, an application that uses the TELNET Synch signal should perform the following steps:

1. Send the TELNET IP character.

2. Send the TELNET Sync sequence. That is, transmit DATA MARK (DM) as the only character in a TCP urgent-mode send operation.

3. Send the other protocol's urgent-data command—the FTP abort (ABOR) command, for example.

4. Send the other protocol's equivalent to the TELNET DATA MARK, if any such equivalent exists.

As you will learn, this is precisely how FTP interrupts a file-transfer process.

MANAGING THE CONNECTIONS

As you have learned, FTP-based client programs use the control connection to send commands to, and receive replies from, the FTP server. Typically, the FTP service commands the client sends across the control connection ask the server to either perform some file-related action on the server's system or to transfer information across the data connection. The FTP client creates the control connection in the same way that previous clients that you have examined in *Internet Programming* created a connection to a remote host. In other words, the client creates a socket and then connects it to the server's well-known port. The client sends FTP commands to the FTP server across the control connection just like the SMTP and POP3 clients transmitted commands to their respective servers.

In other words, for the FTP control connection, there is nothing new for you to learn. You have seen the same TCP connection process repeated numerous times for the other client programs *Internet Programming* presents. However, the FTP data connection is a different matter. As you will learn in the following section, the FTP client follows a different procedure to create the FTP data connection. Although the procedure to create a data connection (as described in the following section) is new in terms of the programming statements used, previous chapters have presented all the concepts you need to understand the procedure. In other words, in previous chapters of *Internet Programming*, you have not written any programs that create a connection like the data connection. However, you will have no trouble understanding the process.

REVIEWING A TYPICAL FTP SESSION

A typical FTP session goes through four stages. First, an FTP client program connects to an FTP server. Second, the user logs into the FTP server host. Third, the FTP client and server exchange command and reply messages similar to those SMTP and POP3 servers and clients exchange. (Typically, some commands will result in a file transfer between the communicating host computers.) Fourth, the FTP client closes the connection with the FTP server. The FTP protocol uses TCP connections for all communications. FTP clients establish a TCP connection to an FTP server in the same way as they establish any other TCP connection. FTP clients contact FTP servers at well-known port number 21. FTP servers typically accept a connection and then transmit a 220 reply code as shown here:

```
220 Service ready
```

In many cases, the 220 reply message will be multiline, with several lines of text that tell the user how to login. After the FTP client receives a 220 reply code, the FTP login process begins. Typically, the FTP server host will require the FTP client to transmit a username and a password. The FTP server, in turn, will send a reply message for each transmission. A typical FTP-command-and-server-reply exchange during the login process looks like this:

```
USER username
331 User name ok, need password
PASS secret
230 User logged in
```

After logging in, the user may send FTP commands to change the working directory on the FTP server host. After the user finds a file they want to retrieve, FTP requires the client and server to establish a second TCP connection to carry the data for the file-transfer operation. To tell the server which protocol port on the FTP client host to contact, the client transmits an FTP PORT command. Next, to initiate the file-transfer operation, the client transmits the retrieve (RETR) command. The server, in turn, responds as shown here:

```
RETR filename
150 File status okay; about to open data connection
```

After the FTP server transmits the 150 reply code, the server establishes a TCP connection with the FTP client host. The server contacts the client host at the protocol port the client specified in the FTP PORT command. After the FTP client accepts the connection from the FTP server, the server immediately begins to transfer the requested file. If the file transfer completes successfully, the server transmits a 226 reply code, as shown here:

```
226 Closing data connection, file transfer successful
```

The FTP client uses a similar process to transfer files from the client host to the server host. However, instead of the retrieve (RETR) command, the client transmits the store (STOR) command. For an anonymous FTP login, the server typically will not accept file transfers from the client. As such, the client and server exchange would look something like this:

```
STOR filename
550 Access denied
```

When the user decides to terminate the FTP session, the client will transmit the quit (QUIT) command and the server will respond as shown here:

```
QUIT
221 Good-bye
```

CREATING THE DATA CONNECTION

FTP-based programs use the data connection for three basic purposes:

- To send a listing of files or directories from the server to the client
- To send a file from the client to the server
- To send a file from the server to the client

FTP servers use the FTP data connection to send file listings to the FTP client. Although the server could use a multiline response to a file-list query, the data connection offers a couple of advantages. First, an FTP implementation may limit the number of lines that a multiline response can include. Second, sending file listings through the data connection makes it easier for a terminal-based FTP user to capture and save file listings in a file. When either the client or server uses the data connection to transfer files (or other information, such as a file listing), they usually follow the procedure described next. First, the client creates the data connection. Because the client initiates all commands that require use of the data connection, the client must also create the connection to receive the requested data. However, also remember that the client transmits its requests across the control connection—not the data connection itself. This distinction highlights an important difference between the FTP client and previous clients that you have examined in *Internet Programming*.

With previous client programs discussed in *Internet Programming*, the client also created the connection. However, in previous cases, the client performed an active open on the connection. That is, the client created a socket and then actively connected it to the remote host. In effect, the client and server exchanged messages across a socket connected to the server's well-known protocol port. The FTP control connection remains open during the entire FTP session with the server. However, the FTP client creates and maintains the data connection only as long as a transfer operation is in progress. After a transfer operation completes, the client closes the data connection. In other words, the FTP client maintains the data connection only for the duration of a particular transfer operation. Each time the client needs to exchange data with the server (across the data connection), the client creates a new data connection. The key point to note here is that the FTP data transfers do not occur at a well-known port—they occur on a port that the client's host selects.

As such, an FTP client must perform a passive open on the data-connection socket and then tell the server which port on the client's host to contact. Otherwise, the FTP server has no idea where to send the data the client requested through the control connection. After the client tells the FTP server which protocol port to use, the server performs an active open, and the client's host uses the socket and protocol port the FTP client specified. In other words, for the data connection, the FTP client acts like a server. The client creates a socket, binds the socket to a local address, tells the server which address to contact, and then listens for an incoming connection. However, the difference between an FTP client and a real server is that an FTP client only accepts a connection from the FTP server on the other end of the control connection. As you may recall from the concurrent and iterative server discussions in previous chapters, a server socket typically stores a wildcard for the remote host address. In other words, the server socket accepts connections from any remote host. An FTP client stores the address of the FTP server in the socket created for the data connection. As such, the socket will accept only connections from the FTP server. The same process to create the data connection occurs regardless of whether the client wants to send or receive a file. In both cases, the client creates the socket, binds it to a local address, tells the FTP server which port to contact, and then listens for a connection from the FTP server. In other words, in both cases (for sending and receiving files), the FTP client performs a passive open and the FTP server performs the active open.

Aborting a File Transfer

As previously discussed, the FTP client uses the TELNET protocol across the control connection to communicate with the FTP server. In actuality, the SMTP and POP3 clients discussed in the previous chapter (as well as most other application protocols not discussed in *Internet Programming*) also use the TELNET protocol to communicate with their respective servers. In effect, TELNET is TCP/IP's virtual-terminal protocol. As you have learned, the TELNET protocol defines the network virtual-terminal (NVT) ASCII that SMTP, POP3, FTP, and other application protocols use. Most application protocols, such as SMTP and POP3, use the TELNET protocol to transmit their own protocol-defined commands to their protocol servers.

The difference between FTP and the other application protocols discussed in *Internet Programming* is that FTP also actually uses some of the TELNET protocol commands. That is, SMTP and POP3 use the TELNET protocol to transmit commands to their servers. However, the only commands that SMTP and POP3 transmit are the command strings defined by their respective protocols. The FTP protocol also defines command strings similar to the SMTP and POP3 command strings. However, as discussed in the section *Understanding the FTP/TELNET Relationship*, FTP also uses the TELNET Synch signal, which is actually a TELNET-defined command.

FTP commands fall into three categories: access-control identifiers, data transfer parameters, and FTP service requests. An FTP client can send certain commands (such as ABOR, STAT, QUIT) over the control connection while a data transfer is in progress. Some servers may not be able to monitor the control and data connections at the same time. Such servers require special action to get the server's attention during the transfer process. The FTP specification (RFC 959) outlines the following procedure to get an FTP server's attention during a file-transfer operation. As you will see, the procedure is essentially identical to the procedure defined by the TELNET specification as described in this chapter's section *Understanding the TELNET Synch Signal*. FTP tentatively recommends the following procedure:

1. The user system inserts the TELNET *Interrupt Process* (IP) signal in the TELNET stream (across the control connection).

2. The user system sends the TELNET *Synch* signal—a segment that contains the TELNET DATA MARK command byte only.

3. The user system inserts the FTP command (ABOR, for example) in the TELNET stream (across the control connection).

4. The server protocol interpreter (PI), after receiving the IP command byte, scans the TELNET stream *for exactly one FTP* command.

In other words, during a file transfer operation, FTP uses TCP urgent data to place the FTP server in urgent mode. After placing the FTP server in urgent mode, the client transmits the FTP command to which the client wants a response. When an FTP server is in urgent mode, it scans the control connection data stream until it finds an FTP command string and then responds. If the server host cannot manage two TCP connections at the same time, the FTP server will pause the file transfer operation, respond to the urgent data request from the client, and then resume file transfer operations.

As the specification mentions, this procedure may be unnecessary for some servers but the actions listed should have no unusual effect on such servers. In other words, if the server is capable of managing two TCP connections at the same time, the server will respond to the urgent data command request while continuing the file transfer operations without pause. In either case, the net effect is the same. The FTP server responds to the client's request during the file transfer operation without aborting the file transfer. Obviously, if the client's urgent data request is to abort the file transfer, the server will do so. However, the aborted file transfer occurs as a direct result of the client's request. The interruption (on the control connection) does not cause the FTP server to abort the file transfer.

DEFINING THE *FTP* COMMANDS

The File Transfer Protocol includes over thirty commands that an FTP-based program can use to manage file-transfer operations. The FTP commands fall into three categories: access-control commands, transfer-parameter commands, and service commands. The access-control commands transmit information that either identifies the user to the server or tells the server what locations (directories) the client program wishes to access. The transfer-parameter commands let the client define the FTP options previously discussed: file types, file formats, file structures, and transmission modes. The FTP service commands define the file-transfer operation that the user wants to perform. The following sections discuss the FTP commands currently defined for each category. Each of the command descriptions include possible reply status values. Table 16.9 (presented later in this chapter) describes the possible reply codes in detail.

DEFINING THE ACCESS-CONTROL COMMANDS

Access-control commands either identify the user to the FTP server or tell the server what locations the client program wishes to access. Before you examine the access-control commands in detail, you should understand that FTP users can transmit the USER, PASS, and ACCT access-control commands several times during a single FTP session. The USER command transmits a username, the PASS command transmits a password, and the ACCT command transmits an account name or number. Some FTP servers let a client transmit a new USER command at any point during the FTP session. A client might do so to change the access control and/or accounting information. Essentially, a new USER command starts the login sequence all over again. However, all transfer parameters remain unchanged and the server will complete any file transfer operations already in progress.

In effect, a new USER command lets you change who the server believes is using the FTP client program without forcing the user to close the FTP command and log back into the system with a new username. Obviously, a new username will probably require a new password, so the server will permit a new PASS command also. FTP does not associate the ACCT command with the USER command. Some networks may require accounting information only when the user performs certain operations, such as storing files. As such, FTP does not restrict the ACCT command's usage. In other words, the client may transmit the ACCT command (and argument) at any time during the FTP session (that is, whenever it is appropriate to do so).

USERNAME (USER)

As you have learned, before you can access the files at an FTP site, you must first log into the site by specifying a username and password. The USER command requires an argument that identifies the user to the server. The parameter can contain whatever value the server requires for access. For example, in the case of anonymous FTP, the user parameter would be *anonymous*. Typically, the USER command is the first command the client transmits after it establishes the control connection. The USER command does not guarantee access to the server. In other words, the server may require additional identification information in the form of a password and/or an account. Possible reply codes are: 230, 331, 332, 421, 500, 501, 530.

PASSWORD (PASS)

After you specify a username to the FTP site, you must specify a password. The PASS command requires an argument that specifies the user's password. A client can only transmit this command immediately after the USER command. Most FTP-based client programs mask or hide the user's password—the client does not display the password on the client's computer screen. However, the client transmits the password as an ordinary ASCII character string—unencoded. Possible reply codes are: 202, 230, 332, 421, 500, 501, 503, 530.

ACCOUNT (ACCT)

The ACCT command requires an argument that identifies the user's account. Typically, user accounts let the remote system track accounting information. In other words, suppose a company has a large data processing center. Employees in the center may work for several different departments or divisions within the company. In such cases, a company may require computer users to enter a charge account when they log into the company's computer network. The company can use the accounting information to track hours and costs associated with particular projects or business operations. Possible reply codes are: 202, 230, 421, 500, 501, 503, 530.

CHANGE WORKING DIRECTORY (CWD)

Like most computer systems, FTP server hosts store files in subdirectories. Most file-related FTP commands, such as those that retrieve or store files, operate in the working directory on the remote host. As users retrieve files from an FTP site, they may need to move from one directory to another. The CWD command lets the user move to a different directory on the remote host. CWD requires an argument that specifies a path to directory. Possible reply codes are: 250, 421, 500, 501, 502, 530, 550.

CHANGE TO PARENT DIRECTORY (CDUP)

Frequently, while changing the working directory on a remote host, a user will simply want to change to the next higher subdirectory. CDUP is a special case of CWD. CDUP changes the default directory to the next level above the current directory. FTP includes CDUP primarily to simplify the implementation of programs that transfer entire directory trees between operating systems that use different syntax for naming parent directories. Possible reply codes are: 250, 421, 500, 501, 502, 530, 550.

STRUCTURE MOUNT (SMNT)

As you may know, the UNIX operating system lets privileged users mount multiple file systems (disks) which, in effect, add files and directories to the UNIX computer. In a similar way, the SMNT command lets an FTP user mount a file system data structure. SMNT requires an argument that specifies a path to a directory or some other system-dependent file group designator. Possible reply codes are: 202, 250, 421, 500, 501, 502, 530, 550.

REINITIALIZE (REIN)

The REIN returns the client to the state that immediately follows the establishment of the control connection. In other words, after receiving a REIN command, the server probably expects a USER command as the next transmission across the control connection. The client can use the REIN command to transfer files for several users without having to close and reopen a connection for each user. In other words, the REIN command terminates a USER. The command flushes all I/O and account information. However, the command lets any transfers-in-progress complete without interruption. FTP resets all parameters to the default settings but keeps the control connection open. Possible reply codes are: 120, 220, 421, 500, 502.

LOGOUT (QUIT)

When a user finishes all file transfers, the user can use the QUIT command to end the FTP session. If a file transfer is not in progress, the server closes the control connection. If a file transfer is in progress, the connection remains open long enough to transmit a reply code. However, the server immediately closes the connection after transmitting the reply code. An unexpected close on the control connection will cause the FTP server to take the effective action of an abort (ABOR) and a logout (QUIT). Possible reply codes are: 221, 500.

DEFINING THE TRANSFER-PARAMETER COMMANDS

As you have learned, FTP users can specify file types, file formats, file structures, and transmission modes. The transfer-parameter commands let the client define these FTP options for the server. All data-transfer parameters have default values that the client can use without change. In other words, unless the client wants to change a particular parameter, the client does not have to issue any transfer-parameter commands. FTP clients can specify transfer-parameter commands in any order. However, the transfer-parameter commands must precede any FTP service request. The commands shown in Table 16.3 specify data-transfer parameters.

Command	Description
PORT	data port
PASV	passive
TYPE	representation type
STRU	file structure
MODE	transfer mode

Table 16.3 The FTP transfer-parameter commands.

DATA PORT (PORT)

As you have learned, FTP requires the client and server to establish a new TCP connection for each file-transfer operation. The file-transfer operations do not occur at the well-known protocol port for FTP. Instead, the server contacts the client at a protocol port the client specifies. The client uses the PORT command to tell the server which port to contact. The PORT command requires an argument that specifies a protocol port the data connection can use. The PORT argument is the combination of a 32-bit Internet host address and a 16-bit TCP port address. The client must break this address information into 8-bit fields and transmit each field value (separated by a comma) as a decimal number in NVT ASCII. For example, suppose your client program is running on jamsa.com (IP address 168.158.20.102) and you want to use protocol port 1150 (0x047E) to receive data. Your program would transmit the PORT command as shown:

```
PORT 168,158,20,102,4,126
```

Possible reply codes are: 220, 421, 500, 501, 530.

PASSIVE (PASV)

Normally, an FTP client tells the server which port on the client host to contact, and the server initiates the TCP connection for the data channel. However, the client can use the PASV command to ask the server's data-transfer process to *listen* on a data port (which is not its default data port) and to wait for a connection rather than initiate one upon receipt of a transfer command. The server responds to this command with its host address and the protocol port on which it will listen. Possible reply codes are: 227, 421, 500, 501, 502, 530.

REPRESENTATION TYPE (TYPE)

The TYPE command tells FTP how to represent a file during a file-transfer operation. FTP can manage four different file-types: local, image, EBCDIC, and ASCII. For ASCII and EBCDIC file transfers, the user can also specify one of three format controls: nonprint, TELNET format control, and FORTRAN carriage control. Table 16.4 lists the various parameter combinations that are available for the TYPE command.

TYPE	Description
A N	Use ASCII file-type with Nonprint format control—the default.
A T	Use ASCII file-type with TELNET format control.
A C	Use ASCII file-type with (FORTRAN) carriage control.
E N	Use EBCDIC file-type with Nonprint format control.
E T	Use EBCDIC file-type with TELNET format control.
E C	Use EBCDIC file-type with (FORTRAN) carriage control.
I	Use Image file-type.
L 8	Use Local file-type (with eight-bit bytes).

Table 16.4 The FTP parameters for the TYPE command.

Possible reply codes are: 200, 421, 500, 501, 504, 530.

FILE STRUCTURE (STRU)

FTP defines three types of structures: file, record, and page. FTP clients use the STRU command to specify which structure to use for file-transfer operations. The STRU command requires a single character as a parameter. As shown in Table 16.5, the parameter specifies one of the FTP structures previously discussed. Possible reply codes are: 200, 421, 500, 501, 504, 530.

STRU Parameter	Description
F	File (no record structure)—the default
R	Record structure
P	Page structure

Table 16.5 The FTP parameters for the STRU command.

TRANSFER MODE (MODE)

FTP also defines three types of file-transfer modes. FTP clients use the MODE command to specify which mode to use. Like the STRU command, MODE also requires a single character as a parameter. As shown in Table 16.6, the parameter specifies one of the FTP transmission modes previously discussed.

MODE Parameter	Description
S	Stream—the default
B	Block
C	Compressed

Table 16.6 The FTP parameters for the MODE command.

Possible reply codes are: 200, 421, 500, 501, 504, 530.

DEFINING THE *FTP* SERVICE COMMANDS

The FTP service commands specify the file-transfer operations that the user wants to perform. As you might expect, the service commands represent the largest category of commands the FTP protocol defines. The argument to an FTP service command will normally be a pathname. The syntax of pathnames must conform to server site conventions. An FTP client can specify service commands in any order, with the exception of the *rename to* command, which must follow a *rename from* command. Also, the client must follow the restart command with the interrupted service command (STOR or RETR, for example). Except for certain informative replies, the FTP server always transfers data in response to a service command across the data connection.

RETRIEVE (RETR)

FTP exists to help users transfer files between a remote host and their local host computer. FTP clients use the RETR command to tell a server to send a file to another host computer (typically, although not necessarily, the client's local host). The RETR command causes the server-DTP (data transfer process) to transfer a copy of the file, specified in the pathname, to the server- or user-DTP at the other end of the data connection. Possible reply codes are: 110, 125, 150, 226, 250, 421, 425, 426, 450, 451, 500, 501, 530, 550.

STORE (STOR)

Just as the RETR command retrieves a file from a remote host, the STOR command lets a user transmit a file to the remote host. STOR causes the server-DTP to accept the data transferred across the data connection and to store the data as a file at the server site. If the file specified in the pathname exists at the server site, the FTP implementation overwrites the file contents with the transferred data. If the file specified in the pathname does not already exist, the file-transfer operation creates a new file at the server site. Possible reply codes are: 110, 125, 150, 226, 250, 421, 425, 426, 450, 451, 452, 500, 501, 530, 532, 551, 552, 553.

STORE UNIQUE (STOU)

The STOU command behaves like STOR except that the file it creates is in the current directory under a name unique to that directory. The FTP server's 250 (Transfer Started) reply code will include the server-generated name. Possible reply codes are: 110, 125, 150, 226, 250, 421, 425, 426, 450, 451, 452, 500, 501, 530, 532, 551, 552, 553.

APPEND (WITH CREATE) (APPE)

The APPE command also behaves like STOR except that APPE will not overwrite an existing file. APPE causes the server-DTP to accept the data transferred across the data connection and to store the data in a file at the server site. If the file specified in the pathname exists at the server site, then the server appends the data to that file. If the file specified in the pathname does not already exist, the file transfer operation creates a new file at the server site. Possible reply codes are: 110, 120, 150, 226, 250, 331, 332, 350, 421, 425, 426, 450, 451, 452, 500, 501, 502, 530, 532, 550, 551, 552, 553.

ALLOCATE (ALLO)

Like any other computer, FTP server hosts have a finite amount of disk storage space. Some servers may require the ALLO command to reserve sufficient storage for the new file that the user wants to transfer. ALLO requires a decimal integer argument (an ASCII text representation of a decimal number) that represents the number of storage bytes that the server needs to reserve for the file. Typically, the client will follow ALLO with a STOR or APPE command. Servers that do not require the ALLO command treat it as a NOOP (no operation). Possible reply codes are: 200, 202, 421, 500, 501, 504, 530.

RESTART (REST)

Occasionally, a user may have to temporarily stop a file-transfer operation. The REST command lets the user restart the file transfer without having to re-transmit previously transferred data. REST requires an argument that tells the server where to restart a transfer. REST does not cause the file transfer to actually resume. REST causes the server to skip over the file to the specified data checkpoint. The client should follow this command with an appropriate FTP service command that causes file transfer to resume. Possible reply codes are: 350, 421, 500, 501, 502, 530.

RENAME FROM (RNFR)

Just as a user can transfer files to a remote host, users can rename existing files on the remote host computer. RNFR specifies the old pathname of a file that the user wants to rename. The client must immediately follow the RNFR command with a *rename to* (RNTO) command that specifies the new file pathname. Possible reply codes are: 350, 421, 450, 500, 501, 502, 530, 550.

RENAME TO (RNTO)

The RNTO command works in conjunction with the RNFR command. RNTO specifies the new pathname of the file identified in the immediately preceding *rename from* (RNFR) command. Together, RNTO and RNFR cause the FTP server to rename a file. Possible reply codes are: 250, 421, 500, 501, 502, 503, 530, 532, 553.

ABORT (ABOR)

Occasionally, a user may need or want to abort a file-transfer operation before it completes. The ABOR command tells the server to abort the previous FTP service command and any associated data transfer in progress. To force the server to recognize this request, FTP may have to use the TELNET Synch signal discussed previously. The server takes no action if the previous command has already completed. Although the server closes the data connection in response to this command, the control connection remains open. An FTP server must handle two conditions under which the ABOR command arrives. First, the FTP service command may have already completed. Second, the FTP service command may still be in progress. In the first case, the server closes the data connection (if it is open) and responds with a 226 reply code. The 226 reply code tells the client that the server successfully processed the abort command. In the second case, the server aborts the FTP service in progress and closes the data connection. In this case, the server returns a 426 reply code to indicate that the service request terminated abnormally. The server then sends a 226 reply code, which indicates that the server successfully processed the abort command. Possible reply codes are: 225, 226, 421, 500, 501, 502.

DELETE (DELE)

Just as users can rename files on a remote host, users can also delete remote host files. The DELE command causes the server to delete the file specified in the command's pathname argument. It is important to note that FTP does not ask for confirmation of this request. In other words, if you want users to conform their request to delete a file, your program must include the confirmation request. Possible reply codes are: 250, 421, 450, 500, 501, 502, 530, 550.

REMOVE DIRECTORY (RMD)

Just as users can delete files on a remote host, users can also remove directories on a remote host. The RMD command causes the server to remove the directory specified in the pathname. Possible reply codes are: 250, 421, 500, 501, 502, 530, 550.

MAKE DIRECTORY (MKD)

If a user is storing a file on the remote host, they may need to create (make) a directory to hold the file. Likewise, users can use the MKD command to cause the server to create the directory that the command's pathname argument specifies. Possible reply codes are: 257, 421, 450, 500, 501, 502, 530, 550.

PRINT WORKING DIRECTORY (PWD)

As users change directories on a remote host, it's possible to forget which directory is the working directory. PWD causes the server to return the name of the working directory as part of the server's reply code. The PWD command is more valuable to users of Ftp command-line programs (which may not always display the working directory) than to users of Windows-based Ftp programs. Typically, a Windows-based Ftp program will maintain a visual display of the working directory. Possible reply codes are: 257, 421, 500, 501, 502, 550.

LIST (LIST)

As a user traverses the directory tree of a remote host, he or she can have the FTP client transmit the LIST command to see the files located in each directory on the remote host. The LIST command causes the server to send a file list. If the pathname specifies a directory or other group of files, the server transfers a list of files in the specified directory. If the pathname specifies a file, the server sends current information about the file. A null argument implies the user's working or default directory. The data transfer occurs across the data connection in type ASCII or type EBCDIC. (The user must ensure that the TYPE is appropriately ASCII or EBCDIC.) Since the information on a file may vary widely from system to system, this information may be hard to automatically use in a program, but may be quite useful to a human user. Possible reply codes are: 125, 150, 226, 250, 421, 425, 426, 450, 451, 500, 501, 502, 530.

NAME LIST (NLST)

The NLST command is similar to LIST. However, NLST returns information that a program can use to further process files automatically. Like the LIST command, NLST causes the server to send a directory listing to the client. The pathname argument should specify a directory or other system-specific file group descriptor. A null argument implies the current directory. The server returns a stream of filenames and no other information. The server will transfer the data in ASCII or EBCDIC type over the data connection as valid pathname strings separated by <CRLF> or <NL>. (Again, the user must ensure that the TYPE is correct.) Possible reply codes are: 125, 150, 226, 250, 257, 421, 425, 426, 450, 451, 500, 501, 502, 530.

SITE PARAMETERS (SITE)

Sometimes a server may provide services (essential to file transfer) that are specific to the server's local system. However, such services may not be sufficiently universal for FTP to include them as commands in the protocol. Typically, the server states the nature of these services and the specification of their syntax in reply to the HELP SITE command. Possible reply codes are: 200, 202, 500, 501, 530.

SYSTEM (SYST)

Users can transmit the SYST command to determine the type of operating system in use at the remote host. As its first word, the server's reply to this command must be one of the system names that the current version of the Internet Assigned Numbers Authority (IANA) RFC lists. Possible reply codes are: 215, 421, 500, 501, 502.

STATUS (STAT)

During unusually long file-transfer operations, a user may want to check the status of the FTP server. The STAT command causes the server to send a status response over the control connection in the form of a reply. The client can send a STAT command during a file transfer (using the TELNET Synch signal, if necessary). The server may respond with the status of the operation in progress, or it may send the information between file transfers. In the latter case, the command may have an argument field. If the argument is a pathname, the command is similar to the LIST command except that the server transfers the data across the control connection. If the user specifies a partial pathname, the server may respond with a list of file names or attributes associated with that specification. If the user gives no argument, the server returns general status information about the server FTP process. Typically, such information includes the current values for all transfer parameters and the status of connections. Possible reply codes are: 211, 212, 213, 421, 450, 500, 501, 502, 530.

HELP (HELP)

If a user has questions about a particular FTP command or possibly about a particular FTP server, the client can transmit the HELP command. HELP causes the server to send helpful information about its implementation status over the control connection to the user. The HELP command may take an argument (any command name, for example) and return more specific information as a response. The reply code is type 211 or 214. The FTP specification suggests that FTP implementations permit users to use the HELP command before entering a USER command. The server may use this reply to specify site-dependent parameters. Possible reply codes are: 211, 214, 421, 500, 501, 502.

NO OPERATION (NOOP)

Well-designed FTP client programs can use the NOOP command to test the connection to the FTP server. NOOP does not affect any parameters or previously entered commands. It specifies no action other than that the server send an OK reply. Possible reply codes are: 200, 421, 500.

DEFINING THE FTP REPLY CODES

The FTP protocol uses a reply-code scheme that is practically identical to the one described in Chapter 17 for SMTP. In other words, each digit in the reply code has special significance. Table 16.7 briefly describes the significance of the first digit in an FTP reply code.

Code	Description
1yz	Positive Preliminary reply: The server initiated the requested action; expect another reply before proceeding with a new command.
2yz	Positive Completion reply: The server successfully completed the requested action. The client can initiate a new request.
3yz	Positive Intermediate reply: The server accepted the command but the requested action requires more information.
4yz	Transient (temporary) Negative Completion reply: The server did not accept the command, and the requested action did not occur.
5yz	Permanent Negative Completion reply: The server did not accept the command and the requested action did not occur.

Table 16.7 The significance of the first digit in FTP reply codes.

Likewise, the second digit in the FTP reply codes refines the message slightly more, as shown in Table 16.8.

Code	Description
x0z	Syntax: These replies refer to syntax errors, syntactically correct commands that don't fit any functional category.
x1z	Information: These are replies to requests for information, such as status or help.
x2z	Connections: These replies refer to the control and data connections.
x3z	Authentication and accounting: These replies are for the login process and accounting procedures.
x4z	Unspecified as yet.
x5z	File system: These replies indicate the status of the Server file system vis-à-vis the requested transfer or other file system action.

Table 16.8 The significance of the second digit in FTP reply codes.

Table 16.9 lists the control codes the FTP specification currently defines.

Code	Description
110	Restart marker reply. In this case, the text is exact and not left to the particular implementation.
120	Service ready in nnn minutes.
125	Data connection already open; transfer starting.
150	File status okay; about to open data connection.
200	Command okay.

Table 16.9 Currently defined FTP reply codes. (continued on the next page)

Code	Description
202	Command not implemented, superfluous at this site.
211	System status, or system help reply.
212	Directory status.
213	File status.
214	Help message.
215	NAME system type.
220	Service ready for new user.
221	Service closing control connection. Logged out if appropriate.
225	Data connection open; no transfer in progress.
226	Closing data connection. Requested file action successful.
227	Entering Passive Mode
230	User logged in, proceed.
250	Requested file action okay, completed.
257	"PATHNAME" created.
331	User name okay, need password.
332	Need account for login.
350	Requested file action pending further information.
421	Service not available, closing control connection.
425	Can't open data connection.
426	Connection closed; transfer aborted.
450	Requested file action not taken. File unavailable.
451	Requested action aborted: local error in processing.
452	Requested action not taken. Insufficient storage space in system.
500	Syntax error, command unrecognized.
501	Syntax error in parameters or arguments.
502	Command not implemented.
503	Bad sequence of commands.
504	Command not implemented for that parameter.
530	Not logged in.
532	Need account for storing files.
550	Requested action not taken. File unavailable.
551	Requested action aborted: page type unknown.
552	Requested file action aborted. Exceeded storage allocation.
553	Requested action not taken. File name not allowed.

Table 16.9 Currently defined FTP reply codes. (continued from the previous page)

PUTTING IT ALL TOGETHER

In this chapter, you learned that the Internet defines three file-transfer protocols. Although Internet users predominately use one protocol (the File Transfer Protocol), other file-transfer protocols, such as the Trivial File Transfer Protocol, offer capabilities you can use in custom applications or custom protocols. This chapter discussed the FTP model for file-transfer operations, which uses two separate but cooperating TCP connections to pass data between an FTP client and server. This chapter also examined FTP options that support various file types, formats, structures, and transmission modes. As you learned, many FTP options are holdovers from the Internet's early years, and many hosts no longer support many of the options the FTP specification defines.

This chapter discussed how FTP uses the TELNET protocol across its control connection. You also learned how an FTP client uses the TELNET DATA MARK interpretation of TCP urgent data to communicate with an FTP server in the middle of a file-transfer operation. This chapter also discussed each of the FTP command strings and presented tables with the FTP reply codes to these commands. In Section 3 of *Internet Programming*, you will learn how to use visual-programming techniques to develop Internet programs and see examples of programs that access the Internet's WorldWide Web. Section 3 will also walk through the creation of a hypothetical custom protocol. Before you continue with Section 3 and the next chapter, make sure you understand the following key concepts:

✓ Simple protocols, such as the Trivial File Transfer Protocol, provide excellent frameworks from which you can build a custom protocol.

✓ The FTP file-transfer model uses two TCP connections for file transfer operations: one channel carries command and control information and the other carries data, such as files and directory information.

✓ TELNET represents a network-virtual-terminal (NVT) protocol.

✓ FTP defines over 30 NVT ASCII-based commands that include access-control identifiers, file-transfer parameters, and file-transfer service requests.

✓ TELNET defines its commands as special escape sequences.

✓ FTP clients use the TELNET Synch signal to send commands to an FTP server during a file-transfer operation.

Chapter 17
Programming the Internet with DLLs

As your knowledge of Internet programming grows, you will begin to develop your own collection of functions that perform key tasks. In fact, throughout the last few chapters, you have already started your collection of useful Internet-based functions. By placing these functions within your own custom dynamic link library (DLL), you make it easier for your future programs to use them. For example, WINSOCK.DLL is a Windows dynamic link library whose functions provide your programs with access to the TCP/IP-based sockets. To have your programs use a WINSOCK.DLL function, you only need to understand what task the function performs, not how the function actually performs the task.

In this chapter, you will develop a simple Windows DLL that you can use with practically any visual-programming tool to create FTP-based client programs. Within this Windows DLL, you will encapsulate your core network algorithms and thereby build your own "programming layer" that hides the network I/O details and lets you focus on the visual aspects of your Internet programs. By the time you finish this chapter, you will understand the following key concepts:

- How to create and manage an FTP control connection

- How to create a client socket that listens for connection

- How to create a simple yet powerful DLL that encapsulates Winsock-based functions that perform FTP-client operations

REVIEWING THE GAME PLAN

Chapters 17 and 18 use the quick-program model to develop a fully-functional, FTP-based program. *Internet Programming* builds the Ftp program in four stages. Stage one (QFTP1) sets up the framework for managing the FTP control channel. Stage two (QFTP2) adds the data channel. Stage three (QFTP3) modifies and adds functions to create a Winsock back-end. And stage four creates QFTPLIB (which is actually a dynamic link library) and a Visual Basic front-end called SOCKFTP. This chapter will cover stages one, two, and three. Chapter 18 will cover stage four. You will find complete source code for all four stages of the Quick FTP (QFTP) program (as well as the SOCKFTP program) on *Internet Programming's* companion disk.

FTP: A QUICK REVIEW

As explained in the previous chapter, the File Transfer Protocol (FTP) uses two TCP connections: a control channel and a data channel. The control channel remains open during the entire session with a remote host. Your program uses the control channel to tell the server what file operations you want the server to perform. The QFTP1 (quick FTP, stage 1) program establishes a control connection to an FTP server. QFTP2 (quick FTP, stage 2) opens a data channel (the other TCP connection). However, as explained in the last chapter, FTP clients open and close the data channel for each transaction. In other words, each time the client needs to perform a file-transfer operation (either to or from the server), the client opens a new data channel. In most cases, the server closes the data channel immediately after the file-transfer operation completes.

The server uses the data channel to transfer and receive data, such as files and directory listings. Through the control channel, the server receives commands from, and transmits reply codes to, the client. In other words, with FTP, you may have two full-duplex communication processes occurring at the same time. As explained in the next section, to start, QFTP1 ignores the data channel and focuses strictly on the control channel.

STAGE ONE: CONTROLLING THE SERVER

As discussed, unless a file transfer (or directory listing) operation occurs, an FTP client does not need to open (or use) the FTP data channel. To keep matters simple, this chapter implements the control-channel functions and the data-channel function in two separate steps. This section builds QFTP1—a quick program model for an FTP client that uses the FTP control channel only.

DESIGNING THE PROGRAM

In previous quick programs, typically, you used only one or two program functions. For example, the early quick programs used only the WinMain function. In later quick programs, a separate function contained the program statements that establish client/server connections. Although previous programs in this book could have consisted of many smaller function definitions, *Internet Programming* collected all or most of the program statements together into larger groups. By doing so, *Internet Programming* did not force you to jump from one function to another during the discussions. Although QFTP1 uses six functions, you will find that you have encountered similar or identical program statements in previous chapters. In other words, QFTP1 performs network communication in a familiar way.

REVIEWING FTP REPLY CODES

As you learned in the previous chapter, the FTP protocol defines a flexible yet unambiguous system of reply codes. FTP reply codes (like those the Simple Mail Transfer Protocol uses) consist of a three-digit number. Each digit in the reply-code number is significant. For example, the first digit defines a general level of success or failure. The second and third digits provide more refined success and failure definitions. Depending on whether you need a sophisticated client or simple client, your programs may never need to examine any digit of the reply code other than the first. The GetReplyCode function accepts a pointer to a buffer that contains a reply-code character string from an FTP server. As shown next, the function converts the three text characters in the reply code to an integer value and then returns the reply code (as an integer) to your programs:

```
UINT GetReplyCode(LPSTR lpszServerReply)
{
  UINT nCode;                                  // Reply code as a number
  char c;                                      // Temporary storage

  c = *(lpszServerReply+3);                     // Save the character
  *(lpszServerReply+3) = '\0';                  // Terminate the code

  nCode = atoi((const char *)lpszServerReply);  // Convert code to number
  *(lpszServerReply+3) = c;                     // Restore the character

  return(nCode);                                // Return the reply code
}
```

Note that the atoi function requires a NULL-terminated string. As such, the GetReplyCode function inserts a NULL character into the string immediately after the reply code. However, the lpszServerReply buffer contains the full text of the server's reply—not just the reply code. Before inserting the NULL, the GetReplyCode function saves, in variable c, the character that the NULL will overwrite. As you can see, after the atoi function returns, GetReplyCode restores the character that it previously overwrote with the null-terminator. As discussed, the server reply contains the reply code and a descriptive task-string message. In some cases, your programs may also want to use the text portion of the FTP server's replies. (To do so, your programs examine the reply buffer.) However, convert reply code text characters into integers.

TRAPPING ERRORS

As you may have noticed, the previous quick programs did not perform a lot of error checking. Although error checking is extremely necessary for production programs, error checks tend to clutter a program and obscure implementation details. The assumption underlying the program examples *Internet Programming* uses is that you bought this book primarily to learn from the program examples, not necessarily to use the examples (unmodified) in your own programs (although you are certainly welcome to do so). If, in the program examples, you encounter flaws that result from insufficient error checking, keep in mind our goal to produce easy-to-understand examples that illustrate important Internet programming concepts. Although *Internet Programming's* goal does not change in this chapter, the QFTP programs herein do contain significantly more error trapping than the earlier quick programs. Because later sections of this chapter incorporate the program functions into a DLL, more error checking is both appropriate and necessary. In the program source files, you will find error checks that typically look something like this:

```
if ((result = function()) == ERROR_CONDITION)
{
  int iWinsockErr = WSAGetLastError();
  wsprintf(szBuffer,
        "Error #%d occurred while doing this operation.", iWinsockErr);
  MessageBeep(MB_ICONHAND);
  MessageBox(NULL, szCommandBuffer, lpszFunctionName,
```

```
        MB_OK|MB_ICONSTOP);
    return(ERROR_CONDITION);
}
```

Note the use of the lpszFunctionName variable in the MessageBox function call. Another feature of the QFTP programs is that each function contains a statement similar to the one shown here:

```
lpszFunctionName = "ConnectFTPControlSocket";
```

The lpszFunctionName variable is a global pointer (LPSTR). Throughout the QFTP programs, a program statement at the beginning of each function assigns the function name to the lpszFunctionName pointer. As shown in the previous MessageBox statement, each function can use the lpszFunctionName pointer in MessageBox statements to show you where different activities occur within the QFTP programs. You may find such information extremely helpful when you troubleshoot DLL problems from another environment (such as Visual Basic).

If-Else versus Multiple Return Paths

As you may have noticed, the later programs in this book often use multiple return paths when sound programming practice calls for nested if-else constructs. We chose to avoid the wider nested-if statements because of the fixed width of our pages and because wrapped code is difficult to read. If you dislike multiple return paths and prefer nested if-else constructs, you can easily re-write the function definitions.

Reviewing the Big Picture

Like previous quick programs, QFTP1 uses symbolic constants to eliminate user-interface requirements. In other words, rather than adding statements to perform user I/O to get site information, the program assigns specific site information to the symbolic constants. To change the site information, you must change these constants and then recompile your program. As previously discussed, Internet host NIC.DDN.MIL maintains an online archive of RFCs and other useful Internet documentation. As you have learned, many FTP sites permit anonymous FTP access. NIC.DDN.MIL is one such host. NIC.DDN.MIL is also a convenient test site since the FTP login instructions request that you use the password *guest* instead of your Internet e-mail address. The QFTP programs use the following symbolic constants to connect to NIC.DDN.MIL:

```
#define HOST_NAME "NIC.DDN.MIL"
#define PASSWORD "PASS guest\r\n"
```

The following statements implement the WinMain function for QFTP1:

```
int PASCAL WinMain(HANDLE hInstance, HANDLE hPrevInstance,
    LPSTR lpszCmdParam, int nCmdShow)
{
```

```
    WSADATA wsaData;
    SOCKET hControlChannel;
    UINT nReplyCode;

    lpszFunctionName = "WinMain";

    if (WSAStartup(WINSOCK_VERSION, &wsaData))
      // ...Handle the error and return.

    hControlChannel = ConnectFTPControlSocket((LPSTR)HOST_NAME);

    if (hControlChannel != INVALID_SOCKET)
      {
        // If the control sockek is valid, then login.
        nReplyCode = AnonymousFTPLogIn(hControlChannel);

        if (nReplyCode == 230) // User logged in; okay to proceed.
          {
            SendFTPCommand(hControlChannel, "QUIT\r\n");
            closesocket(hControlChannel);
          }
      }

  WSACleanup();
  MessageBeep(MB_ICONEXCLAMATION);
  MessageBox(NULL, "THE END!!", PROG_NAME, MB_OK|MB_ICONEXCLAMATION);
  return(NULL);
}
```

As you can see, after initializing Winsock with the WSAStartup function, WinMain calls ConnectFTPControlSocket and stores the returned socket handle in the hControlChannel variable. As its name implies, ConnectFTPControlSocket creates and connects a socket to the FTP server. This socket represents the control channel for all other QFTP functions that must talk to the server. After making sure ConnectFTPControlSocket returned a valid handle, WinMain calls the AnonymousFTPLogIn function to perform an anonymous login. As you can see, WinMain expects to see a reply code 230 from the login process. If you refer to the FTP specification, you will find that reply code 230 means that the computer logged the user in and that it's okay to proceed. In this case, after successfully logging in, the program will simply log out and end. To log out, WinMain sends the FTP "QUIT" command and then closes the control socket.

OPENING THE CONTROL CHANNEL

To open the control channel, the ConnectFTPControlSocket function creates and connects a socket to the FTP server. First, ConnectFTPControlSocket uses the gethostbyname function to resolve a host name. Second, ConnectFTPControlSocket uses the socket function to create a socket.

Third, ConnectFTPControlSocket uses getservbyname to retrieve service information (for FTP in this case) from the network services database. Fourth, ConnectFTPControlSocket constructs a socket address by assigning port and address information to an Internet socket-address structure (SOCKADDR_IN). Fifth, ConnectFTPControlSocket uses the connect function to connect the socket to the remote host. And sixth, ConnectFTPControlSocket uses the ReadFTPServerReply function to read the server's greeting.

The ConnectFTPControlSocket function definition in QFTP1 remains the same for all QFTP versions. The following program statements show the complete function definition for ConnectFTPControlSocket (minus error-handling):

```
SOCKET ConnectFTPControlSocket(LPSTR lpszHost)
{
  LPHOSTENT lpHostEnt;          // Internet host information structure
  SOCKADDR_IN sockAddr;         // Socket address structure
  LPSERVENT lpServEnt;          // Service information structure
  short nProtocolPort;          // Protocol port
  int nConnect;                 // Socket connection results

  SOCKET hControlSocket = INVALID_SOCKET;

  lpszFunctionName = "ConnectFTPControlSocket";

  if (!(lpHostEnt = gethostbyname(lpszHost)))
    // ...Handle the error and return.

  if ((hControlSocket = socket(PF_INET, SOCK_STREAM, IPPROTO_TCP))
      == INVALID_SOCKET)
    // ...Handle the error and return.

  lpServEnt = getservbyname("ftp", DEFAULT_PROTOCOL);

  if (lpServEnt == NULL)
    nProtocolPort = htons(IPPORT_FTP);
  else
    nProtocolPort = lpServEnt->s_port;

  // Define the socket address
  sockAddr.sin_family = AF_INET;
  sockAddr.sin_port = nProtocolPort;
  sockAddr.sin_addr = *((LPIN_ADDR)*lpHostEnt->h_addr_list);

  // Connect the socket
  if (nConnect = connect(hControlSocket, (LPSOCKADDR)&sockAddr,
      sizeof(sockAddr)))
    // ...Handle the error and return.
```

```
  if (ReadFTPServerReply(hControlSocket) >= 400)
    return(INVALID_SOCKET);
  else
    return(hControlSocket);
}
```

As you may recall from previous quick programs, many protocols require a client program to send some type of message to the server after the client establishes a connection. In contrast, an FTP server sends the client a greeting after the client establishes the connection. As shown in step six of the function outline, just before the ConnectFTPControlSocket function returns, it calls the ReadFTPServerReply function, which reads the server's reply from the control channel. If the server reply code is 400 or greater (indicating an error), ConnectFTPControlSocket returns INVALID_SOCKET. Otherwise, ConnectFTPControlSocket returns the socket handle for the control channel.

READING THE SERVER'S REPLIES

In the stage two modifications (QFTP2), you will make significant changes to the ReadFTPServerReply function. However, for stage one (QFTP1), the function is not much more that a single call to the Winsock recv function. Notice that the function adds a null-terminator to the end of the buffer before it calls the Windows MessageBox function to display the server's reply. Also note that the value ReadFTPServerReply returns is the reply code as passed by the GetReplyCode function discussed earlier. In other words, the primary purpose of the ReadFTPServerReply function is to read the control channel and report the server's reply code to a function that calls ReadFTPServerReply:

```
UINT ReadFTPServerReply(SOCKET hControlChannel)
{
  char sReceiveBuffer[1024];
  int iLength;

  lpszFunctionName = "ReadFTPServerReply";

  if ((iLength = recv(hControlChannel, (LPSTR)sReceiveBuffer,
         sizeof(sReceiveBuffer), NO_FLAGS)) == SOCKET_ERROR)
    // ...Handle the error and return.

  sReceiveBuffer[iLength] = '\0';
  MessageBeep(MB_ICONASTERISK);
  MessageBox(NULL, (LPSTR)sReceiveBuffer, lpszFunctionName,
         MB_OK|MB_ICONINFORMATION);

  return(GetReplyCode(sReceiveBuffer));
}
```

Normally, programs that send commands to an FTP server will also call the ReadFTPServerReply function to get the server's reply. In other words, program functions that communicate with the FTP server and make decisions based on the server's replies depend very heavily on ReadFTPServerReply, which makes the ReadFTPServerReply function an important player in the final QFTP design.

SENDING COMMANDS TO THE FTP SERVER

Before an FTP server will accept requests for file transfers, the user must log into the FTP server's host system. The AnonymousFTPLogIn function is not essential it's only purpose is to provide a convenient program structure for experimenting with FTP commands that return replies through the FTP control channel. As shown next, AnonymousFTPLogIn simply includes the USER command and the PASSWORD constant defined at the beginning of the program:

```
UINT AnonymousFTPLogIn(SOCKET hControlSocket)
{
   int nReplyCode;                    // FTP server reply code
     int iMsg = 0;                    // Index subscript for FTP commands

   lpszFunctionName = "AnonymousFTPLogIn";

   char *LoginCommand[] =
      {
      "USER anonymous\r\n",
      PASSWORD,
      NULL
      };

   do {
      nReplyCode = SendFTPCommand(hControlSocket,
           (LPSTR)LoginCommand[iMsg++]);
   } while (LoginCommand[iMsg] && nReplyCode < 400);

   return(nReplyCode);
}
```

To experiment with other commands such as PWD and SYST, simply insert the command strings in the LoginCommand[] array before the NULL entry. If you experiment with QFTP1, do not transmit any commands that use the data channel. (If you are unsure which commands require your program to use the data channel, refer back to the FTP command descriptions in the previous chapter). As you can see, the core program statement in AnonymousFTPLogIn is the call to SendFTPCommand. Just as the ReadFTPServerReply function is a "wrapper" around the Winsock recv function, the SendFTPCommand function is a wrapper around the Winsock send function. As shown next, SendFTPCommand transmits a command string to the FTP server through the control channel (which the control socket handle, hControlHandle, identifies):

```
UINT SendFTPCommand(SOCKET hControlChannel, LPSTR szCommandBuffer)
{
  lpszFunctionName = "SendFTPCommand";

  // Send the FTP command
  if ((send(hControlChannel, (LPSTR)szCommandBuffer,
       lstrlen(szCommandBuffer), NO_FLAGS)) == SOCKET_ERROR)
    {
      int iWinsockErr = WSAGetLastError();
      wsprintf(szCommandBuffer, "Error %d from the send() function!!",
           iWinsockErr);
      MessageBeep(MB_ICONHAND);
      MessageBox(NULL, szCommandBuffer, lpszFunctionName,
           MB_OK|MB_ICONSTOP);
      // Return 999 to indicate an error has occurred
      return(999);
    }

  return(ReadFTPServerReply(hControlChannel));
}
```

As you will learn in Chapter 18, the final version of QFTP uses the same SendFTPCommand function as QFTP1. In other words, the program statements in the QFTP2 and QFTPLIB versions of SendFTPCommand are the same as shown here. As such, the previous code listing shows the complete function definition, including the SOCKET_ERROR handling code. As indicated by the program comment about the 999 return value, the SendFTPCommand function returns 999 when an error occurs. If you design a production version of a program based on the QFTP example programs, you should define an error code for each different error that your program handles. However, for the QFTP example programs, *Internet Programming* uses 999 as a generic return value to indicate that an error occurred within a QFTP function.

UNDERSTANDING THE CONTROL CHANNEL

Although QFTP1 includes twice as many function definitions as previous quick programs, the functions really contain no new program constructs. Likewise, QFTP1 does not use the Winsock API in any unconventional way. In other words, as previously stated, your programs manage the FTP control channel in the same way as they manage most other Internet socket connections. In summary, QFTP1 defines three important functions for later use in other programs: the ConnectFTPControlSocket, SendFTPCommand, and ReadFTPServerReply functions. The ConnectFTPControlSocket function establishes an active connection to the FTP server's well-known protocol port. This connection will serve as a control channel between your client and the FTP server. To send commands through the control channel, your program functions call SendFTPCommand. To read server replies through the control channel, your program functions call ReadFTPServerReply.

The only other important (yet simple) function discussed in this section was the GetReplyCode function, which extracts the FTP reply code from the server's reply string and converts the code into a numeric value. To simplify the design of any program module that must seriously analyze server replies, use the GetReplyCode function to convert all reply codes into integers. If you have not already done so, compile and run QFTP1. To see the relationship between the various program modules, use your compiler's debugger to step through the program statements.

STAGE TWO: TRANSFERRING THE DATA

This section reviews QFTP2—the second development stage of the FTP client program. Like QFTP1, you can find the complete source code for QFTP2 on *Internet Programming's* companion disk. Of the six functions the first version of QFTP defines, QFTP2 uses four without change: ConnectFTPControlSocket, AnonymousFTPLogin, SendFTPCommand, and GetReplyCode. Because these functions are identical to their counterparts in QFTP1, this section will not discuss them further. QFTP2's WinMain function has one more program statement than QFTP1's WinMain. As shown in the following program fragment, if the reply code from the anonymous login is okay, QFTP2's WinMain function calls the DemonstrateCommand function:

```
// If the control channel is valid, then login.
nReplyCode = AnonymousFTPLogIn(hControlChannel);

if (nReplyCode == 230) // User logged in; okay to proceed.
{
   DemonstrateCommand(hControlChannel);
   SendFTPCommand(hControlChannel, "QUIT\r\n");
   closesocket(hControlChannel);
}
```

Other than the call to the DemonstrateCommand function, the WinMain function in QFTP2 is identical to the one in QFTP1. As explained in the next section, DemonstrateCommand illustrates the Winsock process your programs must follow to use an FTP command that returns data through the FTP data channel.

REVIEWING THE DATA CHANNEL

As discussed in the previous chapter, FTP-based client programs use the data channel to receive directory listings and files from the FTP server. Likewise, FTP clients use the data channel to send files to the server. As you may know, the data your programs receive from the data channel normally requires little or no interpretation. In most cases, the FTP-client simple writes the incoming data to a file. Unfortunately, the data channel is a little more complicated to set up than the control channel. As explained in the previous chapter, the difficulty with the data channel is that the client must temporarily act like a server. In other words, the client must listen for and identify connection requests *from* the FTP server.

The FTP control connection remains open during the entire FTP session. However, the client and server maintain the data connection only for the duration of each data transfer. As such, for each transfer operation, the client and server programs must establish a new data connection. As previously mentioned, the key point to note here is that the FTP data transfers do not occur at a well-known port—they occur on a port that the Winsock implementation (on the client's host) selects. Since the FTP client initiates all transfer operations, the client must perform a passive open on a socket and then tell the server to which port on the client's host it must connect. In other words, before the client tells the server to perform a file transfer, the client must tell the server to which port the server should send the file data.

After the client tells the server which socket address (IP address plus protocol port) will receive file data, the client must listen at that port address and accept the incoming connection request from the server. To let the server know which address to use, the client sends the FTP PORT command. The PORT command asks the server to establish a data connection at the address that the PORT command's parameters specify. In effect, the FTP client must act like a server until the FTP server establishes the connection and opens the data channel. As you will learn when you create a World Wide Web server program in Chapter 19, the only difference between the FTP client and a real server is that the client only accepts a connection from the FTP server on the other end of its control connection.

USING THE DATA CHANNEL

FTP client and server programs use the same process to create a data connection regardless of whether the client wants to send or receive a file. In both cases, the client creates a socket, binds it to a local address, tells the FTP server which port to contact, and then listens for a connection from the FTP server. In other words, in both cases (sending and receiving files), the FTP client performs a passive open and the FTP server performs an active open.

To use the data channel, the FTP client program first creates a socket to listen for connections from the FTP server. Next, the FTP client asks the FTP server to establish a data connection and tells the server which client socket address to contact—the client program's listener socket. Then, the FTP client sends a command to the FTP server that requires a data-transfer operation through the data channel. After the FTP client accepts an incoming connection from the FTP server, the client closes the listener socket (In Winsock, accepting the connection creates a new socket.) and uses the data channel. When the transmission is complete, the client closes the data socket and thus the data channel.

IDENTIFYING THE *FTP* SOCKETS

During an FTP session with a remote host computer, you essentially have three different sockets at play. The first socket connects your program to the control channel. The second socket, which your program creates each time it needs a data channel, listens for server connections. The third socket, which the Winsock implementation creates each time your program accepts a connection from an FTP server, receives file data. *Internet Programming* will use the following terms to distinguish between the three sockets. The book will refer to the first socket as the *control socket*. Depending on the program context and its usage, either the variable hControlSocket or hControlChannel will represent this socket. *Internet Programming* will refer to second socket as the *listener socket*. The program examples will use the variable hListenSocket to identify the listener socket. *Internet Programming* will refer to the third socket as the *data socket*. The program examples will use hDataSocket or hDataChannel to represent the data socket.

OPENING THE DATA CHANNEL

As shown next, the DemonstrateCommand function provides the program structure to perform the steps that the previous outline describes. First, DemonstrateCommand calls the CreateListenSocket function. As you will learn, the CreateListenSocket function creates the listener socket and tells the server (using the control channel) which address to contact. Second, DemonstrateCommand transmits (using SendFTPCommand) an FTP command to the FTP server that requires the server to establish a data connection. As shown in the DemonstrateCommand program statements, QFTP2 transmits the NLST command (which directs the server to transmit a list of filenames that reside in the working directory on the server's host). If you decide to experiment with QFTP2, you can substitute any command that requires the server to use the data channel. Third, DemonstrateCommand calls the AcceptDataConnection function to accept a data connection from the server. As you can see, the AcceptDataConnection function requires the listener-socket handle as a parameter and returns a data-socket handle. As noted in the comments, AcceptDataConnection closes the listener socket after it accepts a connection from the FTP server:

```
VOID DemonstrateCommand(SOCKET hControlChannel)
{
  SOCKET hDataChannel;
  SOCKET hListenSocket;
  UINT nReplyCode;

  lpszFunctionName = "DemonstrateCommand";

  if ((hListenSocket = CreateListenSocket(hControlChannel))
      == INVALID_SOCKET)
    return;

  // Hard code the NLST command for testing.
  if (nReplyCode = SendFTPCommand(hControlChannel,
      "NLST\r\n") >= 400)
    return;

  // Accept the data connection from the server. Note that
  // AcceptDataConnection() closes the hListenSocket for us.
```

```
    if ((hDataChannel = AcceptDataConnection(hListenSocket))
         == INVALID_SOCKET)
      return;

    ReadDataChannel(hDataChannel, "NLST.CMD");
    closesocket(hDataChannel);
    return;
}
```

In effect, when the AcceptDataConnection function returns with the handle to the data socket, the FTP data channel is open and ready for business. The DemonstrateCommand function, in turn, calls the ReadDataChannel function to exercise the data connection. The ReadDataChannel function requires the data-socket handle. (ReadDataChannel needs to know which socket to read). ReadDataChannel also requires a second parameter that represents the name of a data file. As discussed, during most transactions that occur on the data channel, the client will write incoming data to a local file (typically, the incoming data represents a file). Likewise, QFTP2 writes to a file any data it receives from the data channel. Typically, a client FTP program displays the results from the NLST command in a window (a list box, perhaps) or prints the results to the user's screen if the user's workstation is a text-based terminal. By writing the server's results to a target file in this way, you can change this program to use the FTP RETR command to retrieve a file from the server. After the ReadDataChannel function returns, DemonstrateCommand closes the data socket and exits. After the DemonstrateCommand function returns to WinMain, QFTP2 terminates program execution in the same way as QFTP1.

LISTENING FOR THE SERVER

As discussed, an FTP client must prepare to receive an incoming connection request from the FTP server before the client transmits a command that requires use of a data connection. The CreateListenSocket function performs this task for QFTP2. As you will learn, the socket-address parameters that CreateListenSocket uses are different from those all previous quick program functions use. The following program statements show the CreateListenSocket function definition (minus error handling code):

```
SOCKET CreateListenSocket(SOCKET hControlSocket)
{
   SOCKADDR_IN sockAddr;
   SOCKET hListenSocket;

   lpszFunctionName = "CreateListenSocket";

   if ((hListenSocket = socket(PF_INET, SOCK_STREAM, IPPROTO_TCP))
        == INVALID_SOCKET)
     // ...Handle the error and return.
```

```
    // Let the system assign a socket address
    sockAddr.sin_family = AF_INET;
    sockAddr.sin_port = htons(0);             // htons() is just a reminder.
    sockAddr.sin_addr.s_addr = INADDR_ANY;

    // Bind the socket
    if (bind(hListenSocket, (LPSOCKADDR)&sockAddr, sizeof(sockAddr)))
        // ...Handle the error and return.

    // Listen for the FTP server connection
    if (listen(hListenSocket, QUEUE_SIZE))
        // ...Handle the error and return.

    return(RequestDataConnection(hControlSocket, hListenSocket));
}
```

The CreateListenSocket function uses the familiar Winsock socket function to create a listener socket. However, note the values the function assigns to the socket-address structure following the socket function. Previous quick programs assigned a well-known port to sockAddr.sin_port that specifies the protocol server to contact. As you can see, CreateListenSocket assigns a value of zero to the protocol-port field in the socket-address structure and the Winsock symbolic constant INADDR_ANY to the address field. By using zero as a port address, the CreateListenSocket function lets the Winsock implementation (WINSOCK.DLL) assign a port address. Strictly speaking, your program could assign the FTP server address to the address field in the socket-address structure. Doing so would prevent the TCP software module from forwarding any other connection requests to your listener socket. However, the odds are rather remote that another host (besides the FTP server) would request a connection to your IP address and to a port assigned by your Winsock implementation. As such, specifying INADDR_ANY as a remote host address is fine for this implementation.

UNDERSTANDING SOCKET NAMES

The CreateListenSocket function uses two Winsock functions that programs in previous chapters have not used: bind and listen. As discussed in Chapters 7 and 8, programs typically use the bind and listen functions to create server applications. Since an FTP client must temporarily act like a server when it opens the data channel, an FTP client program must also use the bind and listen functions. A socket name consists of three components: a host (IP) address, a protocol number (a symbolic constant for either UDP or TCP), and a protocol port that identifies an application. Typically, you don't care which port your client applications use. However, a server program must listen at a specific port—the one a client program will use to contact the server program.

The Winsock bind function associates a *name* (combination of IP address, protocol number, and protocol port) with a socket. In CreateListenSocket's case, the function doesn't care which protocol port the system assigns to the listener socket. Instead, the QFTP2 program will tell the FTP server to contact whichever port the host system assigns. The listen function places a socket in a passive-listening mode. In other words, listen tells the socket to listen for incoming connection requests. A listener socket acknowledges connection requests and places those requests in an in-coming-connection queue. The first parameter to the listen function tells Winsock which port to monitor. The second parameter specifies the maximum number of incoming connections to stack in the connection queue. The maximum number permitted in Winsock version 1.1 is five.

The listen function does not accept connections—it only tells a socket to listen for connections and to send the requester an acknowledgment. In other words, a listener socket monitors the specified address and acknowledges requests for your program. To actually accept a connection, your program must call the accept function. However, an FTP-based client, like QFTP2, must tell the server which protocol port to contact before the client tries to accept a data connection from the FTP server. If you examine the return statement in the CreateListenSocket function, you will find that CreateListenSocket calls the RequestDataConnection function. As you will learn, the RequestDataConnection function reads the socket name (combination of IP address, protocol number, and protocol port) that the CreateListenSocket function's listen function assigns. RequestDataConnection then reports the name to the FTP server.

USING THE *FTP PORT* COMMAND

As mentioned, the RequestDataConnection function tells the FTP server which client address to contact to create a connection for the FTP data channel. RequestDataConnection uses the Winsock getsockname function to determine which protocol port Winsock assigned to the listener socket. RequestDataConnection uses the FTP PORT command to transmit the client IP address and protocol port to the server through the control channel. However, before you examine the FTP port command, you need to understand some peculiar Winsock behavior. As you have learned, TCP/IP protocols associate an IP address with a network interface card—not a host computer. A computer can contain multiple network interface cards. (As you have learned, network professionals refer to such computers as multihomed.)

When you bind a socket to a local address and specify INADDR_ANY as a valid address for a socket, Winsock will not immediately assign your IP address to the socket (even if your computer only contains one interface card and thus one IP address). In other words, assume you use create a socket and specify INADDR_ANY as a socket address. Next, assume you call the bind function to give the socket a local name (combination of IP address, protocol number, and protocol port). Winsock will immediately assign a port to the socket but not an IP address. Winsock will not assign an IP address until after it establishes a network connection with the socket. The fact that Winsock does not immediately assign your IP address to the socket structure can be a major surprise and cost you valuable troubleshooting time if you are unaware of Winsock's behavior (as noted in the Winsock specification). The following program statements show the function definition for RequestDataConnection. As you can see, RequestDataConnection uses getsockname to retrieve the port assignment Winsock made when CreateListenSocket called the bind function.

```
SOCKET RequestDataConnection(SOCKET hControlSocket,
    SOCKET hListenSocket)
{
  SOCKADDR_IN sockAddr;          // Socket address structure
  int iLength;                   // Length of the address structure
  UINT nLocalPort;               // Local port for listening
  UINT nReplyCode;               // FTP server reply code

  lpszFunctionName = "RequestDataConnection";

  // Get the address for the hListenSocket
  iLength = sizeof(sockAddr);
  if (getsockname(hListenSocket, (LPSOCKADDR)&sockAddr,
      &iLength) == SOCKET_ERROR)
    {
      int iWinsockErr = WSAGetLastError();
      wsprintf(gszCommandBuffer,
          "Error #%d occurred while getting listen socket name!!",
          iWinsockErr);
      MessageBeep(MB_ICONSTOP);
      MessageBox(NULL, gszCommandBuffer, lpszFunctionName,
          MB_OK|MB_ICONSTOP);
      return(INVALID_SOCKET);
    }


  // Extract the local port from the hListenSocket
  nLocalPort = sockAddr.sin_port;

  // Now, reuse the socket address structure to
  // get the IP address from the control socket.
  if (getsockname(hControlSocket, (LPSOCKADDR)&sockAddr,
      &iLength) == SOCKET_ERROR)
    {
      int iWinsockErr = WSAGetLastError();
      wsprintf(gszCommandBuffer,
          "Error #%d occurred while getting control socket name!!",
          iWinsockErr);
      MessageBeep(MB_ICONSTOP);
      MessageBox(NULL, gszCommandBuffer, lpszFunctionName,
          MB_OK|MB_ICONSTOP);
      return(INVALID_SOCKET);
    }

  // Format the PORT command with the correct numbers.
  wsprintf(gszCommandBuffer, "PORT %d,%d,%d,%d,%d,%d\r\n",
        sockAddr.sin_addr.S_un.S_un_b.s_b1,
        sockAddr.sin_addr.S_un.S_un_b.s_b2,
        sockAddr.sin_addr.S_un.S_un_b.s_b3,
        sockAddr.sin_addr.S_un.S_un_b.s_b4,
```

```
            // Remember, the port is in network byte order. The FTP server
            // expects to see the high-order byte from the port (in terms of
            // the network byte order) first. As such, from a PC,(which uses
            // little endian byte order) the program must transmit the low-
            // order byte first and then the high-order. (If this is
            // confusing, see the "Internet Programming" chapter entitled
            // "Time and the Network Byte Order".
            nLocalPort & 0xFF,
            nLocalPort >> 8);

    // Tell the server which port to use for data.
    if (nReplyCode = SendFTPCommand(hControlSocket, gszCommandBuffer)
            != 200)
        {
        wsprintf(gszCommandBuffer,
                "Error %d from PORT command to server!",
                nReplyCode);
        MessageBeep(MB_ICONSTOP);
        MessageBox(NULL, gszCommandBuffer, lpszFunctionName,
                MB_OK|MB_ICONSTOP);
        return(INVALID_SOCKET);
        }
    else
        return(hListenSocket);
    }
```

If you step through this function using a debugger and examine the contents of the sockAddr structure after the getsockname function call, the results may surprise you. You will find that the socket-address structure contains a protocol port but the address may be invalid. In other words, Winsock assigned (and stored) the port address in the internal socket-data structure but not the IP address. This behavior presents a minor problem. You need to transmit your IP address and your local port address to the FTP server. To obtain the local IP address, your program can call the gethostname function, which returns the DNS name of the local machine. However, if you choose this option, your program will also have to perform a DNS lookup—a lot of work and unnecessary network traffic just to find out your local IP address. The RequestDataConnection function offers a much simpler solution than performing a DNS lookup. First, as shown in the following program statements, RequestDataConnection obtains the name for the listener socket. Remember, the getsockname function retrieves the socket name from the socket data-structure and stores the values in the local socket-address structure pointed to by getsockname's second parameter:

```
// Get the address for the hListenSocket
iLength = sizeof(sockAddr);
if (getsockname(hListenSocket, (LPSOCKADDR)&sockAddr,
    &iLength) == SOCKET_ERROR)
```

```
// ...Handle the error
```

As shown next, the function then extracts and stores the port address from the listener socket so that the program knows which port to tell the server to contact:

```
// Extract the local port from the hListenSocket
nLocalPort = sockAddr.sin_port;
```

Finally, RequestDataConnection calls the getsockname function a second time but with the control-socket handle instead of the listener-socket handle. Since the control-socket connection is active, the control socket contains the local IP address in its data structures. The second getsockname function call (shown next) causes Winsock to fill the sockAddr structure with the IP address for the local host:

```
// Now, reuse the socket address structure to
// get the IP address from the control socket.
if (getsockname(hControlSocket, (LPSOCKADDR)&sockAddr, &iLength)
    == SOCKET_ERROR)
```

Winsock will also fill the port-address field with the port number for the control channel. However, as previously shown, RequestDataConnection has already stored the port address for the listener socket in the local variable nLocalPort. The next several lines in RequestDataConnection format the string in the command buffer as an FTP PORT command. This PORT command looks something like the following (note that the command should not use spaces between commas).

```
PORT 168,158,20,192,150,4
```

As discussed in the program comments, you must be careful to place the eight-bit port values in the correct positions in the PORT command string. Reversing the port-byte values is an easy mistake to make and a hard one to spot. The big problem is that you can transmit the PORT command with the port bytes reversed and no one will complain. No one, that is, until the server tries to connect to the wrong port. In other words, if you reverse the port bytes in the PORT command, your listener socket will listen on one port while the server will try to contact your program on a different port. The server will probably transmit a 425 reply code on the control channel to tell you that it can't open the data connection. Unfortunately, the server doesn't know why. The server doesn't know the client is not listening on the port that the server tried to contact. After RequestDataConnection formats the PORT command, it uses SendFTPCommand to transmit the port command (across the control connection) to the server. Finally, the RequestDataConnection function ends and returns either the handle of the listener socket or an error value (INVALID_SOCKET).

ACCEPTING SERVER CONNECTIONS

As previously shown, the return statement in the CreateListenSocket function embeds a call to the RequestDataConnection function. In other words, when RequestDataConnection returns with the listener-socket handle (assuming no errors occurred), the listener-socket handle returns all the way to the DemonstrateCommand function. If the listener-socket handle is valid, the DemonstrateCommand function transmits the test command (NLST) and then calls the AcceptDataConnection function. With the error handling removed, AcceptDataConnection is a small function, as shown in the following program lines:

```
SOCKET AcceptDataConnection(SOCKET hListenSocket)
{
  SOCKET hDataSocket;
  SOCKADDR_IN sockAddr;
  int iAddrLength;

  lpszFunctionName = "AcceptDataConnection";

  hDataSocket = accept(hListenSocket, (LPSOCKADDR)&sockAddr,
      &iAddrLength);

  // Close the listener socket since it is no longer needed.
  closesocket(hListenSocket);

  if (hDataSocket == INVALID_SOCKET)
    // ...Handle the error and return.
  else
    return(hDataSocket);
}
```

As you can see, the AcceptDataConnection function calls the Winsock accept function and waits for the FTP server connection. As previously mentioned, when a connection request arrives at the monitored port address, Winsock creates a new socket and returns the new socket handle from the accept function. The AcceptDataConnection function stores the new data-socket handle in hDataSocket and returns the handle, in this case, to the caller. This new handle represents the FTP data channel that the FTP client and server can use to transfer data.

READING THE DATA CHANNEL

When AcceptDataConnection returns to DemonstrateCommand with a valid data-socket handle, DemonstrateCommand calls the ReadDataChannel function. The ReadDataChannel function shown next is primarily a wrapper for the Winsock recv function:

```
BOOL ReadDataChannel(SOCKET hDataSocket, LPSTR lpszFileName)
{
  char sDataBuffer[4096];   // Data-storage buffer for the data channel
  int nBytesRecv;           // Bytes received from the data channel
  HFILE hFile;              // File handle for data file
  OFSTRUCT openFileBuff;    // The Windows open file data structure
  LONG lData = 0L;          // Bytes received and written to the file
```

```
lpszFunctionName = "ReadDataChannel";

if ((hFile = OpenFile(lpszFileName, (OFSTRUCT far *)&openFileBuff,
      OF_CREATE)) == HFILE_ERROR)
   // ...Handle the error and return.

do
   {
     nBytesRecv = recv(hDataSocket, (LPSTR)&sDataBuffer,
           sizeof(sDataBuffer), NO_FLAGS);

     lData += nBytesRecv;
     if (nBytesRecv > 0 )
       {
         if (HFILE_ERROR == _lwrite (hFile, sDataBuffer, nBytesRecv))
           // ...Handle the error and return.
       }
   }
while (nBytesRecv > 0);

// Close the file and check for error returns.
_lclose(hFile);
if (nBytesRecv == SOCKET_ERROR)
   // ...Handle the error and return.
else
   {
     wsprintf(gszCommandBuffer,"%lu bytes written to %s\n", lData,
           lpszFileName);
     MessageBeep(MB_ICONINFORMATION);
     MessageBox(NULL, gszCommandBuffer, lpszFunctionName,
           MB_OK|MB_ICONINFORMATION);
   }

return(TRUE);
}
```

As you can see, the ReadDataChannel function uses a do-while loop to read data from the specified socket. This loop is very similar to the ones you have encountered in previous quick programs. However, ReadDataChannel also uses the Windows OpenFile and _write functions to create a file and write the incoming data to your local hard drive. When ReadDataChannel exits the do-while loop, it immediately closes the file.

The ReadDataChannel function uses its second parameter to name the file for the incoming data. In other words, your program modules must determine the name and location of the file before they call ReadDataChannel. The QFTPLIB program modules (developed in stage 3) use the ReadDataChannel function definition (plus error handling).

IDENTIFYING THE FILE-NAMING PROBLEM

File-naming conventions, as well as directory-naming (file location) conventions, vary from one operating system to the next. DOS- and 16-bit Windows-based PCs use an eight-dot-three file-naming convention (an eight-character filename plus a dot plus a three-character extension). UNIX systems and 32-bit Windows (Windows NT and Windows 95) systems are not so restrictive. A program that reads and stores files that other systems create must translate foreign filenames into a convention the local file-naming system accepts. The previously shown ReadDataChannel function design separates the program logic for filenames from the task of reading and writing data from the data channel. To avoid complicating the program modules with filename and location logic, QFTP uses a simple file-naming system that names incoming data after the command used to retrieve the data. For example, QFTP writes NLST data to "NLST.CMD." Of course, each transfer operation will overwrite the file that stored the previous transfer.

Stage three (QFTPLIB) of the QFTP development adds three functions that handle file I/O for an FTP-client program: ExtractFileName, CreateTransferFile, and TransferFile. The ExtractFileName function extracts a valid DOS filename from a UNIX-style filename or path string. The CreateTransferFile function simply creates a file from a valid DOS filename and returns a file handle. The TransferFile function reads data from the data channel and writes it to a file on your hard disk. As you will learn, the TransferFile function is very similar to the ReadDataChannel function. However, the TransferFile function does not enter a do-while loop. Instead, the TransferFile function calls the recv function one time and returns the number of bytes read from the data channel.

Other program modules can create their own do-while loop and call the TransferFile function from within it. A program module that calls the TransferFile function in this way can display status information for the program user. Since the TransferFile function returns the number of bytes read, the caller can maintain a running total of the bytes transferred and display the running total for the user. Note that the ReadDataChannel function does not provide this capability since it reads the data channel from within its own internal do-while loop—calling functions have no way to receive status information while the ReadDataChannel function reads the data channel.

REVISITING THE SERVER REPLY CODES

When the ReadDataChannel function returns control to the DemonstrateCommand function, DemonstrateCommand closes the data socket and returns to WinMain. As previously shown, WinMain, in turn, transmits the FTP QUIT command to the server, closes the control socket, and exits—the QFTP2 program ends. Before moving on to stage three of the QFTP development, you need to examine the ReadFTPServerReply function in QFTP2. As discussed, the ReadFTPServerReply function performs the critical task of parsing FTP server reply strings for FTP reply codes. Keep in mind that your FTP-based programs cannot depend on the recv function to retrieve entire server replies in a single function call. In other words, a robust, FTP-based client typically executes some type of loop (similar to the do-while construct used to read the data channel) that reads data from the control channel. There are some important caveats to note with regard to such loops.

As you have learned, the control channel remains open during the entire FTP session. As such, if your program calls the recv function for a blocking socket but the server does not transmit any data, the recv function will block and wait forever to receive data—essentially hanging your program. The recv function has blocked your only communication link to the server. The recv function needs a server reply before it unblocks the socket, but your program cannot access the control channel to tell the server to send a reply until after recv unblocks the socket. You must carefully design ReadFTPServerReply to avoid any occurrence of this condition. Because the ReadFTPServerReply design in QFTP1 did not read server replies in a loop, QFTP1 avoids this problem. However, if you design a program based on QFTP1 and one of your program modules calls ReadFTPServerReply when the server is not transmitting replies, even the non-loop version of ReadFTPServerReply will hang your program. As shown next, the QFTP2 version of ReadFTPServerReply implements a simple loop that avoids a couple of conditions that would hang the QFTP2 program:

```
UINT ReadFTPServerReply(SOCKET hControlChannel)
{
    // Note that the function now uses a global receive buffer so
    // in the future other program modules can access the full
    // text of the server's reply rather than just the
    // server's reply code (which this function returns.)

    int iBytesRead;          // Bytes read from the control channel
    int iBufferLength;       // Length of the server reply buffer
    int iEnd;                // Index into the server reply buffer
    int iSpaceRemaining;     // Space remaining in the buffer

    lpszFunctionName = "ReadFTPServerReply";

    iEnd = 0;
    iBufferLength = iSpaceRemaining = sizeof(gsServerReplyBuffer);
    do
      {
        iSpaceRemaining -= iEnd;
        iBytesRead = recv(hControlChannel,
              (LPSTR)(gsServerReplyBuffer+iEnd), iSpaceRemaining,
              NO_FLAGS);

        iEnd+=iBytesRead;

        // Make sure CRLF was not the the last byte pair received.
        // Otherwise, recv() will wait forever for the next packet.
```

```
        if (*(gsServerReplyBuffer+(iEnd-2)) == '\r' &&
          *(gsServerReplyBuffer+(iEnd-1)) == '\n')
              break;
    }
    while (iBytesRead > 0 && iEnd < iBufferLength);

    if (iBytesRead == SOCKET_ERROR)
      // ...Handle the error and return.

    gsServerReplyBuffer[iEnd] = '\0';
    MessageBeep(MB_ICONINFORMATION);
    MessageBox(NULL, (LPSTR)gsServerReplyBuffer, lpszFunctionName,
          MB_OK|MB_ICONINFORMATION);

    // Extract reply code from the server reply and return as an integer
    return(GetReplyCode(gsServerReplyBuffer));
}
```

For reasons that will become obvious in the QFTPLIB version of QFTP, the QFTP2 version of
ReadFTPServerReply uses a global receive buffer rather than a local one. As you can see, QFTP2
also adds a do-while loop to ReadFTPServerReply. This loop is similar to the ones you've seen in
previous quick programs. The *while* statement checks to make sure that the recv function received
data (meaning that more data may arrive) and that the loop does not pass the end of the receive
buffer (overwriting memory that it does not own). The only new feature of the loop is the following *if* construct:

```
if (*(gsServerReplyBuffer+(iEnd-2)) == '\r' &&
      *(gsServerReplyBuffer+(iEnd-1)) == '\n')
      break;
```

One condition that might cause the loop to hang is when the receive buffer contains the server's
complete reply. In other words, the server sends a reply terminated by the NVT ASCII end-of-
line marker (a carriage-return line-feed—CRLF). In previous quick programs, the do-while loop
continued to call the recv function to read data from the socket until recv returned with zero bytes.
When the recv function returned with zero bytes, the test condition for the do-while loop caused
the program to exit the loop as it does here also. However, in the previous quick programs, recv
always returned with zero bytes because the server closed the TCP connection after transmitting
the last block of data.

In this case, the server does not close the FTP control channel after transmitting a reply (the control channel remains open during the entire FTP session). Instead, the server marks the end of
each reply line with a CRLF. The *if* statement shown here tests the last byte-pair in the receive
buffer for a carriage-return and line-feed and causes the program to break out of the loop when it
finds one. If the do-while loop did not contain a test for this condition and instead called the recv
function again, the recv function would wait forever for a reply (and hang the program) because

the server has no more data to send—the CRLF indicates that the server has finished. If you step through the ReadFTPServerReply program loop with a debugger while the program receives data from the control channel, you will see that this condition usually causes the program to exit from the do-while loop. In other words, the server typically sends a reply that ReadFTPServerReply collects in a single call to recv.

As you will learn in stage 3, you must add additional logic to the ReadFTPServerReply function to handle multiline replies correctly. However, for the QFTP2 version of the program, the do-while loop previously shown is sufficient. You might want to run QFTP2 against various FTP sites on the Internet and note the various multiline reply formats that you encounter. Understand that capturing multiline replies (which QFTP2 does) is not the problem. The problem is that your program must parse the correct reply code for each multiline reply. Under real-world scenarios, your FTP client may encounter not only multiline replies in its receive buffer, but also a multiline reply (or part of a multiline reply) mixed with other single-line replies. In other words, under actual operation, your program may encounter multiple replies from the server in the control-channel receive buffer—some of the replies may be multiline replies. In such cases, analyzing the control-channel receive buffer to determine the correct reply code rapidly becomes a messy process. Stage 3 adds program logic to help resolve this problem.

STAGE THREE: IMPLEMENTING THE DLL

In developing QFTP1 and QFTP2, you have laid the foundation for a small, custom dynamic link library (DLL). As discussed, Winsock is not a visually-oriented API. One approach to visually programming the Internet is to create generic, back-end, Winsock-based routines that remain hidden during the development process. After you define and create them, your Winsock routines become a part of your own custom network API. Using this DLL you can use your preferred visual-programming tools to develop software as usual. When your visual program modules need to perform network I/O, they call the pre-defined API functions in your custom perform network I/O.

If you have previously avoided creating Windows DLLs, you have missed a powerful Windows development tool. As you will see, by slightly modifying the function prototypes defined in QFTP1 and QFTP2, you can place the quick-program function definitions into a DLL virtually unchanged. This section discusses the QFTPLIB dynamic-link library (QFTPLIB.DLL). You can find the complete source code for the DLL in the source-file QFTPLIB.CPP on the *Internet Programming* companion disk. *Internet Programming* will not discuss Windows DLL development issues. If you are unfamiliar with Windows DLLs or need more explanation related to Windows DLLs, see the dynamic-link-libraries chapter (Chapter 19) in *Programming Windows 3.1, Third Edition*, Charles Petzold, Microsoft Press, 1992, or some other book that discusses DLLs in detail. For now, you can simply change the QFTP function prototypes as shown next:

```
extern "C" UINT FAR PASCAL GetReplyCode(LPSTR lpszServerReply)
extern "C" LPSTR _export FAR PASCAL GetFTPServerReplyText(VOID)
extern "C" UINT FAR PASCAL ReadFTPServerReply(SOCKET hControlChannel)
extern "C" UINT _export FAR PASCAL SendFTPCommand(SOCKET
    hControlChannel, LPSTR gszCommandBuffer)
extern "C" UINT _export FAR PASCAL ReadDataChannel(SOCKET
    hControlSocket,
extern "C" SOCKET _export FAR PASCAL ConnectFTPControlSocket(LPSTR
    lpszHost)
extern "C" SOCKET FAR PASCAL RequestDataConnection(SOCKET
    hControlSocket, SOCKET hListenSocket)
extern "C" SOCKET _export FAR PASCAL CreateListenSocket(SOCKET
    hControlSocket)
extern "C" SOCKET _export FAR PASCAL AcceptDataConnection(SOCKET
    hListenSocket)
extern "C" UINT _export FAR PASCAL TransferFile(SOCKET hControlSocket,
    SOCKET hDataSocket, HFILE hFile)
extern "C" void _export FAR PASCAL ExtractFileName(LPSTR lpPathString,
    LPSTR lpszFileName)
extern "C" HFILE _export FAR PASCAL  CreateTransferFile(LPSTR
    lpszFileName)
```

As you can see, each function now contains the extern "C" qualifier, which prevents name-mangling by a C++ compiler. (As you may know, within the linker-information portion of an object file, C++ compilers alter function names with codes that indicate the parameters to the function and the return value. These codes permit function overloading and some error checking during the link process). QFTPLIB declares each function to have a FAR PASCAL return as required by Windows. Some function prototypes also include the _export keyword. Windows program modules that load the DLL can call exported functions (when prototypes include the _export modifier). In other words, your compiler exports these function definitions. Functions that do not include the _export modifier can only be called by functions that reside within the DLL itself. Again, if this is new to you, please see a Windows programming book that discusses Windows dynamic link libraries. For now, simply note that functions without the _export prefix are for internal use by the DLL only. In other words, functions in QFTPLIB.DLL can call other functions (that are in the calling function's scope) in QFTPLIB.DLL. However, other programs (such as Visual Basic or your Visual C++ programs) can only access the QFTPLIB.DLL function definitions with the _export prefix.

The following sections discuss some minor changes to the QFTP2 function definitions you must make to use the functions in QFTPLIB. The following paragraphs also discuss ten new QFTPLIB functions (most of which are trivial and easy to understand). Note that the QFTPLIB DLL does not include the QFTP2 functions: WinMain, AnonymousFTPLogin, and DemonstrateCommand. Instead, LibMain replaces WinMain in a DLL. The other two functions (AnonymousFTPLogin and DemonstrateCommand) provided an experimental framework for understanding FTP use on the Internet. Instead of AnonymousFTPLogin and DemonstrateCommand, you can use the visual front-end defined in QFTP stage four for FTP experimentation with the QFTPLIB implementation.

ADDING THE EASY STUFF

As mentioned in the previous section, QFTPLIB adds ten new functions. This section discusses five of the functions that are trivial. First, just as every C program needs a main function and every Windows program needs a WinMain, every DLL needs a LibMain. The LibMain function shown next is about as simple as a LibMain function can be:

```
int _export FAR PASCAL LibMain(HANDLE hInstance, WORD wDataSeg,
    WORD wHeapSize, LPSTR lpszCmdParam)
{
  if (wHeapSize > 0)   // Heap size defined in the DEF file.
    UnlockData(0);     // Unlocks the current data segment.

  return(1);
}
```

LibMain initialization routines can be quite complex depending on the sophistication of the routines stored in the library. The LibMain function in QFTPLIB simply unlocks the data segment which your compiler's startup routine (LIBENTRY.OBJ for Microsoft and CODS.OBJ for Borland, for example) locks on entry into the DLL. (For more details about DLL startup and initialization, see Charles Petzold's *Programming Windows 3.1, Third Edition*, Microsoft Press, 1992, or your compiler manual.) The WEP (Windows exit procedure) function is a Windows callback function that performs cleanup operations for a DLL before Windows unloads the library. Early versions of Windows (before version 3.1) required a WEP function for every DLL. In Windows version 3.1, the WEP function is optional. However, most DLLs use a WEP function, and QFTPLIB includes a simple function definition that you can modify as required if you decide to build on the QFTPLIB.DLL implementation:

```
int _export FAR PASCAL WEP(int nParam)
{
  return(1);
}
```

As you have learned, Winsock requires your program to call the WSAStartup function to initialize the WINSOCK.DLL. As shown next, QFTPLIB includes a simple function named LoadWinsock that is nothing more than a wrapper for WSAStartup:

```
extern "C" BOOL _export FAR PASCAL LoadWinsock(VOID)
{
```

```
   WSADATA wsaData;                // Winsock implementation details

   if (WSAStartup(WINSOCK_VERSION, &wsaData))
     {
       MessageBeep(MB_ICONSTOP);
       MessageBox(NULL, "Could not load Windows Sockets DLL.",
             PROG_NAME, MB_OK|MB_ICONSTOP);
       return(FALSE);
     }
   else
     return(TRUE);
}
```

As you can see, LoadWinsock displays a message box if it cannot find the WINSOCK.DLL. If the WINSOCK.DLL is not in memory when your QFTPLIB-based programs start, you can modify the LoadWinsock function to perform a path search (or perhaps a disk-wide search) for WINSOCK.DLL. Then, you can have LoadWinsock use the LoadLibrary function to manually load WINSOCK.DLL. In keeping with the *quick* program model, QFTPLIB simply reports the error and exits. If you are creating production-quality programs, you would want the function to return the Winsock data structure so your programs could verify version number support and so on. Likewise, as you have learned, a well-written Winsock-based program should call WSACleanup before it exits. As shown next, QFTPLIB includes CloseWinsock as the counterpart to LoadWinsock:

```
extern "C" BOOL _export FAR PASCAL CloseWinsock(VOID)
{
   if (WSACleanup())
     {
       int iWinsockErr = WSAGetLastError();
       wsprintf(gszCommandBuffer, "WSACleanup() caused error# %d",
           iWinsockErr);
       MessageBeep(MB_ICONSTOP);
       MessageBox(NULL, gszCommandBuffer, PROG_NAME, MB_OK|MB_ICONSTOP);
       return(FALSE);
     }
   else
     return(TRUE);
}
```

If WSACleanup fails, there is not much your program can do about it. However, by calling the CloseWinsock function instead of WSACleanup directly, CloseWinsock will retrieve the Winsock error code using WSAGetLastError and display the error for your program users. The other trivial function addition to QFTPLIB is GetFTPServerReplyText. As previously discussed, the QFTP2 version of ReadFTPServerReply used a global variable named gsServerReplyBuffer to store the FTP server's reply strings. By using a global variable, QFTPLIB lets other functions have access to the full text of server's replies. (Remember, as a rule, QFTP functions only report the reply codes as numbers.) GetFTPServerReplyText (shown next) simply returns a pointer to the variable that stores the server's replies. (Note that QFTPLIB changed the name of the DLL global-variable buffer from gsServerReplyBuffer to gsServerReplyText):

```
extern "C" LPSTR _export FAR PASCAL GetFTPServerReplyText(VOID)
{
    return((LPSTR)gsServerReplyText);
}
```

In some cases, in addition to noting the server's reply codes, a program may want to extract a text string from the server's reply. For example, the FTP PWD (print working directory) command returns the server's working directory as a string value following the reply code. Likewise, the FTP SYST command returns the server system-type as a string in the reply code. Whenever a program needs access to the full text of a server's reply, the program can call GetFTPServerReplyText to obtain a pointer to the reply buffer. The calling module can then copy the server's reply text into local memory and analyze it as required (extract the current working directory or system type, for example). The key point to note about this simple design implementation is that QFTPLIB repeatedly uses the same global buffer to store server replies. As such, if your program module needs the server's reply text, the module should call GetFTPServerReplyText immediately after sending the command to the server. Otherwise, an intervening reply might overwrite the server reply text of interest to your program module.

UNBLOCKING THE FTP CHANNELS

A blocking function on your control-channel socket is potentially fatal to your program. As previously discussed, if your control socket can block, the recv function can lockup (or hang) your program. Such blocking might occur when your program calls recv for the control socket and the FTP server does not need to send a reply. In such cases, the recv function will wait forever. One solution to this blocking problem is a timer that controls how long the recv function waits. However, the recv function, itself, provides no such capability. If you call recv for a blocking socket, recv will always block and wait for a reply. If no reply ever comes, your program hangs. To avoid this problem, you can use a non-blocking socket for your control socket. As discussed in previous chapters, your programs can use the Winsock select function to make a socket non-blocking. QFTPLIB adds a simple function named IsReadyToRead (shown next) that performs this service for any program module that needs a non-blocking socket:

```
extern "C" BOOL FAR PASCAL IsReadyToRead(SOCKET hSocket)
{
    FD_SET setReadyToRead;      // Socket set to test ready-to-read status
    TIMEVAL timeTimeOut;        // Amount of time to wait for status change
    int nReady;                 // Ready-to-read flag
```

```
    lpszFunctionName = "IsReadyToRead";

    timerclear(&timeTimeOut);
    FD_ZERO(&setReadyToRead);
    FD_SET(hSocket, &setReadyToRead);

    if ((nReady = select(NULL, (LPFD_SET)&setReadyToRead, NULL, NULL,
        &timeTimeOut)) == SOCKET_ERROR)
      {
        int iWinsockErr = WSAGetLastError();
        wsprintf(gszCommandBuffer,
            "Error %d from the select() function!!", iWinsockErr);
        MessageBeep(MB_ICONSTOP);
        MessageBox(NULL, gszCommandBuffer, lpszFunctionName,
            MB_OK|MB_ICONSTOP);
        return(FALSE);
      }

    return(nReady ? TRUE : FALSE);
}
```

The following paragraphs discuss the IsReadyToRead function's implementation details. If necessary, you can review *Internet Programming's* previous discussions of the select function and blocking and non-blocking sockets—particularly the blocking and non-blocking socket discussions in Chapter 8. The following discussions assume you are familiar with the information already presented. As previously discussed, the select function lets your programs determine the state of one or more sockets. For this purpose, Winsock uses the fd_set structure shown here:

```
#define FD_SETSIZE 64              // The maximum number of sockets per SET

typedef struct fd_set
 {
   u_int fd_count;                 // The number of sockets in the SET
   SOCKET fd_array[FD_SETSIZE]; // An array of socket handles
 } fd_set;

typedef struct fd_set FD_SET;  // Extended type definition for Windows
```

You can find these definitions in the winsock.h header file. A *set* is really nothing more than a list of socket handles stored in an array. If you use a debugger to step through a program that uses fd_set structures and the macros (discussed next) that manipulate these structures, you will discover that the operations are very simple. In fact, most explanations make the process much more complicated than it actually is. The fd_set structure simply stores a list of socket handles. When your program modules call the select function, your program passes one or pointers to an fd_set structure. Winsock consults the list of sockets in the fd_set structure to see which sockets your program wants to examine. Winsock then examines the actual sockets the list (or set) identifies. For each socket in the list, Winsock checks to see if the socket's state corresponds to the state requested. As discussed in previous chapters, you can ask for read, write, and error state checks. Winsock counts the number of sockets in all the lists pointed to by the select function and returns the total number of sockets that match. For the sake of clarity, Table 17.1 lists the FD_SET macros previously presented in Chapter 8. As you can see, Winsock defines four macros to manipulate the FD_SET sockets.

Macro Name	Function
FD_CLR	Removes a socket handle from a set.
FD_ISSET	Returns a non-zero value (true) if the socket handle is set and a zero (false) if the socket handle is not set.
FD_SET	Adds a socket handle to a set.
FD_ZERO	Initializes a set of socket handles.

Table 17.1 Macros that manipulate sets of socket handles for the select function.

The contents of an FD_SET structure remain undefined after its declaration. In other words, Winsock does not initialize the structure elements to any specific value. As such, you should always call the FD_ZERO macro to initialize an FD_SET structure. Winsock defines a TIMEVAL structure that you can use with the select function also. The TIMEVAL argument tells the select function how long to wait, if necessary, before a socket in the specified sets matches the requested status condition:

```
struct timeval
{
   long tv_sec;            // Seconds
   long tv_usec;           // Microseconds
};

typedef struct timeval TIMEVAL;
```

If the TIMEVAL structure elements equal zero, the select function will evaluate the current state of each socket in the combined sets and immediately return without waiting. Note that setting the TIMEVAL structure elements to zero is different than passing a NULL pointer to the select function. If you pass select a NULL pointer instead of a pointer to a valid TIMEVAL structure, the select function assumes blocking operations and will wait (block) until one of the sockets in the sets matches the requested status. The key point to note here is what happens when you pass the select function a pointer to a TIMEVAL structure that has both elements set to zero. When the TIMEVAL elements equal zero, the select function assumes you want to perform non-blocking operations with all the sockets listed in the FD_SET structures. In other words, to change a socket from one that can block (the default when you use the socket function to create a socket) to a non-blocking socket, you call the select function with a pointer to a TIMEVAL structure that contains both elements set to zero. Thereafter, the specified sockets will assume non-blocking operations.

As previously discussed in Chapter 8, a non-blocking socket presents other problems that your program must handle. However, changing your control socket to a non-blocking socket prevents an inadvertent recv call on the control channel from hanging your program. In other words, if the socket is not ready for read operations, the recv function will return with an error rather than wait forever. (These error returns are problems that your program modules that use non-blocking sockets must expect and handle.) Winsock.h defines a macro named timerclear that sets both TIMEVAL elements to zero. As shown in the following program statements, the IsReadyToRead function calls timerclear to set the TIMEVAL structure timeTimeOut to zero:

```
timerclear(&timeTimeOut);
FD_ZERO(&setReadyToRead);
FD_SET(hSocket, &setReadyToRead);
```

Next, IsReadyToRead calls the FD_ZERO macro to initialize the FD_SET structure setReadyToRead to zero. Then, IsReadyToRead calls the FD_SET macro to add the socket handle (passed to it as a parameter) to the setReadyToRead structure. Finally, IsReadyToRead calls the select function as shown here:

```
if ((nReady = select(NULL, (LPFD_SET)&setReadyToRead, NULL, NULL,
      &timeTimeOut)) == SOCKET_ERROR)
```

If no errors occur, IsReadyToRead returns a true or false value, depending on whether the socket is ready to read. The QFTPLIB functions that call the IsReadyToRead function actually ignore the return value. The primary purpose of the IsReadyToRead function is to demonstrate how to change a socket from blocking operations to non-blocking operations.

MAKING SOME MINOR ADJUSTMENTS

Now that you know how QFTPLIB changes a socket from blocking to non-blocking, you can understand why QFTPLIB makes minor adjustments to three function definitions included in the QFTP2 version of the program. As you have learned, the QFTP modules use the ConnectFTPControlSocket function to create and connect a socket for use as the FTP control channel. Likewise, the AcceptDataConnection function returns the socket handle for the data channel. Just before both functions (ConnectFTPControlSocket and AcceptDataConnection) return their respective socket handles, they call the IsReadyToRead function. The following program statements show the return statement for ConnectFTPControlSocket:

```
// Make the control socket non-blocking before returning.
```

```
IsReadyToRead(hControlSocket);

if (ReadFTPServerReply(hControlSocket) >= 400)
   return(INVALID_SOCKET);
else
   return(hControlSocket);
```

The following program fragment shows the return statement for AcceptDataConnection. As you can see, AcceptDataConnection also calls the IsReadyToRead function before returning a socket handle (for the data channel) to its caller:

```
if (hDataSocket == INVALID_SOCKET)
// ...Handle the error and return.
else
{
   // Make the data channel non-blocking before returning
   IsReadyToRead(hDataSocket);
   return(hDataSocket);
}
```

Before the ConnectFTPControlSocket function returns the socket handle that the next program module will use, ConnectFTPControlSocket sets up the control-channel socket for non-blocking operations. AcceptDataConnection performs the same service for the data channel socket. Since the data socket is now non-blocking, QFTPLIB modifies the ReadDataChannel function to alert you (and your program users) when the program tries to read the data channel and no incoming data exists. You could simply let such an occurrence fail silently. However, theoretically, your program modules should never call the ReadDataChannel function when no incoming data exists. Rather than let the occurrence go by unnoticed, a better solution is to simply display a message box that alerts you and the user that a problem occurred. During program testing, you can monitor these occurrences to see if perhaps you need to modify your program logic. In QFTPLIB, the final program statements for ReadDataChannel are now as shown here:

```
if (nBytesRecv == SOCKET_ERROR)
// ...Handle the error and return.
else if (lData == 0)
{
   MessageBeep(MB_ICONINFORMATION);
   MessageBox(NULL, (LPSTR)"Nothing on the data channel to read!",
      lpszFunctionName, MB_OK|MB_ICONINFORMATION);
   return(FALSE);
}
else
{
   wsprintf(gszCommandBuffer,"%lu bytes written to %s\n", lData,
      lpszFileName);
```

```
    MessageBeep(MB_ICONINFORMATION);
    MessageBox(NULL, gszCommandBuffer, lpszFunctionName,
        MB_OK|MB_ICONINFORMATION);
}
// Read the control channel to see what the server thought about it.
return(ReadFTPServerReply(hControlSocket));
```

If the byte count (as recorded by lData) is zero, ReadDataChannel displays a message box that reports the occurrence. Also, just before returning, ReadDataChannel reads the control channel (using ReadFTPServerReply) to see how the server reports the termination of the read operation. Typically, after a successful file transfer operation (or successfully aborting a file transfer), an FTP server will transmit a reply code 226: *Closing data connection. Requested file action successful.* As you can see, the ReadDataChannel function now returns the reply code from ReadFTPServerReply instead of a Boolean True or False, as was the case for QFTP1 and QFTP2.

GETTING SERIOUS WITH THE SERVER REPLIES

The major change in QFTPLIB occurs in the ReadFTPServerReply function. However, these changes have nothing to do with the fact that the function is moving into a DLL. Rather, the earlier design does not perform a sufficient server-reply parsing. As you will learn, parsing real-world server replies is somewhat more complicated that the earlier designs would lead you to believe. As you will learn, a lot of detail goes into developing a stable function such as ReadFTPServerReply. To develop a function, you must always start with the protocol specification—study it and try to understand every word. Don't let the typical prose in an RFC intimidate you. The professionals that write the RFCs are knowledgeable specialists—and they don't like to waste words. Be assured, if an author discusses something in an RFC, there is an important reason for the discussion. Also, don't write a program that makes assumptions about a subject not discussed in the RFC.

The following ReadFTPServerReply implementation appears to work with most FTP sites. However, you may encounter FTP replies that ReadFTPServerReply does not correctly process. If this occurs, you may want to modify QFTP2 to use QFTPLIB's version of ReadFTPServerReply. You can then run QFTP2 against the problem server. The most effective way to find such problems is to step through a program like QFTP2 with your debugger. The objective of the *quick* program model design is to keep program operation so simple that you can understand everything that happens. If you encounter problems the ReadFTPServerReply function causes, in all probability, you will discover that the server complies with the FTP specification and the ReadFTPServerReply function does not properly handle behavior that the specification permits. After you determine the cause of the problem, you can modify the function to handle the previously unencountered server reply.

REVISITING THE DO-WHILE LOOP IN READFTPSERVERREPLY

As you have learned, QFTP2 added a do-while loop to the ReadFTPServerReply function. As shown next, the QFTPLIB design retains the same basic structure. However, note that the

QFTPLIB design has the ReadFTPServerReply function analyze the contents of the server reply-buffer before entering the do-while loop and just before exiting:

```c
extern "C" UINT FAR PASCAL ReadFTPServerReply(SOCKET hControlChannel)
{
    int iBytesRead;          // Bytes read from the control channel
    int iBufferLength;       // Length of the server reply buffer
    int iEnd;                // Index into the server reply buffer
    int iSpaceRemaining;     // Space remaining in the buffer
    int iReplySize;          // Length of first reply in the buffer

    lpszFunctionName = "ReadFTPServerReply";

    // Be cautious and zero fill the buffer
    _fmemset(gsReplyBuffer, 0, sizeof(gsReplyBuffer));

    // Be tricky and peek ahead to see what's in the buffer.
    if ((iBytesRead = recv(hControlChannel,
        (LPSTR)(gsReplyBuffer), sizeof(gsReplyBuffer), MSG_PEEK)) > 0)
      //
      // ...Analyze the reply buffer before retrieving the data
      //

    iEnd = 0; // Start with zero bytes.
    do
       {
         iSpaceRemaining -= iEnd;
         iBytesRead = recv(hControlChannel,
             (LPSTR)(gsServerReplyText+iEnd), iSpaceRemaining, NO_FLAGS);

                     // Make sure CRLF was not the last byte pair received.
                     // Otherwise, recv() will wait forever for next packet.
                     if (*(gsServerReplyText+(iEND-2)) == '\r' &&
                         *(gsServerReplyText+(iEND-1)) == '\n')
                        //
                        // ...Analyze the reply buffer before returning
                        //
       }
    while (iBytesRead > 0 && iEnd < iBufferLength);

    if (iBytesRead == SOCKET_ERROR)
       // ...Handle the error and return.

    gsServerReplyText[iEnd] = '\0';

    MessageBeep(MB_ICONINFORMATION);
    MessageBox(NULL, (LPSTR)gsServerReplyText, lpszFunctionName,
        MB_OK|MB_ICONINFORMATION);
```

```
    return(GetReplyCode(gsServerReplyText));
}
```

Also, the ReadFTPServerReply function now uses an intermediate buffer (gsReplyBuffer) to peek at the reply from the server. As shown, ReadFTPServerReply uses the _fmemset function to fill gsReplyBuffer with zeros. As a result, the buffer does not contain data from a previous read, which makes things easier for any programmer that needs to visually examine the buffer contents from within a debugger.

USING THE MSG_PEEK FLAG

The pre-loop analysis (shown next) uses the MSG_PEEK flag with the recv function. As discussed in Chapter 8, the MSG_PEEK flag lets your programs preview the data in the incoming-data queue. The MSG_PEEK flag tells Winsock to copy data from the incoming-data queue to your message buffer. However, the MSG_PEEK flag also tells the transport layer not to remove the copied data from the incoming-data queue—which normally happens immediately after a process retrieves data from the queue:

```
// Be tricky and peek ahead to see what's in the buffer.
if ((iBytesRead = recv(hControlChannel,
        (LPSTR)(gsReplyBuffer), sizeof(gsReplyBuffer), MSG_PEEK)) > 0)
  {
    if ((iReplySize = ReadReplyLine(gsReplyBuffer)) == 0)
      iBufferLength = iSpaceRemaining = sizeof(gsServerReplyText);
    else
      iBufferLength = iSpaceRemaining = iReplySize;
  }
else
  {
    MessageBeep(MB_ICONINFORMATION);
    MessageBox(NULL,
          (LPSTR)"Nothing on the control channel to read!",
          lpszFunctionName, MB_OK|MB_ICONINFORMATION);
    return(999); // Return 999 to indicate an error has occurred
  }
```

As you can see, ReadFTPServerReply calls a new function named ReadReplyLine to actually perform the analysis on the previewed data. If recv returns zero bytes, the function displays a message box that tells the user that nothing is on the control channel to read. If data exists, ReadFTPServerReply passes ReadReplyLine a pointer to the buffer (gsReplyBuffer).

REVIEWING THE READREPLYLINE FUNCTION

The ReadReplyLine function (shown next) examines the reply buffer for several conditions:

```
extern "C" UINT FAR PASCAL ReadReplyLine(LPSTR lpszReplyBuffer)
{
  LPSTR lpEOL;                    // End of line
  UINT nLimitReplyBytes;          // End of reply
  PSTR pLastLineCode = "123?";
  LPSTR lpLastLine;
  int i;

  // lpszFunctionName = "ReadReplyLine";

  nLimitReplyBytes = 0;

  if (*(lpszReplyBuffer+3) == MULTILINE_REPLY)
    {
      // Get the code from the reply buffer
      for (i = 0; i <3; i++ )
        *(pLastLineCode+i) = *(lpszReplyBuffer+i);

      // Use a trailing space to look for the last line
      *(pLastLineCode+i) = ' ';

      // Search the buffer for the last line
      if ((lpLastLine = _fstrstr(lpszReplyBuffer, pLastLineCode)))
        {
          // Okay, be cautious and make sure a CRLF exists
          lpEOL = (LPSTR)_fstrstr(lpLastLine, EOL_MARKER);
          // Note length to read if more than one reply is in the buffer
          nLimitReplyBytes = lpEOL ?
              (UINT)((lpEOL - lpszReplyBuffer)+2) : 0;
        }
      else
        nLimitReplyBytes = 0;
    }
  else
    {
      // If the reply is not multiline then find the end of the line.
      lpEOL = (LPSTR)_fstrstr(lpszReplyBuffer, EOL_MARKER);

      // If an end-of-line marker was not found, read everything
      // (i.e. don't limit the reply size). Otherwise, only read to the
      // end of line marker.
      nLimitReplyBytes = lpEOL ? (UINT)((lpEOL - lpszReplyBuffer)+2) : 0;
    }
  return(nLimitReplyBytes);
}
```

As explained in the following paragraphs, ReadReplyLine has one primary objective and one secondary objective. Primarily, the ReadReplyLine function ensures that ReadFTPServerReply does not inadvertently read two different replies as one. In other words, if the receive buffer contains more than one reply code, ReadReplyLine finds the end of the first reply code and tells the ReadFTPServerReply function to read up to that point in the buffer only. To do so, ReadReplyLine determines how many bytes ReadFTPServerReply should read and returns that value to ReadFTPServerReply. The ReadReplyLine function's secondary objective is to help make sure ReadFTPServerReply does not inadvertently treat a partial reply from the server as though it were a complete reply. The keys to these two objectives are the end-of-line and multiline definitions the protocol specification contains.

ADDING DOS FILE-NAMING CAPABILITIES

As previously discussed, because most FTP sites use UNIX-based computers for FTP-server hosts, many filenames on the Internet will not comply with the DOS eight-dot-three file-naming convention. The ExtractFileName function (shown next) solves the file-naming compatibility problem for a Windows-based FTP client program. The ExtractFileName function creates an (8.3) DOS filename from a character string that contains a UNIX filename. First, the function searches for the last forward slash in the path. (In other words, the function finds the last directory in the path string, if any.) The function then enters a for-loop to store up to the next eight characters in the path string. The for-loop also tests for the end of the string (null-terminator) and a period (which indicates the beginning of a file extension). Finally, the function adds a period and then stores up to the next three characters in the path string to create a file extension. The following program statements define the ExtractFileName function:

```
extern "C" void _export FAR PASCAL ExtractFileName(LPSTR lpPathString,
    LPSTR lpszFileName)
{
  LPSTR lp;                  // General purpose pointer
  UINT i;                    // General purpose index
  UINT iExtLength = 0;       // Length of file extension (after the dash)

  // Find the last forward slash (assume UNIX/NT directory conventions)
  if (lp = _fstrrchr(lpPathString, '/'))
    lp++;
  else
    lp = lpPathString;

  // Loop while the length of the name is less than 8 characters
  // (a valid DOS length), the character is not a dot and the
  // pointer is valid
  for (i = 0; i < 8 && *lp != '.' && lp; i++)
    *(lpszFileName+i) = *(lp++);

  // Add a dot to mark the start of the file extension
  *(lpszFileName+i) = '.';
  i++;
```

```
    // Find the last dot and use up to the next three characters for
    // the new file name.
    if (lp = _fstrrchr(lpPathString, '.'))
        for (iExtLength = 0; iExtLength < 3 && (*(lp)); iExtLength++)
            *(lpszFileName+(i++)) = *(++lp);

    // Null-terminate the new file name
    *(lpszFileName+i) = '\0';

    return;
}
```

Note: The ExtractFileName function expects the caller to allocate enough memory to store up to thirteen characters—the eight-dot-three filename plus the null-terminator.

To open (create) a file to store file data it receives from an FTP-server host, the SockFTP client program (which you will learn more about in the next chapter) uses the filename the ExtractFileName function creates. The SockFTP client will use the CreateTransferFile function shown here:

```
extern "C" HFILE _export FAR PASCAL CreateTransferFile(LPSTR
    lpszFileName)
{
  HFILE hFile;              // File handle for data file
  OFSTRUCT openFileBuff;    // The Windows open file data structure

  lpszFunctionName = "CreateTransferFile";

  if ((hFile = OpenFile(lpszFileName, (OFSTRUCT far *)&openFileBuff,
      OF_CREATE)) == HFILE_ERROR)
    {
      _lclose(hFile);
      wsprintf(gszCommandBuffer,"Error creating file: %s\n",
          lpszFileName);
      MessageBeep(MB_ICONSTOP);
      MessageBox(NULL, gszCommandBuffer, lpszFunctionName,
          MB_OK|MB_ICONSTOP);
    }
  return(hFile);
}
```

As you can see, to create a file, the CreateTransferFile function calls the Windows OpenFile function with an OF_CREATE flag. If the file creation causes an error, the CreateTransferFile function displays an error message in a Windows message box. Otherwise, the CreateTransferFile function returns a file handle for the newly created file. The SockFTP client program discussed in the chapter will pass the file handle returned by the CreateTransferFile function to the TransferFile function shown here:

```
extern "C" UINT _export FAR PASCAL TransferFile(SOCKET hControlSocket,
    SOCKET hDataSocket, HFILE hFile)
{
  char szFileData[1024];       // Buffer to hold file data
  int nCharRecv;               // Number of characters received
  char szMsg[100];             // General purpose buffer for messages

  nCharRecv = recv(hDataSocket, (LPSTR)&szFileData, sizeof(szFileData),
        NO_FLAGS);
  if (nCharRecv > 0 )
    {
      if (HFILE_ERROR == _lwrite (hFile, szFileData, nCharRecv))
        {
          _lclose(hFile);
          wsprintf(szMsg,"%d Error occurred during recv()!", nCharRecv);
          MessageBox(NULL, szMsg, PROG_NAME, MB_OK|MB_ICONSTOP);
          return(HFILE_ERROR);
        }
    }
  else if (nCharRecv == SOCKET_ERROR)
    {
      _lclose(hFile);
      nCharRecv = WSAGetLastError();
      wsprintf(szMsg,"%d Error occurred during recv()!", nCharRecv);
      MessageBox(NULL, szMsg, PROG_NAME, MB_OK|MB_ICONSTOP);
      return(SOCKET_ERROR);
    }

  if (nCharRecv == 0)
    {
      _lclose(hFile);
      ReadFTPServerReply(hControlSocket);
    }

  return(nCharRecv);
}
```

As you can see, the TransferFile function is very similar to the ReadDataChannel function discussed earlier in this chapter. However, as previously noted, the TransferFile function does not enter a do-while loop like the ReadDataChannel function. Instead, the TransferFile function calls the recv function one time and returns the number of bytes read from the data channel. The TransferFile function writes any received data to the file that corresponds to the file handle passed to it as its third parameter (hFile). When the recv function returns with zero bytes from the data channel (indicating that the server closed the data channel), the TransferFile function closes the file and reads the server's reply from the control channel. To determine when the server has finished, the calling program module can test the byte count the TransferFile function returns. When the TransferFile function returns zero bytes, the calling program knows that the server finished the transfer and that the TransferFile function closed the data file on the local hard disk.

PUTTING IT ALL TOGETHER

In this chapter, you have learned how to create a *quick* program that effectively demonstrates the key features of a rather sophisticated Internet protocol—the File Transfer Protocol. You have also learned how to move the functions that comprise this program into a Windows DLL. One important point to note is that none of these program functions used any of the asynchronous Windows-specific Winsock functions. As you will discover in the next chapter, by limiting the custom Winsock-based DLL to the synchronous Winsock functions, you have created a tool that you can use within the Visual Basic environment, as well as a C/C++ environment. Visual-programming environments offer many benefits, particularly for testing and experimentation. You can use simple DLLs, such as QFTPLIB, to rapidly prototype and test program logic and network operations.

Key elements of an application will become more clear from testing and real-world experimentation on the Internet. If you are a C/C++ programmer, from such results, you can begin to develop more sophisticated programs and DLLs that effectively use the asynchronous Windows-specific functions. If you primarily use other environments (such as Visual Basic) where the asynchronous Windows functions are of limited value, you can continue to build sophisticated network programs that rely on simple DLL implementations, such as QFTPLIB. In the next chapter, you will create an FTP-based client program that uses Visual Basic to access the QFTPLIB functions created in this chapter. You will learn that you can combine a visual programming environment with a simple Winsock-based DLL to rapidly create applications and tools that help you understand the Internet. Before you move on to the next chapter, make sure you understand the following key concepts:

- ✓ FTP clients initiate TCP connections for the FTP control channel.
- ✓ FTP servers initiate TCP connections for the FTP data channel.
- ✓ FTP clients use a listener socket to detect data-channel connection requests from FTP servers.
- ✓ Programs configure an FTP listener socket that acts like a server socket.
- ✓ You can easily encapsulate Winsock-based program routines in a Windows DLL and build a solid programming layer your other programs can use.

Chapter 18
Visual Programming on the Internet

As discussed in Chapter 17, most programmers call a visual-programming tool any product that lets them draw objects, such as dialog boxes, rather than write equivalent code. Normally, visual tools are event-driven rather than procedure-oriented. In other words, visual tools lend themselves to the asynchronous *point-and-click* environment of Windows. Due to the growing popularity of asynchronous operating systems and their typical *graphical user-interfaces* (GUI), more and more application designers are using visual-programming tools.

Microsoft's Visual Basic is probably one of the most popular visual-programming tools in existence. Although this chapter will focus on how you can use Visual Basic to write Internet programs, this chapter is not about Visual Basic programming. As such, you can use the techniques this chapter presents with whatever visual programming tools you normally prefer to use. This chapter shows you how to integrate FTP-based DLL functions with a graphical user-interface create a fully functional FTP client program.

- ◆ How to effectively use Winsock-based functions encapsulated in a Windows DLL

- ◆ How to define several simple routines that work together to perform complex Internet operations

- ◆ How to integrate extremely simple Windows DLLs with other program modules to create fully functional and sophisticated client programs

- ◆ How to use visual tools to develop other tools for testing and experimental purposes on the Internet

WATCHING SOCKFTP IN ACTION

To better understand the FTP client-program design discussed in the following sections, you may want to run the SockFTP program first. After you have seen the program in operation, you will more easily recognize and understand the purpose of many SockFTP program functions.

To run the SockFTP program, double-click your mouse on the SockFTP icon that appears in the Internet Programming program-group window. The SockFTP program window will appear as shown in Figure 18.1.

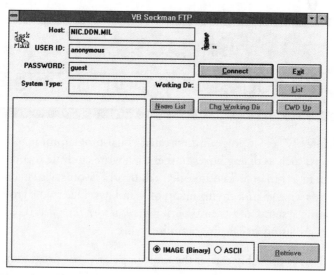

Figure 18.1 SockFTP program window.

At startup, SockFTP defaults to the FTP login parameters for FTP site NIC.DDN.MIL—an FTP repository for all online Internet RFC documents. To begin, click your mouse on the Connect button. SockFTP, in turn, will try to establish a connection to port 21 (the FTP protocol port) on the host NIC.DDN.MIL.

After SockFTP connects, SockFTP uses the parameters in the USER ID and PASSWORD text-boxes to automatically log you in. If the login is successful, SockFTP transmits, in succession, the PWD, SYST, and NLST commands.

If the FTP server accepts the NLST command (File Name List command), you may see disk activity on your computer. To keep the SockFTP design simple, yet useful, SockFTP reads all data your system receives through the data channel and writes the data to your hard drive. The filename that SockFTP uses for each write operation is the FTP command that caused the data transfer. For example, after the NLST transfer completes, you will find a new file named NLST.CMD on your hard drive.

If this sounds familiar to you, it should. SockFTP is simply using the ReadDataChannel function that you created in the QFTPLIB program in Chapter 17. After the server closes the data channel, SockFTP reads NLST.CMD from your hard drive and displays the filenames in the directory list-box located on the right side of the SockFTP program window.

After displaying the NLST results, SockFTP enables five command buttons (Name List, Chg Working Dir, CWD Up, List, and Retrieve) that manage server operations for you, as shown in Figure 18.2.

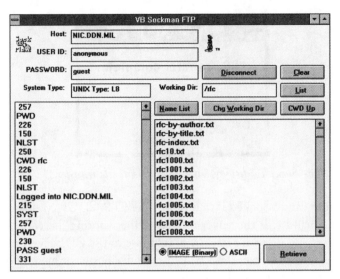

Figure 18.2 *SockFTP program window.*

Use the scroll bar to scroll through the directory list and locate the rfc directory. Click your mouse on the rfc directory name to highlight it and then click your mouse on the Chg Working Dir button. SockFTP, in turn, will use the selected item in the directory list-box (the rfc directory) as a parameter for the FTP CWD command. In other words, when you click your mouse on the Chg Working Dir button as just described, SockFTP will transmit the FTP CWD command with "rfc" as its parameter.

If the server accepts the command, the server will change its working directory for your FTP session to the rfc directory. If SockFTP receives an okay reply code from the server, SockFTP transmits another NLST command to display the contents of the rfc directory. In other words, each time you click on the Chg Working Dir button and SockFTP receives an *okay* reply from the server, SockFTP automatically transmits the NLST command to display the contents of the new working directory.

Use the directory list-box's scroll bar to locate a file named RFC-INDEX.TXT. When you find the file RFC-INDEX.TXT, click your mouse on it to select it and then click your mouse on the Retrieve button. SockFTP, in turn, will initiate a file-transfer operation to transfer RFC-INDEX.TXT to your hard disk. (RFC-INDEX.TXT contains the most current list of RFCs for the Internet.)

After you click your mouse on the Retrieve button, SockFTP uses the Host, USER ID, PASSWORD, and System Type text-boxes to give you file-transfer progress reports. When the file transfer completes, SockFTP will display a message box, as shown in Figure 18.3.

Figure 18.3 *Message box SockFTPdisplays after a successful file transfer.*

The CWD Up button causes SockFTP to transmit the FTP CDUP command. As you may recall, the CDUP command tells the server to change the working directory to the next higher subdirectory in the server's directory tree. If, in response to the CDUP command, SockFTP receives an *okay* reply from the server, SockFTP automatically transmits the NLST command to display the contents of the new default directory.

At any time, you can manually transmit the NLST command by clicking your mouse on the Name List button. The List button causes SockFTP to transmit the FTP LIST command, which provides more details about the files and subdirectories in the server's working directory. The Retrieve button causes SockFTP to transmit the FTP RETR command to retrieve the filename currently selected in the directory list-box. When you have finished taking SockFTP for a spin around the Internet, click your mouse on the Disconnect button (if you are still connected to an FTP server) and then click the Exit button to quit the program.

UNDERSTANDING THE DESIGN GOALS

Although SockFTP is fully functional, its implementation focuses on demonstrating visual programming techniques and FTP protocol operations. In other words, SockFTP does not implement all the typical error checking a commercial-quality FTP client requires. For example, when you click your mouse on the Retrieve button, SockFTP simply extracts the currently selected item from the directory list-box and transmits the value as a parameter with the FTP RETR command. If you have previously clicked the List button to receive a detailed file and directory listing, the FTP server will not understand the parameter that SockFTP transmits with the RETR command. (That is, the parameter will be the detailed file entry from the directory list-box.)

In other words, such behavior is not a flaw in the SockFTP design—it's a by-product of rapid prototyping. As you may know, one of the strengths of visual programming is that you can quickly develop or change programs. The visual design of SockFTP is no exception. You can easily experiment with different commands and operations against different FTP servers. In many cases, you can learn more about a protocol by watching how a server handles erroneous commands and parameters. Sometimes you can predict the results. In other cases, you cannot. You can test your understanding of a protocol by transmitting various commands and reviewing the results. If a server responds in a way that you did not expect, you may not understand some of the subtle points related to the protocol.

For example, a minor detail in one of Click procedures in the initial SockFTP implementation caused an FTP server to report that it did not understand the CDUP command. Close examination of the module revealed that the CDUP command string included a single space between "CDUP" and the CRLF. The FTP specification clearly disallows this. However, with a different protocol that did not clearly specify server results, you could easily modify your command strings, transmit them, and observe the server's behavior.

As you have learned, all the example programs in *Internet Programming* make extensive use of message boxes. Message boxes are easy to use and make great teaching aids. However, they can severely handicap a program's usefulness. To make the SockFTP program more useful without decreasing its tutorial value, the source files on the Internet Programming companion disk encapsulate two QFTPLIB message boxes inside #IFDEF statements. The first #IFDEF statement occurs near the end of the ReadFTPServerReply function, as shown here:

```
#ifdef _DEBUG
   MessageBeep(MB_ICONINFORMATION);
   MessageBox(NULL, (LPSTR)gsServerReplyText, lpszFunctionName,
        MB_OK|MB_ICONINFORMATION);
#endif
```

If you have a lot of experience with the Microsoft Visual C++ compiler, you may know that Visual C++ lets you store makefile options for both *release* and *debug* versions of your source code. When you choose the project option to build a debug version of your program, Visual C++ automatically defines the _DEBUG symbolic constant. In effect, when you compile a debug version of your program, you enable any code residing within the #IFDEF construct. The other #IFDEF statement occurs near the end of the ReadDataChannel function, as shown here:

```
#ifdef _DEBUG
   else
     {
       wsprintf(gszCommandBuffer,"%lu bytes written to %s\n", lData,
            lpszFileName);
       MessageBeep(MB_ICONINFORMATION);
       MessageBox(NULL, gszCommandBuffer, lpszFunctionName,
            MB_OK|MB_ICONINFORMATION);
     }
#endif
```

The message boxes encapsulated in ReadFTPServerReply and ReadDataChannel report every occurrence of a recv operation for the FTP control and data channels. If you modify the SockFTP program or you encounter problems, you will want to recompile the QFTPLIB source code with _DEBUG defined. Doing so will both enable message boxes and help you monitor activity within the DLL. However, for normal program operation, these two message boxes are not necessary.

Note: All compilers let you define constants like _DEBUG. If you use a compiler other than Microsoft Visual C++ (such as Borland C++), see your compiler manuals for instructions on how to define constants such as _DEBUG to control program compilation.

If you run the SockFTP program, you will notice that the message list-box on the left side of the SockFTP program window contains a running log of the dialog between SockFTP and the FTP server. SockFTP also adds other information to the log during the FTP session. SockFTP inserts each new log entry at the top of the message list-box. At first, you may find this behavior odd. It may seem more logical to add each new log entry to the bottom of the message list-box. However, if you add new log entries to the bottom of the message list-box, you must constantly scroll through the list-box to find the results of the last server command. By inserting the commands at the top of the message list-box, the most recent command results are clearly visible at all times.

The key point to note is that visual-programming products make it easy for you to rapidly prototype and test not only applications, but the behavior of Internet servers and protocols. While SockFTP is not a fully functional FTP client, its design provides the framework for you to build a powerful testing tool for experimenting with the Internet.

Throughout the book, the *quick* program model provided an excellent teaching model. Also, as you have learned, you can easily convert the *quick* programs into functions for a custom DLL. From the custom DLL, you can build even more powerful tools that teach you about, and make it easy for you to experiment with, different program designs on the Internet.

You can build experimentation tools with any programming product. However, typically, visual programming products will let you prototype and experiment more rapidly. The Visual Basic product is especially powerful due to its interpretative nature. Using a solid underlying DLL that performs low-level network operations, you can use Visual Basic to rapidly test program designs and network operations with very little programming effort. The combination of the two (custom DLL and Visual Basic) let you focus on the big picture and the design of your ultimate program application—whatever that may be.

For example, to make SockFTP appear to be an FTP client, user-friendly command buttons automatically transmit FTP commands with the correct syntax. To provide more flexibility, you could modify SockFTP and add another text-box that accepts commands you type during an FTP session. In other words, SockFTP implements only a few of the available FTP commands. You could add a command string text-box to SockFTP, experiment with the other FTP commands, and then decide which ones, if any, to add to SockFTP.

You can also easily modify SockFTP to connect to different server ports. In other words, you can use the SockFTP design to create a general purpose Internet utility for use with multiple protocols and servers. To do so, however. you will also need to modify a few functions in the QFTPLIB dynamic link library. However, the *quick* program models in previous chapters have demonstrated how to do just about anything you might need to do.

How you use SockFTP is up to you. However, if you are serious about programming the Internet, you can find a lot of imaginative uses for SockFTP or some derivative of its design. As you encounter new requirements that QFTPLIB.DLL does not handle, you can develop a *quick* program that models the new requirement. Next, you can add the *quick* program functions to your own custom version of the DLL.

If you are primarily a Visual Basic programmer, you will probably derive Visual Basic applications from the experimental designs of the *quick* programs. However, if you are primarily a C/C++ programmer, you can derive powerful software-development tools from the *quick* programs. In other words, regardless of how you develop your final target applications, you can use visual-programming tools, such as Visual Basic, to boost your programming productivity.

For example, run SockFTP, examine the program statements that comprise the program, and experiment with various changes to the program. Then, ask yourself how long it would take to perform the same programming tasks in a C/C++ environment. Especially consider the possibility that you might not know at the beginning of the effort precisely how an Internet server or protocol would respond to your testing.

The following sections discuss the SockFTP implementation details. As you examine the various components, don't view SockFTP as an FTP client only. If you do, you will miss the real value of the program. You can buy (or freely obtain) better FTP clients. However, you probably can't find an Internet experimentation tool like SockFTP with complete source code that you can easily adapt to your own personal needs. The primary objective of the SockFTP design is to make such a tool available to you. The goal of the following sections is to explain the tool in sufficient detail so you can modify it, as required, to meet your needs. In other words, SockFTP is a work in progress— you can complete the work to satisfy your own personal requirements.

REVIEWING YOUR OPTIONS

This chapter discusses a Visual Basic program design for an FTP client based on the DLL (QFTPLIB) that you developed in the previous chapter. If you prefer to use a visual-programming tool other than Visual Basic, simply implement the algorithms this chapter discusses with your preferred tool. As you will learn, the program code this chapter presents is relatively simple.

Although most experienced Visual Basic programmers are familiar with the techniques for using DLLs, many do not frequently take advantage of DLLs. Instead, most Visual Basic programmers prefer to use VBX (Visual Basic Extensions) files. VBX files are Windows DLLs with a few features specially designed for Visual Basic programmers. Unfortunately, 32-bit versions of Windows do not support VBXs. All versions of Windows support and will continue to support a standard Windows DLL. To port a VBX-based program to 32-bit Windows, programmers must convert VBXs to the new Microsoft standard—OLE controls.

In other words, as you will learn, you can use DLLs with visual products (such as Visual Basic) with very little extra effort. You can also easily move a DLL-based Visual Basic program to 32-bit Windows. However, if you want to develop VBX-based programs and move them to 32-bit Windows, you must first learn how to use OLE controls in Visual Basic. In addition, you must learn how to convert all your VBXs into OLE controls. If you want to plan for the future, you should either use OLE controls or design new Visual Basic programs around standard Windows DLLs.

If you prefer to temporarily avoid the rather steep OLE learning curve, you can design a custom DLL interface that will simultaneously support Visual Basic and C/C++ programs. In fact, if you use the Windows DLL approach to Winsock development, you can easily (and simultaneously) support a wide mix of Visual Basic and C/C++ network-based programs that run on a mix of 16-bit and 32-bit platforms.

This chapter does not discuss Visual Basic programming with VBX or OLE controls. The focus of this chapter is strictly on Visual Basic's use of Windows DLLs (particularly the QFTPLIB.DLL). As discussed, you can use Visual Basic or any other visually-oriented programming tool to create the same implementation discussed here.

QFTP STAGE FOUR: GETTING A VISUAL ON THE TARGET

As you may know, Visual Basic provides programmers with a tremendous productivity boost when they design user-interfaces. It can take a typical C/C++ programmer a staggering amount of time and code lines to implement a design that you can create in a few hours with Visual Basic. Although many Visual Basic programmers design front-end (user-interface) and back-end (file, hardware, and network input/output) products with Visual Basic, you can use Visual Basic for your user-interface and use a custom DLL for the back-end to your programs.

If nothing else, you can use Visual Basic to prototype your user-interface and a lot of the program logic that typically goes into designing a fully-functional product. The beauty of using Visual Basic for the front-end is that you may discover that the Visual Basic front-end meets all your program requirements. If so, you can completely eliminate the development time required for the C/C++ user-interface. If necessary, you can later replace the Visual Basic front-end with a C/C++ interface—or any other interface that lets you access functions in Windows DLLs.

In other words, placing the core of your Internet programs in a standard Windows DLL provides you with tremendous flexibility. In short, you can completely replace the front-ends to your Internet applications without affecting other parts of your program. By encapsulating your Winsock-based routines in a DLL, you can continually refine the visual side of your application without modifying stable network-algorithms that you can evolve over time.

REVIEWING THE VISUAL BASIC-TO-DLL INTERFACE

This chapter uses Visual Basic to develop an FTP-client program (named SockFTP). The program uses the QFTPLIB dynamic link library that you developed in the previous chapter. However, before discussing the SockFTP's design details, you may find it helpful to review the Visual Basic-to-DLL interface.

UNDERSTANDING THE DECLARE STATEMENT

In many cases, you can simplify your Visual Basic program designs by encapsulating frequently used routines in a DLL. Likewise, there may be times when your programs require functions that are easier for you to code in C or C++. By placing such functions in a DLL, you can easily call them from Visual Basic. As is the case for C/C++, your Visual Basic programs can call any exported function located in the DLL. The key to using DLLs in Visual Basic is the *Declare* statement. The Visual Basic Declare statement declares a reference to an external procedure located in a DLL. For DLLs, the Visual Basic Declare statement is the equivalent of a function prototype in C/C++. In other words, the Declare statement defines the Visual Basic interface to a function located in a DLL. As shown in the following list, the Declare statement can contain up to six parts:

- The Visual Basic procedure type (function or subroutine) represented by the DLL function

- The name of the function

- The name of the DLL that contains the function

- An optional alias name for the function

- An optional list of arguments

- A declaration of the returned variable type if the procedure returns a value—Visual Basic does not require the procedure to do so.

For example, the SockFTP program declares the Windows lstrcpy function to be an external procedure:

```
Declare Function lstrcpy Lib "KERNEL.DLL" (ByVal lpToString As Any,
    ByVal lpFromString As Any) As Long
```

Likewise, SockFTP declares the Winsock closesocket function and QFTPLIB's ReadDataChannel function to be external procedures:

```
Declare Function closesocket Lib "WINSOCK.DLL" (ByVal hSocket
     As Integer) As Integer

Declare Function ReadDataChannel Lib "QFTPLIB.DLL" (ByVal hCtrlSocket
     As Integer, ByVal hDataSocket As Integer, ByVal lpszFileName
     As String) As Integer
```

You can write a Visual Basic Declare statement for practically any C/C++ function prototype that you want to create. However, it is absolutely critical that you correctly define the variable definitions in the Declare statement. If you do not, you can expect Windows to generate a General Protection Fault (GPF)!

Internet Programming will use the generic term *procedure* to refer to Visual Basic functions and subroutines unless referring to a specific function or subroutine by name. A *function* (for which Visual Basic uses the *Function* keyword) declares a procedure that returns a value. A subroutine (for which Visual Basic uses the *Sub* keyword) declares a procedure that does not return a value.

Although the syntax is slightly different between a Visual Basic subroutine and a Visual Basic function, you can, in general, use either as your program requires. However, if you declare a procedure to be a function (one that returns a value), Visual Basic requires you to store the return value. In other words, with Visual Basic, you cannot ignore the return value from a function like you can in C/C++. (Actually, you can ignore the return value but you must store it first.) In general, *Internet Programming's* use of the term *function* in this chapter will refer to a C/C++ function in a DLL.

After you properly define a Declare statement for a function in a DLL, you can use the function like any other Visual Basic procedure. For example, the following Visual Basic code fragment calls QFTPLIB's AcceptDataConnection and ReadDataChannel functions, the Winsock closesocket function, and a locally defined Visual Basic subroutine named subShowServerReplyCode:

```
If intServerReplyCode < 400 Then

  intDataSocket = AcceptDataConnection(intListenSocket)

  If intDataSocket <> INVALID_SOCKET Then
    intServerReplyCode = ReadDataChannel(glbintControlSocket,
         intDataSocket, "NLST.CMD")
  End If

  subShowServerReplyCode (intServerReplyCode)
  intWinsockReplyCode = closesocket(intDataSocket)
End If
```

As you can see, the program uses the DLL function and Visual Basic subroutine within the *If* statement. To use the DLL function, the program simply declares and then calls the function. Although SockFTP does not use any "subroutine-type" functions, you declare them in exactly the same way as a function—except with the Sub keyword and no return type. The source file SOCKFTP.BAS contains complete declarations for all DLL-based functions that SockFTP uses.

USING VISUAL BASIC CALLING CONVENTIONS

Visual Basic documentation typically uses the term *argument* to refer to variable values passed to functions and subroutines. Windows documentation, on the other hand, typically uses the term *parameter*. In the context of this chapter, arguments and parameters are the same.

As a C/C++ programmer, you can pass parameters to a function by value or by reference (a pointer value). Visual Basic provides the same flexibility; however, Visual Basic syntax is quite different. By default, Visual Basic passes all parameters as pointers. Unless you specify otherwise, when Visual Basic passes a variable to a procedure, Visual Basic passes a pointer to the variable in the calling procedure.

This means, by default, any operations that a Visual Basic procedure performs on a variable will reflect in the variable located in the caller. If you want to pass a copy of a variable's contents to a Visual Basic procedure, you must use Visual Basic's ByVal keyword in the procedure declaration.

Handling string variables with Visual Basic requires careful attention to detail. As you may know, C/C++ handles character strings as a simple series of bytes. Visual Basic handles string values as a special data type called HLSTR (a handle to a Visual Basic string). The implementation details about HLSTR are unimportant. The key point to note is that a normal Windows DLL does not know how to handle an HLSTR data type.

Since *Internet Programming's* objective is to design program modules Visual Basic and C/C++ programs can use without modification, you need to know how to avoid the HLSTR data type. As you will learn, Visual Basic provides a way to bypass the HLSTR data type.

When you pass Visual Basic a string variable to a DLL using ByVal, Visual Basic null-terminates the value before passing it to the DLL function. However, in the case of a string parameter, the ByVal keyword tells Visual Basic to obtain a copy of the string modified by the DLL. Visual Basic does not really pass the DLL a pointer to a Visual Basic memory location. However, Visual Basic will retrieve a copy of the modified string for use in your program.

To change a Visual Basic string within a DLL function, you must explicitly allocate memory space to hold the string buffer passed to the DLL. If you are primarily a C programmer, you may not realize the significance of this stipulation. As you know, in a C program, you must always allocate string space. However, Visual Basic programmers rarely need to do so.

A Visual Basic programmer can simply assign a string value to a variable of type String, and Visual Basic automatically handles the memory allocation. However, because Visual Basic does not automatically handle memory allocation for a string parameter passed to a DLL, your program must explicitly do so.

Again, the Visual Basic implementation details are unimportant. However, there are two key points to note. One, you cannot pass a Visual Basic string to a DLL unless you specially design a DLL to handle Visual Basic HLSTR data types. Two, if you use the ByVal keyword with a string parameter to a DLL, you must explicitly allocate space for the string (including the null-terminator). By doing so, you can use DLL-based functions to modify Visual Basic string variables. Later in this chapter, you will follow these guidelines to change a Visual Basic character string within a DLL.

Understanding Visual Basic Parameter Types

C/C++ can handle a much wider variety of data types than Visual Basic. As a result, you must treat certain types of parameters required by DLL functions with caution. Although Visual Basic includes 32-bit and 16-bit data types for numbers, Visual Basic does not distinguish between signed and unsigned numbers. All integer values in Visual Basic are signed-values. Visual Basic refers to its 16-bit numeric data type as data type Integer. Like the syntax for all Visual Basic variable declarations, you use the following syntax to declare an integer variable:

```
intVariableName As Integer
```

You can use the Visual Basic Integer data type to represent the following Windows and C/C++ data types: int, short, unsigned int, unsigned short, BOOL, and WORD.

Using LPSTR Values in Visual Basic

As you may know, many functions in the Windows API return an LPSTR value. LPSTR is simply a long (far or 32-bit) pointer to an address in your computer's memory. The memory address pointed to by an LPSTR variable holds character data which may or may not be null-terminated.

Since the pointer variable itself is actually a 32-bit value, you can use a Visual Basic Long data type to store an LPSTR pointer. Windows API functions that require an LPSTR parameter actually expect to receive a 32-bit value that represents a memory address. Typically, Windows functions use LPSTR pointer variables to pass references to character data.

As previously discussed, in effect, you can pass DLL functions a pointer (such as LPSTR) to string data by declaring the string parameter as ByVal As String. Doing so lets the DLL operate on the string data, and your Visual Basic program can use the string that results from such operations. This process actually uses a specially formatted copy of the data that both the DLL and Visual Basic can access. As you have learned, however, the Visual Basic program must explicitly allocate memory for the string.

Visual Basic cannot access memory allocated outside the Visual Basic environment. As such, to access string data that does not originate in a Visual Basic program module, you can use the Long data type as a far pointer. When a DLL returns an LPSTR pointer to Visual Basic, you should store the value in a Long data type. In turn, you can pass this pointer value to a Windows API function that can access memory locations based on the pointer's contents.

Another way to access non-Visual Basic string data is to use the Windows lstrcpy function. As you may know, the Windows lstrcpy function works like the C/C++ strcpy function. In other words, the function accepts two pointer variables and copies data from the memory location pointed to by one variable to the memory location pointed to by the other variable.

Understanding SockFTP

Like C/C++-based Windows programs, Visual Basic programs consist of various types of program objects. Probably the most fundamental object in Visual Basic is the *Form* object.

A Visual Basic Form is very similar to a Windows dialog box. A Visual Basic Form can contain various object types, such as text-boxes, list-boxes, command buttons, and so on. The SockFTP program uses a single form named frmSockFTP and builds the FTP client around objects located on this form. The following sections discuss the various objects the SockFTP project defines and includes.

Understanding Objects, Properties, and Events

Just as most activity in a Windows program revolves around Windows messages, most activity in a Visual Basic program revolves around *events*. In Visual Basic, when an object recognizes an action, the object triggers a Visual Basic event. For example, when you click your mouse on a Visual Basic command button, you trigger an event for that command button. Likewise, pressing a key with your program cursor in a text-box triggers an event for the text-box. Visual Basic events can occur as a result of a user's action or a program statement. In addition, the Windows operating system may trigger an event.

If you are unfamiliar with Visual Basic, this section provides a quick introduction to Visual Basic concepts related to objects, properties, and events. In doing so, this section also presents all the Visual Basic objects that comprise the SockFTP client program.

The essence of creating a sophisticated Windows program is managing Windows messages. Likewise, event-programming is at the core of a well-designed Visual Basic program. Visual Basic provides a programmer with access to each event recognized by a Visual Basic object. A programmer can let Visual Basic perform some default action as the result of an event, or the programmer can define a Visual Basic procedure that executes each time the event occurs.

This event-driven programming model is extremely powerful. It also lends itself to visual programming. You draw objects on a form and use a point-and-click strategy to set various properties related to the form. Visual Basic provides list-boxes that automatically identify all objects and available properties.

Note: Similar tools exist for C/C++ programmers, but such tools are not as popular as Visual Basic.

The SockFTP program barely scratches the surface of Visual Basic's event-programming model. In fact, SockFTP only works with eleven events. As discussed, Windows can trigger an event just like a user. Two of the events SockFTP uses are system-generated. For example, each time the user starts SockFTP, the program loads a main SockFTP form, and Windows triggers a Form Load event. Likewise, when a user exits the program, Visual Basic closes (or unloads) the form and Windows triggers a Form Unload event. The other nine events occur when a user clicks their mouse on one of the command buttons SockFTP defines.

If you refer back to Figure 18.1, you will discover that only seven command buttons are visible. *Visibility* is a property Visual Basic associates with many Visual Basic objects. When the Visible property is True, the object is visible—when the Visible property is False, Visual Basic hides the object. SockFTP defines two of its command buttons with the Visible property equal to False. In other words, by default, the command buttons are invisible to you. The two hidden buttons are the Disconnect and Clear command buttons.

Another way to control which options a user may choose is to change the Enabled property. For example, examine Figure 18.1 again and take special note of the List, Name List, Retrieve, Chg Working Dir, and CWD Up command buttons. You will see that all four buttons are grayed-out—in other words, not enabled. Although a user can see and click their mouse on disabled objects like the disabled command buttons, Visual Basic prevents any object-recognized events from occurring as a result of such actions.

The only command buttons enabled at startup are the Connect and Exit buttons. When the SockFTP user clicks their mouse on the Connect button, a Connect button Click event occurs. As you will learn, when the Connect button Click event occurs, SockFTP uses the Host and User ID information from the SockFTP form to initiate an FTP session with an Internet host.

The procedure that executes when the Connect button Click event occurs uses the Visual Basic program statements shown next to toggle the Visible property for the Connect and Exit buttons to False:

```
frmSockFTP.cmdConnect.Visible = False
frmSockFTP.cmdExit.Visible = False
```

In other words, when you click the Connect button, the Connect and Exit buttons disappear.

By design, event-driven programs prevent a user from initiating potentially dangerous combinations of events or prevent unnecessary events that cause an additional and unnecessary process load on the operating system or program.

For example, since the SockFTP design uses one FTP site connection at a time, SockFTP disables the Connect button while you remain logged into an FTP site. Likewise, SockFTP hides the Exit button to remind you to disconnect your FTP connection before you exit the program. SockFTP does not prevent you from exiting (in fact, the program automatically disconnects the socket when you exit). However, as a general practice, you should gracefully terminate an FTP connection (by transmitting the QUIT command discussed in Chapter 16). The SockFTP design encourages that behavior.

Refer back to Figure 18.2 to see how the SockFTP program window appears after SockFTP successfully logs you into an FTP site. As you will discover, the Connect and Exit buttons are invisible, and Visual Basic now displays the Disconnect and Clear buttons. Likewise, the other five command buttons are no longer grayed-out—their Enabled property is True.

Just as setting the Visible property to False hides an object, setting the Visible property equal to True displays the object. SockFTP uses the program statements shown next to display the Disconnect and Clear buttons:

```
frmSockFTP.cmdDisconnect.Visible = True
frmSockFTP.cmdClear.Visible = True
```

If you use SockFTP to connect to an FTP site, SockFTP temporarily disables most of the command buttons each time it initiates a network operation that may take a little time (such as when looking up a host address). SockFTP defines a Visual Basic subroutine named subShowButtons (shown next) that sets the Enabled property for each button to True or False, as the program requires:

```
Sub subShowButtons (intButtonToggle As Integer)
   frmSockFTP.cmdListDir.Enabled = intButtonToggle
   frmSockFTP.cmdRetrieve.Enabled = intButtonToggle
   frmSockFTP.cmdChgWorkingDir.Enabled = intButtonToggle
   frmSockFTP.cmdCwdUp.Enabled = intButtonToggle
   frmSockFTP.cmdNameList.Enabled = intButtonToggle
End Sub
```

As you can see, the subShowButtons subroutine accepts an Integer parameter that it uses as a Boolean value to toggle the Enabled property for each of the five command buttons. To use the subShowButtons subroutine, a program module simply calls the subroutine with a True or False parameter. As you will learn, a program module that needs to prevent you from pressing these command buttons typically includes a subShowButtons program statement at the beginning and end of its definition.

As discussed, Visual Basic automatically defines events and properties for objects that you add to your program modules. For example, when you add a command button to a form, Visual Basic automatically adds a Click procedure that you can define to handle the Click events that occur when a user clicks on the command button. The following sections discuss the event procedures in more detail.

Understanding the Event Procedures

As you have learned, Visual Basic objects recognize certain program or system related actions called *events*. As a Visual Basic programmer, you manage program operations by initiating or responding to object events. Visual Basic automatically associates procedures with object events. In other words, you do not have to declare or name event procedures. You simply create a procedure definition that meets the requirements of your program.

Table 18.1 lists objects (with event procedures) defined for the SockFTP program. As you may know, with the exception of Form events, Visual Basic creates event-procedure names by concatenating the object name (such as cmdConnect) with an underscore and the event name (such as Click). Visual Basic always names form-event procedures with the name Form instead of the form-object name—for example, Form_Load not frmSockFTP_Load.

Object	Event	Procedure Name and Description
frmSockFTP	Load	Form_Load toggles command buttons off and loads the WINSOCK.DLL.
frmSockFTP	Unload	Form_Unload calls cmdExit_Click, which, unloads WINSOCK.DLL.
cmdChgWorkingDir	Click	cmdChgWorkingDir_Click changes the working directory on the FTP server to the value currently selected in the directory list-box. (Uses CWD.)
cmdClear	Click	cmdClear_Click clears all list-box entries.
cmdConnect	Click	cmdConnect_Click executes procedures that login to an FTP site using parameters specified in the SockFTP text-boxes.
cmdCwdUp	Click	cmdCwdUp_Click changes the working directory to the next higher level in the server's directory tree.
cmdDisconnect	Click	cmdDisconnect_Click disconnects from an FTP server site.
cmdExit	Click	cmdExit_Click calls the DLL function CloseWinsock to deallocate WINSOCK.DLL resources and terminates program execution.

Table 18.1 SockFTP event procedure descriptions. *(continued on the next page)*

Object	Event	Procedure Name and Description
cmdListDir	Click	cmdListDir_Click displays server files located in the server's working directory.
cmdNameList	Click	cmdNameList_Click displays a detailed list of server files located in the server's working directory.
cmdRetrieve	Click	cmdRetrieve_Click retrieves the filename value currently selected in the directory list-box.

Table 18.1 SockFTP event procedure descriptions. (continued from the previous page)

The following sections discuss each of the SockFTP event procedures in detail.

DEFINING FORM_LOAD

As discussed, each time you start the SockFTP program, the program loads the main SockFTP window (or form), which causes a Form Load event. Visual Basic calls the Form_Load event sub-routine just before the system displays the SockFTP form (frmSockFTP):

```
Sub Form_Load ()
  Dim intSuccess As Integer

  subCenterForm frmSockFTP
  subShowButtons (False)
  intSuccess = LoadWinsock()
End Sub
```

Form_Load calls the subCenterForm subroutine to center the form and then calls the subShowButtons subroutine to disable all server command buttons. Finally, Form_Load calls the QFTPLIB LoadWinsock function to initialize the Winsock DLL.

DEFINING FORM_UNLOAD

When you exit the SockFTP program, Visual Basic will close and unload the SockFTP form. Visual Basic calls Form_Unload just before it unloads the form and releases all resources. When the Unload event occurs, as shown next, SockFTP simply calls the procedure defined for the Exit command button to execute the SockFTP shutdown procedures:

```
Sub Form_Unload (Cancel As Integer)
  cmdExit_Click
End Sub
```

Note: Setting the Cancel parameter to any non-zero value prevents the form from being removed but does not stop other events, such as exiting from Windows.

DEFINING CMDCHGWORKINGDIR_CLICK

When you click on the Chg Working Dir command button, Visual Basic generates a Click event that executes the cmdChgWorkingDir_Click subroutine. The cmdChgWorkingDir_Click subroutine uses the Visual Basic ListIndex method to obtain the index number of the currently selected item in the directory list-box. The cmdChgWorkingDir_Click subroutine uses this index to obtain the string value from the list-box entry. The string entry currently selected in the directory list-box may contain the name of a subdirectory or a file in the working directory on the server. SockFTP does not test the value in anyway to determine which type of value the string contains. The cmdChgWorkingDir_Click subroutine simply passes the string to the SockFTP strDoCWDCommand procedure, which initiates a process to transmit the CWD command to the server. The strDoCWDCommand function returns the new working directory, which, as shown next, cmdChgWorkingDir_Click stores in the WorkingDir text-box:

```
Sub cmdChgWorkingDir_Click ()
   Dim intServerReplyCode As Integer
   Dim intListIndex As Integer
   Dim strDir As String

   intListIndex = frmSockFTP.lstServerFiles.ListIndex
   strDir = frmSockFTP.lstServerFiles.List(intListIndex)

   txtWorkingDir.Text = strDoCWDCommand(strDir)
End Sub
```

DEFINING CMDCLEAR_CLICK

The SockFTP window contains a message list-box that displays a running list of messages exchanged by SockFTP and the FTP server. Each time you connect to a new FTP site, you may want to erase the messages to, and replies from, the previous FTP server. Rather than automatically make that choice for you, SockFTP defines a Clear button. The Clear button directs SockFTP to erase all entries in the message list-box. You can use this button at any time during an FTP session with SockFTP. When you click your mouse on the Clear command button, Visual Basic generates a Click event that results in a call to the cmdClear_Click subroutine. As shown next, the cmdClear_Click procedure uses the Visual Basic Clear method to erase all entries in the message list-box:

```
Sub cmdClear_Click ()
   frmSockFTP.lstServerDialog.Clear
End Sub
```

DEFINING CMDCONNECT_CLICK

As discussed in the section, *Watching SockFTP in Action*, to start an FTP session with an FTP server, you click your mouse on the SockFTP Connect button. The Connect button directs SockFTP to initiate a network connection between the SockFTP client and the host specified in the Host text-box. When you click your mouse on the Connect command button, Visual Basic generates a Click event which causes SockFTP to execute cmdConnect_Click. The cmdConnect_Click procedure establishes a TCP connection to the FTP port on the host system that you specify in the Host text-box. At each step of the connection process, cmdConnect_Click calls the procedure, subShowServerCommand, to display either the command sent to the server or the reply code.

To establish the connection, first, the cmdConnect_Click procedure calls the QFTPLIB ConnectFTPControlSocket function (which you developed in the last chapter). As you may recall, ConnectFTPControlSocket simply performs the typical socket connection process that you have used in most of the programs throughout *Internet Programming*. ConnectFTPControlSocket returns a socket handle that your program must use to access the control channel to the FTP server.

If ConnectFTPControlSocket returns a valid socket handle, cmdConnect_Click updates the message list-box and transmits the USER command by calling intDoUSERCommand. If the server returns a reply code 331 (User name okay, need password), cmdConnect_Click transmits the PASS command by calling intDoPASSCommand.

The cmdConnect_Click procedure expects to receive a reply code 230 from the PASS command. Reply code 230 means that the server logged you in and has given you permission to proceed.

If the server indicates that you logged in okay, cmdConnect_Click calls two more SockFTP procedures to obtain useful information from the server and to store the return values in the SockFTP text-boxes. For example, the cmdConnect_Click procedure calls strDoPWDCommand to obtain the server's working directory and stores the value in the Working Directory text-box. Likewise cmdConnect_Click calls strDoSYSTCommand to obtain the server's system type and stores the value in the System Type text-box.

Finally, the cmdConnect_Click procedure makes the Disconnect and Clear command buttons visible and tells intDoListCommand to transmit the NLST command to obtain a filename list for the server's working directory. After intDoListCommand returns, cmdConnect_Click enables the server command buttons for your use. To enable the command buttons, cmdConnect_Click calls the subShowButtons procedure discussed previously.

If the QFTPLIB ConnectFTPControlSocket function cannot obtain a valid socket handle, cmdConnect_Click unhides the Connect and Exit buttons and then exits.

If the ConnectFTPControlSocket function obtains a valid socket handle and either the USER or PASS commands fail, cmdConnect_Click calls the SockFTP subCloseIncompleteConnection procedure. The subCloseIncompleteConnection procedure, in turn, closes the control socket, hides the Disconnect and Clear buttons, and then unhides the Connect and Exit buttons. Shown next is the complete Visual Basic source code to perform this connection process:

```
Sub cmdConnect_Click ()
  Dim intServerReplyCode As Integer
  Dim strCommand As String

  frmSockFTP.cmdConnect.Visible = False
  frmSockFTP.cmdExit.Visible = False
  frmSockFTP.lstServerFiles.Clear

  glbintControlSocket = ConnectFTPControlSocket(frmSockFTP.txtHostName)

  If glbintControlSocket <> INVALID_SOCKET Then

    subShowServerCommand ("CONNECTED to: " & frmSockFTP.txtHostName)
    intServerReplyCode = intDoUSERCommand()

    If intServerReplyCode = 331 Then
      intServerReplyCode = intDoPASSCommand()

      If intServerReplyCode = 230 Then
        frmSockFTP.txtWorkingDir = strDoPWDCommand()
        frmSockFTP.txtSystemType = strDoSYSTCommand()
        frmSockFTP.cmdDisconnect.Visible = True
        frmSockFTP.cmdClear.Visible = True
        subShowServerCommand ("Logged into " & frmSockFTP.txtHostName)
        intServerReplyCode  = intDoListCommand("NLST")
        subShowButtons (True)
      Else
        subCloseIncompleteConnection
      End If
    Else
      subCloseIncompleteConnection
    End If

  Else
    ' Make buttons visible if we failed to connect. Otherwise, let
    ' cmdDisconnect_Click make it visible when we disconnect.
    frmSockFTP.cmdConnect.Visible = True
    frmSockFTP.cmdExit.Visible = True
  End If
End Sub
```

DEFINING CMDCWDUP_CLICK

The CWD Up button directs SockFTP to tell the server to change the working directory on the server host to the next higher directory in the server's directory tree. When you click your mouse on the CWD Up command button, Visual Basic generates a Click event that executes cmdCwdUp_Click. As shown next, the cmdCwdUp_Click procedure calls strDoCDUPCommand and stores the return value in the Working Directory text-box:

```
Sub cmdCwdUp_Click ()
   Dim intServerReplyCode As Integer

   txtWorkingDir.Text = strDoCDUPCommand()
End Sub
```

The strDoCDUPCommand procedure transmits the FTP CDUP to the FTP server and returns the name of the new working directory on the server.

Defining cmdDisconnect_Click

The Disconnect button directs SockFTP to close the TCP connection to the FTP server host (but does not cause the SockFTP program to end). When you click your mouse on the Disconnect command button, Visual Basic generates a Click event which executes cmdDisconnect_Click, as shown here:

```
Sub cmdDisconnect_Click ()
   Dim intServerReplyCode As Integer
   Dim intWinsockReplyCode As Integer
   Dim strCommand As String

   frmSockFTP.cmdDisconnect.Visible = False
   frmSockFTP.cmdClear.Visible = False
   subShowButtons (False)

   strCommand = "QUIT" & Chr(13) & Chr(10) ' Add the CRLF
   subShowServerCommand (strCommand)
   intServerReplyCode = SendFTPCommand(glbintControlSocket, strCommand)
   subShowServerReplyCode (intServerReplyCode)

   intWinsockReplyCode = closesocket(glbintControlSocket)

   frmSockFTP.txtWorkingDir = ""
   frmSockFTP.txtSystemType = ""
   frmSockFTP.cmdConnect.Visible = True
   frmSockFTP.cmdExit.Visible = True
   frmSockFTP.lstServerFiles.Clear

End Sub
```

The cmdDisconnect_Click procedure calls subShowButtons to hide the Disconnect and Clear buttons and disable the server command buttons. The cmdDisconnect_Click procedure uses the

QFTPLIB SendFTPCommand function to transmit the QUIT command to the server. The cmdDisconnect_Click procedure then makes a direct call to the Winsock DLL to close the control socket (using the Winsock closesocket function).

Before exiting, cmdDisconnect_Click erases the Working Directory and System Type text-boxes, unhides the Connect and Exit command buttons, and clears the directory list-box. However, cmdDisconnect_Click does not clear the entries in the message list-box. In other words, when you disconnect from an FTP server, SockFTP leaves you with a complete history of your FTP session with the server. You can analyze this server dialog off-line to identify any problems that have occurred during the session. Of course, if you plan to connect to a different FTP server, you may not want to retain the logged information from the previous session. If so, you can click your mouse on the Clear button to clear the message list-box.

DEFINING CMDEXIT_CLICK

To exit the SockFTP program, you can click your mouse on the Exit button. When you click your mouse on the Exit command button, Visual Basic generates a Click event that executes the cmdExit_Click procedure. Also, as previously shown, SockFTP executes cmdExit_Click when Visual Basic signals the Form Unload event. As shown next, the cmdExit_Click procedure calls the QFTPLIB CloseWinsock function, which deallocates Winsock resources for the program. Next, cmdExit_Click calls the Visual Basic End command, which terminates program execution:

```
Sub cmdExit_Click ()
  Dim intSuccess As Integer

  intSuccess = CloseWinsock()
  End
End Sub
```

DEFINING CMDLISTDIR_CLICK

When you click your mouse on the List command button, Visual Basic generates a Click event that executes cmdListDir_Click. The cmdListDir_Click procedure calls the SockFTP procedure intDoListCommand, which executes procedures that transmit the LIST command to the server and display the results in the directory list-box:

```
Sub cmdListDir_Click ()
  Dim intServerReplyCode As Integer

  intServerReplyCode = intDoListCommand("LIST")
End Sub
```

Defining cmdRetrieve_Click

When you click your mouse on the Retrieve command button, Visual Basic generates a Click event which executes the cmdRetrieve_Click procedure. The cmdRetrieve_Click procedure is similar to the cmdChgWorkingDir_Click procedure. Both procedures use the Visual Basic ListIndex method to obtain the index number of the item currently selected in the directory list-box. Next, both procedures use this index to obtain the string value that corresponds to the item.

As in the event that initiates cmdChgWorkingDir_Click, the string value in the directory list-box may contain the name of a subdirectory or a file. As previously noted, SockFTP does not test the list-box value in anyway to determine which type of value the string contains. The cmdRetrieve_Click procedure simply passes the string to the intDoRETRCommand procedure.

Using the string value from the directory list-box as a parameter, the intDoRETRCommand procedure initiates a process to transmit the RETR command to the server. In addition to passing intDoRETRCommand the list-box string value (a filename), cmdRetrieve_Click also passes either a True or False value, depending on whether you selected the IMAGE option button or the ASCII option button before clicking your mouse on the Retrieve button.

If the image file-type value is True (meaning that you selected the IMAGE option button), the intDoRETRCommand procedure will transmit the FTP TYPE command with an "I" parameter. If the image file-type value is False (meaning that you selected the ASCII option button), intDoRETRCommand will automatically transmit the FTP TYPE command with an "A N" parameter value. As you may recall, the "A N" parameters in the TYPE command tell the server to use the ASCII file-type with a nonprint format:

```
Sub cmdRetrieve_Click ()
   Dim intServerReplyCode As Integer
   Dim intListIndex, optImage As Integer
   Dim strFile As String

   intListIndex = frmSockFTP.lstServerFiles.ListIndex
   strFile = frmSockFTP.lstServerFiles.List(intListIndex)
   optImage = optImageFileType.Value

   intServerReplyCode = intDoRETRCommand(strFile, optImage)
End Sub
```

Reviewing SockFTP Objects that Store Information

As you have learned, many Visual Basic objects recognize and respond to various type of actions called events. The Visual Basic response to an event is to call the appropriate event procedure like the ones described in the previous section. As you have learned, you can define exactly what you want to happen each time an event occurs.

Several of the event procedures use objects located on the SockFTP form. Table 18.2 lists the various SockFTP objects that store either the information you type or the data the server returns.

Object Name	Description
lstServerDialog	Contains a running list of transmitted FTP commands and server-reply codes.
lstServerFiles	Contains file and directory information for the working directory on the server.
optAsciiFileType	Directs the server to use the ASCII file-type when transferring files. Mutually exclusive with the optImageFileType option button.
optImageFileType	Directs the server to use the image file-type when transferring files.
txtHostName	SockFTP uses the host name that this text-box stores to establish a TCP connection to the host's FTP port.
txtPassword	SockFTP uses the value that this text-box stores as a parameter to the FTP PASS (password) command.
txtSystemType	Stores the host system type code the server returns in response to the SYST command.
txtUserID	SockFTP uses the value this text-box stores as a parameter to the FTP USER command.
txtWorkingDir	Stores the working directory that the server returns in response to the PWD command.

Table 18.2 SockFTP objects that contain data you type or the FTP server returns.

Reviewing Miscellaneous Objects in SockFTP

Other than the form object itself (frmSockFTP), the objects listed in Table 18.3 are non-essential to the SockFTP program. In other words, they are either labels or add aesthetic appeal (pictures or icons, for example). The table includes a brief description of each object.

Object Type	Object Name	Description
Form	frmSockFTP	Represents the SockFTP program as a Form object in Visual Basic.
Frame	fraFileType	Encapsulates the two file-type option buttons, enabling you to conveniently move both buttons at the same time.

Table 18.3 Miscellaneous SockFTP objects. (continued on the next page)

Object Type	Object Name	Description
Label	lblFTP	Displays the text string "FTP."
Label	lblInternetProgramming	Displays the text string "Internet Programming."
Label	lblHostName	Labels the Host text-box.
Label	lblPassword	Labels the PASSWORD text-box.
Label	lblSystemType	Labels the System Type text-box.
Label	lblUserId	Labels the USER ID text-box.
Label	lblWorkingDir	Labels the Working Directory text-box.
PictureBox	picJPLogo	Contains the Jamsa Press logo picture.
PictureBox	picSockman	Contains the Sockman icon picture.

Table 18.3 Miscellaneous SockFTP objects. (continued from the previous page)

DEFINING THE SOCKFTP PROCEDURES

As you have learned, most program activity in a Visual Basic program results from some type of event that either a user, the system, or a program statement triggers. Previous sections in this chapter have reviewed the custom event procedures that respond to Visual Basic events of interest to the SockFTP program. As you learned, many of those event procedures call functions and subroutines that SockFTP defines. The following sections discuss all the remaining procedures SockFTP defines.

DEFINING INTDOLISTCOMMAND

The intDoListCommand procedure establishes a data connection with the FTP server in preparation to receive the server's reply to either an NLST or LIST command. (The string parameter received by intDoListCommand specifies which command to transmit.) The intDoListCommand procedure primarily uses functions QFTPLIB.DLL contains to perform this procedure. Throughout the procedure, intDoListCommand uses subShowServerReplyCode to display the commands transmitted to the server and the server's reply codes.

To begin, intDoListCommand uses subShowButtons to disable the server command buttons. Next, intDoListCommand calls the QFTPLIB CreateListenSocket function. As you may recall, CreateListenSocket creates a socket that listens for a connection request from the FTP server. If CreateListenSocket successfully creates the listener socket, intDoListCommand uses the QFTPLIB

SendFTPCommand function to transmit a list command (either NLST or LIST) to the server. The calling procedure specifies which list command to transmit in the string parameter that the caller passes to intDoListCommand in strListCommand.

If the server's reply code to the list command does not indicate an error (it must be less than 400), intDoListCommand calls the QFTPLIB AcceptDataConnection function to accept the incoming-connection request from the server. AcceptDataConnection returns a handle to the data socket, which represents the data channel to the FTP server. If the data socket handle is valid, intDoListCommand calls the QFTPLIB ReadDataChannel function to read the data channel. Otherwise, intDoListCommand closes the listener socket and adds a message to the message listbox that reports the error.

If all goes well, intDoListCommand calls the SockFTP subReadListFile procedure to read the server directory listing from the file on your hard disk and add the entries to the directory list-box. As you may recall, ReadDataChannel stores incoming data in a filename that your programs specify as one of the ReadDataChannel parameters. QFTP programs and SockFTP use the FTP command that initiated the data-transfer process for the filename parameter. The program statements shown next define intDoListCommand:

```
Function intDoListCommand (strListCommand As String) As Integer
   Dim intListenSocket As Integer
   Dim intDataSocket As Integer
   Dim strCommand As String
   Dim intServerReplyCode, intWinsockReply  As Integer

   subShowButtons (False)

   intListenSocket = CreateListenSocket(glbintControlSocket)

   If intListenSocket <> INVALID_SOCKET Then
      strCommand = strListCommand & Chr(13) & Chr(10) ' Add the CRLF
      subShowServerCommand (strCommand)
      intServerReplyCode = SendFTPCommand(glbintControlSocket, strCommand)
      subShowServerReplyCode (intServerReplyCode)

      If intServerReplyCode < 400 Then
        intDataSocket = AcceptDataConnection(intListenSocket)

        If intDataSocket <> INVALID_SOCKET Then
          intServerReplyCode = ReadDataChannel(glbintControlSocket,
                 intDataSocket, strListCommand)
          subShowServerReplyCode (intServerReplyCode)
          intServerReplyCode = closesocket(intDataSocket)

          ' Read the command results and add the files to the list box.
          subReadListFile (strListCommand)
```

```
      Else
        intWinsockReply = closesocket(intListenSocket)
        intServerReplyCode = 999
        subShowServerReplyCode (intServerReplyCode)
        subShowServerCommand ("INVALID DATA SOCKET!")
      End If

    Else
      subShowServerCommand ("UNEXPECTED Reply Code " &
          intServerReplyCode)
    End If

  Else
    intServerReplyCode = 999
    subShowServerReplyCode (intServerReplyCode)
    subShowServerCommand ("INVALID LISTEN SOCKET!")
  End If

  intDoListCommand = intServerReplyCode
  subShowButtons (True)
End Function
```

DEFINING *INTDOPASSCOMMAND*

The intDoPASSCommand procedure uses the FTP PASS command to log a SockFTP user into the FTP host. To do so, intDoPASSCommand calls the QFTPLIB SendFTPCommand function to transmit the PASS command to the FTP server. The intDoPASSCommand procedure passes the value from the password text-box (frmSockFTP.txtPassword) to the server as the parameter for the PASS command. As shown in the following procedure listing, the intDoPASSCommand procedure reports the server's reply code back to the calling procedure:

```
Function intDoPASSCommand () As Integer
  Dim strCommand As String
  Dim intServerReplyCode As Integer

  strCommand = "PASS " & frmSockFTP.txtPassword & Chr(13) & Chr(10)
  subShowServerCommand (strCommand)
    intServerReplyCode = SendFTPCommand(glbintControlSocket, strCommand)
  subShowServerReplyCode (intServerReplyCode)

  If intServerReplyCode <> 230 Then
    subShowServerCommand ("EXPECTED Reply Code 230")
  End If

  intDoPASSCommand = intServerReplyCode
End Function
```

DEFINING *INTDORETRCOMMAND*

The intDoRETRCommand procedure uses the FTP RETR (retrieve) command to "get" a file from the FTP server. If you examine the intDoRETRCommand procedure (shown next), you will discover that it is similar to the intDoListCommand procedure previously described. However, the intDoRETRCommand procedure transmits two FTP commands instead of just one. Also, to perform data transfers, intDoRETRCommand calls strTransferFile (a Visual Basic procedure) instead of the QFTPLIB.DLL ReadDataChannel function.

The intDoRETRCommand procedure receives two parameters. The first parameter (strFileName) specifies the name of the file to retrieve—intDoRETRCommand concatenates this value with the RETR command. The second parameter (optImage) is actually a Boolean value that tells intDoRETRCommand whether to tell the server to use an image or an ASCII file transfer. If optImage is True, intDoRETRCommand transmits the TYPE command with an "I" parameter to tell the server to use an image file transfer. If optImage is False (which means that the selected option button for file types is ASCII), intDoRETRCommand transmits the TYPE command with an "A N" parameter—ASCII file-type, nonprint format. After the AcceptDataConnection function returns a valid data-socket handle, the intDoRETRCommand function calls strTransferFile, which performs the actual data transfer that results from the FTP RETR command:

```
Function intDoRETRCommand (strFileName As String, optImage As Integer)
    As Integer
  Dim intListenSocket As Integer
  Dim intDataSocket As Integer
  Dim strCommand As String
  Dim strType As String
  Dim strServerReply As String
  Dim intServerReplyCode, intWinsockReply  As Integer

  subShowButtons (False)

  intListenSocket = CreateListenSocket(glbintControlSocket)

  If intListenSocket <> INVALID_SOCKET Then
    If optImage = True Then
      strType = "I"
    Else
      strType = "A N"
      End If

      strCommand = "TYPE " & strType & Chr(13) & Chr(10) ' Add the CRLF
      subShowServerCommand (strCommand)
      intServerReplyCode = SendFTPCommand(glbintControlSocket,
          strCommand)
      subShowServerReplyCode (intServerReplyCode)
```

```
        strCommand = "RETR " & strFileName & Chr(13) & Chr(10)
        subShowServerCommand (strCommand)
        intServerReplyCode = SendFTPCommand(glbintControlSocket, strCommand)
        subShowServerReplyCode (intServerReplyCode)

        If intServerReplyCode < 400 Then
          intDataSocket = AcceptDataConnection(intListenSocket)

          If intDataSocket <> INVALID_SOCKET Then
            strServerReply = strTransferFile(intDataSocket, strFileName)
            subShowServerCommand (strServerReply)
            intServerReplyCode = CInt(Left$(strServerReply, 3))
            Beep
            intWinsockReply = closesocket(intDataSocket)
          Else
            intWinsockReply = closesocket(intListenSocket)
            intServerReplyCode = 999
            subShowServerReplyCode (intServerReplyCode)
            subShowServerCommand ("INVALID DATA SOCKET!")
          End If

        Else
          subShowServerCommand ("UNEXPECTED Reply Code " & _
                intServerReplyCode)
        End If
      Else
        intServerReplyCode = 999
        subShowServerReplyCode (intServerReplyCode)
        subShowServerCommand ("INVALID LISTEN SOCKET!")
      End If

      intDoRETRCommand = intServerReplyCode
      subShowButtons (True)
End Function
```

REVIEWING INTDoUSERCOMMAND

The intDoUSERCommand procedure (shown next) uses the FTP USER command as part of the SockFTP procedure for logging into an FTP site. Other than transmitting the USER command instead of the PASS command and expecting a different reply code from the server, intDoUSERCommand is identical to intDoPASSCommand. You could easily combine both procedures into one and require the caller to specify which command to transmit:

```
Function intDoUSERCommand () As Integer
   Dim strCommand As String
   Dim intServerReplyCode As Integer
```

```
    strCommand = "USER " & frmSockFTP.txtUserID & Chr(13) & Chr(10)
    subShowServerCommand (strCommand)
    intServerReplyCode = SendFTPCommand(glbintControlSocket, strCommand)
    subShowServerReplyCode (intServerReplyCode)

    If intServerReplyCode <> 331 Then
      subShowServerCommand ("EXPECTED Reply Code 331")
    End If

    intDoUSERCommand = intServerReplyCode
End Function
```

As you continue to review the SockFTP procedures, you will discover that a number of procedures are very similar. Typically, *Internet Programming* maintains similar procedures as separate program modules. However, the only reason for doing so is to simplify discussions of the program statements.

In other words, to ensure the program statements clearly illustrate the tasks performed in a procedure, *Internet Programming* does not typically combine similar procedures. However, as you adapt SockFTP for your own purposes, there is no reason why you should not combine procedures, such as intDoUSERCommand and intDoPASSCommand, into a single general purpose function.

Note: The intDoListCommand procedure illustrates how you would design a general purpose procedure that handles multiple commands. As previously shown, intDoListCommand can transmit either the NLST or the LIST commands.

Defining strCutCrLf

As you have learned, most servers require a CRLF character pair to identify the end of a line. As you saw in the Form_Load function discussion, SockFTP defines a global variable that the SockFTP modules can easily use when concatenating string values for transmission to the FTP server.

Server replies also typically include the CRLF character pairs. Unfortunately, these characters appear as black symbols in a Visual Basic text-box. Although they cause no harm, they are visually distracting. The strCutCrLf procedure provides a convenient way to eliminate any trailing CRLFs from a text string before you pass the string to a Visual Basic function for display. As shown next, the strCutCrLf procedure uses the Visual Basic InStr function to search for the CRLF pair and returns a value that excludes any CRLF endings. Note that despite its name, strCutCrLf does not actually perform any destructive operations on the text string passed to it as a parameter. In effect, you can use strCutCrLf to parse lines of text ending with a CRLF in a non-destructive way:

```
Function strCutCrLf (strText As String) As String
```

```
    Dim intCrLfLocation As Integer

    intCrLfLocation = InStr(1, strText, Chr(13) & Chr(10))   ' Add the CRLF

    If intCrLfLocation > 0 Then
      intCrLfLocation = intCrLfLocation - 1
    Else
      intCrLfLocation = Len(strText)
    End If

    strCutCrLf = Left(strText, intCrLfLocation)
End Function
```

DEFINING STRDOCDUPCOMMAND AND STRDOCWDCOMMAND

As you have learned, the FTP commands CWD and CDUP tell the server to change its working directory for the current FTP session. CWD requires a parameter that tells the server which directory to make current. CDUP does not require a parameter. CDUP simply tells the server to make the next higher directory in the server's directory tree structure the current directory.

As shown in the following program listings, the strDoCDUPCommand procedure and the strDoCWDCommand procedure are nearly identical. As shown here, strDoCDUPCommand transmits the CDUP command without any parameters:

```
Function strDoCDUPCommand () As String
  Dim strCommand As String           ' The command string to transmit
  Dim intServerReplyCode As Integer  ' The server's reply

  subShowButtons (False)                 ' Turn the buttons off

  strCommand = "CDUP" & Chr(13) & Chr(10)
  subShowServerCommand (strCommand) ' Display the command for the user
  intServerReplyCode = SendFTPCommand(glbintControlSocket, strCommand)
  subShowServerReplyCode (intServerReplyCode)

  If intServerReplyCode = 250 Then   ' If okay display the file list
    intServerReplyCode = intDoListCommand("NLST")
  End If

  strDoCDUPCommand = strDoPWDCommand()
  subShowButtons (True)
End Function
```

The strDoCWDCommand procedure concatenates the strDirectory value received as a parameter with the CWD command and then follows the same procedure as strDoCDUPCommand to transmit the command string:

```
Function strDoCWDCommand (strDirectory As String) As String
   Dim strCommand As String
   Dim intServerReplyCode As Integer

   subShowButtons (False)
   strCommand = "CWD " & strDirectory & Chr(13) & Chr(10) ' Add the CRLF
   subShowServerCommand (strCommand)
   intServerReplyCode = SendFTPCommand(glbintControlSocket, strCommand)
   subShowServerReplyCode (intServerReplyCode)

   If intServerReplyCode = 250 Then
      intServerReplyCode = intDoListCommand("NLST")
   End If

   strDoCWDCommand = strDoPWDCommand()
   subShowButtons (True)
End Function
```

Both functions expect to receive a reply code 250 from the server if the server successfully changes the working directory. If the functions receive a reply code 250, both functions call SockFTP's intDoListCommand function to display the list of files in the new working directory on the server.

DEFINING STRDOPWDCOMMAND

The strDoPWDCommand procedure (shown next) uses the FTP PWD command to obtain the name of the server's working directory. The strDoPWDCommand procedure follows the same steps used by most other SockFTP procedures that must transmit a command to the server—it calls the QFTPLIB function SendFTPCommand:

```
Function strDoPWDCommand () As String
   Dim strCommand As String
   Dim strDirectory As String
   Dim intServerReplyCode As Integer

   subShowButtons (False)
   strCommand = "PWD" & Chr(13) & Chr(10) ' Add the CRLF
   subShowServerCommand (strCommand)
   intServerReplyCode = SendFTPCommand(glbintControlSocket, strCommand)
   subShowServerReplyCode (intServerReplyCode)

   If intServerReplyCode = 257 Then
      strDirectory = strGetServerReplyText()
      strDirectory = strCutCrLf(strDirectory)
      strDirectory = strExtractQuotedExpression(strDirectory)
   Else
      strDirectory = ""
   End If
```

```
    strDoPWDCommand = strDirectory
    subShowButtons (True)
End Function
```

As you have learned, the QFTPLIB functions typically rely on the numeric value in the server's reply codes. As such, in most cases, the QFTPLIB functions do not examine the *text* included in the server's reply.

The PWD command causes the server to return a reply code 257 that includes a specially formatted string that identifies the name of the working directory. The server encapsulates the directory name in double quotes. For the FTP PWD command to have any value, a program module must be able to examine the actual string contents of the server's reply. SockFTP defines several functions that perform this service for Visual Basic program modules.

To extract the working directory from the server's reply, first, strDoPWDCommand calls strGetServerReplyText. The strGetServerReplyText procedure returns the full text of a server reply minus the reply-code prefix—in other words, only the text portion of the server's reply. After strGetServerReplyText returns the server's reply text, strDoPWDCommand passes the server's reply text to strCutCrLf, which, as previously discussed, removes the trailing CRLF. Finally, the strDoPWDCommand procedure passes the string that results from all this processing to strExtractQuotedExpression.

The strExtractQuotedExpression procedure searches the string parameter for a value encapsulated in double quotes. If it finds a quoted value, strExtractQuotedExpression returns only the quoted portion of the string. If it can't find a quoted value, it returns the entire string parameter originally passed to it. Regardless of whether strExtractQuotedExpression finds a quoted value, strDoPWDCommand passes, back to its caller, the string value strExtractQuotedExpression returns. In the event that the PWD command fails (meaning the server does not return a reply code 257), strDoPWDCommand returns an empty string to its caller.

DEFINING STRDOSYSTCOMMAND

As shown next, to extract the system type from the server's reply to the SYST command, strDoSYSTCommand follows a process similar to strDoPWDCommand. However, strDoSYSTCommand expects a reply code 215 instead of 257 and transmits the SYST command instead of PWD. Also, strDoSYSTCommand does not call strExtractQuotedExpression.

Note: The server reply does not encapsulate the system type in quotes—the entire reply text describes the system type.

```
Function strDoSYSTCommand () As String
    Dim strCommand As String
```

```
      Dim strSystemType As String
      Dim intServerReplyCode As Integer

      subShowButtons False

      strCommand = "SYST" & glbstrCRLF
      subShowServerCommand (strCommand)
      intServerReplyCode = SendFTPCommand(glbintControlSocket, strCommand)
      subShowServerReplyCode (intServerReplyCode)

      If intServerReplyCode = 215 Then
         strSystemType = strGetServerReplyText()
         strSystemType = strCutCrLf(strSystemType)
      Else
         strSystemType = ""
      End If
      strDoSYSTCommand = strSystemType

      subShowButtons True
   End Function
```

DEFINING STREXTRACTQUOTEDEXPRESSION

In some cases, an FTP server responds to a command with a reply code that contains specially marked text that an FTP client may find valuable or interesting. For example, FTP servers respond to the PWD command with a reply code string that looks something like this:

```
257 "PATHNAME" created.
```

The strExtractQuotedExpression procedure, shown next, searches the string parameter passed to it for the existence of a quoted value:

```
Function strExtractQuotedExpression (strValue As String) As String
   Dim int1stQuoteLocation As Integer
   Dim int2ndQuoteLocation As Integer
   Dim strQuotedValue As String

   ' Use the caller's value if two quotes are not found
   strQuotedValue = strValue

   int1stQuoteLocation = InStr(1, strValue, Chr(34)) ' Double quote

   If int1stQuoteLocation > 0 Then
      int2ndQuoteLocation = InStr(int1stQuoteLocation + 1, _
            strValue, Chr(34))
      If int2ndQuoteLocation > 0 Then
         strQuotedValue = Mid$(strValue, int1stQuoteLocation + 1, _
            int2ndQuoteLocation - int1stQuoteLocation - 1)
```

```
        End If
    End If

    strExtractQuotedExpression = strQuotedValue
End Function
```

The procedure uses the Visual Basic InStr function to locate the first occurrence of the double-quote character. If the procedure finds a double-quote, it uses the InStr function again. However, it starts the second search one character past the location of the first double-quote.

If the procedure finds a second double-quote, it uses the Visual Basic Mid function to extract the string between the first and second double quotes. If the procedure fails to find both quotes, it returns the entire string parameter originally passed to it. As such, the caller can use the entire string by default or the quoted value if one exists.

Depending on your program's requirements, you might prefer to have the procedure return an empty string if it can't find a quoted value. However, for the SockFTP program, the current implementation is preferable.

DEFINING STRGETSERVERREPLY AND STRGETSERVERREPLYTEXT

The strGetServerReply procedure uses the technique described earlier for calling the Windows lstrcpy function to obtain a copy of string data that does not originate within the Visual Basic environment. As you may recall, the QFTPLIB revision to the QFTP programs added the GetFTPServerReplyText function. GetFTPServerReplyText returns a LPSTR pointer to the global buffer that stores the FTP server's reply text. The following program statements define the strGetServerReply procedure:

```
Function strGetServerReply () As String
    Dim lpReplyTextAddress As Long
    Dim strReply As String

    lpReplyTextAddress = GetFTPServerReplyText()
    strReply = Space$(2048)

    lpReplyTextAddress = lstrcpy(strReply, lpReplyTextAddress)

    strGetServerReply = strReply
End Function
```

The strGetServerReply procedure calls GetFTPServerReplyText and stores the returned pointer value in a Long (32-bit) variable named lpReplyTextAddress. Next, strGetServerReply allocates space (as Visual Basic requires) to store the maximum size of the reply buffer QFTPLIB.DLL allocates. Finally, strGetServerReply calls the Windows lstrcpy function to copy the data in the DLL's buffer into the Visual Basic allocated space that strReply represents. The strGetServerReply procedure returns the server's reply string, which now exists within memory space Visual Basic allocates and owns.

Note: *The Visual Basic Space function allocates bytes of memory space as specified by its numeric parameter.*

DEFINING STRGETSERVERREPLYTEXT

As shown next, the strGetServerReplyText function depends on strGetServerReply to perform most of its work. The key difference between strGetServerReplyText and strGetServerReply is that strGetServerReply returns the server's entire reply string, including the reply code—strGetServerReplyText does not:

```
Function strGetServerReplyText () As String
   Dim strReplyText As String

   strReplyText = strGetServerReply()
   strGetServerReplyText = Right(strReplyText, Len(strReplyText) - 4)

End Function
```

The strGetServerReplyText function uses the Visual Basic Right and Len functions to return only the text portion of the server's reply. In other words, strGetServerReplyText excludes the first four characters (which contain the three-digit reply code and either a space or a hyphen) in the server's reply text.

DEFINING STRTRANSFERFILE

The strTransferFile function performs data-transfer operations for the intDoRETRCommand procedure. SockFTP could eliminate strTransferFile and let intDoRETRCommand call the QFTPLIB ReadDataChannel function just as you saw the intDoListCommand do. However, file-transfer operations have the potential to take much more time to complete than either a directory-list or a name-list transfer.

As you may recall, the ReadDataChannel function uses a single do-while loop to read data from the data channel. As such, when SockFTP uses the ReadDataChannel function for file transfers, SockFTP has no way to keep the user informed about the progress of the data transfer. The QFTPLIB TransferFile function provides a better alternative.

The TransferFile function performs a single recv and returns the number of bytes received from the data channel. As such, SockFTP can call the TransferFile function from within a Visual Basic do-while loop and display a running total of the number of bytes transferred from the FTP server.

Rather than add any additional text-boxes to display status information, the strTransferFile function temporarily uses the Host, USER ID, PASSWORD, and System Type text-boxes. In fact, the majority of the program statements in strTransferFile either reset or restore properties and values associated with the four text-boxes that display file-transfer status information. The following program statements show the essential flow of activities within the strTransferFile function:

```
Function strTransferFile (hDataSocket As Integer, strFileName As String)
     As String
' Declare local variables
' ...More program statements

' Create a valid DOS filename from the user's selection
strLocalFile = Space$(13)
lngPointerAddress = ExtractFileName(strFileName, strLocalFile)
hFile = CreateTransferFile(strLocalFile)

If hFile <> HFILE_ERROR Then
   ' Save text-box values and reset properties for file transfer
   ' ...More program statements

   ' Initialize the total byte counter and enter the read loop
   lngTotalBytes = 0
   Do
      ' Read data from the data channel and update the byte count
      intBytes = TransferFile(glbintControlSocket, hDataSocket, hFile)
      lngTotalBytes = lngTotalBytes + intBytes
      frmSockFTP.txtSystemType.Text = Str$(lngTotalBytes)
   Loop While intBytes > 0

   ' Read the server's reply
   strServerReply = strGetServerReply()
   MsgBox strServerReply, , "SockFTP"

   ' Restore text-box values and default properties
   ' ...More program statements

   strTransferFile = strServerReply
Else
   MsgBox "Unable to create " & strLocalFile, , "SockFTP"
   strTransferFile = "File creation error."
End If

End Function
```

If you review the complete definition for strTransferFile (found in source file SOCKFTP.BAS), you will find that the function is rather long. However, as previously noted, the majority of the statements are simple assignment statements that save and restore values for the text-boxes.

DEFINING subCENTERFORM

The subCenterForm prodder is a non-Internet related procedure that simply calculates the size of the user's computer screen and centers a form on the screen. In SockFTP, the Form_Load event procedure calls subCenterForm before Visual Basic displays the SockFTP form. In other words, before Visual Basic displays the SockFTP form, the program executes this procedure to center itself on the computer user's screen, regardless of the user's screen size:

```
Sub subCenterForm (frm As Form)
  ' Center form horizontally
  frm.Left = (Screen.Width - frm.Width) / 2
  ' Center form vertically
  frm.Top = (Screen.Height - frm.Height) / 2
End Sub
```

DEFINING subCLOSEINCOMPLETECONNECTION

SockFTP uses the subCloseIncompleteConnection procedure to close the control-channel socket in the event that the program does not successfully login to an FTP site. The only procedure in SockFTP that uses subCloseIncompleteConnection is cmdConnect_Click. However, cmdConnect_Click calls subCloseIncompleteConnection for two events that occur at different points within the cmdConnect_Click procedure.

In one case, SockFTP may successfully open a control socket only to have CreateListenSocket fail to open a listener socket. In the other case, the program may successfully open the control socket and the listener socket only to have AcceptDataConnection fail to return a valid handle for the data socket. For both these events, cmdConnect_Click calls subCloseIncompleteConnection to close the control socket. In the following procedure listing, subCloseIncompleteConnection also assumes the responsibility for resetting the Disconnect, Clear, Connect, and Exit buttons to their initial state:

```
Sub subCloseIncompleteConnection ()
  Dim intWinsockReplyCode As Integer

  intWinsockReplyCode = closesocket(glbintControlSocket)

  frmSockFTP.cmdDisconnect.Visible = False
  frmSockFTP.cmdClear.Visible = False

  frmSockFTP.cmdConnect.Visible = True
  frmSockFTP.cmdExit.Visible = True

  subShowServerCommand ("Socket closed--incomplete connection!")
End Sub
```

DEFINING subREADLISTFILE

The subReadListFile procedure is another non-Internet related procedure in SockFTP. The subReadListFile procedure uses standard, Visual Basic, file I/O functions to open and read a file that contains values for the directory list-box. In other words, subReadListFile opens and reads the list file ReadDataChannel creates. The subReadListFile procedure uses the Visual Basic AddItem method to add each line in the file to the directory list-box.

```
Sub subReadListFile (strFileName As String)
  Dim intFileHandle As Integer

  intFileHandle = FreeFile

  frmSockFTP.lstServerFiles.Clear

  On Error GoTo ErrorHandler

  Open strFileName For Input Access Read Lock Write As intFileHandle

  Do While Not EOF(intFileHandle)
    Line Input #intFileHandle, strFileName
    frmSockFTP.lstServerFiles.AddItem strFileName
  Loop

Closefile:
  Close #intFileHandle
  Exit Sub

ErrorHandler:
  Resume Closefile
End Sub
```

DEFINING subSHOWSERVERCOMMAND AND subSHOWSERVERREPLYCODE

Both subShowServerCommand and subShowServerReplyCode add items to the message list-box. The difference is that subShowServerReplyCode expects an integer value (the actual numeric value for the reply code) and it also expects a string. The subShowServerReplyCode procedure uses the Visual Basic Str function to convert the reply code from a numeric value to a string. The following statements define the subShowServerCommand and subShowServerReplyCode procedures:

```
Sub subShowServerCommand (ByVal strCommand As String)
Dim strListBox As String

strListBox = strCutCrLf(strCommand)

frmSockFTP.lstServerDialog.AddItem strListBox, 0
End Sub
```

```
Sub subShowServerReplyCode (intReplyCode As Integer)
   Dim strListBox As String


   strListBox = Str$(intReplyCode)
   frmSockFTP.lstServerDialog.AddItem strListBox, 0
End Sub
```

DEFINING *subShowButtons*

As previously discussed, the subShowButtons procedure toggles the Enabled property for the five command buttons that control file operations for the FTP session. Other SockFTP procedures call the subShowButtons procedure with a True value to enable the buttons and a False value to disable them:

```
Sub subShowButtons (intButtonToggle As Integer)
   frmSockFTP.cmdListDir.Enabled = intButtonToggle
   frmSockFTP.cmdRetrieve.Enabled = intButtonToggle
   frmSockFTP.cmdChgWorkingDir.Enabled = intButtonToggle
   frmSockFTP.cmdCwdUp.Enabled = intButtonToggle
End Sub
```

PUTTING IT ALL TOGETHER

If you review all the Visual Basic functions and subroutines discussed in this chapter, you will realize that most of the procedures consisted of only a few program statements. In other words, although this chapter presented a lot of procedures, each procedure, taken by itself, was easy to understand. The chapter demonstrated how you can use Winsock and custom DLLs from a visual environment. You can use the SockFTP procedures this chapter defines to model the functions and procedures you design for a similar FTP client. In the next chapter, you will learn how to use similar programming techniques to master the World Wide Web. Before you move on to the next chapter, make sure you understand the following key concepts:

✓ The Visual Basic Declare statement lets you use almost any function in the Windows API or any DLL written for the Windows operating system.

✓ Visual programming tools provide a valuable mechanism for rapid prototyping and testing.

✓ A Winsock-based DLL combined with a visual-programming environment creates a powerful tool for developing Internet applications.

Chapter 19
Spiders on the Web

For a long time, scientists and engineers have explored the idea of creating a universal information database. However, not until just recently have they had the means to create such a database. Many people view the Internet's *World Wide Web* (WWW, W3, or Web) as a prototype for just such a database. The technology that network professionals are developing for the Web places the idea of a global information database within the realm of possibility.

The *Internet Programming* companion disk includes a help file (WEBHELP.HLP) that introduces the essential components that comprise the Web. The Web Help file explains basic Web concepts such as hypertext and hyperlinks. The Help file also describes the Web's Hypertext Markup Language (HTML) and shows examples of HTML use. To use the Web Help file, double-click your mouse on the Web Help icon within the Internet Programming group window.

This chapter focuses on programming issues related to the Web. This chapter assumes you are familiar with Web operations—at least from a user viewpoint. If you are not familiar with the Web, you may want to browse through the Web Help file before you read this chapter. By the time you finish this chapter, you will understand the following key concepts:

- How the World Wide Web defines locations and access methods for practically any type of file that you might find on the Internet

- How hypertext documents let you retrieve large quantities of diverse information without worrying about the retrieval process

- How hypertext documents use Hypertext Markup Language (HTML) to define hyperlinks, which connect related information stored at locations around the world

- How the Hypertext Transfer Protocol (HTTP) lets World-Wide-Web client programs retrieve information from the Internet

- How to create a Web client program that forms the foundation for a Web spider program that can perform autonomous file retrieval

- How to create a simple Web server program that you can easily modify to act as a server for other protocols beside HTTP

REVIEWING THE HYPERTEXT TRANSFER PROTOCOL

Like everything else on the Internet, Web operations depend on a protocol—the Hypertext Transfer Protocol (HTTP). Like the FTP, POP, and SMTP protocols, HTTP defines a set of commands and uses ASCII text strings for its command language. An HTTP transaction is actually much simpler than the FTP transactions discussed in the previous three chapters. An HTTP transaction consists of four parts: a connection, a request, a response, and a close. In general, an HTTP client program establishes a TCP connection to the well-known port for HTTP (port 80) on a remote host. Next, the client sends a request to the HTTP server. After the HTTP server sends a response, either the client or the server closes the connection. Every HTTP transaction follows the same basic pattern.

A Winsock-based HTTP client uses the same procedure to establish an HTTP connection as it uses to establish any other TCP connection. In most cases, an HTTP client will request that the HTTP server send a file (such as an HTML file) or a hypermedia file (such as an image, video, audio, or animation file). As such, in most cases, the server's response simply consists of a byte-stream file transfer to the client's local protocol-port. Likewise, HTTP does not require any special closing operations. Either the client or the server (or both) can close the TCP connection.

UNDERSTANDING HTTP CLIENT REQUESTS

The principle reason for the Web's existence is to provide network users with easy access to a large body of resource files located on the Internet. As discussed, after establishing a connection, an HTTP client can send an HTTP request. An HTTP client request typically asks the HTTP server to transfer a resource file (another hypertext document, an image, audio, animation, or video file) from the server's host to the client's host. The file requests Web client programs transmit specify a filename, an Internet location (host address), and a method (typically a protocol such as HTTP or FTP) to retrieve the requested file. The combination of these elements form something called a *universal resource identifier (URI)*.

REVIEWING URIS AND URLS

To retrieve a resource file from the Internet, a Web browser must know where to find the file and how to talk to the host that owns the file. Today, Web browsers use the HTTP protocol and several other common Internet protocols, such as FTP, GOPHER, ARCHIE, VERONICA, and WAIS. URIs define the information a Web browser requires to use any of these access protocols for file retrieval. The Web Help file contains additional information about URIs and *uniform resource locators (URLs)*—a closely related concept. However, the following paragraphs provide a quick overview. At first, you may find it a little difficult to distinguish between URIs and URLs. In general, you can view a specific URI as an identifier for a specific object, such as an HTML or image file. A URI represents a generic name for any object on the Internet. However, if you want to use existing protocols to retrieve an object from the Internet, you need to know the Internet address (or something which approximates an address) of the host that stores the object. A URL is a URI that includes location (address) information encoded in the URI.

UNDERSTANDING URLS

Although the Web pioneered the use of URLs, Internet professionals plan to develop URLs into an Internet standard that other Internet professionals can use. As you read the following paragraphs (and especially if you decide to review RFC 1738, *Uniform Resource Locators (URL)*, Berners-Lee, Masinter, and McCahill, 1994), keep in mind that the purpose of the URL specification is to define a generic syntax for accessing a wide-variety of Internet objects.

UNDERSTANDING URL SYNTAX

As discussed, the URL form of a URI includes location or address information. The sole purpose of a URL is to encapsulate information that a network program can use to locate an object on the Internet. The URL serves no function after the program locates an object.

In other words, for all practical purposes, you can treat a URL as a special type of network address. However, rather than simply identifying a host computer, the URL identifies a specific object on a specific host computer. A URL also contains one other important characteristic that makes it unlike previously discussed network entities or concepts—the URL identifies an access method for the referenced object.

RFC 1738 refers to access methods as *schemes*. In other words, a URL scheme describes how a program will access or retrieve a specific Internet object. Today, for all practical purposes, you can view an *access* method as a protocol. Table 19.1 lists the currently defined access schemes for URLs.

As you can see, several URL access schemes are protocols previously discussed in *Internet Programming*.

URL Scheme	Description
ftp	File Transfer Protocol
http	Hypertext Transfer Protocol
gopher	The Gopher Protocol
mailto	Electronic mail address
news	USENET news
nntp	USENET news using NNTP access
telnet	Reference to interactive sessions
wais	Wide Area Information Servers
file	Host-specific filenames
prospero	Prospero Directory Service

Table 19.1 Currently defined URL access schemes.

The basic syntax for a URL is simple—it only contains two parts, as shown here:

```
<scheme>:<scheme-specific-part>
```

The first part of the URL contains the name of the scheme (which typically is a protocol name) you will use to access an object. The second part contains scheme-specific information, such as the name and location of an object, and information the specific access method requires. For example, many Internet users are familiar with the TELNET protocol. As you probably know, you can use TELNET client programs to log into practically any host on the Internet. However, depending on how you want to login, you may need to supply a username and password. The URL scheme for TELNET makes provisions for this information, as shown here:

```
telnet://<user>:<password>@<host>:<port>/
```

Since this chapter focuses on the Web, it will use the Hypertext Transfer Protocol (HTTP) scheme for most URL examples. As previously mentioned, HTTP is the Web's own special protocol. For detailed information about the other URL schemes, you should read RFC 1738.

DEFINING THE *HTTP* URL SCHEME

The HTTP URL scheme simply identifies Internet resources you can use the Hypertext Transfer Protocol (HTTP) to access. The syntax for the HTTP URL scheme (shown next) is similar to the TELNET scheme previously shown:

```
http://<host>:<port>/<path>?<search_part>
```

As you can see, the scheme portion of the URL is "http" and the scheme-specific portion identifies a host, port, path, and search_part. If your programs omit the port element in the URL, the URL will default to protocol port 80 (the well-known port for the HTTP). Note that the HTTP URL scheme does not let you specify a username or password. As you may know, the Web does not currently require usernames or passwords. Also, be aware that the HTTP protocol does not currently implement the "search_part" of the URL. Although RFC 1738 includes the search_part within the syntax for HTTP URL schemes, you will not find any use for the search_part and thus can ignore it. *Internet Programming* will examine the path element of the HTTP URL scheme in a later section that discusses HTTP in general. For now, simply understand that, in general, the path element identifies a Internet host directory path to an object (typically an HTML document) HTTP retrieves.

UNDERSTANDING *HTTP* METHODS

As discussed, an HTTP client request (typically a request to transfer a resource file) is the second part of an HTPP transaction. HTTP client requests fall into two basic categories: a simple request and a full request. HTTP refers to its commands as *methods*. The only method (or command) a simple request uses is the GET method. As you can see from the syntax for a simple HTTP request (shown next), your program simply transmits a URI and a carriage-return line-feed (CRLF) after the GET command:

```
GET <uri> CRLF
```

This simple request will cause the HTTP server to locate and transfer the object that the specified URI identifies. The resource object may be an HTML document, image, audio, video, or animation file. Since the client transmits a request for a specific object, the client should know how to handle the returned object. For example, a client that requests an image file should know how to display an image file. For simple HTTP requests, the HTTP server is not much more than a file server.

An HTTP full request also begins with an HTTP method. Unfortunately, because the definitions of many proposed HHTP methods for full requests are incomplete, such methods currently are not very useful. After the method, the full request's syntax includes the URI and the HTTP protocol version. A full request can also include header-request fields (similar to MIME header fields associated with SMTP). However, the client transmits the header-request fields on their own lines with each header-request field terminated by a CRLF.

An HTTP server uses reply codes similar to those SMTP, POP, and FTP servers use. However, the reply code (or status code, as the HTTP specification calls it) is not the first element on the reply line. Instead, HTTP servers include their version numbers as the first element on the reply line:

```
<http version>  <status code>  <reason line> <CRLF>
```

For more details about the HTTP protocol, its methods, and request fields, you need to locate the latest specification. The best place to start looking for current Web information is the Web server at CERN. (CERN is the European Laboratory for Particle physics. CERN is based in Switzerland, where the Web project started.) If you own a Web browser, start with URL *http:// www.w3.org/* and follow the hyperlinks to the latest information. If you don't have a Web browser, you can still find the latest Web information at CERN. However, you will need to login to their FTP server (using anonymous FTP) on host *ftp.www.w3.org*.

UNDERSTANDING THE OPPORTUNITY

HTML documents contain a lot of information that a Web client must interpret. However, actual network operations on the Web using URIs, URLs, and HTTP are relatively simple. In fact, Web operations are much easier than FTP operations. To perform a Web operation, your program only needs to manage one TCP connection. Furthermore, your program has to maintain this connection only for the duration of the file transfer. As a result, developing programs that traverse the Web and retrieve documents is a trivial process.

In contrast, creating a browser program that properly interprets and displays the contents of an HTML document is a difficult process. However, most of the programming challenges that browsers create are not network-related. As such, *Internet Programming* will not discuss Web browsers beyond their ability to retrieve Web documents. Today, the Web represents the cutting edge in Internet technology. As the number of businesses that connect to the Internet each day continues to increase, the Web will evolve rapidly. In fact, this evolution is already occurring. If you want to become involved with the Web phenomenon, you may start by writing your own Web browser. Although a number of excellent browsers already exist—Cello and Mosaic, to mention a couple of the more well-known—there's certainly room for something better. You might very well be able to sit down and write a better browser. However, before you do so, consider the fact that you will be competing with some well-financed companies that already have a huge head start in the marketplace.

However, the Web does present some tremendous opportunities. One area that is virtually untouched (and surprisingly so) is automated-search tools for the Web. (Automated-search tools are programs that traverse or explore the Web, retrieving and recording information without human intervention).What's more, automatic search tools are an area that very likely will always require a high-degree of customization. In other words, regardless of whether you are self-employed or work for somebody else, the demand for new and evolving Web-exploration programs should grow—especially as more and more businesses discover the Web.

UNDERSTANDING THE PROBLEMS

Unfortunately, in the few short years that the Web has been in existence, a number of problems have arisen related to automated exploration of the Web. Web professionals typically refer to automated Web exploration tools as spiders, robots, or Web wanderers. In other words, a Web *spider* (or robot or wanderer) is a program that traverses or explores the World Wide Web automatically—without human intervention. The possibilities Web spider programs present generate a lot of enthusiasm and excitement—particularly for programmers that enjoy creating interesting applications. Because the rapidly growing number of documents on the Web contain a wealth of information, the Web is a prime target for exploration. Likewise, the Web's size and the resources the Web connects make automated exploration very desirable. However, before you create any Web exploration programs, you may want to do your own research using the resources the following sections identify.

COMING UP TO SPEED

If you want to jump to rapidly accumulate background information on Web spiders and related programming topics, load your Web browser and head for the United Kingdom. A company named NEXOR maintains a Web home page dedicated to Web robots, wanderers, and spiders. You can find the NEXOR home page at URL *http://web.nexor.co.uk/mak/doc/robots/robots.html.*

The NEXOR home page will lead you to a lot of useful and important information. Although not all the information resides on their server, hypertext documents on the NEXOR server contain hyperlinks to most of the places you need to visit to rapidly accumulate background information on the Web spiders. On the NEXOR home page, you will find hyperlinks to a list of existing Web robots and other automated tools. In addition, you will discover a Web mailing list dedicated to discussions of technical aspects of Web robots. However, the two most important documents you can access through the NEXOR home page are *Guidelines for Robot Writers* and *Ethical Web Agents.*

First, read the white paper on *Ethical Web Agents.* The paper (in HTML form) is by David Eichmann, an assistant professor of software engineering at the University of Houston—Clear Lake. Eichmann's paper provides valuable background information about, and some important history related to, automated search tools (or spiders) on the Web. Eichmann describes the benefits and hazards associated with Web spiders. Next, read the *Guidelines for Robot Writers* (also in HTML form) by Martijn Koster at NEXOR. Koster's document describes a general design philosophy for the Web spider and outlines essential do's and don'ts for programmers that develop Web spiders. By the time you finish reviewing these documents and others found on the NEXOR server (or on documents linked to the NEXOR server), you'll understand many issues you need to consider before you create a Web spider.

PROGRAMMING THE WEB

The companion disk that accompanies *Internet Programming* includes a program named SockWEB that implements a simple Web-based program that retrieves Web files. SockWEB is a Visual Basic program similar to the SockFTP program discussed in the previous chapter—only much simpler. Like the SockFTP program, SockWEB also uses a simple DLL file to perform network I/O. However, SockWEB uses the dynamic link library QWEBLIB.DLL instead of QFTPLIB.DLL.

The following sections discuss the QWEBLIB dynamic link library and the Visual Basic program SockWEB. If, after reviewing the information the previous section references, you decide to design a Web spider, you may be able to use the SockWEB program as a foundation on which to build your search-agent software.

REVIEWING THE *QWEBLIB* DYNAMIC LINK LIBRARY

The QWEBLIB dynamic link library contains very little that you have not already seen in previous *Internet Programming* program examples. Table 19.2 lists the functions the QWEBLIB dynamic link library defines.

Function	Description
ConnectWebServerSocket	Creates and connects a communication socket to a Web server.
ExtractFileName	Extracts a valid DOS filename from a Web URL.
SendWebQuery	Transmits a simple Web query (using the GET command) to retrieve a Web resource file.
RecvWebFile	Reads data from the Web socket connection and writes the data to a local data file.
LibMain	Initializes the QWEBLIB dynamic link library.
WEP	Represents an empty shell that you can use to create a custom Windows exit procedure.

Table 19.2 Program functions the QWEBLIB dynamic link library defines.

The WEP, LibMain, and ExtractFileName functions in the QWEBLIB dynamic link library are identical to the same-named functions in QFTPLIB. The ConnectWebServerSocket function creates and connects a socket to a remote host's port 80 (the well-known port for the Web's HTTP protocol). The SendWebQuery function transmits a query to a remote host. As shown next, the SendWebQuery function calls the ExtractFileName function and creates a local data file to store the data transferred from the Web server:

```
extern "C" HFILE _export FAR PASCAL SendWebQuery(SOCKET nSocket,
    LPSTR lpszQuery)
{
  HFILE hFile;                  // File handle for data-stroage file
  OFSTRUCT openFileBuff;        // Windows open file structure
```

```
char szFileName[13];          // Storage buffer for the new filename
char szWebQuery[100];         // Buffer to hold the Web query
int nCharSent;                // Number of characters transmitted
char szMsg[100];              // General purpose buffer for messages

wsprintf(szWebQuery,"GET %s\n", (LPSTR)lpszQuery);
nCharSent = send(nSocket, szWebQuery, lstrlen(szWebQuery), NO_FLAGS);

if (nCharSent == SOCKET_ERROR)
  {
    nCharSent = WSAGetLastError();
    wsprintf(szMsg,"%d Error occurred during send()!", nCharSent);
    MessageBox(NULL, szMsg, PROG_NAME, MB_OK|MB_ICONSTOP);
    hFile = SOCKET_ERROR;
  }

else
  {
    ExtractFileName(lpszQuery, szFileName);

    hFile = OpenFile(szFileName, (OFSTRUCT far *)&openFileBuff,
         OF_CREATE);
    if (hFile == HFILE_ERROR)
      {
        wsprintf(szMsg,"Error occurred opening file: %s",
             (LPSTR)szFileName);
        MessageBox(NULL, szMsg, PROG_NAME, MB_OK|MB_ICONSTOP);
      }
  }
  return(hFile);
}
```

The SendWebQuery function returns the file handle for the local data file. After the RecvWebFile function (shown next) completes the data transfer, it closes the data file that the SendWebQuery function created:

```
extern "C" UINT _export FAR PASCAL RecvWebFile(SOCKET nSocket,
    HFILE hFile)
{
  char szWebInfo[5000];       // Buffer to hold Web information
  int nCharRecv;              // Number of characters received
  char szMsg[1000];           // General purpose buffer for messages
  static LONG lTotalData;     // Tracks the total bytes transferred

  nCharRecv = recv(nSocket, (LPSTR)&szWebInfo, sizeof(szWebInfo),
       NO_FLAGS);
  lTotalData += nCharRecv;
  if (nCharRecv > 0 )
```

```
    {
       if (HFILE_ERROR == _lwrite (hFile, szWebInfo, nCharRecv))
         {
            lTotalData = 0;
            _lclose(hFile);
            wsprintf(szMsg,"%d Error occurred during recv()!", nCharRecv);
            MessageBox(NULL, szMsg, PROG_NAME, MB_OK|MB_ICONSTOP);
            return(HFILE_ERROR);
         }

       if (nCharRecv == lTotalData)
         {
            if (*(szWebInfo+0) == '<')
              {
                 *(szWebInfo+nCharRecv) = '\0';
                 wsprintf(szMsg,"%s", (LPSTR)szWebInfo);
                 MessageBox(NULL, szMsg, PROG_NAME, MB_OK|MB_ICONSTOP);
              }
         }
    }
  else if (nCharRecv == SOCKET_ERROR)
    {
       lTotalData = 0;
       _lclose(hFile);
       nCharRecv = WSAGetLastError();
       wsprintf(szMsg,"%d Error occurred during recv()!", nCharRecv);
       MessageBox(NULL, szMsg, PROG_NAME, MB_OK|MB_ICONSTOP);
       return(SOCKET_ERROR);
    }

  if (nCharRecv == 0)
    {
       lTotalData = 0;
       _lclose(hFile);
    }

  return(nCharRecv);
}
```

As you can see, the RecvWebFile function reads data from a socket and writes it to a local data file in practically the same way as other program examples discussed previously in *Internet Programming*. However, you may not understand the purpose of the program statements shown here:

```
if (nCharRecv == lTotalData)
 {
   if (*(szWebInfo+0) == '<')
     {
        *(szWebInfo+nCharRecv) = '\0';
```

```
        wsprintf(szMsg,"%s", (LPSTR)szWebInfo);
        MessageBox(NULL, szMsg, PROG_NAME, MB_OK|MB_ICONSTOP);
    }
}
```

The *if* construct tests the initial data received from the socket to determine whether the incoming-data transfer is HTML-based data (an HTML file or possibly an HTML-based message). If the incoming data is HTML-based, the RecvWebFile function displays the initial block of data in a message box for the user to review. By doing so, the program lets the user abort the transfer if the incoming data is not what the user expected.

To understand how this *if* construct works, note that the RecvWebFile function stores the number of bytes received from each call to the recv function in the nCharRecv variable. Next, note that the RecvWebFile function uses the static variable lTotalData to track the *total* number of bytes received. (Since the lTotalData variable is static, the lTotalData variable retains its value from one RecvWebFile function call to next.) The only time that nCharRecv will equal lTotalData (the condition for which the *if* construct tests) is the first time that the recv function reads data from the socket connection.

The Visual Basic SockWEB program uses the QWEBLIB dynamic link library to perform network I/O. You can use the SockWEB program to read hypertext files or multimedia files, such as image, audio, video, and animation files. As discussed in the Web Help file on the *Internet Programming* companion disk, the Web's HTML files use the greater-than (>) and less-than (<) signs to delimit (encapsulate) HTML tags.

Typically, the first character in an HTML file will be the less-than sign that marks the beginning of an HTML tag. The *if* construct shown here tests the first character of the first data block from the socket:

```
if (*(szWebInfo+0) == '<')
```

If the first character is the less-than (<) sign, the RecvWebFile function assumes the incoming data is an HTML file and displays the data block in a message box. Regardless of whether the incoming data is HTML-based, the RecvWebFile function writes it into a local data file.

REVIEWING THE SOCKWEB PROGRAM OPERATION

The primary purpose of the QWEBLIB dynamic link library discussed in the previous section is to perform network I/O for the SockWEB program. The SockWEB program is a very simple Web file reader. As shown in Figure 19.1, the SockWEB File Reader dialog box (a Visual Basic form) initially displays two text-boxes and a single command button.

Figure 19.1 The initial SockWEB File Reader dialog box.

When a user clicks their mouse on the Read command button, the program tries to establish a connection to the host that the Web Server text-box specifies. Then, the program reads the URL file that the Universal Resource Locator text-box specifies. Also, when the user clicks the Read command button, the program hides the Read command button and displays a Cancel button and two more text-boxes. As shown in Figure 19.2, one text-box displays the number of bytes transferred and the other text-box displays the local data file where the program will write the incoming data.

Figure 19.2 The SockWEB File Reader dialog box during a data transfer.

When the data-transfer operation completes, the SockWEB File Reader dialog box reverts back to the state previously shown in Figure 19.1. The following section explains how the SockWEB program performs the data-transfer operations, as well as how the program manages the Visual Basic form.

REVIEWING THE SOCKWEB PROGRAM DEFINITION

As discussed in Chapter 18, to call functions that dynamic link libraries store, your Visual Basic programs use the Declare statement to specify DLL function prototypes. The SockWEB program declares three functions found in the Winsock DLL and four functions found in the QWEBLIB DLL. In addition to defining the SockWEB form (named frmSockWeb) shown in the previous section, the SockWEB program defines three event procedures. First, SockWEB defines the Form_load procedure, which simply centers the SockWEB form on the user's screen in the same way as the SockFTP subCenterForm procedure. Also, as shown in the previous section, the SockWEB program defines two command buttons: Read and Cancel. SockWEB defines the Click-event procedure for the Cancel button as shown here:

```
Sub cmdCancel_Click ()
   Dim intStatus As Integer
   intStatus = WSACancelBlockingCall()
```

```
End Sub
```

As you can see, the cmdCancel_Click procedure simply calls the Winsock WSACancelBlockingCall function to cancel any blocking function calls in progress. The following section discusses the Click-event procedure for the Read button. The following section also explains what happens to a file-transfer operation if the user clicks the Cancel button in the middle of the file transfer.

UNDERSTANDING THE CLICK-EVENT FOR THE READ BUTTON

The Click-event procedure (cmdRead_Click) for the Read button contains most of the SockWEB program's functionality. If you examine the SOCKWEB.FRM source file, you will discover the cmdRead_Click procedure is rather long. However, if you also examine the program statements that define the cmdRead_Click procedure, you will discover that the procedure is quite simple. Since the cmdRead_Click procedure is rather long, the following paragraphs will discuss the procedure in fragments. To start, note that the cmdRead_Click procedure declares several variables, as shown here:

```
Sub cmdRead_Click ()
   Dim intStatus As Integer        ' Status value returned by DLL
   Dim nSocket As Integer          ' Socket handle for the connection
   Dim hFile  As Integer           ' File handle for the local data file
   Dim nTotalBytes As Long         ' Counter for total bytes transferred
   Dim nBytes As Integer           ' Byte-count for each call to recv
   Dim lpszLocalFileName As String ' Filename for the local data file
   Dim lpszPath As String          ' Path string for the URL
   Dim PointerAddress As Long      ' Memory addresses from DLL functions
```

The purpose of these variables will become more clear in the following paragraphs. After declaring its local variables, the cmdCancel_Click procedure tests the contents of the URL and Web Server text-boxes to make sure the user entered some data. If either text-box is empty (zero length text), the procedure displays a message box and exits, as shown here:

```
If Len(txtURL.Text) = 0 Or Len(txtWebServer.Text) = 0 Then
   MsgBox "Please enter a server name and a Web URL.",
   MB_ICONSTOP + MB_OK, "WEB File Reader"
   Exit Sub
End If
```

After making sure that the user has entered something into both the URL and Web Server text-boxes, the procedure disables and hides the Read command button, as shown here:

```
cmdRead.Enabled = 0
cmdRead.Visible = 0
```

and then proceeds to display the other SockWEB text-boxes and the Cancel command button, as shown here:

```
lblBytesTransferred.Visible = 1
txtBytesTransferred.Visible = 1
txtBytesTransferred.Text = "CONNECTING"
cmdCancel.Visible = 1
txtLocalFileName.Visible = 1
txtLocalFileName.Enabled = 1
lblLocalFileName.Visible = 1
```

Next, the following program statements extract a valid DOS filename from the URL that the user entered. As you can see, the procedure calls the ExtractFileName function found in the QWEBLIB dynamic link library:

```
lpszPath = txtURL.Text
lpszLocalFileName = String$(13, " ")
PointerAddress = ExtractFileName(lpszPath, lpszLocalFileName)
```

As previously discussed, the ExtractFileName function stores a valid DOS filename in the buffer area pointed to by its second parameter (in this case, the Visual Basic variable lpszLocalFileName). As shown next, the procedure stores the valid filename in the local filename text-box (txtLocalFileName):

```
txtLocalFileName.Text = lpszLocalFileName
```

At this point, the procedure has now performed all its initial setup operations and can now begin network operations. First, the procedure calls the ConnectWebServerSocket function in QWEBLIB.DLL to create and connect a socket to the remote host that the user specifies:

```
' Connect to the Web server
nSocket = ConnectWebServerSocket(txtWebServer.Text)
```

As previously shown, if the ConnectWebServerSocket function successfully creates and connects the socket to a Web server on the remote host, the ConnectWebServerSocket function will return a valid socket handle. As shown next, the procedure tests the value that ConnectWebServerSocket stores in the nSocket variable to make sure the value is valid. If the socket handle is valid, the procedure displays the text "SENDING QUERY" in the BYTES TRANSFERRED text-box and then calls the SendWebQuery function in QWEBLIB.DLL:

```
If nSocket <> INVALID_SOCKET Then
   txtBytesTransferred.Text = "SENDING QUERY"
   hFile = SendWebQuery(nSocket, txtURL.Text)
Else
   ' If the connection failed, reset the command buttons and exit
   cmdRead.Enabled = 1
   cmdRead.Visible = 1
```

```
    lblBytesTransferred.Visible = 0
    txtBytesTransferred.Visible = 0
    txtBytesTransferred.Text = "0"
    cmdCancel.Visible = 0
    txtLocalFileName.Visible = 0
    lblLocalFileName.Visible = 0
    txtLocalFileName.Text = ""
    Exit Sub
End If
```

If the ConnectWebServerSocket function returns an invalid socket handle, the procedure restores the program's text-boxes and command buttons to their default states and then exits. The SockWEB program does not need to display any error messages when ConnectWebServerSocket fails because, as previously shown, the ConnectWebServerSocket function itself displays message boxes when an error occurs.

After connecting the socket to the Web server and successfully opening a local data file, the program updates the BYTES TRANSFERRED text-box to show that the program is now ready to read the data file, as shown here:

```
' Read the data for the Web file and write it to the local hard disk
If hFile <> SOCKET_ERROR And hFile <> HFILE_ERROR Then
    txtBytesTransferred.Text = "READING FILE"
    nTotalBytes = 0
    Do
        nBytes = RecvWebFile(nSocket, hFile)
        nTotalBytes = nTotalBytes + nBytes
        txtBytesTransferred.Text = Str$(nTotalBytes)
    Loop While nBytes > 0
End If
```

As you can see, the procedure enters a do-while loop that calls the RecvWebFile function found in QWEBLIB.DLL to read the data file from the Web server. Two events will cause the procedure to exit the do-while loop. First, when the Web server finishes the transfer, the server will close the TCP connection. Doing so while cause the recv function to return with zero bytes, and the procedure will exit the do-while loop. Second, if the user clicks the Cancel button (which will trigger the Cancel button Click-event previously discussed), the recv function will return with an error value, and the procedure will exit the do-while loop for this event.

The program statements that follow the do-while loop simply reset the program's text-boxes and command buttons to their default state. Doing so leaves the SockWEB form in its initial state, and the program is ready to read another file from the Internet's Web.

```
' Reset the command buttons and exit
```

```
         txtBytesTransferred.Text = "DONE"
         intStatus = closesocket(nSocket)
         intStatus = WSACleanup()
         lblBytesTransferred.Visible = 0
         txtBytesTransferred.Visible = 0
         cmdCancel.Visible = 0
         txtLocalFileName.Visible = 0
         lblLocalFileName.Visible = 0
         txtLocalFileName.Text = ""
         cmdRead.Enabled = 1
         cmdRead.Visible = 1
      End Sub
```

CREATING A WEB SERVER

As you learned in the previous sections, creating a client program to read files from the Web is not too difficult. Creating a Web server application is not much more difficult. This section shows you how to implement a very simple Web server that transmits the same HTML-based message each time a client program connects to the server's port. The server program uses an initialization file (SERVER.INI) to determine the port number to use. You can use the server on any port—not just port 80 for the HTTP protocol.

To change the protocol port, simply change the number 80 in the SERVER.INI file to whatever protocol port you want to monitor. The SERVER.INI file on the Internet Programming companion disk contains the following entries:

```
[ProtocolPort]
Port = 80              ; Well-known port for the World-Wide Web
```

The server application defined in this section is really very bare-bones. For example, the server does not read any commands it receives from the client and always transmits the same response. Nevertheless, the program example demonstrates the steps required to implement practically any type of server that you want to design.

As you read the following sections and review the server-program statements, you may be surprised to learn that you have already encountered nearly all the program statements presented. As such, rather than implement the server program using SDK-style program statements, the following sections describe a server application that uses the C++ application framework that the Microsoft Foundation Classes (MFC) defines. *Internet Programming* does not describe a server program that uses the application framework that Borland's ObjectWindows defines. However, if you carefully review the program statements described in the following sections, you should have little difficulty implementing an ObjectWindows server—assuming you are already familiar with Object Windows.

IDENTIFYING THE INTERNET PROGRAMMING SOURCE CODE

As you may know, the Microsoft Visual C++ compiler (version 1.5) includes an AppWizard utility (similar to Borland's AppExpert) that generates an application shell built on the MFC application framework. The AppWizard lets you take advantage of the power visual programming environments offer you. In a matter of seconds, the AppWizard can generate hundreds of lines of bug-free code that implements several classes defined by the MFC application framework. While the AppWizard can provide a tremendous productivity boost for you, wading through all the AppWizard-generated code to find changes another programmer implemented rapidly becomes tedious. To help you more easily identify the *Internet Programming* changes to the AppWizard code, *Internet Programming* marks any modified or added program statements with the comments shown here:

```
// START CUSTOM CODE: Internet Programming
// END MODIFICATIONS: Internet Programming
```

By simply searching the source-code files for the comments shown, you can rapidly locate and review the *Internet Programming* code modifications to the AppWizard-generated code.

REVIEWING THE SERVER APPLICATION CLASSES

Table 19.3 lists the server application classes that the *Internet Programming* example server program includes. As you will learn, the CServerView class performs the majority of the work for the server application.

MFC Base Class	Server Derived Class	Description
CWinApp	CServerApp	Defines the server application as a Windows object.
CFrameWnd	CMainFrame	Defines the window for use by the server application.
CDocument	CServerDoc	Defines the server's general network connection information.
CScrollView	CServerView	Defines the interface between the user and the network.

Table 19.3 AppWizard generated classes.

Internet Programming does not explain or discuss the MFC base classes or even the AppWizard-generated class information. The following sections only discuss the *Internet Programming* modifications to each of these classes. For a more detailed description of the MFC base classes and an explanation of how the classes interact with each other, see the documentation for the Microsoft Foundation Classes.

REVIEWING THE *CSERVERAPP* CLASS

The CServerApp class defines the server application as a Windows application object. You can find the following program statements in the server1.h header file:

```
#include "..\winsock.h"

const int WINSOCK_VERSION = 0x0101;   // Required Winsock version 1.1
const int DEFAULT_PROTOCOL  = 0;      // No protocol specified, use
default
const int NO_FLAGS = 0;               // No special flags specified
const int MAX_COLUMNS = 80;           // Maximum columns for text display
const int QUEUE_SIZE = 5;             // Maximum number of incoming
                                      // connections to queue
// Server-defined application messages
const int WM_SERVER_ACCEPT = WM_USER+1;
const int WM_CLIENT_CLOSE = WM_USER+2;
const int WM_CLIENT_READ = WM_USER+3;

class CServerApp : public CWinApp
{
  private:
    char chMsgBuffer[100];            // General purpose message buffer

  public:
    WSADATA wsaData;                  // Winsock implementation details

    // Overrides
    virtual BOOL InitInstance();      // Initialize an instance of Server1
    virtual BOOL ExitInstance();      // Exit an instance of Server1
};
```

As you can see, the server1.h header file declares and initializes several constant variables. Also, the header file declares overrides for the default InitInstance and ExitInstance functions. You can the find the definitions for both override functions in the SERVER1.CPP source file. The CServerApp::InitInstance function simply adds Winsock DLL initialization to the InitInstance function, as shown here:

```
BOOL CServerApp::InitInstance()
{
  if (WSAStartup(WINSOCK_VERSION, &wsaData))
    {
      MessageBeep(MB_ICONSTOP);
      MessageBox(NULL,"Winsock could not be initialized!",
            AfxGetAppName(), MB_OK|MB_ICONSTOP);
      WSACleanup();
      return(FALSE);
```

```
    }
  return(TRUE);
}
```

Likewise, the CServerApp::ExitInstance function simply adds Winsock cleanup to the ExitInstance function, as shown here:

```
BOOL CServerApp::ExitInstance()
{
  int iErrorCode;

  if ((iErrorCode = WSACleanup()))
    {
      wsprintf(chMsgBuffer, "Winsock error %d.", iErrorCode);
      MessageBeep(MB_ICONSTOP);
      MessageBox(NULL, chMsgBuffer, AfxGetAppName(),
            MB_OK|MB_ICONSTOP);
    }
  if (m_pMainWnd != NULL)
    VERIFY(m_pMainWnd->DestroyWindow());

  return(CWinApp::ExitInstance());
}
```

REVIEWING THE CMAINFRAME CLASS

The server program only makes a slight modification to the default CMainFrame class. In the MAINFRM1.CPP source file, you will find the following program statements. The Internet programming modifications shown between the START CUSTOM CODE comment and the END MODIFICATIONS comment change the command identifiers associated with the default toolbar:

```
static UINT BASED_CODE buttons[] =
{
  // Same order as in the bitmap 'toolbar.bmp'

  // START CUSTOM CODE: Internet Programming
  // Change File New, Open, and Save options to
  // Server Close, Open, and File Save As.
  ID_SERVER_CLOSE,
  ID_SERVER_OPEN,
  ID_FILE_SAVE_AS,
  // END MODIFICATIONS: Internet Programming
    ID_SEPARATOR,
  ID_EDIT_CUT,
  ID_EDIT_COPY,
  ID_EDIT_PASTE,
    ID_SEPARATOR,
```

```
    ID_FILE_PRINT,
    ID_APP_ABOUT,
};
```

The server application uses the default MFC toolbar shown here:

The default commands associated with the first three buttons are the File menu New, Open, and Save options. The server application changes the first two buttons on the toolbar to the Server menu Close and Open options. In other words, the server program user can use the first two buttons on the toolbar to open and close the server (cause the server to listen for incoming connections or ignore incoming connections). In addition, the server application changes the third button to represent the File menu Save As option instead of the File menu Save option. The server application *Internet Programming* defines does not actually implement the File menu Save As option. However, the idea behind the command change is that a user will probably want to save each server "log file" to a new filename. Figure 19.3 shows the CMainFrame class window that the MFC application framework displays when you execute the server program. As you can see from the window's title bar, the server initially opens in the closed state (not listening for incoming connections).

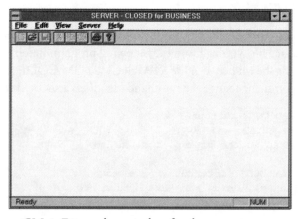

Figure 19.3 The startup CMainFrame class window for the server program.

To open the server (create a listener socket), you can click your mouse on the Open button or the Server menu Open option. Doing so causes the server program to create a listener socket and begin listening for incoming connections. As shown in Figure 19.4, when you open the server for business, the program displays a simple status message that identifies your local host name, specifies the port at which the server will listen, and describes the Winsock implementation in use on your computer.

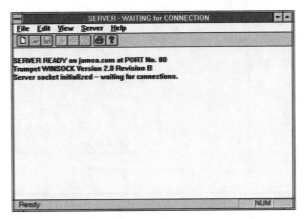

Figure 19.4 *The server program window after creating a listener socket.*

When the server detects and accepts an incoming-client connection, the program will update the server window, as shown in Figure 19.5.

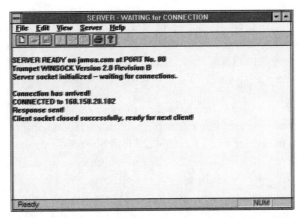

Figure 19.5 *The server program window after detecting and accepting a client connection.*

As discussed, the server program accepts a client connection, transmits an HTML-based reply message, and then closes the client connection. If you use a Web browser, such as Mosaic, to access the server program, you will see the HTML-based response shown in Figure 19.6.

Note: If you do not have a Web browser, see Internet Programming's Web Help file for instructions on how to obtain the NCSA Mosaic Web browser from the Internet.

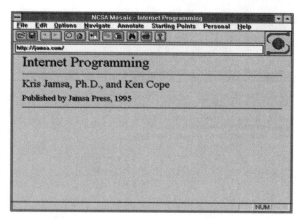

Figure 19.6 The default HTML response from the server program.

USING THE EXAMPLE SERVER PROGRAM

The setup program on the *Internet Programming* companion disk creates a program group that includes an icon named Web Server. (If you have not already done so, run the Setup program on the companion disk to install the book's program examples.) The Web Server icon starts the server program described in this chapter. To start the Web server, double-click your mouse on the Web Server icon. The server, in turn, will start and display its status information. Note that, like all example programs on the *Internet Programming* companion disk, the Web server expects to find the Winsock DLL. If you receive an error message that says the server cannot find WINSOCK.DLL, make sure your WINSOCK.DLL is in your path or start the Trumpet Winsock DLL.

You can start the server program before you connect to the Internet. However, before you can open the server for business, you need to establish your connection to the Internet. After you have started the server and established your connection to the Internet, click your mouse on Server menu Open option or on the toolbar Open button. After you have opened the server, you can use your Web browser to connect to the server. (If you do not own a Web browser, see *Internet Programming's* Web Help file for instructions on how to obtain the NCSA Mosaic Web browser from the Internet.) To connect to the example server program, tell your browser to connect to your PC's IP address, as shown here (substitute your PC's IP address in place of 000.000.000.000):

```
http://000.000.000.000/
```

Note that you should end the Web address with a forward slash. You do not have to specify an HTML filename. The server program transmits the same response to every connection. Immediately after your browser establishes a connection with the server, the server program will transmit an HTML data string that tells your browser to display the title, authors' names, and publisher of *Internet Programming*.

REVIEWING THE CSERVERDOC CLASS

Most of the *Internet Programming* modifications to the CServerDoc class consist of added public-member variables that other classes will use during server operations. You will find the following program statements added by *Internet Programming* in the serv1doc.h source file:

```
const MAX_LINES = 1000;                     // Maximum lines per document

class CServerDoc : public CDocument
{
// Attributes
public:
  CString m_csText[MAX_LINES];              // CString -- one per line
  LONG m_lLineNumber, m_lColumnNumber;      // Current position in document
  UINT m_nServerPort;                       // Server socket handle
  SOCKET m_hServerSocket;                   // Server port
  SOCKADDR_IN m_sockServerAddr;             // Server address structure
  SOCKADDR_IN m_sockClientAddr;             // Client address structure
  LPHOSTENT m_lpHostEntry;                  // Host entry structure
  LPSERVENT m_lpServEntry;                  // Service information
};
```

Once again, you have used similar variables in program examples previously discussed in *Internet Programming*. The only new variable added here is the CString array m_csText. As you may know, the CString class lets you manipulate string data in a way similar to the Basic programming language. In other words, you can concatenate CString variables with the plus sign and compare CString variables with the equal sign.

The CString class has built-in memory allocation, so you don't have to worry about overwriting the end of a CString variable like you do with normal C language string variables. *Internet Programming* uses the m_csText array variable to hold the text displayed in the server's main window.

The CString array lets *Internet Programming* more easily implement scrolling features for the server window. (As you may recall, *Internet Programming* did not implement such features for the Sockman programs.) The only other change to the CServerDoc class occurs in the constructor function for the class, as shown here:

```
CServerDoc::CServerDoc()
{
m_lLineNumber = 0;
m_lColumnNumber = 0;
}
```

As you can see, the server program initializes the line and column number member variables to zero. The CServerView class uses these two variables to manage text output to the server window.

REVIEWING THE CSERVERVIEW CLASS

As previously mentioned, the CServerView class performs most of the work for the server application. *Internet Programming* defines twenty CServerView class member functions. Although several of the member functions are short (consisting of only a few lines of code), the sheer number of functions defined for the CServerView class should give you an idea of how busy this class is for the server application. You can find the definitions for all the CServerView class member functions in the SERV1VW.CPP source file.

You can find the program statements shown next in the serv1vw.h source file. As you can see, the CServerView class definition declares several private variables, four public member functions, and several protected member functions.

```
class CServerView : public CScrollView
{
private:
  char m_chMsgBuffer[100];              // Private message buffer
  SOCKET m_hClientSocket;               // Client socket handle
  SOCKADDR_IN m_sockClientAddr;         // Client address structure
  BOOL m_bServerIsOpen;                 // Open or closed flag
  CServerDoc *m_pDoc;                   // Parent document
  CWnd *m_pParentWnd;                   // Parent window
  CMenu *m_pParentMenu;                 // Parent menu

// Operations
public:
  virtual void ReportWinsockErr(LPSTR lpszErrorMsg);
  virtual void PrintChar(char chChar, BOOL bLastChar);
  virtual void PrintString(LPSTR lpszString);
  virtual void PrintString(CString csString);

// Generated message map functions
protected:
  //{{AFX_MSG(CServerView)
  afx_msg void OnServerClose();
  afx_msg void OnServerOpen();
  afx_msg void OnUpdateServerClose(CCmdUI* pCmdUI);
  afx_msg void OnUpdateServerOpen(CCmdUI* pCmdUI);
  afx_msg void OnUpdateFileNew(CCmdUI* pCmdUI);
  afx_msg void OnUpdateFileOpen(CCmdUI* pCmdUI);
  afx_msg void OnUpdateFileSave(CCmdUI* pCmdUI);
  afx_msg void OnUpdateFileSaveAs(CCmdUI* pCmdUI);
  //}}AFX_MSG

  afx_msg LRESULT OnServerAccept(WPARAM wParam, LPARAM lParam);
  afx_msg LRESULT OnClientClose(WPARAM wParam, LPARAM lParam);
  afx_msg LRESULT OnClientClose(void);
  afx_msg LRESULT OnClientRead(WPARAM wParam, LPARAM lParam);
```

```
    DECLARE_MESSAGE_MAP()
};
```

The following program statements show how the server program maps various menu commands and messages into CServerView class functions. The following sections provide a brief description of the CServerView class functions:

```
BEGIN_MESSAGE_MAP(CServerView, CScrollView)
//{{AFX_MSG_MAP(CServerView)
ON_COMMAND(ID_SERVER_CLOSE, OnServerClose)
ON_COMMAND(ID_SERVER_OPEN, OnServerOpen)
ON_UPDATE_COMMAND_UI(ID_SERVER_CLOSE, OnUpdateServerClose)
ON_UPDATE_COMMAND_UI(ID_SERVER_OPEN, OnUpdateServerOpen)
ON_UPDATE_COMMAND_UI(ID_FILE_NEW, OnUpdateFileNew)
ON_UPDATE_COMMAND_UI(ID_FILE_OPEN, OnUpdateFileOpen)
ON_UPDATE_COMMAND_UI(ID_FILE_SAVE, OnUpdateFileSave)
ON_UPDATE_COMMAND_UI(ID_FILE_SAVE_AS, OnUpdateFileSaveAs)
//}}AFX_MSG_MAP
// Standard printing commands
ON_COMMAND(ID_FILE_PRINT, CScrollView::OnFilePrint)
ON_COMMAND(ID_FILE_PRINT_PREVIEW, CScrollView::OnFilePrintPreview)

// START CUSTOM CODE: Internet Programming
ON_MESSAGE(WM_SERVER_ACCEPT, OnServerAccept)
ON_MESSAGE(WM_CLIENT_CLOSE, OnClientClose)
ON_MESSAGE(WM_CLIENT_READ, OnClientRead)
// END MODIFICATIONS: Internet Programming

END_MESSAGE_MAP()
```

DEFINING THE CSERVERVIEW CONSTRUCTOR

As you may know, a C++ program initializes a class by calling the constructor function for the class each time the program creates a new object of the specified class type. The CServerView class defines the interface between the user and the network. As such, each time you start the server program, the program creates a CServerView class and thus calls the CServerView constructor. The CServerView constructor simply initializes two class member variables: m_bServerIsOpen and m_hClientSocket.

The m_bServerIsOpen variable is a Boolean variable that represents a True or False flag that indicates whether the server is open (listening for incoming connections) or not. Other class functions can examine the m_bServerIsOpen variable to determine the server's state and operate accordingly. A True value for m_bServerIsOpen indicates the server can accept incoming connections. In other words, a listener socket exists and will report incoming connections. The m_hClientSocket variable stores the socket handle for any client programs connected to the server. As shown here,

CServerView initializes the m_bServerIsOpen variable to False and the m_hClientSocket variable to INVALID_SOCKET:

```
CServerView::CServerView()
{
  m_bServerIsOpen = FALSE;
  m_hClientSocket = INVALID_SOCKET;
}
```

DEFINING ~CSERVERVIEW

Just as C++ programs call constructors to initialize a class, C++ programs call a destructor function to destroy a class. As shown next, the CServerView destructor closes the server socket if it is open. The destructor tests the client socket handle m_hClientSocket to see if any clients exist. If so, the destructor closes the client socket also:

```
CServerView::~CServerView()
{
  if (m_bServerIsOpen)
    closesocket(m_pDoc->m_hServerSocket);

  if (m_hClientSocket != INVALID_SOCKET)
    closesocket(m_hClientSocket);
}
```

DEFINING ONINITIALUPDATE

The MFC application framework automatically calls the OnInitialUpdate function for a view class (like CServerView) before displaying the view. You can override the OnInitialUpdate function to perform any one-time initialization that requires information about the document class associated with your view. For example, as shown next, the CServerView::OnInitialUpdate function initializes three private member variables: m_pDoc, m_pParentWnd, and m_pParentMenu.

The m_pDoc variable is a pointer to the view's document class (CServerDoc). You will find that the CServerView member functions use the m_pDoc pointer to access the member variables and functions within the CServerDoc class. Likewise, OnInitialUpdate calls the GetParent function to obtain the address of the parent window for the class. The OnInitialUpdate function immediately uses this pointer with the GetMenu function to obtain the address of the program's menu and store the address in member variable m_pParentMenu.

After initializing the member variables and performing the operations just discussed, the OnInitialUpdate function obtains a device context for the server window and initializes the window. First, the OnInitialUpdate function sets the scroll-bar positions by calling the SetScrollSizes function and then positions the window by calling the GetParentFrame()->MoveWindow function, as shown here:

```
void CServerView::OnInitialUpdate()
{
  m_pDoc = GetDocument();
  m_pDoc->SetTitle("CLOSED for BUSINESS");

  m_pParentWnd = GetParent();
  m_pParentMenu = m_pParentWnd->GetMenu();

  // Setup the server window
  TEXTMETRIC tm;
  CRect rectServerSize;
  CClientDC dc(this);

  dc.GetTextMetrics(&tm);
  SetScrollSizes( MM_TEXT, CSize(0,0), CSize(0,(MAX_LINES*tm.tmHeight)),
      CSize(0, tm.tmHeight));
  GetWindowRect( rectServerSize );
  GetParentFrame()->MoveWindow( rectServerSize.left, rectServerSize.top,
      (MAX_COLUMNS*tm.tmAveCharWidth), (24*tm.tmHeight), FALSE);

  return;
}
```

DEFINING ONDRAW

To paint text on the server window, the program must override the OnDraw function. The MFC
application framework calls the OnDraw function to perform screen display, printing, and print
preview. However, the framework does not define a default implementation. As shown next, the
Web server's implementation paints text on the server window using the TextOut function and
then updates the scroll-bar positions by calling the SetScrollSizes function:

```
void CServerView::OnDraw(CDC* pDC)
{
  TEXTMETRIC tm;
  int iYValue;

  pDC->GetTextMetrics(&tm);
  iYValue = 0;

  for (int iLine = 0; iLine <= m_pDoc->m_lLineNumber; iLine++)
    {
      pDC->TextOut(0,iYValue, m_pDoc->m_csText[iLine],
          m_pDoc->m_csText[iLine].GetLength());
      iYValue += tm.tmHeight;
    }

  SetScrollSizes(MM_TEXT, CSize(0, ((int) m_pDoc->m_lLineNumber+1)
      *tm.tmHeight));
```

```
    return;
}
```

Note that the OnDraw function uses the m_pDoc pointer (discussed in the OnInitialUpdate function) to access the text stored in the CServerDoc array variable m_csText. As you may recall, the server program uses the CString m_csText array variable to hold the text displayed in the server's main window.

DEFINING PRINTSTRING WITH A CSTRING PARAMETER

As you may know, C++ lets you overload function definitions. When you overload a function, you define two or more functions with the same name but with different parameters or return types. For example, the server program overloads the PrintString function. The PrintString function shown next accepts a CString class variable as a parameter. In the next section, you will see a PrintString function that accepts a LPSTR parameter.

Both PrintString functions perform the same operation—they each call the PrintChar function to print an entire string, one character at a time, to the server window. As shown here, the PrintString first makes sure there is data to print and then enters a for-loop to print each character:

```cpp
void CServerView::PrintString(CString csString)
{
  if (csString.GetLength() == 0)
    return;

  // Print each character in the string except the last one
  for (int iChar = 0; iChar < (csString.GetLength()-1); iChar++)
    PrintChar(csString[iChar], FALSE); // Don't update scroll bar

  // Update the scroll bar when reaching the last character
  PrintChar(csString[iChar], TRUE);
  m_pDoc->UpdateAllViews(NULL, 0L, 0);
  return;
}
```

After printing the entire string, the PrintString function uses the m_pDoc pointer and the UpdateAllViews function to update (refresh) the server window with the new text string.

DEFINING PRINTSTRING WITH A LPSTR PARAMETER

The PrintString function shown next is practically identical to the PrintString function in the previous section. However, instead of accepting a CString parameter, the PrintString function shown here accepts a LPSTR parameter:

```
void CServerView::PrintString(LPSTR lpszString)
{
  if (*lpszString == NULL)
    return;

  // Print each character in the string except the last one
  for (int iChar = 0; lpszString[iChar+1] != NULL; iChar++)
    PrintChar(lpszString[iChar], FALSE); // Don't update scroll bar

  // Update the scroll bar when reaching the last character
  PrintChar( lpszString[iChar], TRUE);
  m_pDoc->UpdateAllViews(NULL, 0L, 0);
  return;
}
```

DEFINING PRINTCHAR

As shown in the previous two sections, both the overloaded PrintString functions call the PrintChar function to paint a string to the server window, one character at a time. The PrintChar function uses the m_pDoc pointer to the CServerDoc class to manipulate the m_lColumnNumber and m_lLineNumber variables and keep track of the text displayed within the server's window. Although the PrintChar function is rather long, it uses functions common to many MFC applications and does very little but keep all the variables associated with text output to the server screen properly updated:

```
void CServerView::PrintChar(char chChar, BOOL bLastChar)
{
  // Ignore carriage-returns. The following program
  // statements identify and handle new-lines.
  if (chChar =='\r')
    return;

  CClientDC dc(this);
  TEXTMETRIC tm;
  CPoint pt, ptOrigin;
  CRect rectServerSize;

  OnPrepareDC(&dc);
  dc.GetTextMetrics(&tm);

  if (chChar =='\n')
    {
      // Move to column zero for a new line.
      m_pDoc->m_lColumnNumber = 0;
      if (m_pDoc->m_lLineNumber == (MAX_LINES-1))
        {
          for (int iLine = 0; iLine < MAX_LINES; iLine++)
            m_pDoc->m_csText[iLine] = m_pDoc->m_csText[iLine+1];
```

```
          m_pDoc->m_csText[iLine].Empty;
          m_pDoc->UpdateAllViews(this, 0L, 0);
        }
      else
        m_pDoc->m_lLineNumber++;

      SetScrollSizes( MM_TEXT, CSize(0, ((int) m_pDoc->m_lLineNumber+1)
            * tm.tmHeight));
    }
  else
    {
      if (m_pDoc->m_lColumnNumber++ >= MAX_COLUMNS)
        {
          m_pDoc->m_lColumnNumber = 1;
          if (m_pDoc->m_lLineNumber == (MAX_LINES-1))
            {
              for (int iLine = 0; iLine < MAX_LINES; iLine ++)
                m_pDoc->m_csText[iLine] = m_pDoc->m_csText[iLine+1];

              m_pDoc->m_csText[iLine].Empty;
              m_pDoc->UpdateAllViews(this, 0L, 0);
            }
          else
            m_pDoc->m_lLineNumber++;
        }

      m_pDoc->m_csText[m_pDoc->m_lLineNumber] += chChar;

      if (bLastChar)
        dc.TextOut(0, (int) m_pDoc->m_lLineNumber * tm.tmHeight,
            m_pDoc->m_csText[m_pDoc->m_lLineNumber],
            m_pDoc->m_csText[m_pDoc->m_lLineNumber].GetLength());

    }

// If last character then update the position on the scroll bar
if (bLastChar)
  {
    pt = GetScrollPosition();
    if ((int) m_pDoc->m_lLineNumber * tm.tmHeight < pt.y)
      {
        pt.y = (int) m_pDoc->m_lLineNumber * tm.tmHeight;
        ScrollToPosition(pt);
      }
    else
      {
        CScrollView::GetClientRect( rectServerSize);
        if ((((int)m_pDoc->m_lLineNumber * tm.tmHeight) + tm.tmHeight)
              > rectServerSize.bottom)
```

```
        {
          ptOrigin = dc.GetViewportOrg();
          pt.x = ptOrigin.x;
          pt.y = ((int) m_pDoc->m_lLineNumber * tm.tmHeight) +
                 tm.tmHeight - rectServerSize.bottom;
          ScrollToPosition(pt );
        }
      }
    }
  return;
}
```

The PrintString functions pass a True value in the bLastChar variable to indicate the last character of a string. When PrintChar receives a True value for the bLastChar parameter, the PrintChar
function performs its normal update routines and then calls the TextOut function to update the
text in the window. Also, as shown in the last *if* construct, the PrintChar function updates the
scroll-bars window as required by the amount of text displayed in the server window.

DEFINING REPORTWINSOCKERR

To handle error messages in a consistent manner, the server program defines the ReportWinsockErr
function. The ReportWinsockErr function simply formats the private m_chMsgBuffer character
array with the value from Winsock WSAGetLastError function. Like the other CServerView
member functions, the ReportWinsockErr function calls the PrintString function to print the error
message to the server window. As shown here, the ReportWinsockErr function also notifies the
user of the error by displaying a Windows message box:

```
VOID CServerView::ReportWinsockErr(LPSTR lpszErrorMsg)
{
  wsprintf(m_chMsgBuffer, "\nWinsock error %d: %s\n\n",
          WSAGetLastError(), lpszErrorMsg);
  PrintString((LPSTR)lpszErrorMsg);
  MessageBeep(MB_ICONSTOP);
  MessageBox(m_chMsgBuffer, AfxGetAppName(), MB_OK|MB_ICONSTOP);
  return;
}
```

DEFINING ONSERVERACCEPT

As discussed, the server program transmits a default HTML-based response (shown in Figure 19.6)
to every client connection. The function that performs this task for the server program is
OnServerAccept. As shown in the following program statements, the OnServerAccept function
accepts incoming connections and transmits a default reply. You have encountered most of the
OnServerAccept function program statements in previous programs discussed in *Internet
Programming*:

```
LRESULT CServerView::OnServerAccept(WPARAM wParam, LPARAM lParam)
{
  int iErrorCode;
  int nLength = sizeof(SOCKADDR);

  if (WSAGETSELECTERROR(lParam))
    {
      ReportWinsockErr("Error detected on entry into OnServerAccept.");
      return(0L);
    }

  if (WSAGETSELECTEVENT(lParam) == FD_ACCEPT)
    {
      PrintString("Connection has arrived!\n");

      m_hClientSocket = accept(m_pDoc->m_hServerSocket,
            (LPSOCKADDR)&m_sockClientAddr, (LPINT)&nLength);

      if (m_hClientSocket == INVALID_SOCKET)
        {
          ReportWinsockErr("Server failed to accept connection.");
          return(0L);
        }

      CString csDottedDecimal = "CONNECTED to ";
      csDottedDecimal += inet_ntoa(m_sockClientAddr.sin_addr);
      m_pDoc->SetTitle(csDottedDecimal);
      csDottedDecimal += "\n";

      PrintString(csDottedDecimal);
      CString csText = "<Title>Internet Programming</Title>";
      csText += "<h1>Internet Programming</H1><p><hr>";
      csText += "<H3>Kris Jamsa, Ph.D., and Ken Cope</H3><p>";
      csText += "<H5>Published by Jamsa Press, 1995</H5><p><hr>";
      LPSTR lpszResponse = csText.GetBuffer(1000);

      iErrorCode = send( m_hClientSocket, lpszResponse,
            lstrlen(lpszResponse), NO_FLAGS);
      if (iErrorCode == SOCKET_ERROR)
        ReportWinsockErr("Error sending response to client.");
      else
        PrintString("Response sent!\n");
      OnClientClose();
    }
  return(0L);
}
```

To keep the server as simple as possible, the OnServerAccept function formats an HTML-based reply in memory (rather than reading the reply from disk). As shown, the OnServerAccept function uses a local CString variable named csText to format the reply. In effect, the CString concat-enations shown in the OnServerAccept function format the following HTML document in memory:

```
"<Title>Internet Programming</Title>
<h1>Internet Programming</H1><p><hr>
<H3>Kris Jamsa, Ph.D., and Ken Cope</H3><p>
<H5>Published by Jamsa Press, 1995</H5><p><hr>
```

As shown in Figure 19.6, the text and HTML tags format an HTML reply message that displays the title of this book, followed by a horizontal rule and the authors' names. After the authors' names, a Web browser will display the publisher's name and a copyright date. You can change the CString concatenation statements to create any default reply message that you want. Likewise, if you use the *Internet Programming* example server program as a baseline for developing a fully functional Web server, you will want to modify the program to read HTML files from disk for its default replies. By placing the default response files on disk, you can more easily modify your server's reply messages.

DEFINING ONSERVERCLOSE

When the server-program user closes the server socket by clicking their mouse on the Server menu Close option or on the Close button, Windows will generate a message that causes the MFC ap-plication framework to call the OnServerClose function. As shown next, the OnServerClose function closes the client socket and the server socket by calling the Winsock closesocket func-tion with the appropriate socket handle:

```
void CServerView::OnServerClose()
{
  if (m_hClientSocket != INVALID_SOCKET)
    {
      if (WSAAsyncSelect(m_hClientSocket, m_hWnd, NO_FLAGS, NO_FLAGS))
        ReportWinsockErr("WSAAsyncSelect error in OnServerClose.");

      closesocket(m_hClientSocket);
      m_hClientSocket = INVALID_SOCKET;
    }

  closesocket(m_pDoc->m_hServerSocket);

  m_bServerIsOpen = FALSE;

  m_pDoc->SetTitle("CLOSED for BUSINESS");

  PrintString("\nServer CLOSED for BUSINESS.\n");
  return;
}
```

The OnServerClose function also uses the m_pDoc pointer to call the CServerDoc's SetTitle function (defined by MFC) to change the server program's title bar to the text "CLOSED for BUSINESS." Likewise, the OnServerClose function calls the PrintString function to print a message to the server program's window.

DEFINING ONCLIENTCLOSE WITHOUT PARAMETERS

The server program overloads the OnClientClose function—one OnClientClose function for other member functions and one OnClientClose function that the application framework can call. The OnClientClose function closes the client socket only. Other member functions can call the OnClientClose function shown here:

```
LRESULT CServerView::OnClientClose(void)
{
  int iErrorCode = closesocket(m_hClientSocket);

  m_hClientSocket = INVALID_SOCKET;

  if (iErrorCode == SOCKET_ERROR)
    ReportWinsockErr("Error closing client socket!");
  else
    PrintString("Client socket closed, ready for next client!\n\n");

  m_pDoc->SetTitle("WAITING for CONNECTION");
  return(0L);
}
```

As you can see, the OnClientClose function calls the closesocket function to close the client socket and tests for errors. After closing the socket, the OnClientClose function changes the title bar text to tell the user that the server is waiting for a connection.

DEFINING ONCLIENTCLOSE WITH PARAMETERS

The OnClientClose function shown next also closes the client socket. However, like a call-back function, the OnClientClose function shown here accepts message parameters from Windows:

```
LRESULT CServerView::OnClientClose(WPARAM wParam, LPARAM lParam)
{
  if (WSAGETASYNCERROR(lParam))
    ReportWinsockErr("Error detected on entry into OnClientClose");

  int iErrorCode = closesocket(m_hClientSocket);

  m_hClientSocket = INVALID_SOCKET;

  if (iErrorCode == SOCKET_ERROR)
    ReportWinsockErr("Error closing client socket!");
  else
```

```
      PrintString("Client socket closed successfully, ready for next
client!\n\n");

  m_pDoc->SetTitle("WAITING for CONNECTION");
  return(0L);
}
```

The server implementation on the *Internet Programming* companion disk does not actually use the OnClientClose function shown here. However, the server program does define a message and use the application framework's message-map functions to associate the WM_CLIENT_CLOSE message with the OnClientClose function. The following program fragment shows how the MFC message-map functions associate the OnClientClose function with the WM_CLIENT_CLOSE message. In other words, if Windows sends a WM_CLIENT_CLOSE message, the application framework will call the OnClientClose function. If you decide to modify the server program to use a protocol other than HTTP, you can use this message and the OnClientClose function to close the client sockets connected to the server, as required by your program.

```
BEGIN_MESSAGE_MAP(CServerView, CScrollView)
 ON_MESSAGE(WM_CLIENT_CLOSE, OnClientClose)
END_MESSAGE_MAP()
```

DEFINING ONSERVEROPEN

As you learned in the QFTP programs, to accept connections from other hosts, you must create a listener socket that listens for incoming-connection requests. The OnServerOpen function creates a server socket and places it into a passive-listening mode in the same way that the QFTP programs did. Although the OnServerOpen function shown here is rather long, you have encountered all the network-related program statements in programs previously discussed by *Internet Programming*:

```
void CServerView::OnServerOpen()
{
  WSADATA wsaData;                  // Winsock implementation details
  int iErrorCode;                   // Winsock error code
  char chLocalInfo[64];             // Buffer for Winsock description

  if (WSAStartup(WINSOCK_VERSION, &wsaData))
    {
      MessageBeep(MB_ICONSTOP);
      MessageBox("Winsock could not be initialized!", AfxGetAppName(),
            MB_OK|MB_ICONSTOP);
      WSACleanup();
      return;
    }
  else
    WSACleanup();
```

```
// Resolve the local host name to make sure the user is on-line
if (gethostname(chLocalInfo, sizeof(chLocalInfo)))
  {
    ReportWinsockErr(
          "\nCould not resolve local host!\nAre you on-line?\n");
    return;
  }

// Print the server status including the Winsock DLL description
CString csWinsockID = "\nSERVER READY on ";
csWinsockID += chLocalInfo;
csWinsockID += " at PORT No. ";
csWinsockID += itoa(m_pDoc->m_nServerPort, chLocalInfo, 10);
csWinsockID += "\n";
csWinsockID += wsaData.szDescription;
csWinsockID += "\n";
PrintString(csWinsockID);

// Setup the server using the procedures found in the quick programs.
m_pDoc->m_hServerSocket = socket(PF_INET, SOCK_STREAM,
      DEFAULT_PROTOCOL);

if (m_pDoc->m_hServerSocket == INVALID_SOCKET)
  {
    ReportWinsockErr("Could not create server socket.");
    return;
  }

m_pDoc->m_sockServerAddr.sin_family = AF_INET;
m_pDoc->m_sockServerAddr.sin_addr.s_addr = INADDR_ANY;
m_pDoc->m_sockServerAddr.sin_port = htons(m_pDoc->m_nServerPort);

// Bind the server socket like data socket in the QFTP programs.
if (bind(m_pDoc->m_hServerSocket,
      (LPSOCKADDR)&m_pDoc->m_sockServerAddr,
      sizeof(m_pDoc->m_sockServerAddr)) == SOCKET_ERROR)
  {
    ReportWinsockErr("Could not bind server socket.");
    return;
  }

iErrorCode = WSAAsyncSelect(m_pDoc->m_hServerSocket, m_hWnd,
      WM_SERVER_ACCEPT, FD_ACCEPT);

if (iErrorCode == SOCKET_ERROR)
  {
    ReportWinsockErr("WSAAsyncSelect failed on server socket.");
    return;
  }
```

```
  if (listen(m_pDoc->m_hServerSocket, QUEUE_SIZE) == SOCKET_ERROR)
    {
      ReportWinsockErr("Server socket failed to listen.");
      m_pParentMenu->EnableMenuItem(ID_SERVER_OPEN, MF_ENABLED);
      return;
    }

  PrintString(
        "Server socket initialized -- waiting for connections.\n\n");

  m_bServerIsOpen = TRUE;
  m_pDoc->SetTitle("WAITING for CONNECTION");
  return;
}
```

Defining OnClientRead

The server program implementation on the *Internet Programming* companion disk does not use
the OnClientRead function. However, the OnClientRead function shown here illustrates how to
read data from the server socket should you decide to modify the server program example to do
so:

```
LRESULT CServerView::OnClientRead(WPARAM wParam, LPARAM lParam)
{
  if (WSAGETASYNCERROR(lParam))
    ReportWinsockErr("Error detected on entry into OnClientRead.");

  int iBytesRead;
  int iBufferLength;
  int iEnd;
  int iSpaceRemaining;
  char chIncomingDataBuffer[1024];

  iBufferLength = iSpaceRemaining = sizeof(chIncomingDataBuffer);

  iEnd = 0;

  iSpaceRemaining -= iEnd;
  iBytesRead = recv(m_hClientSocket, (LPSTR)(chIncomingDataBuffer+iEnd),
        iSpaceRemaining, NO_FLAGS);

  iEnd+=iBytesRead;


  if (iBytesRead == SOCKET_ERROR)
    ReportWinsockErr("OnClientRead recv reported a socket error.");

  chIncomingDataBuffer[iEnd] = '\0';
```

```
    if (lstrlen(chIncomingDataBuffer) != 0)
       PrintString(chIncomingDataBuffer);
    else
       OnClientClose();

    return(0L);
}
```

UPDATING THE SERVER MENUS

The remaining functions in the CServerDoc class manage the server program's menu options. The OnUpdateServerClose and OnUpdateServerOpen functions toggle the menu state as the user opens and closes the server's listener socket. The other four functions (OnUpdateFileNew, OnUpdateFileOpen, OnUpdateFileSave, and OnUpdateFileSaveAs) simply disable the File menu options since the server program does not include functions to perform file I/O. You can use these function-shells to define file I/O operations however you want. The message-map functions in the server program already connect the functions to the appropriate menu options. You simply have to define how you want the menu option to perform.

PUTTING IT ALL TOGETHER

This chapter ends your *Internet Programming* tour of the Internet. This chapter presented a lot of information. However, other than the Web-specific details, most of the network operations were previously covered in *Internet Programming*. You should now have a general understanding about how TCP/IP networks function and how the Internet operates. Hopefully, you have enjoyed this book's introduction to Internet programming. You should feel confident that what you don't already know, you can learn armed with the knowledge you have gained from *Internet Programming*. Before you continue on your way, make sure that you understand the following key concepts:

✓ Web URLs tell Web-client programs how to retrieve information-resource files by defining server addresses, file subdirectory locations, and protocols to use for retrieval.

✓ Hypertext documents embed URLs within HTML tags to define hyperlinks between related resource files on the Internet.

✓ The Hypertext Transfer Protocol (HTTP) lets World Wide Web client programs retrieve information from the Internet using NVT ASCII commands similar to those that SMTP, POP, and FTP programs use.

✓ A Web server program is very similar to a file server program that uses the Hypertext Transfer Protocol to transfer files between client and server host-computer systems.

Appendix A
Firewalls and Internet Security

If you ask a wide variety of Internet users to say the first word that pops into their mind when you say "Internet security," many of them will reply "firewall." Those that don't say firewall will probably say "encryption." Today, when network security managers connect their networks to the Internet, they rely on firewalls more than anything else for network security. As you will learn, a firewall can consist of several components. However, in general, a firewall represents a barrier between an internal or local area network (LAN) and external networks, such as the Internet. As an Internet programmer, you have a responsibility to be security conscious. Although network security is primarily the domain of network administrators, you can design your software to complement a network administrator's efforts to establish and maintain security. For example, your Internet programs can include application gateways that prevent unauthorized users from gaining access to sensitive information.

If you don't take security issues into consideration when you design your network applications, computer hackers (the people that try to penetrate network security) may access your programs and steal information, corrupt data, or introduce viruses. If you neglect to provide adequate security in your network programs, you may have to spend a lot of time (and perhaps money) repairing the damage a hacker does. More often than not, hackers are computer programmers. Typically, a hacker not only knows how to program networks, but also thoroughly understands network operating systems. Much of what you've learned from *Internet Programming* is old news to a serious computer hacker. Network professionals have written entire books about various aspects of network security. A small appendix cannot do the subject justice. However, if you know nothing about network security issues or don't exactly understand how a firewall provides network security, this appendix will introduce you to the basic concepts.

PROTECTING DATA INTEGRITY

When someone makes unauthorized changes (either intentional or accidental) to the data a network stores, they ruin the data's integrity. As such, network security must prevent unauthorized persons from tampering or destroying valuable information. To enhance data integrity, many networks include user authorization and file protection that control user access to sensitive information. Using such basic file protections, networks can restrict the amount and type of information a specific user can access.

PROTECTING NETWORK AVAILABILITY

Availability refers to how quickly and easily an authorized user can access the network's resources. The chief threats to network availability are computer viruses and worms. Although network professionals don't agree on precise differences between viruses and worms, most view a program that causes damage to data as a *virus* and one that consumes computer resources (such as CPU processing time) as a *worm*. Worm and virus intruders on a network may not necessarily destroy data. However, worms and viruses usually do load the system down (reduce the available processor time) and reduce the resources available to the authorized system users. As such, to ensure network resources are available to the people who need them, network administrators should run virus detection software on a regular basis.

PROTECTING DATA CONFIDENTIALITY

When a network cannot ensure data confidentiality, unauthorized individuals can obtain copies of sensitive information. To protect confidentiality, many network security managers encrypt sensitive data. Because of the many technical and legal issues associated with data encryption, this appendix does not address data encryption as a security measure. However, if you want to investigate data encryption for e-mail messages, you should read about an encryption scheme called Pretty Good Privacy (PGP). Developed by Philip Zimmermann, PGP is extremely popular and widely-used on the Internet. For more information, get the PGP Frequently Asked Questions (FAQ) document—pgpfaq?.asc, which is available by anonymous FTP from /pub/gb/gbe on Internet host *ftp.netcom.com*. The Internet newsgroup *alt.security.pgp* also focuses on PGP.

UNDERSTANDING A FIREWALL

Network security managers employ firewalls most frequently against threats to data integrity and network availability. Firewalls provide security by placing one or more electronic barriers (packet-filtering, application, and circuit gateways) in the way of unauthorized users. In other words, a firewall is not an entity like a computer (although computers are major components in a firewall). Rather, a firewall is a protection system (or method). The following sections discuss the value and limitations of each of these electronic barriers (or firewall building blocks). As you will learn, each type of electronic barrier functions at a different layer in the network.

UNDERSTANDING PACKET FILTERING

One popular type of electronic barrier filters network packets. In other words, the barrier (a packet-filtering gateway) examines each packet entering and leaving the network. If you have read Chapter 4 of *Internet Programming*, you know that every TCP/IP packet contains routing information in the IP datagram header. Packet filtering uses the capabilities inherent in a router to provide security. As discussed in the first few chapters of *Internet Programming*, a router transfers packets between two different networks. As part of the router's job, it looks at packet headers to determine a packet's destination. In a similar way, a packet filter examines the source- and destination-addresses in a packet header and, based on criteria the network administrator defines, either accepts or rejects the packets. The major advantage of a packet filtering system is that it's cheap. The router software essentially provides most of the capabilities necessary to establish a packet-filtering firewall.

One disadvantage of a packet filter firewall is that it requires a significant amount of time and planning to set up. First, the network- or security-administrator creates a list of acceptable and unacceptable combinations of addresses and port numbers. Next, the administrator configures the router to drop packets that do not meet the established security requirements. To configure a packet filter, a network administrator starts with a set of established guidelines or the organization's security policy. In effect, the guidelines establish to what extent and to which machines the organization will permit outside access. For example, an organization may decide that one particular system will accept connections from any host on the Internet, but only on the SMTP port (25). In other words, the organization decides to set up and configure one host in the LAN to be the organization's mail server. The network administrator will configure the router to accept any incoming packets that have the mail server's IP address, but only if the port that the header specifies is port number 25. If a packet arrives at the router with the mail server's IP address but the packet header specifies a port number other than 25, the router will simply discard the packet.

A network administrator can also set up packet filters that reject or accept all packets from specific hosts. For example, suppose a local college on the Internet has a reputation for being a penetration point for computer hackers. A business might decide to reject all incoming packets with a source address from college's host computer on the Internet. On the surface, a packet filter seems like a good idea. However, before you decide to use this kind of electronic barrier to safeguard your sensitive data, you should understand that a good Internet programmer can write programs that fool a packet filter. If you have already read all of *Internet Programming*, even you have learned enough to construct such a program—a program that transmits IP packets with header information you specify rather than information that the network protocols normally store in the packet.

Network professionals refer to faking packet identification information as *spoofing*. Spoofing has been popular with computer hackers for years. Network administrators can employ a variety of defenses against spoofing. However, the point to note is that packet filtering is not an invincible defense against intruders. In addition, because network administrators must develop complex logic tables that specify who can and who can't do what, holes (omissions) can appear in the requirements used to configure the router. The more flexibility an organization wants to maintain on the Internet, the more complex the configuration requirement and the greater the chance for error.

CIRCUIT GATEWAYS

Just as the packet-filtering gateways operate at the network-layer level of a TCP/IP network, a circuit-gateway firewall operates at the transport-layer level—specifically for TCP connections. As discussed, packet-filtering gateways establish an electronic barrier that examines every network packet as the packet passes through the firewall. A circuit gateway, on the other hand, only creates an electronic barrier when two Internet hosts initially establish a TCP connection. When a client program tries to connect to a server on a host that a circuit gateway protects, the circuit-gateway firewall (rather than the server) actually accepts the connection using a special type of relay software. In other words, a circuit-gateway firewall sits as a barrier between both ends of a TCP connection; the gateway's relay software transfers data between the client and server programs on either side of the gateway. As you might suspect, only client programs that know how to talk to the circuit gateway can reach the server on the other side of the firewall. In other words, circuit-gateways require the use of special client programs.

Clients that want access to the server must negotiate a connection with the circuit-gateway relay that lets the data transfers occur. The relay software intercepts connection requests that occur at all protocol ports the network security manager defines. After a client successfully negotiates a connection with the relay software, the circuit-gateway becomes essentially invisible. In other words, the circuit-gateway firewall establishes a security barrier only during connection negotiations. After the relay software validates the connection request, data transfer proceeds as though the relay software did not exist—the relay does not examine the content of the packets that pass through the firewall. After the security negotiations complete, the relay software acts much like a wire. In other words, the relay software becomes another part of the transmission medium. Remember, the relay software on the circuit gateway handles the security negotiations that initially occur and then essentially makes itself invisible. In other words, after the connection negotiations complete, the circuit gateway becomes invisible. Obviously, since its *your* circuit gateway, you will have the special client software necessary to negotiate the connection. The custom client software makes the security negotiations relatively transparent.

One problem with circuit gateways is that someone inside the network can advertise a protocol port that the circuit gateway software doesn't cover. In other words, an insider can set up a protocol port that incoming callers can use. Unfortunately, it's very difficult to establish network security procedures that protect the network from such internal abuses. However, as you may know, most security measures (whether for a computer network or a local bank) provide only limited protection from an "inside job."

APPLICATION GATEWAYS

As you have learned, packet-filters examine packet header information to keep networks from accepting unauthorized packet transmissions. In a similar way, the circuit-gateway firewall forms an electronic barrier that prevents unauthorized incoming TCP connections. Application gateways (a third type of firewall) form a security barrier for specific network applications. As discussed, packet filters operate at the network-layer level and circuit gateways operate at the transport-layer level. An application gateway works with the top level in the network—the application layer. The application gateway's scheme uses special-purpose code for each application that the network users run. Of course, such an approach requires special application software in the same way that circuit gateways require special client software. However, since the application-gateway software operates at the application level rather than the network or transport level, application gateways do not require special client software.

You need to understand that application gateways are based on a completely different security concept than packet-filtering and circuit gateways. Packet filters and circuit gateways implement security as a general-purpose mechanism. For example, packet filters examine all incoming packets. Although circuit gateways require special client software, in general, anyone with a copy of that software can connect through a circuit gateway. (Network security managers do not restrict the availability of the special client software). In other words, with packet-filter and circuit-gateway firewalls, any application can generally use any protocol or port address authorized by the host without bypassing security.

In contrast, the application-gateway firewall is not a general-purpose security mechanism. Rather, application gateways consist of special-purpose code that builds security into individual programs. To implement the special-purpose code, the application-gateway designer must first analyze the application and determine its security risk. Next, the designer must carefully decide how to implement security. As you can imagine, each application requires new analysis and may represent a completely different set of security risks. Because some programs will represent more significant security threats than others, network security managers should decide which applications pose the biggest security risk and build gateways into those programs first.

For organizations that need tight security, application gateways offer some significant advantages. For example, because each application contains its own custom security measures, holes or omissions in security are unlikely to occur. (However, faulty analysis for, or implementation of, an application gateway can result in security holes.) In other words, an application gateway does not depend on a network administrator to correctly define all possible combinations of authorized and unauthorized access to the network. Additionally, application-gateway designers can easily develop a gateway that includes logging information. For example, military organizations that require tight accountability and traceability can create or use application gateways that automatically log all network transactions that occur with an application. Network security logs (that record predefined network transactions) represent an important component in the security plan for many organizations—military and otherwise.

In Summary

In summary, network security managers must carefully and thoughtfully plan firewalls. In most cases, a network administrator will define the firewall requirements. As an Internet programmer, you may implement the administrator's requirements as a custom security program. As you develop Internet-based programs, you should keep network security in mind. In most cases, the network administrator will not raise security concerns until after the network has experienced a serious security breach. For a more detailed look at firewalls and general Internet security, see *Firewalls and Internet Security*, Cheswick and Bellovin, Addision-Wesley, 1994. If you want to know more about firewalls and FTP, see RFC 1579, *Firewall-Friendly FTP*, Bellovin, 1994. Finally, if you can obtain a copy of the February 1995 issue of the magazine *Internet World*, you can read numerous articles that discuss Internet security in general and firewalls and encryption in particular.

Appendix B
Understanding the Example Programs

The *Internet Programming* companion disk includes example programs with complete source code. This appendix discusses the general design philosophy behind these programs. If you understand the programs' general structure, as well as how we present the programs, you can more rapidly become a proficient Internet programmer. *Internet Programming* primarily focuses on the Internet—not programming per se. This book does not try to teach you the C/C++ programming language or Windows programming techniques. With this in mind, you need to understand two important caveats with regard to the example programs that the *Internet Programming* companion disk contains. First, this book assumes you are already a programmer and have some experience developing Windows-based programs. Second, this book assumes you are familiar with the C/C++ programming language—the language of choice for most Windows programmers. However, you do not have to be an experienced or skilled Windows programmer to take advantage of the example programs on the *Internet Programming* companion disk. In fact, the example programs steer clear of neat tricks in order to keep the Internet programming concepts as simple as possible.

DEFINING THE CATEGORIES

The example programs on the *Internet Programming* companion disk fall into four categories. First, there are example programs that *Internet Programming* refers to as *quick* programs. You can easily identify the quick programs by their "Q" prefix (QLookup, QFinger, and so on). Typically, the quick programs present a single Internet protocol and focus on just a few Winsock functions you can use with that protocol. For day-to-day use, the quick programs have little value. However, they make a powerful teaching tool because there is very little in them to distract you from the key concepts. In addition to the quick programs, the companion disk includes several SDK-style (based on the Software Development Kit) Windows programs that *Internet Programming* will refer to as the *Sockman* programs. In the Sockman program examples, you integrate a variety of Internet-related utilities into a programming template. Using this template's utilities, you can perform network operations, such as looking up a host address or obtaining information about users on other Internet host computers. Additionally, the Sockman template lets you launch other Internet-related programs from the Sockman menus. However, for the purposes of this book, the Sockman utilities themselves are not important. *Internet Programming* includes the Sockman program examples only to illustrate how you can integrate multiple protocols and a variety of Windows Sockets functions into a single program entity.

Internet Programming also includes Visual Basic programs. Each Visual Basic program uses its own custom dynamic link library (DLL) to perform network-related operations based on either the File Transfer Protocol (FTP) or the HyperText Transfer Protocol (HTTP). Each DLL simply encapsulates program concepts that you will learn from *Internet Programming's* quick program examples. The Visual Basic programs demonstrate how you can easily place C/C++ modules into a custom DLL, add a *visual* front-end, and rapidly create fully functional programs or prototypes. (The companion disk includes the complete source code for the DLLs.)

The *Internet Programming* companion disk also includes an example of an Internet server program that uses C++ classes designed around the Microsoft Foundation Classes (MFC). Although *Internet Programming's* server implementation is for the World-Wide Web's HTTP, you can easily modify the program to act as a server for any protocol. In fact, the server program uses an initialization (INI) file to read configuration information. If you understand C++ classes and related concepts (such as *inheritance*), you will understand that *Internet Programming's* server implementation is a model you can use to create a single program that acts as a server for multiple protocols.

REVIEWING THE QUICK PROGRAMS

Strictly speaking, the quick programs on the *Internet Programming* companion disk are not Windows programs at all. Rather, they are bare-bones programs—stripped of everything that might get in the way of the Internet concepts they present. Typically, the quick programs consist of only a few functions. In fact, the first two quick programs use only a single WinMain function. None of the quick programs register a window class and, thus, none handle any Windows messages.

The quick programs show you steps you can follow to perform specific operations on the Internet. Each quick program builds on concepts presented by previous quick programs. Typically, *Internet Programming* builds each quick program around a single Internet protocol (such as FTP, SMTP, and so on). To get the most value from each quick program, first read the corresponding chapter. Second, study the program statements that define the program. Third, run the program and watch the results. Fourth, and most importantly, take time to load the program into the debugger included with your Windows compiler. By running the program within the debugger, you can closely examine the behavior and impact of each program statement.

The quick programs rely on Windows message boxes to communicate information to you. Because the quick programs do not create windows or manage Windows messages, you can use your debugger to easily step through the programs. By doing so, you can see (in detail) how each network operation occurs. If you are unfamiliar with or rarely use your Windows debugger, you will discover that the quick programs provide you with an easy way to learn how to use a debugger. However, for the purposes of this book, the quick programs are most valuable because they let you peek at network operations from within a Windows-based program. For example, if you use your debugger to step through each quick program and examine program variables (especially those that represent socket-data structures), you can see how the contents of the socket-data structures change with each program statement. Additionally, you can observe how the protocols interact with the Windows Sockets API.

Reviewing the Sockman Program Design

The quick programs exist to help you understand key Internet concepts. To help you put these concepts to use within Windows-based programs, *Internet Programming* presents a collection of programs collectively entitled *Sockman* (Socket Manager). Each Sockman program (Sockman1, Sockman2, and so on) on the *Internet Programming* companion disk represents a different stage of development for the same program. In other words, *Internet Programming* builds one Sockman program. However, the book presents the building process in five stages. At each new stage of the process, *Internet Programming* adds a new Internet utility or capability. The Sockman program examples are much more sophisticated than the quick programs. However, Sockman is still rather crude compared to most Windows-based programs. For example, Sockman avoids any kind of Windows memory-management and relies on the use of global variables. Also, while Sockman registers a window class and creates windows and dialog boxes, as necessary, Sockman does not include any functions to manage text output to its main window. Instead, each time a function needs to paint its main window, Sockman clears the window and dumps the contents of a global array variable to the screen—the array contains the text to print.

Understanding the Sockman Filenames

Using the Sockman file-naming scheme, you can easily track the changes that each new stage of the Sockman program's development requires. The basic program (Sockman1, which includes no network I/O capability) consists of two C/C++ modules (.CPP), two header files (.H), a Windows resource file (.RC), and a definition (.DEF) file. Each Sockman program also includes a separate icon (.ICO) file. Each new stage of the Sockman program's development simply adds another CPP file and makes a few modifications to specific functions within some of the existing files.

At each stage of development, Internet Programming renames all modules to show at what stage modifications (if any) occur. For example, *Internet Programming* names the COMMON.CPP module COMMON1.CPP at stage one, COMMON2.CPP at stage two, COMMON3.CPP at stage three, and so on. If you examine all five COMMON.CPP modules, you will discover that they contain the same functions. Likewise, the SOCKMAN.CPP, sockman.h, and global.h modules contain similar information from one stage to the next. However, unlike COMMON.CPP, these three modules include a few changes for each new stage of development. For example, at each new stage of development, *Internet Programming* adds new global variables to the global.h module. In other words, global1.h contains a few global variables. Global2.h contains the same variables plus a few more that the new Lookup module requires. Likewise, global3.h includes the same variables as global2.h and a few more that the new Finger module requires. This appendix does not discuss the LOOKUP.CPP, FINGER.CPP, TIME.CPP, PING.CPP, and sockraw.h modules since the chapters contain detailed discussions. However, the following sections discuss the other Sockman program modules. Although other *Internet Programming* chapters show the modifications these other program modules require, *Internet Programming* does not discuss the modules as a whole anywhere else in the book.

REVIEWING THE *SOCKMAN.CPP* MODULE

The SOCKMAN.CPP module primarily consists of program functions that manage Windows messages. In other words, in addition to WinMain and WndProc (the main Windows procedure function), SOCKMAN.CPP includes two other functions—one processes messages related to Sockman menus (DoMenuCommand) and the other (Do WindsockProgram) processes messages related to network (Winsock) operations.

In some cases, the function definitions (program statements) for the SOCKMAN.CPP functions change slightly at each stage of development, but the overall purpose of each function remains the same. All functions, except AsyncGetServiceInfo, exist in all five SOCKMAN.CPP modules (SOCKMAN1.CPP, SOCKMAN2.CPP, and so on). *Internet Programming* does not include the AsyncGetServiceInfo function in SOCKMAN.CPP until stage three (SOCKMAN3.CPP). You can combine the WndProc, DoMenuCommand, and DoWinsockProgram functions to form a single window-message-handling procedure. In other words, all three functions define procedures for handling messages for the Sockman window class. However, by separating the procedures into three functions, *Internet Programming* can more easily direct you to the appropriate program statements during discussions about Sockman messages.

DEFINING THE WINMAIN FUNCTION

Each new stage of the Sockman program's development requires a few new initialization statements which *Internet Programming* adds to the beginning of the WinMain function definition. However, other than these initialization statements, the WinMain function (like the DoMenuCommand function) remains constant throughout all five versions of the SOCKMAN.CPP. The following program statements define the WinMain function in SOCKMAN1.CPP. As you can see, the Sockman WinMain function is very generic and probably similar to WinMain functions in other Windows programs that you've seen or written:

```
int PASCAL WinMain(HANDLE  hInstance, HANDLE hPrevInstance,
    LPSTR lpszCmdLine, int nCmdShow)
{
  MSG msg ;
  WNDCLASS wndclass ;

  hInstanceSockman = hInstance;
  lstrcpy(szAppName, "SockMan");
  szPrintBuffer[0] = '\0';

  if (!hPrevInstance)
    {
```

```
        wndclass.style         = CS_HREDRAW | CS_VREDRAW;
        wndclass.lpfnWndProc    = WndProc;
        wndclass.cbClsExtra     = 0;
        wndclass.cbWndExtra     = 0;
        wndclass.hInstance      = hInstance;
        wndclass.hIcon          = LoadIcon(hInstance, szAppName);
        wndclass.hCursor        = LoadCursor(NULL, IDC_ARROW);
        wndclass.hbrBackground  = GetStockObject(WHITE_BRUSH);
        wndclass.lpszMenuName   = szAppName;
        wndclass.lpszClassName  = szAppName;

    if (!RegisterClass(&wndclass))
        return FALSE;
    }

hwndSockman = CreateWindow
        (
          szAppName,
          "SockMan rev. 1",
          WS_OVERLAPPEDWINDOW | WS_VSCROLL | WS_HSCROLL,
          CW_USEDEFAULT,
          CW_USEDEFAULT,
          CW_USEDEFAULT,
          CW_USEDEFAULT,
          NULL,
          NULL,
          hInstance,
          NULL
        );

if (!hwndSockman)
   return FALSE;

ShowWindow(hwndSockman, nCmdShow);
UpdateWindow(hwndSockman);
if( StartWinsock())
   {
     while(GetMessage(&msg, NULL, 0, 0))
        {
          TranslateMessage(&msg);
          DispatchMessage(&msg);
        }
   }
WSACleanup();
return(msg.wParam);
}
```

The WinMain function in each version of the SOCKMAN.CPP module is identical, except for a few initialization statements that each new version of SOCKMAN.CPP requires. For example, in addition to initializing hInstanceSockman, szAppName, and szPrintBuffer, the WinMain function in SOCKMAN5.CPP contains the following program statements (which appear immediately after the szPrintBuffer initialization statement):

```
szHostName[0] = '\0';
szPingHost[0] = '\0';
szFingerHost[0] = '\0';
szTimeServer[0] = '\0';
hFingerTask = 0;
hTimeServerTask = 0;
hPingTask = 0;
```

After initializing a few global variables, WinMain registers the Sockman window class. As shown in the following program statement, WinMain declares the WndProc function to be the window-procedure function that handles all messages for the Sockman window class:

```
wndclass.lpfnWndProc  = WndProc;
```

DEFINING THE WNDPROC FUNCTION

In SOCKMAN1.CPP, the WndProc function processes two standard window-class messages: WM_PAINT (a message to update the window) and WM_DESTROY (a message to destroy the window). The WndProc function also contains a *case* statement to process WM_COMMAND messages. However, as you can see, WndProc simply passes all WM_COMMAND messages to the DoMenuCommand function. The following program statements define the WndProc function in SOCKMAN1.CPP:

```
long FAR PASCAL _export WndProc(HWND hwnd, UINT iMessage, UINT wParam,
    LONG lParam)
{
  switch (iMessage)
    {
      case WM_PAINT:
        PAINTSTRUCT ps;
        HDC hdc;
        RECT rect;

        hdc = BeginPaint( hwnd, &ps);

        GetClientRect(hwndSockman, &rect);
        DrawText(hdc, szPrintBuffer, -1, &rect,
            DT_EXPANDTABS|DT_WORDBREAK);
        EndPaint(hwnd, &ps);
        return(0);
```

```
      case WM_COMMAND:
        if (DoMenuCommand(hwnd, iMessage, wParam, lParam))
          return(0);
        else
          break;

      case WM_DESTROY:
        PostQuitMessage(0);
        return(0);
    }

  return(DefWindowProc(hwnd, iMessage, wParam, lParam));
}
```

Throughout the Sockman development that *Internet Programming* describes, the program statements for the previous message cases remain the same. *Internet Programming* modifies WndProc only to add new case statements that process messages that Sockman network operations generate. As you can see, WndProc passes all WM_COMMAND messages to DoMenuCommand.

DEFINING THE DOMENUCOMMAND FUNCTION

The DoMenuCommand function remains constant throughout all five versions of the SOCKMAN.CPP module. As you can see, the DoMenuCommand function processes WM_COMMAND messages for all non-network-related operations. As shown next, the messages the DoMenuCommand function processes occur as a result of Sockman menu selections (such as the File menu Clear, Print, Save As, and Exit options):

```
long DoMenuCommand(HWND hwnd, UINT iMessage, UINT wParam, LONG lParam)
{
  switch (wParam)
    {
      case IDM_FILE_CLEAR:
        szPrintBuffer[0]='\0';
        InvalidateRect(hwndSockman, NULL, TRUE);
        UpdateWindow(hwndSockman);
        return(TRUE);

      case IDM_FILE_PRINT:
      case IDM_FILE_SAVEAS:
        PaintWindow((LPSTR)"Selected function is not yet implemented!");
        MessageBeep(0);
        MessageBox(hwnd, "Sorry! You have to implement this yourself.",
              szAppName, MB_ICONEXCLAMATION | MB_OK);
        return(TRUE);
```

```
        case IDM_FILE_EXIT:
          SendMessage(hwnd, WM_CLOSE, 0, 0L);
          return(TRUE);


        case IDM_HELP_HELP:
          PaintWindow((LPSTR)"Selected function is not yet implemented!");
          MessageBeep(0);
          MessageBox(hwnd, "Help is not yet implemented!", szAppName,
                MB_ICONEXCLAMATION | MB_OK);
          return(TRUE);


        case IDM_HELP_ABOUT:
          MessageBox(hwnd,
                "A programming shell for Windows Sockets programmers.",
                "SockMan - Winsock Program Manager rev. 5",
                MB_ICONINFORMATION | MB_OK);
          return(TRUE);


        default:
          return(DoWinsockProgram(hwnd, wParam, lParam));
      }
  }
```

As you can see from the default case statement, the DoMenuCommand function passes all unidentified WM_COMMAND messages on to the DoWinsockProgram function.

DEFINING THE DOWINSOCKPROGRAM FUNCTION

Like the DoMenuCommand function, the DoWinsockProgram function also processes WM_COMMAND messages that Sockman menu selections trigger. However, as shown next, the DoWinsockProgram function in the SOCKMAN1.CPP module simply displays message boxes for each menu option. As Sockman progresses through its developmental stages, *Internet Programming* modifies these case statements to initiate Sockman network operations related to each menu selection:

```
long DoWinsockProgram(HWND hwnd, UINT wParam, LONG lParam)
{
  switch (wParam)
    {
      case IDM_APP_MAIL:
      case IDM_APP_FTP:
        MessageBeep(0);
        MessageBox(hwnd, "No APPLICATIONS are currently implemented!",
              szAppName, MB_ICONEXCLAMATION | MB_OK);
        return(TRUE);
```

```
      case IDM_LOOKUP_ASYNC:
      case IDM_LOOKUP_BLOCKING:
        MessageBeep(0);
        MessageBox(hwnd, "The LOOKUP utility is not yet implemented!",
              szAppName, MB_ICONEXCLAMATION | MB_OK);
        return(TRUE);

      case IDM_FINGER_ASYNC:
      case IDM_FINGER_BLOCKING:
        MessageBeep(0);
        MessageBox(hwnd, "The FINGER utility is not yet implemented!",
              szAppName, MB_ICONEXCLAMATION | MB_OK);
        return(TRUE);

      case IDM_TIME_UTIL:
        MessageBeep(0);
        MessageBox(hwnd, "The TIME utility is not yet implemented!",
              szAppName, MB_ICONEXCLAMATION | MB_OK);
        return(TRUE);

      case IDM_PING_UTIL:
        MessageBeep(0);
        MessageBox(hwnd, "The PING utility is not yet implemented!",
              szAppName, MB_ICONEXCLAMATION | MB_OK);
        return(TRUE);

    }
  return(FALSE);
}
```

When neither the DoMenuCommand function nor DoWinsockProgram function identifies the WM_COMMAND message, DoMenuCommand will return a false value to the WndProc function. As shown in the following program fragment, when the DoMenuCommand function returns a false value, WndProc passes the WM_COMMAND message to the Windows DefWindowProc function. DefWindowProc, in turn, executes the default procedure for the message:

```
      case WM_COMMAND:
        if (DoMenuCommand(hwnd, iMessage, wParam, lParam))
          return(0);
        else
          break;

      case WM_DESTROY :
        PostQuitMessage(0);
        return(0);
    }

  return(DefWindowProc(hwnd, iMessage, wParam, lParam));
```

The only other function in the SOCKMAN.CPP modules is the AsyncGetServiceInfo function. AsyncGetServiceInfo uses the Winsock WSAAsyncGetServByName function to retrieve information about communication services from the network services database. Chapter 12 discusses the AsyncGetServiceInfo function in detail.

REVIEWING THE COMMON.CPP MODULE

The COMMON.CPP module contains three functions that perform common procedures, such as Winsock initialization, window centering, and text "painting." As previously noted, all five versions of the COMMON.CPP module (COMMON1.CPP, COMMON2.CPP, COMMON3.CPP, and so on) contain the same functions. The following sections discuss the functions contained in the file COMMON.CPP, and show the program statements that define each of these functions. As you will learn, none of the COMMON.CPP functions perform any type of network-related I/O.

DEFINING THE STARTWINSOCK FUNCTION

As previously shown, the WinMain function calls the StartWinsock function just before entering the Sockman program's main message-handling loop. As you may already know, before they can call any Winsock API functions, your programs must call the WSAStartup function to initialize the Winsock dynamic link library. As shown next, the StartWinsock function simply calls the WSAStartup function to initialize the Winsock dynamic link library (DLL) and then reports any Winsock initialization errors that occur. If no errors occur, the StartWinsock function calls the PaintWindow function to display a description of the Winsock DLL:

```
BOOL StartWinsock(VOID)
{
  WSADATA wsaData;                    // Winsock implementation details
  UINT iErr;                          // Error number
  char szErrMessage[MAX_ERR_MESSAGE]; // Error message buffer

  if (iErr = WSAStartup(WINSOCK_VER_11, &wsaData))
    {
      MessageBeep(0);

      switch(iErr)
        {
          case  WSASYSNOTREADY:
            lstrcpy(szErrMessage, WSASYSNOTREADY_MSG);
            break;

          case  WSAVERNOTSUPPORTED:
            lstrcpy(szErrMessage, WSAVERNOTSUPPORTED_MSG);
            break;
```

```
        case  WSAEINVAL:
          lstrcpy(szErrMessage, WSAEINVAL_MSG);
          break;
      }
    MessageBox(NULL, szErrMessage, "SockMan", MB_OK|MB_ICONSTOP);
    return(FALSE);
  }
else
  PaintWindow(wsaData.szDescription);

return(TRUE);
}
```

If WSAStartup initializes the Winsock DLL, the StartWinsock function will return a true value to the WinMain function. A true value from StartWinsock causes WinMain to enter the Sockman program's main message-handling loop. If the Winsock DLL fails to initialize properly, the StartWinsock function will display an error message in a message box and return a false value to the WinMain function. When the Winsock initialization fails, the WinMain function immediately calls the Winsock WSACleanup function (instead of entering the main message-handling loop) and the Sockman program terminates gracefully. Since the Sockman program depends on the Winsock DLL for all network operations, the Sockman program requires a correctly initialized Winsock DLL to function properly.

DEFINING THE CENTERWINDOW FUNCTION

Before Windows displays a dialog box, Windows sends a WM_INITDIALOG message to the function you defined to handle messages for the dialog box. The WM_INITDIALOG message lets your programs perform initialization procedures for the dialog box. The initialization routine for each Sockman dialog box contains a call to the CenterWindow function. The CenterWindow function centers the dialog box over the Sockman window before Windows displays the dialog box. The CenterWindow calls four standard Windows-API functions to center the dialog boxes, regardless of the user's screen size.

The GetWindowRect function retrieves the dimensions (in rectangle coordinates) for the Sockman dialog boxes. The GetClientRect function retrieves the client coordinates for the Sockman window. The following program statements calculate the width and height of the dialog box:

```
nWidth = rect.right - rect.left;
nHeight = rect.bottom - rect.top;
```

Because client coordinates are relative to the upper-left corner of a window's client area, the coordinates of the upper-left corner are (0,0). The next two program statements calculate the x-y coordinates for the center of the Sockman window:

```
point.x = (rectMainWindow.right - rectMainWindow.left) / 2;
point.y = (rectMainWindow.bottom - rectMainWindow.top) / 2;
```

The ClientToScreen function translates the center x-y (client) coordinates of the Sockman window into screen coordinates. In effect, the following two program statements calculate the new x-y coordinates for the upper-left corner of the dialog box that will center the dialog box within the Sockman window:

```
point.x = point.x - (nWidth / 2);
point.y = point.y - (nHeight / 2);
```

Finally, the MoveWindow function moves the dialog box to the x-y coordinates just calculated:

```
MoveWindow(hWnd, point.x, point.y, nWidth, nHeight, FALSE);
```

With MoveWindow's sixth parameter set to False, Windows cannot redraw the window after the move operation. In effect, the CenterWindow function lets Windows repaint the dialog box normally after all other dialog box initialization statements are complete.

DEFINING THE PAINTWINDOW FUNCTION

Most Windows programmers have their own preferred method to paint text to a window and update scroll bars. As previously mentioned, the Sockman program modules do not include any sophisticated functions to manage text output to the main window. Each time a function needs to paint the Sockman main window, Sockman clears the window and dumps the contents of a global array variable to the screen—the array contains the text to print. The Sockman program modules call the PaintWindow function to update the global array variable and paint the Sockman window with any text messages for the user. The PaintWindow function copies its text parameter (lpszTxt) to the szPrintBuffer global variable, invalidates the Sockman window, and then calls the UpdateWindow function to generate a WM_PAINT message.

COMPILING THE EXAMPLE PROGRAMS

After you install the example programs from the *Internet Programming* companion disk to your hard disk, you will find that each program directory contains a MAK file for the Microsoft Visual C++ compiler (version 1.5) and an IDE file for the Borland C++ compiler (version 4.0). If you own and use either of these compilers, you can use the MAK or IDE file to manage each project for the *Internet Programming* example programs.

Index